AND DATA COMMUNICATIONS TECHNOLOGY

WIRELESS COMMUNICATIONS AND NETWORKS

A comprehensive, state-of-the art survey. Covers fundamental wireless communications topics, including antennas and propagation, signal encoding techniques, spread spectrum, and error correction techniques. Examines satellite, cellular, wireless local loop networks and wireless LANs, including Bluetooth and 802.11. Covers Mobile IP and WAP. ISBN 0-13-040864-6

CRYPTOGRAPHY AND NETWORK SECURITY, THIRD EDITION

A tutorial and survey on network security technology. Each of the basic building blocks of network security, including conventional and public-key cryptography, authentication, and digital signatures, are covered. The book covers important network security tools and applications, including S/MIME, IP Security, Kerberos, SSL/TLS, SET, and X509v3. In addition, methods for countering hackers and viruses are explored. **Second edition received the TAA award for the best Computer Science and Engineering Textbook of 1999.** ISBN 0-13- 091429-0

BUSINESS DATA COMMUNICATIONS, FOURTH EDITION

A comprehensive presentation of data communications and telecommunications from a business perspective. Covers voice, data, image, and video communications and applications technology and includes a number of case studies. ISBN 0-13-088263-1

LOCAL AND METROPOLITAN AREA NETWORKS, SIXTH EDITION

An in-depth presentation of the technology and architecture of local and metropolitan area networks. Covers topology, transmission media, medium access control, standards, internetworking, and network management. Provides an up-to-date coverage of LAN/MAN systems, including Fast Ethernet, Fibre Channel, and wireless LANs, plus LAN QoS. **Received the 2001 TAA award for long-term excellence in a Computer Science Textbook.** ISBN 0-13-012939-9

ISDN AND BROADBAND ISDN, WITH FRAME RELAY AND ATM: FOURTH EDITION

An in-depth presentation of the technology and architecture of integrated services digital networks (ISDN). Covers the integrated digital network (IDN), xDSL, ISDN services and architecture, signaling system no. 7 (SS7) and provides detailed coverage of the ITU-T protocol standards. Also provides detailed coverage of protocols and congestion control strategies for both frame relay and ATM. ISBN 0-13-973744-8

Prentice Hall   www.prenhall.com/stallings   telephone: 800-526-0485

PARK LEARNING CENTRE
The Park Cheltenham
Gloucestershire GL50 2RH
Telephone: 01242 714777

THE WILLIAM STALLINGS BOOKS ON COMPUTER

COMPUTER NETWORKS WITH INTERNET PROTOCOLS AND TECHNOLOGY

The objective of this book is to provide an up-to-date survey of developments in the area of Internet-based protocols and algorithms. Using a top-down approach, this book covers applications, transport layer, Internet QoS, Internet routing, data link layer and computer networks, security, and network management. ISBN 0-13-141098-9

COMPUTER ORGANIZATION AND ARCHITECTURE, SIXTH EDITION

A unified view of this broad field. Covers fundamentals such as CPU, control unit, microprogramming, instruction set, I/O, and memory. Also covers advanced topics such as RISC, superscalar, and parallel organization. **Fourth and fifth editions received the TAA award for the best Computer Science and Engineering Textbook of the year.** ISBN 0-13-035119-9

OPERATING SYSTEMS, FOURTH EDITION

A state-of-the art survey of operating system principles. Covers fundamental technology as well as contemporary design issues, such as threads, microkernels, SMPs, real-time systems, multiprocessor scheduling, distributed systems, clusters, security, and object-oriented design. **Third edition received the TAA award for the best Computer Science and Engineering Textbook of 1998.** ISBN 0-13-031999-6

HIGH-SPEED NETWORKS AND INTERNETS, SECOND EDITION

A state-of-the art survey of high-speed networks. Topics covered include TCP congestion control, ATM traffic management, internet traffic management, differentiated and integrated services, internet routing protocols and multicast routing protocols, resource reservation and RSVP, and lossless and lossy compression. Examines important topic of self-similar data traffic. ISBN 0-13-03221-0

NETWORK SECURITY ESSENTIALS, SECOND EDITION

A tutorial and survey on network security technology. The book covers important network security tools and applications, including S/MIME, IP Security, Kerberos, SSL/TLS, SET, and X509v3. In addition, methods for countering hackers and viruses are explored. ISBN 0-13-035128-8

Prentice Hall   www.prenhall.com/stallings   telephone: 800-526-0485

DATA AND COMPUTER COMMUNICATIONS

SEVENTH EDITION

William Stallings

PEARSON
Prentice
Hall

Pearson Education International

Vice President and Editorial Director, ECS: *Marcia Horton*
Publisher: *Alan Apt*
Project Manager: *Jake Warde*
Associate Editor: *Toni D. Holm*
Editorial Assistant: *Patrick Lindner*
Vice President and Director of Production and Manufacturing, ESM: *David W. Riccardi*
Executive Managing Editor: *Vince O'Brien*
Managing Editor: *Camille Trentacoste*
Production Editor: *Rose Kernan*
Director of Creative Services: *Paul Belfanti*
Creative Director: *Carole Anson*
Art Director: *Kenny Beck*
Art Editor: *Gregory Dulles*
Cover Designer: *Kenny Beck*
Manufacturing Manager: *Trudy Pisciotti*
Manufacturing Buyer: *Lisa McDowell*
Marketing Manager: *Pamela Shaffer*
Marketing Assistant: *Barrie Reinhold*

© 2004 by Pearson Education, Inc.
Pearson Prentice Hall
Upper Saddle River, NJ 07458

The author and publisher of this book have used their best efforts in preparing this book. These efforts include
the development, research, and testing of the theories and programs to determine their effectiveness. The author
and publisher make no warranty of any kind, expressed or implied, with regard to these programs or the
documentation contained in this book. The author and publisher shall not be liable in any event for incidental or
consequential damages in connection with, or arising out of, the furnishing, performance, or use of these programs.

If you purchased this book within the United States or Canada you should be aware that it has been wrongfully
imported without the approval of the Publisher or the Author.

Pearson Prentice Hall® is a trademark of Pearson Education, Inc.

Printed in the United States of America

10 9 8 7 6 5 4 3 2 1

ISBN 0-13-183311-1

Pearson Education LTD.
Pearson Education Australia PTY, Limited
Pearson Education Singapore, Pte. Ltd
Pearson Education North Asia Ltd
Pearson Education Canada, Ltd
Pearson Educación de Mexico, S.A. de C.V.
Pearson Education—Japan
Pearson Education Malaysia, Pte. Ltd
Pearson Education, Upper Saddle River, New Jersey

For my scintillating wife
ATS

WEB SITE FOR DATA AND COMPUTER COMMUNICATIONS
Seventh Edition

The Web site at WilliamStallings.com/DCC/DCC7e.html provides support for instructors and students using the book. It includes the following elements.

Course Support Materials

The course support materials include

- Copies of figures from the book in PDF format
- A detailed set of course notes in PDF format suitable for student handout or for use as viewgraphs
- A set of PowerPoint slides for use as lecture aids
- Computer Science Student Support Site: contains a number of links and documents that the student may find useful in his/her ongoing computer science education. The site includes a review of basic, relevant mathematics; advice on research, writing, and doing homework problems; links to computer science research resources, such as report repositories and bibliographies; and other useful links.
- An errata sheet for the book, updated at most monthly

DCC Courses

The DCC7e Web site includes links to Web sites for courses taught using the book. These sites can provide useful ideas about scheduling and topic ordering, as well as a number of useful handouts and other materials.

Useful Web Sites

The DCC7e Web site includes links to relevant Web sites, organized by chapter. The links cover a broad spectrum of topics and will enable students to explore timely issues in greater depth.

Supplemental Documents

The DCC7e Web site includes a number of documents that expand on the treatment in the book. Topics include standards organizations, Sockets, TCP/IP checksum, ASCII, and the sampling theorem.

Internet Mailing List

An Internet mailing list is maintained so that instructors using this book can exchange information, suggestions, and questions with each other and the author. Subscription information is provided at the book's Web site.

Simulation and Modeling Tools

The Web site includes links to the *cnet* Web site and the *modeling tools* Web site. These packages can be used to analyze and experiment with protocol and network design issues. Each site includes downloadable software and background information. The instructor's manual includes more information on loading and using the software and suggested student projects. See Appendix D for more information.

CONTENTS

PART FOUR   LOCAL AREA NETWORKS   463

PREFACE

OBJECTIVES

This book attempts to provide a unified overview of the broad field of data and computer communications. The organization of the book reflects an attempt to break this massive subject into comprehensible parts and to build, piece by piece, a survey of the state of the art. The book emphasizes basic principles and topics of fundamental importance concerning the technology and architecture of this field and provides a detailed discussion of leading-edge topics.

The following basic themes serve to unify the discussion:

- **Principles:** Although the scope of this book is broad, there are a number of basic principles that appear repeatedly as themes and that unify this field. Examples are multiplexing, flow control, and error control. The book highlights these principles and contrasts their application in specific areas of technology.
- **Design approaches:** The book examines alternative approaches to meeting specific communication requirements.
- **Standards:** Standards have come to assume an increasingly important, indeed dominant, role in this field. An understanding of the current status and future direction of technology requires a comprehensive discussion of the related standards.

PLAN OF THE TEXT

The book is divided into five parts:

In addition, the book includes an extensive glossary, a list of frequently used acronyms, and a bibliography. Each chapter includes problems and suggestions for further reading.

The book is intended for both an academic and a professional audience. For the professional interested in this field, the book serves as a basic reference volume and is suitable for self-study. As a textbook, it can be used for a one-semester or two-semester course. It covers the material in the Communication and Networking core course of the joint ACM/IEEE Computing

Curricula 2001. The chapters and parts of the book are sufficiently modular to provide a great deal of flexibility in the design of courses. The following are suggestions for course design:

- **Fundamentals of Data Communications:** Parts One (overview) and Two (data communications) and Chapters 10 and 11 (circuit switching, packet switching, and ATM).
- **Communications Networks:** If the student has a basic background in data communications, then this course could cover Parts One (overview), Three (WAN), and Four (LAN).
- **Computer Networks:** If the student has a basic background in data communications, then this course could cover Part One (overview), Chapters 6 and 7 (data communication techniques and data link control), and Part Five (protocols).

In addition, a more streamlined course that covers the entire book is possible by eliminating certain chapters that are not essential on a first reading. Chapters that could be optional are Chapters 3 (data transmission) and 4 (transmission media), if the student has a basic understanding of these topics; Chapter 8 (multiplexing); Chapter 9 (spread spectrum); Chapters 12 through 14 (routing, congestion control, cellular networks); Chapter 18 (internetworking); and Chapter 21 (network security).

INTERNET SERVICES FOR INSTRUCTORS AND STUDENTS

There is a Web site for this book that provides support for students and instructors. The site includes links to other relevant sites, transparency masters of figures in the book, and sign-up information for the book's Internet mailing list. The Web page is at WilliamStallings.com/DCC/DCC7e.html; see the section, "Web Site for Data and Computer Communications," preceding the Table of Contents, for more information. An Internet mailing list has been set up so that instructors using this book can exchange information, suggestions, and questions with each other and with the author. As soon as typos or other errors are discovered, an errata list for this book will be available at WilliamStallings.com.

PROJECTS FOR TEACHING DATA AND COMPUTER COMMUNICATIONS

For many instructors, an important component of a data communications or networking course is a project or set of projects by which the student gets hands-on experience to reinforce concepts from the text. This book provides an unparalleled degree of support for including a projects component in the course. The instructor's manual not only includes guidance on how to assign and structure the projects, but also includes a set of suggested projects that covers a broad range of topics from the text, including research projects, simulation projects, analytic modeling projects, and reading/report assignments. See Appendix D for details.

SOCKETS PROGRAMMING

The book includes a brief description of Sockets (Appendix C), with a more detailed description available at the book's Web site. The Instructors manual includes a set of programming projects. Sockets programming is an "easy" topic and one that can result in very satisfying hands-on projects for students.

WHAT'S NEW IN THE SEVENTH EDITION

This seventh edition is seeing the light of day less than 4 years after the publication of the sixth edition. During that time, the pace of change in this field continues unabated. In this new edition, I try to capture these changes while maintaining a broad and comprehensive coverage of the entire field. To begin the process of revision, the sixth edition of this book was extensively reviewed by a number of professors who teach the subject. The result is that, in many places, the narrative has been clarified and tightened, and illustrations have been improved. Also, a number of new "field-tested" problems have been added.

Beyond these refinements to improve pedagogy and user-friendliness, there have been major substantive changes throughout the book. Every chapter has been revised, new chapters have been added, and the overall organization of the book has changed. Highlights include:

- **Wireless communications and networking:** There is a significant increase in the amount of material on wireless communications, wireless networks, and wireless standards. The book now devotes one chapter each to spread spectrum technology, cellular wireless networks, and wireless LANs.
- **Gigabit Ethernet:** The discussion on Gigabit Ethernet has been updated and an introduction to 10-Gbps Ethernet has been added.
- **Differentiated services:** There have been substantial developments since the publication of the sixth edition in enhancements to the Internet to support a variety of multimedia and time-sensitive traffic. The most important development, and perhaps the most important vehicle for providing QoS in IP-based networks, is Differentiated Services (DS). This edition provides thorough coverage of DS.
- **Guaranteed frame rate (GFR):** Since the sixth edition, a new ATM service has been standardized: GFR. GFR is designed specifically to support IP backbone subnetworks. This edition provides an explanation of GFR and examines the mechanisms underlying the GFR service.
- **Multiprotocol label switching (MPLS):** MPLS has emerged as a fundamentally important technology in the Internet and is covered in this edition.
- **TCP/IP details:** A new background chapter on TCP and IP has been added, pulling together material scattered throughout the sixth edition. This material is vital to an understanding of QoS and performance issues in IP-based networks.

In addition, throughout the book, virtually every topic has been updated to reflect the developments in standards and technology that have occurred since the publication of the fifth edition.

ACKNOWLEDGMENTS

This new edition has benefited from review by a number of people, who gave generously of their time and expertise. The following people reviewed all or a large part of the manuscript: Michael J. Donahoo (Baylor University), Gary Harkin (Montana State University), Larry Owens (California State U. Fresno), S. Hossein Hosseini (U. of Wisconsin-Milwaukee), and Dr. Charles Baker (Southern Methodist University).

Thanks also to the many people who provided detailed technical reviews of a single chapter: Dave Tweed, Bruce Lane, Denis McMahon, Charles Freund, Paul Hoadley, Stephen Ma, Sandeep Subramaniam, Dragan Cvetkovic, Fernando Gont, Neil Giles, Rajesh Thundil, and Rick Jones.

Finally, I would like to thank the many people responsible for the publication of the book, all of whom did their usual excellent job. This includes the staff at Prentice Hall, particularly my editor Alan Apt, his assistant Patrick Lindner, and production manager Rose Kernan. Also, Jake Warde of Warde Publishers managed the supplements and reviews; and Patricia M. Daly did the copyediting.

CHAPTER 0

READER'S GUIDE

This book, and the accompanying Web site, cover a lot of material. Here we give the reader some basic background information.

0.1   OUTLINE OF THE BOOK

The book is organized into five parts:

Part One. Overview: Provides an introduction to the range of topics covered in the book. This part includes a general overview of data communications and networking, and a discussion of protocols, OSI, and the TCP/IP protocol suite.

Part Two. Data Communications: Concerned primarily with the exchange of data between two directly connected devices. Within this restricted scope, the key aspects of transmission, interfacing, link control, and multiplexing are examined.

Part Three. Wide Area Networks: Examines the internal mechanisms and user-network interfaces that have been developed to support voice, data, and multimedia communications over long-distance networks. The traditional technologies of packet switching and circuit switching are examined, as well as the more recent ATM and wireless WANs. A separate chapter is devoted to congestion control issues.

Part Four. Local Area Networks: Explores the technologies and architectures that have been developed for networking over shorter distances. The transmission media, topologies, and medium access control protocols that are the key ingredients of a LAN design are explored and specific standardized LAN systems examined.

Part Five. Networking Protocols: Explores both the architectural principles and the mechanisms required for the exchange of data among computers, workstations, servers, and other data processing devices. Much of the material in this part relates to the TCP/IP protocol suite.

A more detailed, chapter-by-chapter summary of each part appears at the beginning of that part.

0.2   INTERNET AND WEB RESOURCES

There are a number of resources available on the Internet and the Web to support this book and to help one keep up with developments in this field.

Web Sites for This Book

A special Web page has been set up for this book at WilliamStallings.com/DCC/ DCC7e.html. See the two-page layout at the beginning of this book for a detailed description of that site.

As soon as any typos or other errors are discovered, an errata list for this book will be available at the Web site. Please report any errors that you spot. Errata sheets for my other books, as well as discount ordering information for the books, are at WilliamStallings.com.

I also maintain the Computer Science Student Resource Site, at WilliamStallings.com/StudentSupport.html. The purpose of this site is to provide documents, information, and links for computer science students. Links are organized into four categories:

- **Math:** Includes a basic math refresher, a queuing analysis primer, a number system primer, and links to numerous math sites
- **How-to:** Advice and guidance for solving homework problems, writing technical reports, and preparing technical presentations
- **Research resources:** Links to important collections of papers, technical reports, and bibliographies
- **Miscellaneous:** A variety of useful documents and links

Other Web Sites

There are numerous Web sites that provide information related to the topics of this book. In subsequent chapters, pointers to specific Web sites can be found in the "Recommended Reading" section. Because the URLs for Web sites tend to change frequently, I have not included these in the book. For all of the Web sites listed in the book, the appropriate link can be found at this book's Web site.

The following are Web sites of general interest related to data and computer communications:

- **Network World:** Information and links to resources about data communications and networking.
- **IETF:** Maintains archives that relate to the Internet and IETF activities. Includes keyword-indexed library of RFCs and draft documents as well as many other documents related to the Internet and related protocols.
- **Vendors:** Links to thousands of hardware and software vendors who currently have Web sites, as well as a list of thousands of computer and networking companies in a phone directory.
- **IEEE Communications Society:** Good way to keep up on conferences, publications, and so on.
- **ACM Special Interest Group on Communications (SIGCOMM):** Good way to keep up on conferences, publications, and so on.
- **International Telecommunications Union:** Contains a listing of ITU-T recommendations, plus information on obtaining ITU-T documents in hard copy or on CD-ROM.
- **International Organization for Standardization:** Contains a listing of ISO standards, plus information on obtaining ISO documents in hard copy or on CD-ROM.
- **CommWeb:** Links to vendors, tutorials and other useful information.

USENET Newsgroups

A number of USENET newsgroups are devoted to some aspect of data communications, networks, and protocols. As with virtually all USENET groups, there is a high noise-to-signal ratio, but it is worth experimenting to see if any meet your needs. The most relevant are as follows:

- **comp.dcom.lans, comp.dcom.lans.misc:** General discussions of LANs
- **comp.dcom.lans.ethernet:** Covers Ethernet, Ethernet-like systems, and the IEEE 802.3 CSMA/CD standards
- **comp.std.wireless:** General discussion of wireless networks including wireless LANs
- **comp.security.misc:** Computer security and encryption
- **comp.dcom.cell-relay:** Covers ATM and ATM LANs
- **comp.dcom.frame-relay:** Covers frame relay networks
- **comp.dcom.net-management:** Discussion of network management applications, protocols, and standards
- **comp.protocols.tcp-ip:** The TCP/IP protocol suite

0.3   STANDARDS

It has long been accepted in the telecommunications industry that standards are required to govern the physical, electrical, and procedural characteristics of communication equipment. In the past, this view has not been embraced by the computer industry. Whereas communication equipment vendors recognize that their equipment will generally interface to and communicate with other vendors' equipment, computer vendors have traditionally attempted to monopolize their customers. The proliferation of computers and distributed processing has made that an untenable position. Computers from different vendors must communicate with each other and, with the ongoing evolution of protocol standards, customers will no longer accept special-purpose protocol conversion software development. The result is that standards now permeate all of the areas of technology discussed in this book.

There are a number of advantages and disadvantages to the standards-making process. We list here the most striking ones. The principal advantages of standards are as follows:

- A standard assures that there will be a large market for a particular piece of equipment or software. This encourages mass production and, in some cases, the use of large-scale-integration (LSI) or very-large-scale-integration (VLSI) techniques, resulting in lower costs.
- A standard allows products from multiple vendors to communicate, giving the purchaser more flexibility in equipment selection and use.

The principal disadvantages are as follows:

- A standard tends to freeze the technology. By the time a standard is developed, subjected to review and compromise, and promulgated, more efficient techniques are possible.
- There are multiple standards for the same thing. This is not a disadvantage of standards per se, but of the current way things are done. Fortunately, in recent years the various standards-making organizations have begun to cooperate more closely. Nevertheless, there are still areas where multiple conflicting standards exist.

Throughout this book, we describe the most important standards in use or being developed for various aspects of data and computer communications. Various organizations have been involved in the development or promotion of these standards. The most important (in the current context) of these organizations are as follows:

- **Internet Society:** The Internet SOCiety (ISOC) is a professional membership society with more than 150 organizational and 6000 individual members in over 100 countries. It provides leadership in addressing issues that confront the future of the Internet and is the organization home for the groups responsible for Internet infrastructure standards, including the Internet Engineering Task Force (IETF) and the Internet Architecture Board (IAB). All of the RFCs and Internet standards are developed through these organizations.
- **IEEE 802:** The IEEE (Institute of Electrical and Electronics Engineers) 802 LAN/MAN Standards Committee develops local area network standards and metropolitan area network standards. The most widely used standards are for the Ethernet family, token ring, wireless LAN, bridging, and virtual bridged LANs. An individual working group provides the focus for each area.
- **ITU-T:** The International Telecommunication Union (ITU) is an international organization within the United Nations System where governments and the private sector coordinate global telecom networks and services. The ITU Telecommunication Standardization Sector (ITU-T) is one of the three sectors of the ITU. ITU-T's mission is the production of standards covering all fields of telecommunications.
- **ATM Forum:** The ATM Forum is an international nonprofit organization formed with the objective of accelerating the use of ATM (asynchronous transfer mode) products and services through a rapid convergence of interoperability specifications. In addition, the Forum promotes industry cooperation and awareness.
- **ISO:** The International Organization for Standardization (ISO)[1] is a worldwide federation of national standards bodies from more than 140 countries, one from each country. ISO is a nongovernmental organization that promotes

---

[1]ISO is not an acronym (in which case it would be IOS), but a word, derived from the Greek, meaning *equal*.

the development of standardization and related activities with a view to facilitating the international exchange of goods and services, and to developing cooperation in the spheres of intellectual, scientific, technological, and economic activity. ISO's work results in international agreements that are published as International Standards.

A more detailed discussion of these organizations is contained in a supporting document at this book's Web site.

PART ONE Overview

ISSUES FOR PART ONE

The purpose of Part One is to provide a background and context for the remainder of this book. The broad range of topics that are encompassed in the field of data and computer communications is introduced, and the fundamental concepts of protocols and protocol architectures are examined.

ROAD MAP FOR PART ONE

Chapter 1 Introduction

Chapter 1 provides an overview of Parts Two through Four of the book, giving the "big picture." In essence, the book deals with four topics: data communications over a transmission link; wide area networks; local area networks; and protocols and the TCP/IP protocol architecture. Chapter 1 provides a preview of the first three of these topics.

Chapter 2 Protocols and Architecture

Chapter 2 discusses the concept protocol architectures. This chapter can be read immediately following Chapter 1 or deferred until the beginning of Part Three, Four, or Five.

After a general introduction, the chapter deals with the two most important protocol architectures: the Open Systems Interconnection (OSI) model and TCP/IP. Although the OSI model is often used as the framework for discourse in this area, it is the TCP/IP protocol suite that is the basis for most commercially available interoperable products and that is the focus of Part Five of this book.

CHAPTER 1

DATA COMMUNICATIONS AND NETWORKING OVERVIEW

KEY POINTS

- The scope of this book is broad, covering three general areas: data communications, networking, and protocols; the first two are introduced in this chapter.
- Data communications deals with the transmission of signals in a reliable and efficient manner. Topics covered include signal transmission, transmission media, signal encoding, interfacing, data link control, and multiplexing.
- Networking deals with the technology and architecture of the communications networks used to interconnect communicating devices. This field is generally divided into the topics of local area networks (LANs) and wide area networks (WANs).

The 1970s and 1980s saw a merger of the fields of computer science and data communications that profoundly changed the technology, products, and companies of the now combined computer-communications industry. The computer-communications revolution has produced several remarkable facts:

- There is no fundamental difference between data processing (computers) and data communications (transmission and switching equipment).
- There are no fundamental differences among data, voice, and video communications.
- The distinction among single-processor computer, multiprocessor computer, local network, metropolitan network, and long-haul network has blurred.

One effect of these trends has been a growing overlap of the computer and communications industries, from component fabrication to system integration. Another result is the development of integrated systems that transmit and process all types of data and information. Both the technology and the technical standards organizations are driving toward integrated public systems that make virtually all data and information sources around the world easily and uniformly accessible.

This book aims to provide a unified view of the broad field of data and computer communications. The organization of the book reflects an attempt to break this massive subject into comprehensible parts and to build, piece by piece, a survey of the state of the art. This introductory chapter begins with a general model of communications. Then, a brief discussion introduces each of the Parts Two through Four of this book. Chapter 2 provides an overview to Part Five.

1.1 A COMMUNICATIONS MODEL

We begin our study with a simple model of communications, illustrated by the block diagram in Figure 1.1a.

The fundamental purpose of a communications system is the exchange of data between two parties. Figure 1.1b presents one particular example, which is communication between a workstation and a server over a public telephone network.

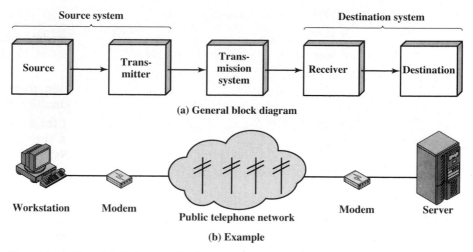

Figure 1.1 Simplified Communications Model

Another example is the exchange of voice signals between two telephones over the same network. The key elements of the model are as follows:

- **Source.** This device generates the data to be transmitted; examples are telephones and personal computers.
- **Transmitter:** Usually, the data generated by a source system are not transmitted directly in the form in which they were generated. Rather, a transmitter transforms and encodes the information in such a way as to produce electromagnetic signals that can be transmitted across some sort of transmission system. For example, a modem takes a digital bit stream from an attached device such as a personal computer and transforms that bit stream into an analog signal that can be handled by the telephone network.
- **Transmission system:** This can be a single transmission line or a complex network connecting source and destination.
- **Receiver:** The receiver accepts the signal from the transmission system and converts it into a form that can be handled by the destination device. For example, a modem will accept an analog signal coming from a network or transmission line and convert it into a digital bit stream.
- **Destination:** Takes the incoming data from the receiver.

This simple narrative conceals a wealth of technical complexity. To get some idea of the scope of this complexity, Table 1.1 lists some of the key tasks that must be performed in a data communications system. The list is somewhat arbitrary: Elements could be added; items on the list could be merged; and some items represent several tasks that are performed at different "levels" of the system. However, the list as it stands is suggestive of the scope of this book.

The first item, **transmission system utilization**, refers to the need to make efficient use of transmission facilities that are typically shared among a number of communicating devices. Various techniques (referred to as multiplexing) are used to

Table 1.1   Communications Tasks

Transmission system utilization	Addressing
Interfacing	Routing
Signal generation	Recovery
Synchronization	Message formatting
Exchange management	Security
Error detection and correction	Network management
Flow control	

allocate the total capacity of a transmission medium among a number of users. Congestion control techniques may be required to assure that the system is not overwhelmed by excessive demand for transmission services.

To communicate, a device must **interface** with the transmission system. All the forms of communication discussed in this book depend on the use of electromagnetic signals propagated over a transmission medium. Thus, once an interface is established, **signal generation** is required for communication. The properties of the signal, such as form and intensity, must be such that the signal is (1) capable of being propagated through the transmission system, and (2) interpretable as data at the receiver.

Not only must the signals be generated to conform to the requirements of the transmission system and receiver, but also there must be some form of **synchronization** between transmitter and receiver. The receiver must be able to determine when a signal begins to arrive and when it ends. It must also know the duration of each signal element.

Beyond the basic matter of deciding on the nature and timing of signals, there is a variety of requirements for communication between two parties that might be collected under the term **exchange management**. If data are to be exchanged in both directions over a period of time, the two parties must cooperate. For example, for two parties to engage in a telephone conversation, one party must dial the number of the other, causing signals to be generated that result in the ringing of the called phone. The called party completes a connection by lifting the receiver. For data processing devices, more will be needed than simply establishing a connection; certain conventions must be decided on. These conventions may include whether both devices may transmit simultaneously or must take turns, the amount of data to be sent at one time, the format of the data, and what to do if certain contingencies such as an error arise.

The next two items might have been included under exchange management, but they seem important enough to list separately. In all communications systems, there is a potential for error; transmitted signals are distorted to some extent before reaching their destination. **Error detection and correction** are required in circumstances where errors cannot be tolerated. This is usually the case with data processing systems. For example, in transferring a file from one computer to another, it is simply not acceptable for the contents of the file to be accidentally altered. **Flow control** is required to assure that the source does not overwhelm the destination by sending data faster than they can be processed and absorbed.

Next are the related but distinct concepts of **addressing** and **routing**. When more than two devices share a transmission facility, a source system must indicate the identity of the intended destination. The transmission system must assure that the destination system, and only that system, receives the data. Further, the transmission system may itself be a network through which various paths may be taken. A specific route through this network must be chosen.

Recovery is a concept distinct from that of error correction. Recovery techniques are needed in situations in which an information exchange, such as a database transaction or file transfer, is interrupted due to a fault somewhere in the system. The objective is either to be able to resume activity at the point of interruption or at least to restore the state of the systems involved to the condition prior to the beginning of the exchange.

Message formatting has to do with an agreement between two parties as to the form of the data to be exchanged or transmitted, such as the binary code for characters.

Frequently, it is important to provide some measure of **security** in a data communications system. The sender of data may wish to be assured that only the intended receiver actually receives the data. And the receiver of data may wish to be assured that the received data have not been altered in transit and that the data actually come from the purported sender.

Finally, a data communications facility is a complex system that cannot create or run itself. **Network management** capabilities are needed to configure the system, monitor its status, react to failures and overloads, and plan intelligently for future growth.

Thus, we have gone from the simple idea of data communication between source and destination to a rather formidable list of data communications tasks. In this book, we elaborate this list of tasks to describe and encompass the entire set of activities that can be classified under data and computer communications.

1.2 DATA COMMUNICATIONS

Following Part One, this book is organized into four parts. Part Two deals with the must fundamental aspects of the communications function, focusing on the transmission of signals in a reliable and efficient manner. For want of a better name, we have given Part Two the title "Data Communications," although that term arguably encompasses some or even all of the topics of Parts Three through Five.

To get some flavor for the focus of Part Two, Figure 1.2 provides a new perspective on the communications model of Figure 1.1a. We trace the details of this figure using electronic mail as an example.

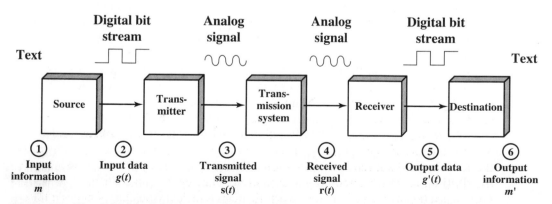

Figure 1.2 Simplified Data Communications Model

Suppose that the input device and transmitter are components of a personal computer. The user of the PC wishes to send a message m to another user. The user activates the electronic mail package on the PC and enters the message via the keyboard (input device). The character string is briefly buffered in main memory. We can view it as a sequence of bits (g) in memory. The personal computer is connected to some transmission medium, such as a local network or a telephone line, by an I/O device (transmitter), such as a local network transceiver or a modem. The input data are transferred to the transmitter as a sequence of voltage shifts $[g(t)]$ representing bits on some communications bus or cable. The transmitter is connected directly to the medium and converts the incoming stream $[g(t)]$ into a signal $[s(t)]$ suitable for transmission; specific alternatives will be described in Chapter 5.

The transmitted signal $s(t)$ presented to the medium is subject to a number of impairments, discussed in Chapter 3, before it reaches the receiver. Thus, the received signal $r(t)$ may differ from $s(t)$. The receiver will attempt to estimate the original $s(t)$, based on $r(t)$ and its knowledge of the medium, producing a sequence of bits $g'(t)$. These bits are sent to the output personal computer, where they are briefly buffered in memory as a block of bits (g'). In many cases, the destination system will attempt to determine if an error has occurred and, if so, cooperate with the source system to eventually obtain a complete, error-free block of data. These data are then presented to the user via an output device, such as a printer or screen. The message (m') as viewed by the user will usually be an exact copy of the original message (m).

Now consider a telephone conversation. In this case the input to the telephone is a message (m) in the form of sound waves. The sound waves are converted by the telephone into electrical signals of the same frequency. These signals are transmitted without modification over the telephone line. Hence the input signal $g(t)$ and the transmitted signal $s(t)$ are identical. The signal $s(t)$ will suffer some distortion over the medium, so that $r(t)$ will not be identical to $s(t)$. Nevertheless, the signal $r(t)$ is converted back into a sound wave with no attempt at correction or improvement of signal quality. Thus, m' is not an exact replica of m. However, the received sound message is generally comprehensible to the listener.

The discussion so far does not touch on other key aspects of data communications, including data link control techniques for controlling the flow of data and detecting and correcting errors, and multiplexing techniques for transmission efficiency. All of these topics are explored in Part Two.

1.3   DATA COMMUNICATION NETWORKING

It is often impractical for two communicating devices to be directly, point-to-point connected. This is so for one (or both) of the following contingencies:

- The devices are very far apart. It would be inordinately expensive, for example, to string a dedicated link between two devices thousands of kilometers apart.
- There is a set of devices, each of which may require a link to many of the others at various times. Examples are all of the telephones in the world and all of the terminals and computers owned by a single organization. Except for the case of a very few devices, it is impractical to provide a dedicated wire between each pair of devices.

The solution to this problem is to attach each device to a communication network. There are two major categories into which communications networks are traditionally classified: wide area networks (WANs) and local area networks (LANs). The distinction between the two, both in terms of technology and application, has become somewhat blurred in recent years, but it remains a useful way of organizing the discussion.

Wide Area Networks

Wide area networks generally cover a large geographical area, require the crossing of public right-of-ways, and rely at least in part on circuits provided by a common carrier. Typically, a WAN consists of a number of interconnected switching nodes. A transmission from any one device is routed through these internal nodes to the specified destination device. These nodes (including the boundary nodes) are not concerned with the content of the data; rather, their purpose is to provide a switching facility that will move the data from node to node until they reach their destination.

Traditionally, WANs have been implemented using one of two technologies: circuit switching and packet switching. More recently, frame relay and ATM networks have assumed major roles.

Circuit Switching

In a circuit-switching network, a dedicated communications path is established between two stations through the nodes of the network. That path is a connected sequence of physical links between nodes. On each link, a logical channel is dedicated to the connection. Data generated by the source station are transmitted along the dedicated path as rapidly as possible. At each node, incoming data are routed or switched to the appropriate outgoing channel without delay. The most common example of circuit switching is the telephone network.

Packet Switching

A quite different approach is used in a packet-switching network. In this case, it is not necessary to dedicate transmission capacity along a path through the network. Rather, data are sent out in a sequence of small chunks, called packets. Each packet is passed through the network from node to node along some path leading from source to destination. At each node, the entire packet is received, stored briefly, and then transmitted to the next node. Packet-switching networks are commonly used for terminal-to-computer and computer-to-computer communications.

Frame Relay

Packet switching was developed at a time when digital long-distance transmission facilities exhibited a relatively high error rate compared to today's facilities. As a result, there is a considerable amount of overhead built into packet-switching schemes to compensate for errors. The overhead includes additional bits added to each packet to introduce redundancy and additional processing at the end stations and the intermediate switching nodes to detect and recover from errors.

With modern high-speed telecommunications systems, this overhead is unnecessary and counterproductive. It is unnecessary because the rate of errors has been dramatically lowered and any remaining errors can easily be caught in the end systems by logic that operates above the level of the packet-switching logic. It is counterproductive because the overhead involved soaks up a significant fraction of the high capacity provided by the network.

Frame relay was developed to take advantage of these high data rates and low error rates. Whereas the original packet-switching networks were designed with a data rate to the end user of about 64 kbps, frame relay networks are designed to operate efficiently at user data rates of up to 2 Mbps. The key to achieving these high data rates is to strip out most of the overhead involved with error control.

ATM

Asynchronous transfer mode (ATM), sometimes referred to as cell relay, is a culmination of developments in circuit switching and packet switching. ATM can be viewed as an evolution from frame relay. The most obvious difference between frame relay and ATM is that frame relay uses variable-length packets, called frames, and ATM uses fixed-length packets, called cells. As with frame relay, ATM provides little overhead for error control, depending on the inherent reliability of the transmission system and on higher layers of logic in the end systems to catch and correct errors. By using a fixed packet length, the processing overhead is reduced even further for ATM compared to frame relay. The result is that ATM is designed to work in the range of 10s and 100s of Mbps, and in the Gbps range.

ATM can also be viewed as an evolution from circuit switching. With circuit switching, only fixed-data-rate circuits are available to the end system. ATM allows the definition of multiple virtual channels with data rates that are dynamically defined at the time the virtual channel is created. By using small, fixed-size cells, ATM is so efficient that it can offer a constant-data-rate channel even though it is using a packet-switching technique. Thus, ATM extends circuit switching to allow multiple channels with the data rate on each channel dynamically set on demand.

Local Area Networks

As with WANs, a LAN is a communications network that interconnects a variety of devices and provides a means for information exchange among those devices. There are several key distinctions between LANs and WANs:

1. The scope of the LAN is small, typically a single building or a cluster of buildings. This difference in geographic scope leads to different technical solutions, as we shall see.
2. It is usually the case that the LAN is owned by the same organization that owns the attached devices. For WANs, this is less often the case, or at least a significant fraction of the network assets are not owned. This has two implications. First, care must be taken in the choice of LAN, because there may be a substantial capital investment (compared to dial-up or leased charges for WANs) for both purchase and maintenance. Second, the network management responsibility for a LAN falls solely on the user.
3. The internal data rates of LANs are typically much greater than those of WANs.

LANs come in a number of different configurations. The most common are switched LANs and wireless LANs. The most common switched LAN is a switched Ethernet LAN, which may consist of a single switch with a number of attached devices, or a number of interconnected switches. Two other prominent examples are ATM LANs, which simply use an ATM network in a local area, and Fibre Channel. Wireless LANs use a variety of wireless transmission technologies and organizations. LANs are examined in depth in Part Four.

Wireless Networks

As was just mentioned, wireless LANs are common, being widely used in business environments. Wireless technology is also common for both wide area voice and data networks. Wireless networks provide advantages in the areas of mobility and ease of installation and configuration. Chapters 14 and 17 deal with wireless WANs and LANs, respectively.

Metropolitan Area Networks

As the name suggests, a MAN occupies a middle ground between LANs and WANs. Interest in MANs has come about as a result of a recognition that the traditional point-to-point and switched network techniques used in WANs may be inadequate for the growing needs of organizations. While frame relay and ATM promise to meet a wide range of high-speed needs, there is a requirement now for both private and public networks that provide high capacity at low costs over a large area. A number of approaches have been implemented, including wireless networks and metropolitan extensions to Ethernet.

The primary market for MANs is the customer that has high-capacity needs in a metropolitan area. A MAN is intended to provide the required capacity at lower cost and greater efficiency than obtaining an equivalent service from the local telephone company.

1.4 AN EXAMPLE CONFIGURATION

To give some feel for the scope of concerns of Parts Two through Four, Figure 1.3 illustrates some of the typical communications and network elements in use today. In the upper left-hand portion of the figure, we see an individual residential user connected to an Internet service provider (ISP) through some sort of subscriber connection. Common examples of such a connection are the public telephone network, for which the user requires a dial-up modem (e.g., a 56-kbps modem); a digital subscriber line (DSL), which provides a high-speed link over telephone lines and requires a special DSL modem; and a cable TV facility, which requires a cable modem. In each case, there are separate issues concerning signal encoding, error control, and the internal structure of the subscriber network.

Typically, an ISP will consist of a number of interconnected servers (only a single server is shown) connected to the Internet through a high-speed link. One example of such a link is a SONET (synchronous optical network) line, described in Chapter 8. The Internet consists of a number of interconnected routers that span the globe. The routers forward packets of data from source to destination through the Internet.

The lower portion of Figure 1.3 shows a LAN implemented using a single Ethernet switch. This is a common configuration at a small business or other small

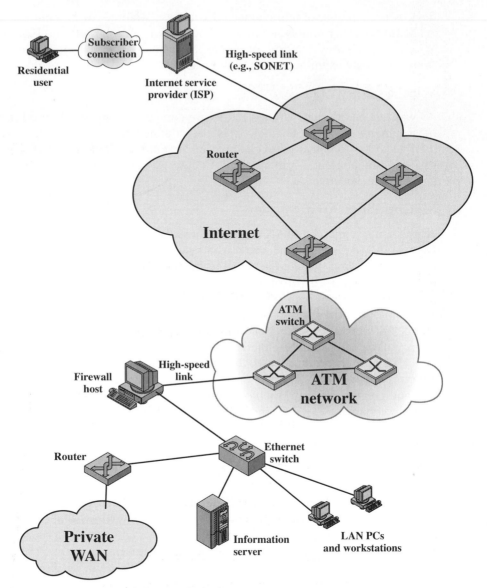

Figure 1.3 A Networking Configuration

organization. The LAN is connected to the Internet through a firewall host that provides security services. In this example the firewall connects to the Internet through
an ATM network. There is also a router off of the LAN hooked into a private WAN,
which might be a private ATM or frame relay network.

A variety of design issues, such as signal encoding and error control, relate to the
links between adjacent elements, such as between routers on the Internet or between
switches in the ATM network, or between a subscriber and an ISP. The internal structure
of the various networks (telephone, ATM, Ethernet) raises additional issues. We will be
occupied in Parts Two through Four with the design features suggested by Figure 1.3.

CHAPTER 2

PROTOCOL ARCHITECTURE

KEY POINTS

- A protocol architecture is the layered structure of hardware and software that supports the exchange of data between systems and supports distributed applications, such as electronic mail and file transfer.
- At each layer of a protocol architecture, one or more common protocols are implemented in communicating systems. Each protocol provides a set of rules for the exchange of data between systems.
- The most widely used protocol architecture is the TCP/IP protocol suite, which consists of the following layers: physical, network access, internet, transport, and application.
- Another important protocol architecture is the seven-layer Open Systems Interconnection (OSI) model.

This chapter provides a context for the detailed material that follows. It shows how the concepts of Parts Two through Five fit into the broader area of computer networks and computer communications. This chapter may be read in its proper sequence or it may be deferred until the beginning of Part Three, Four, or Five.[1]

We begin this chapter by introducing the concept of a layered protocol architecture and looking at a simple example. Next, the chapter introduces the Open Systems Interconnection (OSI) reference model. OSI is a standardized architecture that is often used to describe communications functions but that is now rarely implemented. We then examine the most important protocol architecture, the TCP/IP protocol suite. TCP/IP is an Internet-based concept and is the framework for developing a complete range of computer communications standards. Virtually all computer vendors now provide support for this architecture.

2.1 THE NEED FOR A PROTOCOL ARCHITECTURE

When computers, terminals, and/or other data processing devices exchange data, the procedures involved can be quite complex. Consider, for example, the transfer of a file between two computers. There must be a data path between the two computers, either directly or via a communication network. But more is needed. Typical tasks to be performed include the following:

1. The source system must either activate the direct data communication path or inform the communication network of the identity of the desired destination system.

2. The source system must ascertain that the destination system is prepared to receive data.

3. The file transfer application on the source system must ascertain that the file management program on the destination system is prepared to accept and store the file for this particular user.

---

[1] The reader may find it helpful just to skim this chapter on a first reading and then reread it more carefully just before embarking on Part Five.

4. If the file formats used on the two systems are incompatible, one or the other system must perform a format translation function.

It is clear that there must be a high degree of cooperation between the two computer systems. Instead of implementing the logic for this as a single module, the task is broken up into subtasks, each of which is implemented separately. In a protocol architecture, the modules are arranged in a vertical stack. Each layer in the stack performs a related subset of the functions required to communicate with another system. It relies on the next lower layer to perform more primitive functions and to conceal the details of those functions. It provides services to the next higher layer. Ideally, layers should be defined so that changes in one layer do not require changes in other layers.

Of course, it takes two to communicate, so the same set of layered functions must exist in two systems. Communication is achieved by having the corresponding, or **peer**, layers in two systems communicate. The peer layers communicate by means of formatted blocks of data that obey a set of rules or conventions known as a **protocol**. The key features of a protocol are as follows:

- **Syntax:** Concerns the format of the data blocks
- **Semantics:** Includes control information for coordination and error handling
- **Timing:** Includes speed matching and sequencing

Appendix 2A provides a specific example of a protocol, the Internet standard Trivial File Transfer Protocol (TFTP).

2.2 A SIMPLE PROTOCOL ARCHITECTURE

Having introduced the concept of a protocol, we can now introduce the concept of a protocol architecture. As an example, Figure 2.1 suggests the way in which a file transfer facility could be implemented. Three modules are used. A file transfer module could perform tasks 3 and 4 in the preceding list. The two modules on the two systems exchange files and commands. However, rather than requiring the file transfer module to deal with the details of actually transferring data and commands, the file transfer modules each rely on a communications service module. This module is responsible for making sure that the file transfer commands and data are reliably exchanged between systems. Among other things, this module would perform task 2. We observe that the nature of the exchange between systems is independent of the nature of the network that interconnects them. Therefore, rather than building details of the network interface into the communications service module, it makes sense to have a third module, a network access module, that performs task 1 by interacting with the network.

To summarize, the file transfer module contains all of the logic that is unique to the file transfer application, such as transmitting passwords, file commands, and file records. There is a need to transmit these files and commands reliably. However, the same sorts of reliability requirements are relevant to a variety of applications

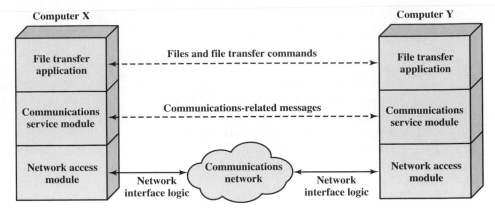

Figure 2.1   A Simplified Architecture for File Trasfer

(e.g., electronic mail, document transfer). Therefore, a separate communications service module that can be used by a variety of applications meets these requirements. The communications service module is concerned with assuring that the two computer systems are active and ready for data transfer and for keeping track of the data that are being exchanged to assure delivery. However, these tasks are independent of the type of network that is being used. Therefore, the logic for actually dealing with the network is placed in a separate network access module. That way, if the network to be used is changed, only the network access module is affected.

Thus, instead of a single module for performing communications, there is a structured set of modules that implements the communications function. That structure is referred to as a **protocol architecture**. An analogy might be useful at this point. Suppose an executive in office X wishes to send a document to an executive in office Y. The executive in X prepares the document and perhaps attaches a note. This corresponds to the actions of the file transfer application in Figure 2.1. Then the executive in X hands the document to a secretary or administrative assistant (AA). The AA in X puts the document in an envelope and puts Y's address and X's return address on the outside. Perhaps the envelope is also marked "confidential." The AA's actions correspond to the communications service module in Figure 2.1. The AA in X then gives the package to the shipping department. Someone in the shipping department decides how to send the package: mail, UPS, or express courier. The shipping department attaches the appropriate postage or shipping documents to the package and ships it out. The shipping department corresponds to the network access module of Figure 2.1. When the package arrives at Y, a similar layered set of actions occurs. The shipping department at Y receives the package and delivers it to the appropriate AA or secretary based on the name on the package. The AA opens the package and hands the enclosed document to the executive to whom it is addressed.

In the remainder of this section, we generalize the preceding example to present a simplified protocol architecture. Following that, we look at more complex, real-world examples: OSI and TCP/IP.

A Three-Layer Model

In very general terms, communications can be said to involve three agents: applications, computers, and networks. Applications execute on computers that typically support multiple simultaneous applications. Computers are connected to networks, and the data to be exchanged are transferred by the network from one computer to another. Thus, the transfer of data from one application to another involves first getting the data to the computer in which the application resides and then getting it to the intended application within the computer.

With these concepts in mind, it appears natural to organize the communication task into three relatively independent layers: network access layer, transport layer, and application layer.

The **network access layer** is concerned with the exchange of data between a computer and the network to which it is attached. The sending computer must provide the network with the address of the destination computer, so that the network may route the data to the appropriate destination. The sending computer may wish to invoke certain services, such as priority, that might be provided by the network. The specific software used at this layer depends on the type of network to be used; different standards have been developed for circuit switching, packet switching, LANs, and others. Thus, it makes sense to separate those functions having to do with network access into a separate layer. By doing this, the remainder of the communications software, above the network access layer, need not be concerned about the specifics of the network to be used. The same higher-layer software should function properly regardless of the particular network to which the computer is attached.

Regardless of the nature of the applications that are exchanging data, there is usually a requirement that data be exchanged reliably. That is, we would like to be assured that all of the data arrive at the destination application and that the data arrive in the same order in which they were sent. As we shall see, the mechanisms for providing reliability are essentially independent of the nature of the applications. Thus, it makes sense to collect those mechanisms in a common layer shared by all applications; this is referred to as the **transport layer**.

Finally, the **application layer** contains the logic needed to support the various user applications. For each different type of application, such as file transfer, a separate module is needed that is peculiar to that application.

Figures 2.2 and 2.3 illustrate this simple architecture. Figure 2.2 shows three computers connected to a network. Each computer contains software at the network access and transport layers and software at the application layer for one or more applications. For successful communication, every entity in the overall system must have a unique address. Actually, two levels of addressing are needed. Each computer on the network must have a unique network address; this allows the network to deliver data to the proper computer. Each application on a computer must have an address that is unique within that computer; this allows the transport layer to support multiple applications at each computer. These latter addresses are known as **service access points** (SAPs), or **ports**, connoting the fact that each application is individually accessing the services of the transport layer.

Figure 2.3 indicates that modules at the same level on different computers communicate with each other by means of a protocol. Let us trace a simple operation. Suppose that an application, associated with SAP 1 at computer X, wishes

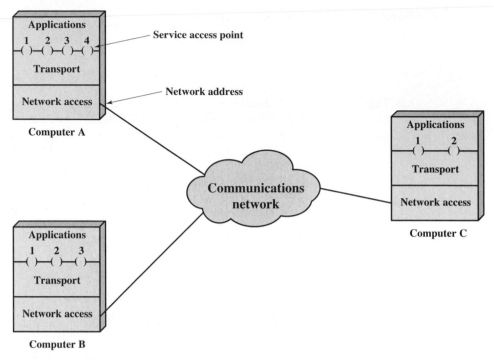

Figure 2.2   Protocol Architectures and Networks

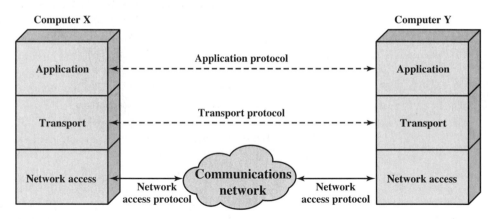

Figure 2.3   Protocols in a Simplified Architecture

to send a message to another application, associated with SAP 2 at computer Y. The application at X hands the message over to its transport layer with instructions to send it to SAP 2 on computer Y. The transport layer hands the message over to the network access layer, which instructs the network to send the message to computer Y. Note that the network need not be told the identity of the destination service access point. All that it needs to know is that the data are intended for computer Y.

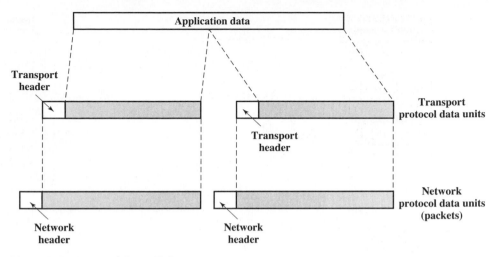

Figure 2.4 Protocol Data Units

To control this operation, control information, as well as user data, must be transmitted, as suggested in Figure 2.4. Let us say that the sending application generates a block of data and passes this to the transport layer. The transport layer may break this block into two smaller pieces to make it more manageable. To each of these pieces the transport layer appends a transport header, containing protocol control information. The combination of data from the next higher layer and control information is known as a **protocol data unit** (PDU); in this case, it is referred to as a **transport PDU**. The header in each transport PDU contains control information to be used by the peer transport protocol at computer B. Examples of items that may be stored in this header include the following:

- **Destination SAP:** When the destination transport layer receives the transport PDU, it must know to whom the data are to be delivered.
- **Sequence number:** Because the transport protocol is sending a sequence of PDUs, it numbers them sequentially so that if they arrive out of order, the destination transport entity may reorder them.
- **Error-detection code:** The sending transport entity may include a code that is a function of the contents of the remainder of the PDU. The receiving transport protocol performs the same calculation and compares the result with the incoming code. A discrepancy results if there has been some error in transmission. In that case, the receiver can discard the PDU and take corrective action.

The next step is for the transport layer to hand each PDU over to the network layer, with instructions to transmit it to the destination computer. To satisfy this request, the network access protocol must present the data to the network with a request for transmission. As before, this operation requires the use of control information. In this case, the network access protocol appends a network access header

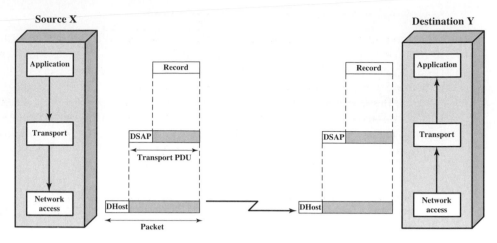

Figure 2.5 Operation of a Protocol Architecture

to the data it receives from the transport layer, creating a network access PDU. Examples of the items that may be stored in the header include the following:

- **Destination computer address:** The network must know to whom (which computer on the network) the data are to be delivered.
- **Facilities requests:** The network access protocol might want the network to make use of certain facilities, such as priority.

Figure 2.5 puts all of these concepts together, showing the interaction between modules to transfer one block of data. Let us say that the file transfer module in computer X is transferring a file one record at a time to computer Y. Each record is handed over to the transport layer module. We can picture this action as being in the form of a command or procedure call. The arguments of this procedure call include the destination computer address, the destination service access point, and the record. The transport layer appends the destination service access point and other control information to the record to create a transport PDU. This is then handed down to the network access layer by another procedure call. In this case, the arguments for the command are the destination computer address and the transport PDU. The network access layer uses this information to construct a network PDU. The transport PDU is the data field of the network PDU, and the network PDU header includes information concerning the source and destination computer addresses. Note that the transport header is not "visible" at the network access layer; the network access layer is not concerned with the contents of the transport PDU.

The network accepts the network PDU from X and delivers it to Y. The network access module in Y receives the PDU, strips off the header, and transfers the enclosed transport PDU to Y's transport layer module. The transport layer examines the transport PDU header and, on the basis of the SAP field in the header, delivers the enclosed record to the appropriate application, in this case the file transfer module in Y.

Standardized Protocol Architectures

When communication is desired among computers from different vendors, the software development effort can be a nightmare. Different vendors use different data formats and data exchange protocols. Even within one vendor's product line, different model computers may communicate in unique ways.

As the use of computer communications and computer networking proliferates, a one-at-a-time special-purpose approach to communications software development is too costly to be acceptable. The only alternative is for computer vendors to adopt and implement a common set of conventions. For this to happen, standards are needed. Such standards would have two benefits:

- Vendors feel encouraged to implement the standards because of an expectation that, because of wide usage of the standards, their products would be less marketable without them.
- Customers are in a position to require that any vendor wishing to propose equipment to them implement the standards.

Two protocol architectures have served as the basis for the development of interoperable protocol standards: the TCP/IP protocol suite and the OSI reference model. TCP/IP is by far the most widely used interoperable architecture. OSI, though well known, has never lived up to its early promise. There is also a widely used proprietary scheme: IBM's System Network Architecture (SNA). The remainder of this chapter looks at OSI and TCP/IP.

2.3 OSI

Standards are needed to promote interoperability among vendor equipment and to encourage economies of scale. Because of the complexity of the communications task, no single standard will suffice. Rather, the functions should be broken down into more manageable parts and organized as a communications architecture. The architecture would then form the framework for standardization. This line of reasoning led the International Organization for Standardization (ISO) in 1977 to establish a subcommittee to develop such an architecture. The result was the Open Systems Interconnection (OSI) reference model. Although the essential elements of the model were in place quickly, the final ISO standard, ISO 7498, was not published until 1984. A technically compatible version was issued by CCITT (now ITU-T) as X.200.

The Model

A widely accepted structuring technique, and the one chosen by ISO, is layering. The communications functions are partitioned into a hierarchical set of layers. Each layer performs a related subset of the functions required to communicate with another system. It relies on the next lower layer to perform more primitive functions and to conceal the details of those functions. It provides services to the next higher layer. Ideally, the layers should be defined so that changes in one layer do not require changes in the other layers. Thus, we have decomposed one problem into a number of more manageable subproblems.

The task of ISO was to define a set of layers and the services performed by each layer. The partitioning should group functions logically and should have enough layers to make each layer manageably small, but should not have so many layers that the processing overhead imposed by the collection of layers is burdensome. The principles that guided the design effort are summarized in Table 2.1. The resulting reference model has seven layers, which are listed with a brief definition in Figure 2.6. Table 2.2 provides ISO's justification for the selection of these layers.

Figure 2.7 illustrates the OSI architecture. Each system contains the seven layers. Communication is between applications in the two computers, labeled application X and application Y in the figure. If application X wishes to send a message to application Y, it invokes the application layer (layer 7). Layer 7 establishes a peer relationship with layer 7 of the target computer, using a layer-7 protocol (application protocol). This protocol requires services from layer 6, so the two layer-6 entities use

Table 2.1 Principles Used in Defining the OSI Layers (X.200)

1. Do not create so many layers as to make the system engineering task of describing and integrating the layers more difficult than necessary.

2. Create a boundary at a point where the description of services can be small and the number of interactions across the boundary are minimized.

3. Create separate layers to handle functions that are manifestly different in the process performed or the technology involved.

4. Collect similar functions into the same layer.

5. Select boundaries at a point which past experience has demonstrated to be successful.

6. Create a layer of easily localized functions so that the layer could be totally redesigned and its protocols changed in a major way to take advantage of new advances in architecture, hardware, or software technology without changing the services expected from and provided to the adjacent layers.

7. Create a boundary where it may be useful at some point in time to have the corresponding interface standardized.

8. Create a layer where there is a need for a different level of abstraction in the handling of data, for example morphology, syntax, semantic.

9. Allow changes of functions or protocols to be made within a layer without affecting other layers.

10. Create for each layer boundaries with its upper and lower layer only.

   Similar principles have been applied to sublayering:

11. Create further subgrouping and organization of functions to form sublayers within a layer in cases where distinct communication services need it.

12. Create, where needed, two or more sublayers with a common, and therefore minimal functionality to allow interface operation with adjacent layers.

13. Allow bypassing of sublayers.

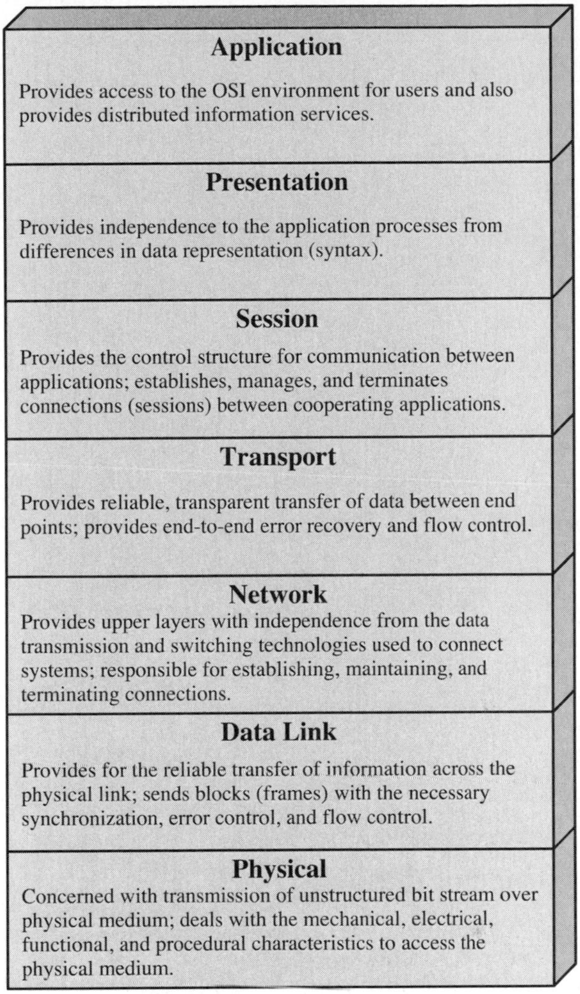

Application
Provides access to the OSI environment for users and also provides distributed information services.

Presentation
Provides independence to the application processes from differences in data representation (syntax).

Session
Provides the control structure for communication between applications; establishes, manages, and terminates connections (sessions) between cooperating applications.

Transport
Provides reliable, transparent transfer of data between end points; provides end-to-end error recovery and flow control.

Network
Provides upper layers with independence from the data transmission and switching technologies used to connect systems; responsible for establishing, maintaining, and terminating connections.

Data Link
Provides for the reliable transfer of information across the physical link; sends blocks (frames) with the necessary synchronization, error control, and flow control.

Physical
Concerned with transmission of unstructured bit stream over physical medium; deals with the mechanical, electrical, functional, and procedural characteristics to access the physical medium.

Figure 2.6 The OSI Layers

a protocol of their own, and so on down to the physical layer, which actually transmits bits over a transmission medium.

Note that there is no direct communication between peer layers except at the physical layer. That is, above the physical layer, each protocol entity sends data down to the next lower layer to get the data across to its peer entity. Even at the physical layer, the OSI model does not stipulate that two systems be directly connected. For example, a packet-switched or circuit-switched network may be used to provide the communication link.

Figure 2.7 also highlights the use of protocol data units (PDUs) within the OSI architecture. First, consider the most common way in which protocols are realized. When application X has a message to send to application Y, it transfers those data to an application entity in the application layer. A header is appended to the data that

Table 2.2 Justification of the OSI Layers (X.200)

1. It is essential that the architecture permits usage of a realistic variety of physical media for interconnection with different control procedures (for example, V.24, V.25, etc.). Application of principles 3, 5, and 8 (Table 2.1) leads to identification of a **physical layer** as the lowest layer in the architecture.

2. Some physical communication media (for example, telephone line) require specific techniques to be used in order to transmit data between systems despite a relatively high error rate (i.e., an error rate not acceptable for the great majority of applications). These specific techniques are used in data link control procedures, which have been studied and standardized for a number of years. It must also be recognized that new physical communication media (for example, fiber optics) will require different data link control procedures. Application of principles 3, 5, and 8 leads to identification of a **data link layer** on top of the physical layer in the architecture.

3. In the open systems architecture, some open systems will act as the final destination of data. Some open systems may act only as intermediate nodes (forwarding data to other systems). Application of principles 3, 5, and 7 leads to identification of a **network layer** on top of the data link layer. Network-oriented protocols such as routing, for example, will be grouped in this layer. Thus, the network layer will provide a connection path (network connection) between a pair of transport entities, including the case where intermediate nodes are involved.

4. Control of data transportation from source end open system to destination end open system (which is not performed in intermediate nodes) is the last function to be performed in order to provide the totality of the transport service. Thus, the upper layer in the transport service part of the architecture is the **transport layer**, on top of the network layer. This transport layer relieves higher-layer entities from any concern with the transportation of data between them.

5. There is a need to organize and synchronize dialogue and to manage the exchange of data. Application of principles 3 and 4 leads to the identification of a **session layer** on top of the transport layer.

6. The remaining set of general interest functions are those related to representation and manipulation of structured data for the benefit of application programs. Application of principles 3 and 4 leads to the identification of a **presentation layer** on top of the session layer.

7. Finally, there are applications consisting of application processes that perform information processing. An aspect of these application processes and the protocols by which they communicate comprise the **application layer** as the highest layer of the architecture.

contains the required information for the peer layer 7 protocol (encapsulation). The original data plus the header are now passed as a unit to layer 6. The presentation entity treats the whole unit as data and appends its own header (a second encapsulation). This process continues down through layer 2, which generally adds both a header and a trailer. This layer 2 unit, called a frame, is then passed onto the transmission medium by the physical layer. When the frame is received by the target system, the reverse process occurs. As the data ascend, each layer strips off the outermost header, acts on the protocol information contained therein, and passes the remainder up to the next layer.

At each stage of the process, a layer may segment the data unit it receives from the next higher layer into several parts, to accommodate its own requirements. These data units must then be reassembled by the corresponding peer layer before being passed up.

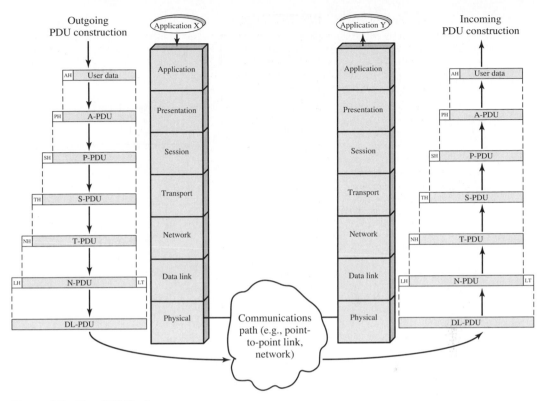

Figure 2.7   The OSI Environment

Standardization within the OSI Framework[2]

The principal motivation for the development of the OSI model was to provide a framework for standardization. Within the model, one or more protocol standards can be developed at each layer. The model defines in general terms the functions to be performed at that layer and facilitates the standards-making process in two ways:

- Because the functions of each layer are well defined, standards can be developed independently and simultaneously for each layer. This speeds up the standards-making process.
- Because the boundaries between layers are well defined, changes in standards in one layer need not affect already existing software in another layer. This makes it easier to introduce new standards.

---

[2] The concepts introduced in this subsection apply as well to the TCP/IP architecture.

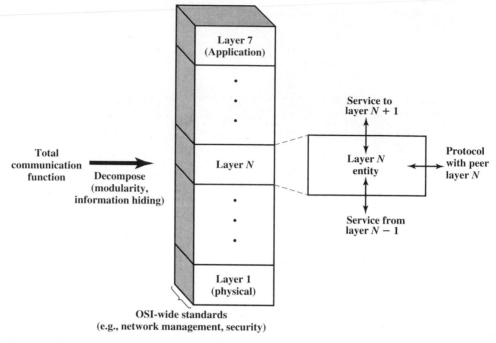

Figure 2.8 The OSI Architecture as a Framework for Standardization

Figure 2.8 illustrates the use of the OSI model as such a framework. The overall communications function is decomposed into seven distinct layers, using the principles outlined in Table 2.1. These principles essentially amount to using modular design. That is, the overall function is broken up into a number of modules, making the interfaces between modules as simple as possible. In addition, the design principle of information hiding is used: Lower layers are concerned with greater levels of detail; upper layers are independent of these details. Each layer provides services to the next higher layer and implements a protocol to the peer layer in other systems.

Figure 2.9 shows more specifically the nature of the standardization required at each layer. Three elements are key:

- **Protocol specification:** Two entities at the same layer in different systems cooperate and interact by means of a protocol. Because two different open systems are involved, the protocol must be specified precisely. This includes the format of the protocol data units exchanged, the semantics of all fields, and the allowable sequence of PDUs.

- **Service definition:** In addition to the protocol or protocols that operate at a given layer, standards are needed for the services that each layer provides to the next higher layer. Typically, the definition of services is equivalent to a functional description that defines what services are provided, but not how the services are to be provided.

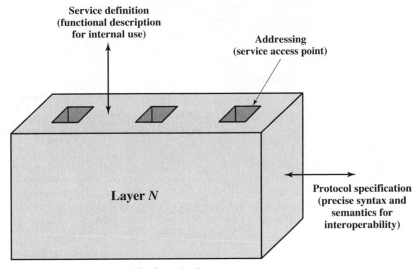

Figure 2.9 Layer-Specific Standards

- **Addressing:** Each layer provides services to entities at the next higher layer. These entities are referenced by means of a service access point (SAP). Thus, a network service access point (NSAP) indicates a transport entity that is a user of the network service.

The need to provide a precise protocol specification for open systems is self-evident. The other two items listed warrant further comment. With respect to service definitions, the motivation for providing only a functional definition is as follows. First, the interaction between two adjacent layers takes place within the confines of a single open system and is not the concern of any other open system. Thus, as long as peer layers in different systems provide the same services to their next higher layers, the details of how the services are provided may differ from one system to another without loss of interoperability. Second, it will usually be the case that adjacent layers are implemented on the same processor. In that case, we would like to leave the system programmer free to exploit the hardware and operating system to provide an interface that is as efficient as possible.

With respect to addressing, the use of an address mechanism at each layer, implemented as a service access point, allows each layer to multiplex multiple users from the next higher layer. Multiplexing may not occur at each layer, but the model allows for that possibility.

Service Primitives and Parameters

The services between adjacent layers in the OSI architecture are expressed in terms of primitives and parameters. A primitive specifies the function to be performed, and the parameters are used to pass data and control information. The actual form of a primitive is implementation dependent. An example is a procedure call.

Table 2.3 Service Primitive Types

REQUEST	A primitive issued by a service user to invoke some service and to pass the parameters needed to specify fully the requested service
INDICATION	A primitive issued by a service provider either to 1. indicate that a procedure has been invoked by the peer service user on the connection and to provide the associated parameters, or 2. notify the service user of a provider-initiated action
RESPONSE	A primitive issued by a service user to acknowledge or complete some procedure previously invoked by an indication to that user
CONFIRM	A primitive issued by a service provider to acknowledge or complete some procedure previously invoked by a request by the service user

Four types of primitives are used in standards to define the interaction between adjacent layers in the architecture (X.210). These are defined in Table 2.3. The layout of Figure 2.10a suggests the time ordering of these events. For example, consider the transfer of data from an (N) entity to a peer (N) entity in another system. The following steps occur:

1. The source (N) entity invokes its $(N - 1)$ entity with a *request* primitive. Associated with the primitive are the parameters needed, such as the data to be transmitted and the destination address.
2. The source $(N - 1)$ entity prepares an $(N - 1)$ PDU to be sent to its peer $(N - 1)$ entity.
3. The destination $(N - 1)$ entity delivers the data to the appropriate destination (N) entity via an *indication* primitive, which includes the data and source address as parameters.
4. If an acknowledgment is called for, the destination (N) entity issues a *response* primitive to its $(N - 1)$ entity.

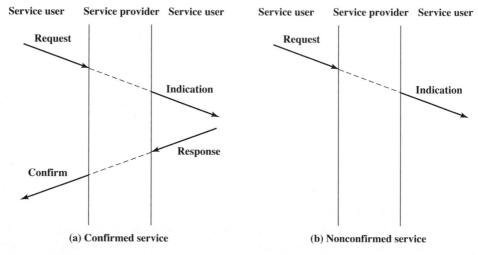

(a) Confirmed service   (b) Nonconfirmed service

Figure 2.10 Time Sequence Diagrams for Service Primitives

5. The $(N - 1)$ entity conveys the acknowledgment in an $(N - 1)$ PDU.

6. The acknowledgment is delivered to the (N) entity as a *confirm* primitive.

This sequence of events is referred to as a **confirmed service**, as the initiator receives confirmation that the requested service has had the desired effect at the other end. If only request and indication primitives are involved (corresponding to steps 1 through 3), then the service dialogue is a **nonconfirmed service**; the initiator receives no confirmation that the requested action has taken place (Figure 2.10b).

The OSI Layers

In this section we discuss briefly each of the layers and, where appropriate, give examples of standards for protocols at those layers.

Physical Layer

The physical layer covers the physical interface between devices and the rules by which bits are passed from one to another. The physical layer has four important characteristics:

- **Mechanical:** Relates to the physical properties of the interface to a transmission medium. Typically, the specification is of a pluggable connector that joins one or more signal conductors, called circuits.
- **Electrical:** Relates to the representation of bits (e.g., in terms of voltage levels) and the data transmission rate of bits.
- **Functional:** Specifies the functions performed by individual circuits of the physical interface between a system and the transmission medium.
- **Procedural:** Specifies the sequence of events by which bit streams are exchanged across the physical medium.

Physical layer protocols are discussed in some detail in Chapter 6. Examples of standards at this layer are EIA-232-F and portions of wireless and LAN standards.

Data Link Layer

Whereas the physical layer provides only a raw bit stream service, the data link layer attempts to make the physical link reliable and provides the means to activate, maintain, and deactivate the link. The principal service provided by the data link layer to higher layers is that of error detection and control. Thus, with a fully functional data link layer protocol, the next higher layer may assume error-free transmission over the link. However, if communication is between two systems that are not directly connected, the connection will comprise a number of data links in tandem, each functioning independently. Thus, the higher layers are not relieved of an error control responsibility.

Chapter 7 is devoted to data link protocols. Examples of standards at this layer are HDLC and LLC.

Network Layer

The network layer provides for the transfer of information between end systems across some sort of communications network. It relieves higher layers of the need to know anything about the underlying data transmission and switching technologies used to connect systems. At this layer, the computer system engages in a dialogue with the network to specify the destination address and to request certain network facilities, such as priority.

There is a spectrum of possibilities for intervening communications facilities to be managed by the network layer. At one extreme, there is a direct point-to-point link between stations. In this case, there may be no need for a network layer because the data link layer can perform the necessary function of managing the link.

Next, the systems could be connected across a single network, such as a circuit-switching or packet-switching network. As an example, the packet level of the X.25 standard is a network layer standard for this situation. Figure 2.11 shows how the OSI architecture accommodates the presence of a network. The lower three layers are concerned with attaching to and communicating with the network. The packets that are created by the end system pass through one or more network nodes that act as relays between the two end systems. The network nodes implement layers 1 through 3 of the architecture. In the figure, two end systems are connected through a single network node. Layer 3 in the node performs a switching and routing function. Within the node, there are two data link layers and two physical layers, corresponding to the links to the two end systems. Each data link (and physical) layer operates independently to provide service to the network layer over its respective link. The upper four layers are "end-to-end" protocols between the attached end systems.

At the other extreme, two end systems might wish to communicate but are not even connected to the same network. Rather, they are connected to networks that,

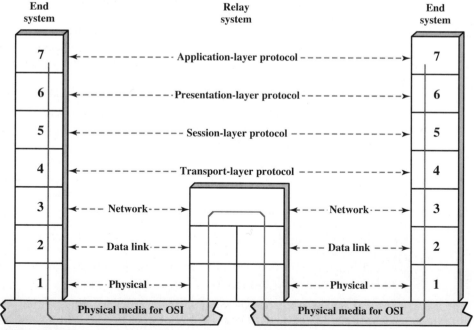

Figure 2.11   The Use of a Relay

directly or indirectly, are connected to each other. This case requires the use of some sort of internetworking technique; we explore this approach in Chapter 18.

Transport Layer

The transport layer provides a mechanism for the exchange of data between end systems. The connection-oriented transport service ensures that data are delivered error free, in sequence, with no losses or duplications. The transport layer may also be concerned with optimizing the use of network services and providing a requested quality of service to session entities. For example, the session entity may specify acceptable error rates, maximum delay, priority, and security.

The size and complexity of a transport protocol depend on how reliable or unreliable the underlying network and network layer services are. Accordingly, ISO has developed a family of five transport protocol standards, each oriented toward a different underlying service. In the TCP/IP protocol suite, there are two common transport-layer protocols: the connection-oriented TCP (Transmission Control Protocol) and the connectionless UDP (User Datagram Protocol).

Session Layer

The lowest four layers of the OSI model provide the means for the reliable exchange of data and may provide various quality of service options. For some applications, this basic service is insufficient. For example, a remote terminal access application might require a half-duplex dialogue. A transaction-processing application might require checkpoints in the data transfer stream to permit backup and recovery. A message-processing application might require the ability to interrupt a dialogue to prepare a new portion of a message and later to resume the dialogue where it was left off.

All these capabilities could be embedded in specific applications at layer 7. However, because these types of dialogue-structuring tools have widespread applicability, it makes sense to organize them into a separate layer: the session layer.

The session layer provides the mechanism for controlling the dialogue between applications in end systems. In many cases, there will be little or no need for session-layer services, but for some applications, such services are used. The key services provided by the session layer include the following:

- **Dialogue discipline:** This can be two-way simultaneous (full duplex) or two-way alternate (half duplex).
- **Grouping:** The flow of data can be marked to define groups of data. For example, if a retail store is transmitting sales data to a regional office, the data can be marked to indicate the end of the sales data for each department. This would signal the host computer to finalize running totals for that department and start new running counts for the next department.
- **Recovery:** The session layer can provide a checkpointing mechanism, so that if a failure of some sort occurs between checkpoints, the session entity can retransmit all data since the last checkpoint.

ISO has issued a standard for the session layer that includes, as options, services such as those just described.

Presentation Layer

The presentation layer defines the format of the data to be exchanged between applications and offers application programs a set of data transformation services. The presentation layer defines the syntax used between application entities and provides for the selection and subsequent modification of the representation used. Examples of specific services that may be performed at this layer include data compression and encryption.

Application Layer

The application layer provides a means for application programs to access the OSI environment. This layer contains management functions and generally useful mechanisms to support distributed applications. In addition, general-purpose applications such as file transfer, electronic mail, and terminal access to remote computers are considered to reside at this layer.

2.4 THE TCP/IP PROTOCOL ARCHITECTURE

The TCP/IP protocol architecture is a result of protocol research and development conducted on the experimental packet-switched network, ARPANET, funded by the Defense Advanced Research Projects Agency (DARPA), and is generally referred to as the TCP/IP protocol suite. This protocol suite consists of a large collection of protocols that have been issued as Internet standards by the Internet Architecture Board (IAB).

The TCP/IP Layers

The TCP/IP model organizes the communication task into five relatively independent layers:

- Physical layer
- Network access layer
- Internet layer
- Host-to-host, or transport layer
- Application layer

The **physical layer** covers the physical interface between a data transmission device (e.g., workstation, computer) and a transmission medium or network. This layer is concerned with specifying the characteristics of the transmission medium, the nature of the signals, the data rate, and related matters.

The **network access layer** is concerned with the exchange of data between an end system (server, workstation, etc.) and the network to which it is attached. The sending computer must provide the network with the address of the destination computer, so that the network may route the data to the appropriate destination. The sending computer may wish to invoke certain services, such as priority, that might be provided by the network. The specific software used at this layer depends on the type of network to be used; different standards have been developed for circuit switching, packet switching (e.g., frame relay), LANs (e.g., Ethernet), and others. Thus it makes sense to separate those functions having to do with network access into a separate layer. By doing this, the remainder of the communications software, above the network access layer, need not be concerned about the specifics of the network to be used. The same higher-layer software should function properly regardless of the particular network to which the computer is attached.

The network access layer is concerned with access to and routing data across a network for two end systems attached to the same network. In those cases where two devices are attached to different networks, procedures are needed to allow data to traverse multiple interconnected networks. This is the function of the **internet layer**. The Internet Protocol (IP) is used at this layer to provide the routing function across multiple networks. This protocol is implemented not only in the end systems but also in routers. A router is a processor that connects two networks and whose primary function is to relay data from one network to the other on its route from the source to the destination end system.

Regardless of the nature of the applications that are exchanging data, there is usually a requirement that data be exchanged reliably. That is, we would like to be assured that all of the data arrive at the destination application and that the data arrive in the same order in which they were sent. As we shall see, the mechanisms for providing reliability are essentially independent of the nature of the applications. Thus, it makes sense to collect those mechanisms in a common layer shared by all applications; this is referred to as the **host-to-host layer**, or **transport layer**. The Transmission Control Protocol (TCP) is the most commonly used protocol to provide this functionality.

Finally, the **application layer** contains the logic needed to support the various user applications. For each different type of application, such as file transfer, a separate module is needed that is peculiar to that application.

Figure 2.12 illustrates the layers of the TCP/IP and OSI architectures, showing roughly the correspondence in functionality between the two.

TCP and UDP

For most applications running as part of the TCP/IP protocol architecture, the transport layer protocol is TCP. TCP provides a reliable connection for the transfer of data between applications. A connection is simply a temporary logical association between two entities in different systems. Each TCP PDU, called a **TCP segment**, includes a source port and destination port value in the segment header, which serve the same function as the service access point (SAP) in the OSI architecture. These port values identify the respective users (applications) of the two

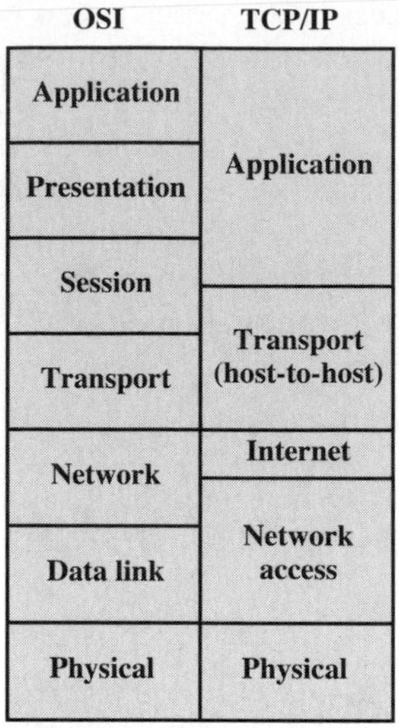

OSI	TCP/IP
Application	Application
Presentation	
Session	
Transport	Transport (host-to-host)
Network	Internet
Data link	Network access
Physical	Physical

Figure 2.12 A Comparison of the OSI and TCP/IP Protocol Architectures

TCP entities. A logical connection refers to a given pair of port values. For the duration of the connection each entity keeps track of TCP segments coming and going to the other entity, in order to regulate the flow of segments and to recover from lost or damaged segments.

In addition to TCP, there is one other transport-level protocol that is in common use as part of the TCP/IP protocol suite: the User Datagram Protocol (UDP). UDP does not guarantee delivery, preservation of sequence, or protection against duplication. UDP enables a procedure to send messages to other procedures with a minimum of protocol mechanism. Some transaction-oriented applications make use of UDP; one example is SNMP (Simple Network Management Protocol), the standard network management protocol for TCP/IP networks. Because it is connectionless, UDP has very little to do. Essentially, it adds a port addressing capability to IP.

Operation of TCP and IP

Figure 2.13 indicates how these protocols are configured for communications. To make clear that the total communications facility may consist of multiple networks, the constituent networks are usually referred to as **subnetworks**. Some sort of network access protocol, such as the Ethernet logic, is used to connect a computer to a subnetwork. This protocol enables the host to send data across the subnetwork to another host or, if the target host is on another subnetwork, to a router that will forward the data. IP is implemented in all of the end systems and the routers. It acts as a relay to move a block of data from one host, through one or more routers, to another host. TCP is implemented only in the end systems; it keeps track of the blocks of data to assure that all are delivered reliably to the appropriate application.

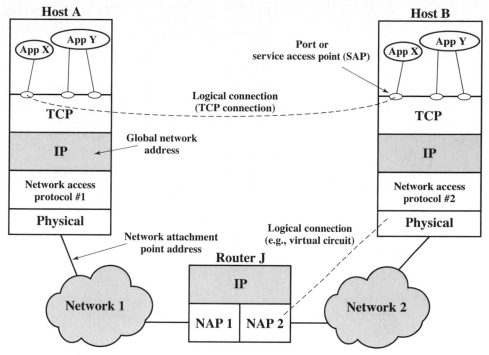

Figure 2.13 TCP/IP Concepts

For successful communication, every entity in the overall system must have a unique address. Actually, two levels of addressing are needed. Each host on a subnetwork must have a unique global internet address; this allows the data to be delivered to the proper host. Each process with a host must have an address that is unique within the host; this allows the host-to-host protocol (TCP) to deliver data to the proper process. These latter addresses are known as ports.

Let us trace a simple operation. Suppose that a process, associated with port 1 at host A, wishes to send a message to another process, associated with port 3 at host B. The process at A hands the message down to TCP with instructions to send it to host B, port 2. TCP hands the message down to IP with instructions to send it to host B. Note that IP need not be told the identity of the destination port. All it needs to know is that the data are intended for host B. Next, IP hands the message down to the network access layer (e.g., Ethernet logic) with instructions to send it to router J (the first hop on the way to B).

To control this operation, control information as well as user data must be transmitted, as suggested in Figure 2.14. Let us say that the sending process generates a block of data and passes this to TCP. TCP may break this block into smaller pieces to make it more manageable. To each of these pieces, TCP appends control information known as the TCP header, forming a **TCP segment**. The control information is to be used by the peer TCP protocol entity at host B. Examples of items in this header include the following:

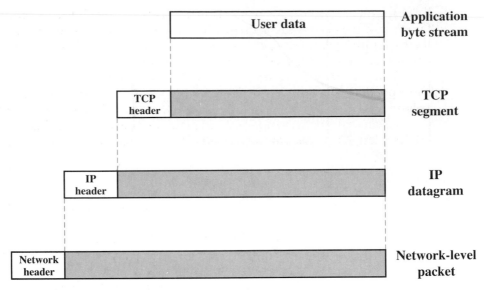

Figure 2.14 Protocol Data Units in the TCP/IP Architecture

- **Destination port:** When the TCP entity at B receives the segment, it must know to whom the data are to be delivered.
- **Sequence number:** TCP numbers the segments that it sends to a particular destination port sequentially, so that if they arrive out of order, the TCP entity at B can reorder them.
- **Checksum:** The sending TCP includes a code that is a function of the contents of the remainder of the segment. The receiving TCP performs the same calculation and compares the result with the incoming code. A discrepancy results if there has been some error in transmission.

Next, TCP hands each segment over to IP, with instructions to transmit it to B. These segments must be transmitted across one or more subnetworks and relayed through one or more intermediate routers. This operation, too, requires the use of control information. Thus IP appends a header of control information to each segment to form an **IP datagram**. An example of an item stored in the IP header is the destination host address (in this example, B).

Finally, each IP datagram is presented to the network access layer for transmission across the first subnetwork in its journey to the destination. The network access layer appends its own header, creating a packet, or frame. The packet is transmitted across the subnetwork to router J. The packet header contains the information that the subnetwork needs to transfer the data across the subnetwork. Examples of items that may be contained in this header include the following:

- **Destination subnetwork address:** The subnetwork must know to which attached device the packet is to be delivered.
- **Facilities requests:** The network access protocol might request the use of certain subnetwork facilities, such as priority.

At router J, the packet header is stripped off and the IP header examined. On the basis of the destination address information in the IP header, the IP module in the router directs the datagram out across subnetwork 2 to B. To do this, the datagram is again augmented with a network access header.

When the data are received at B, the reverse process occurs. At each layer, the corresponding header is removed, and the remainder is passed on to the next higher layer, until the original user data are delivered to the destination process.

As an aside, the generic name for a block of data exchanged at any protocol level is referred to as a **protocol data unit** (PDU). Thus, a TCP segment is a TCP PDU.

TCP/IP Applications

A number of applications have been standardized to operate on top of TCP. We mention three of the most common here.

The **Simple Mail Transfer Protocol (SMTP)** provides a basic electronic mail facility. It provides a mechanism for transferring messages among separate hosts. Features of SMTP include mailing lists, return receipts, and forwarding. The SMTP protocol does not specify the way in which messages are to be created; some local editing or native electronic mail facility is required. Once a message is created, SMTP accepts the message and makes use of TCP to send it to an SMTP module on another host. The target SMTP module will make use of a local electronic mail package to store the incoming message in a user's mailbox.

The **File Transfer Protocol (FTP)** is used to send files from one system to another under user command. Both text and binary files are accommodated, and the protocol provides features for controlling user access. When a user wishes to engage in file transfer, FTP sets up a TCP connection to the target system for the exchange of control messages. This connection allows user ID and password to be transmitted and allows the user to specify the file and file actions desired. Once a file transfer is approved, a second TCP connection is set up for the data transfer. The file is transferred over the data connection, without the overhead of any headers or control information at the application level. When the transfer is complete, the control connection is used to signal the completion and to accept new file transfer commands.

TELNET provides a remote logon capability, which enables a user at a terminal or personal computer to logon to a remote computer and function as if directly connected to that computer. The protocol was designed to work with simple scroll-mode terminals. TELNET is actually implemented in two modules: User TELNET interacts with the terminal I/O module to communicate with a local terminal. It converts the characteristics of real terminals to the network standard and vice versa. Server TELNET interacts with an application, acting as a surrogate terminal handler so that remote terminals appear as local to the application. Terminal traffic between User and Server TELNET is carried on a TCP connection.

Protocol Interfaces

Each layer in the TCP/IP protocol suite interacts with its immediate adjacent layers. At the source, the application layer makes use of the services of the end-to-end layer and provides data down to that layer. A similar relationship exists at the interface of

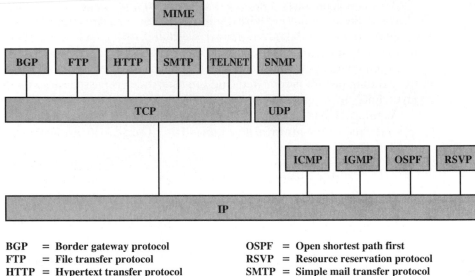

BGP   = Border gateway protocol
FTP   = File transfer protocol
HTTP = Hypertext transfer protocol
ICMP = Internet control message protocol
IGMP = Internet group management protocol
IP   = Internet protocol
MIME = Multipurpose internet mail extension

OSPF = Open shortest path first
RSVP = Resource reservation protocol
SMTP = Simple mail transfer protocol
SNMP = Simple network management protocol
TCP   = Transmission control protocol
UDP   = User datagram protocol

Figure 2.15   Some Protocols in the TCP/IP Protocol Suite

the end-to-end and internet layers and at the interface of the internet and network access layers. At the destination, each layer delivers data up to the next higher layer.

This use of each individual layer is not required by the architecture. As Figure 2.15 suggests, it is possible to develop applications that directly invoke the services of any one of the layers. Most applications require a reliable end-to-end protocol and thus make use of TCP. Some special-purpose applications do not need the services of TCP. Some of these applications, such as the Simple Network Management Protocol (SNMP), use an alternative end-to-end protocol known as the User Datagram Protocol (UDP); others may make use of IP directly. Applications that do not involve internetworking and that do not need TCP have been developed to invoke the network access layer directly.

2.5 RECOMMENDED READING AND WEB SITE

For the reader interested in greater detail on TCP/IP, there are two three-volume works that are more than adequate. The works by Comer and Stevens have become classics and are considered definitive [COME00, COME99, COME01]. The works by Stevens and Wright are equally worthwhile and more detailed with respect to protocol operation [STEV94, STEV96, WRIG95]. A more compact and very useful reference work is [RODR02], which covers the spectrum of TCP/IP-related protocols in a technically concise but thorough fashion, including coverage of some protocols not found in the other two works.

COME99   Comer, D., and Stevens, D. *Internetworking with TCP/IP, Volume II: Design Implementation, and Internals.* Upper Saddle River, NJ: Prentice Hall, 1994.

COME00   Comer, D. *Internetworking with TCP/IP, Volume I: Principles, Protocols, and Architecture.* Upper Saddle River, NJ: Prentice Hall, 2000.

COME01   Comer, D., and Stevens, D. *Internetworking with TCP/IP, Volume III: Client-Server Programming and Applications.* Upper Saddle River, NJ: Prentice Hall, 2001.

RODR02   Rodriguez, A., et al., *TCP/IP Tutorial and Technical Overview.* Upper Saddle River: NJ: Prentice Hall, 2002.

STEV94   Stevens, W. *TCP/IP Illustrated, Volume 1: The Protocols.* Reading, MA: Addison-Wesley, 1994.

STEV96   Stevens, W. *TCP/IP Illustrated, Volume 3: TCP for Transactions, HTTP, NNTP, and the UNIX(R) Domain Protocol.* Reading, MA: Addison-Wesley, 1996.

WRIG95   Wright, G., and Stevens, W. *TCP/IP Illustrated, Volume 2: The Implementation.* Reading, MA: Addison-Wesley, 1995.

Recommended Web Site:

- **Networking Links:** Excellent collection of links related to TCP/IP

2.6 KEY TERMS, REVIEW QUESTIONS, AND PROBLEMS

Key Terms

application layer	peer layer	subnetwork
checksum	physical layer	Transmission Control Protocol
data link layer	port	(TCP)
header	presentation layer	transport layer
internet	protocol	Uscr Datagram Protocol
Internet Protocol (IP)	protocol architecture	(UDP)
internetworking	protocol data unit (PDU)	
network layer	router	
Open Systems	service access point (SAP)	
Interconnection (OSI)	session layer	

Review Questions

2.1 What is the major function of the network access layer?

2.2 What tasks are performed by the transport layer?

2.3 What is a protocol?

2.4 What is a protocol data unit (PDU)?

2.5 What is a protocol architecture?

2.6 What is TCP/IP?

2.7 What are some advantages to layering as seen in the TCP/IP architecture?

2.8 What is a router?

Problems

2.1 Using the layer models in Figure 2.16, describe the ordering and delivery of a pizza, indicating the interactions at each level.

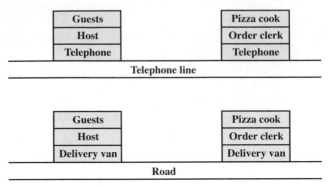

Figure 2.16 Architecture for Problem 2.1

2.2 **a.** The French and Chinese prime ministers need to come to an agreement by telephone, but neither speaks the other's language. Further, neither has on hand a translator that can translate to the language of the other. However, both prime ministers have English translators on their staffs. Draw a diagram similar to Figure 2.16 to depict the situation, and describe the interaction and each level.

　　b. Now suppose that the Chinese prime minister's translator can translate only into Japanese and that the French prime minister has a German translator available. A translator between German and Japanese is available in Germany. Draw a new diagram that reflects this arrangement and describe the hypothetical phone conversation.

2.3 List the major disadvantages with the layered approach to protocols.

2.4 Two blue armies are each poised on opposite hills preparing to attack a single red army in the valley. The red army can defeat either of the blue armies separately but will fail to defeat both blue armies if they attack simultaneously. The blue armies communicate via an unreliable communications system (a foot soldier). The commander with one of the blue armies would like to attack at noon. His problem is this: If he sends a message to the other blue army, ordering the attack, he cannot be sure it will get through. He could ask for acknowledgment, but that might not get through. Is there a protocol that the two blue armies can use to avoid defeat?

2.5 A broadcast network is one in which a transmission from any one attached station is received by all other attached stations over a shared medium. Examples are a bus-topology local area network, such as Ethernet, and a wireless radio network. Discuss the need or lack of need for a network layer (OSI layer 3) in a broadcast network.

2.6 Based on the principles enunciated in Table 2.1
　　a. Design an architecture with eight layers and make a case for it.
　　b. Design one with six layers and make a case for that.

2.7 In Figure 2.14, exactly one protocol data unit (PDU) in layer N is encapsulated in a PDU at layer $(N - 1)$. It is also possible to break one N-level PDU into multiple $(N - 1)$-level PDUs (segmentation) or to group multiple N-level PDUs into one $(N - 1)$-level PDU (blocking).

    a. In the case of segmentation, is it necessary that each $(N - 1)$-level segment contain a copy of the N-level header?

    b. In the case of blocking, is it necessary that each N-level PDU retain its own header, or can the data be consolidated into a single N-level PDU with a single N-level header?

2.8 The previous version of the TFTP specification, RFC 783, included the following statement:

> All packets other than those used for termination are acknowledged individually unless a timeout occurs.

The RFC 1350 specification revises this to say

> All packets other than duplicate ACK's and those used for termination are acknowledged unless a timeout occurs.

The change was made to fix a problem referred to as the "Sorcerer's Apprentice." Deduce and explain the problem.

2.9 What is the limiting factor in the time required to transfer a file using TFTP?

APPENDIX 2A   THE TRIVIAL FILE TRANSFER PROTOCOL

This appendix provides an overview of the Internet standard Trivial File Transfer Protocol (TFTP), defined in RFC 1350. Our purpose is to give the reader some flavor for the elements of a protocol.

Introduction to TFTP

TFTP is far simpler than the Internet standard FTP (RFC 959). There are no provisions for access control or user identification, so TFTP is only suitable for public access file directories. Because of its simplicity, TFTP is easily and compactly implemented. For example, some diskless devices use TFTP to download their firmware at boot time.

TFTP runs on top of UDP. The TFTP entity that initiates the transfer does so by sending a read or write request in a UDP segment with a destination port of 69 to the target system. This port is recognized by the target UDP module as the identifier of the TFTP module. For the duration of the transfer, each side uses a transfer identifier (TID) as its port number.

TFTP Packets

TFTP entities exchange commands, responses, and file data in the form of packets, each of which is carried in the body of a UDP segment. TFTP supports five types of packets (Figure 2.17); the first two bytes contains an opcode that identifies the packet type:

* **RRQ:** The read request packet requests permission to transfer a file from the other system. The packet includes a file name, which is a sequence of ASCII[3]

---

[3] ASCII is the American Standard Code for Information Interchange, a standard of the American National Standards Institute. It designates a unique 7-bit pattern for each letter, with an eighth bit used for parity. ASCII is equivalent to the International Reference Alphabet (IRA), defined in ITU-T Recommendation T.50.

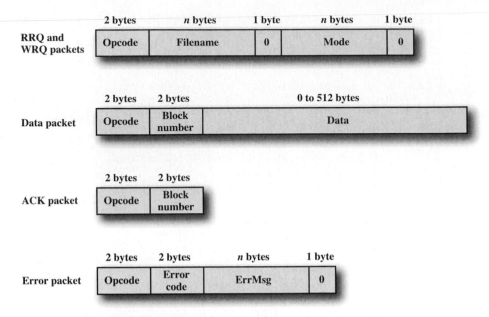

Figure 2.17 TFTP Packet Formats

bytes terminated by a zero byte. The zero byte is the means by which the receiving TFTP entity knows when the file name is terminated. The packet also includes a mode field, which indicates whether the data file is to be interpreted as a string of ASCII bytes or as raw 8-bit bytes of data.

- **WRQ:** The write request packet requests permission to transfer a file to the other system.
- **Data:** The block numbers on data packets begin with one and increase by one for each new block of data. This convention enables the program to use a single number to discriminate between new packets and duplicates. The data field is from zero to 512 bytes long. If it is 512 bytes long, the block is not the last block of data; if it is from zero to 511 bytes long, it signals the end of the transfer.
- **ACK:** This packet is used to acknowledge receipt of a data packet or a WRQ packet. An ACK of a data packet contains the block number of the data packet being acknowledged. An ACK of a WRQ contains a block number of zero.
- **Error:** An error packet can be the acknowledgment of any other type of packet. The error code is an integer indicating the nature of the error (Table 2.4). The error message is intended for human consumption, and should be in ASCII. Like all other strings, it is terminated with a zero byte.

All packets other than duplicate ACKs (explained subsequently) and those used for termination are to be acknowledged. Any packet can be acknowledged by an error packet. If there are no errors, then the following conventions apply. A WRQ or a data packet is acknowledged by an ACK packet. When a RRQ is sent, the other side responds (in the absence of error) by beginning to transfer the file; thus, the first data block serves as an acknowledgment of the RRQ packet. Unless a file transfer is

Table 2.4 TFTP Error Codes

Value	Meaning
0	Not defined, see error message (if any)
1	File not found
2	Access violation
3	Disk full or allocation exceeded
4	Illegal TFTP operation
5	Unknown transfer ID
6	File already exists
7	No such user

complete, each ACK packet from one side is followed by a data packet from the other, so that the data packet functions as an acknowledgment. An error packet can be acknowledged by any other kind of packet, depending on the circumstance.

Overview of a Transfer

The example illustrated in Figure 2.18 is of a simple file transfer operation from A to B. No errors occur, and the details of the option specification are not explored.

The operation begins when the TFTP module in system A sends a write request (WRQ) to the TFTP module in system B. The WRQ packet is carried as the body of a UDP segment. The write request includes the name of the file (in this case, XXX) and a mode of octet, or raw data. In the UDP header, the destination port number is 69, which alerts the receiving UDP entity that this message is intended for the TFTP application. The source port number is a TID selected by A, in this case 1511. System B is prepared to accept the file and so responds with an ACK with a block number of 0. In the UDP header, the destination port is 1511, which enables the UDP entity at A to route the incoming packet to the TFTP module, which can match this TID with the TID in the WRQ. The source port is a TID selected by B for this file transfer, in this case 1660.

Following this initial exchange, the file transfer proceeds. The transfer consists of one or more data packets from A, each of which is acknowledged by B. The final data packet contains less than 512 bytes of data, which signals the end of the transfer.

Errors and Delays

If TFTP operates over a network or internet (as opposed to a direct data link), it is possible for packets to be lost. Because TFTP operates over UDP, which does not provide a reliable delivery service, there needs to be some mechanism in TFTP to deal with lost packets. TFTP uses the common technique of a timeout mechanism. Suppose that A sends a packet to B that requires an acknowledgment (i.e., any packet other than duplicate ACKs and those used for termination). When A has transmitted the packet, it starts a timer. If the timer expires before the acknowledgment is received from B, A retransmits the same packet. If in fact the original packet was lost, then the retransmission will be the first copy of this packet received by B.

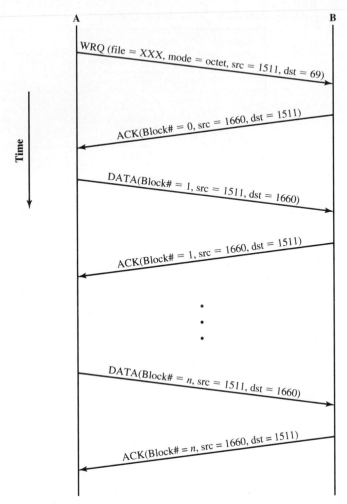

Figure 2.18 Example TFTP Operation

If the original packet was not lost but the acknowledgment from B was lost, then B will receive two copies of the same packet from A and simply acknowledges both copies. Because of the use of block numbers, this causes no confusion. The only exception to this rule is for duplicate ACK packets. The second ACK is ignored.

Syntax, Semantics, and Timing

In Section 2.1, it was mentioned that the key features of a protocol can be classified as syntax, semantics, and timing. These categories are easily seen in TFTP. The formats of the various TFTP packets form the **syntax** of the protocol. The **semantics** of the protocol are shown in the definitions of each of the packet types and the error codes. Finally, the sequence in which packets are exchanged, the use of block numbers, and the use of timers are all aspects of the **timing** of TFTP.

PART TWO Data Communications

ISSUES FOR PART TWO

Part Two deals with the transfer of data between two devices that are directly connected; that is, the two devices are linked by a single transmission path rather than a network. There are a host of technical and design issues raised in even this simple context. First, we need to understand something about the process of transmitting signals across a communications link. Both analog and digital transmission techniques are used. In both cases, the signal can be described as consisting of a spectrum of components across a range of electromagnetic frequencies. The transmission properties of the signal depend on which frequencies are involved. Also, the types of impairments, such as attenuation, that a signal suffers are dependent on frequency. A separate concern is the transmission medium used to transmit signals, which is a factor in determining what performance can be achieved, in terms of data rate and distance. Closely tied to considerations of the signal and the medium is the way in which data are encoded on the signal. Again, the encoding technique is a factor in transmission performance.

Beyond the fundamental concepts of signal, medium, and encoding, Part Two deals with two other important aspects of data communications: reliability and efficiency. In any communications scheme, there will be a certain rate of errors suffered during transmission. A data link control protocol provides mechanisms for detecting and recovering from such errors, so that a potentially unreliable transmission path is turned into a reliable data communications link. Finally, if the capacity of the link is greater than the requirements for a single transmission, then a variety of multiplexing techniques can be used to provide for efficient use of the medium.

ROAD MAP FOR PART TWO

Chapter 3 Data Transmission

The principles of data transmission underlie all of the concepts and techniques presented in this book. To understand the need for encoding, multiplexing, switching, error control, and so on, the reader should understand the behavior of data signals propagated through a transmission medium. Chapter 3 discusses the distinction between digital and analog data and digital and analog transmission. Concepts of attenuation and noise are also examined.

Chapter 4 Transmission Media

Transmission media can be classified as either guided or wireless. The most commonly used guided transmission media are twisted pair, coaxial cable, and optical fiber. Wireless techniques include terrestrial and satellite microwave, broadcast radio, and infrared. Chapter 4 covers all of these topics.

Chapter 5 Data Encoding

Data come in both analog (continuous) and digital (discrete) form. For transmission, input data must be encoded as an electrical signal that is tailored to the characteristics of the transmission medium. Both analog and digital data can be represented by either analog or digital signals; each of the four cases is discussed in Chapter 5.

Chapter 6 The Data Communication Interface

In Chapter 6, the emphasis shifts from data transmission to data communications. For two devices linked by a transmission medium to exchange digital data, a high degree of cooperation is required. Typically, data are transmitted one bit at a time over the medium. The timing (rate, duration, spacing) of these bits must be the same for transmitter and receiver. Two common communication techniques—asynchronous and synchronous—are explored. Following this, the chapter examines the topics of transmission errors and error detection and correction techniques. This chapter also looks at transmission line interfaces. Typically, digital data devices do not attach to and signal across a transmission medium directly. Rather, this process is mediated through a standardized interface.

Chapter 7 Data Link Control

True cooperative exchange of digital data between two devices requires some form of data link control. Chapter 7 examines the fundamental techniques common to all data link control protocols, including flow control and error control, and then examines the most commonly used protocol, HDLC.

Chapter 8 Multiplexing

Transmission facilities are, by and large, expensive. It is often the case that two communication stations will not utilize the full capacity of a data link. For efficiency, it should be possible to share that capacity. The generic term for such sharing is *multiplexing*.

Chapter 8 concentrates on the three most common types of multiplexing techniques. The first, frequency division multiplexing (FDM), is the most widespread and is familiar to anyone who has ever used a radio or television set. The second is a particular case of time division multiplexing (TDM), often known as synchronous TDM. This is commonly used for multiplexing digitized voice streams. The third type is another form of TDM that is more complex but potentially more efficient than synchronous TDM; it is referred to as statistical or asynchronous TDM.

Chapter 9 Spread Spectrum

An increasingly popular form of wireless communications is known as spread spectrum. Two general approaches are used: frequency hopping and direct sequence spread spectrum. Chapter 9 provides an overview of both techniques. The chapter also looks at the concept of code division multiple access (CDMA), which is an application of spread spectrum to provide multiple access.

CHAPTER **3**

DATA TRANSMISSION

KEY POINTS

- All of the forms of information that are discussed in this book (voice, data, image, video) can be represented by electromagnetic signals. Depending on the transmission medium and the communications environment, either analog or digital signals can be used to convey information.

- Any electromagnetic signal, analog or digital, is made up of a number of constituent frequencies. A key parameter that characterizes the signal is bandwidth, which is the width of the range of frequencies that comprises the signal. In general, the greater the bandwidth of the signal, the greater its information-carrying capacity.

- A major problem in designing a communications facility is transmission impairment. The most significant impairments are attenuation, attenuation distortion, delay distortion, and the various types of noise. The various forms of noise include thermal noise, intermodulation noise, crosstalk, and impulse noise. For analog signals, transmission impairments introduce random effects that degrade the quality of the received information and may affect intelligibility. For digital signals, transmission impairments may cause bit errors at the receiver.

- The designer of a communications facility must deal with four factors: the bandwidth of the signal, the data rate that is used for digital information, the amount of noise and other impairments, and the level of error rate that is acceptable. The bandwidth is limited by the transmission medium and the desire to avoid interference with other nearby signals. Because bandwidth is a scarce resource, we would like to maximize the data rate that is achieved in a given bandwidth. The data rate is limited by the bandwidth, the presence of impairments, and the error rate that is acceptable.

The successful transmission of data depends principally on two factors: the quality of the signal being transmitted and the characteristics of the transmission medium. The objective of this chapter and the next is to provide the reader with an intuitive feeling for the nature of these two factors.

The first section presents some concepts and terms from the field of electrical engineering. This should provide sufficient background to deal with the remainder of the chapter. Section 3.2 clarifies the use of the terms *analog* and *digital*. Either analog or digital data may be transmitted using either analog or digital signals. Furthermore, it is common for intermediate processing to be performed between source and destination, and this processing has either an analog or digital character.

Section 3.3 looks at the various impairments that may introduce errors into the data during transmission. The chief impairments are attenuation, attenuation distortion, delay distortion, and the various forms of noise. Finally, we look at the important concept of channel capacity.

3.1 CONCEPTS AND TERMINOLOGY

In this section we introduce some concepts and terms that will be referred to throughout the rest of the chapter and, indeed, throughout Part Two.

Transmission Terminology

Data transmission occurs between transmitter and receiver over some transmission medium. Transmission media may be classified as guided or unguided. In both cases, communication is in the form of electromagnetic waves. With **guided media**, the waves are guided along a physical path; examples of guided media are twisted pair, coaxial cable, and optical fiber. **Unguided media**, also called **wireless**, provide a means for transmitting electromagnetic waves but do not guide them; examples are propagation through air, vacuum, and seawater.

The term **direct link** is used to refer to the transmission path between two devices in which signals propagate directly from transmitter to receiver with no intermediate devices, other than amplifiers or repeaters used to increase signal strength. Note that this term can apply to both guided and unguided media.

A guided transmission medium is **point to point** if it provides a direct link between two devices and those are the only two devices sharing the medium. In a **multipoint** guided configuration, more than two devices share the same medium.

A transmission may be simplex, half duplex, or full duplex. In **simplex** transmission, signals are transmitted in only one direction; one station is transmitter and the other is receiver. In **half-duplex** operation, both stations may transmit, but only one at a time. In **full-duplex** operation, both stations may transmit simultaneously. In the latter case, the medium is carrying signals in both directions at the same time. How this can be is explained in due course. We should note that the definitions just given are the ones in common use in the United States (ANSI definitions). Elsewhere (ITU-T definitions), the term *simplex* is used to correspond to half duplex as defined previously, and duplex is used to correspond to full duplex as just defined.

Frequency, Spectrum, and Bandwidth

In this book, we are concerned with electromagnetic signals used as a means to transmit data. At point 3 in Figure 1.2, a signal is generated by the transmitter and transmitted over a medium. The signal is a function of time, but it can also be expressed as a function of frequency; that is, the signal consists of components of different frequencies. It turns out that the **frequency domain** view of a signal is more important to an understanding of data transmission than a **time domain** view. Both views are introduced here.

Time Domain Concepts

Viewed as a function of time, an electromagnetic signal can be either analog or digital. An **analog signal** is one in which the signal intensity varies in a smooth fashion over time. In other words, there are no breaks or discontinuities in the signal.[1]

---

[1] A mathematical definition: a signal $s(t)$ is continuous if $\lim_{t \to a} s(t) = s(a)$ for all a.

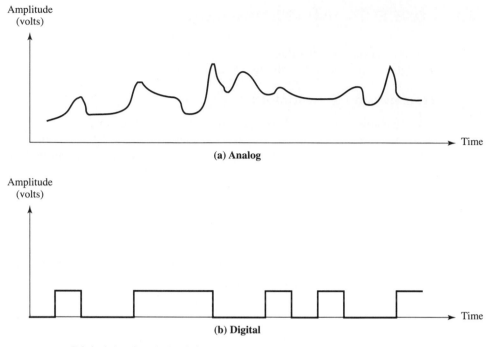

Figure 3.1 Digital Analog and Digital Waveforms

A **digital signal** is one in which the signal intensity maintains a constant level for some period of time and then changes to another constant level.[2] Figure 3.1 shows an example of each kind of signal. The continuous signal might represent speech, and the discrete signal might represent binary 1s and 0s.

The simplest sort of signal is a **periodic signal**, in which the same signal pattern repeats over time. Figure 3.2 shows an example of a periodic continuous signal (sine wave) and a periodic discrete signal (square wave). Mathematically, a signal $s(t)$ is defined to be periodic if and only if

$$s(t + T) = s(t) \qquad -\infty < t < +\infty$$

where the constant T is the period of the signal (T is the smallest value that satisfies the equation). Otherwise, a signal is **aperiodic**.

The sine wave is the fundamental periodic signal. A general sine wave can be represented by three parameters: peak amplitude (A), frequency (f), and phase (ϕ). The **peak amplitude** is the maximum value or strength of the signal over time; typically, this value is measured in volts. The **frequency** is the rate [in cycles per second, or Hertz (Hz)] at which the signal repeats. An equivalent parameter is the

---

[2] This is an idealized definition. In fact, the transition from one voltage level to another will not be instantaneous, but there will be a small transition period. Nevertheless, an actual digital signal approximates closely the ideal model of constant voltage levels with instantaneous transitions.

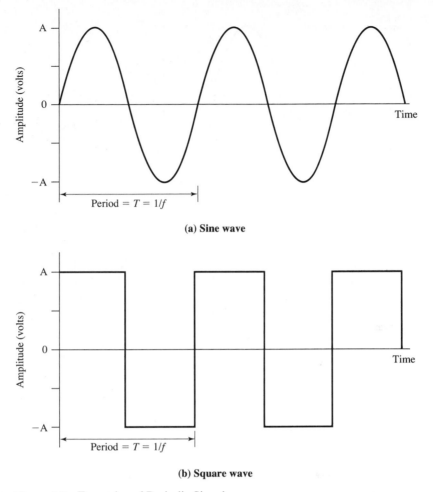

Figure 3.2 Examples of Periodic Signals

period (T) of a signal, which is the amount of time it takes for one repetition; therefore, $T = 1/f$. **Phase** is a measure of the relative position in time within a single period of a signal, as is illustrated later. More formally, for a periodic signal $f(t)$, phase is the fractional part t/T of the period T through which t has advanced relative to an arbitrary origin. The origin is usually taken as the last previous passage through zero from the negative to the positive direction.

The general sine wave can be written

$$s(t) = A \sin(2\pi f t + \phi)$$

Figure 3.3 shows the effect of varying each of the three parameters. In part (a) of the figure, the frequency is 1 Hz; thus the period is $T = 1$ second. Part (b) has the same frequency and phase but a peak amplitude of 0.5. In part (c) we have $f = 2$, which

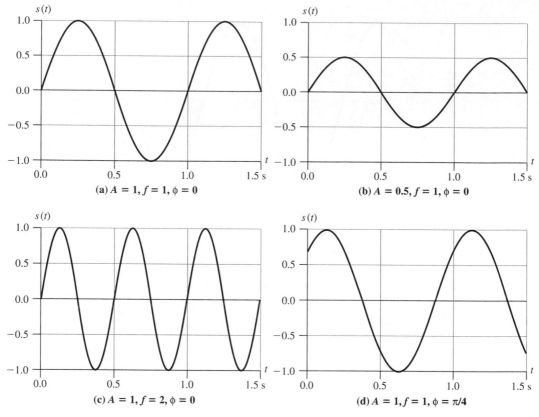

Figure 3.3 $s(t) = A \sin(2\pi ft + \phi)$

is equivalent to $T = 0.5$. Finally, part (d) shows the effect of a phase shift of $\pi/4$ radians, which is 45 degrees (2π radians $= 360° = 1$ period).

In Figure 3.3, the horizontal axis is time; the graphs display the value of a signal at a given point in space as a function of time. These same graphs, with a change of scale, can apply with horizontal axes in space. In this case, the graphs display the value of a signal at a given point in time as a function of distance. For example, for a sinusoidal transmission (say an electromagnetic radio wave some distance from a radio antenna, or sound some distance from loudspeaker), at a particular instant of time, the intensity of the signal varies in a sinusoidal way as a function of distance from the source.

There is a simple relationship between the two sine waves, one in time and one in space. Define the **wavelength**, λ, of a signal as the distance occupied by a single cycle or, put another way, the distance between two points of corresponding phase of two consecutive cycles. Assume that the signal is traveling with a velocity v. Then the wavelength is related to the period as follows: $\lambda = vT$. Equivalently, $\lambda f = v$. Of particular relevance to this discussion is the case where $v = c$, the speed of light in free space, which is approximately 3×10^8 m/s.

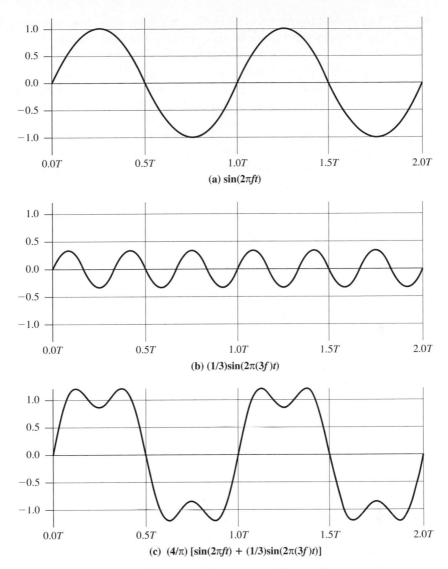

Figure 3.4 Addition of Frequency Components $(T = 1/f)$

Frequency Domain Concepts

In practice, an electromagnetic signal will be made up of many frequencies. For example, the signal

$$s(t) = (4/\pi) \times (\sin(2\pi ft) + (1/3) \sin(2\pi(3f)t))$$

is shown in Figure 3.4c. The components of this signal are just sine waves of frequencies f and $3f$; parts (a) and (b) of the figure show these individual components. There are two interesting points that can be made about this figure:

- The second frequency is an integer multiple of the first frequency. When all of the frequency components of a signal are integer multiples of one frequency, the latter frequency is referred to as the **fundamental frequency**.
- The period of the total signal is equal to the period of the fundamental frequency. The period of the component $\sin(2\pi ft)$ is $T = 1/f$, and the period of $s(t)$ is also T, as can be seen from Figure 3.4c.

It can be shown, using a discipline known as Fourier analysis, that any signal is made up of components at various frequencies, in which each component is a sinusoid. By adding together enough sinusoidal signals, each with the appropriate amplitude, frequency, and phase, any electromagnetic signal can be constructed. Put another way, any electromagnetic signal can be shown to consist of a collection of periodic analog signals (sine waves) at different amplitudes, frequencies, and phases. The importance of being able to look at a signal from the frequency perspective (frequency domain) rather than a time perspective (time domain) should become clear as the discussion proceeds. For the interested reader, the subject of Fourier analysis is introduced in Appendix B.

So we can say that for each signal, there is a time domain function $s(t)$ that specifies the amplitude of the signal at each instant in time. Similarly, there is a frequency domain function $S(f)$ that specifies the peak amplitude of the constituent frequencies of the signal. Figure 3.5a shows the frequency domain function for the signal of Figure 3.4c. Note that, in this case, $S(f)$ is discrete. Figure 3.5b shows the frequency domain function for a single square pulse that has the value 1 between $-X/2$ and $X/2$, and is 0 elsewhere.[3] Note that in this case $S(f)$ is continuous and that it has nonzero values indefinitely, although the magnitude of the frequency components rapidly becomes smaller for larger f. These characteristics are common for real signals.

The **spectrum** of a signal is the range of frequencies that it contains. For the signal of Figure 3.4c, the spectrum extends from f to $3f$. The **absolute bandwidth** of a signal is the width of the spectrum. In the case of Figure 3.4c, the bandwidth is $2f$. Many signals, such as that of Figure 3.5b, have an infinite bandwidth. However, most of the energy in the signal is contained in a relatively narrow band of frequencies. This band is referred to as the **effective bandwidth**, or just **bandwidth**.

One final term to define is **dc component**. If a signal includes a component of zero frequency, that component is a direct current (dc) or constant component. For example, Figure 3.6 shows the result of adding a dc component to the signal of Figure 3.4c. With no dc component, a signal has average amplitude of zero, as seen in the time domain. With a dc component, it has a frequency term at $f = 0$ and a nonzero average amplitude.

Relationship between Data Rate and Bandwidth

We have said that effective bandwidth is the band within which most of the signal energy is concentrated. The term *most* in this context is somewhat arbitrary.

---

[3]In fact, the function $S(f)$ for this case is symmetric around $f = 0$ and so has values for negative frequencies. The presence of negative frequencies is a mathematical artifact whose explanation is beyond the scope of this book.

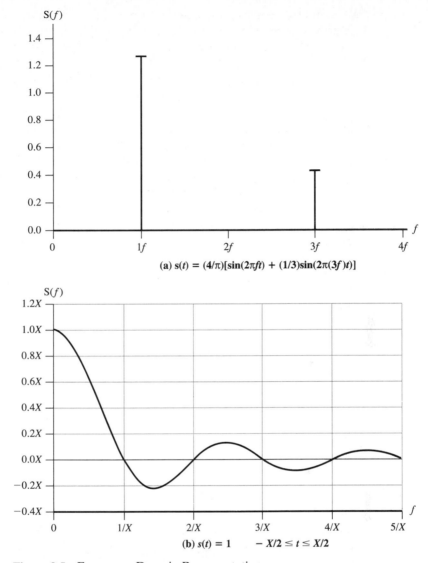

(a) $s(t) = (4/\pi)[\sin(2\pi ft) + (1/3)\sin(2\pi(3f)t)]$

(b) $s(t) = 1 \quad -X/2 \leq t \leq X/2$

Figure 3.5 Frequency Domain Representations

The important issue here is that, although a given waveform may contain frequencies over a very broad range, as a practical matter any transmission system (transmitter plus medium plus receiver) will be able to accommodate only a limited band of frequencies. This, in turn, limits the data rate that can be carried on the transmission medium.

To try to explain these relationships, consider the square wave of Figure 3.2b. Suppose that we let a positive pulse represent binary 0 and a negative pulse represent binary 1. Then the waveform represents the binary stream 0101 . . . . The duration of each pulse is $1/(2f)$; thus the data rate is $2f$ bits per second (bps). What are the frequency components of this signal? To answer this question, consider again

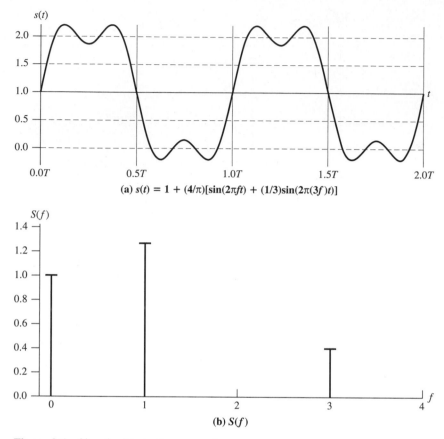

(a) $s(t) = 1 + (4/\pi)[\sin(2\pi ft) + (1/3)\sin(2\pi(3f)t)]$

(b) $S(f)$

Figure 3.6   Signal with dc Component

Figure 3.4. By adding together sine waves at frequencies f and $3f$, we get a wave-form that begins to resemble the original square wave. Let us continue this process by adding a sine wave of frequency $5f$, as shown in Figure 3.7a, and then adding a sine wave of frequency $7f$, as shown in Figure 3.7b. As we add additional odd multi-ples of f, suitably scaled, the resulting waveform approaches that of a square wave more and more closely.

Indeed, it can be shown that the frequency components of the square wave with amplitudes A and $-A$ can be expressed as follows:

$$s(t) = A \times \frac{4}{\pi} \times \sum_{k \text{ odd}, k=1}^{\infty} \frac{\sin(2\pi kft)}{k}$$

Thus, this waveform has an infinite number of frequency components and hence an infinite bandwidth. However, the peak amplitude of the kth frequency component, kf, is only $1/k$, so most of the energy in this waveform is in the first few frequency components. What happens if we limit the bandwidth to just the first three fre-quency components? We have already seen the answer, in Figure 3.7a. As we can

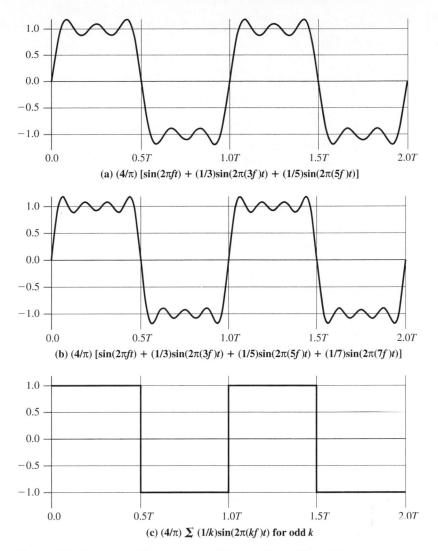

Figure 3.7   Frequency Components of Square Wave ($T = 1/f$)

see, the shape of the resulting waveform is reasonably close to that of the original square wave.

We can use Figures 3.4 and 3.7 to illustrate the relationship between data rate and bandwidth. Suppose that we are using a digital transmission system that is capable of transmitting signals with a bandwidth of 4 MHz. Let us attempt to transmit a sequence of alternating 1s and 0s as the square wave of Figure 3.7c. What data rate can be achieved? We look at three cases.

Case I. Let us approximate our square wave with the waveform of Figure 3.7a. Although this waveform is a "distorted" square wave, it is sufficiently close to the square wave that a receiver should be able to discriminate between a binary

0 and a binary 1. If we let $f = 10^6$ cycles/second $= 1$ MHz, then the bandwidth of the signal

$$s(t) = \frac{4}{\pi} \times \left[\sin((2\pi \times 10^6)t) + \frac{1}{3}\sin((2\pi \times 3 \times 10^6)t) + \frac{1}{5}\sin((2\pi \times 5 \times 10^6)t) \right]$$

is $(5 \times 10^6) - 10^6 = 4$ MHz. Note that for $f = 1$ MHz, the period of the fundamental frequency is $T = 1/10^6 = 10^{-6} = 1$ μs. If we treat this waveform as a bit string of 1s and 0s, one bit occurs every 0.5 μs, for a data rate of $2 \times 10^6 = 2$ Mbps. Thus, for a bandwidth of 4 MHz, a data rate of 2 Mbps is achieved.

Case II. Now suppose that we have a bandwidth of 8 MHz. Let us look again at Figure 3.7a, but now with $f = 2$ MHz. Using the same line of reasoning as before, the bandwidth of the signal is $(5 \times 2 \times 10^6) - (2 \times 10^6) = 8$ MHz. But in this case $T = 1/f = 0.5$ μs. As a result, one bit occurs every 0.25 μs for a data rate of 4 Mbps. Thus, other things being equal, by doubling the bandwidth, we double the potential data rate.

Case III. Now suppose that the waveform of Figure 3.4c is considered adequate for approximating a square wave. That is, the difference between a positive and negative pulse in Figure 3.4c is sufficiently distinct that the waveform can be successfully used to represent a sequence of 1s and 0s. Assume as in Case II that $f = 2$ MHz and $T = 1/f = 0.5$ μs, so that one bit occurs every 0.25 μs for a data rate of 4 Mbps. Using the waveform of Figure 3.4c, the bandwidth of the signal is $(3 \times 2 \times 10^6) - (2 \times 10^6) = 4$ MHz. Thus, a given bandwidth can support various data rates depending on the ability of the receiver to discern the difference between 0 and 1 in the presence of noise and other impairments.

To summarize,

- **Case I:** Bandwidth $= 4$ MHz; data rate $= 2$ Mbps
- **Case II:** Bandwidth $= 8$ MHz; data rate $= 4$ Mbps
- **Case III:** Bandwidth $= 4$ MHz; data rate $= 4$ Mbps

We can draw the following conclusions from the preceding discussion. In general, any digital waveform will have infinite bandwidth. If we attempt to transmit this waveform as a signal over any medium, the transmission system will limit the bandwidth that can be transmitted. Furthermore, for any given medium, the greater the bandwidth transmitted, the greater the cost. Thus, on the one hand, economic and practical reasons dictate that digital information be approximated by a signal of limited bandwidth. On the other hand, limiting the bandwidth creates distortions, which makes the task of interpreting the received signal more difficult. The more limited the bandwidth, the greater the distortion, and the greater the potential for error by the receiver.

One more illustration should serve to reinforce these concepts. Figure 3.8 shows a digital bit stream with a data rate of 2000 bits per second. With a bandwidth of 2500 Hz, or even 1700 Hz, the representation is quite good. Furthermore, we can

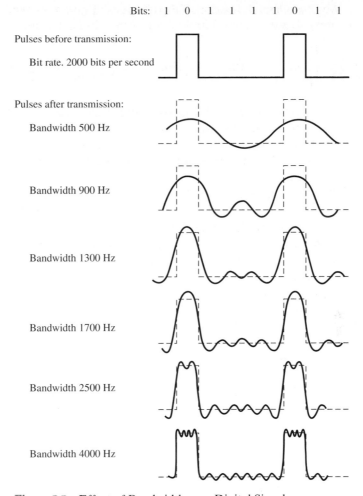

Figure 3.8   Effect of Bandwidth on a Digital Signal

generalize these results. If the data rate of the digital signal is W bps, then a very good representation can be achieved with a bandwidth of $2W$ Hz. However, unless noise is very severe, the bit pattern can be recovered with less bandwidth than this (see the discussion of channel capacity in Section 3.4).

Thus, there is a direct relationship between data rate and bandwidth: The higher the data rate of a signal, the greater is its required effective bandwidth. Looked at the other way, the greater the bandwidth of a transmission system, the higher is the data rate that can be transmitted over that system.

Another observation worth making is this: If we think of the bandwidth of a signal as being centered about some frequency, referred to as the **center frequency**, then the higher the center frequency, the higher the potential bandwidth and therefore the higher the potential data rate. For example, if a signal is centered at 2 MHz, its maximum bandwidth is 4 MHz.

We return to a discussion of the relationship between bandwidth and data rate in Section 3.4, after a consideration of transmission impairments.

3.2 ANALOG AND DIGITAL DATA TRANSMISSION

The terms *analog* and *digital* correspond, roughly, to *continuous* and *discrete*, respectively. These two terms are used frequently in data communications in at least three contexts: data, signaling, and transmission.

Briefly, we define **data** as entities that convey meaning, or information. **Signals** are electric or electromagnetic representations of data. **Signaling** is the physical propagation of the signal along a suitable medium. **Transmission** is the communication of data by the propagation and processing of signals. In what follows, we try to make these abstract concepts clear by discussing the terms *analog* and *digital* as applied to data, signals, and transmission.

Analog and Digital Data

The concepts of analog and digital data are simple enough. Analog data take on continuous values in some interval. For example, voice and video are continuously varying patterns of intensity. Most data collected by sensors, such as temperature and pressure, are continuous valued. Digital data take on discrete values; examples are text and integers.

The most familiar example of analog data is **audio**, which, in the form of acoustic sound waves, can be perceived directly by human beings. Figure 3.9 shows

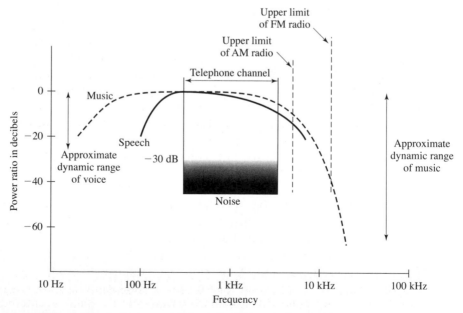

Figure 3.9   Acoustic Spectrum of Speech and Music [CARN99a]

the acoustic spectrum for human speech and for music.[4] Frequency components of typical speech may be found between approximately 100 Hz and 7 kHz. Although much of the energy in speech is concentrated at the lower frequencies, tests have shown that frequencies below 600 or 700 Hz add very little to the intelligibility of speech to the human ear. Typical speech has a dynamic range of about 25 dB;[5] that is, the power produced by the loudest shout may be as much as 300 times greater than the least whisper. Figure 3.9 also shows the acoustic spectrum and dynamic range for music.

Another common example of analog data is **video**. Here it is easier to characterize the data in terms of the viewer (destination) of the TV screen rather than the original scene (source) that is recorded by the TV camera. To produce a picture on the screen, an electron beam scans across the surface of the screen from left to right and top to bottom. For black-and-white television, the amount of illumination produced (on a scale from black to white) at any point is proportional to the intensity of the beam as it passes that point. Thus at any instant in time the beam takes on an analog value of intensity to produce the desired brightness at that point on the screen. Further, as the beam scans, the analog value changes. Thus the video image can be thought of as a time-varying analog signal.

Figure 3.10 depicts the scanning process. At the end of each scan line, the beam is swept rapidly back to the left (horizontal retrace). When the beam reaches the bottom, it is swept rapidly back to the top (vertical retrace). The beam is turned off (blanked out) during the retrace intervals.

To achieve adequate resolution, the beam produces a total of 483 horizontal lines at a rate of 30 complete scans of the screen per second. Tests have shown that this rate will produce a sensation of flicker rather than smooth motion. To provide a flicker-free image without increasing the bandwidth requirement, a technique known as **interlacing** is used. As Figure 3.10 shows, the odd numbered scan lines and the even numbered scan lines are scanned separately, with odd and even fields alternating on successive scans. The odd field is the scan from A to B and the even field is the scan from C to D. The beam reaches the middle of the screen's lowest line after 241.5 lines. At this point, the beam is quickly repositioned at the top of the screen and recommences in the middle of the screen's topmost visible line to produce an additional 241.5 lines interlaced with the original set. Thus the screen is refreshed 60 times per second rather than 30, and flicker is avoided.

A familiar example of digital data is **text** or character strings. While textual data are most convenient for human beings, they cannot, in character form, be easily stored or transmitted by data processing and communications systems. Such systems are designed for binary data. Thus a number of codes have been devised by which characters are represented by a sequence of bits. Perhaps the earliest common example of this is the Morse code. Today, the most commonly used text code is

---

[4]Note the use of a log scale for the *x*-axis. Because the *y*-axis is in units of decibels, it is effectively a log scale also. A basic review of log scales is in the math refresher document at the Computer Science Student Resource Site at WilliamStallings.com/StudentSupport.html.

[5]The concept of decibels is explained in Appendix 3A.

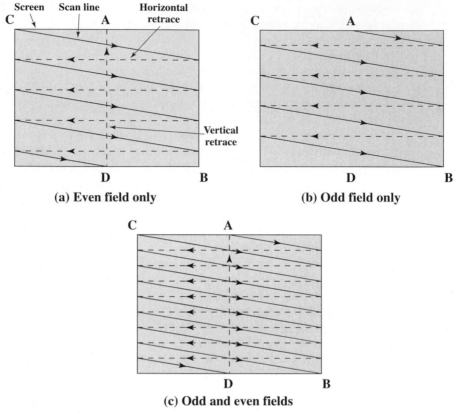

Figure 3.10   Video Interlaced Scanning

the International Reference Alphabet (IRA).[6] Each character in this code is represented by a unique 7-bit pattern; thus 128 different characters can be represented.
This is a larger number than is necessary, and some of the patterns represent invisi-
ble *control characters*. IRA-encoded characters are almost always stored and transmitted using 8 bits per character. The eighth bit is a parity bit used for error
detection. This bit is set such that the total number of binary 1s in each octet is
always odd (odd parity) or always even (even parity). Thus a transmission error that
changes a single bit, or any odd number of bits, can be detected.

Analog and Digital Signals

In a communications system, data are propagated from one point to another by
means of electromagnetic signals. An analog signal is a continuously varying electromagnetic wave that may be propagated over a variety of media, depending on
spectrum; examples are wire media, such as twisted pair and coaxial cable; fiber

---

[6] IRA is defined in ITU-T Recommendation T.50 and was formerly known as International Alphabet
Number 5 (IA5). The U.S. national version of IRA is referred to as the American Standard Code for
Information Interchange (ASCII). A description and table of the IRA code is contained in a supporting
document at this book's Web site.

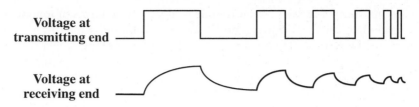

Figure 3.11 Attenuation of Digital Signals

optic cable; and unguided media, such as atmosphere or space propagation. A digital signal is a sequence of voltage pulses that may be transmitted over a wire medium; for example, a constant positive voltage level may represent binary 0 and a constant negative voltage level may represent binary 1.

The principal advantages of digital signaling are that it is generally cheaper than analog signaling and is less susceptible to noise interference. The principal disadvantage is that digital signals suffer more from attenuation than do analog signals. Figure 3.11 shows a sequence of voltage pulses, generated by a source using two voltage levels, and the received voltage some distance down a conducting medium. Because of the attenuation, or reduction, of signal strength at higher frequencies, the pulses become rounded and smaller. It should be clear that this attenuation can lead rather quickly to the loss of the information contained in the propagated signal.

In what follows, we first look at some specific examples of signal types and then discuss the relationship between data and signals.

Examples

Let us return to our three examples of the preceding subsection. For each example, we will describe the signal and estimate its bandwidth.

The most familiar example of analog information is audio, or acoustic, information, which, in the form of sound waves, can be perceived directly by human beings. One form of acoustic information, of course, is human speech, which has frequency components in the range 20 Hz to 20 kHz. This form of information is easily converted to an electromagnetic signal for transmission (Figure 3.12). In essence, all of the

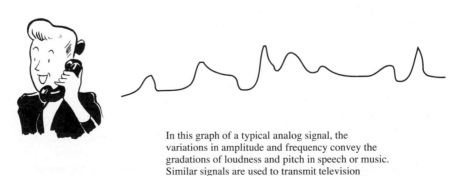

In this graph of a typical analog signal, the variations in amplitude and frequency convey the gradations of loudness and pitch in speech or music. Similar signals are used to transmit television pictures, but at much higher frequencies.

Figure 3.12 Conversion of Voice Input to Analog Signal

sound frequencies, whose amplitude is measured in terms of loudness, are converted into electromagnetic frequencies, whose amplitude is measured in volts. The telephone handset contains a simple mechanism for making such a conversion.

In the case of acoustic data (voice), the data can be represented directly by an electromagnetic signal occupying the same spectrum. However, there is a need to compromise between the fidelity of the sound as transmitted electrically and the cost of transmission, which increases with increasing bandwidth. As mentioned, the spectrum of speech is approximately 100 Hz to 7 kHz, although a much narrower bandwidth will produce acceptable voice reproduction. The standard spectrum for a voice channel is 300 to 3400 Hz. This is adequate for speech transmission, minimizes required transmission capacity, and allows the use of rather inexpensive telephone sets. The telephone transmitter converts the incoming acoustic voice signal into an electromagnetic signal over the range 300 to 3400 Hz. This signal is then transmitted through the telephone system to a receiver, which reproduces it as acoustic sound.

Now let us look at the video signal. To produce a video signal, a TV camera, which performs similar functions to the TV receiver, is used. One component of the camera is a photosensitive plate, upon which a scene is optically focused. An electron beam sweeps across the plate from left to right and top to bottom, in the same fashion as depicted in Figure 3.10 for the receiver. As the beam sweeps, an analog electric signal is developed proportional to the brightness of the scene at a particular spot. We mentioned that a total of 483 lines are scanned at a rate of 30 complete scans per second. This is an approximate number taking into account the time lost during the vertical retrace interval. The actual U.S. standard is 525 lines, but of these about 42 are lost during vertical retrace. Thus the horizontal scanning frequency is (525 lines) $\times$ (30 scan/s) = 15,750 lines per second, or 63.5 μs/line. Of this 63.5 μs, about 11 μs are allowed for horizontal retrace, leaving a total of 52.5 μs per video line.

Now we are in a position to estimate the bandwidth required for the video signal. To do this we must estimate the upper (maximum) and lower (minimum) frequency of the band. We use the following reasoning to arrive at the maximum frequency: The maximum frequency would occur during the horizontal scan if the scene were alternating between black and white as rapidly as possible. We can estimate this maximum value by considering the resolution of the video image. In the vertical dimension, there are 483 lines, so the maximum vertical resolution would be 483. Experiments have shown that the actual subjective resolution is about 70% of that number, or about 338 lines. In the interest of a balanced picture, the horizontal and vertical resolutions should be about the same. Because the ratio of width to height of a TV screen is 4:3, the horizontal resolution should be about $4/3 \times 338 = 450$ lines. As a worst case, a scanning line would be made up of 450 elements alternating black and white. The scan would result in a wave, with each cycle of the wave consisting of one higher (black) and one lower (white) voltage level. Thus there would be $450/2 = 225$ cycles of the wave in 52.5 μs, for a maximum frequency of about 4.2 MHz. This rough reasoning, in fact, is fairly accurate. The lower limit is a dc or zero frequency, where the dc component corresponds to the average illumination of the scene (the average value by which the brightness exceeds the reference black level). Thus the bandwidth of the video signal is approximately 4 MHz − 0 = 4 MHz.

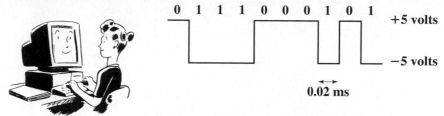

0 1 1 1 0 0 0 1 0 1   **+5 volts**

                                 −5 volts

                                 0.02 ms

User input at a PC is converted into a stream of binary
digits (1s and 0s). In this graph of a typical digital signal,
binary one is represented by −5 volts and binary zero is
represented by +5 volts. The signal for each bit has a duration
of 0.02 ms, giving a data rate of 50,000 bits per second (50 kbps).

Figure 3.13   Conversion of PC Input to Digital Signal

The foregoing discussion did not consider color or audio components of the signal. It turns out that, with these included, the bandwidth remains about 4 MHz.

Finally, the third example described is the general case of binary digital data. Binary information is generated by terminals, computers, and other data processing equipment and then converted into digital voltage pulses for transmission, as illustrated in Figure 3.13. A commonly used signal for such data uses two constant (dc) voltage levels, one level for binary 1 and one level for binary 0. (In Chapter 5, we shall see that this is but one alternative, referred to as NRZ.) Again, we are interested in the bandwidth of such a signal. This will depend, in any specific case, on the exact shape of the waveform and the sequence of 1s and 0s. We can obtain some understanding by considering Figure 3.8 (compare Figure 3.7). As can be seen, the greater the bandwidth of the signal, the more faithfully it approximates a digital pulse stream.

Data and Signals

In the foregoing discussion, we have looked at analog signals used to represent analog data and digital signals used to represent digital data. Generally, analog data are a function of time and occupy a limited frequency spectrum; such data can be represented by an electromagnetic signal occupying the same spectrum. Digital data can be represented by digital signals, with a different voltage level for each of the two binary digits.

As Figure 3.14 illustrates, these are not the only possibilities. Digital data can also be represented by analog signals by use of a modem (modulator/demodulator). The modem converts a series of binary (two-valued) voltage pulses into an analog signal by encoding the digital data onto a carrier frequency. The resulting signal occupies a certain spectrum of frequency centered about the carrier and may be propagated across a medium suitable for that carrier. The most common modems represent digital data in the voice spectrum and hence allow those data to be propagated over ordinary voice-grade telephone lines. At the other end of the line, another modem demodulates the signal to recover the original data.

In an operation very similar to that performed by a modem, analog data can be represented by digital signals. The device that performs this function for voice

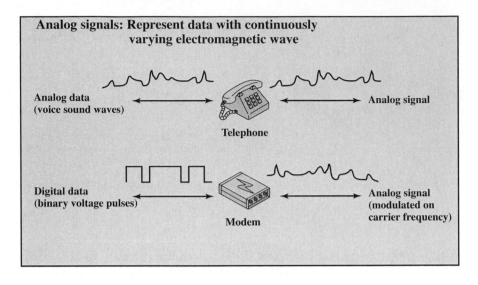

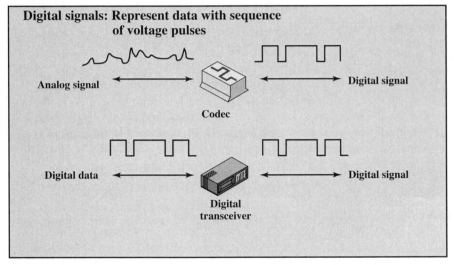

Figure 3.14 Analog and Digital Signaling of Analog and Digital Data

data is a codec (coder-decoder). In essence, the codec takes an analog signal that directly represents the voice data and approximates that signal by a bit stream. At the receiving end, the bit stream is used to reconstruct the analog data.

Thus Figure 3.14 suggests that data may be encoded into signals in a variety of ways. We will return to this topic in Chapter 5.

Analog and Digital Transmission

Both analog and digital signals may be transmitted on suitable transmission media. The way these signals are treated is a function of the transmission system. Table 3.1 summarizes the methods of data transmission. **Analog transmission** is a means of transmitting analog signals without regard to their content; the signals may represent analog data (e.g., voice) or digital data (e.g., binary data that pass through a modem). In either case, the analog signal will become weaker (attenuate) after a certain distance. To achieve longer distances, the analog transmission system includes amplifiers that boost the energy in the signal. Unfortunately, the amplifier also boosts the noise components. With amplifiers cascaded to achieve long distances, the signal becomes more and more distorted. For analog data, such as voice, quite a bit of distortion can be tolerated and the data remain intelligible. However, for digital data, cascaded amplifiers will introduce errors.

Digital transmission, in contrast, is concerned with the content of the signal. A digital signal can be transmitted only a limited distance before attenuation, noise, and other impairments endanger the integrity of the data. To achieve

Table 3.1   Analog and Digital Transmission

(a) Data and Signals

	Analog Signal	Digital Signal
Analog Data	Two alternatives: (1) signal occupies the same spectrum as the analog data; (2) analog data are encoded to occupy a different portion of spectrum.	Analog data are encoded using a codec to produce a digital bit stream.
Digital Data	Digital data are encoded using a modem to produce analog signal.	Two alternatives: (1) signal consists of a two voltage levels to represent the two binary values; (2) digital data are encoded to produce a digital signal with desired properties.

(b) Treatment of Signals

	Analog Transmission	Digital Transmission
Analog Signal	Is propagated through amplifiers; same treatment whether signal is used to represent analog data or digital data.	Assumes that the analog signal represents digital data. Signal is propagated through repeaters; at each repeater, digital data are recovered from inbound signal and used to generate a new analog outbound signal.
Digital Signal	Not used	Digital signal represents a stream of 1s and 0s, which may represent digital data or may be an encoding of analog data. Signal is propagated through repeaters; at each repeater, stream of 1s and 0s is recovered from inbound signal and used to generate a new digital outbound signal.

greater distances, repeaters are used. A repeater receives the digital signal, recovers the pattern of 1s and 0s, and retransmits a new signal. Thus the attenuation is overcome.

The same technique may be used with an analog signal if it is assumed that the signal carries digital data. At appropriately spaced points, the transmission system has repeaters rather than amplifiers. The repeater recovers the digital data from the analog signal and generates a new, clean analog signal. Thus noise is not cumulative.

The question naturally arises as to which is the preferred method of transmission. The answer being supplied by the telecommunications industry and its customers is digital. Both long-haul telecommunications facilities and intrabuilding services have moved to digital transmission and, where possible, digital signaling techniques. The most important reasons are as follows:

- **Digital technology:** The advent of large-scale integration (LSI) and very-large-scale integration (VLSI) technology has caused a continuing drop in the cost and size of digital circuitry. Analog equipment has not shown a similar drop.

- **Data integrity:** With the use of repeaters rather than amplifiers, the effects of noise and other signal impairments are not cumulative. Thus it is possible to transmit data longer distances and over lower quality lines by digital means while maintaining the integrity of the data.

- **Capacity utilization:** It has become economical to build transmission links of very high bandwidth, including satellite channels and optical fiber. A high degree of multiplexing is needed to utilize such capacity effectively, and this is more easily and cheaply achieved with digital (time division) rather than analog (frequency division) techniques. This is explored in Chapter 8.

- **Security and privacy:** Encryption techniques can be readily applied to digital data and to analog data that have been digitized.

- **Integration:** By treating both analog and digital data digitally, all signals have the same form and can be treated similarly. Thus economies of scale and convenience can be achieved by integrating voice, video, and digital data.

3.3 TRANSMISSION IMPAIRMENTS

With any communications system, the signal that is received may differ from the signal that is transmitted due to various transmission impairments. For analog signals, these impairments can degrade the signal quality. For digital signals, bit errors may be introduced: A binary 1 is transformed into a binary 0 and vice versa. In this section, we examine the various impairments and how they may affect the information-carrying capacity of a communication link; Chapter 5 looks at measures that can be taken to compensate for these impairments.

The most significant impairments are

- Attenuation and attenuation distortion
- Delay distortion
- Noise

Attenuation

The strength of a signal falls off with distance over any transmission medium. For guided media, this reduction in strength, or attenuation, is generally exponential and thus is typically expressed as a constant number of decibels per unit distance. For unguided media, attenuation is a more complex function of distance and the make-up of the atmosphere. Attenuation introduces three considerations for the transmission engineer. First, a received signal must have sufficient strength so that the electronic circuitry in the receiver can detect the signal. Second, the signal must maintain a level sufficiently higher than noise to be received without error. Third, attenuation is often an increasing function of frequency.

The first and second problems are dealt with by attention to signal strength and the use of amplifiers or repeaters. For a point-to-point link, the signal strength of the transmitter must be strong enough to be received intelligibly, but not so strong as to overload the circuitry of the transmitter or receiver, which would cause distortion. Beyond a certain distance, the attenuation becomes unacceptably great, and repeaters or amplifiers are used to boost the signal at regular intervals. These problems are more complex for multipoint lines where the distance from transmitter to receiver is variable.

The third problem is particularly noticeable for analog signals. Because the attenuation varies as a function of frequency, the received signal is distorted, reducing intelligibility. To overcome this problem, techniques are available for equalizing attenuation across a band of frequencies. This is commonly done for voice-grade telephone lines by using loading coils that change the electrical properties of the line; the result is to smooth out attenuation effects. Another approach is to use amplifiers that amplify high frequencies more than lower frequencies.

An example is provided in Figure 3.15a, which shows attenuation as a function of frequency for a typical leased line. In the figure, attenuation is measured relative to the attenuation at 1000 Hz. Positive values on the y-axis represent attenuation greater than that at 1000 Hz. A 1000-Hz tone of a given power level is applied to the input, and the power, P_{1000}, is measured at the output. For any other frequency f, the procedure is repeated and the relative attenuation in decibels is[7]

$$N_f = -10 \log_{10} \frac{P_f}{P_{1000}}$$

The solid line in Figure 3.15a shows attenuation without equalization. As can be seen, frequency components at the upper end of the voice band are attenuated

---

[7] In the remainder of this book, unless otherwise indicated, we use $\log(x)$ to mean $\log_{10}(x)$.

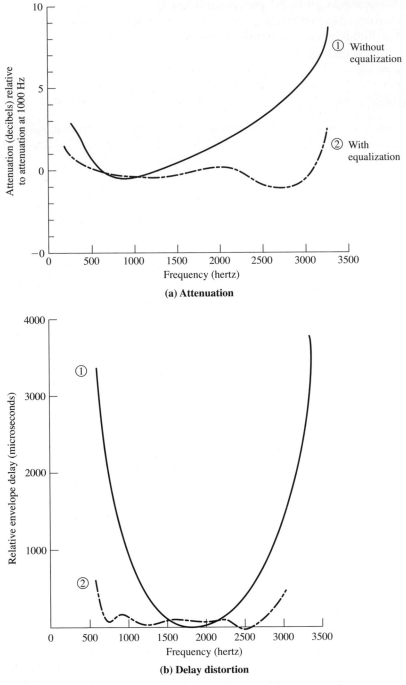

Figure 3.15   Attenuation and Delay Distortion Curves for a Voice Channel

much more than those at lower frequencies. It should be clear that this will result in a distortion of the received speech signal. The dashed line shows the effect of equalization. The flattened response curve improves the quality of voice signals. It also allows higher data rates to be used for digital data that are passed through a modem.

Attenuation distortion can present less of a problem with digital signals. As we have seen, the strength of a digital signal falls off rapidly with frequency (Figure 3.5b); most of the content is concentrated near the fundamental frequency or bit rate of the signal.

Delay Distortion

Delay distortion occurs because the velocity of propagation of a signal through a guided medium varies with frequency. For a bandlimited signal, the velocity tends to be highest near the center frequency and fall off toward the two edges of the band. Thus various frequency components of a signal will arrive at the receiver at different times, resulting in phase shifts between the different frequencies.

This effect is referred to as delay distortion because the received signal is distorted due to varying delays experienced at its constituent frequencies. Delay distortion is particularly critical for digital data. Consider that a sequence of bits is being transmitted, using either analog or digital signals. Because of delay distortion, some of the signal components of one bit position will spill over into other bit positions, causing intersymbol interference, which is a major limitation to maximum bit rate over a transmission channel.

Equalizing techniques can also be used for delay distortion. Again using a leased telephone line as an example, Figure 3.15b shows the effect of equalization on delay as a function of frequency.

Noise

For any data transmission event, the received signal will consist of the transmitted signal, modified by the various distortions imposed by the transmission system, plus additional unwanted signals that are inserted somewhere between transmission and reception. The latter, undesired signals are referred to as noise. It is noise that is the major limiting factor in communications system performance.

Noise may be divided into four categories:

- Thermal noise
- Intermodulation noise
- Crosstalk
- Impulse noise

Thermal noise is due to thermal agitation of electrons. It is present in all electronic devices and transmission media and is a function of temperature. Thermal noise is uniformly distributed across the bandwidths typically used in communications systems and hence is often referred to as white noise. Thermal noise cannot be eliminated and therefore places an upper bound on communications system performance. Because of the weakness of the signal received by satellite earth stations, thermal noise is particularly significant for satellite communication.

The amount of thermal noise to be found in a bandwidth of 1 Hz in any device or conductor is

$$N_0 = kT \, (\text{W/Hz})$$

where[8]

N_0 = noise power density in watts per 1 Hz of bandwidth

k = Boltzmann's constant = 1.38×10^{-23} J/K

T = temperature, in kelvins (absolute temperature), where the symbol K is used to represent 1 kelvin

Example 3.1 Room temperature is usually specified as $T = 17°C$, or 290 K. At this temperature, the thermal noise power density is:

$$N_0 = (1.38 \times 10^{-23}) \times 290 = 4 \times 10^{-21} \, \text{W/Hz} = -204 \, \text{dBW/Hz}$$

where dBW is the decibel-watt, defined in Appendix 3A.

The noise is assumed to be independent of frequency. Thus the thermal noise in watts present in a bandwidth of B Hertz can be expressed as

$$N = kTB$$

or, in decibel-watts,

$$N = 10 \log k + 10 \log T + 10 \log B$$
$$= -228.6 \, \text{dBW} + 10 \log T + 10 \log B$$

Example 3.2 Given a receiver with an effective noise temperature of 294 K and a 10-MHz bandwidth, the thermal noise level at the receiver's output is

$$N = -228.6 \, \text{dBW} + 10 \log(294) + 10 \log 10^7$$
$$= -228.6 + 24.7 + 70$$
$$= -133.9 \, \text{dBW}$$

When signals at different frequencies share the same transmission medium, the result may be **intermodulation noise**. The effect of intermodulation noise is to produce signals at a frequency that is the sum or difference of the two original

---

[8]A Joule (J) is the International System (SI) unit of electrical, mechanical, and thermal energy. A Watt is the SI unit of power, equal to one Joule per second. The kelvin (K) is the SI unit of thermodynamic temperature. For a temperature in kelvins of T, the corresponding temperature in degrees Celsius is equal to $T - 273.15$.

frequencies or multiples of those frequencies. For example, the mixing of signals at frequencies f_1 and f_2 might produce energy at the frequency $f_1 + f_2$. This derived signal could interfere with an intended signal at the frequency $f_1 + f_2$.

Intermodulation noise is produced by nonlinearities in the transmitter, receiver, and/or intervening transmission medium. Ideally, these components behave as linear systems; that is, the output is equal to the input times a constant. However, in any real system, the output is a more complex function of the input. Excessive nonlinearity can be caused by component malfunction or overload from excessive signal strength. It is under these circumstances that the sum and difference frequency terms occur.

Crosstalk has been experienced by anyone who, while using the telephone, has been able to hear another conversation; it is an unwanted coupling between signal paths. It can occur by electrical coupling between nearby twisted pairs or, rarely, coax cable lines carrying multiple signals. Crosstalk can also occur when microwave antennas pick up unwanted signals; although highly directional antennas are used, microwave energy does spread during propagation. Typically, crosstalk is of the same order of magnitude as, or less than, thermal noise.

All of the types of noise discussed so far have reasonably predictable and relatively constant magnitudes. Thus it is possible to engineer a transmission system to cope with them. **Impulse noise**, however, is noncontinuous, consisting of irregular pulses or noise spikes of short duration and of relatively high amplitude. It is generated from a variety of causes, including external electromagnetic disturbances, such as lightning, and faults and flaws in the communications system.

Impulse noise is generally only a minor annoyance for analog data. For example, voice transmission may be corrupted by short clicks and crackles with no loss of intelligibility. However, impulse noise is the primary source of error in digital data communication. For example, a sharp spike of energy of 0.01 s duration would not destroy any voice data but would wash out about 560 bits of data being transmitted at 56 kbps. Figure 3.16 is an example of the effect of noise on a digital signal. Here the noise consists of a relatively modest level of thermal noise plus occasional spikes of impulse noise. The digital data can be recovered from the signal by sampling the received waveform once per bit time. As can be seen, the noise is occasionally sufficient to change a 1 to a 0 or a 0 to a 1.

3.4 CHANNEL CAPACITY

We have seen that there are a variety of impairments that distort or corrupt a signal. For digital data, the question that then arises is to what extent these impairments limit the data rate that can be achieved. The maximum rate at which data can be transmitted over a given communication path, or channel, under given conditions, is referred to as the **channel capacity**.

There are four concepts here that we are trying to relate to one another.

- **Data rate:** This is the rate, in bits per second (bps), at which data can be communicated.

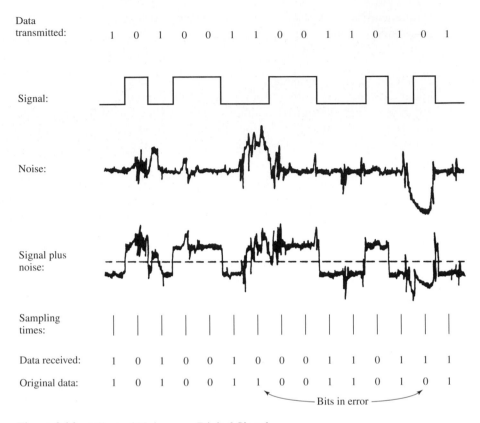

Figure 3.16 Effect of Noise on a Digital Signal

- **Bandwidth:** This is the bandwidth of the transmitted signal as constrained by the transmitter and the nature of the transmission medium, expressed in cycles per second, or Hertz.
- **Noise:** This is the average level of noise over the communications path.
- **Error rate:** This is the rate at which errors occur, where an error is the reception of a 1 when a 0 was transmitted or the reception of a 0 when a 1 was transmitted.

The problem we are addressing is this: Communications facilities are expensive and, in general, the greater the bandwidth of a facility, the greater the cost. Furthermore, all transmission channels of any practical interest are of limited bandwidth. The limitations arise from the physical properties of the transmission medium or from deliberate limitations at the transmitter on the bandwidth to prevent interference from other sources. Accordingly, we would like to make as efficient use as possible of a given bandwidth. For digital data, this means that we would like to get as high a data rate as possible at a particular limit of error rate for a given bandwidth. The main constraint on achieving this efficiency is noise.

Nyquist Bandwidth

To begin, let us consider the case of a channel that is noise free. In this environment, the limitation on data rate is simply the bandwidth of the signal. A formulation of this limitation, due to Nyquist, states that if the rate of signal transmission is $2B$, then a signal with frequencies no greater than B is sufficient to carry the signal rate. The converse is also true: Given a bandwidth of B, the highest signal rate that can be carried is $2B$. This limitation is due to the effect of intersymbol interference, such as is produced by delay distortion. The result is useful in the development of digital-to-analog encoding schemes and is derived in a supporting document at this book's web site.

Note that in the preceding paragraph, we referred to signal rate. If the signals to be transmitted are binary (two voltage levels), then the data rate that can be supported by B Hz is $2B$ bps. As an example, consider a voice channel being used, via modem, to transmit digital data. Assume a bandwidth of 3100 Hz. Then the capacity, C, of the channel is $2B = 6200$ bps. However, as we shall see in Chapter 5, signals with more than two levels can be used; that is, each signal element can represent more than one bit. For example, if four possible voltage levels are used as signals, then each signal element can represent two bits. With multilevel signaling, the Nyquist formulation becomes

$$C = 2B \log_2 M$$

where M is the number of discrete signal or voltage levels. Thus, for $M = 8$, a value used with some modems, C becomes 18,600 bps, for a bandwidth of 3100 Hz.

So, for a given bandwidth, the data rate can be increased by increasing the number of different signal elements. However, this places an increased burden on the receiver: Instead of distinguishing one of two possible signal elements during each signal time, it must distinguish one of M possible signal elements. Noise and other impairments on the transmission line will limit the practical value of M.

Shannon Capacity Formula

Nyquist's formula indicates that, all other things being equal, doubling the bandwidth doubles the data rate. Now consider the relationship among data rate, noise, and error rate. The presence of noise can corrupt one or more bits. If the data rate is increased, then the bits become "shorter" so that more bits are affected by a given pattern of noise. Thus, at a given noise level, the higher the data rate, the higher the error rate.

Figure 3.16 illustrates this relationship. If the data rate is increased, then more bits will occur during the interval of a noise spike and hence more errors will occur.

All of these concepts can be tied together neatly in a formula developed by the mathematician Claude Shannon. As we have just illustrated, the higher the data rate, the more damage that unwanted noise can do. For a given level of noise, we would expect that a greater signal strength would improve the ability to receive data correctly in the presence of noise. The key parameter involved in this reasoning is the signal-to-noise ratio (SNR, or S/N),[9] which is the ratio of the power in a signal to the power contained in the noise that is present at a particular point in the transmission. Typically, this ratio is measured at a receiver, because it is at this point that an attempt is made to process the signal and recover the data. For convenience, this ratio is often reported in decibels:

$$\text{SNR}_{dB} = 10 \log_{10} \frac{\text{signal power}}{\text{noise power}}$$

This expresses the amount, in decibels, that the intended signal exceeds the noise level. A high SNR will mean a high-quality signal and a low number of required intermediate repeaters.

The signal-to-noise ratio is important in the transmission of digital data because it sets the upper bound on the achievable data rate. Shannon's result is that the maximum channel capacity, in bits per second, obeys the equation

$$C = B \log_2(1 + \text{SNR}) \tag{2.1}$$

where C is the capacity of the channel in bits per second and B is the bandwidth of the channel in Hertz. The Shannon formula represents the theoretical maximum that can be achieved. In practice, however, only much lower rates are achieved. One reason for this is that the formula assumes white noise (thermal noise). Impulse noise is not accounted for, nor are attenuation distortion or delay distortion.

The capacity indicated in the preceding equation is referred to as the error-free capacity. Shannon proved that if the actual information rate on a channel is less than the error-free capacity, then it is theoretically possible to use a suitable signal code to achieve error-free transmission through the channel. Shannon's theorem unfortunately does not suggest a means for finding such codes, but it does provide a yardstick by which the performance of practical communication schemes may be measured.

Several other observations concerning the preceding equation may be instructive. For a given level of noise, it would appear that the data rate could be increased by increasing either signal strength or bandwidth. However, as the signal strength increases, so do the effects of nonlinearities in the system, leading to an increase in intermodulation noise. Note also that, because noise is assumed to be white, the wider the bandwidth, the more noise is admitted to the system. Thus, as B increases, SNR decreases.

---

[9]Some of the literature uses SNR; others use S/N. Also, in some cases the dimensionless quantity is referred to as SNR or S/N. and the quantity in decibels is referred to as SNR_{dB} or $(\text{S/N})_{dB}$. Others use just SNR or S/N to mean the dB quantity. This text uses SNR and SNR_{dB}.

Example 3.3 Let us consider an example that relates the Nyquist and Shannon formulations. Suppose that the spectrum of a channel is between 3 MHz and 4 MHz and $\text{SNR}_{dB} = 24$ dB. Then

$$B = 4\,\text{MHz} - 3\,\text{MHz} = 1\,\text{MHz}$$
$$\text{SNR}_{dB} = 24\,\text{dB} = 10\log_{10}(\text{SNR})$$
$$\text{SNR} = 251$$

Using Shannon's formula,

$$C = 10^6 \times \log_2(1 + 251) \approx 10^6 \times 8 = 8\,\text{Mbps}$$

This is a theoretical limit and, as we have said, is unlikely to be reached. But assume we can achieve the limit. Based on Nyquist's formula, how many signaling levels are required? We have:

$$C = 2B\log_2 M$$
$$8 \times 10^6 = 2 \times (10^6) \times \log_2 M$$
$$4 = \log_2 M$$
$$M = 16$$

The Expression E_b/N_0

Finally, we mention a parameter related to SNR that is more convenient for determining digital data rates and error rates and that is the standard quality measure for digital communication system performance. The parameter is the ratio of signal energy per bit to noise power density per Hertz, E_b/N_0. Consider a signal, digital or analog, that contains binary digital data transmitted at a certain bit rate R. Recalling that 1 Watt = 1 J/s, the energy per bit in a signal is given by $E_b = ST_b$, where S is the signal power and T_b is the time required to send one bit. The data rate R is just $R = 1/T_b$. Thus

$$\frac{E_b}{N_0} = \frac{S/R}{N_0} = \frac{S}{kTR}$$

or, in decibel notation,

$$\left(\frac{E_b}{N_0}\right)_{dB} = S_{dBW} - 10\log R - 10\log k - 10\log T$$
$$= S_{dBW} - 10\log R + 228.6\,\text{dBW} - 10\log T$$

The ratio E_b/N_0 is important because the bit error rate for digital data is a (decreasing) function of this ratio. Given a value of E_b/N_0 needed to achieve a desired error rate, the parameters in the preceding formula may be selected. Note that as the bit rate R increases, the transmitted signal power, relative to noise, must increase to maintain the required E_b/N_0.

Let us try to grasp this result intuitively by considering again Figure 3.16. The signal here is digital, but the reasoning would be the same for an analog signal. In several instances, the noise is sufficient to alter the value of a bit. If the data rate were doubled, the bits would be more tightly packed together, and the same passage of noise might destroy two bits. Thus, for constant signal and noise strength, an increase in data rate increases the error rate.

The advantage of E_b/N_0 over SNR is that the latter quantity depends on the bandwidth.

Example 3.4 For binary phase shift keying (defined in Chapter 5), $E_b/N_0 = 8.4$ dB is required for a bit error rate of 10^{-4} (one bit error out of every 10,000). If the effective noise temperature is 290°K (room temperature) and the data rate is 2400 bps, what received signal level is required?

We have

$$
\begin{aligned}
8.4 &= S(\text{dBW}) - 10\log 2400 + 228.6\,\text{dBW} - 10\log 290 \\
&= S(\text{dBW}) - (10)(3.38) + 228.6 - (10)(2.46) \\
S &= -161.8\,\text{dBW}
\end{aligned}
$$

We can relate E_b/N_0 to SNR as follows. We have

$$\frac{E_b}{N_0} = \frac{S}{N_0 R}$$

The parameter N_0 is the noise power density in Watts/Hertz. Hence, the noise in a signal with bandwidth B_T is $N = N_0 B_T$. Substituting, we have

$$\frac{E_b}{N_0} = \frac{S}{N} \frac{B_T}{R} \tag{2.2}$$

Another formulation of interest relates to E_b/N_0 spectral efficiency. Shannon's result [Equation (2.1)] can be rewritten as

$$\frac{S}{N} = 2^{C/B} - 1$$

Using Equation (2.2), and equating B_T with B and R with C, we have

$$\frac{E_b}{N_0} = \frac{B}{C}(2^{C/B} - 1)$$

This is a useful formula that relates the achievable spectral efficiency C/B to E_b/N_0.

> **Example 3.5** Suppose we want to find the minimum E_b/N_0 required to achieve a spectral efficiency of 6 bps/Hz. Then $E_b/N_0 = (1/6)(2^6 - 1) = 10.5 = 10.21$ dB.

3.5 RECOMMENDED READING

There are many books that cover the fundamentals of analog and digital transmission. [COUC01] is quite thorough. Other good reference works are [FREE99], which includes some of the examples used in this chapter, and [HAYK01].

COUC01   Couch, L. *Digital and Analog Communication Systems.* Upper Saddle River, NJ: Prentice Hall, 2001.

FREE99   Freeman, R. *Fundamentals of Telecommunications.* New York: Wiley, 1999.

HAYK01   Haykin, S. *Communication Systems.* New York: Wiley, 2001.

3.6 KEY TERMS, REVIEW QUESTIONS, AND PROBLEMS

Key Terms

absolute bandwidth	digital data	peak amplitude
analog data	digital signal	period
analog signal	digital transmission	periodic signal
analog transmission	direct link	point-to-point link
aperiodic	effective bandwidth	phase
attenuation	frequency	signal
attenuation distortion	frequency domain	signaling
bandwidth	full duplex	simplex
center frequency	fundamental frequency	spectrum
channel capacity	guided media	thermal noise
crosstalk	half duplex	time domain
data	impulse noise	transmission
dc component	intermodulation noise	unguided media
decibel (dB)	multipoint link	wavelength
delay distortion	noise	wireless

Review Questions

3.1 Differentiate between guided media and unguided media.
3.2 Differentiate between an analog and a digital electromagnetic signal.
3.3 What are three important characteristics of a periodic signal?
3.4 How many radians are there in a complete circle of 360 degrees?
3.5 What is the relationship between the wavelength and frequency of a sine wave?
3.6 What is the relationship between a signal's spectrum and its bandwidth?
3.7 What is attenuation?
3.8 Define channel capacity.
3.9 What key factors affect channel capacity?

Problems

3.1 **a.** For multipoint configuration, only one device at a time can transmit. Why?
   b. There are two methods of enforcing the rule that only one device can transmit. In the centralized method, one station is in control and can either transmit or allow a specified other station to transmit. In the decentralized method, the stations jointly cooperate in taking turns. What do you see as the advantages and disadvantages of the two methods?

3.2 A signal has a fundamental frequency of 1000 Hz. What is its period?

3.3 Express the following in the simplest form you can:
   a. $\sin(2\pi ft - \pi) + \sin(2\pi ft + \pi)$
   b. $\sin 2\pi ft + \sin(2\pi ft - \pi)$

3.4 Sound may be modeled as sinusoidal functions. Compare the relative frequency and wavelength of musical notes. Use 330 m/s as the speed of sound and the following frequencies for the musical scale.

Note	C	D	E	F	G	A	B	C
Frequency	264	297	330	352	396	440	495	528

3.5 If the solid curve in Figure 3.17 represents $\sin(2\pi t)$, what does the dotted curve represent? That is, the dotted curve can be written in the form $A \sin(2\pi ft + \phi)$; what are $A, f,$ and ϕ?

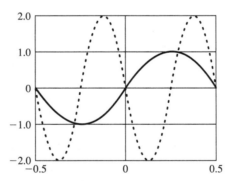

Figure 3.17 Figure for Problem 3.5

3.6 Decompose the signal $(1 + 0.1 \cos 5t) \cos 100t$ into a linear combination of sinusoidal function, and find the amplitude, frequency, and phase of each component. *Hint:* Use the identity for $\cos a \cos b$.

3.7 Find the period of the function $f(t) = (10 \cos t)^2$.

3.8 Consider two periodic functions $f_1(t)$ and $f_2(t)$, with periods T_1 and T_2, respectively. Is it always the case that the function $f(t) = f_1(t) + f_2(t)$ is periodic? If so, demonstrate this fact. If not, under what conditions is $f(t)$ periodic?

3.9 Figure 3.4 shows the effect of eliminating higher-harmonic components of a square wave and retaining only a few lower harmonic components. What would the signal look like in the opposite case; that is, retaining all higher harmonics and eliminating a few lower harmonics?

3.10 Figure 3.5b shows the frequency domain function for a single square pulse. The single pulse could represent a digital 1 in a communication system. Note that an infinite number of higher frequencies of decreasing magnitudes is needed to represent the single pulse. What implication does that have for a real digital transmission system?

3.11 IRA is a 7-bit code that allows 128 characters to be defined. In the 1970s, many newspapers received stories from the wire services in a 6-bit code called TTS. This code carried upper- and lowercase characters as well as many special characters and formatting commands. The typical TTS character set allowed over 100 characters to be defined. How do you think this could be accomplished?

3.12 For a video signal, what increase in horizontal resolution is possible if a bandwidth of 5 MHz is used? What increase in vertical resolution is possible? Treat the two questions separately; that is, the increased bandwidth is to be used to increase either horizontal or vertical resolution, but not both.

3.13 **a.** Suppose that a digitized TV picture is to be transmitted from a source that uses a matrix of 480 × 500 picture elements (pixels), where each pixel can take on one of 32 intensity values. Assume that 30 pictures are sent per second. (This digital source is roughly equivalent to broadcast TV standards that have been adopted.) Find the source rate R (bps).
   b. Assume that the TV picture is to be transmitted over a channel with 4.5-MHz bandwidth and a 35-dB signal-to-noise ratio. Find the capacity of the channel (bps).
   c. Discuss how the parameters given in part (a) could be modified to allow transmission of color TV signals without increasing the required value for R.

3.14 Given an amplifier with an effective noise temperature of 10,000°K and a 10-MHz bandwidth, what thermal noise level may we expect at its output?

3.15 What is the channel capacity for a teleprinter channel with a 300-Hz bandwidth and a signal-to-noise ratio of 3 dB, where the noise is white thermal noise?

3.16 A digital signaling system is required to operate at 9600 bps.
   a. If a signal element encodes a 4-bit word, what is the minimum required bandwidth of the channel?
   b. Repeat part (a) for the case of 8-bit words.

3.17 What is the thermal noise level of a channel with a bandwidth of 10 kHz carrying 1000 watts of power operating at 50°C?

3.18 Study the works of Shannon and Nyquist on channel capacity. Each places an upper limit on the bit rate of a channel based on two different approaches. How are the two related?

3.19 Given a channel with an intended capacity of 20 Mbps, the bandwidth of the channel is 3 MHz. Assuming white thermal noise, what signal to noise ratio is required to achieve this capacity?

3.20 The square wave of Figure 3.7c, with $T = 1$ ms, is passed through a lowpass filter that passes frequencies up to 8 kHz with no attenuation.
   a. Find the power in the output waveform.
   b. Assuming that at the filter input there is a thermal noise voltage with $N_0 = 0.1 \, \mu\text{Watt/Hz}$, find the output signal to noise ratio in dB.

3.21 If the received signal level for a particular digital system is -151 dBW and the receiver system effective noise temperature is 1500 K, what is E_b/N_0 for a link transmitting 2400 bps?

3.22 Fill in the missing elements in the following table of approximate power ratios for various dB levels.

Decibels	1	2	3	4	5	6	7	8	9	10
Losses			0.5							0.1
Gains			2							10

3.23 If an amplifier has a 30 dB voltage gain, what voltage ratio does the gain represent?

3.24 An amplifier has an output of 20 W. What is its output in dBW?

APPENDIX 3A DECIBELS AND SIGNAL STRENGTH

An important parameter in any transmission system is the signal strength. As a signal propagates along a transmission medium, there will be a loss, or *attenuation*, of signal strength. To compensate, amplifiers may be inserted at various points to impart a gain in signal strength.

It is customary to express gains, losses, and relative levels in decibels because

- Signal strength often falls off exponentially, so loss is easily expressed in terms of the decibel, which is a logarithmic unit.
- The net gain or loss in a cascaded transmission path can be calculated with simple addition and subtraction.

The decibel is a measure of the ratio between two signal levels. The decibel gain is given by

$$G_{dB} = 10 \log_{10} \frac{P_{out}}{P_{in}}$$

where

G_{dB} = gain, in decibels
P_{in} = input power level
P_{out} = output power level
$\log_{10}$ = logarithm to the base 10

Table 3.2 shows the relationship between decibel values and powers of 10.

There is some inconsistency in the literature over the use of the terms *gain* and *loss*. If the value of G_{dB} is positive, this represents an actual gain in power. For example, a gain of 3 dB means that the power has doubled. If the value of G_{dB} is negative, this represents an actual loss in power. For example, a gain of −3 dB means that the power has halved, and this is a loss of power. Normally, this is expressed by saying there is a loss of 3 dB. However, some of the literature would say that this is a loss of −3 dB. It makes more sense to say that a negative gain corresponds to a positive loss. Therefore, we define a decibel loss as

Table 3.2 Decibel Values

Power Ratio	dB	Power Ratio	dB
10^1	10	10^{-1}	−10
10^2	20	10^{-2}	−20
10^3	30	10^{-3}	−30
10^4	40	10^{-4}	−40
10^5	50	10^{-5}	−50
10^6	60	10^{-6}	−60

$$L_{dB} = -10 \log_{10} \frac{P_{out}}{P_{in}} = 10 \log_{10} \frac{P_{in}}{P_{out}} \qquad (2.2)$$

Example 3.6 If a signal with a power level of 10 mW is inserted onto a transmission line and the measured power some distance away is 5 mW, the loss can be expressed as $L_{dB} = 10 \log(10/5) = 10(0.3) = 3$ dB.

Note that the decibel is a measure of relative, not absolute, difference. A loss from 1000 mW to 500 mW is also a loss of 3 dB.

The decibel is also used to measure the difference in voltage, taking into account that power is proportional to the square of the voltage:

$$P = \frac{V^2}{R}$$

where

P = power dissipated across resistance R

V = voltage across resistance R

Thus

$$L_{dB} = 10 \log \frac{P_{in}}{P_{out}} = 10 \log \frac{V_{in}^2/R}{V_{out}^2/R} = 20 \log \frac{V_{in}}{V_{out}}$$

Example 3.7 Decibels are useful in determining the gain or loss over a series of transmission elements. Consider a series in which the input is at a power level of 4 mW, the first element is a transmission line with a 12-dB loss (−12-dB gain), the second element is an amplifier with a 35-dB gain, and the third element is a transmission line with a 10-dB loss. The net gain is (−12 + 35 − 10) = 13 dB. To calculate the output power P_{out},

$$G_{dB} = 13 = 10 \log(P_{out}/4 \, mW)$$
$$P_{out} = 4 \times 10^{1.3} \, mW = 79.8 \, MW$$

Decibel values refer to relative magnitudes or changes in magnitude, not to an absolute level. It is convenient to be able to refer to an absolute level of power or voltage in decibels so that gains and losses with reference to an initial signal level may be calculated easily. The **dBW (decibel-Watt)** is used extensively in microwave applications. The value of 1 W is selected as a reference and defined to be 0 dBW. The absolute decibel level of power in dBW is defined as

$$Power_{dBW} = 10 \log \frac{Power_W}{1 \, W}$$

Example 3.8   A power of 1000 W is 30 dBW, and a power of 1 mW is -30 dBW.

Another common unit is the **dBm (decibel-milliWatt)**, which uses 1 mW as the reference. Thus 0 dBM = 1 mW. The formula is

$$\text{Power}_{\text{dBW}} = 10 \log \frac{\text{Power}_{\text{mW}}}{1 \text{ mW}}$$

Note the following relationships:

$$+30 \text{ dBm} = 0 \text{ dBW}$$
$$0 \text{ dBm} = -30 \text{ dBW}$$

A unit in common use in cable television and broadband LAN applications is the dBmV (decibel-millivolt). This is an absolute unit with 0 dBmV equivalent to 1 mV. Thus

$$\text{Voltage}_{\text{dBmV}} = 20 \log \frac{\text{Voltage}_{\text{mV}}}{1 \text{ mV}}$$

In this case, the voltage levels are assumed to be across a 75-ohm resistance.

CHAPTER 4

TRANSMISSION MEDIA

KEY POINTS

- The transmission media that are used to convey information can be classified as guided or unguided. Guided media provide a physical path along which the signals are propagated; these include twisted pair, coaxial cable, and optical fiber. Unguided media employ an antenna for transmitting through air, vacuum, or water.

- Traditionally, twisted pair has been the workhorse for communications of all sorts. Higher data rates over longer distances can be achieved with coaxial cable, and so coaxial cable has often been used for high-speed local area network and for high-capacity long-distance trunk applications. However, the tremendous capacity of optical fiber has made that medium more attractive than coaxial cable, and thus optical fiber has taken over much of the market for high-speed LANs and for long-distance applications.

- Unguided transmission techniques commonly used for information communications include broadcast radio, terrestrial microwave, and satellite. Infrared transmission is used in some LAN applications.

In a data transmission system, the **transmission medium** is the physical path between transmitter and receiver. Recall from Chapter 3 that for **guided media**, electromagnetic waves are guided along a solid medium, such as copper twisted pair, copper coaxial cable, and optical fiber. For unguided media, wireless transmission occurs through the atmosphere, outer space, or water.

The characteristics and quality of a data transmission are determined both by the characteristics of the medium and the characteristics of the signal. In the case of guided media, the medium itself is more important in determining the limitations of transmission.

For unguided media, the bandwidth of the signal produced by the transmitting antenna is more important than the medium in determining transmission characteristics. One key property of signals transmitted by antenna is directionality. In general, signals at lower frequencies are omnidirectional; that is, the signal propagates in all directions from the antenna. At higher frequencies, it is possible to focus the signal into a directional beam.

In considering the design of data transmission systems, key concerns are data rate and distance: the greater the data rate and distance the better. A number of design factors relating to the transmission medium and the signal determine the data rate and distance:

- **Bandwidth:** All other factors remaining constant, the greater the bandwidth of a signal, the higher the data rate that can be achieved.

- **Transmission impairments:** Impairments, such as attenuation, limit the distance. For guided media, twisted pair generally suffers more impairment than coaxial cable, which in turn suffers more than optical fiber.

- **Interference:** Interference from competing signals in overlapping frequency bands can distort or wipe out a signal. Interference is of particular concern for unguided media but is also a problem with guided media. For guided media,

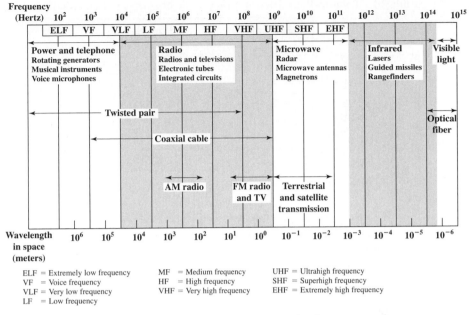

Figure 4.1 Electromagnetic Spectrum for Telecommunications

interference can be caused by emanations from nearby cables. For example, twisted pairs are often bundled together and conduits often carry multiple cables. Interference can also be experienced from unguided transmissions. Proper shielding of a guided medium can minimize this problem.

- **Number of receivers:** A guided medium can be used to construct a point-to-point link or a shared link with multiple attachments. In the latter case, each attachment introduces some attenuation and distortion on the line, limiting distance and/or data rate.

Figure 4.1 depicts the electromagnetic spectrum and indicates the frequencies at which various guided media and unguided transmission techniques operate. In this chapter we examine these guided and unguided alternatives. In all cases, we describe the systems physically, briefly discuss applications, and summarize key transmission characteristics.

4.1 GUIDED TRANSMISSION MEDIA

For guided transmission media, the transmission capacity, in terms of either data rate or bandwidth, depends critically on the distance and on whether the medium is point-to-point or multipoint. Table 4.1 indicates the characteristics typical for the common guided media for long-distance point-to-point applications; we defer a discussion of the use of these media for multipoint LANs to Part Four.

Table 4.1 Point-to-Point Transmission Characteristics of Guided Media [GLOV98]

	Frequency Range	Typical Attenuation	Typical Delay	Repeater Spacing
Twisted pair (with loading)	0 to 3.5 kHz	0.2 dB/km @ 1kHz	50 μs/km	2 km
Twisted pairs (multi-pair cables)	0 to 1 MHz	3 dB/km @ 1kHz	5 μs/km	2 km
Coaxial cable	0 to 500 MHz	7 dB/km @ 10 MHz	4 μs/km	1 to 9 km
Optical fiber	180 to 370 THz	0.2 to 0.5 dB/km	5 μs/km	40 km

THz = TeraHerz = 10^{12} Hz.

The three guided media commonly used for data transmission are twisted pair, coaxial cable, and optical fiber (Figure 4.2). We examine each of these in turn.

Twisted Pair

The least expensive and most widely used guided transmission medium is twisted pair.

Physical Description

A twisted pair consists of two insulated copper wires arranged in a regular spiral pattern. A wire pair acts as a single communication link. Typically, a number of these pairs are bundled together into a cable by wrapping them in a tough protective sheath. Over longer distances, cables may contain hundreds of pairs. The twisting tends to decrease the crosstalk interference between adjacent pairs in a cable. Neighboring pairs in a bundle typically have somewhat different twist lengths to reduce the crosstalk interference. On long-distance links, the twist length typically varies from 5 to 15 cm. The wires in a pair have thicknesses of from 0.4 to 0.9 mm.

Applications

By far the most common transmission medium for both analog and digital signals is twisted pair. It is the most commonly used medium in the telephone network and is the workhorse for communications within buildings.

In the telephone system, individual residential telephone sets are connected to the local telephone exchange, or "end office," by twisted-pair wire. These are referred to as **subscriber loops**. Within an office building, each telephone is also connected to a twisted pair, which goes to the in-house private branch exchange (PBX) system or to a Centrex facility at the end office. These twisted-pair installations were designed to support voice traffic using analog signaling. However, by means of a modem, these facilities can handle digital data traffic at modest data rates.

Twisted pair is also the most common medium used for digital signaling. For connections to a digital data switch or digital PBX within a building, a data rate of 64 kbps is common. Twisted pair is also commonly used within a building for local area networks supporting personal computers. Data rates for such products are typically in the neighborhood of 10 Mbps. However, twisted-pair networks with data rates of to 1 Gbps have been developed, although these are quite limited in terms of

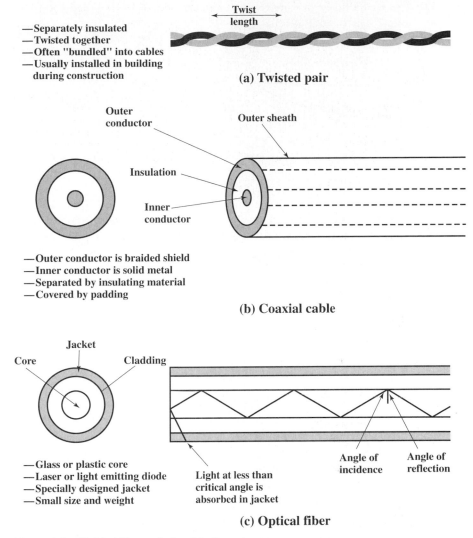

—Separately insulated
—Twisted together
—Often "bundled" into cables
—Usually installed in building
   during construction

(a) Twisted pair

—Outer conductor is braided shield
—Inner conductor is solid metal
—Separated by insulating material
—Covered by padding

(b) Coaxial cable

—Glass or plastic core
—Laser or light emitting diode
—Specially designed jacket
—Small size and weight

(c) Optical fiber

Figure 4.2 Guided Transmission Media

the number of devices and geographic scope of the network. For long-distance applications, twisted pair can be used at data rates of 4 Mbps or more.

Twisted pair is much less expensive than the other commonly used guided transmission media (coaxial cable, optical fiber) and is easier to work with.

Transmission Characteristics

Twisted pair may be used to transmit both analog and digital transmission. For analog signals, amplifiers are required about every 5 to 6 km. For digital transmission (using either analog or digital signals), repeaters are required every 2 or 3 km.

Compared to other commonly used guided transmission media (coaxial cable, optical fiber), twisted pair is limited in distance, bandwidth, and data rate. As

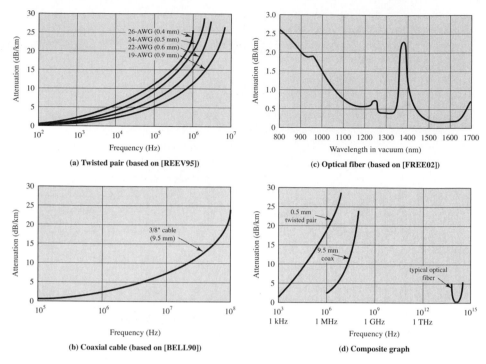

Figure 4.3 Attenuation of Typical Guided Media

Figure 4.3a shows, the attenuation for twisted pair is a very strong function of frequency. Other impairments are also severe for twisted pair. The medium is quite susceptible to interference and noise because of its easy coupling with electromagnetic fields. For example, a wire run parallel to an ac power line will pick up 60-Hz energy. Impulse noise also easily intrudes into twisted pair. Several measures are taken to reduce impairments. Shielding the wire with metallic braid or sheathing reduces interference. The twisting of the wire reduces low-frequency interference, and the use of different twist lengths in adjacent pairs reduces crosstalk.

For point-to-point analog signaling, a bandwidth of up to about 1 MHz is possible. This accommodates a number of voice channels. For long-distance digital point-to-point signaling, data rates of up to a few Mbps are possible; for very short distances, data rates of up to 1 Gbps have been achieved in commercially available products.

Unshielded and Shielded Twisted Pair

Twisted pair comes in two varieties: unshielded and shielded. Unshielded twisted pair (UTP) is ordinary telephone wire. Office buildings, by universal practice, are prewired with excess unshielded twisted pair, more than is needed for simple telephone support. This is the least expensive of all the transmission media commonly used for local area networks and is easy to work with and easy to install.

Unshielded twisted pair is subject to external electromagnetic interference, including interference from nearby twisted pair and from noise generated in the environment. A way to improve the characteristics of this medium is to shield the twisted pair with a metallic braid or sheathing that reduces interference. This shielded twisted pair (STP) provides better performance at higher data rates. However, it is more expensive and more difficult to work with than unshielded twisted pair.

Category 3 and Category 5 UTP

Most office buildings are prewired with a type of 100-ohm twisted pair cable commonly referred to as voice grade. Because voice-grade twisted pair is already installed, it is an attractive alternative for use as a LAN medium. Unfortunately, the data rates and distances achievable with voice-grade twisted pair are limited.

In 1991, the Electronic Industries Association published standard EIA-568, *Commercial Building Telecommunications Cabling Standard*, which specifies the use of voice-grade unshielded twisted pair as well as shielded twisted pair for in-building data applications. At that time, the specification was felt to be adequate for the range of frequencies and data rates found in office environments. Up to that time, the principal interest for LAN designs was in the range of data rates from 1 Mbps to 16 Mbps. Subsequently, as users migrated to higher-performance workstations and applications, there was increasing interest in providing LANs that could operate up to 100 Mbps over inexpensive cable. In response to this need, EIA-568-A was issued in 1995. The new standard reflects advances in cable and connector design and test methods. It covers 150-ohm shielded twisted pair and 100-ohm unshielded twisted pair.

EIA-568-A recognizes three categories of UTP cabling:

- **Category 3:** UTP cables and associated connecting hardware whose transmission characteristics are specified up to 16 MHz
- **Category 4:** UTP cables and associated connecting hardware whose transmission characteristics are specified up to 20 MHz
- **Category 5:** UTP cables and associated connecting hardware whose transmission characteristics are specified up to 100 MHz

Of these, it is Category 3 and Category 5 cable that have received the most attention for LAN applications. Category 3 corresponds to the voice-grade cable found in abundance in most office buildings. Over limited distances, and with proper design, data rates of up to 16 Mbps should be achievable with Category 3. Category 5 is a data-grade cable that is becoming increasingly common for preinstallation in new office buildings. Over limited distances, and with proper design, data rates of up to 100 Mbps should be achievable with Category 5.

A key difference between Category 3 and Category 5 cable is the number of twists in the cable per unit distance. Category 5 is much more tightly twisted, with a typical twist length of 0.6 to 0.85 cm, compared to 7.5 to 10 cm for Category 3. The tighter twisting of Category 5 is more expensive but provides much better performance than Category 3.

Table 4.2 summarizes the performance of Category 3 and 5 UTP, as well as the STP specified in EIA-568-A. The first parameter used for comparison, attenuation, is fairly straightforward. The strength of a signal falls off with distance over any transmission medium. For guided media attenuation is generally exponential and therefore is typically expressed as a constant number of decibels per unit distance.

Table 4.2 Comparison of Shielded and Unshielded Twisted Pair

Frequency (MHz)	Attenuation (dB per 100 m)			Near-end Crosstalk (dB)		
	Category 3 UTP	Category 5 UTP	150-ohm STP	Category 3 UTP	Category 5 UTP	150-ohm STP
1	2.6	2.0	1.1	41	62	58
4	5.6	4.1	2.2	32	53	58
16	13.1	8.2	4.4	23	44	50.4
25	—	10.4	6.2	—	41	47.5
100	—	22.0	12.3	—	32	38.5
300	—	—	21.4	—	—	31.3

Near-end crosstalk as it applies to twisted pair wiring systems is the coupling of the signal from one pair of conductors to another pair. These conductors may be the metal pins in a connector or wire pairs in a cable. The near end refers to coupling that takes place when the transmit signal entering the link couples back to the receiving conductor pair at that same end of the link (i.e., the near transmitted signal is picked up by the near receive pair).

Since the publication of EIA-568-A, there has been ongoing work on the development of standards for premises cabling, driven by two issues. First, the Gigabit Ethernet specification requires the definition of parameters that are not specified completely in any published cabling standard. Second, there is a desire to specify cabling performance to higher levels, namely Enhanced Category 5 (Cat 5E), Category 6, and Category 7. Tables 4.3 and 4.4 summarize these new cabling schemes and compare them to the existing standards.

Coaxial Cable

Physical Description

Coaxial cable, like twisted pair, consists of two conductors, but is constructed differently to permit it to operate over a wider range of frequencies. It consists of a hollow outer cylindrical conductor that surrounds a single inner wire conductor (Figure 4.2b). The inner conductor is held in place by either regularly spaced insulating

Table 4.3 Twisted Pair Categories and Classes

	Category 3 Class C	Category 5 Class D	Category 5E	Category 6 Class E	Category 7 Class F
Bandwidth	16 MHz	100 MHz	100 MHz	200 MHz	600 MHz
Cable Type	UTP	UTP/FTP	UTP/FTP	UTP/FTP	SSTP
Link Cost (Cat 5 = 1)	0.7	1	1.2	1.5	2.2

UTP = Unshielded twisted pair
FTP = Foil twisted pair
SSTP = Shielded screen twisted pair

Table 4.4 High-Performance LAN Copper Cabling Alternatives [JOHN98]

Name	Construction	Expected Performance	Cost
Category 5 UTP	Cable consists of 4 pairs of 24 AWG (0.50 mm) copper with thermoplastic polyolefin or fluorinated ethylene propylene (FEP) jacket. Outside sheath consists of polyvinylchlorides (PVC), a fire-retardant polyolefin or fluoropolymers.	Mixed and matched cables and connecting hardware from various manufacturers that have a reasonable chance of meeting TIA Cat 5 Channel and ISO Class D requirements. No manufacturer's warranty is involved.	1
Enhanced Cat 5 UTP (Cat 5E)	Cable consists of 4 pairs of 24 AWG (0.50 mm) copper with thermoplastic polyolefin or fluorinated ethylene propylene (FEP) jacket. Outside sheath consists of polyvinylchlorides (PVC), a fire-retardant polyolefin or fluoropolymers. Higher care taken in design and manufacturing.	Category 5 components from one supplier or from multiple suppliers where components have been deliberately matched for improved impedance and balance. Offers ACR performance in excess of Cat 5 Channel and Class D as well as a 10-year or greater warranty.	1.2
Category 6 UTP	Cable consists of 4 pairs of 0.50 to 0.53 mm copper with thermoplastic polyolefin or fluorinated ethylene propylene (FEP) jacket. Outside sheath consists of polyvinylchlorides (PVC), a fire-retardant polyolefin or fluoropolymers. Extremely high care taken in design and manufacturing. Advanced connector designs.	Category 6 components from one supplier that are extremely well matched. Channel zero ACR point (effective bandwidth) is guaranteed to 200 MHz or beyond. Best available UTP. Performance specifications for Category 6 UTP to 250 MHz are under development.	1.5
Foil Twisted Pair	Cable consists of 4 pairs of 24 AWG (0.50 mm) copper with thermoplastic polyolefin or fluorinated ethylene propylene (FEP) jacket. Pairs are surrounded by a common metallic foil shield. Outside sheath consists of polyvinylchlorides (PVC), a fire-retardant polyolefin, or fluoropolymers.	Category 5 components from one supplier or from multiple suppliers where components have been deliberately designed to minimize EMI susceptibility and maximize EMI immunity. Various grades may offer increased ACR performance.	1.3
Shielded Foil Twisted Pair	Cable consists of 4 pairs of 24 AWG (0.50 mm) copper with thermoplastic polyolefin or fluorinated ethylene propylene (FEP) jacket. Pairs are surrounded by a common metallic foil shield, followed by a braided metallic shield. Outside sheath consists of polyvinylchlorides (PVC), a fire-retardant polyolefin, or fluoropolymers.	Category 5 components from one supplier or from multiple suppliers where components have been deliberately designed to minimize EMI susceptibility and maximize EMI immunity. Offers superior EMI protection to FTP.	1.4
Category 7 Shielded-Screen Twisted Pair	Also called PiMF (for Pairs in Metal Foil), SSTP of 4 pairs of 22-23AWG copper with a thermoplastic polyolefin or fluorinated ethylenepropylene (FEP) jacket. Pairs are individually surrounded by a helical or longitudinal metallic foil shield, followed by a braided metallic shield. Outside sheath of polyvinylchlorides (PVC), a fire-retardant polyolefin, or fluoropolymers.	Category 7 cabling provides positive ACR to 600 to 1200 MHz. Shielding on the individual pairs gives it phenomenal ACR.	2.2

ACR = Attenuation to crosstalk ratio
EMI = Electromagnetic interference

101

rings or a solid dielectric material. The outer conductor is covered with a jacket or shield. A single coaxial cable has a diameter of from 1 to 2.5 cm. Coaxial cable can be used over longer distances and support more stations on a shared line than twisted pair.

Applications

Coaxial cable is perhaps the most versatile transmission medium and is enjoying widespread use in a wide variety of applications. The most important of these are

- Television distribution
- Long-distance telephone transmission
- Short-run computer system links
- Local area networks

Coaxial cable is widely used as a means of distributing TV signals to individual homes—cable TV. From its modest beginnings as Community Antenna Television (CATV), designed to provide service to remote areas, cable TV reaches almost as many homes and offices as the telephone. A cable TV system can carry dozens or even hundreds of TV channels at ranges up to a few tens of kilometers.

Coaxial cable has traditionally been an important part of the long-distance telephone network. Today, it faces increasing competition from optical fiber, terrestrial microwave, and satellite. Using frequency division multiplexing (FDM, see Chapter 8), a coaxial cable can carry over 10,000 voice channels simultaneously.

Coaxial cable is also commonly used for short-range connections between devices. Using digital signaling, coaxial cable can be used to provide high-speed I/O channels on computer systems.

Transmission Characteristics

Coaxial cable is used to transmit both analog and digital signals. As can be seen from Figure 4.3b, coaxial cable has frequency characteristics that are superior to those of twisted pair, and can hence be used effectively at higher frequencies and data rates. Because of its shielded, concentric construction, coaxial cable is much less susceptible to interference and crosstalk than twisted pair. The principal constraints on performance are attenuation, thermal noise, and intermodulation noise. The latter is present only when several channels (FDM) or frequency bands are in use on the cable.

For long-distance transmission of analog signals, amplifiers are needed every few kilometers, with closer spacing required if higher frequencies are used. The usable spectrum for analog signaling extends to about 500 MHz. For digital signaling, repeaters are needed every kilometer or so, with closer spacing needed for higher data rates.

Optical Fiber

Physical Description

An optical fiber is a thin (2 to 125 μm), flexible medium capable of guiding an optical ray. Various glasses and plastics can be used to make optical fibers. The lowest losses have been obtained using fibers of ultrapure fused silica. Ultrapure fiber is difficult to manufacture; higher-loss multicomponent glass fibers are more economical and still provide good performance. Plastic fiber is even less costly and can be used for short-haul links, for which moderately high losses are acceptable.

An optical fiber cable has a cylindrical shape and consists of three concentric sections: the core, the cladding, and the jacket (Figure 4.2c). The **core** is the innermost section and consists of one or more very thin strands, or fibers, made of glass or plastic; the core has a diameter in the range of 8 to 100 μm. Each fiber is surrounded by its own **cladding**, a glass or plastic coating that has optical properties different from those of the core. The interface between the core and cladding acts as a reflector to confine light that would otherwise escape the core. The outermost layer, surrounding one or a bundle of cladded fibers, is the **jacket**. The jacket is composed of plastic and other material layered to protect against moisture, abrasion, crushing, and other environmental dangers.

Applications

One of the most significant technological breakthroughs in data transmission has been the development of practical fiber optic communications systems. Optical fiber already enjoys considerable use in long-distance telecommunications, and its use in military applications is growing. The continuing improvements in performance and decline in prices, together with the inherent advantages of optical fiber, have made it increasingly attractive for local area networking. The following characteristics distinguish optical fiber from twisted pair or coaxial cable:

- **Greater capacity:** The potential bandwidth, and hence data rate, of optical fiber is immense; data rates of hundreds of Gbps over tens of kilometers have been demonstrated. Compare this to the practical maximum of hundreds of Mbps over about 1 km for coaxial cable and just a few Mbps over 1 km or up to 100 Mbps to 1 Gbps over a few tens of meters for twisted pair.

- **Smaller size and lighter weight:** Optical fibers are considerably thinner than coaxial cable or bundled twisted-pair cable—at least an order of magnitude thinner for comparable information transmission capacity. For cramped conduits in buildings and underground along public rights-of-way, the advantage of small size is considerable. The corresponding reduction in weight reduces structural support requirements.

- **Lower attenuation:** Attenuation is significantly lower for optical fiber than for coaxial cable or twisted pair (Figure 4.3c) and is constant over a wide range.

- **Electromagnetic isolation:** Optical fiber systems are not affected by external electromagnetic fields. Thus the system is not vulnerable to interference, impulse noise, or crosstalk. By the same token, fibers do not radiate energy, so there is little interference with other equipment and there is a high degree of security from eavesdropping. In addition, fiber is inherently difficult to tap.

- **Greater repeater spacing:** Fewer repeaters mean lower cost and fewer sources of error. The performance of optical fiber systems from this point of view has been steadily improving. Repeater spacing in the tens of kilometers for optical fiber is common, and repeater spacings of hundreds of kilometers have been demonstrated. Coaxial and twisted-pair systems generally have repeaters every few kilometers.

Five basic categories of application have become important for optical fiber:

- Long-haul trunks
- Metropolitan trunks
- Rural exchange trunks
- Subscriber loops
- Local area networks

Long-haul fiber transmission is becoming increasingly common in the telephone network. Long-haul routes average about 1500 km in length and offer high capacity (typically 20,000 to 60,000 voice channels). These systems compete economically with microwave and have so underpriced coaxial cable in many developed countries that coaxial cable is rapidly being phased out of the telephone network in such countries. Undersea optical fiber cables have also enjoyed increasing use.

Metropolitan trunking circuits have an average length of 12 km and may have as many as 100,000 voice channels in a trunk group. Most facilities are installed in underground conduits and are repeaterless, joining telephone exchanges in a metropolitan or city area. Included in this category are routes that link long-haul microwave facilities that terminate at a city perimeter to the main telephone exchange building downtown.

Rural exchange trunks have circuit lengths ranging from 40 to 160 km and link towns and villages. In the United States, they often connect the exchanges of different telephone companies. Most of these systems have fewer than 5000 voice channels. The technology used in these applications competes with microwave facilities.

Subscriber loop circuits are fibers that run directly from the central exchange to a subscriber. These facilities are beginning to displace twisted pair and coaxial cable links as the telephone networks evolve into full-service networks capable of handling not only voice and data, but also image and video. The initial penetration of optical fiber in this application is for the business subscriber, but fiber transmission into the home will soon begin to appear.

A final important application of optical fiber is for local area networks. Standards have been developed and products introduced for optical fiber networks that have a total capacity of 100 Mbps to 10 Gbps and can support hundreds or even thousands of stations in a large office building or a complex of buildings.

The advantages of optical fiber over twisted pair and coaxial cable become more compelling as the demand for all types of information (voice, data, image, video) increases.

Transmission Characteristics

Optical fiber transmits a signal-encoded beam of light by means of **total internal reflection**. Total internal reflection can occur in any transparent medium that has a higher index of refraction than the surrounding medium. In effect, the optical fiber acts as a waveguide for frequencies in the range of about 10^{14} to 10^{15} Hertz; this covers portions of the infrared and visible spectra.

Figure 4.4 shows the principle of optical fiber transmission. Light from a source enters the cylindrical glass or plastic core. Rays at shallow angles are reflected and propagated along the fiber; other rays are absorbed by the surrounding

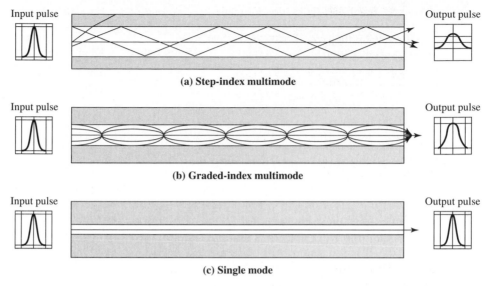

Figure 4.4 Optical Fiber Transmission Modes

material. This form of propagation is called **step-index multimode**, referring to the variety of angles that will reflect. With multimode transmission, multiple propagation paths exist, each with a different path length and hence time to traverse the fiber. This causes signal elements (light pulses) to spread out in time, which limits the rate at which data can be accurately received. Put another way, the need to leave spacing between the pulses limits data rate. This type of fiber is best suited for transmission over very short distances. When the fiber core radius is reduced, fewer angles will reflect. By reducing the radius of the core to the order of a wavelength, only a single angle or mode can pass: the axial ray. This **single-mode** propagation provides superior performance for the following reason. Because there is a single transmission path with single-mode transmission, the distortion found in multimode cannot occur. Single-mode is typically used for long-distance applications, including telephone and cable television. Finally, by varying the index of refraction of the core, a third type of transmission, known as **graded-index multimode**, is possible. This type is intermediate between the other two in characteristics. The higher refractive index (discussed subsequently) at the center makes the light rays moving down the axis advance more slowly than those near the cladding. Rather than zigzagging off the cladding, light in the core curves helically because of the graded index, reducing its travel distance. The shortened path and higher speed allows light at the periphery to arrive at a receiver at about the same time as the straight rays in the core axis. Graded-index fibers are often used in local area networks.

Two different types of light source are used in fiber optic systems: the light-emitting diode (LED) and the injection laser diode (ILD). Both are semiconductor devices that emit a beam of light when a voltage is applied. The LED is less costly, operates over a greater temperature range, and has a longer operational life. The ILD, which operates on the laser principle, is more efficient and can sustain greater data rates.

Table 4.5 Frequency Utilization for Fiber Applications

Wavelength (in vacuum) Range (nm)	Frequency Range (THz)	Band Label	Fiber Type	Application
820 to 900	366 to 333		Multimode	LAN
1280 to 1350	234 to 222	S	Single mode	Various
1528 to 1561	196 to 192	C	Single mode	WDM
1561 to 1620	192 to 185	L	Single mode	WDM

WDM = wavelength division multiplexing (see Chapter 8)

There is a relationship among the wavelength employed, the type of transmission, and the achievable data rate. Both single mode and multimode can support several different wavelengths of light and can employ laser or LED light sources. In optical fiber, based on the attenuation characteristics of the medium and on properties of light sources and receivers, four transmission windows are appropriate, shown in Table 4.5.

Note the tremendous bandwidths available. For the four windows, the respective bandwidths are 33 THz, 12 THz, 4 THz, and 7 THz. This is several orders of magnitude greater than the bandwidth available in the radio-frequency spectrum.

One confusing aspect of reported attenuation figures for fiber optic transmission is that, invariably, fiber optic performance is specified in terms of wavelength rather than frequency. The wavelengths that appear in graphs and tables are the wavelengths corresponding to transmission in a vacuum. However, on the fiber, the velocity of propagation is less than the speed of light in a vacuum (c); the result is that although the frequency of the signal is unchanged, the wavelength is changed.

Example 4.1 For a wavelength in vacuum of 1550 nm, the corresponding frequency is $f = c/\lambda = (3 \times 10^8)/(1550 \times 10^{-9}) = 193.4 \times 10^{12} = 193.4$ THz. For a typical single mode fiber, the velocity of propagation is approximately $v = 2.04 \times 10^8$. In this case, a frequency of 193.4 THz corresponds to a wavelength of $\lambda = v/f = (2.04 \times 10^8)/(193.4 \times 10^{12}) = 1055$ nm. Therefore, on this fiber, when a wavelength of 1550 nm is cited, the actual wavelength on the fiber is 1055 nm.

The four transmission windows are in the infrared portion of the frequency spectrum, below the visible-light portion, which is 400 to 700 nm. The loss is lower at higher wavelengths, allowing greater data rates over longer distances. Many local applications today use 850-nm LED light sources. Although this combination is relatively inexpensive, it is generally limited to data rates under 100 Mbps and distances of a few kilometers. To achieve higher data rates and longer distances, a 1300-nm LED or laser source is needed. The highest data rates and longest distances require 1500-nm laser sources.

Figure 4.3c shows attenuation versus wavelength for a typical optical fiber. The unusual shape of the curve is due to the combination of a variety of factors that contribute to attenuation. The two most important of these are absorption and scattering. In this context, the term *scattering* refers to the change in direction of light rays after they strike small particles or impurities in the medium.

4.2   WIRELESS TRANSMISSION

Three general ranges of frequencies are of interest in our discussion of wireless transmission. Frequencies in the range of about 1 GHz (gigahertz = 10^9 Hertz) to 40 GHz are referred to as **microwave frequencies**. At these frequencies, highly directional beams are possible, and microwave is quite suitable for point-to-point transmission. Microwave is also used for satellite communications. Frequencies in the range of 30 MHz to 1 GHz are suitable for omnidirectional applications. We refer to this range as the **radio** range.

Another important frequency range, for local applications, is the infrared portion of the spectrum. This covers, roughly, from 3×10^{11} to 2×10^{14} Hz. Infrared is useful to local point-to-point and multipoint applications within confined areas, such as a single room.

For unguided media, transmission and reception are achieved by means of an antenna. Before looking at specific categories of wireless transmission, we provide a brief introduction to antennas.

Antennas

An antenna can be defined as an electrical conductor or system of conductors used either for radiating electromagnetic energy or for collecting electromagnetic energy. For transmission of a signal, electrical energy from the transmitter is converted into electromagnetic energy by the antenna and radiated into the surrounding environment (atmosphere, space, water). For reception of a signal, electromagnetic energy impinging on the antenna is converted into electrical energy and fed into the receiver.

In two-way communication, the same antenna can be and often is used for both transmission and reception. This is possible because any antenna transfers energy from the surrounding environment to its input receiver terminals with the same efficiency that it transfers energy from the output transmitter terminals into the surrounding environment, assuming that the same frequency is used in both directions. Put another way, antenna characteristics are essentially the same whether an antenna is sending or receiving electromagnetic energy.

An antenna will radiate power in all directions but, typically, does not perform equally well in all directions. A common way to characterize the performance of an antenna is the radiation pattern, which is a graphical representation of the radiation properties of an antenna as a function of space coordinates. The simplest pattern is produced by an idealized antenna known as the isotropic antenna. An

isotropic antenna is a point in space that radiates power in all directions equally. The actual radiation pattern for the isotropic antenna is a sphere with the antenna at the center.

Parabolic Reflective Antenna

An important type of antenna is the **parabolic reflective antenna**, which is used in terrestrial microwave and satellite applications. You may recall from your precollege geometry studies that a parabola is the locus of all points equidistant from a fixed line and a fixed point not on the line. The fixed point is called the *focus* and the fixed line is called the *directrix* (Figure 4.5a). If a parabola is revolved about its axis, the surface generated is called a *paraboloid*. A cross section through the paraboloid parallel to its axis forms a parabola and a cross section perpendicular to the axis forms a circle. Such surfaces are used in headlights, optical and radio telescopes, and microwave antennas because of the following property: If a source of electromagnetic energy (or sound) is placed at the focus of the paraboloid, and if the paraboloid is a reflecting surface, then the wave will bounce back in lines parallel to the axis of the paraboloid; Figure 4.5b shows this effect in cross section. In theory, this effect creates a parallel beam without dispersion. In practice, there will be some dispersion, because the source of energy must occupy more than one point. The larger the diameter of the antenna, the more tightly directional is the beam. On reception, if incoming waves are parallel to the axis of the reflecting paraboloid, the resulting signal will be concentrated at the focus.

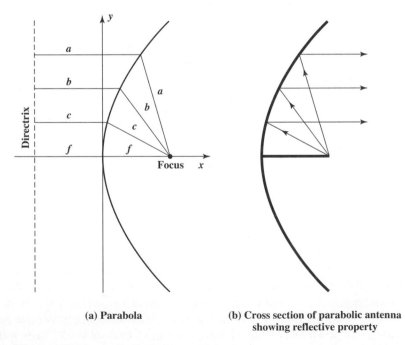

(a) Parabola

(b) Cross section of parabolic antenna
showing reflective property

Figure 4.5 Parabolic Reflective Antenna

Antenna Gain

Antenna gain is a measure of the directionality of an antenna. Antenna gain is defined as the power output, in a particular direction, compared to that produced in any direction by a perfect omnidirectional antenna (isotropic antenna). For example, if an antenna has a gain of 3 dB, that antenna improves upon the isotropic antenna in that direction by 3 dB, or a factor of 2. The increased power radiated in a given direction is at the expense of other directions. In effect, increased power is radiated in one direction by reducing the power radiated in other directions. It is important to note that antenna gain does not refer to obtaining more output power than input power but rather to directionality.

A concept related to that of antenna gain is the **effective area** of an antenna. The effective area of an antenna is related to the physical size of the antenna and to its shape. The relationship between antenna gain and effective area is

$$G = \frac{4\pi A_e}{\lambda^2} = \frac{4\pi f^2 A_e}{c^2} \tag{4.1}$$

where

G = antenna gain
A_e = effective area
f = carrier frequency
c = speed of light ($\approx 3 \times 10^8$ m/s)
λ = carrier wavelength

For example, the effective area of an ideal isotropic antenna is $\lambda^2/4\pi$, with a power gain of 1; the effective area of a parabolic antenna with a face area of A is $0.56A$, with a power gain of $7A/\lambda^2$.

Example 4.2   For a parabolic reflective antenna with a diameter of 2 m, operating at 12 GHz, what is the effective area and the antenna gain? We have an area of $A = \pi r^2 = \pi$ and an effective area of $A_e = 0.56\pi$. The wavelength is $\lambda = c/f = (3 \times 10^8)/(12 \times 10^9) = 0.025$ m. Then

$$G = (7A)/\lambda^2 = (7 \times \pi)/(0.025)^2 = 35{,}186$$
$$G_{dB} = 45.46 \text{ dB}$$

Terrestrial Microwave

Physical Description

The most common type of microwave antenna is the parabolic "dish." A typical size is about 3 m in diameter. The antenna is fixed rigidly and focuses a narrow beam to achieve line-of-sight transmission to the receiving antenna. Microwave antennas are usually located at substantial heights above ground level to extend the range between antennas and to be able to transmit over intervening obstacles. To achieve long-distance transmission, a series of microwave relay towers is used, and point-to-point microwave links are strung together over the desired distance.

Applications

The primary use for terrestrial microwave systems is in long haul telecommunications service, as an alternative to coaxial cable or optical fiber. The microwave facility requires far fewer amplifiers or repeaters than coaxial cable over the same distance but requires line-of-sight transmission. Microwave is commonly used for both voice and television transmission.

Another increasingly common use of microwave is for short point-to-point links between buildings. This can be used for closed-circuit TV or as a data link between local area networks. Short-haul microwave can also be used for the so-called bypass application. A business can establish a microwave link to a long-distance telecommunications facility in the same city, bypassing the local telephone company.

Another important use of microwave is in cellular systems, examined in Chapter 14.

Transmission Characteristics

Microwave transmission covers a substantial portion of the electromagnetic spectrum. Common frequencies used for transmission are in the range 1 to 40 GHz. The higher the frequency used, the higher the potential bandwidth and therefore the higher the potential data rate. Table 4.6 indicates bandwidth and data rate for some typical systems.

As with any transmission system, a main source of loss is attenuation. For microwave (and radio frequencies), the loss can be expressed as

$$L = 10 \log\left(\frac{4\pi d}{\lambda}\right)^2 \text{dB} \tag{4.2}$$

where d is the distance and λ is the wavelength, in the same units. Thus, loss varies as the square of the distance. In contrast, for twisted-pair and coaxial cable, loss varies exponentially with distance (linear in decibels). Thus repeaters or amplifiers may be placed farther apart for microwave systems—10 to 100 km is typical. Attenuation is increased with rainfall. The effects of rainfall become especially noticeable above 10 GHz. Another source of impairment is interference. With the growing popularity of microwave, transmission areas overlap and interference is always a danger. Thus the assignment of frequency bands is strictly regulated.

The most common bands for long-haul telecommunications are the 4-GHz to 6-GHz bands. With increasing congestion at these frequencies, the 11-GHz band is

Table 4.6 Typical Digital Microwave Performance

Band (GHz)	Bandwidth (MHz)	Data Rate (Mbps)
2	7	12
6	30	90
11	40	135
18	220	274

now coming into use. The 12-GHz band is used as a component of cable TV systems. Microwave links are used to provide TV signals to local CATV installations; the signals are then distributed to individual subscribers via coaxial cable. Higher-frequency microwave is being used for short point-to-point links between buildings; typically, the 22-GHz band is used. The higher microwave frequencies are less useful for longer distances because of increased attenuation but are quite adequate for shorter distances. In addition, at the higher frequencies, the antennas are smaller and cheaper.

Satellite Microwave

Physical Description

A communication satellite is, in effect, a microwave relay station. It is used to link two or more ground-based microwave transmitter/receivers, known as earth stations, or ground stations. The satellite receives transmissions on one frequency band (uplink), amplifies or repeats the signal, and transmits it on another frequency (downlink). A single orbiting satellite will operate on a number of frequency bands, called **transponder channels**, or simply **transponders**.

Figure 4.6 depicts in a general way two common configurations for satellite communication. In the first, the satellite is being used to provide a point-to-point link between two distant ground-based antennas. In the second, the satellite provides communications between one ground-based transmitter and a number of ground-based receivers.

For a communication satellite to function effectively, it is generally required that it remain stationary with respect to its position over the earth. Otherwise, it would not be within the line of sight of its earth stations at all times. To remain stationary, the satellite must have a period of rotation equal to the earth's period of rotation. This match occurs at a height of 35,863 km at the equator.

Two satellites using the same frequency band, if close enough together, will interfere with each other. To avoid this, current standards require a 4° spacing (angular displacement as measured from the earth) in the 4/6-GHz band and a 3° spacing at 12/14 GHz. Thus the number of possible satellites is quite limited.

Applications

The communication satellite is a technological revolution as important as fiber optics. Among the most important applications for satellites are the following:

- Television distribution
- Long-distance telephone transmission
- Private business networks

Because of their broadcast nature, satellites are well suited to television distribution and are being used extensively in the United States and throughout the world for this purpose. In its traditional use, a network provides programming from a central location. Programs are transmitted to the satellite and then broadcast down to a number of stations, which then distribute the programs to individual

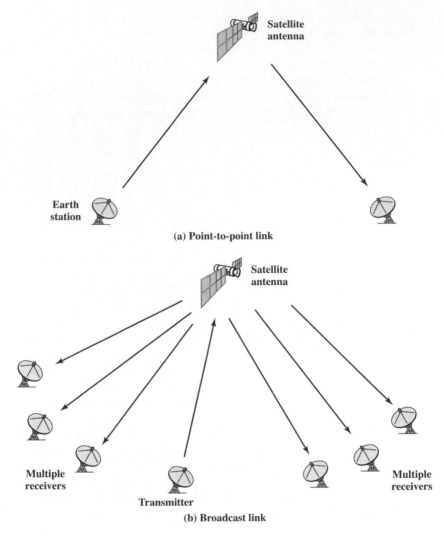

Figure 4.6 Satellite Communication Configurations

viewers. One network, the Public Broadcasting Service (PBS), distributes its television programming almost exclusively by the use of satellite channels. Other commercial networks also make substantial use of satellite, and cable television systems are receiving an ever-increasing proportion of their programming from satellites. The most recent application of satellite technology to television distribution is direct broadcast satellite (DBS), in which satellite video signals are transmitted directly to the home user. The decreasing cost and size of receiving antennas have made DBS economically feasible, and a number of channels are either already in service or in the planning stage.

Satellite transmission is also used for point-to-point trunks between telephone exchange offices in public telephone networks. It is the optimum medium for high-usage international trunks and is competitive with terrestrial systems for many long-distance intranational links.

Finally, there are a number of business data applications for satellite. The satellite provider can divide the total capacity into a number of channels and lease these channels to individual business users. A user equipped with the antennas at a number of sites can use a satellite channel for a private network. Traditionally, such applications have been quite expensive and limited to larger organizations with high-volume requirements. A recent development is the very small aperture terminal (VSAT) system, which provides a low-cost alternative. Figure 4.7 depicts a typical VSAT configuration. A number of subscriber stations are equipped with low-cost VSAT antennas. Using some discipline, these stations share a satellite transmission capacity for transmission to a hub station. The hub station can exchange messages with each of the subscribers and can relay messages between subscribers.

Transmission Characteristics

The optimum frequency range for satellite transmission is in the range 1 to 10 GHz. Below 1 GHz, there is significant noise from natural sources, including galactic, solar, and atmospheric noise, and human-made interference from various electronic devices. Above 10 GHz, the signal is severely attenuated by atmospheric absorption and precipitation.

Most satellites providing point-to-point service today use a frequency bandwidth in the range 5.925 to 6.425 GHz for transmission from earth to satellite (uplink) and a bandwidth in the range 3.7 to 4.2 GHz for transmission from satellite to earth (downlink). This combination is referred to as the 4/6-GHz band. Note that the uplink and downlink frequencies differ. For continuous operation without interference, a satellite cannot transmit and receive on the same frequency. Thus signals received from a ground station on one frequency must be transmitted back on another.

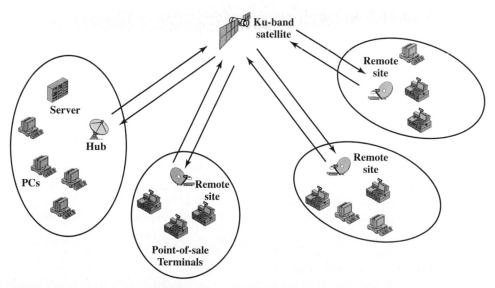

Figure 4.7   Typical VSAT Configuration

The 4/6-GHz band is within the optimum zone of 1 to 10 GHz but has become saturated. Other frequencies in that range are unavailable because of sources of interference operating at those frequencies, usually terrestrial microwave. Therefore, the 12/14-GHz band has been developed (uplink: 14 to 14.5 GHz; downlink: 11.7 to 12.2 GHz). At this frequency band, attenuation problems must be overcome. However, smaller and cheaper earth-station receivers can be used. It is anticipated that this band will also saturate, and use is projected for the 20/30-GHz band (uplink: 27.5 to 30.0 GHz; downlink: 17.7 to 20.2 GHz). This band experiences even greater attenuation problems but will allow greater bandwidth (2500 MHz versus 500 MHz) and even smaller and cheaper receivers.

Several properties of satellite communication should be noted. First, because of the long distances involved, there is a propagation delay of about a quarter second from transmission from one earth station to reception by another earth station. This delay is noticeable in ordinary telephone conversations. It also introduces problems in the areas of error control and flow control, which we discuss in later chapters. Second, satellite microwave is inherently a broadcast facility. Many stations can transmit to the satellite, and a transmission from a satellite can be received by many stations.

Broadcast Radio

Physical Description

The principal difference between broadcast radio and microwave is that the former is omnidirectional and the latter is directional. Thus broadcast radio does not require dish-shaped antennas, and the antennas need not be rigidly mounted to a precise alignment.

Applications

Radio is a general term used to encompass frequencies in the range of 3 kHz to 300 GHz. We are using the informal term **broadcast radio** to cover the VHF and part of the UHF band: 30 MHz to 1 GHz. This range covers FM radio and UHF and VHF television. This range is also used for a number of data networking applications.

Transmission Characteristics

The range 30 MHz to 1 GHz is an effective one for broadcast communications. Unlike the case for lower-frequency electromagnetic waves, the ionosphere is transparent to radio waves above 30 MHz. Thus transmission is limited to the line of sight, and distant transmitters will not interfere with each other due to reflection from the atmosphere. Unlike the higher frequencies of the microwave region, broadcast radio waves are less sensitive to attenuation from rainfall.

As with microwave, the amount of attenuation due to distance obeys Equation (4.2), namely $10 \log\left(\dfrac{4\pi d}{\lambda}\right)^2$ dB. Because of the longer wavelength, radio waves suffer relatively less attenuation.

A prime source of impairment for broadcast radio waves is multipath interference. Reflection from land, water, and natural or human-made objects can create multiple paths between antennas. This effect is frequently evident when TV reception displays multiple images as an airplane passes by.

Infrared

Infrared communications is achieved using transmitters/receivers (transceivers) that modulate noncoherent infrared light. Transceivers must be within the line of sight of each other either directly or via reflection from a light-colored surface such as the ceiling of a room.

One important difference between infrared and microwave transmission is that the former does not penetrate walls. Thus the security and interference problems encountered in microwave systems are not present. Furthermore, there is no frequency allocation issue with infrared, because no licensing is required.

4.3 WIRELESS PROPAGATION

A signal radiated from an antenna travels along one of three routes: ground wave, sky wave, or line of sight (LOS). Table 4.7 shows in which frequency range each predominates. In this book, we are almost exclusively concerned with LOS communication, but a short overview of each mode is given in this section.

Ground Wave Propagation

Ground wave propagation (Figure 4.8a) more or less follows the contour of the earth and can propagate considerable distances, well over the visual horizon. This effect is found in frequencies up to about 2 MHz. Several factors account for the tendency of electromagnetic wave in this frequency band to follow the earth's curvature. One factor is that the electromagnetic wave induces a current in the earth's surface, the result of which is to slow the wavefront near the earth, causing the wavefront to tilt downward and hence follow the earth's curvature. Another factor is diffraction, which is a phenomenon having to do with the behavior of electromagnetic waves in the presence of obstacles.

Electromagnetic waves in this frequency range are scattered by the atmosphere in such a way that they do not penetrate the upper atmosphere.

The best-known example of ground wave communication is AM radio.

Sky Wave Propagation

Sky wave propagation is used for amateur radio, CB radio, and international broadcasts such as BBC and Voice of America. With sky wave propagation, a signal from an earth-based antenna is reflected from the ionized layer of the upper atmosphere (ionosphere) back down to earth. Although it appears the wave is reflected from the ionosphere as if the ionosphere were a hard reflecting surface, the effect is in fact caused by refraction. Refraction is described subsequently.

A sky wave signal can travel through a number of hops, bouncing back and forth between the ionosphere and the earth's surface (Figure 4.8b). With this propagation mode, a signal can be picked up thousands of kilometers from the transmitter.

Table 4.7 Frequency Bands

Band	Frequency Range	Free-Space Wavelength Range	Propagation Characteristics	Typical Use
ELF (extremely low frequency)	30 to 300 Hz	10,000 to 1000 km	GW	Power line frequencies; used by some home control systems
VF (voice frequency)	300 to 3000 Hz	1000 to 100 km	GW	Used by the telephone system for analog subscriber lines
VLF (very low frequency)	3 to 30 kHz	100 to 10 km	GW; low attenuation day and night; high atmospheric noise level	Long-range navigation; submarine communication
LF (low frequency)	30 to 300 kHz	10 to 1 km	GW; slightly less reliable than VLF; absorption in daytime	Long-range navigation; marine communication radio beacons
MF (medium frequency)	300 to 3000 kHz	1000 to 100 m	GW and night SW; attenuation low at night, high in day; atmospheric noise	Maritime radio; direction finding; AM broadcasting
HF (high frequency)	3 to 30 MHz	100 to 10 m	SW; quality varies with time of day, season, and frequency	Amateur radio; international broadcasting, military communication; long-distance aircraft and ship communication
VHF (very high frequency)	30 to 300 MHz	10 to 1 m	LOS; scattering because of temperature inversion; cosmic noise	VHF television; FM broadcast and two-way radio, AM aircraft communication; aircraft navigational aids
UHF (ultra high frequency)	300 to 3000 MHz	100 to 10 cm	LOS; cosmic noise	UHF television; cellular telephone; radar; microwave links; personal communications systems
SHF (super high frequency)	3 to 30 GHz	10 to 1 cm	LOS; rainfall attenuation above 10 GHz; atmospheric attenuation due to oxygen and water vapor	Satellite communication; radar; terrestrial microwave links; wireless local loop
EHF (extremely high frequency)	30 to 300 GHz	10 to 1 mm	LOS; atmospheric attenuation due to oxygen and water vapor	Experimental; wireless local loop
Infrared	300 GHz to 400 THz	1 mm to 770 nm	LOS	Infrared LANs; consumer electronic applications
Visible light	400 THz to 900 THz	770 nm to 330 nm	LOS	Optical communication

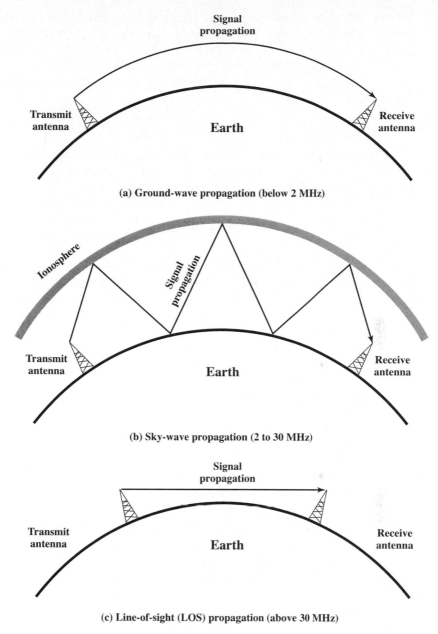

(a) Ground-wave propagation (below 2 MHz)

(b) Sky-wave propagation (2 to 30 MHz)

(c) Line-of-sight (LOS) propagation (above 30 MHz)

Figure 4.8   Wireless Propagation Modes

Line-of-Sight Propagation

Above 30 MHz, neither ground wave nor sky wave propagation modes operate, and communication must be by line of sight (Figure 4.8c). For satellite communication, a signal above 30 MHz is not reflected by the ionosphere and therefore a signal can be transmitted between an earth station and a satellite overhead that is not beyond the horizon. For ground-based communication, the transmitting and receiving antennas must be within an *effective* line of sight of each other. The term *effective* is used because microwaves are bent or refracted by the atmosphere. The amount and even the direction of the bend depends on conditions, but generally microwaves are bent with the curvature of the earth and will therefore propagate farther than the optical line of sight.

Refraction

Before proceeding, a brief discussion of refraction is warranted. Refraction occurs because the velocity of an electromagnetic wave is a function of the density of the medium through which it travels. In a vacuum, an electromagnetic wave (such as light or a radio wave) travels at approximately 3×10^8 m/s. This is the constant, c, commonly referred to as the speed of light, but actually referring to the speed of light in a vacuum.[1] In air, water, glass, and other transparent or partially transparent media, electromagnetic waves travel at speeds less than c.

When an electromagnetic wave moves from a medium of one density to a medium of another density, its speed changes. The effect is to cause a one-time bending of the direction of the wave at the boundary between the two media. Moving from a less dense to a more dense medium, the wave will bend toward the more dense medium. This phenomenon is easily observed by partially immersing a stick in water.

The **index of refraction**, or **refractive index**, of one medium relative to another is the sine of the angle of incidence divided by the sine of the angle of refraction. The index of refraction is also equal to the ratio of the respective velocities in the two media. The absolute index of refraction of a medium is calculated in comparison with that of a vacuum. Refractive index varies with wavelength, so that refractive effects differ for signals with different wavelengths.

Although an abrupt, one-time change in direction occurs as a signal moves from one medium to another, a continuous, gradual bending of a signal will occur if it is moving through a medium in which the index of refraction gradually changes. Under normal propagation conditions, the refractive index of the atmosphere decreases with height so that radio waves travel more slowly near the ground than at higher altitudes. The result is a slight bending of the radio waves toward the earth.

Optical and Radio Line of Sight

With no intervening obstacles, the optical line of sight can be expressed as:

$$d = 3.57\sqrt{h}$$

where d is the distance between an antenna and the horizon in kilometers and h is the antenna height in meters. The effective, or radio, line of sight to the horizon is expressed as (Figure 4.9)

$$d = 3.57\sqrt{Kh}$$

---

[1]The exact value is 299,792,458 m/s.

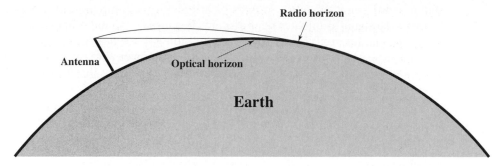

Figure 4.9 Optical and Radio Horizons

where K is an adjustment factor to account for the refraction. A good rule of thumb is $K = 4/3$. Thus, the maximum distance between two antennas for LOS propagation is $3.57\left(\sqrt{Kh_1} + \sqrt{Kh_2}\right)$, where h_1 and h_2 are the heights of the two antennas.

Example 4.3   The maximum distance between two antennas for LOS transmission if one antenna is 100 m high and the other is at ground level is

$$d = 3.57\sqrt{Kh} = 3.57\sqrt{133} = 41 \text{ km}$$

Now suppose that the receiving antenna is 10 m high. To achieve the same distance, how high must the transmitting antenna be? The result is

$$41 = 3.57\left(\sqrt{Kh_1} + \sqrt{13.3}\right)$$
$$\sqrt{Kh_1} = \frac{41}{3.57} - \sqrt{13.3} = 7.84$$
$$h_1 = 7.84^2/1.33 = 46.2 \text{ m}$$

This is a savings of over 50 m in the height of the transmitting antenna. This example illustrates the benefit of raising receiving antennas above ground level to reduce the necessary height of the transmitter.

4.4 LINE-OF-SIGHT TRANSMISSION

Section 3.3 discussed various transmission impairments common to both guided and wireless transmission. In this section, we extend the discussion to examine some impairments specific to wireless line-of-sight transmission.

Free Space Loss

For any type of wireless communication the signal disperses with distance. Therefore, an antenna with a fixed area will receive less signal power the farther it is from the transmitting antenna. For satellite communication this is the primary mode of signal loss. Even if no other sources of attenuation or impairment are assumed, a transmitted signal attenuates over distance because the signal is being spread over a larger and larger area. This form of attenuation is known as **free space loss**, which can be express in terms of the ratio of the radiated power P_t to the power P_r received by the antenna or, in decibels, by taking 10 times the log of that ratio. For the ideal isotropic antenna, free space loss is

$$\frac{P_t}{P_r} = \frac{(4\pi d)^2}{\lambda^2} = \frac{(4\pi f d)^2}{c^2}$$

where

P_t = signal power at the transmitting antenna

P_r = signal power at the receiving antenna

λ = carrier wavelength

d = propagation distance between antennas

c = speed of light $(3 \times 10^8 \, \text{m/s})$

where d and λ are in the same units (e.g., meters).

This can be recast as

$$L_{dB} = 10 \log \frac{P_t}{P_r} = 20 \log \sqrt{\frac{4\pi d}{\lambda}} = -20 \log(\lambda) + 20 \log(d) + 21.98 \, \text{dB}$$

$$= 20 \log \sqrt{\frac{4\pi f d}{c}} = 20 \log(f) + 20 \log(d) - 147.56 \, \text{dB}$$

(4.3)

Figure 4.10 illustrates the free space loss equation.[2]

For other antennas, we must take into account the gain of the antenna, which yields the following free space loss equation:

$$\frac{P_t}{P_r} = \frac{(4\pi)^2(d)^2}{G_r G_t \lambda^2} = \frac{(\lambda d)^2}{A_r A_t} = \frac{(cd)^2}{f^2 A_r A_t}$$

where

G_t = gain of the transmitting antenna

G_r = gain of the receiving antenna

A_t = effective area of the transmitting antenna

A_r = effective area of the receiving antenna

---

[2]As was mentioned in Appendix 3A, there is some inconsistency in the literature over the use of the terms *gain* and *loss*. Equation (4.3) follows the convention of Equation (2.2).

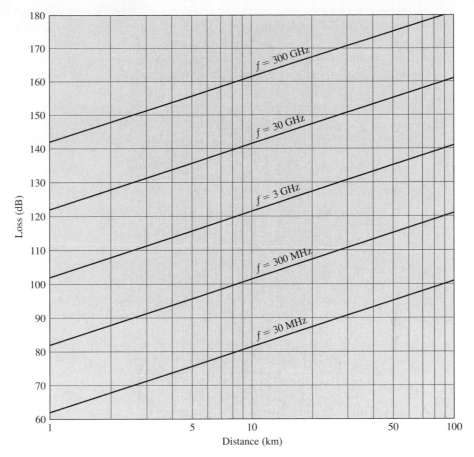

Figure 4.10   Free Space Loss

The third fraction is derived from the second fraction using the relationship between antenna gain and effective area defined in Equation (4.1). We can recast the loss equation as

$$
\begin{aligned}
L_{dB} &= 20\log(\lambda) + 20\log(d) - 10\log(A_t A_r) \\
&= -20\log(f) + 20\log(d) - 10\log(A_t A_r) + 169.54\,\text{dB}
\end{aligned}
\tag{4.4}
$$

Thus, for the same antenna dimensions and separation, the longer the carrier wavelength (lower the carrier frequency f), the higher is the free space path loss. It is interesting to compare Equations (4.3) and (4.4). Equation (4.3) indicates that as the frequency increases, the free space loss also increases, which would suggest that at higher frequencies, losses become more burdensome. However, Equation (4.4) shows that we can easily compensate for this increased loss with antenna gains.

In fact, there is a net gain at higher frequencies, other factors remaining constant. Equation (4.3) shows that at a fixed distance an increase in frequency results in an increased loss measured by $20\log(f)$. However, if we take into account antenna gain, and fix antenna area, then the change in loss is measured by $-20\log(f)$; that is, there is actually a decrease in loss at higher frequencies.

Example 4.4 Determine the isotropic free space loss at 4 GHz for the shortest path to a synchronous satellite from earth (35,863 km). At 4 GHz, the wavelength is $(3 \times 10^8)/(4 \times 10^9) = 0.075$ m. Then,

$$L_{dB} = -20\log(0.075) + 20\log(35.853 \times 10^6) + 21.98 = 195.6\,dB$$

Now consider the antenna gain of both the satellite- and ground-based antennas. Typical values are 44 dB and 48 dB, respectively. The free space loss is

$$L_{dB} = 195.6 - 44 - 48 = 103.6\,dB$$

Now assume a transmit power of 250 W at the earth station. What is the power received at the satellite antenna? A power of 250 W translates into 24 dBW, so the power at the receiving antenna is $24 - 103.6 = -79.6$ dBW.

Atmospheric Absorption

An additional loss between the transmitting and receiving antennas is atmospheric absorption. Water vapor and oxygen contribute most to attenuation. A peak attenuation occurs in the vicinity of 22 GHz due to water vapor. At frequencies below 15 GHz, the attenuation is less. The presence of oxygen results in an absorption peak in the vicinity of 60 GHz but contributes less at frequencies below 30 GHz. Rain and fog (suspended water droplets) cause scattering of radio waves that results in attenuation. In this context, the term *scattering* refers to the production of waves of changed direction or frequency when radio waves encounter matter. This can be a major cause of signal loss. Thus, in areas of significant precipitation, either path lengths have to be kept short or lower-frequency bands should be used.

Multipath

For wireless facilities where there is a relatively free choice of where antennas are to be located, they can be placed so that if there are no nearby interfering obstacles, there is a direct line-of-sight path from transmitter to receiver. This is generally the case for many satellite facilities and for point-to-point microwave. In other cases, such as mobile telephony, there are obstacles in abundance. The signal can be reflected by such obstacles so that multiple copies of the signal with varying delays

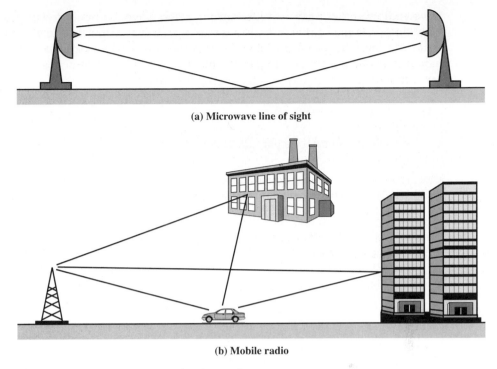

(a) Microwave line of sight

(b) Mobile radio

Figure 4.11 Examples of Multipath Interference

can be received. In fact, in extreme cases, there may be no direct signal. Depending on the differences in the path lengths of the direct and reflected waves, the composite signal can be either larger or smaller than the direct signal. Reinforcement and cancellation of the signal resulting from the signal following multiple paths can be controlled for communication between fixed, well-sited antennas, and between satellites and fixed ground stations. One exception is when the path goes across water, where the wind keeps the reflective surface of the water in motion. For mobile telephony and communication to antennas that are not well sited, multipath considerations can be paramount.

Figure 4.11 illustrates in general terms the types of multipath interference typical in terrestrial, fixed microwave and in mobile communications. For fixed microwave, in addition to the direct line of sight, the signal may follow a curved path through the atmosphere due to refraction and the signal may also reflect from the ground. For mobile communications, structures and topographic features provide reflection surfaces.

Refraction

Radio waves are refracted (or bent) when they propagate through the atmosphere. The refraction is caused by changes in the speed of the signal with altitude or by other spatial changes in the atmospheric conditions. Normally, the speed of the signal increases with altitude, causing radio waves to bend downward. However, on occasion, weather conditions may lead to variations in speed with height that differ significantly from the typical variations. This may result in a situation in which only a fraction or no part of the line-of-sight wave reaches the receiving antenna.

4.5 RECOMMENDED READING AND WEB SITES

Detailed descriptions of the transmission characteristics of the transmission media discussed in this chapter can be found in [FREE98]. [REEV95] provides an excellent treatment of twisted pair and optical fiber. [BORE97] is a thorough treatment of optical fiber transmission components. Another good paper on the subject is [WILL97]. [FREE02] is a detailed technical reference on optical fiber. [STAL00] discusses the characteristics of transmission media for LANs in greater detail.

For a more thorough treatment on wireless transmission and propagation, see [STAL02] and [RAPP96]. [FREE97] is an excellent detailed technical reference on wireless topics.

BORE97   Borella, M., et al., "Optical Components for WDM Lightwave Networks." *Proceedings of the IEEE*, August 1997.

FREE97   Freeman, R. *Radio System Design for Telecommunications*. New York: Wiley, 1997.

FREE98   Freeman, R. *Telecommunication Transmission Handbook*. New York: Wiley, 1998.

FREE02   Freeman, R. *Fiber-Optic Systems for Telecommunications*. New York: Wiley, 2002.

RAPP96   Rappaport, T. *Wireless Communications*. Upper Saddle River, NJ: Prentice Hall, 1996.

REEV95   Reeve, W. *Subscriber Loop Signaling and Transmission Handbook*. Piscataway, NJ: IEEE Press, 1995.

STAL00   Stallings, W. *Local and Metropolitan Area Networks, 4th Edition*. Upper Saddle River, NJ: Prentice Hall, 2000.

STAL02   Stallings, W. *Wireless Communications and Networks*. Upper Saddle River, NJ: Prentice Hall, 2002.

WILL97   Willner, A. "Mining the Optical Bandwidth for a Terabit per Second." *IEEE Spectrum*, April 1997.

Recommended Web Sites:

- **Siemon Company:** Good collection of technical articles on cabling, plus information about cabling standards
- **Wireless Developer Network:** News, tutorials, and discussions on wireless topics

4.6   KEY TERMS, REVIEW QUESTIONS, AND PROBLEMS

Key Terms

antenna	line of sight (LOS)	satellite
antenna gain	microwave frequencies	shielded twisted pair (STP)
atmospheric absorption	multipath	sky wave propagation
attenuation	omnidirectional antenna	terrestrial microwave
coaxial cable	optical fiber	transmission medium
directional antenna	optical LOS	twisted pair
effective area	parabolic reflective antenna	unguided media
free space loss	radio	unshielded twisted pair (UTP)
ground wave propagation	radio LOS	wavelength division
guided media	reflection	multiplexing (WDM)
index of refraction	refraction	wireless transmission
infrared	refractive index	
isotropic antenna	scattering	

Review Questions

4.1 Why are the wires twisted in twisted-pair copper wire?

4.2 What are some major limitations of twisted-pair wire?

4.3 What is the difference between unshielded twisted pair and shielded twisted pair?

4.4 Describe the components of optical fiber cable.

4.5 What are some major advantages and disadvantages of microwave transmission?

4.6 What is direct broadcast satellite (DBS)?

4.7 Why must a satellite have distinct uplink and downlink frequencies?

4.8 Indicate some significant differences between broadcast radio and microwave.

4.9 What two functions are performed by an antenna?

4.10 What is an isotropic antenna?

4.11 What is the advantage of a parabolic reflective antenna?

4.12 What factors determine antenna gain?

4.13 What is the primary cause of signal loss in satellite communications?

4.14 What is refraction?

4.15 What is the difference between diffraction and scattering?

Problems

4.1 Suppose that data are stored on 1.4-Mbyte floppy diskettes that weigh 30 g each. Suppose that an airliner carries 10^4 kg of these floppies at a speed of 1000 km/h over a distance of 5000 km. What is the data transmission rate in bits per second of this system?

4.2 A telephone line is known to have a loss of 20 dB. The input signal power is measured as 0.5 W, and the output noise level is measured as 4.5 μW. Using this information, calculate the output signal-to-noise ratio in dB.

4.3 Given a 100-Watt power source, what is the maximum allowable length for the following transmission media if a signal of 1 watt is to be received?
    a. 24-gauge (0.5 mm) twisted pair operating at 300 kHz
    b. 24-gauge (0.5 mm) twisted pair operating at 1 MHz
    c. 0.375-inch (9.5 mm) coaxial cable operating at 1 MHz
    d. 0.375-inch (9.5 mm) coaxial cable operating at 25 MHz
    e. optical fiber operating at its optimal frequency

4.4 Coaxial cable is a two-wire transmission system. What is the advantage of connecting the outer conductor to ground?

4.5 Show that doubling the transmission frequency or doubling the distance between transmitting antenna and receiving antenna attenuates the power received by 6 dB.

4.6 It turns out that the depth in the ocean to which airborne electromagnetic signals can be detected grows with the wavelength. Therefore, the military got the idea of using very long wavelengths corresponding to about 30 Hz to communicate with submarines throughout the world. It is desirable to have an antenna that is about one-half wavelength long. How long would that be?

4.7 The audio power of the human voice is concentrated at about 300 Hz. Antennas of the appropriate size for this frequency are impracticably large, so that to send voice by radio the voice signal must be used to modulate a higher (carrier) frequency for which the natural antenna size is smaller.
    a. What is the length of an antenna one-half wavelength long for sending radio at 300 Hz?
    b. An alternative is to use a modulation scheme, as described in Chapter 5, for transmitting the voice signal by modulating a carrier frequency, so that the bandwidth of the signal is a narrow band centered on the carrier frequency. Suppose we would like a half-wave antenna to have a length of 1 meter. What carrier frequency would we use?

4.8 Stories abound of people who receive radio signals in fillings in their teeth. Suppose you have one filling that is 2.5 mm (0.0025 m) long that acts as a radio antenna. That is, it is equal in length to one-half the wavelength. What frequency do you receive?

4.9 You are communicating between two satellites. The transmission obeys the free space law. The signal is too weak. Your vendor offers you two options. The vendor can use a higher frequency that is twice the current frequency or can double the effective area of both of the antennas. Which will offer you more received power or will both offer the same improvement, all other factors remaining equal? How much improvement in the received power do you obtain from the best option?

4.10 For radio transmission in free space, signal power is reduced in proportion to the square of the distance from the source, whereas in wire transmission, the attenuation is a fixed number of dB per kilometer. The following table is used to show the dB reduction relative to some reference for free space radio and uniform wire. Fill in the missing numbers to complete the table.

Distance (km)	Radio (dB)	Wire (dB)
1	−6	−3
2		
4		
8		
16		

4.11 Section 4.2 states that if a source of electromagnetic energy is placed at the focus of the paraboloid, and if the paraboloid is a reflecting surface, then the wave will bounce back in lines parallel to the axis of the paraboloid. To demonstrate this, consider the parabola $y^2 = 2px$ shown in Figure 4.12. Let $P(x_1, y_1)$ be a point on the parabola, and PF be the line from P to the focus. Construct the line L through P parallel to the x-axis and the line M tangent to the parabola at P. The angle between L and M is β, and the angle between PF and M is α. The angle α is the angle at which a ray from F strikes the parabola at P. Because the angle of incidence equals the angle of reflection, the ray reflected from P must be at an angle α to M. Thus, if we can show that $\alpha = \beta$, we have demonstrated that rays reflected from the parabola starting at F will be parallel to the x-axis.

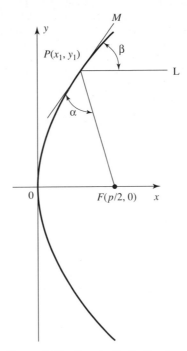

Figure 4.12 Parabolic Reflection

a. First show that $\tan \beta = (p/y_1)$. *Hint:* Recall from trigonometry that the slope of a line is equal to the tangent of the angle the line makes with the positive x-direction. Also recall that the slope of the line tangent to a curve at a given point is equal to the derivative of the curve at that point.

b. Now show that $\tan \alpha = (p/y_1)$, which demonstrates that $\alpha = \beta$. *Hint:* Recall from trigonometry that the formula for the tangent of the difference between two angles α_1 and α_2 is $\tan(\alpha_2 - \alpha_1) = (\tan \alpha_2 - \tan \alpha_1)/(1 + \tan \alpha_2 \times \tan \alpha_1)$.

4.12 It is often more convenient to express distance in km rather than m and frequency in MHz rather than Hz. Rewrite Equation (4.3) using these dimensions.

4.13 Suppose a transmitter produces 50 W of power.
    a. Express the transmit power in units of dBm and dBW.
    b. If the transmitter's power is applied to a unity gain antenna with a 900-MHz carrier frequency, what is the received power in dBm at a free space distance of 100 m?
    c. Repeat (b) for a distance of 10 km.
    d. Repeat (c) but assume a receiver antenna gain of 2.

4.14 A microwave transmitter has an output of 0.1 W at 2 GHz. Assume that this transmitter is used in a microwave communication system where the transmitting and receiving antennas are parabolas, each 1.2 m in diameter.

    a. What is the gain of each antenna in decibels?

    b. Taking into account antenna gain, what is the effective radiated power of the transmitted signal?

    c. If the receiving antenna is located 24 km from the transmitting antenna over a free space path, find the available signal power out of the receiving antenna in dBm units.

4.15 Section 4.3 states that with no intervening obstacles, the optical line of sight can be expressed as $d = 3.57\sqrt{h}$, where d is the distance between an antenna and the horizon in kilometers and h is the antenna height in meters. Using a value for the earth's radius of 6370 km, derive this equation. *Hint:* Assume that the antenna is perpendicular to the earth's surface, and note that the line from the top of the antenna to the horizon forms a tangent to the earth's surface at the horizon. Draw a picture showing the antenna, the line of sight, and the earth's radius to help visualize the problem.

4.16 Determine the height of an antenna for a TV station that must be able to reach customers up to 80 km away.

4.17 Suppose a ray of visible light passes from the atmosphere into water at an angle to the horizontal of 30°. What is the angle of the ray in the water? *Note:* At standard atmospheric conditions at the earth's surface, a reasonable value for refractive index is 1.0003. A typical value of refractive index for water is 4/3.

CHAPTER 5

SIGNAL ENCODING TECHNIQUES

KEY POINTS

- Both analog and digital information can be encoded as either analog or digital signals. The particular encoding that is chosen depends on the specific requirements to be met and the media and communications facilities available.
- **Digital data, digital signals:** The simplest form of digital encoding of digital data is to assign one voltage level to binary one and another to binary zero. More complex encoding schemes are used to improve performance, by altering the spectrum of the signal and providing synchronization capability.
- **Digital data, analog signal:** A modem converts digital data to an analog signal so that it can be transmitted over an analog line. The basic techniques are amplitude shift keying (ASK), frequency shift keying (FSK), and phase shift keying (PSK). All involve altering one or more characteristics of a carrier frequency to represent binary data.
- **Analog data, digital signals:** Analog data, such as voice and video, are often digitized to be able to use digital transmission facilities. The simplest technique is pulse code modulation (PCM), which involves sampling the analog data periodically and quantizing the samples.
- **Analog data, analog signals:** Analog data are modulated by a carrier frequency to produce an analog signal in a different frequency band, which can be utilized on an analog transmission system. The basic techniques are amplitude modulation (AM), frequency modulation (FM), and phase modulation (PM).

In Chapter 3 a distinction was made between analog and digital data and analog and digital signals. Figure 3.13 suggested that either form of data could be encoded into either form of signal.

Figure 5.1 is another depiction that emphasizes the process involved. For **digital signaling**, a data source $g(t)$, which may be either digital or analog, is encoded into a digital signal $x(t)$. The actual form of $x(t)$ depends on the encoding

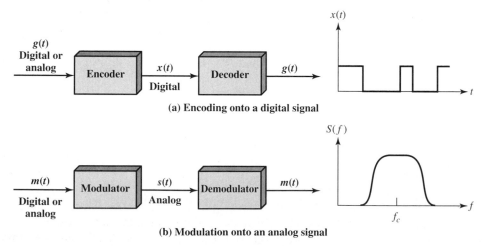

(a) Encoding onto a digital signal

(b) Modulation onto an analog signal

Figure 5.1   Encoding and Modulation Techniques

technique and is chosen to optimize use of the transmission medium. For example, the encoding may be chosen to conserve bandwidth or to minimize errors.

The basis for **analog signaling** is a continuous constant-frequency signal known as the **carrier signal**. The frequency of the carrier signal is chosen to be compatible with the transmission medium being used. Data may be transmitted using a carrier signal by modulation. **Modulation** is the process of encoding source data onto a carrier signal with frequency f_c. All modulation techniques involve operation on one or more of the three fundamental frequency domain parameters: amplitude, frequency, and phase.

The input signal $m(t)$ may be analog or digital and is called the modulating signal or **baseband signal**. The result of modulating the carrier signal is called the modulated signal $s(t)$. As Figure 5.1b indicates, $s(t)$ is a bandlimited (bandpass) signal. The location of the bandwidth on the spectrum is related to f_c and is often centered on f_c. Again, the actual form of the encoding is chosen to optimize some characteristic of the transmission.

Each of the four possible combinations depicted in Figure 5.1 is in widespread use. The reasons for choosing a particular combination for any given communication task vary. We list here some representative reasons:

- **Digital data, digital signal:** In general, the equipment for encoding digital data into a digital signal is less complex and less expensive than digital-to-analog modulation equipment.
- **Analog data, digital signal:** Conversion of analog data to digital form permits the use of modern digital transmission and switching equipment. The advantages of the digital approach were outlined in Section 3.2.
- **Digital data, analog signal:** Some transmission media, such as optical fiber and unguided media, will only propagate analog signals.
- **Analog data, analog signal:** Analog data in electrical form can be transmitted as baseband signals easily and cheaply. This is done with voice transmission over voice-grade lines. One common use of modulation is to shift the bandwidth of a baseband signal to another portion of the spectrum. In this way multiple signals, each at a different position on the spectrum, can share the same transmission medium. This is known as frequency division multiplexing.

We now examine the techniques involved in each of these four combinations.

5.1 DIGITAL DATA, DIGITAL SIGNALS

A digital signal is a sequence of discrete, discontinuous voltage pulses. Each pulse is a signal element. Binary data are transmitted by encoding each data bit into signal elements. In the simplest case, there is a one-to-one correspondence between bits and signal elements. An example is shown in Figure 3.15, in which binary 1 is represented by a lower voltage level and binary 0 by a higher voltage level. We show in this section that a variety of other encoding schemes are also used.

First, we define some terms. If the signal elements all have the same algebraic sign, that is, all positive or negative, then the signal is **unipolar**. In **polar** signaling,

Table 5.1 Key Data Transmission Terms

Term	Units	Definition
Data element	Bits	A single binary one or zero
Data rate	Bits per second (bps)	The rate at which data elements are transmitted
Signal element	Digital: a voltage pulse of constant amplitude Analog: a pulse of constant frequency, phase, and amplitude	That part of a signal that occupies the shortest interval of a signaling code
Signaling rate or modulation rate	Signal elements per second (baud)	The rate at which signal elements are transmitted

one logic state is represented by a positive voltage level, and the other by a negative voltage level. The **data signaling rate**, or just **data rate**, of a signal is the rate, in bits per second, that data are transmitted. The duration or length of a bit is the amount of time it takes for the transmitter to emit the bit; for a data rate R, the bit duration is $1/R$. The **modulation rate**, in contrast, is the rate at which the signal level is changed. This will depend on the nature of the digital encoding, as explained later. The modulation rate is expressed in baud, which means signal elements per second. Finally, the terms mark and space, for historical reasons, refer to the binary digits 1 and 0, respectively. Table 5.1 summarizes key terms; these should be clearer when we see an example later in this section.

The tasks involved in interpreting digital signals at the receiver can be summarized by again referring to Figure 3.15. First, the receiver must know the timing of each bit. That is, the receiver must know with some accuracy when a bit begins and ends. Second, the receiver must determine whether the signal level for each bit position is high (0) or low (1). In Figure 3.15, these tasks are performed by sampling each bit position in the middle of the interval and comparing the value to a threshold. Because of noise and other impairments, there will be errors, as shown.

What factors determine how successful the receiver will be in interpreting the incoming signal? We saw in Chapter 3 that three factors are important: the signal-to-noise ratio (or, better, E_b/N_0), the data rate, and the bandwidth. With other factors held constant, the following statements are true:

- An increase in data rate increases bit error rate (BER).[1]
- An increase in SNR decreases bit error rate.
- An increase in bandwidth allows an increase in data rate.

---

[1] The BER is the most common measure of error performance on a data circuit and is defined as the probability that a bit is received in error. It is also called the *bit error ratio*. This latter term is clearer, because the term *rate* typically refers to some quantity that varies with time. Unfortunately, most books and standards documents refer to the R in BER as *rate*.

Table 5.2 Definition of Digital Signal Encoding Formats

Nonreturn to Zero-Level (NRZ-L)
0 = high level
1 = low level

Nonreturn to Zero Inverted (NRZI)
0 = no transition at beginning of interval (one bit time)
1 = transition at beginning of interval

Bipolar-AMI
0 = no line signal
1 = positive or negative level, alternating for successive ones

Pseudoternary
0 = positive or negative level, alternating for successive zeros
1 = no line signal

Manchester
0 = transition from high to low in middle of interval
1 = transition from low to high in middle of interval

Differential Manchester
Always a transition in middle of interval
0 = transition at beginning of interval
1 = no transition at beginning of interval

B8ZS
Same as bipolar AMI, except that any string of eight zeros is replaced by a string with two code violations

HDB3
Same as bipolar AMI, except that any string of four zeros is replaced by a string with one code violation

There is another factor that can be used to improve performance, and that is the encoding scheme. The encoding scheme is simply the mapping from data bits to signal elements. A variety of approaches have been tried. In what follows, we describe some of the more common ones; they are defined in Table 5.2 and depicted in Figure 5.2.

Before describing these techniques, let us consider the following ways of evaluating or comparing the various techniques.

- **Signal spectrum:** Several aspects of the signal spectrum are important. A lack of high-frequency components means that less bandwidth is required for transmission. In addition, lack of a direct-current (dc) component is also desirable. With a dc component to the signal, there must be direct physical attachment of transmission components. With no dc component, ac coupling via transformer is possible; this provides excellent electrical isolation, reducing interference. Finally, the magnitude of the effects of signal distortion and interference depend on the spectral properties of the transmitted signal. In practice, it usually happens that the transmission characteristics of a channel are worse near the band edges. Therefore, a good signal design should concentrate the transmitted power in the middle of the transmission bandwidth.

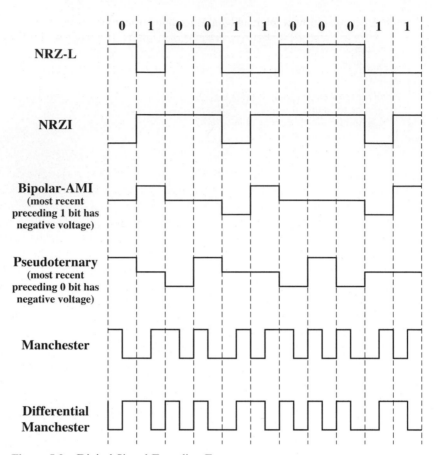

Figure 5.2 Digital Signal Encoding Formats

In such a case, a smaller distortion should be present in the received signal. To meet this objective, codes can be designed with the aim of shaping the spectrum of the transmitted signal.

- **Clocking:** We mentioned the need to determine the beginning and end of each bit position. This is no easy task. One rather expensive approach is to provide a separate clock lead to synchronize the transmitter and receiver. The alternative is to provide some synchronization mechanism that is based on the transmitted signal. This can be achieved with suitable encoding.

- **Error detection:** We will discuss various error-detection techniques in Chapter 6 and show that these are the responsibility of a layer of logic above the signaling level that is known as data link control. However, it is useful to have some error detection capability built into the physical signaling encoding scheme. This permits errors to be detected more quickly.

- **Signal interference and noise immunity:** Certain codes exhibit superior performance in the presence of noise. Performance is usually expressed in terms of a BER.

- **Cost and complexity:** Although digital logic continues to drop in price, this factor should not be ignored. In particular, the higher the signaling rate to achieve a given data rate, the greater the cost. We will see that some codes require a signaling rate that is in fact greater than the actual data rate.

We now turn to a discussion of various techniques.

Nonreturn to Zero (NRZ)

The most common, and easiest, way to transmit digital signals is to use two different voltage levels for the two binary digits. Codes that follow this strategy share the property that the voltage level is constant during a bit interval; there is no transition (no return to a zero voltage level). For example, the absence of voltage can be used to represent binary 0, with a constant positive voltage used to represent binary 1. More commonly, a negative voltage represents one binary value and a positive voltage represents the other. This latter code, known as **Nonreturn to Zero-Level** (NRZ-L), is illustrated[2] in Figure 5.2. NRZ-L is generally the code used to generate or interpret digital data by terminals and other devices. If a different code is to be used for transmission, it is typically generated from an NRZ-L signal by the transmission system [in terms of Figure 5.1, NRZ-L is $g(t)$ and the encoded signal is $x(t)$].

A variation of NRZ is known as **NRZI** (Nonreturn to Zero, invert on ones). As with NRZ-L, NRZI maintains a constant voltage pulse for the duration of a bit time. The data themselves are encoded as the presence or absence of a signal transition at the beginning of the bit time. A transition (low to high or high to low) at the beginning of a bit time denotes a binary 1 for that bit time; no transition indicates a binary 0.

NRZI is an example of **differential encoding**. In differential encoding, the information to be transmitted is represented in terms of the changes between successive signal elements rather than the signal elements themselves. In general, the encoding of the current bit is determined as follows: if the current bit is a binary 0, then the current bit is encoded with the same signal as the preceding bit; if the current bit is a binary 1, then the current bit is encoded with a different signal than the preceding bit. One benefit of differential encoding is that it may be more reliable to detect a transition in the presence of noise than to compare a value to a threshold. Another benefit is that with a complex transmission layout, it is easy to lose the sense of the polarity of the signal. For example, on a multidrop twisted-pair line, if the leads from an attached device to the twisted pair are accidentally inverted, all 1s and 0s for NRZ-L will be inverted. This cannot happen with differential encoding.

The NRZ codes are the easiest to engineer and, in addition, make efficient use of bandwidth. This latter property is illustrated in Figure 5.3, which compares the spectral density of various encoding schemes. In the figure, frequency is normalized

---

[2] In this figure, a negative voltage is equated with binary 1 and a positive voltage with binary 0. This is the opposite of the definition used in virtually all other textbooks. The definition here conforms to the use of NRZ-L in data communications interfaces and the standards that govern those interfaces.

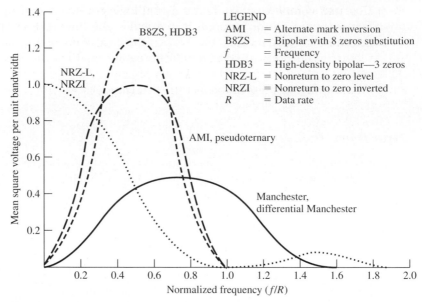

Figure 5.3 Spectral Density of Various Signal Encoding Schemes

to the data rate. As can be seen, most of the energy in NRZ and NRZI signals is between dc and half the bit rate. For example, if an NRZ code is used to generate a signal with data rate of 9600 bps, most of the energy in the signal is concentrated between dc and 4800 Hz.

The main limitations of NRZ signals are the presence of a dc component and the lack of synchronization capability. To picture the latter problem, consider that with a long string of 1s or 0s for NRZ-L or a long string of 0s for NRZI, the output is a constant voltage over a long period of time. Under these circumstances, any drift between the timing of transmitter and receiver will result in loss of synchronization between the two.

Because of their simplicity and relatively low frequency response characteristics, NRZ codes are commonly used for digital magnetic recording. However, their limitations make these codes unattractive for signal transmission applications.

Multilevel Binary

A category of encoding techniques known as multilevel binary addresses some of the deficiencies of the NRZ codes. These codes use more than two signal levels. Two examples of this scheme are illustrated in Figure 5.2, bipolar-AMI (alternate mark inversion) and pseudoternary.[3]

In the case of the **bipolar-AMI** scheme, a binary 0 is represented by no line signal, and a binary 1 is represented by a positive or negative pulse. The binary 1 pulses

---

[3] These terms are not used consistently in the literature. In some books, these two terms are used for different encoding schemes than those defined here, and a variety of terms have been used for the two schemes illustrated in Figure 5.2. The nomenclature used here corresponds to the usage in various ITU-T standards documents.

must alternate in polarity. There are several advantages to this approach. First, there will be no loss of synchronization if a long string of 1s occurs. Each 1 introduces a transition, and the receiver can resynchronize on that transition. A long string of 0s would still be a problem. Second, because the 1 signals alternate in voltage from positive to negative, there is no net dc component. Also, the bandwidth of the resulting signal is considerably less than the bandwidth for NRZ (Figure 5.3). Finally, the pulse alternation property provides a simple means of error detection. Any isolated error, whether it deletes a pulse or adds a pulse, causes a violation of this property.

The comments of the previous paragraph also apply to **pseudoternary**. In this case, it is the binary 1 that is represented by the absence of a line signal, and the binary 0 by alternating positive and negative pulses. There is no particular advantage of one technique versus the other, and each is the basis of some applications.

Although a degree of synchronization is provided with these codes, a long string of 0s in the case of AMI or 1s in the case of pseudoternary still presents a problem. Several techniques have been used to address this deficiency. One approach is to insert additional bits that force transitions. This technique is used in ISDN for relatively low data rate transmission. Of course, at a high data rate, this scheme is expensive, because it results in an increase in an already high signal transmission rate. To deal with this problem at high data rates, a technique that involves scrambling the data is used. We examine two examples of this technique later in this section.

Thus, with suitable modification, multilevel binary schemes overcome the problems of NRZ codes. Of course, as with any engineering design decision, there is a tradeoff. With multilevel binary coding, the line signal may take on one of three levels, but each signal element, which could represent $\log_2 3 = 1.58$ bits of information, bears only one bit of information. Thus multilevel binary is not as efficient as NRZ coding. Another way to state this is that the receiver of multilevel binary signals has to distinguish between three levels $(+A, -A, 0)$ instead of just two levels in the signaling formats previously discussed. Because of this, the multilevel binary signal requires approximately 3 dB more signal power than a two-valued signal for the same probability of bit error. This is illustrated in Figure 5.4. Put another way, the bit error rate for NRZ codes, at a given signal-to-noise ratio, is significantly less than that for multilevel binary.

Biphase

There is another set of coding techniques, grouped under the term *biphase*, that overcomes the limitations of NRZ codes. Two of these techniques, Manchester and differential Manchester, are in common use.

In the **Manchester** code, there is a transition at the middle of each bit period. The midbit transition serves as a clocking mechanism and also as data: a low-to-high transition represents a 1, and a high-to-low transition represents a 0.[4] In **differential Manchester**, the midbit transition is used only to provide clocking. The encoding of

---

[4] The definition of Manchester presented here is the opposite of that used in a number of respectable textbooks (e.g., [TANE03], [KURO01], [LEON00], [WALR00], and [PETE00]), in which a low-to-high transition represents a binary 0 and a high-to-low transition represents a binary 1. Here, we conform to industry practice and to the definition used in the various LAN standards, such as IEEE 802.3.

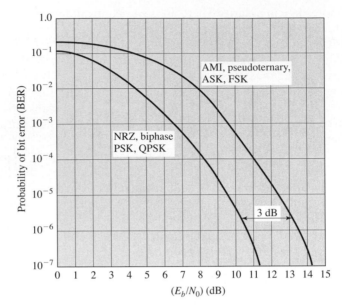

Figure 5.4   Theoretical Bit Error Rate for Various Encoding Schemes

a 0 is represented by the presence of a transition at the beginning of a bit period, and a 1 is represented by the absence of a transition at the beginning of a bit period. Differential Manchester has the added advantage of employing differential encoding.

All of the biphase techniques require at least one transition per bit time and may have as many as two transitions. Thus, the maximum modulation rate is twice that for NRZ; this means that the bandwidth required is correspondingly greater. On the other hand, the biphase schemes have several advantages:

- **Synchronization:** Because there is a predictable transition during each bit time, the receiver can synchronize on that transition. For this reason, the biphase codes are known as self-clocking codes.
- **No dc component:** Biphase codes have no dc component, yielding the benefits described earlier.
- **Error detection:** The absence of an expected transition can be used to detect errors. Noise on the line would have to invert both the signal before and after the expected transition to cause an undetected error.

As can be seen from Figure 5.3, the bandwidth for biphase codes is reasonably narrow and contains no dc component. However, it is wider than the bandwidth for the multilevel binary codes.

Biphase codes are popular techniques for data transmission. The more common Manchester code has been specified for the IEEE 802.3 (Ethernet) standard for baseband coaxial cable and twisted-pair CSMA/CD bus LANs. Differential Manchester has been specified for the IEEE 802.5 token ring LAN, using shielded twisted pair.

Modulation Rate

When signal-encoding techniques are used, a distinction needs to be made between data rate (expressed in bits per second) and modulation rate (expressed in baud). The data rate, or bit rate, is $1/T_b$, where T_b = bit duration. The modulation rate is the rate at which signal elements are generated. Consider, for example, Manchester encoding. The minimum size signal element is a pulse of one-half the duration of a bit interval. For a string of all binary zeroes or all binary ones, a continuous stream of such pulses is generated. Hence the maximum modulation rate for Manchester is $2/T_b$. This situation is illustrated in Figure 5.5, which shows the transmission of a stream of binary 1s at a data rate of 1 Mbps using NRZI and Manchester. In general,

$$D = \frac{R}{L} = \frac{R}{\log_2 M} \tag{5.1}$$

where

D = modulation rate, baud
R = data rate, bps
M = number of different signal elements = 2^L
L = number of bits per signal element

One way of characterizing the modulation rate is to determine the average number of transitions that occur per bit time. In general, this will depend on the exact sequence of bits being transmitted. Table 5.3 compares transition rates for various techniques. It indicates the signal transition rate in the case of a data stream of

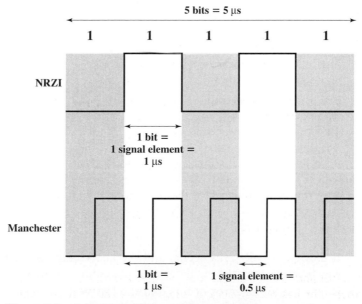

Figure 5.5 A Stream of Binary Ones at 1 Mbps

Table 5.3   Normalized Signal Transition Rate of Various Digital Signal Encoding Schemes

	Minimum	**101010. . .**	**Maximum**
NRZ-L	0 (all 0s or 1s)	1.0	1.0
NRZI	0 (all 0s)	0.5	1.0 (all 1s)
Bipolar-AMI	0 (all 0s)	1.0	1.0
Pseudoternary	0 (all 1s)	1.0	1.0
Manchester	1.0 (1010...)	1.0	2.0 (all 0s or 1s)
Differential Manchester	1.0 (all 1s)	1.5	2.0 (all 0s)

alternating 1s and 0s, and for the data stream that produces the minimum and maximum modulation rate.

Scrambling Techniques

Although the biphase techniques have achieved widespread use in local area network applications at relatively high data rates (up to 10 Mbps), they have not been widely used in long-distance applications. The principal reason for this is that they require a high signaling rate relative to the data rate. This sort of inefficiency is more costly in a long-distance application.

Another approach is to make use of some sort of scrambling scheme. The idea behind this approach is simple: Sequences that would result in a constant voltage level on the line are replaced by filling sequences that will provide sufficient transitions for the receiver's clock to maintain synchronization. The filling sequence must be recognized by the receiver and replaced with the original data sequence. The filling sequence is the same length as the original sequence, so there is no data rate penalty. The design goals for this approach can be summarized as follows:

* No dc component
* No long sequences of zero-level line signals
* No reduction in data rate
* Error-detection capability

Two techniques are commonly used in long-distance transmission services; these are illustrated in Figure 5.6.

A coding scheme that is commonly used in North America is known as **bipolar with 8-zeros substitution (B8ZS)**. The coding scheme is based on a bipolar-AMI. We have seen that the drawback of the AMI code is that a long string of zeros may result in loss of synchronization. To overcome this problem, the encoding is amended with the following rules:

* If an octet of all zeros occurs and the last voltage pulse preceding this octet was positive, then the eight zeros of the octet are encoded as $000 + - 0 - +$.
* If an octet of all zeros occurs and the last voltage pulse preceding this octet was negative, then the eight zeros of the octet are encoded as $000 - + 0 + -$.

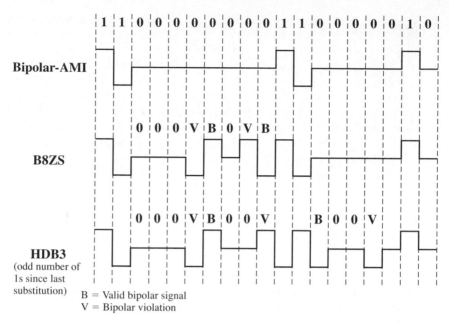

Figure 5.6 Encoding Rules for B8ZS and HDB3

This technique forces two code violations (signal patterns not allowed in AMI) of the AMI code, an event unlikely to be caused by noise or other transmission impairment. The receiver recognizes the pattern and interprets the octet as consisting of all zeros.

A coding scheme that is commonly used in Europe and Japan is known as the **high-density bipolar-3 zeros (HDB3)** code (Table 5.4). As before, it is based on the use of AMI encoding. In this case, the scheme replaces strings of four zeros with sequences containing one or two pulses. In each case, the fourth zero is replaced with a code violation. In addition, a rule is needed to ensure that successive violations are of alternate polarity so that no dc component is introduced. Thus, if the last violation was positive, this violation must be negative and vice versa. Table 5.4 shows that this condition is tested for by determining (1) whether the number of pulses since the last violation is even or odd and (2) the polarity of the last pulse before the occurrence of the four zeros.

Figure 5.3 shows the spectral properties of these two codes. As can be seen, neither has a dc component. Most of the energy is concentrated in a relatively sharp spectrum around a frequency equal to one-half the data rate. Thus, these codes are well suited to high data rate transmission.

Table 5.4 HDB3 Substitution Rules

	Number of Bipolar Pulses (ones) since Last Substitution	
Polarity of Preceding Pulse	**Odd**	**Even**
−	000−	+00+
+	000+	−00−

5.2 DIGITAL DATA, ANALOG SIGNALS

We turn now to the case of transmitting digital data using analog signals. The most familiar use of this transformation is for transmitting digital data through the public telephone network. The telephone network was designed to receive, switch, and transmit analog signals in the voice-frequency range of about 300 to 3400 Hz. It is not at present suitable for handling digital signals from the subscriber locations (although this is beginning to change). Thus digital devices are attached to the network via a modem (modulator-demodulator), which converts digital data to analog signals, and vice versa.

For the telephone network, modems are used that produce signals in the voice-frequency range. The same basic techniques are used for modems that produce signals at higher frequencies (e.g., microwave). This section introduces these techniques and provides a brief discussion of the performance characteristics of the alternative approaches.

We mentioned that modulation involves operation on one or more of the three characteristics of a carrier signal: amplitude, frequency, and phase. Accordingly, there are three basic encoding or modulation techniques for transforming digital data into analog signals, as illustrated in Figure 5.7: amplitude shift keying (ASK),

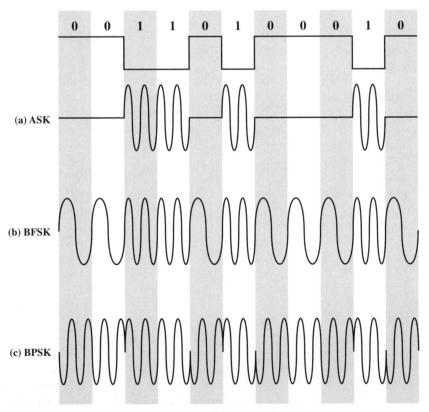

Figure 5.7   Modulation of Analog Signals for Digital Data

frequency shift keying (FSK), and phase shift keying (PSK). In all these cases, the resulting signal occupies a bandwidth centered on the carrier frequency.

Amplitude Shift Keying

In ASK, the two binary values are represented by two different amplitudes of the carrier frequency. Commonly, one of the amplitudes is zero; that is, one binary digit is represented by the presence, at constant amplitude, of the carrier, the other by the absence of the carrier (Figure 5.7a). The resulting transmitted signal for one bit time is

$$\textbf{ASK} \qquad s(t) = \begin{cases} A\cos(2\pi f_c t) & \text{binary 1} \\ 0 & \text{binary 0} \end{cases} \qquad (5.2)$$

where the carrier signal is $A\cos(2\pi f_c t)$. ASK is susceptible to sudden gain changes and is a rather inefficient modulation technique. On voice-grade lines, it is typically used only up to 1200 bps.

The ASK technique is used to transmit digital data over optical fiber. For LED (light-emitting diode) transmitters, Equation (5.2) is valid. That is, one signal element is represented by a light pulse while the other signal element is represented by the absence of light. Laser transmitters normally have a fixed "bias" current that causes the device to emit a low light level. This low level represents one signal element, while a higher-amplitude lightwave represents another signal element.

Frequency Shift Keying

The most common form of FSK is binary FSK (BFSK), in which the two binary values are represented by two different frequencies near the carrier frequency (Figure 5.7b). The resulting transmitted signal for one bit time is

$$\textbf{BFSK} \qquad s(t) = \begin{cases} A\cos(2\pi f_1 t) & \text{binary 1} \\ A\cos(2\pi f_2 t) & \text{binary 0} \end{cases} \qquad (5.3)$$

where f_1 and f_2 are typically offset from the carrier frequency f_c by equal but opposite amounts.

Figure 5.8 shows an example of the use of BFSK for full-duplex operation over a voice-grade line. The figure is a specification for the Bell System 108 series modems. Recall that a voice-grade line will pass frequencies in the approximate range 300 to 3400 Hz, and that *full duplex* means that signals are transmitted in both directions at the same time. To achieve full-duplex transmission, this bandwidth is split. In one direction (transmit or receive), the frequencies used to represent 1 and 0 are centered on 1170 Hz, with a shift of 100 Hz on either side. The effect of alternating between those two frequencies is to produce a signal whose spectrum is indicated as the shaded area on the left in Figure 5.8. Similarly, for the other direction (receive or transmit) the modem uses frequencies shifted 100 Hz to each side of a center frequency of 2125 Hz. This signal is indicated by the shaded area on the right in Figure 5.8. Note that there is little overlap and thus little interference.

BFSK is less susceptible to error than ASK. On voice-grade lines, it is typically used up to 1200 bps. It is also commonly used for high-frequency (3 to 30 MHz)

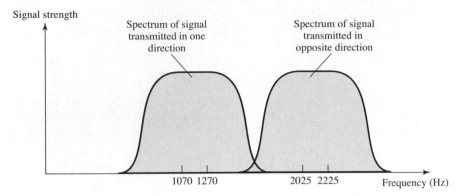

Figure 5.8 Full-Duplex FSK Transmission on a Voice-Grade Line

radio transmission. It can also be used at even higher frequencies on local area networks that use coaxial cable.

A signal that is more bandwidth efficient, but also more susceptible to error, is multiple FSK (MFSK), in which more than two frequencies are used. In this case each signaling element represents more than one bit. The transmitted MFSK signal for one signal element time can be defined as follows:

$$\textbf{MFSK} \qquad s_i(t) = A \cos 2\pi f_i t, \qquad 1 \leq i \leq M \qquad (5.4)$$

where

$$f_i = f_c + (2i - 1 - M)f_d$$
f_c = the carrier frequency
f_d = the difference frequency
M = number of different signal elements = 2^L
L = number of bits per signal element

To match the data rate of the input bit stream, each output signal element is held for a period of $T_s = LT$ seconds, where T is the bit period (data rate = $1/T$). Thus, one signal element, which is a constant-frequency tone, encodes L bits. The total bandwidth required is $2Mf_d$. It can be shown that the minimum frequency separation required is $2f_d = 1/T_s$. Therefore, the modulator requires a bandwidth of $W_d = 2Mf_d = M/T_s$.

Example 5.1 With $f_c = 250\,\text{kHz}$, $f_d = 25\,\text{kHz}$, and $M = 8\,(L = 3\,\text{bits})$, we have the following frequency assignments for each of the eight possible 3-bit data combinations:

$f_1 = 75\,\text{kHz}$ 000 $f_2 = 125\,\text{kHz}$ 001 $f_3 = 175\,\text{kHz}$ 010 $f_4 = 225\,\text{kHz}$ 011
$f_5 = 275\,\text{kHz}$ 100 $f_6 = 325\,\text{kHz}$ 101 $f_7 = 375\,\text{kHz}$ 110 $f_8 = 425\,\text{kHz}$ 111

This scheme can support a data rate of $2f_d = 1/T_s = 50\,\text{kbps}$.

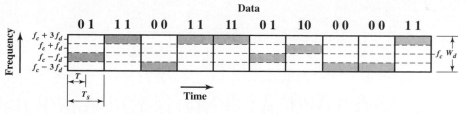

Figure 5.9   MFSK Frequency Use (M = 4)

Figure 5.9 shows an example of MFSK with M = 4. An input bit stream is encoded 2 bits at a time, with each of the four possible 2-bit combinations transmitted as a different frequency.

Phase Shift Keying

In PSK, the phase of the carrier signal is shifted to represent data.

Two-Level PSK

The simplest scheme uses two phases to represent the two binary digits (Figure 5.7c) and is known as binary phase shift keying. The resulting transmitted signal for one bit time is

$$\textbf{BPSK} \qquad s(t) = \begin{cases} A\cos(2\pi f_c t) \\ A\cos(2\pi f_c t + \pi) \end{cases} = \begin{cases} A\cos(2\pi f_c t) & \text{binary } 1 \\ -A\cos(2\pi f_c t) & \text{binary } 0 \end{cases} \qquad (5.5)$$

Because a phase shift of 180° (π) is equivalent to flipping the sine wave or multiplying it by −1, the rightmost expressions in Equation (5.5) can be used. This leads to a convenient formulation. If we have a bit stream, and we define $d(t)$ as the discrete function that takes on the value of +1 for one bit time if the corresponding bit in the bit stream is 1 and the value of −1 for one bit time if the corresponding bit in the bit stream is 0, then we can define the transmitted signal as

$$\textbf{BPSK} \qquad s_d(t) = A\,d(t)\cos(2\pi f_c t) \qquad (5.6)$$

An alternative form of two-level PSK is differential PSK (DPSK). Figure 5.10 shows an example. In this scheme, a binary 0 is represented by sending a signal burst of the same phase as the previous signal burst sent. A binary 1 is represented by sending a signal burst of opposite phase to the preceding one. This term *differential* refers to the fact that the phase shift is with reference to the previous bit transmitted rather than to some constant reference signal. In differential encoding, the information to be transmitted is represented in terms of the changes between successive data symbols rather than the signal elements themselves. DPSK avoids the requirement for an accurate local oscillator phase at the receiver that is matched with the transmitter. As long as the preceding phase is received correctly, the phase reference is accurate.

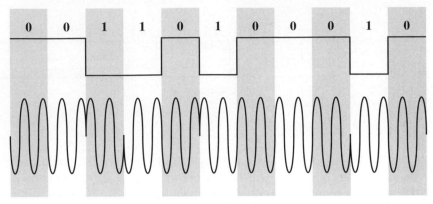

Figure 5.10 Differential Phase Shift Keying (DPSK)

Four-Level PSK

More efficient use of bandwidth can be achieved if each signaling element represents more than one bit. For example, instead of a phase shift of 180°, as allowed in BPSK, a common encoding technique, known as quadrature phase shift keying (QPSK), uses phase shifts of multiples of $\pi/2$ (90°).

$$\text{QPSK} \qquad s(t) = \begin{cases} A\cos\left(2\pi f_c t + \dfrac{\pi}{4}\right) & 11 \\[2ex] A\cos\left(2\pi f_c t + \dfrac{3\pi}{4}\right) & 01 \\[2ex] A\cos\left(2\pi f_c t - \dfrac{3\pi}{4}\right) & 00 \\[2ex] A\cos\left(2\pi f_c t - \dfrac{\pi}{4}\right) & 10 \end{cases} \qquad (5.7)$$

Thus each signal element represents two bits rather than one.

Figure 5.11 shows the QPSK modulation scheme in general terms. The input is a stream of binary digits with a data rate of $R = 1/T_b$, where T_b is the width of each bit. This stream is converted into two separate bit streams of $R/2$ bps each, by taking alternate bits for the two streams. The two data streams are referred to as the I (in-phase) and Q (quadrature phase) streams. In the diagram, the upper stream is modulated on a carrier of frequency f_c by multiplying the bit stream by the carrier. For convenience of modulator structure we map binary 1 to $\sqrt{1/2}$ and binary 0 to $-\sqrt{1/2}$. Thus, a binary 1 is represented by a scaled version of the carrier wave and a binary 0 is represented by a scaled version of the negative of the carrier wave, both at a constant amplitude. This same carrier wave is shifted by 90° and used for modulation of the lower binary stream. The two modulated signals are then added together and transmitted. The transmitted signal can be expressed as follows:

$$\text{QPSK} \qquad s(t) = \frac{1}{\sqrt{2}} I(t) \cos 2\pi f_c t - \frac{1}{\sqrt{2}} Q(t) \sin 2\pi f_c t$$

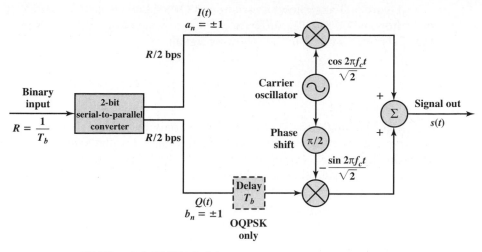

Figure 5.11   QPSK and OQPSK Modulators

Figure 5.12 shows an example of QPSK coding. Each of the two modulated streams is a BPSK signal at half the data rate of the original bit stream. Thus, the combined signals have a symbol rate that is half the input bit rate. Note that from one symbol time to the next, a phase change of as much as $180°$ (π) is possible.

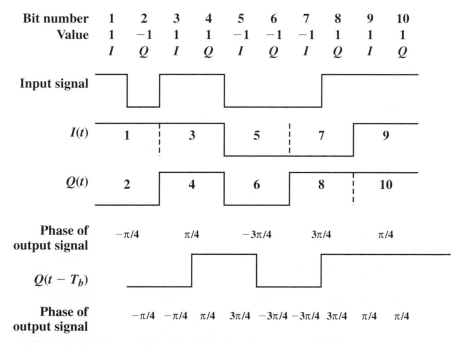

Figure 5.12   Example of QPSK and OQPSK Waveforms

Figure 5.11 also shows a variation of QPSK known as offset QPSK (OQPSK), or orthogonal QPSK. The difference is that a delay of one bit time is introduced in the Q stream, resulting in the following signal:

$$s(t) = \frac{1}{\sqrt{2}} I(t) \cos 2\pi f_c t - \frac{1}{\sqrt{2}} Q(t - T_b) \sin 2\pi f_c t$$

Because OQPSK differs from QPSK only by the delay in the Q stream, its spectral characteristics and bit error performance are the same as that of QPSK. From Figure 5.12, we can observe that only one of two bits in the pair can change sign at any time and thus the phase change in the combined signal never exceeds $90°$ $(\pi/2)$. This can be an advantage because physical limitations on phase modulators make large phase shifts at high transition rates difficult to perform. OQPSK also provides superior performance when the transmission channel (including transmitter and receiver) has significant nonlinear components. The effect of nonlinearities is a spreading of the signal bandwidth, which may result in adjacent channel interference. It is easier to control this spreading if the phase changes are smaller; hence the advantage of OQPSK over QPSK.

Multilevel PSK

The use of multiple levels can be extended beyond taking bits two at a time. It is possible to transmit bits three at a time using eight different phase angles. Further, each angle can have more than one amplitude. For example, a standard 9600 bps modem uses 12 phase angles, four of which have two amplitude values, for a total of 16 different signal elements.

This latter example points out very well the difference between the data rate R (in bps) and the modulation rate D (in baud) of a signal. Let us assume that this scheme is being employed with digital input in which each bit is represented by a constant voltage pulse, one level for binary one and one level for binary zero. The data rate is $R = 1/T_b$. However, the encoded signal contains $L = 4$ bits in each signal element using $M = 16$ different combinations of amplitude and phase. The modulation rate can be seen to be $R/4$, because each change of signal element communicates four bits. Thus the line signaling speed is 2400 baud, but the data rate is 9600 bps. This is the reason that higher bit rates can be achieved over voice-grade lines by employing more complex modulation schemes.

Performance

In looking at the performance of various digital-to-analog modulation schemes, the first parameter of interest is the bandwidth of the modulated signal. This depends on a variety of factors, including the definition of bandwidth used and the filtering technique used to create the bandpass signal. We will use some straightforward results from [COUC01].

The transmission bandwidth B_T for ASK is of the form

$$\textbf{ASK} \quad B_T = (1 + r)R \tag{5.8}$$

where R is the bit rate and r is related to the technique by which the signal is filtered to establish a bandwidth for transmission; typically $0 < r < 1$. Thus the bandwidth is directly related to the bit rate. The preceding formula is also valid for PSK.

For FSK, the bandwidth can be expressed as

$$\text{FSK} \qquad B_T = 2\Delta F + (1 + r)R \qquad\qquad (5.9)$$

where $\Delta F = f_2 - f_c = f_c - f_1$ is the offset of the modulated frequency from the carrier frequency. When very high frequencies are used, the ΔF term dominates. For example, one of the standards for FSK signaling on a coaxial cable multipoint local network uses $\Delta F = 1.25\,\text{MHz}$, $f_c = 5\,\text{MHz}$, and $R = 1\,\text{Mbps}$; in this case the $2\Delta F = 2.5\,\text{MHz}$ term dominates. In the example of the preceding section for the Bell 108 modem, $\Delta F = 100\,\text{Hz}$, $f_c = 1170\,\text{Hz}$ (in one direction), and $R = 300\,\text{bps}$; in this case the $(1 + r)R$ term dominates.

With multilevel PSK (MPSK), significant improvements in bandwidth can be achieved. In general,

$$\text{MPSK} \qquad B_T = \left(\frac{1 + r}{L}\right)R = \left(\frac{1 + r}{\log_2 M}\right)R \qquad (5.10)$$

where L is the number of bits encoded per signal element and M is the number of different signal elements.

For multilevel FSK (MFSK), we have

$$\text{MFSK} \qquad B_T = \left(\frac{(1 + r)M}{\log_2 M}\right)R \qquad\qquad (5.11)$$

Table 5.5 shows the ratio of data rate, R, to transmission bandwidth for various schemes. This ratio is also referred to as the **bandwidth efficiency**. As the name suggests, this parameter measures the efficiency with which bandwidth can be used to transmit data. The advantage of multilevel signaling methods now becomes clear.

Table 5.5 Data Rate to Transmission Bandwidth Ratio for Various Digital-to-Analog Encoding Schemes

	$r = 0$	$r = 0.5$	$r = 1$
ASK	1.0	0.67	0.5
FSK			
Wideband ($\Delta F \gg R$)	~0	~0	~0
Narrowband ($\Delta F \approx f_c$)	1.0	0.67	0.5
PSK	1.0	0.67	0.5
Multilevel signaling			
$L = 4, b = 2$	2.00	1.33	1.00
$L = 8, b = 3$	3.00	2.00	1.50
$L = 16, b = 4$	4.00	2.67	2.00
$L = 32, b = 5$	5.00	3.33	2.50

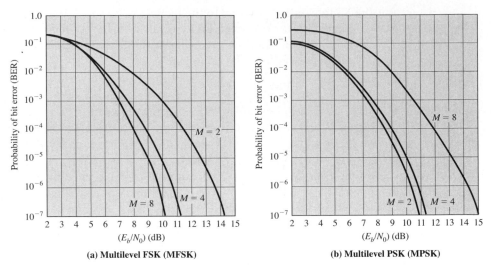

Figure 5.13 Theoretical Bit Error Rate for Multilevel FSK and PSK

Of course, the preceding discussion refers to the spectrum of the input signal to a communications line. Nothing has yet been said of performance in the presence of noise. Figure 5.4 summarizes some results based on reasonable assumptions concerning the transmission system [COUC01]. Here bit error rate is plotted as a function of the ratio E_b/N_0 defined in Chapter 3. Of course, as that ratio increases, the bit error rate drops. Further, DPSK and BPSK are about 3 dB superior to ASK and BFSK.

Figure 5.13 shows the same information for various levels of M for MFSK and MPSK. There is an important difference. For MFSK, the error probability for a given value E_b/N_0 decreases as M increases, while the opposite is true for MPSK. On the other hand, comparing Equations (6.10) and (6.11), the bandwidth efficiency of MFSK decreases as M increases, while the opposite is true of MPSK.

Example 5.2 What is the bandwidth efficiency for FSK, ASK, PSK, and QPSK for a bit error rate of 10^{-7} on a channel with an SNR of 12 dB?

Using Equation (2.2), we have

$$\frac{E_b}{N_0} = 12 \text{ dB} - \left(\frac{R}{B_T}\right)_{dB}$$

For FSK and ASK, from Figure 5.4,

$$\frac{E_b}{N_0} = 14.2 \text{ dB}$$

$$\left(\frac{R}{B_T}\right)_{dB} = -2.2 \text{ dB}$$

$$\frac{R}{B_T} = 0.6$$

For PSK, from Figure 5.4

$$\frac{E_b}{N_0} = 11.2 \, \text{dB}$$

$$\left(\frac{R}{B_T}\right)_{\text{dB}} = 0.8 \, \text{dB}$$

$$\frac{R}{B_T} = 1.2$$

The result for QPSK must take into account that the baud rate $D = R/2$. Thus

$$\frac{R}{B_T} = 2.4$$

As the preceding example shows, ASK and FSK exhibit the same bandwidth efficiency, PSK is better, and even greater improvement can be achieved with multi-level signaling.

It is worthwhile to compare these bandwidth requirements with those for digital signaling. A good approximation is

$$B_T = 0.5(1 + r)D$$

where D is the modulation rate. For NRZ, $D = R$, and we have

$$\frac{R}{B_T} = \frac{2}{1 + r}$$

Thus digital signaling is in the same ballpark, in terms of bandwidth efficiency, as ASK, FSK, and PSK. A significant advantage for analog signaling is seen with multi-level techniques.

Quadrature Amplitude Modulation

QAM is a popular analog signaling technique that is used in the asymmetric digital subscriber line (ADSL), described in Chapter 8, and in some wireless standards. This modulation technique is a combination of ASK and PSK. QAM can also be considered a logical extension of QPSK. QAM takes advantage of the fact that it is possible to send two different signals simultaneously on the same carrier frequency, by using two copies of the carrier frequency, one shifted by 90° with respect to the other. For QAM, each carrier is ASK modulated. The two independent signals are simultaneously transmitted over the same medium. At the receiver, the two signals are demodulated and the results combined to produce the original binary input.

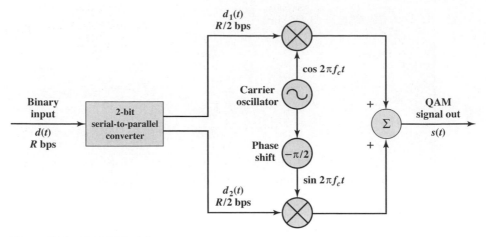

Figure 5.14 QAM Modulator

Figure 5.14 shows the QAM modulation scheme in general terms. The input is a stream of binary digits arriving at a rate of R bps. This stream is converted into two separate bit streams of $R/2$ bps each, by taking alternate bits for the two streams. In the diagram, the upper stream is ASK modulated on a carrier of frequency f_c by multiplying the bit stream by the carrier. Thus, a binary zero is represented by the absence of the carrier wave and a binary one is represented by the presence of the carrier wave at a constant amplitude. This same carrier wave is shifted by 90° and used for ASK modulation of the lower binary stream. The two modulated signals are then added together and transmitted. The transmitted signal can be expressed as follows:

$$\textbf{QAM} \qquad s(t) = d_1(t) \cos 2\pi f_c t + d_2(t) \sin 2\pi f_c t$$

If two-level ASK is used, then each of the two streams can be in one of two states and the combined stream can be in one of $4 = 2 \times 2$ states. This is essentially QPSK. If four-level ASK is used (i.e., four different amplitude levels), then the combined stream can be in one of $16 = 4 \times 4$ states. Systems using 64 and even 256 states have been implemented. The greater the number of states, the higher the data rate that is possible within a given bandwidth. Of course, as discussed previously, the greater the number of states, the higher the potential error rate due to noise and attenuation.

5.3 ANALOG DATA, DIGITAL SIGNALS

In this section we examine the process of transforming analog data into digital signals. Strictly speaking, it might be more correct to refer to this as a process of converting analog data into digital data; this process is known as digitization. Once analog data have been converted into digital data, a number of things can happen. The three most common are as follows:

1. The digital data can be transmitted using NRZ-L. In this case, we have in fact gone directly from analog data to a digital signal.

Figure 5.15 Digitizing Analog Data

2. The digital data can be encoded as a digital signal using a code other than NRZ-L. Thus an extra step is required.
3. The digital data can be converted into an analog signal, using one of the modulation techniques discussed in Section 5.2.

This last, seemingly curious, procedure is illustrated in Figure 5.15, which shows voice data that are digitized and then converted to an analog ASK signal. This allows digital transmission in the sense defined in Chapter 3. The voice data, because they have been digitized, can be treated as digital data, even though transmission requirements (e.g., use of microwave) dictate that an analog signal be used.

The device used for converting analog data into digital form for transmission, and subsequently recovering the original analog data from the digital, is known as a **codec** (coder-decoder). In this section we examine the two principal techniques used in codecs, pulse code modulation and delta modulation. The section closes with a discussion of comparative performance.

Pulse Code Modulation

Pulse code modulation (PCM) is based on the sampling theorem:

> **Sampling Theorem:** If a signal $f(t)$ is sampled at regular intervals of time and at a rate higher than twice the highest signal frequency, then the samples contain all the information of the original signal. The function $f(t)$ may be reconstructed from these samples by the use of a lowpass filter.

For the interested reader, a proof is provided in a supporting document at this book's Web site. If voice data are limited to frequencies below 4000 Hz, a conservative procedure for intelligibility, 8000 samples per second would be sufficient to characterize the voice signal completely. Note, however, that these are analog samples, called **pulse amplitude modulation (PAM)** samples. To convert to digital, each of these analog samples must be assigned a binary code.

Figure 5.16 shows an example in which the original signal is assumed to be bandlimited with a bandwidth of B. PAM samples are taken at a rate of $2B$, or once every $T_s = 1/2B$ seconds. Each PAM sample is approximated by being *quantized* into one of 16 different levels. Each sample can then be represented by 4 bits. But because the quantized values are only approximations, it is impossible to recover the original signal exactly. By using an 8-bit sample, which allows 256 quantizing levels, the quality of the recovered voice signal is comparable with that achieved via

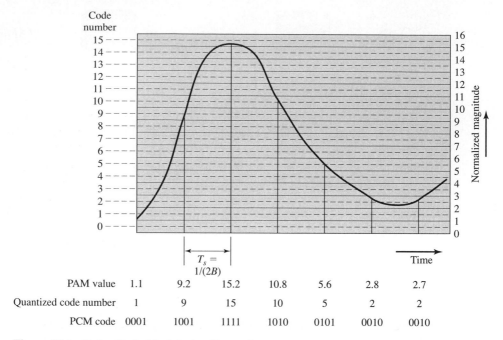

Figure 5.16   Pulse Code Modulation Example

analog transmission. Note that this implies that a data rate of 8000 samples per second $\times$ 8 bits per sample = 64 kbps is needed for a single voice signal.

Thus, PCM starts with a continuous-time, continuous-amplitude (analog) signal, from which a digital signal is produced (Figure 5.17). The digital signal consists of blocks of n bits, where each n-bit number is the amplitude of a PCM pulse. On reception, the process is reversed to reproduce the analog signal. Notice, however, that this process violates the terms of the sampling theorem. By quantizing the PAM pulse, the original signal is now only approximated and cannot be recovered exactly. This effect is known as quantizing error or quantizing noise. The signal-to-noise ratio for quantizing noise can be expressed as [GIBS93]

$$SNR_{dB} = 20 \log 2^n + 1.76 \, dB = 6.02n + 1.76 \, dB$$

Thus each additional bit used for quantizing increases SNR by about 6 dB, which is a factor of 4.

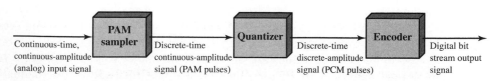

Figure 5.17   PCM Block Diagram

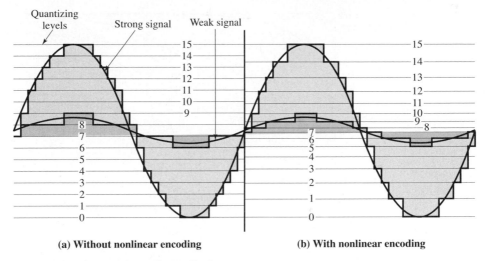

(a) Without nonlinear encoding   (b) With nonlinear encoding

Figure 5.18 Effect of Nonlinear Coding

Typically, the PCM scheme is refined using a technique known as nonlinear encoding, which means, in effect, that the quantization levels are not equally spaced. The problem with equal spacing is that the mean absolute error for each sample is the same, regardless of signal level. Consequently, lower amplitude values are relatively more distorted. By using a greater number of quantizing steps for signals of low amplitude, and a smaller number of quantizing steps for signals of large amplitude, a marked reduction in overall signal distortion is achieved (e.g., see Figure 5.18).

The same effect can be achieved by using uniform quantizing but companding (compressing-expanding) the input analog signal. Companding is a process that compresses the intensity range of a signal by imparting more gain to weak signals than to strong signals on input. At output, the reverse operation is performed. Figure 5.19 shows typical companding functions. Note that the effect on the input side is to compress the sample so that the higher values are reduced with respect to the lower values. Thus, with a fixed number of quantizing levels, more levels are available for lower-level signals. On the output side, the compander expands the samples so the compressed values are restored to their original values.

Nonlinear encoding can significantly improve the PCM SNR ratio. For voice signals, improvements of 24 to 30 dB have been achieved.

Delta Modulation (DM)

A variety of techniques have been used to improve the performance of PCM or to reduce its complexity. One of the most popular alternatives to PCM is delta modulation (DM).

With delta modulation, an analog input is approximated by a staircase function that moves up or down by one quantization level (δ) at each sampling interval (T_s). An example is shown in Figure 5.20, where the staircase function is overlaid on the original analog waveform. The important characteristic of this staircase function is that its behavior is binary: At each sampling time, the function moves up or down

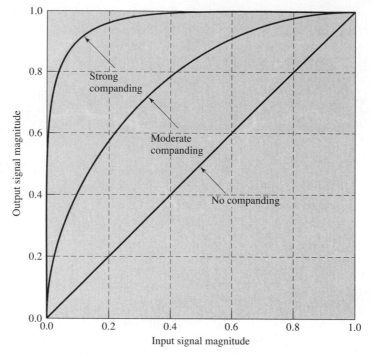

Figure 5.19 Typical Companding Functions

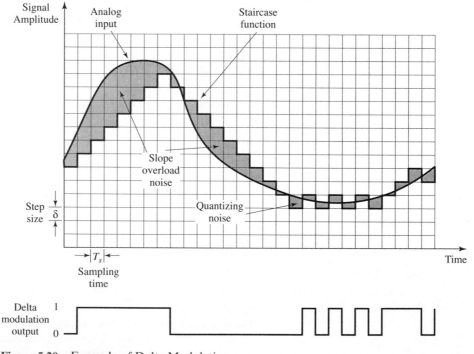

Figure 5.20 Example of Delta Modulation

a constant amount δ. Thus, the output of the delta modulation process can be represented as a single binary digit for each sample. In essence, a bit stream is produced by approximating the derivative of an analog signal rather than its amplitude: A 1 is generated if the staircase function is to go up during the next interval; a 0 is generated otherwise.

The transition (up or down) that occurs at each sampling interval is chosen so that the staircase function tracks the original analog waveform as closely as possible. Figure 5.21 illustrates the logic of the process, which is essentially a feedback mechanism. For transmission, the following occurs: At each sampling time, the analog input is compared to the most recent value of the approximating staircase function. If the value of the sampled waveform exceeds that of the staircase function, a 1 is generated; otherwise, a 0 is generated. Thus, the staircase is always changed in the direction of the input signal. The output of the DM process is therefore a binary sequence that can be used at the receiver to reconstruct the staircase function. The staircase function can then be smoothed by some type of integration process or by passing it through a lowpass filter to produce an analog approximation of the analog input signal.

There are two important parameters in a DM scheme: the size of the step assigned to each binary digit, δ, and the sampling rate. As Figure 5.20 illustrates,

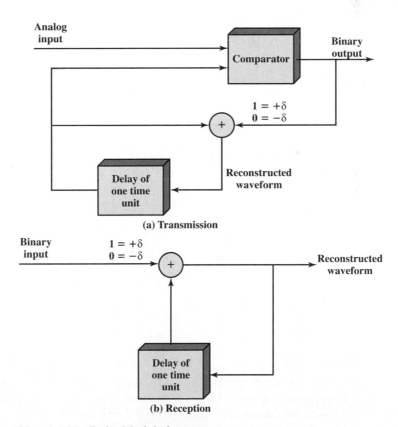

Figure 5.21   Delta Modulation

δ must be chosen to produce a balance between two types of errors or noise. When the analog waveform is changing very slowly, there will be quantizing noise. This noise increases as δ is increased. On the other hand, when the analog waveform is changing more rapidly than the staircase can follow, there is slope overload noise. This noise increases as δ is decreased.

It should be clear that the accuracy of the scheme can be improved by increasing the sampling rate. However, this increases the data rate of the output signal.

The principal advantage of DM over PCM is the simplicity of its implementation. In general, PCM exhibits better SNR characteristics at the same data rate.

Performance

Good voice reproduction via PCM can be achieved with 128 quantization levels, or 7-bit coding ($2^7 = 128$). A voice signal, conservatively, occupies a bandwidth of 4 kHz. Thus, according to the sampling theorem, samples should be taken at a rate of 8000 samples per second. This implies a data rate of $8000 \times 7 = 56$ kbps for the PCM-encoded digital data.

Consider what this means from the point of view of bandwidth requirement. An analog voice signal occupies 4 kHz. Using PCM this 4-kHz analog signal can be converted into a 56-kbps digital signal. But using the Nyquist criterion from Chapter 3, this digital signal could require on the order of 28 kHz of bandwidth. Even more severe differences are seen with higher bandwidth signals. For example, a common PCM scheme for color television uses 10-bit codes, which works out to 92 Mbps for a 4.6-MHz bandwidth signal. In spite of these numbers, digital techniques continue to grow in popularity for transmitting analog data. The principal reasons for this are as follows:

- Because repeaters are used instead of amplifiers, there is no additive noise.
- As we shall see, time division multiplexing (TDM) is used for digital signals instead of the frequency division multiplexing (FDM) used for analog signals. With TDM, there is no intermodulation noise, whereas we have seen that this is a concern for FDM.
- The conversion to digital signaling allows the use of the more efficient digital switching techniques.

Furthermore, techniques have been developed to provide more efficient codes. In the case of voice, a reasonable goal appears to be in the neighborhood of 4 kbps. With video, advantage can be taken of the fact that from frame to frame, most picture elements will not change. Interframe coding techniques should allow the video requirement to be reduced to about 15 Mbps, and for slowly changing scenes, such as found in a video teleconference, down to 64 kbps or less.

As a final point, we mention that in many instances, the use of a telecommunications system will result in both digital-to-analog and analog-to-digital processing. The overwhelming majority of local terminations into the telecommunications network is analog, and the network itself uses a mixture of analog and digital techniques. Thus digital data at a user's terminal may be converted to analog by a modem, subsequently digitized by a codec, and perhaps suffer repeated conversions before reaching its destination.

Thus, telecommunication facilities handle analog signals that represent both voice and digital data. The characteristics of the waveforms are quite different. Whereas voice signals tend to be skewed to the lower portion of the bandwidth (Figure 3.9), analog encoding of digital signals has a more uniform spectral content over the bandwidth and therefore contains more high-frequency components. Studies have shown that, because of the presence of these higher frequencies, PCM-related techniques are preferable to DM-related techniques for digitizing analog signals that represent digital data.

5.4 ANALOG DATA, ANALOG SIGNALS

Modulation has been defined as the process of combining an input signal $m(t)$ and a carrier at frequency f_c to produce a signal $s(t)$ whose bandwidth is (usually) centered on f_c. For digital data, the motivation for modulation should be clear: When only analog transmission facilities are available, modulation is required to convert the digital data to analog form. The motivation when the data are already analog is less clear. After all, voice signals are transmitted over telephone lines at their original spectrum (referred to as baseband transmission). There are two principal reasons for analog modulation of analog signals:

- A higher frequency may be needed for effective transmission. For unguided transmission, it is virtually impossible to transmit baseband signals; the required antennas would be many kilometers in diameter.
- Modulation permits frequency division multiplexing, an important technique explored in Chapter 8.

In this section we look at the principal techniques for modulation using analog data: amplitude modulation (AM), frequency modulation (FM), and phase modulation (PM). As before, the three basic characteristics of a signal are used for modulation.

Amplitude Modulation

Amplitude modulation (AM) is the simplest form of modulation and is depicted in Figure 5.22. Mathematically, the process can be expressed as

$$\textbf{AM} \qquad s(t) = [1 + n_a x(t)] \cos 2\pi f_c t \qquad (5.12)$$

where $\cos 2\pi f_c t$ is the carrier and $x(t)$ is the input signal (carrying data), both normalized to unity amplitude. The parameter n_a, known as the **modulation index**, is the ratio of the amplitude of the input signal to the carrier. Corresponding to our previous notation, the input signal is $m(t) = n_a x(t)$. The "1" in the Equation (5.12) is a dc component that prevents loss of information, as explained subsequently. This scheme is also known as double sideband transmitted carrier (DSBTC).

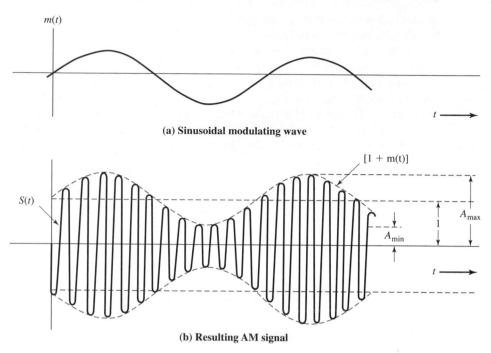

(a) Sinusoidal modulating wave

(b) Resulting AM signal

Figure 5.22   Amplitude Modulation

Example 5.3   Derive an expression for $s(t)$ if $x(t)$ is the amplitude-modulating signal $\cos 2\pi f_m t$.
   We have

$$s(t) = [1 + n_a \cos 2\pi f_m t] \cos 2\pi f_c t$$

By trigonometric identity, this may be expanded to

$$s(t) = \cos 2\pi f_c t + \frac{n_a}{2} \cos 2\pi (f_c - f_m)t + \frac{n_a}{2} \cos 2\pi (f_c + f_m)t$$

The resulting signal has a component at the original carrier frequency plus a pair of components each spaced f_m hertz from the carrier.

From Equation (5.12) and Figure 5.22, it can be seen that AM involves the multiplication of the input signal by the carrier. The envelope of the resulting signal is $[1 + n_a x(t)]$ and, as long as $n_a < 1$, the envelope is an exact reproduction of the original signal. If $n_a > 1$, the envelope will cross the time axis and information is lost.
   It is instructive to look at the spectrum of the AM signal. An example is shown in Figure 5.23. The spectrum consists of the original carrier plus the spectrum of the input signal translated to f_c. The portion of the spectrum for $|f| > |f_c|$ is the *upper sideband*, and the portion of the spectrum for $|f| < |f_c|$ is *lower sideband*. Both the

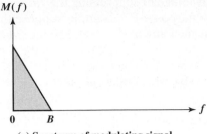

(a) Spectrum of modulating signal

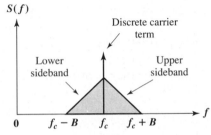

(b) Spectrum of AM signal with carrier at f_c

Figure 5.23   Spectrum of an AM Signal

upper and lower sidebands are replicas of the original spectrum $M(f)$, with the lower sideband being frequency reversed. As an example, consider a voice signal with a bandwidth that extends from 300 to 3000 Hz being modulated on a 60-kHz carrier. The resulting signal contains an upper sideband of 60.3 to 63 kHz, a lower sideband of 57 to 59.7 kHz, and the 60-kHz carrier. An important relationship is

$$P_t = P_c\left(1 + \frac{n_a^2}{2}\right)$$

where P_t is the total transmitted power in $s(t)$ and P_c is the transmitted power in the carrier. We would like n_a as large as possible so that most of the signal power is used to carry information. However, n_a must remain below 1.

It should be clear that $s(t)$ contains unnecessary components, because each of the sidebands contains the complete spectrum of $m(t)$. A popular variant of AM, known as single sideband (SSB), takes advantage of this fact by sending only one of the sidebands, eliminating the other sideband and the carrier. The principal advantages of this approach are as follows:

- Only half the bandwidth is required, that is, $B_T = B$, where B is the bandwidth of the original signal. For DSBTC, $B_T = 2B$.
- Less power is required because no power is used to transmit the carrier or the other sideband. Another variant is double sideband suppressed carrier (DSBSC), which filters out the carrier frequency and sends both sidebands. This saves some power but uses as much bandwidth as DSBTC.

The disadvantage of suppressing the carrier is that the carrier can be used for synchronization purposes. For example, suppose that the original analog signal is an ASK waveform encoding digital data. The receiver needs to know the starting point of each bit time to interpret the data correctly. A constant carrier provides a clocking mechanism by which to time the arrival of bits. A compromise approach is vestigial sideband (VSB), which uses one sideband and a reduced-power carrier.

Angle Modulation

Frequency modulation (FM) and phase modulation (PM) are special cases of angle modulation. The modulated signal is expressed as

$$\textbf{Angle Modulation} \qquad s(t) = A_c \cos[2\pi f_c t + \phi(t)] \qquad (5.13)$$

For phase modulation, the phase is proportional to the modulating signal:

$$\textbf{PM} \qquad \phi(t) = n_p m(t) \qquad (5.14)$$

where n_p is the phase modulation index.

For frequency modulation, the derivative of the phase is proportional to the modulating signal:

$$\textbf{FM} \qquad \phi'(t) = n_f m(t) \qquad (5.15)$$

where n_f is the frequency modulation index.

For those who wish a more detailed mathematical explanation of the preceding, consider the following. The phase of $s(t)$ at any instant is just $2\pi f_c t + \phi(t)$. The instantaneous phase deviation from the carrier signal is $\phi(t)$. In PM, this instantaneous phase deviation is proportional to $m(t)$. Because frequency can be defined as the rate of change of phase of a signal, the instantaneous frequency of $s(t)$ is

$$2\pi f_i(t) = \frac{d}{dt}[2\pi f_c t + \phi(t)]$$

$$f_i(t) = f_c + \frac{1}{2\pi}\phi'(t)$$

and the instantaneous frequency deviation from the carrier frequency is $\phi'(t)$, which in FM is proportional to $m(t)$.

Figure 5.24 illustrates amplitude, phase, and frequency modulation by a sine wave. The shapes of the FM and PM signals are very similar. Indeed, it is impossible to tell them apart without knowledge of the modulation function.

Several observations about the FM process are in order. The peak deviation ΔF can be seen to be

$$\Delta F = \frac{1}{2\pi} n_f A_m \, \text{Hz}$$

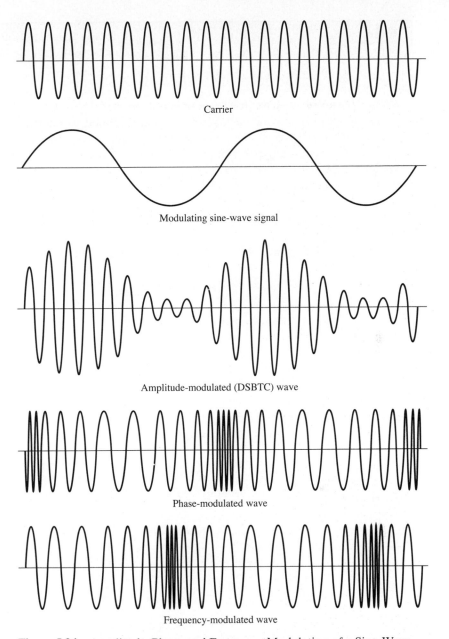

Carrier

Modulating sine-wave signal

Amplitude-modulated (DSBTC) wave

Phase-modulated wave

Frequency-modulated wave

Figure 5.24 Amplitude, Phase, and Frequency Modulation of a Sine-Wave Carrier by a Sine-Wave Signal

where A_m is the maximum value of $m(t)$. Thus an increase in the magnitude of $m(t)$ will increase ΔF, which, intuitively, should increase the transmitted bandwidth B_T. However, as should be apparent from Figure 5.24, this will not increase the average power level of the FM signal, which is $A_c^2/2$. This is distinctly different from AM, where the level of modulation affects the power in the AM signal but does not affect its bandwidth.

Example 5.4   Derive an expression for $s(t)$ if $\phi(t)$ is the phase-modulating signal $n_p \cos 2\pi f_m t$. Assume that $A_c = 1$. This can be seen directly to be

$$s(t) = \cos[2\pi f_c t + n_p \cos 2\pi f_m t]$$

The instantaneous phase deviation from the carrier signal is $n_p \cos 2\pi f_m t$. The phase angle of the signal varies from its unmodulated value in a simple sinusoidal fashion, with the peak phase deviation equal to n_p.

The preceding expression can be expanded using Bessel's trigonometric identities:

$$s(t) = \sum_{n=-\infty}^{\infty} J_n(n_p) \cos\left(2\pi f_c t + 2\pi n f_m t + \frac{n\pi}{2}\right)$$

where $J_n(n_p)$ is the nth-order Bessel function of the first kind. Using the property

$$J_{-n}(x) = (-1)^n J_n(x)$$

this can be rewritten as

$$s(t) = J_0(n_p) \cos 2\pi f_c t +$$
$$\sum_{n=1}^{\infty} J_n(n_p)\left[\cos\left(2\pi(f_c + n f_m)t + \frac{n\pi}{2}\right) + \cos\left(2\pi(f_c - n f_m)t + \frac{(n+2)\pi}{2}\right)\right]$$

The resulting signal has a component at the original carrier frequency plus a set of sidebands displaced from f_c by all possible multiples of f_m. For $n_p \ll 1$, the higher-order terms fall off rapidly.

Example 5.5   Derive an expression for $s(t)$ if $\phi'(t)$ is the frequency modulating signal $-n_f \sin 2\pi f_m t$. The form of $\phi'(t)$ was chosen for convenience. We have

$$\phi(t) = -\int n_f \sin 2\pi f_m t \, dt = \frac{n_f}{2\pi f_m} \cos 2\pi f_m t$$

Thus

$$s(t) = \cos\left[2\pi f_c t + \frac{n_f}{2\pi f_m} \cos 2\pi f_m t\right]$$
$$= \cos\left[2\pi f_c t + \frac{\Delta F}{f_m} \cos 2\pi f_m t\right]$$

The instantaneous frequency deviation from the carrier signal is $-n_f \sin 2\pi f_m t$. The frequency of the signal varies from its unmodulated value in a simple sinusoidal fashion, with the peak frequency deviation equal to n_f radians/second.

The equation for the FM signal has the identical form as for the PM signal, with $\Delta F/f_m$ substituted for n_p. Thus the Bessel expansion is the same.

As with AM, both FM and PM result in a signal whose bandwidth is centered at f_c. However, we can now see that the magnitude of that bandwidth is very different. Amplitude modulation is a linear process and produces frequencies that are the sum and difference of the carrier signal and the components of the modulating signal. Hence, for AM,

$$B_T = 2B$$

However, angle modulation includes a term of the form $\cos(\phi(t))$ which is nonlinear and will produce a wide range of frequencies. In essence, for a modulating sinusoid of frequency f_m, $s(t)$ will contain components at $f_c + f_m$, $f_c + 2f_m$, and so on. In the most general case, infinite bandwidth is required to transmit an FM or PM signal. As a practical matter, a very good rule of thumb, known as Carson's rule [COUC01], is

$$B_T = 2(\beta + 1)B$$

where

$$\beta = \begin{cases} n_p A_m & \text{for PM} \\ \dfrac{\Delta F}{B} = \dfrac{n_f A_m}{2\pi B} & \text{for FM} \end{cases}$$

We can rewrite the formula for FM as

$$B_T = 2\Delta F + 2B \tag{5.16}$$

Thus both FM and PM require greater bandwidth than AM.

5.5 RECOMMENDED READING

It is difficult, for some reason, to find solid treatments of digital-to-digital encoding schemes. Useful treatments include [SKLA01] and [BERG96].

There are many good references on analog modulation schemes for digital data. Good choices are [COUC01], [XION00], and [PROA02]; these three also provide comprehensive treatment of digital and analog modulation schemes for analog data.

An exceptionally clear exposition that covers digital-to-analog, analog-to-digital, and analog-to-analog techniques is [PEAR92].

An instructive treatment of the concepts of bit rate, baud, and bandwidth is [FREE98]. A recommended tutorial that expands on the concepts treated in the past few chapters relating to bandwidth efficiency and encoding schemes is [SKLA93].

BERG96   Bergmans, J. *Digital Baseband Transmission and Recording.* Boston: Kluwer, 1996.

COUC01   Couch, L. *Digital and Analog Communication Systems.* Upper Saddle River, NJ: Prentice Hall, 2001.

FREE98   Freeman, R. "Bits, Symbols, Baud, and Bandwidth." *IEEE Communications Magazine,* April 1998.

PEAR92   Pearson, J. *Basic Communication Theory.* Upper Saddle River, NJ: Prentice Hall, 1992.

PROA02   Proakis, J. *Communication Systems Engineering.* Upper Saddle River, NJ: Prentice Hall, 2002.

SKLA01   Sklar, B. *Digital Communications: Fundamentals and Applications.* Upper Saddle River, NJ: Prentice Hall, 2001.

SKLA93   Sklar, B. "Defining, Designing, and Evaluating Digital Communication Systems." *IEEE Communications Magazine,* November 1993.

XION00   Xiong, F. *Digital Modulation Techniques.* Boston: Artech House, 2000.

5.6 KEY TERMS, REVIEW QUESTIONS, AND PROBLEMS

Key Terms

alternate mark inversion (AMI)	differential encoding	nonreturn to zero-level (NRZ-L)
amplitude modulation (AM)	differential Manchester	phase modulation (PM)
amplitude shift keying (ASK)	differential PSK (DPSK)	phase shift keying (PSK)
angle modulation	frequency modulation (FM)	polar
bandwidth efficiency	frequency shift keying (FSK)	pseudoternary
baseband signal	high-density bipolar-3 zeros (HDB3)	pulse amplitude modulation (PAM)
biphase	Manchester	pulse code modulation (PCM)
bipolar-AMI	modulation	quadrature amplitude modulation (QAM)
bipolar with 8-zeros substitution (B8ZS)	modulation rate	quadrature PSK (QPSK)
bit error rate (BER)	multilevel binary	scrambling
carrier frequency	nonreturn to zero (NRZ)	unipolar
delta modulation (DM)	nonreturn to zero, inverted (NRZI)	

Review Questions

5.1   List and briefly define important factors that can be used in evaluating or comparing the various digital-to-digital encoding techniques.

5.2   What is differential encoding?

5.3   Explain the difference between NRZ-L and NRZI.

5.4   Describe two multilevel binary digital-to-digital encoding techniques.

5.5 Define *biphase encoding* and describe two biphase encoding techniques.

5.6 Explain the function of scrambling in the context of digital-to-digital encoding techniques.

5.7 What function does a modem perform?

5.8 How are binary values represented in amplitude shift keying, and what is the limitation of this approach?

5.9 What is the difference between QPSK and offset QPSK?

5.10 What is QAM?

5.11 What does the sampling theorem tell us concerning the rate of sampling required for an analog signal?

5.12 What are the differences among angle modulation, PM, and FM?

Problems

5.1 Which of the signals of Table 5.2 use differential encoding?

5.2 Develop algorithms for generating each of the codes of Table 5.2 from NRZ-L.

5.3 A modified NRZ code known as enhanced-NRZ (E-NRZ) is sometimes used for high-density magnetic tape recording. E-NRZ encoding entails separating the NRZ-L data stream into 7-bit words; inverting bits 2, 3, 6, and 7; and adding one parity bit to each word. The parity bit is chosen to make the total number of 1s in the 8-bit word an odd count. What are the advantages of E-NRZ over NRZ-L? Any disadvantages?

5.4 Develop a state diagram (finite state machine) representation of pseudoternary coding.

5.5 Consider the following signal encoding technique. Binary data are presented as input, a_m, for $m = 1, 2, 3, \ldots$ Two levels of processing occur. First, a new set of binary numbers is produced:

$$b_0 = 0$$
$$b_m = (a_m + b_{m-1}) \bmod 2$$

These are then encoded as

$$c_m = b_m - b_{m-1}$$

On reception, the original data are recovered by

$$a_m = c_m \bmod 2$$

  a. Verify that the received values of a_m equal the transmitted values of a_m.
  b. What sort of encoding is this?

5.6 For the bit stream 01001110, sketch the waveforms for each of the codes of Table 5.2. Assume that the signal level for the preceding bit for NRZI was high; the most recent preceding 1 bit (AMI) has a negative voltage; and the most recent preceding 0 bit (pseudoternary) has a negative voltage.

5.7 The waveform of Figure 5.25 belongs to a Manchester encoded binary data stream. Determine the beginning and end of bit periods (i.e., extract clock information) and give the data sequence.

Figure 5.25 A Manchester Stream

5.8 Consider a stream of binary data consisting of a long sequence of 1s followed by a zero followed by a long string of 1s, with the same assumptions as Problem 5.6. Draw the waveform for this sequence using
   a. NRZ-L
   b. Bipolar-AMI
   c. Pseudoternary

5.9 The bipolar-AMI waveform representing the binary sequence 0100101011 is transmitted over a noisy channel. The received waveform is shown in Figure 5.26; it contains a single error. Locate the position of this error and explain your answer.

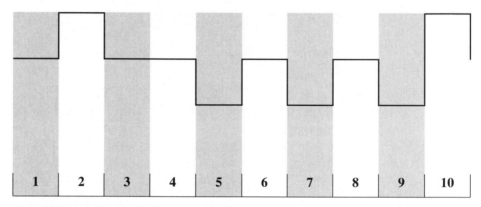

Figure 5.26 A Received Bipolar-AMI Waveform

5.10 One positive side effect of bipolar encoding is that a bipolar violation (two consecutive + pulses or two consecutive − pulses separated by any number of zeros) indicates to the receiver that an error has occurred in transmission. Unfortunately, upon the receipt of such a violation, the receiver does not know which bit is in error (only that an error has occurred). For the received bipolar sequence

$$+ - 0 + - 0 - +$$

which has one bipolar violation, construct two scenarios (each of which involves a different transmitted bit stream with one transmitted bit being converted via an error) that will produce this same received bit pattern.

5.11 Figure 5.27 shows the QAM demodulator corresponding to the QAM modulator of Figure 5.14. Show that this arrangement does recover the two signals $d_1(t)$ and $d_2(t)$, which can be combined to recover the original input.

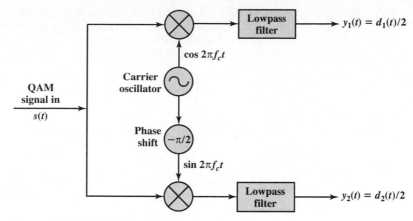

Figure 5.27 QAM Demodulator

5.12 A sine wave is to be used for two different signaling schemes: (a) PSK; (b) QPSK. The duration of a signal element is 10^{-5} s. If the received signal is of the following form:

$$s(t) = 0.005 \sin(2\pi\, 10^6 t + \theta) \text{ volts}$$

and if the measured noise power at the receiver is 2.5×10^{-8} watts, determine the E_b/N_0 (in dB) for each case.

5.13 Derive an expression for baud rate D as a function of bit rate R for QPSK using the digital encoding techniques of Table 5.2.

5.14 What SNR ratio is required to achieve a bandwidth efficiency of 1.0 for ASK, FSK, PSK, and QPSK? Assume that the required bit error rate is 10^{-6}.

5.15 An NRZ-L signal is passed through a filter with $r = 0.5$ and then modulated onto a carrier. The data rate is 2400 bps. Evaluate the bandwidth for ASK and FSK. For FSK assume that the two frequencies used are 50 kHz and 55 kHz.

5.16 Assume that a telephone line channel is equalized to allow bandpass data transmission over a frequency range of 600 to 3000 Hz. The available bandwidth is 2400 Hz. For $r = 1$ evaluate the required bandwidth for 2400 bps QPSK and 4800-bps, eight-level multilevel signaling. Is the bandwidth adequate?

5.17 Why should PCM be preferable to DM for encoding analog signals that represent digital data?

5.18 Are the modem and the codec functional inverses (i.e., could an inverted modem function as a codec, or vice versa)?

5.19 A signal is quantized using 10-bit PCM. Find the signal-to-quantization noise ratio.

5.20 Consider an audio signal with spectral components in the range 300 to 3000 Hz. Assume that a sampling rate of 7000 samples per second will be used to generate a PCM signal.
   a. For SNR = 30 dB, what is the number of uniform quantization levels needed?
   b. What data rate is required?

5.21 Find the step size δ required to prevent slope overload noise as a function of the frequency of the highest-frequency component of the signal. Assume that all components have amplitude A.

5.22 A PCM encoder accepts a signal with a full-scale voltage of 10 V and generates 8-bit codes using uniform quantization. The maximum normalized quantized voltage is $1 - 2^{-8}$. Determine (a) normalized step size, (b) actual step size in volts, (c) actual maximum quantized level in volts, (d) normalized resolution, (e) actual resolution, and (f) percentage resolution.

5.23 The analog waveform shown in Figure 5.28 is to be delta modulated. The sampling period and the step size are indicated by the grid on the figure. The first DM output and the staircase function for this period are also shown. Show the rest of the staircase function and give the DM output. Indicate regions where slope overload distortion exists.

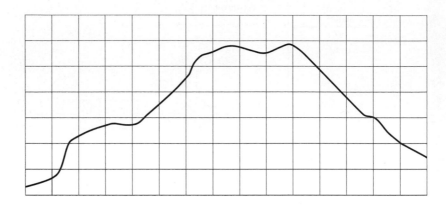

DM output

Figure 5.28 Delta Modulation Example

5.24 Consider the angle-modulated signal

$$s(t) = 10 \cos[(10^8)\pi t + 5 \sin 2\pi(10^3)t]$$

Find the maximum phase deviation and the maximum frequency deviation.

5.25 Consider the angle-modulated signal

$$s(t) = 10 \cos[2\pi(10^6)t + 0.1 \sin(10^3)\pi t]$$

a. Express $s(t)$ as a PM signal with $n_p = 10$.
b. Express $s(t)$ as an FM signal with $n_f = 10\pi$.

5.26 Let $m_1(t)$ and $m_2(t)$ be message signals and let $s_1(t)$ and $s_2(t)$ be the corresponding modulated signals using a carrier frequency of f_c.
a. Show that if simple AM modulation is used, then $m_1(t) + m_2(t)$ produces a modulated signal equal to that of a linear combination of $s_1(t)$ and $s_2(t)$. This is why AM is sometimes referred to as linear modulation.
b. Show that if simple PM modulation is used, then $m_1(t) + m_2(t)$ produces a modulated signal that is not a linear combination of $s_1(t)$ and $s_2(t)$. This is why angle modulation is sometimes referred to as nonlinear modulation.

CHAPTER 6

DIGITAL DATA COMMUNICATION TECHNIQUES

KEY POINTS

- The transmission of a stream of bits from one device to another across a transmission link involves a great deal of cooperation and agreement between the two sides. One of the most fundamental requirements is **synchronization**. The receiver must know the rate at which bits are being received so that it can sample the line at appropriate intervals to determine the value of each received bit. Two techniques are in common use for this purpose. In **asynchronous transmission**, each character of data is treated independently. Each character begins with a start bit that alerts the receiver that a character is arriving. The receiver samples each bit in the character and then looks for the beginning of the next character. This technique would not work well for long blocks of data because the receiver's clock might eventually drift out of synchronization with the transmitter's clock. However, sending data in large blocks is more efficient than sending data one character at a time. For large blocks, **synchronous transmission** is used. Each block of data is formatted as a frame that includes a starting and an ending flag. Some form of synchronization, such as the use of Manchester encoding, is employed.

- **Error detection** is performed by calculating an error-detecting code that is a function of the bits being transmitted. The code is appended to the transmitted bits. The receiver calculates the code based on the incoming bits and compares it to the incoming code to check for errors.

- **Error correction** operates in a fashion similar to error detection but is capable of correcting certain errors in a transmitted bit stream.

- For a device to transmit across a medium, it must be attached through some sort of **interface**. The interface defines not only the electrical characteristics of the signal but also the physical means of attachment and the procedures for sending and receiving bits of data.

The preceding three chapters have been concerned primarily with the attributes of data transmission, such as the characteristics of data signals and transmission media, the encoding of signals, and transmission performance. In this chapter, we shift our emphasis from data transmission to data communications.

For two devices linked by a transmission medium to exchange data, a high degree of cooperation is required. Typically, data are transmitted one bit at a time over the medium. The timing (rate, duration, spacing) of these bits must be the same for transmitter and receiver. Two common techniques for controlling this timing—asynchronous and synchronous—are explored in Section 6.1. Next, we look at the problem of bit errors. As we have seen, data transmission is not an error-free process, and some means of accounting for these errors is needed. After a brief discussion of the distinction between single-bit errors and burst errors, the chapter turns to two approaches to dealing with errors: error detection and error correction.

Next, the chapter provides an overview of the types of line configurations in common use. Finally, we look at the physical interface between data transmitting devices and the transmission line. Typically, digital data devices do not attach to and signal across the medium directly. Instead, this process is mediated through a standardized interface that provides considerable control over the interaction between the transmitting/receiving devices and the transmission line.

6.1 ASYNCHRONOUS AND SYNCHRONOUS TRANSMISSION

In this book, we are primarily concerned with serial transmission of data; that is, data are transferred over a single signal path rather than a parallel set of lines, as is common with I/O devices and internal computer signal paths. With serial transmission, signaling elements are sent down the line one at a time. Each signaling element may be

- **Less than one bit:** This is the case, for example, with Manchester coding.
- **One bit:** NRZ-L and FSK are digital and analog examples, respectively.
- **More than one bit:** QPSK is an example.

For simplicity in the following discussion, we assume one bit per signaling element unless otherwise stated. The discussion is not materially affected by this simplification.

Recall from Figure 3.15 that the reception of digital data involves sampling the incoming signal once per bit time to determine the binary value. One of the difficulties encountered in such a process is that various transmission impairments will corrupt the signal so that occasional errors will occur. This problem is compounded by a timing difficulty: In order for the receiver to sample the incoming bits properly, it must know the arrival time and duration of each bit that it receives.

Suppose that the sender simply transmits a stream of data bits. The sender has a clock that governs the timing of the transmitted bits. For example, if data are to be transmitted at one million bits per second (1 Mbps), then one bit will be transmitted every $1/10^6 = 1$ microsecond (μs), as measured by the sender's clock. Typically, the receiver will attempt to sample the medium at the center of each bit time. The receiver will time its samples at intervals of one bit time. In our example, the sampling would occur once every 1 μs. If the receiver times its samples based on its own clock, then there will be a problem if the transmitter's and receiver's clocks are not precisely aligned. If there is a drift of 1 percent (the receiver's clock is 1% faster or slower than the transmitter's clock), then the first sampling will be 0.01 of a bit time (0.01 μs) away from the center of the bit (center of bit is 0.5 μs from beginning and end of bit). After 50 or more samples, the receiver may be in error because it is sampling in the wrong bit time ($50 \times .01 = 0.5$ μs). For smaller timing differences, the error would occur later, but eventually the receiver will be out of step with the transmitter if the transmitter sends a sufficiently long stream of bits and if no steps are taken to synchronize the transmitter and receiver.

Asynchronous Transmission

Two approaches are common for achieving the desired synchronization. The first is called, oddly enough, asynchronous transmission. The strategy with this scheme is to avoid the timing problem by not sending long, uninterrupted streams of bits.

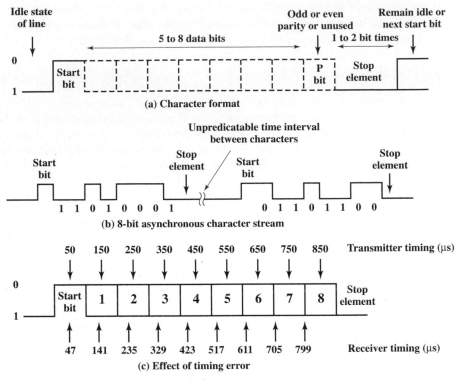

Figure 6.1 Asynchronous Transmission

Instead, data are transmitted one character at a time, where each character is five to eight bits in length.[1] Timing or synchronization must only be maintained within each character; the receiver has the opportunity to resynchronize at the beginning of each new character.

Figure 6.1 illustrates this technique. When no character is being transmitted, the line between transmitter and receiver is in an *idle* state. The definition of *idle* is equivalent to the signaling element for binary 1. Thus, for NRZ-L signaling (see Figure 5.2), which is common for asynchronous transmission, idle would be the presence of a negative voltage on the line. The beginning of a character is signaled by a *start bit* with a value of binary 0. This is followed by the five to eight bits that actually make up the character. The bits of the character are transmitted beginning with the least significant bit. For example, for IRA characters, the data bits are usually followed by a parity bit, which therefore is in the most significant bit position. The parity bit is set by the transmitter such that the total number of ones in the character, including the parity bit, is even (even parity) or odd (odd parity), depending on

---

[1] The number of bits that comprise a character depends on the code used. We have already described one common example, the IRA code, which uses seven bits per character. Another common code is the Extended Binary Coded Decimal Interchange Code (EBCDIC), which is an 8-bit character code used on all IBM machines except for IBM's personal computers and workstations.

the convention being used. This bit is used by the receiver for error detection, as discussed in Section 6.3. The final element is a *stop element*, which is a binary 1. A minimum length for the stop element is specified, and this is usually 1, 1.5, or 2 times the duration of an ordinary bit. No maximum value is specified. Because the stop element is the same as the idle state, the transmitter will continue to transmit the stop element until it is ready to send the next character.

The timing requirements for this scheme are modest. For example, IRA characters are typically sent as 8-bit units, including the parity bit. If the receiver is 5% slower or faster than the transmitter, the sampling of the eighth character bit will be displaced by 45% and still be correctly sampled. Figure 6.1c shows the effects of a timing error of sufficient magnitude to cause an error in reception. In this example we assume a data rate of 10,000 bits per second (10 kbps); therefore, each bit is of 0.1 millisecond (ms), or 100 μs, duration. Assume that the receiver is fast by 6%, or 6 μs per bit time. Thus, the receiver samples the incoming character every 94 μs (based on the transmitter's clock). As can be seen, the last sample is erroneous.

An error such as this actually results in two errors. First, the last sampled bit is incorrectly received. Second, the bit count may now be out of alignment. If bit 7 is a 1 and bit 8 is a 0, bit 8 could be mistaken for a start bit. This condition is termed a *framing error*, as the character plus start bit and stop element are sometimes referred to as a frame. A framing error can also occur if some noise condition causes the false appearance of a start bit during the idle state.

Asynchronous transmission is simple and cheap but requires an overhead of two to three bits per character. For example, for an 8-bit character with no parity bit, using a 1-bit-long stop element, two out of every ten bits convey no information but are there merely for synchronization; thus the overhead is 20%. Of course, the percentage overhead could be reduced by sending larger blocks of bits between the start bit and stop element. However, as Figure 6.1c indicates, the larger the block of bits, the greater the cumulative timing error. To achieve greater efficiency, a different form of synchronization, known as synchronous transmission, is used.

Synchronous Transmission

With synchronous transmission, a block of bits is transmitted in a steady stream without start and stop codes. The block may be many bits in length. To prevent timing drift between transmitter and receiver, their clocks must somehow be synchronized. One possibility is to provide a separate clock line between transmitter and receiver. One side (transmitter or receiver) pulses the line regularly with one short pulse per bit time. The other side uses these regular pulses as a clock. This technique works well over short distances, but over longer distances the clock pulses are subject to the same impairments as the data signal, and timing errors can occur. The other alternative is to embed the clocking information in the data signal. For digital signals, this can be accomplished with Manchester or differential Manchester encoding. For analog signals, a number of techniques can be used; for example, the carrier frequency itself can be used to synchronize the receiver based on the phase of the carrier.

Figure 6.2   Synchronous Frame Format

With synchronous transmission, there is another level of synchronization required, to allow the receiver to determine the beginning and end of a block of data. To achieve this, each block begins with a *preamble* bit pattern and generally ends with a *postamble* bit pattern. In addition, other bits are added to the block that convey control information used in the data link control procedures discussed in Chapter 7. The data plus preamble, postamble, and control information are called a **frame**. The exact format of the frame depends on which data link control procedure is being used.

Figure 6.2 shows, in general terms, a typical frame format for synchronous transmission. Typically, the frame starts with a preamble called a flag, which is 8 bits long. The same flag is used as a postamble. The receiver looks for the occurrence of the flag pattern to signal the start of a frame. This is followed by some number of control fields, then a data field (variable length for most protocols), more control fields, and finally the flag is repeated.

For sizable blocks of data, synchronous transmission is far more efficient than asynchronous. Asynchronous transmission requires 20% or more overhead. The control information, preamble, and postamble in synchronous transmission are typically less than 100 bits. For example, one of the more common schemes, HDLC (described in Chapter 7), contains 48 bits of control, preamble, and postamble. Thus, for a 1000-character block of data, each frame consists of 48 bits of overhead and $1000 \times 8 = 8,000$ bits of data, for a percentage overhead of only $48/8048 \times 100\% = 0.6\%$.

6.2   TYPES OF ERRORS

In digital transmission systems, an error occurs when a bit is altered between transmission and reception; that is, a binary 1 is transmitted and a binary 0 is received, or a binary 0 is transmitted and a binary 1 is received. Two general types of errors can occur: single-bit errors and burst errors. A single-bit error is an isolated error condition that alters one bit but does not affect nearby bits. A burst error of length B is a contiguous sequence of B bits in which the first and last bits and any number of intermediate bits are received in error. More precisely, IEEE Std 100 defines an error burst as follows:

> **Error burst:** A group of bits in which two successive erroneous bits are always separated by less than a given number x of correct bits. The last erroneous bit in the burst and the first erroneous bit in the following burst are accordingly separated by x correct bits or more.

Thus, in an error burst, there is a cluster of bits in which a number of errors occur, although not necessarily all of the bits in the cluster suffer an error.

A single-bit error can occur in the presence of white noise, when a slight random deterioration of the signal-to-noise ratio is sufficient to confuse the receiver's decision of a single bit. Burst errors are more common and more difficult to deal with. Burst errors can be caused by impulse noise, which was described in Chapter 3. Another cause is fading in a mobile wireless environment; fading is described in Chapter 14.

Note that the effects of burst errors are greater at higher data rates.

> **Example 6.1**   An impulse noise event or a fading event of 1 μs occurs. At a data rate of 10 Mbps, there is a resulting error burst of 10 bits. At a data rate of 100 Mbps, there is an error burst of 100 bits.

6.3   ERROR DETECTION

Regardless of the design of the transmission system, there will be errors, resulting in the change of one or more bits in a transmitted frame. In what follows, we assume that data are transmitted as one or more contiguous sequences of bits, called frames. We define these probabilities with respect to errors in transmitted frames:

P_b: Probability that a bit is received in error; also known as the bit error rate (BER)

P_1: Probability that a frame arrives with no bit errors

P_2: Probability that, with an error-detection algorithm in use, a frame arrives with one or more undetected errors

P_3: Probability that, with an error-detection algorithm in use, a frame arrives with one or more detected bit errors but no undetected bit errors

First consider the case in which no means are taken to detect errors. Then the probability of detected errors (P_3) is zero. To express the remaining probabilities, assume the probability that any bit is in error (P_b) is constant and independent for each bit. Then we have

$$P_1 = (1 - P_b)^F$$
$$P_2 = 1 - P_1$$

where F is the number of bits per frame. In words, the probability that a frame arrives with no bit errors decreases when the probability of a single bit error increases, as you would expect. Also, the probability that a frame arrives with no bit errors decreases with increasing frame length; the longer the frame, the more bits it has and the higher the probability that one of these is in error.

178   CHAPTER 6 / DIGITAL DATA COMMUNICATION TECHNIQUES

Example 6.2   A defined objective for ISDN connections is that the BER on a 64-kbps channel should be less than 10^{-6} on at least 90% of observed 1-minute intervals. Suppose now that we have the rather modest user requirement that on average one frame with an undetected bit error should occur per day on a continuously used 64-kbps channel, and let us assume a frame length of 1000 bits. The number of frames that can be transmitted in a day comes out to 5.529×10^{6}, which yields a desired frame error rate of $P_2 = 1/(5.529 \times 10^{6}) = 0.18 \times 10^{-6}$. But if we assume a value of P_b of 10^{-6}, then $P_1 = (0.999999)^{1000} = 0.999$ and therefore $P_2 = 10^{-3}$, which is about three orders of magnitude too large to meet our requirement.

This is the kind of result that motivates the use of error detection techniques. All of these techniques operate on the following principle (Figure 6.3). For a given frame of bits, additional bits that constitute an error-detecting code are added by the transmitter. This code is calculated as a function of the other transmitted bits. Typically, for a data block of k bits, the error-detection algorithm yields an error detection code of $n - k$ bits, where $(n - k) < k$. The error-detection code, also referred to as the **check bits**, is appended to the data block to produce a frame of n bits, which is then transmitted. The receiver separates the incoming frame into the k bits of data and $(n - k)$ bits of the error-detection code. The receiver performs the same error-detection calculation on the data bits and compares this value with the value of the incoming error-detection code. A detected error occurs if and only if there is a mismatch. Thus P_3 is the probability that a frame contains errors and that the error-detection scheme will detect that fact. P_2 is known as the residual error rate and is the probability that an error will be undetected despite the use of an error-detection scheme.

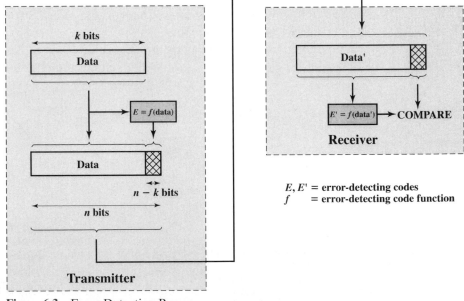

Figure 6.3   Error-Detection Process

Parity Check

The simplest error-detection scheme is to append a parity bit to the end of a block of data. A typical example is character transmission, in which a parity bit is attached to each 7-bit IRA character. The value of this bit is selected so that the character has an even number of 1s (even parity) or an odd number of 1s (odd parity).

> **Example 6.3** If the transmitter is transmitting an IRA G (1110001) and using odd parity, it will append a 1 and transmit 11110001.[2] The receiver examines the received character and, if the total number of 1s is odd, assumes that no error has occurred. If one bit (or any odd number of bits) is erroneously inverted during transmission (for example, 11100001), then the receiver will detect an error.

Note, however, that if two (or any even number) of bits are inverted due to error, an undetected error occurs. Typically, even parity is used for synchronous transmission and odd parity for asynchronous transmission.

The use of the parity bit is not foolproof, as noise impulses are often long enough to destroy more than one bit, particularly at high data rates.

Cyclic Redundancy Check (CRC)

One of the most common, and one of the most powerful, error-detecting codes is the cyclic redundancy check (CRC), which can be described as follows. Given a k-bit block of bits, or message, the transmitter generates an $(n - k)$-bit sequence, known as a frame check sequence (FCS), such that the resulting frame, consisting of n bits, is exactly divisible by some predetermined number. The receiver then divides the incoming frame by that number and, if there is no remainder, assumes there was no error.[3]

To clarify this, we present the procedure in three equivalent ways: modulo 2 arithmetic, polynomials, and digital logic.

Modulo 2 Arithmetic

Modulo 2 arithmetic uses binary addition with no carries, which is just the exclusive-OR (XOR) operation. Binary subtraction with no carries is also interpreted as the XOR operation: For example,

$$
\begin{array}{ccc}
\begin{array}{r} 1111 \\ +1010 \\ \hline 0101 \end{array} &
\begin{array}{r} 1111 \\ -0101 \\ \hline 1010 \end{array} &
\begin{array}{r} 11001 \\ \times\ 11 \\ \hline 11001 \\ 11001 \\ \hline 101011 \end{array}
\end{array}
$$

---

[2] Recall from our discussion in Section 5.1 that the least significant bit of a character is transmitted first and that the parity bit is the most significant bit.

[3] This procedure is slightly different from that of Figure 6.3. As shall be seen, the CRC process could be implemented as follows. The receiver could perform a division operation on the incoming k data bits and compare the result to the incoming $(n - k)$ check bits.

Now define

> $T = n$-bit frame to be transmitted
> $D = k$-bit block of data, or message, the first k bits of T
> $F = (n - k)$-bit FCS, the last $(n - k)$ bits of T
> $P = $ pattern of $n - k + 1$ bits; this is the predetermined divisor

We would like T/P to have no remainder. It should be clear that

$$T = 2^{n-k}D + F$$

That is, by multiplying D by 2^{n-k}, we have in effect shifted it to the left by $n - k$ bits and padded out the result with zeroes. Adding F yields the concatenation of D and F, which is T. We want T to be exactly divisible by P. Suppose that we divide $2^{n-k}D$ by P:

$$\frac{2^{n-k}D}{P} = Q + \frac{R}{P} \qquad (6.1)$$

There is a quotient and a remainder. Because division is modulo 2, the remainder is always at least one bit shorter than the divisor. We will use this remainder as our FCS. Then

$$T = 2^{n-k}D + R \qquad (6.2)$$

Does this R satisfy our condition that T/P have no remainder? To see that it does, consider

$$\frac{T}{P} = \frac{2^{n-k}D + R}{P} = \frac{2^{n-k}D}{P} + \frac{R}{P}$$

Substituting Equation (8.1), we have

$$\frac{T}{P} = Q + \frac{R}{P} + \frac{R}{P}$$

However, any binary number added to itself modulo 2 yields zero. Thus

$$\frac{T}{P} = Q + \frac{R + R}{P} = Q$$

There is no remainder, and therefore T is exactly divisible by P. Thus, the FCS is easily generated: Simply divide $2^{n-k}D$ by P and use the $(n - k)$-bit remainder as the FCS. On reception, the receiver will divide T by P and will get no remainder if there have been no errors.

Example 6.4

1. Given

$$\text{Message } D = 1010001101 \text{ (10 bits)}$$
$$\text{Pattern } P = 110101 \text{ (6 bits)}$$
$$\text{FCR } R = \text{to be calculated (5 bits)}$$

Thus, $n = 15$, $k = 10$, and $(n - k) = 5$.

2. The message is multiplied by 2^5, yielding 101000110100000.

3. This product is divided by P:

```
                                    1 1 0 1 0 1 0 1 1 0 ← Q
P → 1 1 0 1 0 1  / 1 0 1 0 0 0 1 1 0 1 0 0 0 0 0 ← 2ⁿ⁻ᵏD
                  1 1 0 1 0 1
                  1 1 1 0 1 1
                  1 1 0 1 0 1
                    1 1 1 0 1 0
                    1 1 0 1 0 1
                      1 1 1 1 1 0
                      1 1 0 1 0 1
                        1 0 1 1 0 0
                        1 1 0 1 0 1
                          1 1 0 0 1 0
                          1 1 0 1 0 1
                            0 1 1 1 0 ← R
```

4. The remainder is added to $2^5 D$ to give $T = 101000110101110$, which is transmitted.

5. If there are no errors, the receiver receives T intact. The received frame is divided by P:

```
                                    1 1 0 1 0 1 0 1 1 0 ← Q
P → 1 1 0 1 0 1  / 1 0 1 0 0 0 1 1 0 1 0 1 1 1 0 ← T
                  1 1 0 1 0 1
                  1 1 1 0 1 1
                  1 1 0 1 0 1
                    1 1 1 0 1 0
                    1 1 0 1 0 1
                      1 1 1 1 1 0
                      1 1 0 1 0 1
                        1 0 1 1 1 1
                        1 1 0 1 0 1
                          1 1 0 1 0 1
                          1 1 0 1 0 1
                            0 ← R
```

Because there is no remainder, it is assumed that there have been no errors.

The pattern P is chosen to be one bit longer than the desired FCS, and the exact bit pattern chosen depends on the type of errors expected. At minimum, both the high- and low-order bits of P must be 1.

There is a concise method for specifying the occurrence of one or more errors. An error results in the reversal of a bit. This is equivalent to taking the XOR of the bit and 1 (modulo 2 addition of 1 to the bit): $0 + 1 = 1; 1 + 1 = 0$. Thus, the errors in an n-bit frame can be represented by an n-bit field with 1s in each error position. The resulting frame T_r can be expressed as

$$T_r = T \oplus E$$

where

T = transmitted frame

E = error pattern with 1s in positions where errors occur

T_r = received frame

If there is an error ($E \neq 0$), the receiver will fail to detect the error if and only if T_r is divisible by P, which is equivalent to E divisible by P. Intuitively, this seems an unlikely occurrence.

Polynomials

A second way of viewing the CRC process is to express all values as polynomials in a dummy variable X, with binary coefficients. The coefficients correspond to the bits in the binary number. Thus, for $D = 110011$, we have $D(X) = X^5 + X^4 + X + 1$, and for $P = 11001$, we have $P(X) = X^4 + X^3 + 1$. Arithmetic operations are again modulo 2. The CRC process can now be described as:

$$\frac{X^{n-k}D(X)}{P(X)} = Q(X) + \frac{R(X)}{P(X)}$$
$$T(X) = X^{n-k}D(X) + R(X)$$

Compare these equations with Equations (6.1) and (6.2).

Example 6.5   Using the preceding example, for $D = 1010001101$, we have $D(X) = X^9 + X^7 + X^3 + X^2 + 1$, and for $P = 110101$, we have $P(X) = X^5 + X^4 + X^2 + 1$. We should end up with $R = 01110$, which corresponds to $R(X) = X^3 + X^2 + X$. Figure 6.4 shows the polynomial division that corresponds to the binary division in the preceding example.

An error $E(X)$ will only be undetectable if it is divisible by $P(X)$. It can be shown [PETE 61, RAMA88] that all of the following errors are not divisible by a suitably chosen $P(X)$ and hence are detectable:

- All single-bit errors, if $P(X)$ has more than one nonzero term
- All double-bit errors, as long as $P(X)$ has a factor with three terms

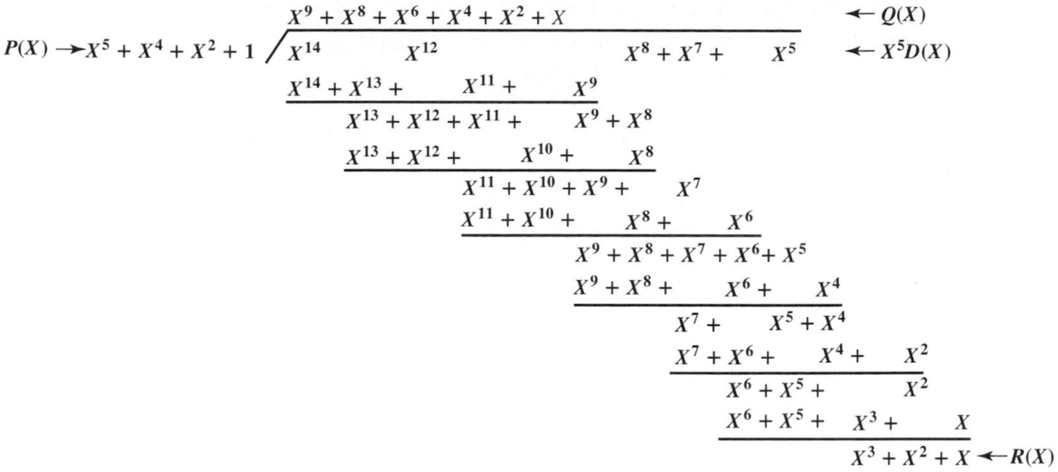

$$P(X) \to X^5 + X^4 + X^2 + 1 \overline{\smash{\big)}\, \begin{array}{l} X^9 + X^8 + X^6 + X^4 + X^2 + X \quad \leftarrow Q(X) \\ \hline X^{14} \qquad X^{12} \qquad\qquad X^8 + X^7 + \quad X^5 \quad \leftarrow X^5 D(X) \end{array}}$$

$$
\begin{array}{l}
\underline{X^{14} + X^{13} + \quad X^{11} + \quad X^9} \\
\quad X^{13} + X^{12} + X^{11} + \quad X^9 + X^8 \\
\quad \underline{X^{13} + X^{12} + \quad X^{10} + \quad X^8} \\
\qquad\qquad X^{11} + X^{10} + X^9 + \quad X^7 \\
\qquad\qquad \underline{X^{11} + X^{10} + \quad X^8 + \quad X^6} \\
\qquad\qquad\qquad X^9 + X^8 + X^7 + X^6 + X^5 \\
\qquad\qquad\qquad \underline{X^9 + X^8 + \quad X^6 + \quad X^4} \\
\qquad\qquad\qquad\qquad X^7 + \quad X^5 + X^4 \\
\qquad\qquad\qquad\qquad \underline{X^7 + X^6 + \quad X^4 + \quad X^2} \\
\qquad\qquad\qquad\qquad\quad X^6 + X^5 + \quad X^2 \\
\qquad\qquad\qquad\qquad\quad \underline{X^6 + X^5 + \quad X^3 + \quad X} \\
\qquad\qquad\qquad\qquad\qquad X^3 + X^2 + X \leftarrow R(X)
\end{array}
$$

Figure 6.4 Example of Polynomial Division

- Any odd number of errors, as long as $P(X)$ contains a factor $(X + 1)$
- Any burst error for which the length of the burst is less than or equal to $n - k$; that is, less than or equal to the length of the FCS
- A fraction of error bursts of length $n - k + 1$; the fraction equals to $1 - 2^{-(n-k-1)}$
- A fraction of error bursts of length greater than $n - k + 1$; the fraction equals to $1 - 2^{-(n-k)}$

In addition, it can be shown that if all error patterns are considered equally likely, then for a burst error of length $r + 1$, the probability of an undetected error ($E(X)$ is divisible by $P(X)$) is $1/2^{r-1}$, and for a longer burst, the probability is $1/2^r$, where r is the length of the FCS.

Four versions of $P(X)$ are widely used:

CRC-12 $= X^{12} + X^{11} + X^3 + X^2 + X + 1$

CRC-16 $= X^{16} + X^{15} + X^2 + 1$

CRC-CCITT $= X^{16} + X^{12} + X^5 + 1$

CRC-32 $= X^{32} + X^{26} + X^{23} + X^{22} + X^{16} + X^{12} + X^{11} + X^{10} + X^8 + X^7 + X^5 + X^4 + X^2 + X + 1$

The CRC-12 system is used for transmission of streams of 6-bit characters and generates a 12-bit FCS. Both CRC-16 and CRC-CCITT are popular for 8-bit characters, in the United States and Europe, respectively, and both result in a 16-bit FCS. This would seem adequate for most applications, although CRC-32 is specified as an option in some point-to-point synchronous transmission standards and is used in IEEE 802 LAN standards.

Digital Logic

The CRC process can be represented by, and indeed implemented as, a dividing circuit consisting of XOR gates and a shift register. The shift register is a string of 1-bit storage devices. Each device has an output line, which indicates the value currently stored, and an input line. At discrete time instants, known as clock times, the value in the storage device is replaced by the value indicated by its input line. The entire register is clocked simultaneously, causing a 1-bit shift along the entire register.

The circuit is implemented as follows:

1. The register contains $n - k$ bits, equal to the length of the FCS.
2. There are up to $n - k$ XOR gates.
3. The presence or absence of a gate corresponds to the presence or absence of a term in the divisor polynomial, $P(X)$, excluding the terms 1 and X^{n-k}.

Example 6.6 The architecture of a CRC circuit is best explained by first considering an example, which is illustrated in Figure 6.5. In this example, we use

$$\text{Data } D = 1010001101; \qquad D(X) = X^9 + X^7 + X^3 + X^2 + 1$$
$$\text{Divisor } P = 110101; \qquad P(X) = X^5 + X^4 + X^2 + 1$$

which were used earlier in the discussion.

Figure 6.5a shows the shift register implementation. The process begins with the shift register cleared (all zeros). The message, or dividend, is then entered, one bit at a time, starting with the most significant bit. Figure 6.5b is a table that shows the step-by-step operation as the input is applied one bit at a time. Each row of the table shows the values currently stored in the five shift-register elements. In addition, the row shows the values that appear at the outputs of the three XOR circuits. Finally, the row shows the value of the next input bit, which is available for the operation of the next step.

Note that the XOR operation affects C_4, C_2, and C_0 on the next shift. This is identical to the binary long division process illustrated earlier. The process continues through all the bits of the message. To produce the proper output, two switches are used. The input data bits are fed in with both switches in the A position. As a result, for the first 10 steps, the input bits are fed into the shift register and also used as output bits. After the last data bit is processed, the shift register contains the remainder (FCS) (shown shaded). As soon as the last data bit is provided to the shift register, both switches are set to the B position. This has two effects: (1) all of the XOR gates become simple pass-throughs; no bits are changed, and (2) as the shifting process continues, the 5 CRC bits are output.

At the receiver, the same logic is used. As each bit of M arrives, it is inserted into the shift register. If there have been no errors, the shift register should contain the bit pattern for R at the conclusion of M. The transmitted bits of R now begin to arrive, and the effect is to zero out the register so that, at the conclusion of reception, the register contains all 0s.

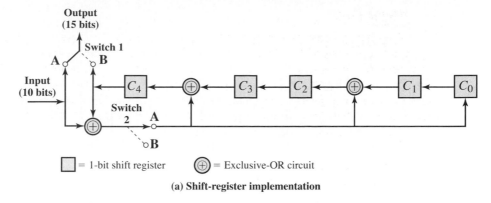

(a) Shift-register implementation

	C_4	C_3	C_2	C_1	C_0	$C_4 \oplus C_3 \oplus I$	$C_4 \oplus C_1 \oplus I$	$C_4 \oplus I$	I = input	
Initial	0	0	0	0	0	1	1	1	1	
Step 1	1	0	1	0	1	1	1	1	0	
Step 2	1	1	1	1	1	1	1	0	1	
Step 3	1	1	1	1	0	0	0	1	0	
Step 4	0	1	0	0	1	1	0	0	0	Message to
Step 5	1	0	0	1	0	1	0	1	0	be sent
Step 6	1	0	0	0	1	0	0	0	1	
Step 7	0	0	0	1	0	1	0	1	1	
Step 8	1	0	0	0	1	1	1	1	0	
Step 9	1	0	1	1	1	0	1	0	1	
Step 10	0	1	1	1	0					

(b) Example with input of 1010001101

Figure 6.5 Circuit with Shift Registers for Dividing by the Polynomial $X^5 + X^4 + X^2 + 1$

Figure 6.6 indicates the general architecture of the shift register implementation of a CRC for the polynomial $P(X) = \sum_{i=0}^{n-k} A_i X^i$, where $A_0 = A_{n-k} = 1$ and all other A_i equal either 0 or 1.[4]

6.4 ERROR CORRECTION

Error detection is a useful technique, found in data link control protocols, such as HDLC, and in transport protocols, such as TCP. However, correction of errors using an error-detection code, requires that block of data be retransmitted, as explained in Chapter 7. For wireless applications this approach is inadequate for two reasons:

1. The bit error rate on a wireless link can be quite high, which would result in a large number of retransmissions.

---

[4] It is common for the CRC register to be shown shifting to the right, which is the reverse of the analogy to binary division. Because binary numbers are usually shown with the most significant bit on the left, a left-shifting register, as is used here, is more appropriate.

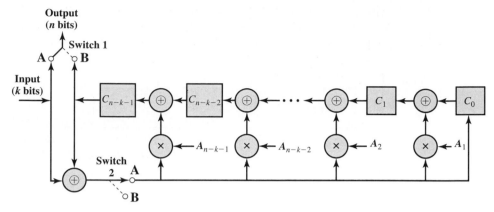

Figure 6.6 General CRC Architecture to Implement Divisor
$(1 + A_1X + A_2X^2 + \ldots + A_{n-1}X^{n-k-1} + X^{n-k})$

2. In some cases, especially satellite links, the propagation delay is very long compared to the transmission time of a single frame. The result is a very inefficient system. As is discussed in Chapter 7, the common approach to retransmission is to retransmit the frame in error plus all subsequent frames. With a long data link, an error in a single frame necessitates retransmitting many frames.

Instead, it would be desirable to enable the receiver to correct errors in an incoming transmission on the basis of the bits in that transmission. Figure 6.7 shows in general how this is done. On the transmission end, each *k*-bit block of data is mapped into an *n*-bit block $(n > k)$ called a **codeword**, using an FEC (forward error correction)

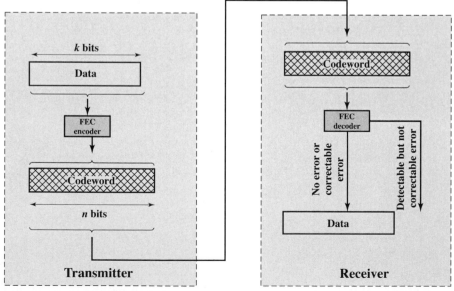

Figure 6.7 Error-Correction Process

encoder. The codeword is then transmitted. During transmission, the signal is subject to impairments, which may produce bit errors in the signal. At the receiver, the incoming signal is demodulated to produce a bit string that is similar to the original codeword but may contain errors. This block is passed through an FEC decoder, with one of four possible outcomes:

1. If there are no bit errors, the input to the FEC decoder is identical to the original codeword, and the decoder produces the original data block as output.
2. For certain error patterns, it is possible for the decoder to detect and correct those errors. Thus, even though the incoming data block differs from the transmitted codeword, the FEC decoder is able to map this block into the original data block.
3. For certain error patterns, the decoder can detect but not correct the errors. In this case, the decoder simply reports an uncorrectable error.
4. For certain, typically rare, error patterns, the decoder does not detect that any errors have occurred and maps the incoming n-bit data block into a k-bit block that differs from the original k-bit block.

How is it possible for the decoder to correct bit errors? In essence, error correction works by adding redundancy to the transmitted message. The redundancy makes it possible for the receiver to deduce what the original message was, even in the face of a certain level of error rate. In this section we look at a widely used form of error-correction code known as a block error-correction code. Our discussion only deals with basic principles; a discussion of specific error-correction codes is beyond our scope.

Before proceeding, we note that in many cases, the error-correction code follows the same general layout as shown for error-detection codes in Figure 6.3. That is, the FEC algorithm takes as input a k-bit block and adds $(n - k)$ check bits to that block to produce an n-bit block; all of the bits in the original k-bit block show up in the n-bit block. For some FEC algorithms, the FEC algorithm maps the k-bit input into an n-bit codeword in such a way that the original k bits do not appear in the codeword.

Block Code Principles

To begin, we define a term that shall be of use to us. The **Hamming distance** $d(\mathbf{v}_1, \mathbf{v}_2)$ between two n-bit binary sequences $\mathbf{v}_1$ and $\mathbf{v}_2$ is the number of bits in which $\mathbf{v}_1$ and $\mathbf{v}_2$ disagree. For example, if

$$\mathbf{v}_1 = 011011, \qquad \mathbf{v}_2 = 110001$$

then

$$d(\mathbf{v}_1, \mathbf{v}_2) = 3$$

Now let us consider the block code technique for error correction. Suppose we wish to transmit blocks of data of length k bits. Instead of transmitting each block as k bits, we map each k-bit sequence into a unique n-bit codeword.

Example 6.7   For $k = 2$ and $n = 5$, we can make the following assignment:

Data block	Codeword
00	00000
01	00111
10	11001
11	11110

Now, suppose that a codeword block is received with the bit pattern 00100. This is not a valid codeword, and so the receiver has detected an error. Can the error be corrected? We cannot be sure which data block was sent because 1, 2, 3, 4, or even all 5 of the bits that were transmitted may have been corrupted by noise. However, notice that it would require only a single bit change to transform the valid codeword 00000 into 00100. It would take two bit changes to transform 00111 to 00100, three bit changes to transform 11110 to 00100, and it would take four bit changes to transform 11001 into 00100. Thus, we can deduce that the most likely codeword that was sent was 00000 and that therefore the desired data block is 00. This is error correction. In terms of Hamming distances, we have

$$d(00000, 00100) = 1; \quad d(00111, 00100) = 2;$$
$$d(11001, 00100) = 4; \quad d(11110, 00100) = 3$$

So the rule we would like to impose is that if an invalid codeword is received, then the valid codeword that is closest to it (minimum distance) is selected. This will only work if there is a unique valid codeword at a minimum distance from each invalid codeword.

For our example, it is not true that for every invalid codeword there is one and only one valid codeword at a minimum distance. There are $2^5 = 32$ possible codewords of which 4 are valid, leaving 28 invalid codewords. For the invalid codewords, we have the following:

Invalid codeword	Minimum distance	Valid codeword	Invalid codeword	Minimum distance	Valid codeword
00001	1	00000	10000	1	00000
00010	1	00000	10001	1	11001
00011	1	00111	10010	2	00000 or 11110
00100	1	00000	10011	2	00111 or 11001
00101	1	00111	10100	2	00000 or 11110
00110	1	00111	10101	2	00111 or 11001
01000	1	00000	10110	1	11110
01001	1	11001	10111	1	00111
01010	2	00000 or 11110	11000	1	11001
01011	2	00111 or 11001	11010	1	11110
01100	2	00000 or 11110	11011	1	11001
01101	2	00111 or 11001	11100	1	11110
01110	1	11110	11101	1	11001
01111	1	00111	11111	1	11110

There are eight cases in which an invalid codeword is at a distance 2 from two different valid codewords. Thus, if one such invalid codeword is received, an error in 2 bits could have caused it and the receiver has no way to choose between the two alternatives. An error is detected but cannot be corrected. However, in every case in which a single bit error occurs, the resulting codeword is of distance 1 from only one valid codeword and the decision can be made. This code is therefore capable of correcting all single-bit errors but cannot correct double bit errors. Another way to see this is to look at the pairwise distances between valid codewords:

$$d(00000, 00111) = 3; \quad d(00000, 11001) = 3; \quad d(00000, 11110) = 4;$$
$$d(00111, 11001) = 4; \quad d(00111, 11110) = 3; \quad d(11001, 11110) = 3;$$

The minimum distance between valid codewords is 3. Therefore, a single bit error will result in an invalid codeword that is a distance 1 from the original valid codeword but a distance at least 2 from all other valid codewords. As a result, the code can always correct a single-bit error. Note that the code also will always detect a double-bit error.

The preceding examples illustrates the essential properties of a block error-correcting code. An (n, k) block code encodes k data bits into n-bit codewords. Typically, each valid codeword reproduces the original k data bits and adds to them $(n - k)$ check bits to form the n-bit codeword. Thus the design of a block code is equivalent to the design of a function of the form $\mathbf{v_c} = f(\mathbf{v_d})$, where $\mathbf{v_d}$ is a vector of k data bits and $\mathbf{v_c}$ is a vector of n codeword bits.

With an (n, k) block code, there are 2^k valid codewords out of a total of 2^n possible codewords. The ratio of redundant bits to data bits, $(n - k)/k$, is called the **redundancy** of the code, and the ratio of data bits to total bits, k/n, is called the **code rate**. The code rate is a measure of how much additional bandwidth is required to carry data at the same data rate as without the code. For example, a code rate of $1/2$ requires double the transmission capacity of an uncoded system to maintain the same data rate. Our example has a code rate of $2/5$ and so requires 2.5 times the capacity of an uncoded system. For example, if the data rate input to the encoder is 1 Mbps, then the output from the encoder must be at a rate of 2.5 Mbps to keep up.

For a code consisting of the codewords $\mathbf{w}_1, \mathbf{w}_2, \dots, \mathbf{w}_s$, where $s = 2^k$, the minimum distance $d_{\min}$ of the code is defined as

$$d_{\min} = \min_{i \neq j} [(\mathbf{w}_i, \mathbf{w}_j)]$$

It can be shown that the following conditions hold. For a given positive integer t, if a code satisfies $d_{\min} \geq 2t + 1$, then the code can correct all bit errors up to and including errors of t bits. If $d_{\min} \geq 2t$, then all errors $\leq t - 1$ bits can be corrected and errors of t bits can be detected but not, in general, corrected. Conversely, any code for which all errors of magnitude $\leq t$ are corrected must satisfy $d_{\min} \geq 2t + 1$, and any code for which all errors of magnitude magnitude $\leq t - 1$ are corrected and all errors of magnitude t are detected must satisfy $d_{\min} \geq 2t$.

Another way of putting the relationship between d_{min} and t is to say that the maximum number of guaranteed correctable errors per codeword satisfies

$$t = \left\lfloor \frac{d_{min} - 1}{2} \right\rfloor$$

where $\lfloor x \rfloor$ means the largest integer not to exceed x (e.g., $\lfloor 6.3 \rfloor = 6$). Furthermore, if we are concerned only with error detection and not error correction, then the number of errors, t, that can be detected satisfies

$$t = d_{min} - 1$$

To see this, consider that if d_{min} errors occur, this could change one valid codeword into another. Any number of errors less than d_{min} can not result in another valid codeword.

The design of a block code involves a number of considerations:

1. For given values of n and k, we would like the largest possible value of d_{min}.
2. The code should be relatively easy to encode and decode, requiring minimal memory and processing time.
3. We would like the number of extra bits, $(n - k)$, to be small, to reduce bandwidth.
4. We would like the number of extra bits, $(n - k)$, to be large, to reduce error rate.

Clearly, the last two objectives are in conflict, and tradeoffs must be made.

It is instructive to examine Figure 6.8, based on one in [LEBO98]. The literature on error-correcting codes frequently includes graphs of this sort to demonstrate

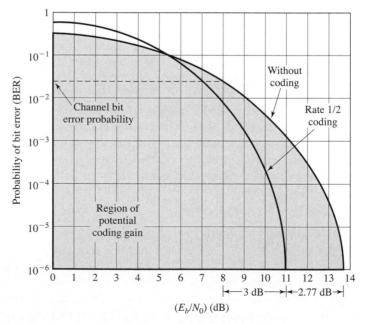

Figure 6.8   How Coding Improves System Performance

the effectiveness of various encoding schemes. Recall from Chapter 5 that coding can be used to reduce the required E_b/N_0 value to achieve a given bit error rate.[5] The coding discussed in Chapter 5 has to do with the definition of signal elements to represent bits. The coding discussed in this chapter also has an effect on E_b/N_0. In Figure 6.8, the curve on the right is for an uncoded modulation system; the shaded region represents the area in which improvement can be achieved. In this region, a smaller BER (bit error rate) is achieved for a given E_b/N_0, and conversely, for a given BER, a smaller E_b/N_0 is required. The other curve is a typical result of a code rate of one-half (equal number of data and check bits). Note that at an error rate of 10^{-5}, the use of coding allows a reduction in E_b/N_0 of 2.77 dB. This reduction is referred to as the **coding gain**, which is defined as the reduction, in decibels, in the required E_b/N_0 to achieve a specified BER of an error-correcting coded system compared to an uncoded system using the same modulation.

It is important to realize that the BER for the second rate 1/2 curve refers to the rate of uncorrected errors and that the E_b value refers to the energy per data bit. Because the rate is 1/2, there are two bits on the channel for each data bit, and the energy per coded bit is half that of the energy per data bit, or a reduction of 3 dB. If we look at the energy per coded bit for this system, then we see that the channel bit error rate is about 2.4×10^{-2}, or 0.024.

Finally, note that below a certain threshold of E_b/N_0, the coding scheme actually degrades performance. In our example of Figure 6.8, the threshold occurs at about 5.4 dB. Below the threshold, the extra check bits add overhead to the system that reduces the energy per data bit causing increased errors. Above the threshold, the error-correcting power of the code more than compensates for the reduced E_b, resulting in a coding gain.

6.5 LINE CONFIGURATIONS

Two characteristics that distinguish various data link configurations are topology and whether the link is half duplex or full duplex.

Topology

The topology of a data link refers to the physical arrangement of stations on a transmission medium. If there are only two stations (e.g., a terminal and a computer or two computers), the link is point to point. If there are more than two stations, then it is a multipoint topology. Traditionally, a multipoint link has been used in the case of a computer (primary station) and a set of terminals (secondary stations). In today's environments, the multipoint topology is found in local area networks.

Traditional multipoint topologies are made possible when the terminals are only transmitting a fraction of the time. Figure 6.9 illustrates the advantages of the multipoint configuration. If each terminal has a point-to-point link to its computer,

---

[5] E_b/N_0 is the ratio of signal energy per bit to noise power density per Hertz; it is defined and discussed in Chapter 3.

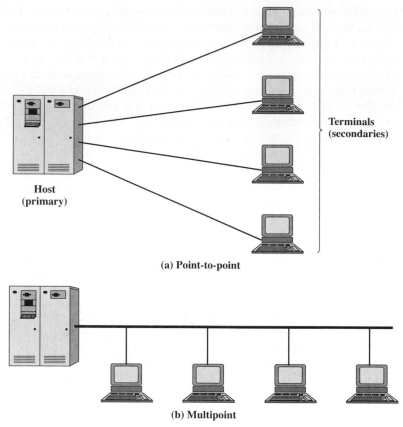

Figure 6.9 Traditional Computer/Terminal Configurations

then the computer must have one I/O port for each terminal. Also there is a separate transmission line from the computer to each terminal. In a multipoint configuration, the computer needs only a single I/O port and a single transmission line, which saves costs.

Full Duplex and Half Duplex

Data exchanges over a transmission line can be classified as full duplex or half duplex. With **half-duplex transmission**, only one of two stations on a point-to-point link may transmit at a time. This mode is also referred to as *two-way alternate*, suggestive of the fact that two stations must alternate in transmitting. This can be compared to a one-lane, two-way bridge. This form of transmission is often used for terminal-to-computer interaction. While a user is entering and transmitting data, the computer is prevented from sending data to the terminal, which would appear on the terminal screen and cause confusion.

For **full-duplex transmission**, two stations can simultaneously send and receive data from each other. Thus, this mode is known as *two-way simultaneous* and may be compared to a two-lane, two-way bridge. For computer-to-computer data exchange, this form of transmission is more efficient than half-duplex transmission.

With digital signaling, which requires guided transmission, full-duplex operation usually requires two separate transmission paths (e.g., two twisted pairs), while half duplex requires only one. For analog signaling, it depends on frequency: If a station transmits and receives on the same frequency, it must operate in half-duplex mode for wireless transmission, although it may operate in full-duplex mode for guided transmission using two separate transmission lines. If a station transmits on one frequency and receives on another, it may operate in full-duplex mode for wireless transmission and in full-duplex mode with a single line for guided transmission.

It is possible to transmit digital signals simultaneously in both directions on a single transmission line using a technique called echo cancellation. This is a signal processing technique whose explanation is beyond the scope of this book.

6.6 INTERFACING

Most digital data processing devices have limited data transmission capability. Typically, they generate a simple digital signal, such as NRZ-L, and the distance across which they can transmit data is limited. Consequently, it is rare for such a device (terminal, computer) to attach directly to a transmission or networking facility. The more common situation is depicted in Figure 6.10. The devices we are discussing, which include terminals and computers, are generically referred to as **data terminal equipment (DTE)**. A DTE makes use of the transmission system through the mediation of **data circuit-terminating equipment (DCE)**. An example of the latter is a modem.

On one side, the DCE is responsible for transmitting and receiving bits, one at a time, over a transmission medium or network. On the other side, the DCE must interact with the DTE. In general, this requires both data and control information to be exchanged. This is done over a set of wires referred to as **interchange circuits**. For this scheme to work, a high degree of cooperation is required. The two DCEs that exchange signals over the transmission line or network must understand each other. That is, the receiver of each must use the same encoding scheme (e.g., Manchester,

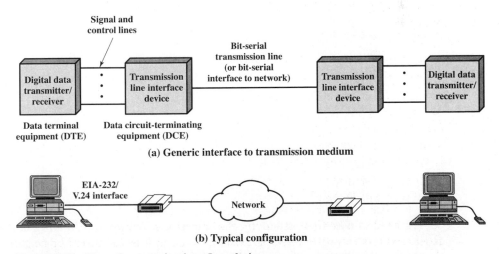

(a) Generic interface to transmission medium

(b) Typical configuration

Figure 6.10 Data Communications Interfacing

PSK) and data rate as the transmitter of the other. In addition, each DTE-DCE pair must be designed to interact cooperatively. To ease the burden on data processing equipment manufacturers and users, standards have been developed that specify the exact nature of the interface between the DTE and the DCE. Such an interface has four important characteristics:

- Mechanical
- Electrical
- Functional
- Procedural

The *mechanical characteristics* pertain to the actual physical connection of the DTE to the DCE. Typically, the signal and control interchange circuits are bundled into a cable with a terminator connector, male or female, at each end. The DTE and DCE must present connectors of opposite genders at one end of the cable, effecting the physical connection. This is analogous to the situation for residential electrical power. Power is provided via a socket or wall outlet, and the device to be attached must have the appropriate male connector (two-pronged, two-pronged polarized, or three-pronged) to match the socket.

The *electrical characteristics* have to do with the voltage levels and timing of voltage changes. Both DTE and DCE must use the same code (e.g., NRZ-L), must use the same voltage levels to mean the same things, and must use the same duration of signal elements. These characteristics determine the data rates and distances that can be achieved.

Functional characteristics specify the functions that are performed by assigning meanings to each of the interchange circuits. Functions can be classified into the broad categories of data, control, timing, and electrical ground.

Procedural characteristics specify the sequence of events for transmitting data, based on the functional characteristics of the interface. The examples that follow should clarify this point.

A variety of standards for interfacing exists. This section presents two of the most important: V.24/EIA-232-F and the ISDN Physical Interface.

V.24/EIA-232-F

One of the most widely used interfaces is specified in the ITU-T standard, V.24. In fact, this standard specifies only the functional and procedural aspects of the interface; V.24 references other standards for the electrical and mechanical aspects. In the United States, there is a corresponding specification, virtually identical, that covers all four aspects: EIA-232-F. The correspondence is as follows:

- Mechanical: ISO 2110
- Electrical: V.28
- Functional: V.24
- Procedural V.24

EIA-232 was first issued by the Electronic Industries Alliance in 1962, as RS-232. It is currently in its sixth revision, EIA-232-F, issued in 1997. The current V.24 and V.28 specifications were issued in 1996 and 1993, respectively. This interface is used to connect DTE devices to voice-grade modems for use on public analog telecommunications systems. It is also widely used for many other interconnection applications.

Mechanical Specification

The mechanical specification for EIA-232-F is illustrated in Figure 6.11. It calls for a 25-pin connector, defined in ISO 2110, with a specific arrangement of leads. This connector is the terminating plug or socket on a cable running from a DTE (e.g., terminal) or DCE (e.g., modem). Though a 25-wire cable could be used to connect the DTE to the DCE, many applications require far fewer wires.

Electrical Specification

The electrical specification defines the signaling between DTE and DCE. Digital signaling is used on all interchange circuits. Depending on the function of the interchange circuit, the electrical values are interpreted either as binary data or as control signals. The convention specifies that, with respect to a common ground, a voltage more negative than -3 volts is interpreted as binary 1 and a voltage more positive than $+3$ volts is interpreted as binary 0. This is the NRZ-L code illustrated in Figure 5.2. The interface is rated at a signal rate of <20 kbps and a distance of <15 meters. Greater distances and data rates are possible with good design, but it is prudent to assume that these limits apply in practice as well as in theory.

The same voltage levels apply to control signals: a voltage more negative than -3 volts is interpreted as an OFF condition and a voltage more positive than $+3$ volts is interpreted as an ON condition.

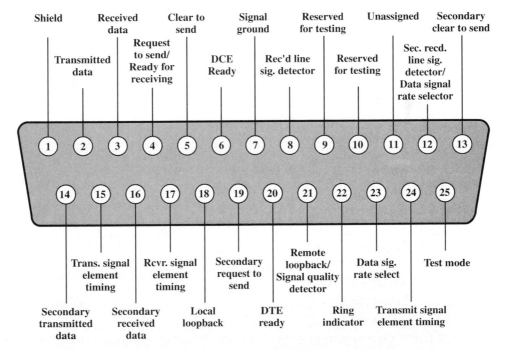

Figure 6.11 Pin Assignments for V.24/EIA-232 (DTE Connector Face)

Functional Specification

Table 6.1 summarizes the functional specification of the interchange circuits, and Figure 6.11 illustrates the placement of these circuits on the connector. The circuits can be grouped into the categories of data, control, timing, and ground. There is one data circuit in each direction, so full-duplex operation is possible. In addition,

Table 6.1 V.24/EIA-232-F Interchange Circuits

V.24	EIA-232	Name	Direction to:	Function
DATA SIGNALS				
103	BA	Transmitted data	DCE	Transmitted by DTE
104	BB	Received data	DTE	Received by DTE
118	SBA	Secondary transmitted data	DCE	Transmitted by DTE
119	SBB	Secondary received data	DTE	Received by DTE
CONTROL SIGNALS				
105	CA	Request to send	DCE	DTE wishes to transmit
106	CB	Clear to send	DTE	DCE is ready to receive; response to Request to send
107	CC	DCE ready	DTE	DCE is ready to operate
108.2	CD	DTE ready	DCE	DTE is ready to operate
125	CE	Ring indicator	DTE	DCE is receiving a ringing signal on the channel line
109	CF	Received line signal detector	DTE	DCE is receiving a signal within appropriate limits on the channel line
110	CG	Signal quality detector	DTE	Indicates whether there is a high probability of error in the data received
111	CH	Data signal rate selector	DCE	Selects one of two data rates
112	CI	Data signal rate selector	DTE	Selects one of two data rates
133	CJ	Ready for receiving	DCE	On/off flow control
120	SCA	Secondary request to send	DCE	DTE wishes to transmit on reverse channel
121	SCB	Secondary clear to send	DTE	DCE is ready to receive on reverse channel
122	SCF	Secondary received line signal detector	DTE	Same as 109, for reverse channel
140	RL	Remote loopback	DCE	Instructs remote DCE to loop back signals
141	LL	Local loopback	DCE	Instructs DCE to loop back signals
142	TM	Test mode	DTE	Local DCE is in a test condition
TIMING SIGNALS				
113	DA	Transmitter signal element timing	DCE	Clocking signal; transitions to ON and OFF occur at center of each signal element
114	DB	Transmitter signal element timing	DTE	Clocking signal; both 113 and 114 relate to signals on circuit 103
115	DD	Receiver signal element timing	DTE	Clocking signal for circuit 104
GROUND				
102	AB	Signal ground/common return		Common ground reference for all circuits

there are two secondary data circuits that are useful when the device operates in a half-duplex fashion. In the case of half-duplex operation, data exchange between two DTEs (via their DCEs and the intervening communications link) is only conducted in one direction at a time. However, there may be a need to send a halt or flow control message to a transmitting device. To accommodate this, the communication link is equipped with a reverse channel, usually at a much lower data rate than the primary channel. At the DTE-DCE interface the reverse channel is carried on a separate pair of data circuits.

There are 16 control circuits. The first 10 of these listed in Table 6.1 relate to the transmission of data over the primary channel. For asynchronous transmission, six of these circuits are used (105, 106, 107, 108.2, 125, 109). The use of these circuits is explained in the subsection on procedural specifications. In addition to these six circuits, three other control circuits are used in synchronous transmission. The Signal Quality Detector circuit is turned ON by the DCE to indicate that the quality of the incoming signal over the telephone line has deteriorated beyond some defined threshold. Most high-speed modems support more than one transmission rate so that they can fall back to a lower speed if the telephone line becomes noisy. The Data Signal Rate Selector circuits are used to change speeds; either the DTE or DCE may initiate the change. Circuit 133 enables a receiver to turn the flow of data on circuit 104 on and off. The next three control circuits (120, 121, 122) are used to control the use of the secondary channel, which may be used as a reverse channel or for some other auxiliary purpose.

The last group of control signals relates to loopback testing. These circuits allow the DTE to cause the DCE to perform a loopback test. These circuits are only valid if the modem or other DCE supports loopback control; this is now a common modem feature. In the local loopback function, the transmitter output of the modem is connected to the receiver input, disconnecting the modem from the transmission line. A stream of data generated by the user device is sent to the modem and looped back to the user device. For remote loopback, the local modem is connected to the transmission facility in the usual fashion, and the receiver output of the remote modem is connected to the modem's transmitter input. During either form of test, the DCE turns ON the Test Mode circuit. Table 6.2 show the settings for all of the circuits related to loopback testing, and Figure 6.12 illustrates the use.

Loopback control is a useful fault isolation tool. For example, suppose that a user at a personal computer is communicating with a server by means of a modem

Table 6.2 Loopback Circuit Settings for V.24/EIA-232

| Local Loopback | | Remote Loopback | | |
Circuit	Condition	Circuit	Local Interface	Remote Interface
DCE Ready	ON	DCE Ready	ON	OFF
Local Loopback	ON	Local Loopback	OFF	OFF
Remote Loopback	OFF	Remote Loopback	ON	OFF
Test Mode	ON	Test Mode	ON	ON

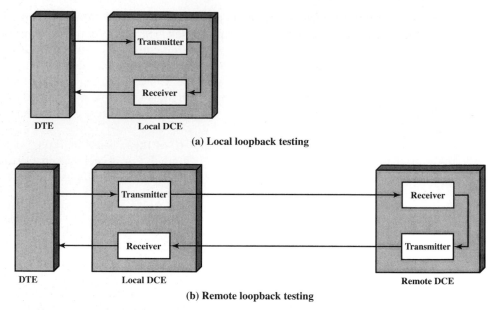

Figure 6.12   Local and Remote Loopback

connection and communication suddenly ceases. The problem could be with the local modem, the communications facility, the remote modem, or the remote server. A network manager can use loopback tests to isolate the fault. Local loopback checks the functioning of the local interface and the local DCE. Remote loopback tests the operation of the transmission channel and the remote DCE.

The timing signals provide clock pulses for synchronous transmission. When the DCE is sending synchronous data over the Received Data circuit (104), it also sends 1-0 and 0-1 transitions on Receiver Element Signal Timing (115), with transitions timed to the middle of each Received Data signal element. When the DTE is sending synchronous data, either the DTE or DCE can provide timing pulses, depending on the circumstances.

Finally, the signal ground/common return (102) serves as the return circuit for all data leads. Hence, transmission is unbalanced, with only one active wire. Balanced and unbalanced transmission are discussed in the section on the ISDN interface.

Procedural Specification

The procedural specification defines the sequence in which the various circuits are used for a particular application. We give a few examples.

The first example is a very common one for connecting two devices over a short distance within a building. It is known as an asynchronous private line modem, or a limited distance modem. As the name suggests, the limited distance modem accepts digital signals from a DTE, such as a terminal or computer, converts these to analog signals, and then transmits these over a short length of medium, such as twisted pair. On the other end of the line is another limited distance modem, which accepts the incoming analog signals, converts them to digital, and passes them on to another terminal or computer. Of course, the exchange of data is two way. For this simple application, only the following interchange circuits are actually required:

- Signal Ground (102)
- Transmitted Data (103)
- Received Data (104)
- Request to Send (105)
- Clear to Send (106)
- DCE Ready (107)
- Received Line Signal Detector (109)

When the modem (DCE) is turned on and is ready to operate, it asserts (applies a constant negative voltage to) the DCE Ready line. When the DTE is ready to send data (e.g., the terminal user has entered a character), it asserts Request to Send. The modem responds, when ready, by asserting Clear to Send, indicating that data may be transmitted over the Transmitted Data line. If the arrangement is half duplex, then Request to Send also inhibits the receive mode. The DTE may now transmit data over the Transmitted Data line. When data arrive from the remote modem, the local modem asserts Received Line Signal Detector to indicate that the remote modem is transmitting and delivers the data on the Received Data line. Note that it is not necessary to use timing circuits, because this is asynchronous transmission.

The circuits just listed are sufficient for private line point-to-point modems, but additional circuits are required to use a modem to transmit data over the telephone network. In this case, the initiator of a connection must call the destination device over the network. Two additional leads are required:

- DTE Ready (108.2)
- Ring Indicator (125)

With the addition of these two lines, the DTE-modem system can effectively use the telephone network in a way analogous to voice telephone usage. Figure 6.13 depicts the steps involved in dial-up half-duplex operation. When a call is made, either manually or automatically, the telephone system sends a ringing signal. A telephone set would respond by ringing its bell; a modem responds by asserting Ring Indicator. A person answers a call by lifting the handset; a DTE answers by asserting DTE Ready. A person who answers a call will listen for another's voice, and if nothing is heard, hang up. A DTE will listen for Received Line Signal Detector, which will be asserted by the modem when a signal is present; if this circuit is not asserted, the DTE will drop DTE Ready. You might wonder how this last contingency might arise. One common way is if a person accidentally dials the number of a modem. This activates the modem's DTE, but when no carrier tone comes through, the problem is resolved.

It is instructive to consider situations in which the distances between devices are so close as to allow two DTEs to signal each other directly. In this case, the

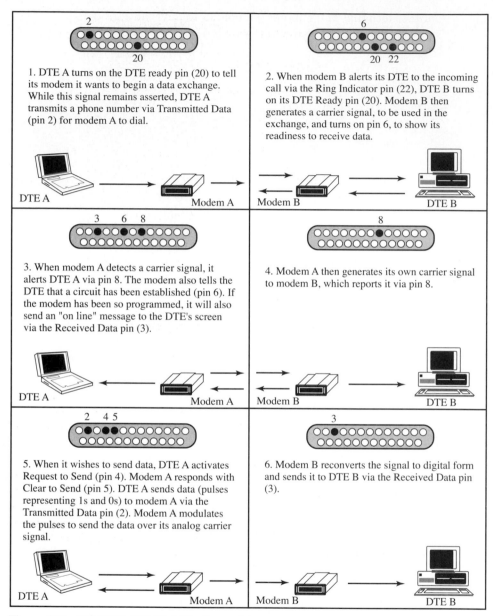

Figure 6.13 V.24/EIA-232 Dial-Up Operation

V.24/EIA-232 interchange circuits can still be used, but no DCE equipment is provided. For this scheme to work, a null modem is needed, which interconnects leads in such a way as to fool both DTEs into thinking that they are connected to modems. Figure 6.14 is an example of a null modem configuration; the reasons for the particular connections should be apparent to the reader who has grasped the preceding discussion.

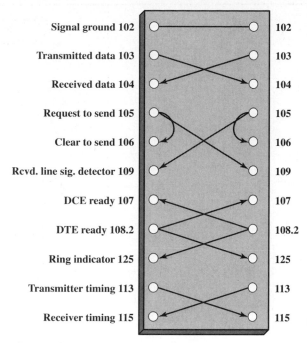

Figure 6.14   Example of a Null Modem

ISDN Physical Interface

The wide variety of functions available with V.24/EIA-232 is provided by the use of a large number of interchange circuits. This is a rather expensive way to achieve results. An alternative would be to provide fewer circuits but to add more logic at the DTE and DCE interfaces. With the dropping costs of logic circuitry, this is an attractive approach. This approach was taken in the X.21 standard for interfacing to public circuit-switched networks, specifying a 15-pin connector. More recently, the trend has been carried further with the specification of an 8-pin physical connector to an Integrated Services Digital Network (ISDN). ISDN is an all-digital replacement for existing public telephone and analog telecommunications networks. In this section, we look at the physical interface defined for ISDN.

Physical Connection

In ISDN terminology, a physical connection is made between terminal equipment (TE) and network-terminating equipment (NT). For purposes of our discussion, these terms correspond, rather closely, to DTE and DCE, respectively. The physical connection, defined in ISO 8877, specifies that the NT and TE cables shall terminate in matching connectors that provide for eight contacts.

Figure 6.15 illustrates the contact assignments for each of the eight lines on both the NT and TE sides. Two pins are used to provide data transmission in each direction. These contact pins are used to connect twisted-pair leads coming from the NT and TE devices. Because there are no specific functional circuits, the transmit/receive circuits are used to carry both data and control signals. The control information is transmitted in the form of messages.

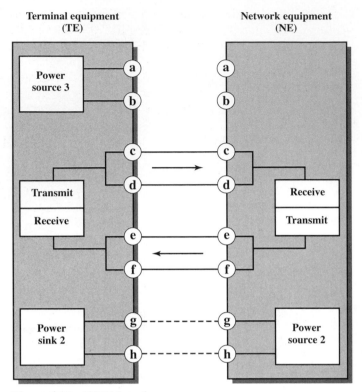

Figure 6.15 ISDN Interface

The specification provides for the capability to transfer power across the interface. The direction of power transfer depends on the application. In a typical application, it may be desirable to provide for power transfer from the network side toward the terminal to, for example, maintain a basic telephony service in the event of failure of the locally provided power. This power transfer can be accomplished using the same leads used for digital signal transmission (c, d, e, f), or on additional wires, using access leads g–h. The remaining two leads are not used in the ISDN configuration but may be useful in other configurations.

Electrical Specification

The ISDN electrical specification dictates the use of balanced transmission. With *balanced transmission*, signals are carried on a line, such as twisted pair, consisting of two conductors. Signals are transmitted as a current that travels down one conductor and returns on the other, the two conductors forming a complete circuit. For digital signals, this technique is known as *differential signaling*,[6] as the binary value depends on the direction of the voltage difference between the two conductors. *Unbalanced transmission*, which is used on older interfaces such as EIA-232, uses a single conductor to carry the signal, with ground providing the return path.

---

[6] Not to be confused with differential encoding; see Section 5.1.

The balanced mode tolerates more, and produces less, noise than unbalanced mode. Ideally, interference on a balanced line will act equally on both conductors and not affect the voltage difference. Because unbalanced transmission does not possess these advantages, it is generally used only on coaxial cable. When it is used on interchange circuits, such as EIA-232, it is limited to very short distances.

The data encoding format used on the ISDN interface depends on the data rate. For the *basic rate* of 192 kbps, the standard specifies the use of pseudoternary coding (Figure 5.2). Binary one is represented by the absence of voltage, and binary zero is represented by a positive or negative pulse of 750 mV$\pm$10%. For the *primary rate*, there are two options: 1.544 Mbps using alternate mark inversion (AMI) with B8ZS (Figure 5.6) and 2.048 Mbps using AMI with HDB3. The reason for the different schemes for the two different primary rates is simply historical; neither has a particular advantage.

6.7 RECOMMENDED READING

The classic treatment of error detecting codes and CRC is [PETE61]. [RAMA88] is an excellent tutorial on CRC.

[STAL02] discusses most of the widely used error-correcting codes. [ADAM91] provides comprehensive treatment of error-correcting codes. [SKLA01] contains a clear, well-written section on the subject. Two useful survey articles are [BERL87] and [BHAR83]. A quite readable theoretical and mathematical treatment of error-correcting codes is [ASH90].

[BLAC96] provides detailed, broad coverage of many physical layer interface standards. [BLAC95] focuses on the ITU-T V series recommendations. These topics are also covered in some detail in [FREE98].

ADAM91	Adamek, J. *Foundations of Coding.* New York: Wiley, 1991.
ASH90	Ash, R. *Information Theory.* New York: Dover, 1990.
BERL87	Berlekamp, E.; Peile, R.; and Pope, S. "The Application of Error Control to Communications." *IEEE Communications Magazine*, April 1987.
BHAR83	Bhargava, V. "Forward Error Correction Schemes for Digital Communications." *IEEE Communications Magazine*, January 1983.
BLAC95	Black, U. *The V Series Recommendations: Standards for Data Communications Over the Telephone Network.* New York: McGraw-Hill, 1996.
BLAC96	Black, U. *Physical Level Interfaces and Protocols.* Los Alamitos, CA: IEEE Computer Society Press, 1996.
FREE98	Freeman, R. *Telecommunication Transmission Handbook.* New York: Wiley, 1998.
PETE61	Peterson, W., and Brown, D. "Cyclic Codes for Error Detection." *Proceedings of the IEEE*, January 1961.
RAMA88	Ramabadran, T., and Gaitonde, S. "A Tutorial on CRC Computations." *IEEE Micro*, August 1988.
SKLA01	Sklar, B. *Digital Communications: Fundamentals and Applications.* Upper Saddle River, NJ: Prentice Hall, 2001.
STAL02	Stallings, W. *Wireless Communications and Networks.* Upper Saddle River, NJ: Prentice Hall, 2001

6.8 KEY TERMS, REVIEW QUESTIONS, AND PROBLEMS

Key Terms

asynchronous transmission	error-correction code (ECC)	interchange circuits
codeword	error detection	Integrated Services Digital
cyclic code	error-detection code	Network (ISDN)
cyclic redundancy check (CRC)	forward error correction (FEC)	modem
data circuit-terminating	frame	parity bit
equipment (DCE)	frame check sequence (FCS)	parity check
data terminal equipment	full duplex	point-to-point
(DTE)	half duplex	synchronous transmission
EIA-232	Hamming code	
error correction	Hamming distance	

Review Questions

6.1 How is the transmission of a single character differentiated from the transmission of the next character in asynchronous transmission?

6.2 What is a major disadvantage of asynchronous transmission?

6.3 How is synchronization provided for synchronous transmission?

6.4 What is a parity bit?

6.5 What is the CRC?

6.6 Why would you expect a CRC to detect more errors than a parity bit?

6.7 List three different ways in which the CRC algorithm can be described.

6.8 Is it possible to design an ECC that will correct some double bit errors but not all double bit errors? Why or why not?

6.9 In an (n, k) block ECC, what do n and k represent?

6.10 What is a DCE and what is its function?

Problems

6.1 Suppose a file of 10,000 bytes is to be sent over a line at 2400 bps.
  a. Calculate the overhead in bits and time in using asynchronous communication. Assume one start bit and a stop element of length one bit, and 8 bits to send the byte itself for each character. The 8-bit character consists of all data bits, with no parity bit.
  b. Calculate the overhead in bits and time using synchronous communication. Assume that the data are sent in frames. Each frame consists of 1000 characters = 8000 bits and an overhead of 48 control bits per frame.
  c. What would the answers to parts (a) and (b) be for a file of 100,000 characters?
  d. What would the answers to parts (a) and (b) be for the original file of 10,000 characters except at a data rate of 9600 bps?

6.2 A data source produces 7-bit IRA characters. Derive an expression of the maximum effective data rate (rate of IRA data bits) over an x-bps line for the following:
  a. Asynchronous transmission, with a 1.5-unit stop element and a parity bit.

    b. Synchronous transmission, with a frame consisting of 48 control bits and 128 information bits. The information field contains 8-bit (parity included) IRA characters.

    c. Same as part b, except that the information field is 1024 bits.

6.3 Demonstrate by example (write down a few dozen arbitrary bit patterns; assume one start bit and a stop element of length one bit) that a receiver that suffers a framing error on asynchronous transmission will eventually become realigned.

6.4 Suppose that a sender and receiver use asynchronous transmission and agree not to use any stop elements. Could this work? If so, explain any necessary conditions.

6.5 An asynchronous transmission scheme uses 8 data bits, an even parity bit, and a stop element of length 2 bits. What percentage of clock inaccuracy can be tolerated at the receiver with respect to the framing error? Assume that the bit samples are taken at the middle of the clock period. Also assume that at the beginning of the start bit the clock and incoming bits are in phase.

6.6 Suppose that a synchronous serial data transmission is clocked by two clocks (one at the sender and one at the receiver) that each have a drift of 1 minute in one year. How long a sequence of bits can be sent before possible clock drift could cause a problem? Assume that a bit waveform will be good if it is sampled within 40% of its center and that the sender and receiver are resynchronized at the beginning of each frame. Note that the transmission rate is not a factor, as both the bit period and the absolute timing error decrease proportionately at higher transmission rates.

6.7 Would you expect that the inclusion of a parity bit with each character would change the probability of receiving a correct message?

6.8 What is the purpose of using modulo 2 arithmetic rather than binary arithmetic in computing an FCS?

6.9 Consider a frame consisting of two characters of four bits each. Assume that the probability of bit error is 10^{-3} and that it is independent for each bit.

    a. What is the probability that the received frame contains at least one error?

    b. Now add a parity bit to each character. What is the probability?

6.10 Using the CRC-CCITT polynomial, generate the 16-bit CRC code for a message consisting of a 1 followed by 15 0s.

    a. Use long division.

    b. Use the shift register mechanism shown in Figure 6.6.

6.11 Explain in words why the shift register implementation of CRC will result in all 0s at the receiver if there are no errors. Demonstrate by example.

6.12 For $P = 110011$ and $M = 11100011$, find the CRC.

6.13 A CRC is constructed to generate a 4-bit FCS for an 11-bit message. The generator polynomial is $X^4 + X^3 + 1$.

    a. Draw the shift register circuit that would perform this task (see Figure 6.6).

    b. Encode the data bit sequence 10011011100 (leftmost bit is the least significant) using the generator polynomial and give the codeword.

    c. Now assume that bit 7 (counting from the LSB) in the codeword is in error and show that the detection algorithm detects the error.

6.14 **a.** In CRC error detection scheme, choose $P(x) = x^4 + x + 1$. Encode the bits 10010011011.

    b. Suppose the channel introduces an error pattern 100010000000000 (i.e., a flip from 1 to 0 or from 0 to 1 in position 1 and 5). What is received? Can the error be detected?

    c. Repeat part (b) with error pattern 100110000000000.

6.15 A modified CRC procedure is commonly used in communications standards. It is defined as follows:

$$\frac{X^{16}M(X) + X^{k}L(X)}{P(X)} = Q + \frac{R(X)}{P(X)}$$

$$FCS = L(X) + R(X)$$

where

$$L(X) = X^{15} + X^{14} + X^{13} + \ldots + X + 1$$

and k is the number of bits being checked (address, control, and information fields).

a. Describe in words the effect of this procedure.

b. Explain the potential benefits.

c. Show a shift register implementation for $P(X) = X^{16} + X^{12} + X^5 + 1$

6.16   Calculate the Hamming pairwise distances among the following codewords:

a. 00000, 10101, 01010

b. 000000, 010101, 101010, 110110

6.17   Section 6.4 discusses block error correction codes that make a decision on the basis of minimum distance. That is, given a code consisting of s equally likely codewords of length n, for each received sequence $\mathbf{v}$, the receiver selects the codeword $\mathbf{w}$ for which the distance $d(\mathbf{w}, \mathbf{v})$ is a minimum. We would like to prove that this scheme is "ideal" in the sense that the receiver always selects the codeword for which the probability of $\mathbf{w}$ given $\mathbf{v}$, $p(\mathbf{w}|\mathbf{v})$, is a maximum. Because all codewords are assumed equally likely, the codeword that maximizes $p(\mathbf{w}|\mathbf{v})$ is the same as the codeword that maximizes $p(\mathbf{v}|\mathbf{w})$.

a. In order that $\mathbf{w}$ be received as $\mathbf{v}$, there must be exactly $d(\mathbf{w}, \mathbf{v})$ errors in transmission, and these errors must occur in those bits where $\mathbf{w}$ and $\mathbf{v}$ disagree. Let β be the probability that a given bit is transmitted incorrectly and n be the length of a codeword. Write an expression for $p(\mathbf{v}|\mathbf{w})$ as a function of β, $d(\mathbf{w}, \mathbf{v})$, and n. *Hint:* The number of bits in error is $d(\mathbf{w}, \mathbf{v})$ and the number of bits not in error is $n - d(\mathbf{w}, \mathbf{v})$.

b. Now compare $p(\mathbf{v}|\mathbf{w}_1)$ and $p(\mathbf{v}|\mathbf{w}_2)$ for two different codewords $\mathbf{w}_1$ and $\mathbf{w}_1$ by $p(\mathbf{v}|\mathbf{w}_1)/p(\mathbf{v}|\mathbf{w}_2)$.

c. Assume that $0 < \beta < 0.5$ and show that $p(\mathbf{v}|\mathbf{w}_1) > p(\mathbf{v}|\mathbf{w}_2)$ if and only if $d(\mathbf{v}, \mathbf{w}_1) < d(\mathbf{v}, \mathbf{w}_1)$. This proves that the codeword $\mathbf{w}$ that gives the largest value of $p(\mathbf{v}|\mathbf{w})$ is that word whose distance from $\mathbf{v}$ is a minimum.

6.18   Section 6.4 states that for a given positive integer t, if a code satisfies $d_{\min} \geq 2t + 1$, then the code can correct all bit errors up to and including errors of t bits. Prove this assertion. *Hint:* Start by observing that for a codeword $\mathbf{w}$ to be decoded as another codeword $\mathbf{w}'$, the received sequence must be at least as close to $\mathbf{w}'$, as to $\mathbf{w}$.

6.19   Draw a timing diagram showing the state of all EIA-232 leads between two DTE-DCE pairs during the course of a data call on the switched telephone network.

6.20   Explain the operation of each null modem connection in Figure 6.14.

6.21   For the V.24/EIA-232 Remote Loopback circuit to function properly, what circuits must be logically connected?

CHAPTER 7

DATA LINK CONTROL PROTOCOLS

KEY POINTS

- Because of the possibility of transmission errors, and because the receiver of data may need to regulate the rate at which data arrive, synchronization and interfacing techniques are insufficient by themselves. It is necessary to impose a layer of control in each communicating device that provides functions such as flow control, error detection, and error control. This layer of control is known as a **data link control protocol**.
- **Flow control** enables a receiver to regulate the flow of data from a sender so that the receiver's buffers do not overflow.
- In a data link control protocol, **error control** is achieved by retransmission of damaged frames that have not been acknowledged or for which the other side requests a retransmission.

Our discussion so far has concerned *sending signals over a transmission link*. For effective digital data communications, much more is needed to control and manage the exchange. In this chapter, we shift our emphasis to that of *sending data over a data communications link*. To achieve the necessary control, a layer of logic is added above the physical interfacing discussed in Chapter 6; this logic is referred to as **data link control** or a **data link control protocol**. When a data link control protocol is used, the transmission medium between systems is referred to as a **data link**.

To see the need for data link control, we list some of the requirements and objectives for effective data communication between two directly connected transmitting-receiving stations:

- **Frame synchronization:** Data are sent in blocks called frames. The beginning and end of each frame must be recognizable. We briefly introduced this topic with the discussion of synchronous frames (Figure 6.2).
- **Flow control:** The sending station must not send frames at a rate faster than the receiving station can absorb them.
- **Error control:** Bit errors introduced by the transmission system should be corrected.
- **Addressing:** On a multipoint line, such as a local area network (LAN), the identity of the two stations involved in a transmission must be specified.
- **Control and data on same link:** It is usually not desirable to have a physically separate communications path for control information. Accordingly, the receiver must be able to distinguish control information from the data being transmitted.
- **Link management:** The initiation, maintenance, and termination of a sustained data exchange require a fair amount of coordination and cooperation among stations. Procedures for the management of this exchange are required.

None of these requirements is satisfied by the physical interfacing techniques described in Chapter 6. We shall see in this chapter that a data link protocol that satisfies these requirements is a rather complex affair. We begin by looking at two key mechanisms that are part of data link control: flow control and error control.

Following this background we look at the most important example of a data link control protocol: HDLC (high level data link control). This protocol is important for two reasons: First, it is a widely used standardized data link control protocol. Second, HDLC serves as a baseline from which virtually all other important data link control protocols are derived. Finally, an appendix to this chapter addresses some performance issues relating to data link control.

7.1 FLOW CONTROL

Flow control is a technique for assuring that a transmitting entity does not overwhelm a receiving entity with data. The receiving entity typically allocates a data buffer of some maximum length for a transfer. When data are received, the receiver must do a certain amount of processing before passing the data to the higher-level software. In the absence of flow control, the receiver's buffer may fill up and overflow while it is processing old data.

To begin, we examine mechanisms for flow control in the absence of errors. The model we will use is depicted in Figure 7.1a, which is a vertical-time sequence diagram. It has the advantages of showing time dependencies and illustrating the correct send-receive relationship. Each arrow represents a single frame transiting a data link between two stations. The data are sent in a sequence of frames, with each

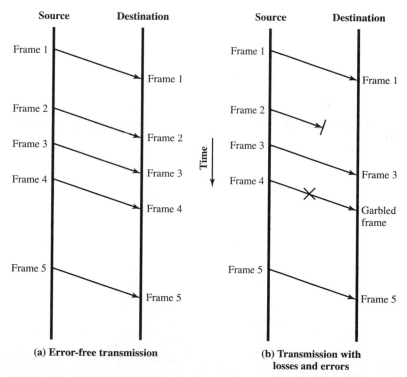

Figure 7.1   Model of Frame Transmission

frame containing a portion of the data and some control information. The time it takes for a station to emit all of the bits of a frame onto the medium is the transmission time; this is proportional to the length of the frame. The propagation time is the time it takes for a bit to traverse the link between source and destination. For this section, we assume that all frames that are transmitted are successfully received; no frames are lost and none arrive with errors. Furthermore, frames arrive in the same order in which they are sent. However, each transmitted frame suffers an arbitrary and variable amount of delay before reception.[1]

Stop-and-Wait Flow Control

The simplest form of flow control, known as stop-and-wait flow control, works as follows. A source entity transmits a frame. After the destination entity receives the frame, it indicates its willingness to accept another frame by sending back an acknowledgment to the frame just received. The source must wait until it receives the acknowledgment before sending the next frame. The destination can thus stop the flow of data simply by withholding acknowledgment. This procedure works fine and, indeed, can hardly be improved upon when a message is sent in a few large frames. However, it is often the case that a source will break up a large block of data into smaller blocks and transmit the data in many frames. This is done for the following reasons:

- The buffer size of the receiver may be limited.
- The longer the transmission, the more likely that there will be an error, necessitating retransmission of the entire frame. With smaller frames, errors are detected sooner, and a smaller amount of data needs to be retransmitted.
- On a shared medium, such as a LAN, it is usually desirable not to permit one station to occupy the medium for an extended period, thus causing long delays at the other sending stations.

With the use of multiple frames for a single message, the stop-and-wait procedure may be inadequate. The essence of the problem is that only one frame at a time can be in transit. To explain we first define the bit length of a link as follows:

$$B = R \times \frac{d}{V} \tag{7.1}$$

where

B = length of the link in bits; this is the number of bits present on the link when a stream of bits fully occupies the link

R = data rate of the link, in bps

d = length, or distance, of the link in meters

V = velocity of propagation, in m/s

---

[1]On a direct point-to-point link, the amount of delay is fixed rather than variable. However, a data link control protocol can be used over a network connection, such as a circuit-switched or ATM network, in which case the delay may be variable.

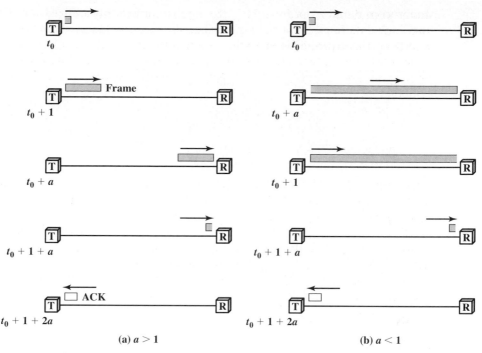

Figure 7.2   Stop-and-Wait Link Utilization (transmission time = 1; propagation time = a)

In situations where the bit length of the link is greater than the frame length, serious inefficiencies result. This is illustrated in Figure 7.2. In the figure, the transmission time (the time it takes for a station to transmit a frame) is normalized to one, and the propagation delay (the time it takes for a bit to travel from sender to receiver) is expressed as the variable a. Thus, we can express a as

$$a = \frac{B}{L} \tag{7.2}$$

where L is the number of bits in the frame (length of the frame in bits).

When a is less than 1, the propagation time is less than the transmission time. In this case, the frame is sufficiently long that the first bits of the frame have arrived at the destination before the source has completed the transmission of the frame. When a is greater than 1, the propagation time is greater than the transmission time. In this case, the sender completes transmission of the entire frame before the leading bits of that frame arrive at the receiver. Put another way, larger values of a are consistent with higher data rates and/or longer distances between stations. Appendix 7A discusses a and data link performance.

Both parts of Figure 7.2 (a and b) consist of a sequence of snapshots of the transmission process over time. In both cases, the first four snapshots show the process of transmitting a frame containing data, and the last snapshot shows the return of a small acknowledgment frame. Note that for $a > 1$, the line is always underutilized and even for $a < 1$, the line is inefficiently utilized. In essence, for very high data rates, for very long distances between sender and receiver, stop-and-wait flow control provides inefficient line utilization.

Example 7.1 Consider a 200-m optical fiber link operating at 1 Gbps. The velocity of propagation of optical fiber is typically about 2×10^8 m/s. Using Equation (7.1), $B = (10^9 \times 200)/(2 \times 10^8) = 1000$. Assume a frame of 1000 octets, or 8000 bits, is transmitted. Using Equation (7.2), $a = (1000/8000) = 0.125$. Using Figure 7.2b as a guide, assume transmission starts at time $t = 0$. After 1 μs (a normalized time of 0.125 frame times), the leading edge (first bit) of the frame has reached R, and the first 1000 bits of the frame are spread out across the link. At time $t = 8$ μs, the trailing edge (final bit) of the frame has just been emitted by T, and the final 1000 bits of the frame are spread out across the link. At $t = 9$ μs, the final bit of the frame arrives at R. R now sends back an ACK frame. If we assume the frame transmission time is negligible (very small ACK frame) and that the ACK is sent immediately, the ACK arrives at T at $t = 10$ μs. At this point, T can begin transmitting a new frame. The actual transmission time for the frame was 8 μs, but the total time to transmit the first frame and receive and ACK is 10 μs.

Now consider a 1-Mbps link between two ground stations that communicate via a satellite relay. A geosynchronous satellite has an altitude of roughly 36,000 km. Then $B = (10^6 \times 2 \times 36,000,000)/(3 \times 10^6) = 240,000$. For a frame length of 8000 bits, $a = (240000/8000) = 30$. Using Figure 7.2a as a guide, we can work through the same steps as before. In this case, it takes 240 ms for the leading edge of the frame to arrive and an additional 8 ms for the entire frame to arrive. The ACK arrives back at T at $t = 488$ ms. The actual transmission time for the first frame was 8 ms, but the total time to transmit the first frame and receive and ACK is 488 ms.

Sliding-Window Flow Control

The essence of the problem described so far is that only one frame at a time can be in transit. In situations where the bit length of the link is greater than the frame length ($a > 1$), serious inefficiencies result. Efficiency can be greatly improved by allowing multiple frames to be in transit at the same time.

Let us examine how this might work for two stations, A and B, connected via a full-duplex link. Station B allocates buffer space for W frames. Thus, B can accept W frames, and A is allowed to send W frames without waiting for any acknowledgments. To keep track of which frames have been acknowledged, each is labeled with a sequence number. B acknowledges a frame by sending an acknowledgment that includes the sequence number of the next frame expected. This acknowledgment also implicitly announces that B is prepared to receive the next W frames, beginning with the number specified. This scheme can also be used to acknowledge multiple frames. For example, B could receive frames 2, 3, and 4, but withhold acknowledgment until frame 4 has arrived. By then returning an acknowledgment with sequence number 5, B acknowledges frames 2, 3, and 4 at one time. A maintains a list of sequence numbers that it is allowed to send, and B maintains a list of sequence numbers that it is prepared to receive. Each of these lists can be thought of as a *window* of frames. The operation is referred to as **sliding-window flow control**.

Several additional comments need to be made. Because the sequence number to be used occupies a field in the frame, it is clearly of bounded size. For example, for a 3-bit field, the sequence number can range from 0 to 7. Accordingly, frames are numbered modulo 8; that is, after sequence number 7, the next number is 0. In general, for a k-bit field the range of sequence numbers is 0 through $2^k - 1$, and frames are numbered modulo 2^k. As will be shown subsequently, the maximum window size is $2^k - 1$.

Figure 7.3 is a useful way of depicting the sliding-window process. It assumes the use of a 3-bit sequence number, so that frames are numbered sequentially from 0 through 7, and then the same numbers are reused for subsequent frames. The shaded rectangle indicates the frames that may be sent; in this figure, the sender may transmit five frames, beginning with frame 0. Each time a frame is sent, the shaded window shrinks; each time an acknowledgment is received, the shaded window grows. Frames between the vertical bar and the shaded window have been sent but not yet acknowledged. As we shall see, the sender must buffer these frames in case they need to be retransmitted.

The window size need not be the maximum possible size for a given sequence number length. For example, using a 3-bit sequence number, a window size of 4 could be configured for the stations using the sliding-window flow control protocol.

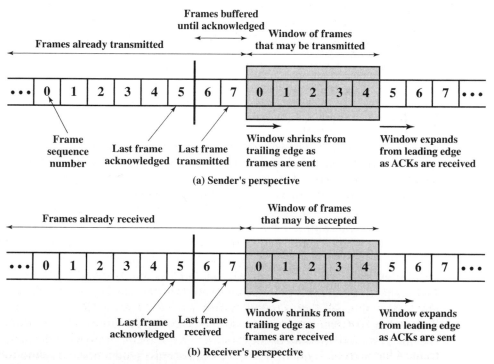

Figure 7.3   Sliding-Window Depiction

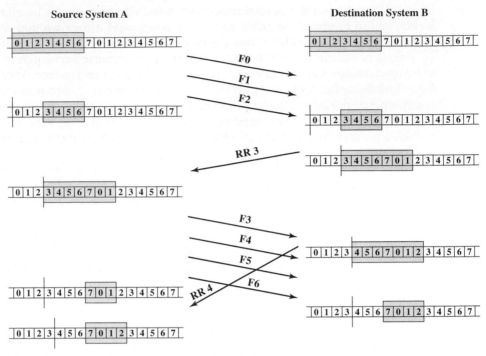

Figure 7.4   Example of a Sliding-Window Protocol

An example is shown in Figure 7.4. The example assumes a 3-bit sequence number field and a maximum window size of seven frames. Initially, A and B have windows indicating that A may transmit seven frames, beginning with frame 0 (F0). After transmitting three frames (F0, F1, F2) without acknowledgment, A has shrunk its window to four frames and maintains a copy of the three transmitted frames. The window indicates that A may transmit four frames, beginning with frame number 3. B then transmits an RR (receive ready) 3, which means "I have received all frames up through frame number 2 and am ready to receive frame number 3; in fact, I am prepared to receive seven frames, beginning with frame number 3." With this , A is back up to permission to transmit seven frames, still beginning with frame 3; also A may discard the buffered frames that have now been acknowledged. A proceeds to transmit frames 3, 4, 5, and 6. B returns RR 4, which acknowledges F3, and allows transmission of F4 through the next instance of F2. By the time this RR reaches A, it has already transmitted F4, F5, and F6, and therefore A may only open its window to permit sending four frames beginning with F7.

The mechanism so far described does indeed provide a form of flow control: The receiver must only be able to accommodate seven frames beyond the one it has last acknowledged. Most protocols also allow a station to cut off the flow of frames from the other side by sending a Receive Not Ready (RNR) message, which acknowledges former frames but forbids transfer of future frames. Thus, RNR 5 means "I have received all frames up through number 4 but am unable to accept any more." At some subsequent point, the station must send a normal acknowledgment to reopen the window.

So far, we have discussed transmission in one direction only. If two stations exchange data, each needs to maintain two windows, one for transmit and one for receive, and each side needs to send the data and acknowledgments to the other. To provide efficient support for this requirement, a feature known as **piggybacking** is typically provided. Each **data frame** includes a field that holds the sequence number of that frame plus a field that holds the sequence number used for acknowledgment. Thus, if a station has data to send and an acknowledgment to send, it sends both together in one frame, saving communication capacity. Of course, if a station has an acknowledgment but no data to send, it sends a separate **acknowledgment frame**, such as RR or RNR. If a station has data to send but no new acknowledgment to send, it must repeat the last acknowledgment sequence number that it sent. This is because the data frame includes a field for the acknowledgment number, and some value must be put into that field. When a station receives a duplicate acknowledgment, it simply ignores it.

Sliding-window flow control is potentially much more efficient than stop-and-wait flow control. The reason is that, with sliding-window flow control, the transmission link is treated as a pipeline that may be filled with frames in transit. In contrast, with stop-and-wait flow control, only one frame may be in the pipe at a time. Appendix 7A quantifies the improvement in efficiency.

Example 7.2   Let us consider the use of sliding-window flow control for the two configurations of Example 7.1. As was calculated in Example 7.1, it takes 10 μs for an ACK to the first frame to be received. It takes 8 μs to transmit one frame, so the sender can transmit one frame and part of a second frame by the time the ACK to the first frame is received. Thus, a window size of 2 is adequate to enable the sender to transmit frames continuously, or a rate of one frame every 8 μs. With stop-and-wait, a rate of only one frame per 10 μs is possible.

For the satellite configuration, it takes 488 ms for an ACK to the first frame to be received. It takes 8 ms to transmit one frame, so the sender can transmit 61 frames by the time the ACK to the first frame is received. With a window size of 6 bits or more, the sender can transmit continuously, or a rate of one frame every 8 ms. If the window size is 7, using a 3-bit window field, then the sender can only send 7 frames and then must wait for an ACK before sending more. In this case, the sender can transmit at a rate of 7 frames per 488 ms, or about one frame every 70 ms. With stop-and-wait, a rate of only one frame per 488 ms is possible.

7.2 ERROR CONTROL

Error control refers to mechanisms to detect and correct errors that occur in the transmission of frames. The model that we will use, which covers the typical case, is illustrated in Figure 7.1b. As before, data are sent as a sequence of frames; frames arrive in the same order in which they are sent; and each transmitted frame suffers an arbitrary and potentially variable amount of delay before reception. In addition, we admit the possibility of two types of errors:

- **Lost frame:** A frame fails to arrive at the other side. For example, a noise burst may damage a frame to the extent that the receiver is not aware that a frame has been transmitted.
- **Damaged frame:** A recognizable frame does arrive, but some of the bits are in error (have been altered during transmission).

The most common techniques for error control are based on some or all of the following ingredients:

- **Error detection:** As discussed in Chapter 6.
- **Positive acknowledgment:** The destination returns a positive acknowledgment to successfully received, error-free frames.
- **Retransmission after timeout:** The source retransmits a frame that has not been acknowledged after a predetermined amount of time.
- **Negative acknowledgment and retransmission:** The destination returns a negative acknowledgment to frames in which an error is detected. The source retransmits such frames.

Collectively, these mechanisms are all referred to as **automatic repeat request** (ARQ); the effect of ARQ is to turn an unreliable data link into a reliable one. Three versions of ARQ have been standardized:

Stop-and-wait ARQ

Go-back-N ARQ

Selective-reject ARQ

All of these forms are based on the use of the flow control techniques discussed in Section 7.1. We examine each in turn.

Stop-and-Wait ARQ

Stop-and-wait ARQ is based on the stop-and-wait flow control technique outlined previously. The source station transmits a single frame and then must await an acknowledgment (ACK). No other data frames can be sent until the destination station's reply arrives at the source station.

Two sorts of errors could occur. First, the frame that arrives at the destination could be damaged. The receiver detects this by using the error-detection technique referred to earlier and simply discards the frame. To account for this possibility, the source station is equipped with a timer. After a frame is transmitted, the source station waits for an acknowledgment. If no acknowledgment is received by the time that the timer expires, then the same frame is sent again. Note that this method requires that the transmitter maintain a copy of a transmitted frame until an acknowledgment is received for that frame.

The second sort of error is a damaged acknowledgment. Consider the following situation. Station A sends a frame. The frame is received correctly by station B, which responds with an acknowledgment (ACK). The ACK is damaged in transit and is not recognizable by A, which will therefore time out and resend the same frame. This duplicate frame arrives and is accepted by B. B has therefore accepted two copies of the same frame as if they were separate. To avoid this problem, frames are alternately labeled with 0 or 1, and positive acknowledgments are of the form ACK0 and ACK1. In keeping with the sliding-window convention, an ACK0 acknowledges receipt of a frame numbered 1 and indicates that the receiver is ready for a frame numbered 0.

Figure 7.5 gives an example of the use of stop-and-wait ARQ, showing the transmission of a sequence of frames from source A to destination B. The figure shows the two types of errors just described. The third frame transmitted by A is lost or damaged and therefore no ACK is returned by B. A times out and retransmits the frame. Later, A transmits a frame labeled 1 but the ACK0 for that frame is lost. A times out and retransmits the same frame. When B receives two frames in a row with the same label, it discards the second frame but sends back an ACK0 to each.

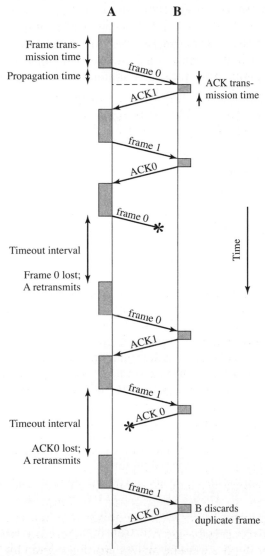

Figure 7.5 Stop-and-Wait ARQ

The principal advantage of stop-and-wait ARQ is its simplicity. Its principal disadvantage, as discussed in Section 7.1, is that stop-and-wait is an inefficient mechanism. The sliding-window flow control technique can be adapted to provide more efficient line use; in this context, it is sometimes referred to as *continuous ARQ*.

Go-Back-N ARQ

The form of error control based on sliding-window flow control that is most commonly used is called go-back-N ARQ. In this method, a station may send a series of frames sequentially numbered modulo some maximum value. The number of unacknowledged frames outstanding is determined by window size, using the sliding-window flow control technique. While no errors occur, the destination will acknowledge incoming frames as usual (RR = receive ready, or piggybacked acknowledgement). If the destination station detects an error in a frame, it may send a negative acknowledgment (REJ = reject) for that frame, as explained in the following rules. The destination station will discard that frame and all future incoming frames until the frame in error is correctly received. Thus, the source station, when it receives a REJ, must retransmit the frame in error plus all succeeding frames that were transmitted in the interim.

Suppose that station A is sending frames to station B. After each transmission, A sets an acknowledgment timer for the frame just transmitted. Suppose that B has previously successfully received frame $(i - 1)$ and A has just transmitted frame i. The go-back-N technique takes into account the following contingencies:

1. **Damaged frame.** If the received frame is invalid (i.e., B detects an error, or the frame is so damaged that B does not even perceive that it has received a frame), B discards the frame and takes no further action as the result of that frame. There are two subcases:

   a. Within a reasonable period of time, A subsequently sends frame $(i + 1)$. B receives frame $(i + 1)$ out of order and sends a REJ i. A must retransmit frame i and all subsequent frames.

   b. A does not soon send additional frames. B receives nothing and returns neither an RR nor a REJ. When A's timer expires, it transmits an RR frame that includes a bit known as the P bit, which is set to 1. B interprets the RR frame with a P bit of 1 as a command that must be acknowledged by sending an RR indicating the next frame that it expects, which is frame i. When A receives the RR, it retransmits frame i. Alternatively, A could just retransmit frame i when its timer expires.

2. **Damaged RR.** There are two subcases:

   a. B receives frame i and sends RR $(i + 1)$, which suffers an error in transit. Because acknowledgments are cumulative (e.g., RR 6 means that all frames through 5 are acknowledged), it may be that A will receive a subsequent RR to a subsequent frame and that it will arrive before the timer associated with frame i expires.

   b. If A's timer expires, it transmits an RR command as in Case 1b. It sets another timer, called the P-bit timer. If B fails to respond to the RR command, or if its response suffers an error in transit, then A's P-bit timer will expire. At this point, A will try again by issuing a new RR command and restarting the P-bit timer. This procedure is tried for a number of iterations. If A fails to obtain an acknowledgment after some maximum number of attempts, it initiates a reset procedure.

3. Damaged REJ. If a REJ is lost, this is equivalent to Case 1b.

Figure 7.6a is an example of the frame flow for go-back-N ARQ. Because of the propagation delay on the line, by the time that an acknowledgment (positive or negative) arrives back at the sending station, it has already sent at least one additional frame beyond the one being acknowledged. In this example, frame 4 is

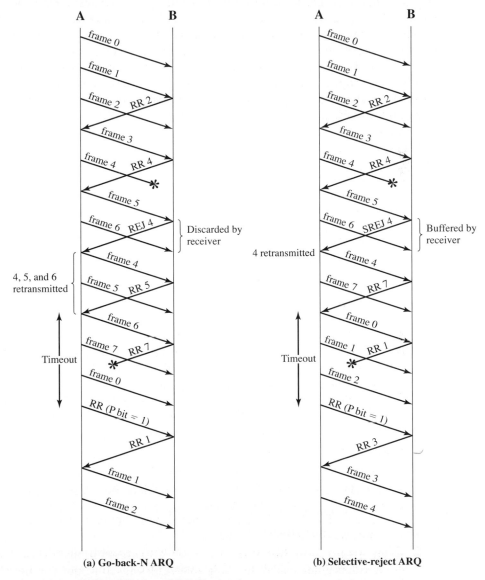

(a) Go-back-N ARQ

(b) Selective-reject ARQ

Figure 7.6   Sliding-Window ARQ Protocols

damaged. Frames 5 and 6 are received out of order and are discarded by B. When frame 5 arrives, B immediately sends a REJ 4. When the REJ to frame 4 is received, not only frame 4 but frames 5 and 6 must be retransmitted. Note that the transmitter must keep a copy of all unacknowledged frames.

In Section 7.1, we mentioned that for a k-bit sequence number field, which provides a sequence number range of 2^k, the maximum window size is limited to $2^k - 1$. This has to do with the interaction between error control and acknowledgment. Consider that if data are being exchanged in both directions, station B must send piggybacked acknowledgments to station A's frames in the data frames being transmitted by B, even if the acknowledgment has already been sent. As we have mentioned, this is because B must put some number in the acknowledgment field of its data frame. As an example, assume a 3-bit sequence number (sequence number space = 8). Suppose a station sends frame 0 and gets back an RR 1, and then sends frames $1, 2, 3, 4, 5, 6, 7, 0$ and gets another RR 1. This could mean that all eight frames were received correctly and the RR 1 is a cumulative acknowledgment. It could also mean that all eight frames were damaged or lost in transit, and the receiving station is repeating its previous RR 1. The problem is avoided if the maximum window size is limited to $7(2^3 - 1)$.

Selective-Reject ARQ

With selective-reject ARQ, the only frames retransmitted are those that receive a negative acknowledgment, in this case called SREJ, or those that time out. Figure 7.6b illustrates this scheme. When frame 5 is received out of order, B sends a SREJ 4, indicating that frame 4 has not been received. However, B continues to accept incoming frames and buffers them until a valid frame 4 is received. At that point, B can place the frames in the proper order for delivery to higher-layer software.

Selective reject would appear to be more efficient than go-back-N, because it minimizes the amount of retransmission. On the other hand, the receiver must maintain a buffer large enough to save post-SREJ frames until the frame in error is retransmitted and must contain logic for reinserting that frame in the proper sequence. The transmitter, too, requires more complex logic to be able to send a frame out of sequence. Because of such complications, select-reject ARQ is much less widely used than go-back-N ARQ. Selective reject is a useful choice for a satellite link because of the long propagation delay involved.

The window size limitation is more restrictive for selective-reject than for go-back-N. Consider the case of a 3-bit sequence number size for selective-reject. Allow a window size of seven, and consider the following scenario [TANE03]:

1. Station A sends frames 0 through 6 to station B.
2. Station B receives all seven frames and cumulatively acknowledges with RR 7.
3. Because of a noise burst, the RR 7 is lost.
4. A times out and retransmits frame 0.
5. B has already advanced its receive window to accept frames $7, 0, 1, 2, 3, 4$, and 5. Thus it assumes that frame 7 has been lost and that this is a new frame 0, which it accepts.

The problem with the foregoing scenario is that there is an overlap between the sending and receiving windows. To overcome the problem, the maximum window size should be no more than half the range of sequence numbers. In the preceding scenario, if only four unacknowledged frames may be outstanding, no confusion can result. In general, for a k-bit sequence number field, which provides a sequence number range of 2^k, the maximum window size is limited to 2^{k-1}.

7.3   HIGH-LEVEL DATA LINK CONTROL (HDLC)

The most important data link control protocol is HDLC (ISO 3009, ISO 4335). Not only is HDLC widely used, but it is the basis for many other important data link control protocols, which use the same or similar formats and the same mechanisms as employed in HDLC.

Basic Characteristics

To satisfy a variety of applications, HDLC defines three types of stations, two link configurations, and three data transfer modes of operation. The three station types are as follows:

- **Primary station:** Responsible for controlling the operation of the link. Frames issued by the primary are called commands.
- **Secondary station:** Operates under the control of the primary station. Frames issued by a secondary are called responses. The primary maintains a separate logical link with each secondary station on the line.
- **Combined station:** Combines the features of primary and secondary. A combined station may issue both commands and responses.

The two link configurations are as follows:

- **Unbalanced configuration:** Consists of one primary and one or more secondary stations and supports both full-duplex and half-duplex transmission.
- **Balanced configuration:** Consists of two combined stations and supports both full-duplex and half-duplex transmission.

The three data transfer modes are as follows:

- **Normal response mode (NRM):** Used with an unbalanced configuration. The primary may initiate data transfer to a secondary, but a secondary may only transmit data in response to a command from the primary.
- **Asynchronous balanced mode (ABM):** Used with a balanced configuration. Either combined station may initiate transmission without receiving permission from the other combined station.
- **Asynchronous response mode (ARM):** Used with an unbalanced configuration. The secondary may initiate transmission without explicit permission of the primary. The primary still retains responsibility for the line, including initialization, error recovery, and logical disconnection.

NRM is used on multidrop lines, in which a number of terminals are connected to a host computer. The computer polls each terminal for input. NRM is also sometimes used on point-to-point links, particularly if the link connects a terminal or other peripheral to a computer. ABM is the most widely used of the three modes; it makes more efficient use of a full-duplex point-to-point link because there is no polling overhead. ARM is rarely used; it is applicable to some special situations in which a secondary may need to initiate transmission.

Frame Structure

HDLC uses synchronous transmission. All transmissions are in the form of frames, and a single frame format suffices for all types of data and control exchanges.

Figure 7.7 depicts the structure of the HDLC frame. The flag, address, and control fields that precede the information field are known as a **header**. The FCS and flag fields following the data field are referred to as a **trailer**.

Flag Fields

Flag fields delimit the frame at both ends with the unique pattern 01111110. A single flag may be used as the closing flag for one frame and the opening flag for the

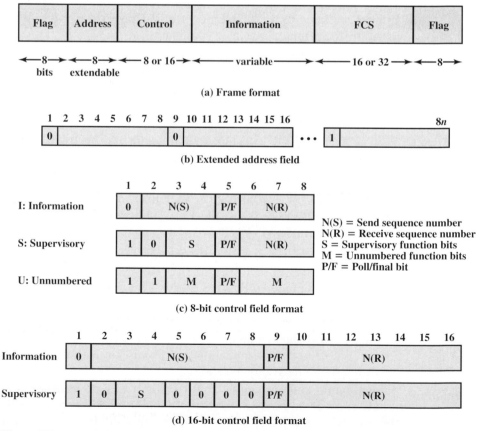

Figure 7.7 HDLC Frame Structure

next. On both sides of the user-network interface, receivers are continuously hunting for the flag sequence to synchronize on the start of a frame. While receiving a frame, a station continues to hunt for that sequence to determine the end of the frame. Because the protocol allows the presence of arbitrary bit patterns (i.e., there are no restrictions on the content of the various fields imposed by the link protocol), there is no assurance that the pattern 01111110 will not appear somewhere inside the frame, thus destroying synchronization. To avoid this problem, a procedure known as *bit stuffing* is used. Between the transmission of the starting and ending flags, the transmitter will always insert an extra 0 bit after each occurrence of five 1s in the frame. After detecting a starting flag, the receiver monitors the bit stream. When a pattern of five 1s appears, the sixth bit is examined. If this bit is 0, it is deleted. If the sixth bit is a 1 and the seventh bit is a 0, the combination is accepted as a flag. If the sixth and seventh bits are both 1, the sender is indicating an abort condition.

With the use of bit stuffing, arbitrary bit patterns can be inserted into the data field of the frame. This property is known as **data transparency**.

Figure 7.8 shows an example of bit stuffing. Note that in the first two cases, the extra 0 is not strictly necessary for avoiding a flag pattern but is necessary for the operation of the algorithm. The pitfalls of bit stuffing are also illustrated in this figure. When a flag is used as both an ending and a starting flag, a 1-bit error merges two frames into one. Conversely, a 1-bit error inside the frame could split it in two.

Original pattern:

111111111111011111101111110

After bit stuffing:

11111011111011011111101011111010

(a) Example

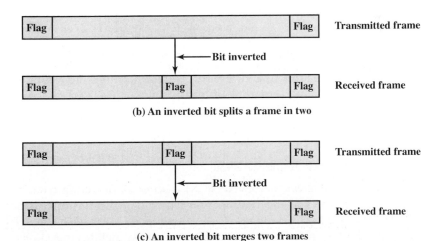

(b) An inverted bit splits a frame in two

(c) An inverted bit merges two frames

Figure 7.8 Bit Stuffing

Address Field

The address field identifies the secondary station that transmitted or is to receive the frame. This field is not needed for point-to-point links but is always included for the sake of uniformity. The address field is usually 8 bits long but, by prior agreement, an extended format may be used in which the actual address length is a multiple of 7 bits. The leftmost bit of each octet is 1 or 0 according as it is or is not the last octet of the address field. The remaining 7 bits of each octet form part of the address. The single-octet address of 11111111 is interpreted as the all-stations address in both basic and extended formats. It is used to allow the primary to broadcast a frame for reception by all secondaries.

Control Field

HDLC defines three types of frames, each with a different control field format. **Information frames** (I-frames) carry the data to be transmitted for the user (the logic above HDLC that is using HDLC). Additionally, flow and error control data, using the ARQ mechanism, are piggybacked on an information frame. **Supervisory frames** (S-frames) provide the ARQ mechanism when piggybacking is not used. **Unnumbered frames** (U-frames) provide supplemental link control functions. The first one or two bits of the control field serve to identify the frame type. The remaining bit positions are organized into subfields as indicated in Figures 7.7c and d. Their use is explained in the discussion of HDLC operation later in this chapter.

All of the control field formats contain the poll/final (P/F) bit. Its use depends on context. Typically, in command frames, it is referred to as the P bit and is set to 1 to solicit (poll) a response frame from the peer HDLC entity. In response frames, it is referred to as the F bit and is set to 1 to indicate the response frame transmitted as a result of a soliciting command.

Note that the basic control field for S- and I-frames uses 3-bit sequence numbers. With the appropriate set-mode command, an extended control field can be used for S- and I-frames that employs 7-bit sequence numbers. U-frames always contain an 8-bit control field.

Information Field

The information field is present only in I-frames and some U-frames. The field can contain any sequence of bits but must consist of an integral number of octets. The length of the information field is variable up to some system-defined maximum.

Frame Check Sequence Field

The frame check sequence (FCS) is an error-detecting code calculated from the remaining bits of the frame, exclusive of flags. The normal code is the 16-bit CRC-CCITT defined in Section 7.2. An optional 32-bit FCS, using CRC-32, may be employed if the frame length or the line reliability dictates this choice.

Operation

HDLC operation consists of the exchange of I-frames, S-frames, and U-frames between two stations. The various commands and responses defined for these frame types are listed in Table 7.1. In describing HDLC operation, we will discuss these three types of frames.

The operation of HDLC involves three phases. First, one side or another initializes the data link so that frames may be exchanged in an orderly fashion. During this phase, the options that are to be used are agreed upon. After initialization, the two sides exchange user data and the control information to exercise flow and error control. Finally, one of the two sides signals the termination of the operation.

Table 7.1   HDLC Commands and Responses

Name	Command/ Response	Description
Information (I)	C/R	Exchange user data
Supervisory (S)		
Receive ready (RR)	C/R	Positive acknowledgment; ready to receive I-frame
Receive not ready (RNR)	C/R	Positive acknowledgment; not ready to receive
Reject (REJ)	C/R	Negative acknowledgment; go back N
Selective reject (SREJ)	C/R	Negative acknowledgment; selective reject
Unnumbered (U)		
Set normal response/extended mode (SNRM/SNRME)	C	Set mode; extended = 7-bit sequence numbers
Set asynchronous response/extended mode (SARM/SARME)	C	Set mode; extended = 7-bit sequence numbers
Set asynchronous balanced/extended mode (SABM, SABME)	C	Set mode; extended = 7-bit sequence numbers
Set initialization mode (SIM)	C	Initialize link control functions in addressed station
Disconnect (DISC)	C	Terminate logical link connection
Unnumbered acknowledgment (UA)	R	Acknowledge acceptance of one of the set-mode commands
Disconnected mode (DM)	R	Responder is in disconnected mode
Request disconnect (RD)	R	Request for DISC command
Request initialization mode (RIM)	R	Initialization needed; request for SIM command
Unnumbered information (UI)	C/R	Used to exchange control information
Unnumbered poll (UP)	C	Used to solicit control information
Reset (RSET)	C	Used for recovery; resets N(R), N(S)
Exchange identification (XID)	C/R	Used to request/report status
Test (TEST)	C/R	Exchange identical information fields for testing
Frame reject (FRMR)	R	Report receipt of unacceptable frame

Initialization

Initialization may be requested by either side by issuing one of the six set-mode commands. This command serves three purposes:

1. It signals the other side that initialization is requested.
2. It specifies which of the three modes (NRM, ABM, ARM) is requested.
3. It specifies whether 3- or 7-bit sequence numbers are to be used.

If the other side accepts this request, then the HDLC module on that end transmits an unnumbered acknowledged (UA) frame back to the initiating side. If the request is rejected, then a disconnected mode (DM) frame is sent.

Data Transfer

When the initialization has been requested and accepted, then a logical connection is established. Both sides may begin to send user data in I-frames, starting with sequence number 0. The N(S) and N(R) fields of the I-frame are sequence numbers that support flow control and error control. An HDLC module sending a sequence of I-frames will number them sequentially, modulo 8 or 128, depending on whether 3- or 7-bit sequence numbers are used, and place the sequence number in N(S). N(R) is the acknowledgment for I-frames received; it enables the HDLC module to indicate which number I-frame it expects to receive next.

S-frames are also used for flow control and error control. The receive ready (RR) frame acknowledges the last I-frame received by indicating the next I-frame expected. The RR is used when there is no reverse user data traffic (I-frames) to carry an acknowledgment. Receive not ready (RNR) acknowledges an I-frame, as with RR, but also asks the peer entity to suspend transmission of I-frames. When the entity that issued RNR is again ready, it sends an RR. REJ initiates the go-back-N ARQ. It indicates that the last I-frame received has been rejected and that retransmission of all I-frames beginning with number N(R) is required. Selective reject (SREJ) is used to request retransmission of just a single frame.

Disconnect

Either HDLC module can initiate a disconnect, either on its own initiative if there is some sort of fault, or at the request of its higher-layer user. HDLC issues a disconnect by sending a disconnect (DISC) frame. The remote entity must accept the disconnect by replying with a UA and informing its layer 3 user that the connection has been terminated. Any outstanding unacknowledged I-frames may be lost, and their recovery is the responsibility of higher layers.

Examples of Operation

To better understand HDLC operation, several examples are presented in Figure 7.9. In the example diagrams, each arrow includes a legend that specifies the frame name, the setting of the P/F bit, and, where appropriate, the values of N(R) and N(S). The setting of the P or F bit is 1 if the designation is present and 0 if absent.

Figure 7.9a shows the frames involved in link setup and disconnect. The HDLC protocol entity for one side issues an SABM command to the other side and starts a timer. The other side, upon receiving the SABM, returns a UA response and sets local variables and counters to their initial values. The initiating entity receives the UA response, sets its variables and counters, and stops the timer. The logical connection is now active, and both sides may begin transmitting frames. Should the timer expire without a response to an SABM, the originator will repeat the SABM, as illustrated. This would be repeated until a UA or DM is received or until, after a given number of tries, the entity attempting initiation gives up and reports failure to a management entity. In such a case, higher-layer intervention is necessary. The same figure (Figure 7.9a) shows the disconnect procedure. One side issues a DISC command, and the other responds with a UA response.

Figure 7.9b illustrates the full-duplex exchange of I-frames. When an entity sends a number of I-frames in a row with no incoming data, then the receive

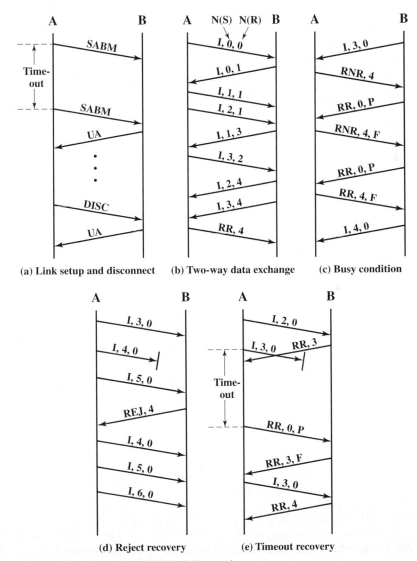

Figure 7.9 Examples of HDLC Operation

sequence number is simply repeated (e.g., I,1,1; I,2.1 in the A-to-B direction). When an entity receives a number of I-frames in a row with no outgoing frames, then the receive sequence number in the next outgoing frame must reflect the cumulative activity (e.g., I,1,3 in the B-to-A direction). Note that, in addition to I-frames, data exchange may involve supervisory frames.

Figure 7.9c shows an operation involving a busy condition. Such a condition may arise because an HDLC entity is not able to process I-frames as fast as they are arriving, or the intended user is not able to accept data as fast as they arrive in I-frames. In either case, the entity's receive buffer fills up and it must halt the incoming flow of I-frames, using an RNR command. In this example, A issues an RNR, which requires B to halt transmission of I-frames. The station receiving the RNR will usually poll the busy station at some periodic interval by sending an RR with the P bit set. This requires the other side to respond with either an RR or an RNR. When the busy condition has cleared, A returns an RR, and I-frame transmission from B can resume.

An example of error recovery using the REJ command is shown in Figure 7.9d. In this example, A transmits I-frames numbered 3, 4, and 5. Number 4 suffers an error and is lost. When B receives I-frame number 5, it discards this frame because it is out of order and sends an REJ with an N(R) of 4. This causes A to initiate retransmission of I-frames previously sent, beginning with frame 4. A may continue to send additional frames after the retransmitted frames.

An example of error recovery using a timeout is shown in Figure 7.9e. In this example, A transmits I-frame number 3 as the last in a sequence of I-frames. The frame suffers an error. B detects the error and discards it. However, B cannot send an REJ, because there is no way to know if this was an I-frame. If an error is detected in a frame, all of the bits of that frame are suspect, and the receiver has no way to act upon it. A, however, would have started a timer as the frame was transmitted. This timer has a duration long enough to span the expected response time. When the timer expires, A initiates recovery action. This is usually done by polling the other side with an RR command with the P bit set, to determine the status of the other side. Because the poll demands a response, the entity will receive a frame containing an N(R) field and be able to proceed. In this case, the response indicates that frame 3 was lost, which A retransmits.

These examples are not exhaustive. However, they should give the reader a good feel for the behavior of HDLC.

7.4 RECOMMENDED READING

An excellent and very detailed treatment of flow control and error control is to be found in [BERT92]. A good survey of data link control protocols is [BLAC93]. [FIOR95] points out some of the real-world reliability problems with HDLC.

There is a large body of literature on the performance of ARQ link control protocols. Three classic papers, well worth reading, are [BENE64], [KONH80], and [BUX80]. A readable survey with simplified performance results is [LIN84]. A more recent analysis is [ZORZ96]. Two books with good coverage of link-level performance are [SPRA91] and [WALR98].

[KLEI92] and [KLEI93] are two key papers that look at the implications of gigabit data rates on performance.

BENE64   Benice, R. "An Analysis of Retransmission Systems." *IEEE Transactions on Communication Technology*, December 1964.

BERT92   Bertsekas, D., and Gallager, R. *Data Networks.* Englewood Cliffs, NJ: Prentice Hall, 1992.

BLAC93   Black, U. *Data Link Protocols.* Englewood Cliffs, NJ: Prentice Hall, 1993.

BUX80   Bux, W.; Kummerle, K.; and Truong, H. "Balanced HDLC Procedures: A Performance Analysis." *IEEE Transactions on Communications*, November 1980.

FIOR95   Fiorini, D.; Chiani, M.; Tralli, V.; and Salati, C. "Can We Trust HDLC?" *Computer Communications Review*, October 1995.

KLEI92   Kleinrock, L. "The Latency/Bandwidth Tradeoff in Gigabit Networks." *IEEE Communications Magazine*, April 1992.

KLEI93   Kleinrock, L. "On the Modeling and Analysis of Computer Networks." *Proceedings of the IEEE*, August 1993.

KONH80   Konheim, A. "A Queuing Analysis of Two ARQ Protocols." *IEEE Transactions on Communications*, July 1980.

LIN84   Lin, S.; Costello, D.; and Miller, M. "Automatic-Repeat-Request Error-Control Schemes." *IEEE Communications Magazine*, December 1984.

SPRA91   Spragins, J.; Hammond, J.; and Pawlikowski, K. *Telecommunications: Protocols and Design.* Reading, MA: Addison-Wesley, 1991.

WALR98   Walrand, J. *Communication Networks: A First Course.* New York: McGraw-Hill, 1998.

ZORZ96   Zorzi, M., and Rao, R. "On the Use of Renewal Theory in the Analysis of ARQ Protocols." *IEEE Transactions on Communications*, September 1996.

7.5 KEY TERMS, REVIEW QUESTIONS, AND PROBLEMS

Key Terms

data frame	flow control	piggybacking
data link	frame synchronization	selective-reject ARQ
data link control protocol	go-back-N ARQ	sliding-window flow control
data transparency	header	stop-and-wait ARQ
error control	high-level data link control	stop-and-wait flow control
flag field	(HDLC)	trailer

Review Questions

7.1 List and briefly define some of the requirements for effective communications over a data link.

7.2 Define flow control.

7.3 Describe stop-and-wait flow control.

7.4 What are reasons for breaking a long data transmission up into a number of frames?

7.5   Describe sliding-window flow control.

7.6   What is the advantage of sliding-window flow control compared to stop-and-wait flow control?

7.7   What is piggybacking?

7.8   Define error control.

7.9   List common ingredients for error control for a link control protocol.

7.10   Describe automatic repeat request (ARQ).

7.11   List and briefly define three versions of ARQ.

7.12   What are the station types supported by HDLC? Describe each.

7.13   What are the transfer modes supported by HDLC? Describe each.

7.14   What is the purpose of the flag field?

7.15   Define *data transparency*.

7.16   What are the three frame types supported by HDLC? Describe each.

Problems

7.1   Consider a half-duplex point-to-point link using a stop-and-wait scheme, in which a series of messages is sent, with each message segmented into a number of frames. Ignore errors and frame overhead.
   a.   What is the effect on line utilization of increasing the message size so that fewer messages will be required? Other factors remain constant.
   b.   What is the effect on line utilization of increasing the number of frames for a constant message size?
   c.   What is the effect on line utilization of increasing frame size?

7.2   A channel has a data rate of 4 kbps and a propagation delay of 20 ms. For what range of frame sizes does stop-and-wait give an efficiency of at least 50%?

7.3   Consider the use of 1000-bit frames on a 1-Mbps satellite channel with a 270-ms delay. What is the maximum link utilization for
   a.   Stop-and-wait flow control?
   b.   Continuous flow control with a window size of 7?
   c.   Continuous flow control with a window size of 127?
   d.   Continuous flow control with a window size of 255?

7.4   In Figure 7.10 frames are generated at node A and sent to node C through node B. Determine the minimum data rate required between nodes B and C so that the buffers of node B are not flooded, based on the following:

   The data rate between A and B is 100 kbps.
   The propagation delay is 5 μs/km for both lines.
   There are full-duplex lines between the nodes.
   All data frames are 1000 bits long; ACK frames are separate frames of negligible length.
   Between A and B, a sliding-window protocol with a window size of 3 is used.
   Between B and C, stop-and-wait is used.
   There are no errors.

   Hint: In order not to flood the buffers of B, the average number of frames entering and leaving B must be the same over a long interval.

Figure 7.10   Configuration for Problem 7.4

7.5 A channel has a data rate of R bps and a propagation delay of t s/km The distance between the sending and receiving nodes is L kilometers. Nodes exchange fixed-size frames of B bits. Find a formula that gives the minimum sequence field size of the frame as a function of $R, t, B,$ and L (considering maximum utilization). Assume that ACK frames are negligible in size and the processing at the nodes is instantaneous.

7.6 No mention was made of reject (REJ) frames in the stop-and-wait ARQ discussion. Why is it not necessary to have REJ0 and REJ1 for stop-and-wait ARQ?

7.7 Suppose that a selective-reject ARQ is used where $W = 4$. Show, by example, that a 3-bit sequence number is needed.

7.8 Using the same assumptions that are used for Figure 7.13 in Appendix 7A, plot line utilization as a function of P, the probability that a single frame is in error for the following error-control techniques:
   a. Stop-and-wait
   b. Go-back-N with $W = 7$
   c. Go-back-N with $W = 127$
   d. Selective reject with $W = 7$
   e. Selective reject with $W = 127$
   Do all of the preceding for the following values of a: 0.1, 1, 10, 100. Draw conclusions about which technique is appropriate for various ranges of a.

7.9 Two neighboring nodes (A and B) use a sliding-window protocol with a 3-bit sequence number. As the ARQ mechanism, go-back-N is used with a window size of 4. Assuming A is transmitting and B is receiving, show the window positions for the following succession of events:
   a. Before A sends any frames
   b. After A sends frames 0, 1, 2 and receives acknowledgment from B for 0 and 1
   c. After A sends frames 3, 4, and 5 and B acknowledges 4 and the ACK is received by A

7.10 Out-of-sequence acknowledgment cannot be used for selective-reject ARQ. That is, if frame i is rejected by station X, all subsequent I-frames and RR frames sent by X must have $N(R) = i$ until frame i is successfully received, even if other frames with $N(S) > i$ are successfully received in the meantime. One possible refinement is the following: $N(R) = j$ in an I-frame or an RR frame is interpreted to mean that frame $j - 1$ and all preceding frames are accepted except for those that have been explicitly rejected using an SREJ frame. Comment on any possible drawback to this scheme.

7.11 The ISO standard for HDLC procedures (ISO 4335) includes the following definitions: (1) An REJ condition is considered cleared upon the receipt of an incoming I-frame with an $N(S)$ equal to the $N(R)$ of the outgoing REJ frame; and (2) a SREJ condition is considered cleared upon the receipt of an I-frame with an $N(S)$ equal to the $N(R)$ of the SREJ frame. The standard includes rules concerning the relationship between REJ and SREJ frames. These rules indicate what is allowable (in terms of transmitting REJ and SREJ frames) if an REJ condition has not yet been cleared and what is allowable if an SREJ condition has not yet been cleared. Deduce the rules and justify your answer.

7.12 Two stations communicate via a 1-Mbps satellite link with a propagation delay of 270 ms. The satellite serves merely to retransmit data received from one station to another, with negligible switching delay. Using HDLC frames of 1024 bits with 3-bit sequence numbers, what is the maximum possible data throughput; that is, what is the throughput of data bits carried in HDLC frames?

7.13 It is clear that bit stuffing is needed for the address, data, and FCS fields of an HDLC frame. Is it needed for the control field?

7.14 Suggest improvements to the bit stuffing-algorithm to overcome the problems of single-bit errors.

7.15 Using the example bit string of Figure 7.8, show the signal pattern on the line using NRZ-L coding. Does this suggest a side benefit of bit stuffing?

7.16 Assume that the primary HDLC station in NRM has sent six I-frames to a secondary. The primary's $N(S)$ count was three (011 binary) prior to sending the six frames. If the poll bit is on in the sixth frame, what will be the N(R) count back from the secondary after the last frame? Assume error-free operation.

7.17 Consider that several physical links connect two stations. We would like to use a "multilink HDLC" that makes efficient use of these links by sending frames on a FIFO basis on the next available link. What enhancements to HDLC are needed?

7.18 A World Wide Web server is usually set up to receive relatively small messages from its clients but to transmit potentially very large messages to them. Explain, then, which type of ARQ protocol (selective reject, go-back-N) would provide less of a burden to a particularly popular WWW server.

APPENDIX 7A PERFORMANCE ISSUES

In this appendix, we examine some of the performance issues related to the use of sliding-window flow control.

Stop-and-Wait Flow Control

Let us determine the maximum potential efficiency of a half-duplex point-to-point line using the stop-and-wait scheme described in Section 7.1. Suppose that a long message is to be sent as a sequence of frames $F_1, F_2, \ldots, F_n$, in the following fashion:

- Station S_1 sends F_1.
- Station S_2 sends an acknowledgment.
- Station S_1 sends F_2.
- Station S_2 sends an acknowledgment.

$$\vdots$$

- Station S_1 sends F_n.
- Station S_2 sends an acknowledgment.

The total time to send the data, T, can be expressed as $t = nT_F$, where T_F is the time to send one frame and receive an acknowledgment. We can express T_F as follows:

$$T_F = t_{prop} + t_{frame} + t_{proc} + t_{prop} + t_{ack} + t_{proc}$$

where

t_{prop} = propagation time from S_1 to S_2

t_{frame} = time to transmit a frame (time for the transmitter to send out all of the bits of the frame)

t_{proc} = processing time at each station to react to an incoming event

t_{ack} = time to transmit an acknowledgment

Let us assume that the processing time is relatively negligible, and that the acknowledgment frame is very small compared to a data frame, both of which are reasonable assumptions. Then we can express the total time to send the data as

$$T = n(2t_{prop} + t_{frame})$$

Of that time, only $n \times t_{frame}$ is actually spent transmitting data and the rest is overhead. The utilization, or efficiency, of the line is

$$U = \frac{n \times t_{frame}}{n(2t_{prop} + t_{frame})} = \frac{t_{frame}}{2t_{prop} + t_{frame}} \tag{7.3}$$

It is useful to define the parameter $a = t_{prop}/t_{frame}$ (see Figure 7.2). Then

$$U = \frac{1}{1 + 2a} \tag{7.4}$$

This is the maximum possible utilization of the link. Because the frame contains overhead bits, actual utilization is lower. The parameter a is constant if both t_{prop} and t_{frame} are constants, which is typically the case: Fixed-length frames are often used for all except the last frame in a sequence, and the propagation delay is constant for point-to-point links.

To get some insight into Equation (7.4), let us derive a different expression for a. We have

$$a = \frac{\text{Propagation Time}}{\text{Transmission Time}} \tag{7.5}$$

The propagation time is equal to the distance d of the link divided by the velocity of propagation V. For unguided transmission through air or space, V is the speed of light, approximately 3×10^8 m/s. For guided transmission, V is approximately 0.67 times the speed of light for optical fiber and copper media. The transmission time is equal to the length of the frame in bits, L, divided by the data rate R. Therefore,

$$a = \frac{d/V}{L/V} = \frac{Rd}{VL}$$

Thus, for fixed-length frames, a is proportional to the data rate times the length of the medium. A useful way of looking at a is that it represents the length of the medium in bits $\left[R \times \left(\frac{d}{V} \right) \right]$ compared to the frame length (L).

With this interpretation in mind, Figure 7.2 illustrates Equation (7.4). In this figure, transmission time is normalized to 1 and hence the propagation time, by Equation (7.5), is a. For the case of $a < 1$, the link's bit length is less than that of the frame. The station T begins transmitting a frame at time t_0. At $t_0 + a$, the leading edge of the frame reaches the receiving station R, while T is still in the process of transmitting the frame. At $t_0 + 1$, T completes transmission. At $t_0 + 1 + a$, R has received the entire frame and immediately transmits a small acknowledgment frame. This acknowledgment arrives back at T at $t_0 + 1 + 2a$. Total elapsed time: $1 + 2a$. Total transmission time: 1. Hence utilization is $1/(1 + 2a)$. The same result is achieved with $a > 1$, as illustrated in Figure 7.2.

> **Example 7.3**   First, consider a wide area network (WAN) using ATM (asynchronous transfer mode, described in Part Three), with the two stations a thousand kilometers apart. The standard ATM frame size (called a cell) is 424 bits and one of the standardized data rates is 155.52 Mbps. Thus, transmission time equals $424/(155.52 \times 10^6) = 2.7 \times 10^{-6}$ seconds. If we assume an optical fiber link, then the propagation time is $(10^6 \text{ meters})/(2 \times 10^8 \text{ m/s}) = 0.5 \times 10^{-2}$ seconds. Thus, $a = (0.5 \times 10^{-2})/(2.7 \times 10^{-6}) \approx 1850$, and efficiency is only $1/3701 = 0.00027$.
>
> At the other extreme, in terms of distance, is the local area network (LAN). Distances range from 0.1 to 10 km, with data rates of 10 Mbps to 1 Gbps; higher data rates tend to be associated with shorter distances. Using a value of $V = 2 \times 10^8$ m/s, a frame size of 1000 bits, and a data rate of 10 Mbps, the value of a is in the range of 0.005 to 0.5. This yields a utilization in the range of 0.5 to 0.99. For a 100-Mbps LAN, given the shorter distances, comparable utilizations are possible.
>
> We can see that LANs are typically quite efficient, whereas high-speed WANs are not. As a final example, let us consider digital data transmission via modem over a voice-grade line. A typical data rate is 56 kbps. Again, let us consider a 1000-bit frame. The link distance can be anywhere from a few tens of meters to thousands of kilometers. If we pick, say, as a short distance $d = 1000$ m, then $a = (56{,}000 \text{ bps} \times 1000 \text{ m})/(2 \times 10^8 \text{ m/s} \times 1000 \text{ bits}) = 2.8 \times 10^{-4}$, and utilization is effectively 1.0. Even in a long-distance case, such as $d = 5000$ km, we have $a = (56{,}000 \times 5 \times 10^6)/(2 \times 10^8 \times 1000 \text{ bits}) = 1.4$ and efficiency equals 0.26.

Error-Free Sliding-Window Flow Control

For sliding-window flow control, the throughput on the line depends on both the window size W and the value of a. For convenience, let us again normalize frame transmission time to a value of 1; thus, the propagation time is a. Figure 7.11 illustrates the efficiency of a full duplex point-to-point line.[2] Station A begins to emit a sequence of frames at time $t = 0$. The leading edge of the first frame reaches station B at $t = a$. The first frame is entirely absorbed by $t = a + 1$. Assuming negligible processing time, B can immediately acknowledge the first frame (ACK). Let us also assume that the acknowledgment frame is so small that transmission time is negligible. Then the ACK reaches A at $t = 2a + 1$. To evaluate performance, we need to consider two cases:

- **Case 1:** $W \geq 2a + 1$. The acknowledgment for frame 1 reaches A before A has exhausted its window. Thus, A can transmit continuously with no pause and normalized throughput is 1.0.

---

[2]For simplicity, we assume that a is an integer, so that an integer number of frames exactly fills the line. The argument does not change for noninteger values of a.

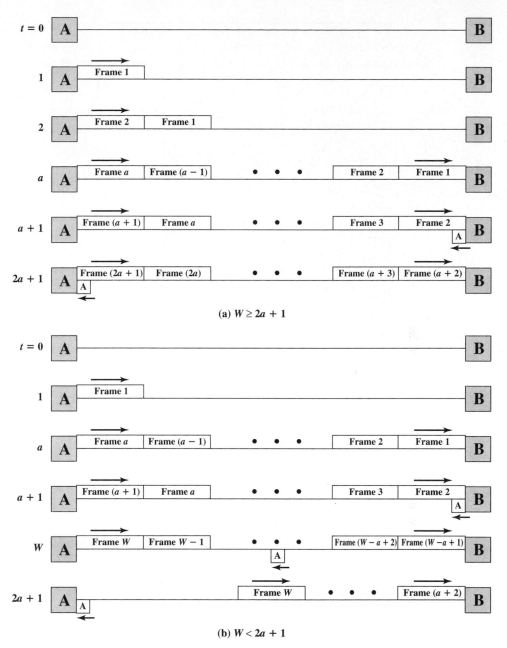

Figure 7.11 Timing of Sliding-Window Protocol

- **Case 2:** $W < 2a + 1$. A exhausts its window at $t = W$ and cannot send additional frames until $t = 2a + 1$. Thus, normalized throughput is W time units out of a period of $(2a + 1)$ time units.

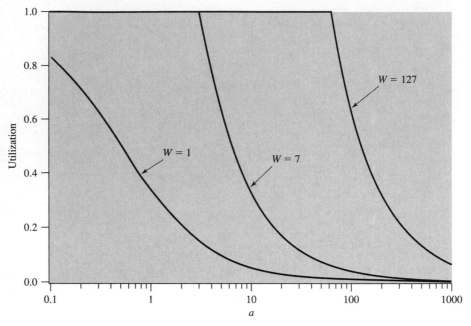

Figure 7.12 Sliding-Window Utilization as a Function of *a*

Therefore, we can express the utilization as

$$U = \begin{cases} 1 & W \geq 2a + 1 \\ \dfrac{W}{2a + 1} & W < 2a + 1 \end{cases} \tag{7.6}$$

Typically, the sequence number is provided for in an n-bit field and the maximum window size is $W = 2^n - 1$ (not 2^n; this is explained in Section 7.2). Figure 7.12 shows the maximum utilization achievable for window sizes of 1, 7, and 127 as a function of a. A window size of 1 corresponds to stop and wait. A window size of 7 (3 bits) is adequate for many applications. A window size of 127 (7 bits) is adequate for larger values of a, such as may be found in high-speed WANs.

ARQ

We have seen that sliding-window flow control is more efficient than stop-and-wait flow control. We would expect that when error control functions are added that this would still be true: that is, that go-back-N and selective-reject ARQ are more efficient than stop-and-wait ARQ. Let us develop some approximations to determine the degree of improvement to be expected.

First, consider stop-and-wait ARQ. With no errors, the maximum utilization is $1/(1 + 2a)$ as shown in Equation (7.4). We want to account for the possibility that some frames are repeated because of bit errors. To start, note that the utilization U can be defined as

$$U = \frac{T_f}{T_t} \tag{7.7}$$

where

T_f = time for transmitter to emit a single frame

T_t = total time that line is engaged in the transmission of a single frame

For error-free operation using stop-and-wait ARQ,

$$U = \frac{T_f}{T_f + 2T_p}$$

where T_p is the propagation time. Dividing by T_f and remembering that $a = T_p/T_f$, we again have Equation (7.4). If errors occur, we must modify Equation (7.7) to

$$U = \frac{T_f}{N_r T_t}$$

where N_r is the expected number of transmissions of a frame. Thus, for stop-and-wait ARQ, we have

$$U = \frac{1}{N_r(1 + 2a)}$$

A simple expression for N_r can be derived by considering the probability P that a single frame is in error. If we assume that ACKs and NAKs are never in error, the probability that it will take exactly k attempts to transmit a frame successfully is $P^{k-1}(1 - P)$. That is, we have $(k - 1)$ unsuccessful attempts followed by one successful attempt; the probability of this occurring is just the product of the probability of the individual events occurring. Then[3]

$$N_r = E[\text{transmissions}] = \sum_{i=1}^{\infty} (i \times \text{Pr}[i \text{ transmissions}])$$

$$= \sum_{i=1}^{\infty} (iP^{i-1}(1 - P)) = \frac{1}{1 - P}$$

So we have:

Stop-and Wait:	$U = \dfrac{1 - P}{1 + 2a}$

---

[3] This derivation uses the equality $\sum_{i=1}^{\infty} (iX^{i-1}) = \dfrac{1}{(1 - X^2)}$ for $(-1 < X < 1)$.

For the sliding-window protocol, Equation (7.6) applies for error-free operation. For selective-reject ARQ, we can use the same reasoning as applied to stop-and-wait ARQ. That is, the error-free equations must be divided by N_r. Again, $N_r = 1/(1 - P)$. So

Selective Reject:
$$U = \begin{cases} 1 - P & W \geq 2a + 1 \\ \dfrac{W(1 - P)}{2a + 1} & W < 2a + 1 \end{cases}$$

The same reasoning applies for go-back-N ARQ, but we must be more careful in approximating N_r. Each error generates a requirement to retransmit K frames rather than just one frame. Thus

$$N_r = \text{E[number of transmitted frames to successfully transmit one frame]}$$

$$= \sum_{i=1}^{\infty} f(i)P^{i-1}(1 - P)$$

where $f(i)$ is the total number of frames transmitted if the original frame must be transmitted i times. This can be expressed as

$$f(i) = 1 + (i - 1)K$$
$$= (1 - K) + Ki$$

Substituting yields[4]

$$N_r = (1 - K) \sum_{i=1}^{\infty} P^{i-1}(1 - P) + K \sum_{i=1}^{\infty} iP^{i-1}(1 - P)$$

$$= 1 - K + \frac{K}{1 - P}$$

$$= \frac{1 - P + KP}{1 - P}$$

By studying Figure 7.11, the reader should conclude that K is approximately equal to $(2a + 1)$ for $W \geq (2a + 1)$, and $K = W$ for $W < (2a + 1)$. Thus

Go-back-N:
$$U = \begin{cases} \dfrac{1 - P}{1 + 2aP} & W \geq 2a + 1 \\ \dfrac{W(1 - P)}{(2a + 1)(1 - P + WP)} & W < 2a + 1 \end{cases}$$

---

[4] This derivation uses the equality $\displaystyle\sum_{i=1}^{\infty} X^{i-1} = \frac{1}{(1 - X)}$ for $(-1 < X < 1)$.

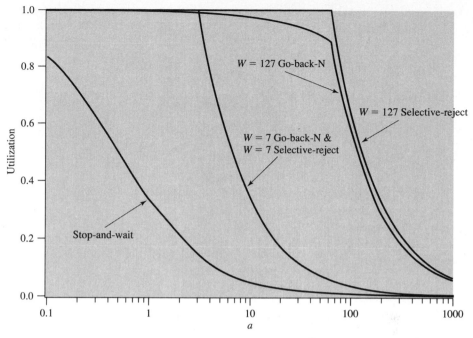

Figure 7.13 ARQ Utilization as a Function of a ($P = 10^{-3}$)

Note that for $W = 1$, both selective-reject and go-back-N ARQ reduce to stop and wait. Figure 7.13[5] compares these three error control techniques for a value of $P = 10^{-3}$. This figure and the equations are only approximations. For example, we have ignored errors in acknowledgment frames and, in the case of go-back-N, errors in retransmitted frames other than the frame initially in error. However, the results do give an indication of the relative performance of the three techniques.

---

[5] For $W = 7$, the curves for go-back-N and selective-reject are so close that they appear to be identical in the figure.

CHAPTER **8**

MULTIPLEXING

KEY POINTS

- To make efficient use of high-speed telecommunications lines, some form of multiplexing is used. Multiplexing allows several transmission sources to share a larger transmission capacity. The two common forms of multiplexing are frequency division multiplexing (FDM) and time division multiplexing (TDM).

- **Frequency division multiplexing** can be used with analog signals. A number of signals are carried simultaneously on the same medium by allocating to each signal a different frequency band. Modulation equipment is needed to move each signal to the required frequency band, and multiplexing equipment is needed to combine the modulated signals.

- **Synchronous time division multiplexing** can be used with digital signals or analog signals carrying digital data. In this form of multiplexing, data from various sources are carried in repetitive frames. Each frame consists of a set of time slots, and each source is assigned one or more time slots per frame. The effect is to interleave bits of data from the various sources.

- **Statistical time division multiplexing** provides a generally more efficient service than synchronous TDM for the support of terminals. With statistical TDM, time slots are not preassigned to particular data sources. Rather, user data are buffered and transmitted as rapidly as possible using available time slots.

In Chapter 7, we described efficient techniques for utilizing a data link under heavy load. Specifically, with two devices connected by a point-to-point link, it is generally desirable to have multiple frames outstanding so that the data link does not become a bottleneck between the stations. Now consider the opposite problem. Typically, two communicating stations will not utilize the full capacity of a data link. For efficiency, it should be possible to share that capacity. A generic term for such sharing is *multiplexing*.

A common application of multiplexing is in long-haul communications. Trunks on long-haul networks are high-capacity fiber, coaxial, or microwave links. These links can carry large numbers of voice and data transmissions simultaneously using multiplexing.

Figure 8.1 depicts the multiplexing function in its simplest form. There are n inputs to a multiplexer. The multiplexer is connected by a single data link to a

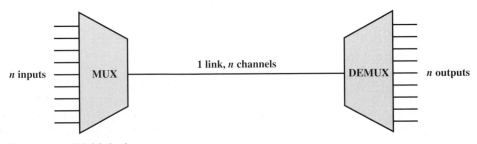

n inputs — MUX   1 link, n channels   DEMUX — n outputs

Figure 8.1 Multiplexing

demultiplexer. The link is able to carry n separate channels of data. The multiplexer combines (multiplexes) data from the n input lines and transmits over a higher-capacity data link. The demultiplexer accepts the multiplexed data stream, separates (demultiplexes) the data according to channel, and delivers them to the appropriate output lines.

The widespread use of multiplexing in data communications can be explained by the following:

- The higher the data rate, the more cost-effective the transmission facility. That is, for a given application and over a given distance, the cost per kbps declines with an increase in the data rate of the transmission facility. Similarly, the cost of transmission and receiving equipment, per kbps, declines with increasing data rate.

- Most individual data communicating devices require relatively modest data rate support. For example, for many terminal and personal computer applications that do not involve Web access or intensive graphics, a data rate of between 9600 bps and 64 kbps is generally adequate.

The preceding statements were phrased in terms of data communicating devices. Similar statements apply to voice communications. That is, the greater the capacity of a transmission facility, in terms of voice channels, the less the cost per individual voice channel, and the capacity required for a single voice channel is modest.

This chapter concentrates on three types of multiplexing techniques. The first, frequency division multiplexing (FDM), is the most heavily used and is familiar to anyone who has ever used a radio or television set. The second is a particular case of time division multiplexing (TDM) known as synchronous TDM. This is commonly used for multiplexing digitized voice streams and data streams. The third type seeks to improve on the efficiency of synchronous TDM by adding complexity to the multiplexer. It is known by a variety of names, including statistical TDM, asynchronous TDM, and intelligent TDM. This book uses the term *statistical TDM*, which highlights one of its chief properties. Finally, we look at the digital subscriber line, which combines FDM and synchronous TDM technologies.

8.1 FREQUENCY DIVISION MULTIPLEXING

Characteristics

FDM is possible when the useful bandwidth of the transmission medium exceeds the required bandwidth of signals to be transmitted. A number of signals can be carried simultaneously if each signal is modulated onto a different carrier frequency and the carrier frequencies are sufficiently separated that the bandwidths of the signals do not significantly overlap. A general case of FDM is shown in Figure 8.2a. Six signal sources are fed into a multiplexer, which modulates each signal onto a different frequency $(f_1, \ldots, f_6)$. Each modulated signal requires a

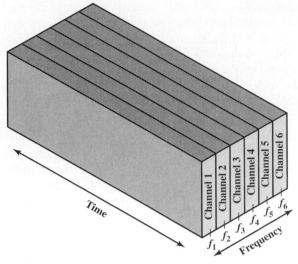

(a) Frequency division multiplexing

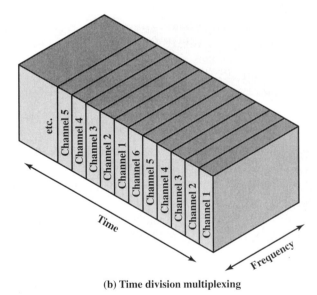

(b) Time division multiplexing

Figure 8.2 FDM and TDM

certain bandwidth centered on its carrier frequency, referred to as a **channel**. To prevent interference, the channels are separated by guard bands, which are unused portions of the spectrum.

The composite signal transmitted across the medium is analog. Note, however, that the input signals may be either digital or analog. In the case of digital input, the input signals must be passed through modems to be converted to analog. In either case, each input analog signal must then be modulated to move it to the appropriate frequency band.

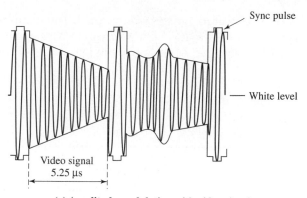

(a) Amplitude modulation with video signal

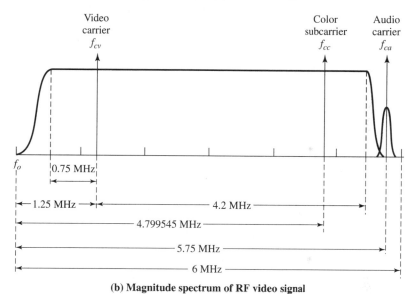

(b) Magnitude spectrum of RF video signal

Figure 8.3 Transmitted TV Signal

Example 8.1 A familiar example of FDM is broadcast and cable television. The television signal discussed in Chapter 3 fits comfortably into a 6-MHz bandwidth. Figure 8.3 depicts the transmitted TV signal and its bandwidth. The black-and-white video signal is AM modulated on a carrier signal f_{cv}. Because the baseband video signal has a bandwidth of 4 MHz, we would expect the modulated signal to have a bandwidth of 8 MHz centered on f_{cv}. To conserve bandwidth, the signal is passed through a sideband filter so that most of the lower sideband is suppressed. The resulting signal extends from about $f_{cv} - 0.75$ MHz to $f_{cv} + 4.2$ MHz. A separate color carrier, f_{cc}, is used to transmit color information. This is spaced far enough from f_{cv} that there is essentially no interference. Finally, the audio portion of the signal is modulated on f_{ca}, outside the effective bandwidth of the other two signals. A bandwidth of 50 kHz is allocated for the audio signal. The composite signal fits into a 6-MHz bandwidth with the video, color, and audio signal carriers at 1.25 MHz, 4.799545 MHz, and 5.75 MHz above the lower edge of the band, respectively. Thus, multiple TV signals can be frequency division multiplexed on a CATV cable, each with a bandwidth of 6 MHz. Given the enormous bandwidth of coaxial cable (as much as 500 MHz), dozens of TV signals can be simultaneously carried using FDM. Of course, using radio-frequency propagation through the atmosphere is also a form of FDM.

A generic depiction of an FDM system is shown in Figure 8.4. A number of analog or digital signals $[m_i(t), i = 1, n]$ are to be multiplexed onto the same transmission

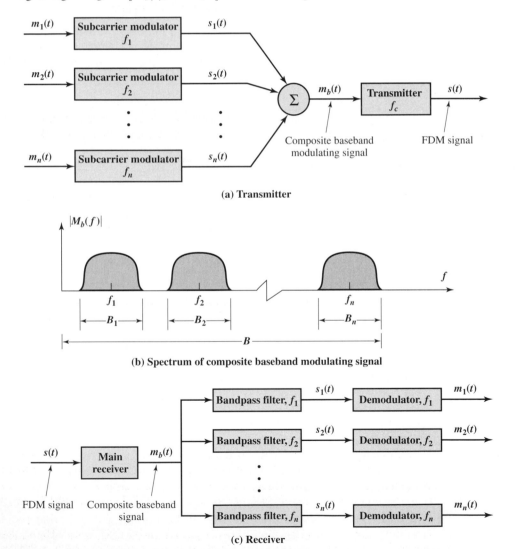

(a) Transmitter

(b) Spectrum of composite baseband modulating signal

(c) Receiver

Figure 8.4 FDM System [COUC01]

medium. Each signal $m_i(t)$ is modulated onto a carrier f_i; because multiple carriers are to be used, each is referred to as a **subcarrier**. Any type of modulation may be used. The resulting analog, modulated signals are then summed to produce a composite baseband[1] signal $m_b(t)$. Figure 8.4b shows the result. The spectrum of signal $m_i(t)$ is shifted to be centered on f_i. For this scheme to work, f_i must be chosen so that the bandwidths of the various signals do not significantly overlap. Otherwise, it will be impossible to recover the original signals.

The composite signal may then be shifted as a whole to another carrier frequency by an additional modulation step. We will see examples of this later. This second modulation step need not use the same modulation technique as the first.

The FDM signal $s(t)$ has a total bandwidth B, where $B > \sum_{i=1}^{n} B_i$. This analog signal may be transmitted over a suitable medium. At the receiving end, the FDM signal is demodulated to retrieve $m_b(t)$, which is then passed through n bandpass filters, each filter centered on f_i and having a bandwidth B_i, for $1 \le i \le n$. In this way, the signal is again split into its component parts. Each component is then demodulated to recover the original signal.

Example 8.2 Let us consider a simple example of transmitting three voice signals simultaneously over a medium. As was mentioned, the bandwidth of a voice signal is generally taken to be 4 kHz, with an effective spectrum of 300 to 3400 Hz (Figure 8.5a). If such a signal is used to amplitude-modulate a 64-kHz carrier, the spectrum of Figure 8.5b results. The modulated signal has a bandwidth of 8 kHz, extending from 60 to 68 kHz. To make efficient use of bandwidth, we elect to transmit only the lower sideband. If three voice signals are used to modulate carriers at 64, 68, and 72 kHz, and only the lower sideband of each is taken, the spectrum of Figure 8.5c results.

This figure points out two problems that an FDM system must cope with. The first is crosstalk, which may occur if the spectra of adjacent component signals overlap significantly. In the case of voice signals, with an effective bandwidth of only 3100 Hz (300 to 3400), a 4-kHz bandwidth is adequate. The spectra of signals produced by modems for voiceband transmission also fit well in this bandwidth. Another potential problem is intermodulation noise, which was discussed in Chapter 3. On a long link, the nonlinear effects of amplifiers on a signal in one channel could produce frequency components in other channels.

Analog Carrier Systems

The long-distance carrier system provided in the United States and throughout the world is designed to transmit voiceband signals over high-capacity transmission links, such as coaxial cable and microwave systems. The earliest, and still a very common, technique for utilizing high-capacity links is FDM. In the United States, AT&T

---

[1]The term *baseband* is used to designate the band of frequencies of the signal delivered by the source and potentially used as a modulating signal. Typically, the spectrum of a baseband signal is significant in a band that includes or is in the vicinity of $f = 0$.

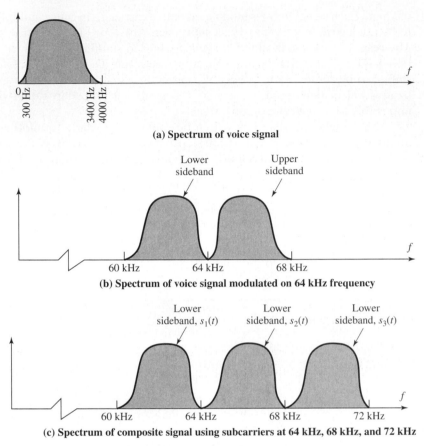

(a) Spectrum of voice signal

(b) Spectrum of voice signal modulated on 64 kHz frequency

(c) Spectrum of composite signal using subcarriers at 64 kHz, 68 kHz, and 72 kHz

Figure 8.5   FDM of Three Voiceband Signals

has designated a hierarchy of FDM schemes to accommodate transmission systems of various capacities. A similar, but unfortunately not identical, system has been adopted internationally under the auspices of ITU-T (Table 8.1).

At the first level of the AT&T hierarchy, 12 voice channels are combined to produce a group signal with a bandwidth of $12 \times 4\,kHz = 48\,kHz$, in the range 60 to 108 kHz. The signals are produced in a fashion similar to that described previously, using subcarrier frequencies of from 64 to 108 kHz in increments of 4 kHz. The next basic building block is the 60-channel supergroup, which is formed by frequency division multiplexing five group signals. At this step, each group is treated as a single signal with a 48 kHz bandwidth and is modulated by a subcarrier. The subcarriers have frequencies from 420 to 612 kHz in increments of 48 kHz. The resulting signal occupies 312 to 552 kHz.

There are several variations to supergroup formation. Each of the five inputs to the supergroup multiplexer may be a group channel containing 12 multiplexed voice signals. In addition, any signal up to 48 kHz wide whose bandwidth is contained within 60 to 108 kHz may be used as input to the supergroup multiplexer. As another variation, it is possible to combine 60 voiceband channels into a super-

Table 8.1 North American and International FDM Carrier Standards

Number of Voice Channels	Bandwidth	Spectrum	AT&T	ITU-T
12	48 kHz	60–108 kHz	Group	Group
60	240 kHz	312–552 kHz	Supergroup	Supergroup
300	1.232 MHz	812–2044 kHz		Mastergroup
600	2.52 MHz	564–3084 kHz	Mastergroup	
900	3.872 MHz	8.516–12.388 MHz		Supermaster group
$N \times 600$			Mastergroup multiplex	
3,600	16.984 MHz	0.564–17.548 MHz	Jumbogroup	
10,800	57.442 MHz	3.124–60.566 MHz	Jumbogroup multiplex	

group. This may reduce multiplexing costs where an interface with existing group multiplexer is not required.

The next level of the hierarchy is the mastergroup, which combines 10 supergroup inputs. Again, any signal with a bandwidth of 240 kHz in the range 312 to 552 kHz can serve as input to the mastergroup multiplexer. The mastergroup has a bandwidth of 2.52 MHz and can support 600 voice frequency (VF) channels. Higher-level multiplexing is defined above the mastergroup, as shown in Table 8.1.

Note that the original voice or data signal may be modulated many times. For example, a data signal may be encoded using QPSK to form an analog voice signal. This signal could then be used to modulate a 76-kHz carrier to form a component of a group signal. This group signal could then be used to modulate a 516-kHz carrier to form a component of a supergroup signal. Each stage can distort the original data; this is so, for example, if the modulator/multiplexer contains nonlinearities or introduces noise.

Wavelength Division Multiplexing

The true potential of optical fiber is fully exploited when multiple beams of light at different frequencies are transmitted on the same fiber. This is a form of frequency division multiplexing (FDM) but is commonly called wavelength division multiplexing (WDM). With WDM, the light streaming through the fiber consists of many colors, or wavelengths, each carrying a separate channel of data. In 1997, a landmark was reached when Bell Laboratories was able to demonstrate a WDM system with 100 beams each operating at 10 Gbps, for a total data rate of 1 trillion bits per second (also referred to as 1 terabit per second or 1 Tbps). Commercial systems with 160 channels of 10 Gbps are now available. In a lab environment, Alcatel has carried 256 channels at 39.8 Gbps each, a total of 10.1 Tbps, over a 100-km span.

A typical WDM system has the same general architecture as other FDM systems. A number of sources generate a laser beam at different wavelengths. These are

Table 8.2   ITU WDM Channel Spacing (G.692)

Frequency (THz)	Wavelength in Vacuum (nm)	50 GHz	100 GHz	200 GHz
196.10	1528.77	X	X	X
196.05	1529.16	X		
196.00	1529.55	X	X	
195.95	1529.94	X		
195.90	1530.33	X	X	X
195.85	1530.72	X		
195.80	1531.12	X	X	
195.75	1531.51	X		
195.70	1531.90	X	X	X
195.65	1532.29	X		
195.60	1532.68	X	X	
...	...			
192.10	1560.61	X	X	X

sent to a multiplexer, which consolidates the sources for transmission over a single fiber line. Optical amplifiers, typically spaced tens of kilometers apart, amplify all of the wavelengths simultaneously. Finally, the composite signal arrives at a demultiplexer, where the component channels are separated and sent to receivers at the destination point.

Most WDM systems operate in the 1550-nm range. In early systems, 200 MHz was allocated to each channel, but today most WDM systems use 50-GHz spacing. The channel spacing defined in ITU-T G.692, which accommodates 80 50-GHz channels, is summarized in Table 8.2.

The term **dense wavelength division multiplexing** (DWDM) is often seen in the literature. There is no official or standard definition of this term. The term connotes the use of more channels, more closely spaced, than ordinary WDM. In general, a channel spacing of 200 GHz or less could be considered dense.

8.2 SYNCHRONOUS TIME DIVISION MULTIPLEXING

Characteristics

Synchronous time division multiplexing is possible when the achievable data rate (sometimes, unfortunately, called bandwidth) of the medium exceeds the data rate of digital signals to be transmitted. Multiple digital signals (or analog signals carrying digital data) can be carried on a single transmission path by interleaving portions of each signal in time. The interleaving can be at the bit level or in blocks of bytes or larger quantities. For example, the multiplexer in Figure 8.2b has six inputs that might each be, say, 9.6 kbps. A single line with a capacity of at least 57.6 kbps (plus overhead capacity) could accommodate all six sources.

A generic depiction of a synchronous TDM system is provided in Figure 8.6. A number of signals $[m_i(t), i = 1, n]$ are to be multiplexed onto the same transmission medium. The signals carry digital data and are generally digital signals. The incoming data from each source are briefly buffered. Each buffer is typically one bit or one character in length. The buffers are scanned sequentially to form a composite digital data stream $m_c(t)$. The scan operation is sufficiently rapid so that each buffer is emptied before more data can arrive. Thus, the data rate of $m_c(t)$ must at least equal the sum of the data rates of the $m_i(t)$. The digital signal $m_c(t)$ may be transmitted directly, or passed through a modem so that an analog signal is transmitted. In either case, transmission is typically synchronous.

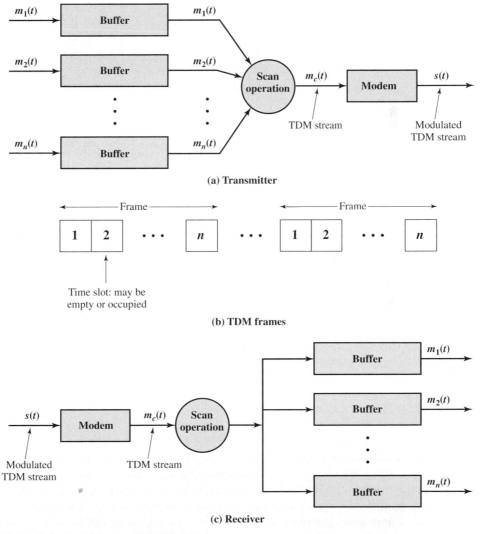

(a) Transmitter

(b) TDM frames

(c) Receiver

Figure 8.6 Synchronous TDM System

The transmitted data may have a format something like Figure 8.6b. The data are organized into **frames**. Each frame contains a cycle of time slots. In each frame, one or more slots are dedicated to each data source. The sequence of slots dedicated to one source, from frame to frame, is called a **channel**. The slot length equals the transmitter buffer length, typically a bit or a byte (character).

The byte-interleaving technique is used with asynchronous and synchronous sources. Each time slot contains one character of data. Typically, the start and stop bits of each character are eliminated before transmission and reinserted by the receiver, thus improving efficiency. The bit-interleaving technique is used with synchronous sources and may also be used with asynchronous sources. Each time slot contains just one bit.

At the receiver, the interleaved data are demultiplexed and routed to the appropriate destination buffer. For each input source $m_i(t)$, there is an identical output destination that will receive the output data at the same rate at which it was generated.

Synchronous TDM is called synchronous not because synchronous transmission is used, but because the time slots are preassigned to sources and fixed. The time slots for each source are transmitted whether or not the source has data to send. This is, of course, also the case with FDM. In both cases, capacity is wasted to achieve simplicity of implementation. Even when fixed assignment is used, however, it is possible for a synchronous TDM device to handle sources of different data rates. For example, the slowest input device could be assigned one slot per cycle, while faster devices are assigned multiple slots per cycle.

TDM Link Control

The reader will note that the transmitted data stream depicted in Figure 8.6b does not contain the headers and trailers that we have come to associate with synchronous transmission. The reason is that the control mechanisms provided by a data link protocol are not needed. It is instructive to ponder this point, and we do so by considering two key data link control mechanisms: flow control and error control. It should be clear that, as far as the multiplexer and demultiplexer (Figure 8.1) are concerned, flow control is not needed. The data rate on the multiplexed line is fixed, and the multiplexer and demultiplexer are designed to operate at that rate. But suppose that one of the individual output lines attaches to a device that is temporarily unable to accept data. Should the transmission of TDM frames cease? Clearly not, because the remaining output lines are expecting to receive data at predetermined times. The solution is for the saturated output device to cause the flow of data from the corresponding input device to cease. Thus, for a while, the channel in question will carry empty slots, but the frames as a whole will maintain the same transmission rate.

The reasoning for error control is the same. It would not do to request retransmission of an entire TDM frame because an error occurs on one channel. The devices using the other channels do not want a retransmission nor would they know that a retransmission has been requested by some other device on another channel. Again, the solution is to apply error control on a per-channel basis.

Flow control and error control can be provided on a per-channel basis by using a data link control protocol such as HDLC on a per-channel basis. A simplified

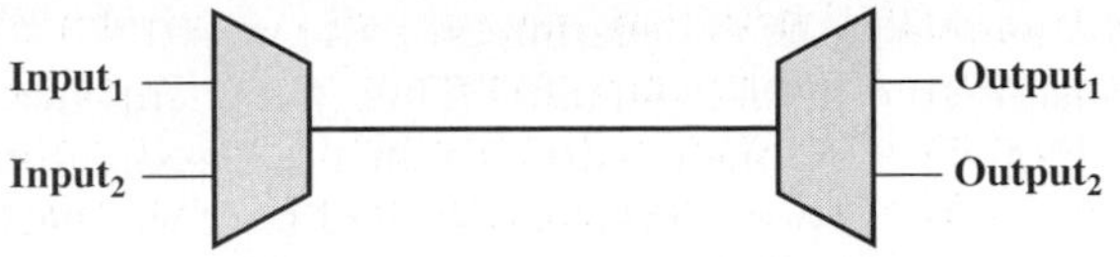

(a) Configuration

Input$_1$ ·········· F$_1$ f$_1$ f$_1$ d$_1$ d$_1$ d$_1$ C$_1$ A$_1$ F$_1$ f$_1$ f$_1$ d$_1$ d$_1$ d$_1$ C$_1$ A$_1$ F$_1$

Input$_2$ ··· F$_2$ f$_2$ f$_2$ d$_2$ d$_2$ d$_2$ d$_2$ C$_2$ A$_2$ F$_2$ f$_2$ f$_2$ d$_2$ d$_2$ d$_2$ d$_2$ C$_2$ A$_2$ F$_2$

(b) Input data streams

··· f$_2$ F$_1$ d$_2$ f$_1$ d$_2$ f$_1$ d$_2$ d$_1$ d$_2$ d$_1$ C$_2$ d$_1$ A$_2$ C$_1$ F$_2$ A$_1$ f$_2$ F$_1$ f$_2$ f$_1$ d$_2$ f$_1$ d$_2$ d$_1$ d$_2$ d$_1$ d$_2$ d$_1$ C$_2$ C$_1$ A$_2$ A$_1$ F$_2$ F$_1$

(c) Multiplexed data stream

Legend: F = flag field   d = one octet of data field
       A = address field f = one octet of FCS field
       C = control field

Figure 8.7   Use of Data Link Control on TDM Channels

example is shown in Figure 8.7. We assume two data sources, each using HDLC. One is transmitting a stream of HDLC frames containing three octets of data each, and the other is transmitting HDLC frames containing four octets of data. For clarity, we assume that character-interleaved multiplexing is used, although bit interleaving is more typical. Notice what is happening. The octets of the HDLC frames from the two sources are shuffled together for transmission over the multiplexed line. The reader may initially be uncomfortable with this diagram, because the HDLC frames have lost their integrity in some sense. For example, each frame check sequence (FCS) on the line applies to a disjointed set of bits. Even the FCS is not in one piece. However, the pieces are reassembled correctly before they are seen by the device on the other end of the HDLC protocol. In this sense, the multiplexing/demultiplexing operation is transparent to the attached stations; to each communicating pair of stations, it appears that they have a dedicated link.

One refinement is needed in Figure 8.7. Both ends of the line need to be a combination multiplexer/demultiplexer with a full-duplex line in between. Then each channel consists of two sets of slots, one traveling in each direction. The individual devices attached at each end can, in pairs, use HDLC to control their own channel. The multiplexer/demultiplexers need not be concerned with these matters.

Framing

We have seen that a link control protocol is not needed to manage the overall TDM link. There is, however, a basic requirement for framing. Because we are not providing flag or SYNC characters to bracket TDM frames, some means is needed to assure frame synchronization. It is clearly important to maintain framing synchronization because, if the source and destination are out of step, data on all channels are lost.

Perhaps the most common mechanism for framing is known as added-digit framing. In this scheme, typically, one control bit is added to each TDM frame. An identifiable pattern of bits, from frame to frame, is used on this "control channel."

A typical example is the alternating bit pattern, 101010 . . . . This is a pattern unlikely to be sustained on a data channel. Thus, to synchronize, a receiver compares the incoming bits of one frame position to the expected pattern. If the pattern does not match, successive bit positions are searched until the pattern persists over multiple frames. Once framing synchronization is established, the receiver continues to monitor the framing bit channel. If the pattern breaks down, the receiver must again enter a framing search mode.

Pulse Stuffing

Perhaps the most difficult problem in the design of a synchronous time division multiplexer is that of synchronizing the various data sources. If each source has a separate clock, any variation among clocks could cause loss of synchronization. Also, in some cases, the data rates of the input data streams are not related by a simple rational number. For both these problems, a technique known as pulse stuffing is an effective remedy. With pulse stuffing, the outgoing data rate of the multiplexer, excluding framing bits, is higher than the sum of the maximum instantaneous incoming rates. The extra capacity is used by stuffing extra dummy bits or pulses into each incoming signal until its rate is raised to that of a locally generated clock signal. The stuffed pulses are inserted at fixed locations in the multiplexer frame format so that they may be identified and removed at the demultiplexer.

Example 8.3   An example, from [COUC01], illustrates the use of synchronous TDM to multiplex digital and analog sources (Figure 8.8). Consider that there are 11 sources to be multiplexed on a single link:

Source 1: Analog, 2-kHz bandwidth
Source 2: Analog, 4-kHz bandwidth
Source 3: Analog, 2-kHz bandwidth
Sources 4–11: Digital, 7200 bps synchronous

As a first step, the analog sources are converted to digital using PCM. Recall from Chapter 5 that PCM is based on the sampling theorem, which dictates that a signal be sampled at a rate equal to twice its bandwidth. Thus, the required sampling rate is 4000 samples per second for sources 1 and 3, and 8000 samples per second for source 2. These samples, which are analog (PAM), must then be quantized or digitized. Let us assume that 4 bits are used for each analog sample. For convenience, these three sources will be multiplexed first, as a unit. At a scan rate of 4 kHz, one PAM sample each is taken from sources 1 and 3, and two PAM samples are taken from source 2 per scan. These four samples are interleaved and converted to 4-bit PCM samples. Thus, a total of 16 bits is generated at a rate of 4000 times per second, for a composite bit rate of 64 kbps.

For the digital sources, pulse stuffing is used to raise each source to a rate of 8 kbps, for an aggregate data rate of 64 kbps. A frame can consist of multiple cycles of 32 bits, each containing 16 PCM bits and two bits from each of the eight digital sources.

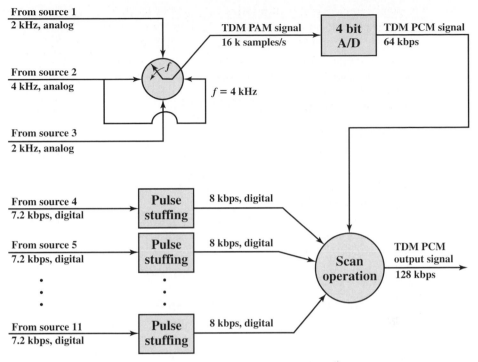

Figure 8.8 TDM of Analog and Digital Sources [COUC01]

Digital Carrier Systems

The long-distance carrier system provided in the United States and throughout the world was designed to transmit voice signals over high-capacity transmission links, such as optical fiber, coaxial cable, and microwave. Part of the evolution of these telecommunications networks to digital technology has been the adoption of synchronous TDM transmission structures. In the United States, AT&T developed a hierarchy of TDM structures of various capacities; this structure is used in Canada and Japan as well as the United States. A similar, but unfortunately not identical, hierarchy has been adopted internationally under the auspices of ITU-T (Table 8.3).

Table 8.3 North American and International TDM Carrier Standards

North American			International (ITU-T)		
Designation	Number of Voice Channels	Data Rate (Mbps)	Level	Number of Voice Channels	Data Rate (Mbps)
DS-1	24	1.544	1	30	2.048
DS-1C	48	3.152	2	120	8.448
DS-2	96	6.312	3	480	34.368
DS-3	672	44.736	4	1920	139.264
DS-4	4032	274.176	5	7680	565.148

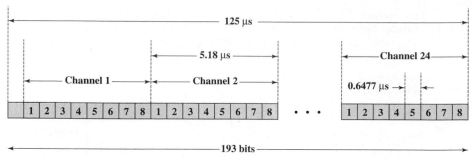

Notes:
1. The first bit is a framing bit, used for synchronization.
2. Voice channels:
   • 8-bit PCM used on five of six frames.
   • 7-bit PCM used on every sixth frame; bit 8 of each channel is a signaling bit.
3. Data channels:
   • Channel 24 is used for signaling only in some schemes.
   • Bits 1–7 used for 56-kbps service
   • Bits 2–7 used for 9.6-, 4.8-, and 2.4-kbps service.

Figure 8.9 DS-1 Transmission Format

The basis of the TDM hierarchy (in North America and Japan) is the DS-1 transmission format (Figure 8.9), which multiplexes 24 channels. Each frame contains 8 bits per channel plus a framing bit for $24 \times 8 + 1 = 193$ bits. For voice transmission, the following rules apply. Each channel contains one word of digitized voice data. The original analog voice signal is digitized using pulse code modulation (PCM) at a rate of 8000 samples per second. Therefore, each channel slot and hence each frame must repeat 8000 times per second. With a frame length of 193 bits, we have a data rate of $8000 \times 193 = 1.544$ Mbps. For five of every six frames, 8-bit PCM samples are used. For every sixth frame, each channel contains a 7-bit PCM word plus a *signaling bit*. The signaling bits form a stream for each voice channel that contains network control and routing information. For example, control signals are used to establish a connection or terminate a call.

The same DS-1 format is used to provide digital data service. For compatibility with voice, the same 1.544-Mbps data rate is used. In this case, 23 channels of data are provided. The twenty-fourth channel position is reserved for a special sync byte, which allows faster and more reliable reframing following a framing error. Within each channel, 7 bits per frame are used for data, with the eighth bit used to indicate whether the channel, for that frame, contains user data or system control data. With 7 bits per channel, and because each frame is repeated 8000 times per second, a data rate of 56 kbps can be provided per channel. Lower data rates are provided using a technique known as subrate multiplexing. For this technique, an additional bit is robbed from each channel to indicate which subrate multiplexing rate is being provided. This leaves a total capacity per channel of $6 \times 8000 = 48$ kbps. This capacity is used to multiplex five 9.6-kbps channels, ten 4.8-kbps channels, or twenty 2.4-kbps channels. For example, if channel 2 is used to provide 9.6-kbps service, then up to five data subchannels share this channel. The data for each subchannel appear as six bits in channel 2 every fifth frame.

Finally, the DS-1 format can be used to carry a mixture of voice and data channels. In this case, all 24 channels are utilized; no sync byte is provided.

Above the DS-1 data rate of 1.544 Mbps, higher-level multiplexing is achieved by interleaving bits from DS-1 inputs. For example, the DS-2 transmission system combines four DS-1 inputs into a 6.312-Mbps stream. Data from the four sources are interleaved 12 bits at a time. Note that $1.544 \times 4 = 6.176$ Mbps. The remaining capacity is used for framing and control bits.

SONET/SDH

SONET (Synchronous Optical Network) is an optical transmission interface originally proposed by BellCore and standardized by ANSI. A compatible version, referred to as Synchronous Digital Hierarchy (SDH), has been published by ITU-T in Recommendation G.707.[2] SONET is intended to provide a specification for taking advantage of the high-speed digital transmission capability of optical fiber.

Signal Hierarchy

The SONET specification defines a hierarchy of standardized digital data rates (Table 8.4). The lowest level, referred to as STS-1 (Synchronous Transport Signal level 1) or OC-1 (Optical Carrier level 1),[3] is 51.84 Mbps. This rate can be used to carry a single DS-3 signal or a group of lower-rate signals, such as DS1, DS1C, DS2, plus ITU-T rates (e.g., 2.048 Mbps).

Multiple STS-1 signals can be combined to form an STS-N signal. The signal is created by interleaving bytes from N STS-1 signals that are mutually synchronized.

For the ITU-T Synchronous Digital Hierarchy, the lowest rate is 155.52 Mbps, which is designated STM-1. This corresponds to SONET STS-3.

Table 8.4 SONET/SDH Signal Hierarchy

SONET Designation	ITU-T Designation	Data Rate	Payload Rate (Mbps)
STS-1/OC-1	STM-0	51.84 Mbps	50.112 Mbps
STS-3/OC-3	STM-1	155.52 Mbps	150.336 Mbps
STS-9/OC-9		466.56 Mbps	451.008 Mbps
STS-12/OC-12	STM-4	622.08 Mbps	601.344 Mbps
STS-18/OC-18		933.12 Mbps	902.016 Mbps
STS-24/OC-24		1.24416 Gbps	1.202688 Gbps
STS-36/OC-36		1.86624 Gbps	1.804032 Gbps
STS-48/OC-48	STM-16	2.48832 Gbps	2.405376 Gbps
STS-96/OC-96		4.87664 Gbps	4.810752 Gbps
STS-192/OC-192	STM-64	9.95328 Gbps	9.621504 Gbps
STS-768	STM-256	39.81312 Gbps	38.486016 Gbps
STS-3072		159.25248 Gbps	1.53944064 Gbps

---

[2] In what follows, we will use the term *SONET* to refer to both specifications. Where differences exist, these will be addressed.

[3] An OC-N rate is the optical equivalent of an STS-N electrical signal. End user devices transmit and receive electrical signals; these must be converted to and from optical signals for transmission over optical fiber.

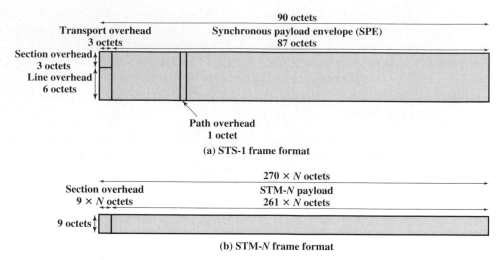

Figure 8.10   SONET/SDH Frame Formats

Frame Format

The basic SONET building block is the STS-1 frame, which consists of 810 octets and is transmitted once every 125 μs, for an overall data rate of 51.84 Mbps (Figure 8.10a). The frame can logically be viewed as a matrix of 9 rows of 90 octets each, with transmission being one row at a time, from left to right and top to bottom.

The first three columns (3 octets × 9 rows = 27 octets) of the frame are devoted to overhead octets. Nine octets are devoted to section-related overhead and 18 octets are devoted to line overhead. Figure 8.11a shows the arrangement of overhead octets, and Table 8.5 defines the various fields.

					Trace J1
Section overhead	Framing A1	Framing A2	STS-ID C1		Trace J1
	BIP-8 B1	Orderwire E1	User F1		BIP-8 B3
	DataCom D1	DataCom D2	DataCom D3		Signal Label C2
Line overhead	Pointer H1	Pointer H2	Pointer Action H3		Path Status G1
	BIP-8 B2	APS K1	APS K2		User F2
	DataCom D4	DataCom D5	DataCom D6		Multiframe H4
	DataCom D7	DataCom D8	DataCom D9		Growth Z3
	DataCom D10	DataCom D11	DataCom D12		Growth Z4
	Growth Z1	Growth Z2	Orderwire E2		Growth Z5

(a) Transport overhead   (b) Path overhead

Figure 8.11   SONET STS-1 Overhead Octets

Table 8.5 STS-1 Overhead Bits

Section Overhead

A1, A2: Framing bytes = F6,28 hex; used to synchronize the beginning of the frame.

C1: STS-1 ID identifies the STS-1 number (1 to N) for each STS-1 within an STS-*N* multiplex.

B1: Bit-interleaved parity byte providing even parity over previous STS-*N* frame after scrambling; the *i*th bit of this octet contains the even parity value calculated from the *i*th bit position of all octets in the previous frame.

E1: Section level 64-kbps PCM orderwire; optional 64-kbps voice channel to be used between section terminating equipment, hubs, and remote terminals.

F1: 64-kbps channel set aside for user purposes.

D1-D3: 192-kbps data communications channel for alarms, maintenance, control, and administration between sections.

Line Overhead

H1-H3: Pointer bytes used in frame alignment and frequency adjustment of payload data.

B2: Bit-interleaved parity for line level error monitoring.

K1, K2: Two bytes allocated for signaling between line level automatic protection switching equipment; uses a bit-oriented protocol that provides for error protection and management of the SONET optical link.

D4-D12: 576-kbps data communications channel for alarms, maintenance, control, monitoring, and administration at the line level.

Z1, Z2: Reserved for future use.

E2: 64-kbps PCM voice channel for line level orderwire.

Path Overhead

J1: 64-kbps channel used to send repetitively a 64-octet fixed-length string so a receiving terminal can continuously verify the integrity of a path; the contents of the message are user programmable.

B3: Bit-interleaved parity at the path level, calculated over all bits of the previous SPE.

C2: STS path signal label to designate equipped versus unequipped STS signals. *Unequipped* means that the line connection is complete but there is no path data to send. For equipped signals, the label can indicate the specific STS payload mapping that might be needed in receiving terminals to interpret the payloads.

G1: Status byte sent from path terminating equipment back to path originating equipment to convey status of terminating equipment and path error performance.

F2: 64-kbps channel for path user.

H4: Multiframe indicator for payloads needing frames that are longer than a single STS frame; multiframe indicators are used when packing lower rate channels (virtual tributaries) into the SPE.

Z3-Z5: Reserved for future use.

The remainder of the frame is payload. The payload includes a column of path overhead, which is not necessarily in the first available column position; the line overhead contains a pointer that indicates where the path overhead starts. Figure 8.11b shows the arrangement of path overhead octets, and Table 8.5 defines these.

Figure 8.10b shows the general format for higher-rate frames, using the ITU-T designation.

8.3   STATISTICAL TIME DIVISION MULTIPLEXING

Characteristics

In a synchronous time division multiplexer, it is generally the case that many of the time slots in a frame are wasted. A typical application of a synchronous TDM involves linking a number of terminals to a shared computer port. Even if all terminals are actively in use, most of the time there is no data transfer at any particular terminal.

An alternative to synchronous TDM is statistical TDM. The statistical multiplexer exploits this common property of data transmission by dynamically allocating time slots on demand. As with a synchronous TDM, the statistical multiplexer has a number of I/O lines on one side and a higher speed multiplexed line on the other. Each I/O line has a buffer associated with it. In the case of the statistical multiplexer, there are n I/O lines, but only k, where $k < n$, time slots available on the TDM frame. For input, the function of the multiplexer is to scan the input buffers, collecting data until a frame is filled, and then send the frame. On output, the multiplexer receives a frame and distributes the slots of data to the appropriate output buffers.

Because statistical TDM takes advantage of the fact that the attached devices are not all transmitting all of the time, the data rate on the multiplexed line is less than the sum of the data rates of the attached devices. Thus, a statistical multiplexer can use a lower data rate to support as many devices as a synchronous multiplexer. Alternatively, if a statistical multiplexer and a synchronous multiplexer both use a link of the same data rate, the statistical multiplexer can support more devices.

Figure 8.12 contrasts statistical and synchronous TDM. The figure depicts four data sources and shows the data produced in four time epochs (t_0, t_1, t_2, t_3). In the case of the synchronous multiplexer, the multiplexer has an effective output rate of four times the data rate of any of the input devices. During each epoch, data are

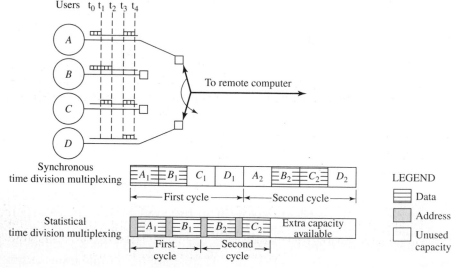

Figure 8.12   Synchronous TDM Contrasted with Statistical TDM

collected from all four sources and sent out. For example, in the first epoch, sources C and D produce no data. Thus, two of the four time slots transmitted by the multiplexer are empty.

In contrast, the statistical multiplexer does not send empty slots if there are data to send. Thus, during the first epoch, only slots for A and B are sent. However, the positional significance of the slots is lost in this scheme. It is not known ahead of time which source's data will be in any particular slot. Because data arrive from and are distributed to I/O lines unpredictably, address information is required to assure proper delivery. Thus, there is more overhead per slot for statistical TDM because each slot carries an address as well as data.

The frame structure used by a statistical multiplexer has an impact on performance. Clearly, it is desirable to minimize overhead bits to improve throughput. Generally, a statistical TDM system will use a synchronous protocol such as HDLC. Within the HDLC frame, the data frame must contain control bits for the multiplexing operation. Figure 8.13 shows two possible formats. In the first case, only one source of data is included per frame. That source is identified by an address. The length of the data field is variable, and its end is marked by the end of the overall frame. This scheme can work well under light load, but is quite inefficient under heavy load.

A way to improve efficiency is to allow multiple data sources to be packaged in a single frame. Now, however, some means is needed to specify the length of data for each source. Thus, the statistical TDM subframe consists of a sequence of data fields, each labeled with an address and a length. Several techniques can be used to make this approach even more efficient. The address field can be reduced by using relative addressing. That is, each address specifies the number of the current source relative to the previous source, modulo the total number of sources. So, for example, instead of an 8-bit address field, a 4-bit field might suffice.

Another refinement is to use a two-bit label with the length field. A value of 00, 01, or 10 corresponds to a data field of one, two, or three bytes; no length field is necessary. A value of 11 indicates that a length field is included.

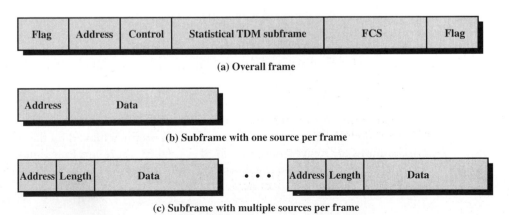

(a) Overall frame

(b) Subframe with one source per frame

(c) Subframe with multiple sources per frame

Figure 8.13 Statistical TDM Frame Formats

Yet another approach is to multiplex one character from each data source that has a character to send in a single data frame. In this case the frame begins with a bit map that has a bit length equal to the number of sources. For each source that transmits a character during a given frame, the corresponding bit is set to one.

Performance

We have said that the data rate of the output of a statistical multiplexer is less than the sum of the data rates of the inputs. This is allowable because it is anticipated that the average amount of input is less than the capacity of the multiplexed line. The difficulty with this approach is that, while the average aggregate input may be less than the multiplexed line capacity, there may be peak periods when the input exceeds capacity.

The solution to this problem is to include a buffer in the multiplexer to hold temporary excess input. Table 8.6 gives an example of the behavior of such systems. We assume 10 sources, each capable of 1000 bps, and we assume that the average input per source is 50% of its maximum. Thus, on average, the input load is 5000 bps. Two cases are shown: multiplexers of output capacity 5000 bps and 7000 bps. The entries in the table show the number of bits input from the 10 devices each millisecond and the output from the multiplexer. When the input exceeds the output, backlog develops that must be buffered.

There is a tradeoff between the size of the buffer used and the data rate of the line. We would like to use the smallest possible buffer and the smallest possible data rate, but a reduction in one requires an increase in the other. Note that we are not so much concerned with the cost of the buffer—memory is cheap—as we are with the fact that the more buffering there is, the longer the delay. Thus, the tradeoff is really one between system response time and the speed of the multiplexed line. In this section, we present some approximate measures that examine this tradeoff. These are sufficient for most purposes.

Let us define the following parameters for a statistical time division multiplexer:

I = number of input sources
R = data rate of each source, bps
M = effective capacity of multiplexed line, bps
α = mean fraction of time each source is transmitting, $0 < \alpha < 1$

$$K = \frac{M}{IR} = \text{ratio of multiplexed line capacity to total maximum input}$$

We have defined M taking into account the overhead bits introduced by the multiplexer. That is, M represents the maximum rate at which data bits can be transmitted.

The parameter K is a measure of the compression achieved by the multiplexer. For example, for a given data rate M, if $K = 0.25$, there are four times as many devices being handled as by a synchronous time division multiplexer using the same link capacity. The value of K can be bounded:

$$\alpha < K < 1$$

Table 8.6 Example of Statistical Multiplexer Performance

Input[a]	Capacity = 5000 bps		Capacity = 7000 bps	
	Output	Backlog	Output	Backlog
6	5	1	6	0
9	5	5	7	2
3	5	3	5	0
7	5	5	7	0
2	5	2	2	0
2	4	0	2	0
2	2	0	2	0
3	3	0	3	0
4	4	0	4	0
6	5	1	6	0
1	2	0	1	0
10	5	5	7	3
7	5	7	7	3
5	5	7	7	1
8	5	10	7	2
3	5	8	5	0
6	5	9	6	0
2	5	6	2	0
9	5	10	7	2
5	5	10	7	0

[a] Input = 10 sources, 1000 bps/source; average input rate = 50% of maximum.

A value of $K = 1$ corresponds to a synchronous time division multiplexer, because the system has the capacity to service all input devices at the same time. If $K < \alpha$, the input will exceed the multiplexer's capacity.

Some results can be obtained by viewing the multiplexer as a single-server queue. A queuing situation arises when a "customer" arrives at a service facility and, finding it busy, is forced to wait. The delay incurred by a customer is the time spent waiting in the queue plus the time for the service. The delay depends on the pattern of arriving traffic and the characteristics of the server. Table 8.7 summarizes results for the case of random (Poisson) arrivals and constant service time. This model is easily related to the statistical multiplexer:

$$\lambda = \alpha IR$$

Table 8.7 Single-Server Queues with Constant Service Times and Poisson (Random) Arrivals

Parameters

λ = mean number of arrivals per second

T_s = service time for each arrival

ρ = utilization; fraction of time server is busy

N = mean number of items in system (waiting and being served)

T_r = residence time; mean time an item spends in system (waiting and being served)

σ_r = standard deviation of T_r

Formulas

$$\rho = \lambda T_s$$

$$N = \frac{\rho^2}{2(1 - \rho)} + \rho$$

$$T_r = \frac{T_s(2 - \rho)}{2(1 - \rho)}$$

$$\sigma_r = \frac{1}{1 - \rho}\sqrt{\rho - \frac{3\rho^2}{2} + \frac{5\rho^3}{6} - \frac{\rho^4}{12}}$$

$$T_s = \frac{1}{M}$$

The average arrival rate λ, in bps, is the total potential input (IR) times the fraction of time α, that each source is transmitting. The service time T_s, in seconds, is the time it takes to transmit one bit, which is $1/M$. Note that

$$\rho = \lambda T_s = \frac{\alpha IR}{M} = \frac{\alpha}{K} = \frac{\lambda}{M}$$

The parameter ρ is the utilization or fraction of total link capacity being used. For example, if the capacity M is 50 kbps and $\rho = 0.5$, the load on the system is 25 kbps. The parameter N in Table 8.7 is a measure of the amount of buffer space being used in the multiplexer. Finally, T_r is a measure of the average delay encountered by an input source.

Figure 8.14 gives some insight into the nature of the tradeoff between system response time and the speed of the multiplexed line. It assumes that data are being transmitted in 1000-bit frames. Figure 8.14a shows the average number of frames that must be buffered as a function of the average utilization of the multiplexed line. The utilization is expressed as a percentage of the total line capacity. Thus, if the average input load is 5000 bps, the utilization is 100% for a line capacity of 5000 bps and about 71% for a line capacity of 7000 bps. Figure 8.14b shows the average delay experienced by a frame as a function of utilization and data rate. Note that as the utilization rises, so do the buffer requirements and the delay. A utilization above 80% is clearly undesirable.

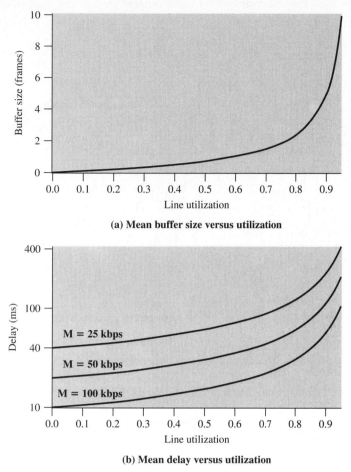

Figure 8.14   Buffer Size and Delay for a Statistical Multiplexer

Note that the average buffer size being used depends only on ρ, and not directly on M. For example, consider the following two cases:

Case I	Case II
$I = 10$	$I = 100$
$R = 100 \text{ bps}$	$R = 100 \text{ bps}$
$\alpha = 0.4$	$\alpha = 0.4$
$M = 500 \text{ bps}$	$M = 5000 \text{ bps}$

In both cases, the value of ρ is 0.8 and the mean buffer size is $N = 2.4$. Thus, proportionately, a smaller amount of buffer space per source is needed for multiplexers that handle a larger number of sources. Figure 8.14b also shows that the average delay will be smaller as the link capacity increases, for constant utilization.

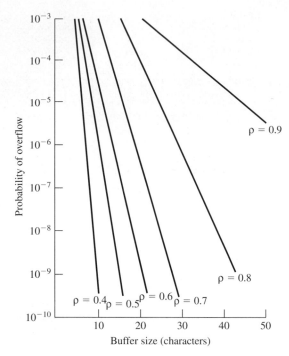

Figure 8.15   Probability of Overflow as a Function of Buffer Size

So far, we have been considering average queue length, and hence the average amount of buffer capacity needed. Of course, there will be some fixed upper bound on the buffer size available. The variance of the queue size grows with utilization. Thus, at a higher level of utilization, a larger buffer is needed to hold the backlog. Even so, there is always a finite probability that the buffer will overflow. Figure 8.15 shows the strong dependence of overflow probability on utilization. This figure and Figure 8.14 suggest that utilization above about 0.8 is undesirable.

Cable Modem

To support data transfer to and from a cable modem, a cable TV provider dedicates two channels, one for transmission in each direction. Each channel is shared by a number of subscribers, and so some scheme is needed for allocating capacity on each channel for transmission. Typically, a form of statistical TDM is used, as illustrated in Figure 8.16. In the downstream direction, cable **headend** to subscriber, a cable scheduler delivers data in the form of small packets. Because the channel is shared by a number of subscribers, if more than one subscriber is active, each subscriber gets only a fraction of the downstream capacity. An individual cable modem subscriber may experience access speeds from 500 kbps to 1.5 Mbps or more, depending on the network architecture and traffic load. The downstream direction is also used to grant time slots to subscribers. When a subscriber has data to transmit, it must first request time slots on the shared upstream channel. Each subscriber is

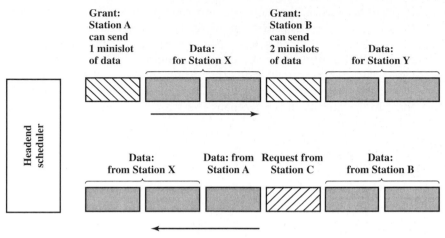

Figure 8.16 Cable Modem Scheme [DUTT99]

given dedicated time slots for this request purpose. The headend scheduler responds to a request packet by sending back an assignment of future time slots to be used by this subscriber. Thus, a number of subscribers can share the same upstream channel without conflict.

8.4 ASYMMETRIC DIGITAL SUBSCRIBER LINE

In the implementation and deployment of a high-speed wide area public digital network, the most challenging part is the link between subscriber and network: the digital subscriber line. With billions of potential endpoints worldwide, the prospect of installing new cable for each new customer is daunting. Instead, network designers have sought ways of exploiting the installed base of twisted-pair wire that links virtually all residential and business customers to telephone networks. These links were installed to carry voice-grade signals in a bandwidth from zero to 4 kHz. However, the wires are capable of transmitting signals over a far broader spectrum—1 MHz or more.

ADSL is the most widely publicized of a family of new modem technologies designed to provide high-speed digital data transmission over ordinary telephone wire. ADSL is now being offered by a number of carriers and is defined in an ANSI standard. In this section, we first look at the overall design of ADSL and then examine the key underlying technology, known as DMT.

ADSL Design

The term *asymmetric* refers to the fact that ADSL provides more capacity downstream (from the carrier's central office to the customer's site) than upstream (from customer to carrier). ADSL was originally targeted at the expected need for video on demand and related services. This application has not materialized. However, since the introduction of ADSL technology, the demand for high-speed access to the

Internet has grown. Typically, the user requires far higher capacity for downstream than for upstream transmission. Most user transmissions are in the form of keyboard strokes or transmission of short e-mail messages, whereas incoming traffic, especially Web traffic, can involve large amounts of data and include images or even video. Thus, ADSL provides a perfect fit for the Internet requirement.

ADSL uses frequency division multiplexing (FDM) in a novel way to exploit the 1-MHz capacity of twisted pair. There are three elements of the ADSL strategy (Figure 8.17):

- Reserve lowest 25 kHz for voice, known as POTS (plain old telephone service). The voice is carried only in the 0 to 4 kHz band; the additional bandwidth is to prevent crosstalk between the voice and data channels.
- Use either echo cancellation[4] or FDM to allocate two bands, a smaller upstream band and a larger downstream band.

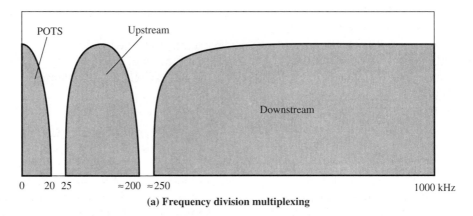

(a) Frequency division multiplexing

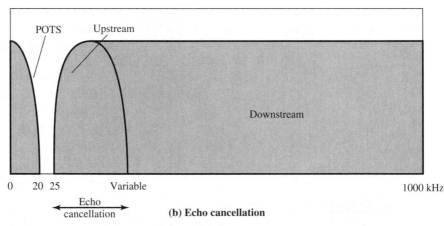

(b) Echo cancellation

Figure 8.17 ADSL Channel Configuration

---

[4] Echo cancellation is a signal processing technique that allows transmission of digital signals in both directions on a single transmission line simultaneously. In essence, a transmitter must subtract the echo of its own transmission from the incoming signal to recover the signal sent by the other side.

- Use FDM within the upstream and downstream bands. In this case, a single bit stream is split into multiple parallel bit streams and each portion is carried in a separate frequency band.

When echo cancellation is used, the entire frequency band for the upstream channel overlaps the lower portion of the downstream channel. This has two advantages compared to the use of distinct frequency bands for upstream and downstream.

- The higher the frequency, the greater the attenuation. With the use of echo cancellation, more of the downstream bandwidth is in the "good" part of the spectrum.
- The echo cancellation design is more flexible for changing upstream capacity. The upstream channel can be extended upward without running into the downstream; instead, the area of overlap is extended.

The disadvantage of the use of echo cancellation is the need for echo cancellation logic on both ends of the line.

The ADSL scheme provides a range of up to 5.5 km, depending on the diameter of the cable and its quality. This is sufficient to cover about 95% of all U.S. subscriber lines and should provide comparable coverage in other nations.

Discrete Multitone

Discrete multitone (DMT) uses multiple carrier signals at different frequencies, sending some of the bits on each channel. The available transmission band (upstream or downstream) is divided into a number of 4-kHz subchannels. On initialization, the DMT modem sends out test signals on each subchannel to determine the signal-to-noise ratio. The modem then assigns more bits to channels with better signal transmission qualities and less bits to channels with poorer signal transmission qualities. Figure 8.18 illustrates this process. Each subchannel can carry a data rate of from 0 to 60 kbps. The figure shows a typical situation in which there is increasing attenuation and hence decreasing signal-to-noise ratio at higher frequencies. As a result, the higher-frequency subchannels carry less of the load.

Figure 8.19 provides a general block diagram for DMT transmission. After initialization, the bit stream to be transmitted is divided into a number of substreams, one for each subchannel that will carry data. The sum of the data rates of the substreams is equal to the total data rate. Each substream is then converted to an analog signal using quadrature amplitude modulation (QAM), described in Chapter 5. This scheme works easily because of QAM's ability to assign different numbers of

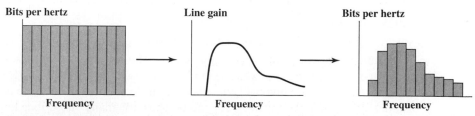

Figure 8.18 DMT Bits per Channel Allocation

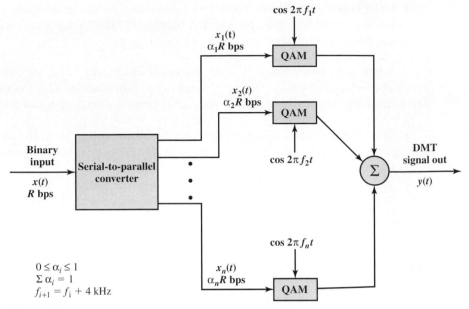

Figure 8.19 DMT Transmitter

bits per transmitted signal. Each QAM signal occupies a distinct frequency band, so these signals can be combined by simple addition to produce the composite signal for transmission.

Present ADSL/DMT designs employ 256 downstream subchannels. In theory, with each 4-kHz subchannel carrying 60 kbps, it would be possible to transmit at a rate of 15.36 Mbps. In practice, transmission impairments prevent attainment of this data rate. Current implementations operate at from 1.5 to 9 Mbps, depending on line distance and quality.

8.5 xDSL

ADSL is one of a number of recent schemes for providing high-speed digital transmission of the subscriber line. Table 8.8 summarizes and compares some of the most important of these new schemes, which collectively are referred to as xDSL.

High Data Rate Digital Subscriber Line

HDSL was developed in the late 1980s by BellCore to provide a more cost-effective means of delivering a T1 data rate (1.544 Mbps). The standard T1 line uses alternate mark inversion (AMI) coding, which occupies a bandwidth of about 1.5 MHz. Because such high frequencies are involved, the attenuation characteristics limit the use of T1 to a distance of about 1 km between repeaters. Thus, for many subscriber lines one or more repeaters are required, which adds to the installation and maintenance expense.

Table 8.8   Comparison of xDSL Alternatives

	ADSL	HDSL	SDSL	VDSL
Bits/second	1.5 to 9 Mbps downstream 16 to 640 kbps upstream	1.544 or 2.048 Mbps	1.544 or 2.048 Mbps	13 to 52 Mbps downstream 1.5 to 2.3 Mbps upstream
Mode	Asymmetric	Symmetric	Symmetric	Asymmetric
Copper Pairs	1	2	1	1
Range (24-gauge UTP)	3.7 to 5.5 km	3.7 km	3.0 km	1.4 km
Signaling	Analog	Digital	Digital	Analog
Line Code	CAP/DMT	2B1Q	2B1Q	DMT
Frequency	1 to 5 MHz	196 kHz	196 kHz	≥10 MHz
Bits/Cycle	Varies	4	4	Varies

UTP = unshielded twisted pair

HDSL uses the 2B1Q coding scheme to provide a data rate of up to 2 Mbps over two twisted-pair lines within a bandwidth that extends only up to about 196 kHz. This enables a range of about 3.7 km to be achieved.

Single Line Digital Subscriber Line

Although HDSL is attractive for replacing existing T1 lines, it is not suitable for residential subscribers because it requires two twisted pair, whereas the typical residential subscriber has a single twisted pair. SDSL was developed to provide the same type of service as HDSL but over a single twisted-pair line. As with HDSL, 2B1Q coding is used. Echo cancellation is used to achieve full-duplex transmission over a single pair.

Very High Data Rate Digital Subscriber Line

One of the newest xDSL schemes is VDSL. As of this writing, many of the details of this signaling specification remain to be worked out. The objective is to provide a scheme similar to ADSL at a much higher data rate by sacrificing distance. The likely signaling technique is DMT/QAM.

VDSL does not use echo cancellation but provides separate bands for different services, with the following tentative allocation:

- POTS: 0–4 kHz
- ISDN: 4–80 kHz
- Upstream: 300–700 kHz
- Downstream: ≥1 MHz

8.6 RECOMMENDED READING AND WEB SITES

A discussion of FDM and TDM carrier systems can be found in [BELL90] and [FREE98]. ISDN interfaces and SONET are treated in greater depth in [STAL99].

[MAXW96] provides a useful a discussion of ADSL. Recommended treatments of xDSL are [HAWL97] and [HUMP97].

BELL90   Bellcore (Bell Communications Research). *Telecommunications Transmission Engineering.* Three volumes. 1990.

FREE98   Freeman, R. *Telecommunications Transmission Handbook.* New York: Wiley, 1998.

HAWL97   Hawley, G. "Systems Considerations for the Use of xDSL Technology for Data Access." *IEEE Communications Magazine*, March 1997.

HUMP97   Humphrey, M., and Freeman, J. "How xDSL Supports Broadband Services to the Home." *IEEE Network*, January/March 1997.

MAXW96   Maxwell, K. "Asymmetric Digital Subscriber Line: Interim Technology for the Next Forty Years." *IEEE Communications Magazine*, October 1996.

STAL99   Stallings, W. *ISDN and Broadband ISDN, with Frame Relay and ATM.* Upper Saddle River, NJ: Prentice Hall, 1999.

Recommended Web Sites:

- **DSL Forum:** Includes a FAQ and technical information about ADSL and other xDSL technologies.
- **Network and Services Integration Forum:** Discusses current products, technology, and standards related to SONET.
- **SONET Home Page:** Useful links, tutorials, white papers, FAQs

8.7 KEY TERMS, REVIEW QUESTIONS, AND PROBLEMS

Key Terms

ADSL	frame	statistical TDM
cable modem	frequency division	subcarrier
channel	multiplexing (FDM)	synchronous TDM
demultiplexer	multiplexer	time division multiplexing
digital carrier system	multiplexing	(TDM)
discrete multitone	pulse stuffing	upstream
downstream	SDH	
echo cancellation	SONET	

Review Questions

8.1 Why is multiplexing so cost-effective?

8.2 How is interference avoided by using frequency division multiplexing?

8.3   What is echo cancellation?

8.4   Define *upstream* and *downstream* with respect to subscriber lines.

8.5   Explain how synchronous time division multiplexing (TDM) works.

8.6   Why is a statistical time division multiplexer more efficient than a synchronous time division multiplexer?

8.7   Using Table 8.3 as a guide, indicate the major difference between North American and International TDM carrier standards.

8.8   Using Figure 8.14 as a guide, indicate the relationship between buffer size and line utilization.

Problems

8.1   The information in four analog signals is to be multiplexed and transmitted over a telephone channel that has a 400- to 3100-Hz bandpass. Each of the analog baseband signals is bandlimited to 500 Hz. Design a communication system (block diagram) that will allow the transmission of these four sources over the telephone channel using
   a. Frequency division multiplexing with SSB (single sideband) subcarriers
   b. Time division multiplexing using PCM; assume 4-bit samples
Show the block diagrams of the complete system, including the transmission, channel, and reception portions. Include the bandwidths of the signals at the various points in the systems.

8.2   To paraphrase Lincoln: . . . all of the channel some of the time, some of the channel all of the time. . . . Refer to Figure 8.2 and relate the preceding to the figure.

8.3   Consider a transmission system using frequency division multiplexing. What cost factors are involved in adding one more pair of stations to the system?

8.4   In synchronous TDM, it is possible to interleave bits, one bit from each channel participating in a cycle. If the channel is using a self-clocking code to assist synchronization, might this bit interleaving introduce problems because there is not a continuous stream of bits from one source?

8.5   Why is it that the start and stop bits can be eliminated when character interleaving is used in synchronous TDM?

8.6   Explain in terms of data link control and physical layer concepts how error and flow control are accomplished in synchronous time division multiplexing.

8.7   One of the 193 bits in the DS-1 transmission format is used for frame synchronization. Explain its use.

8.8   In the DS-1 format, what is the control signal data rate for each voice channel?

8.9   Twenty-four voice signals are to be multiplexed and transmitted over twisted pair. What is the bandwidth required for FDM? Assuming a bandwidth efficiency (ratio of data rate to transmission bandwidth, as explained in Chapter 5) of 1 bps/Hz, what is the bandwidth required for TDM using PCM?

8.10   Draw a block diagram similar to Figure 8.8 for a TDM PCM system that will accommodate four 300-bps, synchronous, digital inputs and one analog input with a bandwidth of 500 Hz. Assume that the analog samples will be encoded into 4-bit PCM words.

8.11   A character-interleaved time division multiplexer is used to combine the data streams of a number of 110-bps asynchronous terminals for data transmission over a 2400-bps digital line. Each terminal sends asynchronous characters consisting of 7 data bits, 1 parity bit, 1 start bit, and 2 stop bits. Assume that one synchronization character is sent every 19 data characters and, in addition, at least 3% of the line capacity is reserved for pulse stuffing to accommodate speed variations from the various terminals.
   a. Determine the number of bits per character.
   b. Determine the number of terminals that can be accommodated by the multiplexer.
   c. Sketch a possible framing pattern for the multiplexer.

8.12 Find the number of the following devices that could be accommodated by a T1-type TDM line if 1% of the T1 line capacity is reserved for synchronization purposes.
   a. 110-bps teleprinter terminals
   b. 300-bps computer terminals
   c. 1200-bps computer terminals
   d. 9600-bps computer output ports
   e. 64-kbps PCM voice-frequency lines
   How would these numbers change if each of the sources were transmitting an average of 10% of the time and a statistical multiplexer was used?

8.13 Ten 9600-bps lines are to be multiplexed using TDM. Ignoring overhead bits in the TDM frame, what is the total capacity required for synchronous TDM? Assuming that we wish to limit average link utilization of 0.8, and assuming that each link is busy 50% of the time, what is the capacity required for statistical TDM?

8.14 A synchronous non-statistical TDM is to be used to combine four 4.8-kbps and one 9.6-kbps signals for transmission over a single leased line. For framing, a block of 7 bits (pattern 1011101) is inserted for each 48 data bits. The reframing algorithm (at the receiving demultiplex) is as follows:
   1. Arbitrarily select a bit position.
   2. Consider the block of 7 contiguous bits starting with that position.
   3. Observe that block of 7 bits each frame for 12 consecutive frames.
   4. If 10 of the 12 blocks match the framing pattern the system is "in-frame"; if not advance one bit position and return to step 2.
   a. Draw the multiplexed bit stream (note that the 9.6-kbps input may be treated as two 4.8-kbps inputs).
   b. What is the % overhead in the multiplexed bit stream?
   c. What is the multiplexed output bit rate?
   d. What is the minimum reframe time? What is the maximum reframe time? What is the Average reframe time?

8.15 A company has two locations: a headquarters and a factory about 25 km away. The factory has four 300-bps terminals that communicate with the central computer facilities over leased voice-grade lines. The company is considering installing TDM equipment so that only one line will be needed. What cost factors should be considered in the decision?

8.16 In synchronous TDM, the I/O lines serviced by the two multiplexers may be either synchronous or asynchronous although the channel between the two multiplexers must be synchronous. Is there any inconsistency in this? Why or why not?

8.17 Assume that you are to design a TDM carrier, say DS-489, to support 30 voice channels using 6-bit samples and a structure similar to DS-1. Determine the required bit rate.

8.18 For a statistical time division multiplexer, define the following parameters:

$$F = \text{frame length, bits}$$
$$OH = \text{overhead in a frame, bits}$$
$$L = \text{load of data in the frame, bps}$$
$$C = \text{capacity of link, bps}$$

   a. Express F as a function of the other parameters. Explain why F can be viewed as a variable rather than a constant.
   b. Plot F versus L for $C = 9.6\,\text{kbps}$ and values of $OH = 40, 80, 120$. Comment on the results and compare to Figure 8.14.
   c. Plot F versus L for $OH = 40$ and values of $C = 9.6\,\text{kbps}$ and 8.2 kbps. Comment on the results and compare to Figure 8.14.

8.19 In statistical TDM, there may be a length field. What alternative could there be to the inclusion of a length field? What problem might this solution cause and how could it be solved?

CHAPTER 9

SPREAD SPECTRUM

KEY POINTS

- Spread spectrum is an increasingly important form of encoding for wireless communications. The use of spread spectrum makes jamming and interception more difficult and improves reception.
- The basic idea of spread spectrum is to modulate the signal so as to increase significantly the bandwidth (spread the spectrum) of the signal to be transmitted.
- **Frequency-hopping spread spectrum** is a form of spread spectrum in which the signal is broadcast over a seemingly random series of radio frequencies, hopping from frequency to frequency at fixed intervals.
- **Direct sequence spread spectrum** is a form of spread spectrum in which each bit in the original signal is represented by multiple bits in the transmitted signal, using a spreading code.
- **Code division multiple access** exploits the nature of spread spectrum transmission to enable multiple users to independently use the same bandwidth with very little interference.

Spread spectrum is an increasingly important form of encoding for wireless communications. This technique does not fit neatly into the categories defined in the Chapter 5, as it can be used to transmit either analog or digital data, using an analog signal.

The spread spectrum technique was developed initially for military and intelligence requirements. The essential idea is to spread the information signal over a wider bandwidth to make jamming and interception more difficult. The first type of spread spectrum developed is known as frequency hopping.[1] A more recent type of spread spectrum is direct sequence. Both of these techniques are used in various wireless communications standards and products.

After a brief overview, we look at these two spread spectrum techniques. We then examine a multiple access technique based on spread spectrum.

9.1 THE CONCEPT OF SPREAD SPECTRUM

Figure 9.1 highlights the key characteristics of any spread spectrum system. Input is fed into a channel encoder that produces an analog signal with a relatively narrow bandwidth around some center frequency. This signal is further modulated using a sequence of digits known as a spreading code or spreading sequence. Typically, but not always, the spreading code is generated by a pseudonoise, or pseudorandom number, generator. The effect of this modulation is to increase significantly the bandwidth (spread the spectrum) of the signal to be transmitted. On the receiving

---

[1] Spread spectrum (using frequency hopping) was invented, believe it or not, by Hollywood screen siren Hedy Lamarr in 1940 at the age of 26. She and a partner who later joined her effort were granted a patent in 1942 (U.S. Patent 2,292,387; 11 August 1942). Lamarr considered this her contribution to the war effort and never profited from her invention.

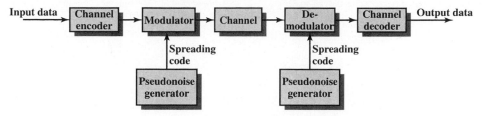

Figure 9.1   General Model of Spread Spectrum Digital Communication System

end, the same digit sequence is used to demodulate the spread spectrum signal. Finally, the signal is fed into a channel decoder to recover the data.

Several things can be gained from this apparent waste of spectrum:

- We can gain immunity from various kinds of noise and multipath distortion. The earliest applications of spread spectrum were military, where it was used for its immunity to jamming.
- It can also be used for hiding and encrypting signals. Only a recipient who knows the spreading code can recover the encoded information.
- Several users can independently use the same higher bandwidth with very little interference. This property is used in cellular telephony applications, with a technique know as code division multiplexing (CDM) or code division multiple access (CDMA).

A comment about pseudorandom numbers is in order. These numbers are generated by an algorithm using some initial value called the seed. The algorithm is deterministic and therefore produces sequences of numbers that are not statistically random. However, if the algorithm is good, the resulting sequences will pass many reasonable tests of randomness. Such numbers are often referred to as pseudorandom numbers.[2] The important point is that unless you know the algorithm and the seed, it is impractical to predict the sequence. Hence, only a receiver that shares this information with a transmitter will be able to decode the signal successfully.

9.2   FREQUENCY-HOPPING SPREAD SPECTRUM

With frequency-hopping spread spectrum (FHSS), the signal is broadcast over a seemingly random series of radio frequencies, hopping from frequency to frequency at fixed intervals. A receiver, hopping between frequencies in synchronization with the transmitter, picks up the message. Would-be eavesdroppers hear only unintelligible blips. Attempts to jam the signal on one frequency succeed only at knocking out a few bits of it.

---

[2] See [STAL02] for a more detailed discussion of pseudorandom numbers.

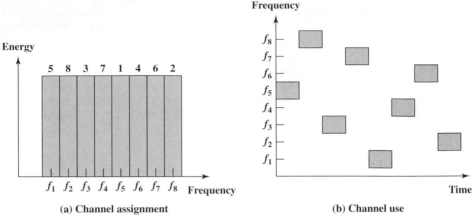

(a) Channel assignment   (b) Channel use

Figure 9.2   Frequency-Hopping Example

Basic Approach

Figure 9.2 shows an example of a frequency-hopping signal. A number of channels are allocated for the FH signal. Typically, there are 2^k carrier frequencies forming 2^k channels. The spacing between carrier frequencies and hence the width of each channel usually corresponds to the bandwidth of the input signal. The transmitter operates in one channel at a time for a fixed interval; for example, the IEEE 802.11 standard uses a 300-ms interval. During that interval, some number of bits (possibly a fraction of a bit, as discussed subsequently) is transmitted using some encoding scheme. The sequence of channels used is dictated by a spreading code. Both transmitter and receiver use the same code to tune into a sequence of channels in synchronization.

A typical block diagram for a frequency-hopping system is shown in Figure 9.3. For transmission, binary data are fed into a modulator using some digital-to-analog encoding scheme, such as frequency shift keying (FSK) or binary phase shift keying (BPSK). The resulting signal is centered on some base frequency. A pseudonoise (PN), or pseudorandom number, source serves as an index into a table of frequencies; this is the spreading code referred to previously. Each k bits of the PN source specifies one of the 2^k carrier frequencies. At each successive interval (each k PN bits), a new carrier frequency is selected. This frequency is then modulated by the signal produced from the initial modulator to produce a new signal with the same shape but now centered on the selected carrier frequency. On reception, the spread spectrum signal is demodulated using the same sequence of PN-derived frequencies and then demodulated to produce the output data.

Figure 9.3 indicates that the two signals are multiplied. Let us give an example of how this works, using BFSK as the data modulation scheme. We can define the FSK input to the FHSS system as [compare to Equation (5.3)]:

$$s_d(t) = A\cos(2\pi(f_0 + 0.5(b_i + 1)\Delta f)t) \quad \text{for } iT < t < (i + 1)T \qquad (9.1)$$

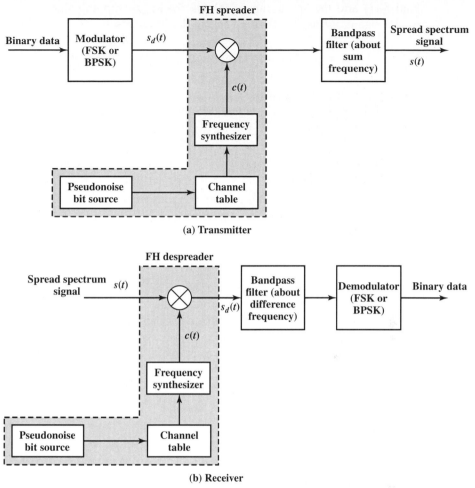

Figure 9.3   Frequency-Hopping Spread Spectrum System

where

A = amplitude of signal

f_0 = base frequency

b_i = value of the ith bit of data (+1 for binary 1, −1 for binary 0)

Δf = frequency separation

T = bit duration; data rate = $1/T$

Thus, during the ith bit interval, the frequency of the data signal is f_0 if the data bit is −1 and $f_0 + \Delta f$ if the data bit is +1.

The frequency synthesizer generates a constant-frequency tone whose frequency hops among a set of 2^k frequencies, with the hopping pattern determined by k bits from the PN sequence. For simplicity, assume the duration of one hop is the same as the duration of one bit and we ignore phase differences between the data signal $s_d(t)$ and the spreading signal, also called a chipping signal, $c(t)$. Then the product signal during the ith hop (during the ith bit) is

$$p(t) = s_d(t)c(t) = A\cos(2\pi(f_0 + 0.5(b_i + 1)\Delta f)t)\cos(2\pi f_i t)$$

where f_i is the frequency of the signal generated by the frequency synthesizer during the ith hop. Using the trigonometric identity[3] $\cos(x)\cos(y) = (1/2)(\cos(x + y) + \cos(x - y))$, we have

$$p(t) = 0.5A[\cos(2\pi(f_0 + 0.5(b_i + 1)\Delta f + f_i)t) + \cos(2\pi(f_0 + 0.5(b_i + 1)\Delta f - f_i)t)]$$

A bandpass filter (Figure 9.3) is used to block the difference frequency and pass the sum frequency, yielding an FHSS signal of

$$s(t) = 0.5A\cos(2\pi(f_0 + 0.5(b_i + 1)\Delta f + f_i)t) \tag{9.2}$$

Thus, during the ith bit interval, the frequency of the data signal is $f_0 + f_i$ if the data bit is -1 and $f_0 + f_i + \Delta f$ if the data bit is $+1$.

At the receiver, a signal of the form $s(t)$ just defined will be received. This is multiplied by a replica of the spreading signal to yield a product signal of the form

$$p(t) = s(t)c(t) = 0.5A\cos(2\pi(f_0 + 0.5(b_i + 1)\Delta f + f_i)t)\cos(2\pi f_i t)$$

Again using the trigonometric identity, we have

$$p(t) = s(t)c(t) = 0.25A[\cos(2\pi(f_0 + 0.5(b_i + 1)\Delta f + f_i + f_i)t) \\ + \cos(2\pi(f_0 + 0.5(b_i + 1)\Delta f)t)]$$

A bandpass filter (Figure 9.3) is used to block the sum frequency and pass the difference frequency, yielding a signal of the form of $s_d(t)$, defined in Equation (9.1):

$$0.25A\cos(2\pi(f_0 + 0.5(b_i + 1)\Delta f)t)$$

FHSS Using MFSK

A common modulation technique used in conjunction with FHSS is multiple FSK (MFSK). Recall from Chapter 5 that MFSK uses $M = 2^L$ different frequencies to encode the digital input L bits at a time. The transmitted signal is of the form (Equation 5.4):

$$s_i(t) = A\cos 2\pi f_i t, \qquad 1 \le i \le M$$

---

[3] See the math refresher document at WilliamStallings.com/StudentSupport.html for a summary of trigonometric identities.

where

$$f_i = f_c + (2i - 1 - M)f_d$$
f_c = denotes the carrier frequency
f_d = denotes the difference frequency
M = number of different signal elements = 2^L
L = number of bits per signal element

For FHSS, the MFSK signal is translated to a new frequency every T_c seconds by modulating the MFSK signal with the FHSS carrier signal. The effect is to translate the MFSK signal into the appropriate FHSS channel. For a data rate of R, the duration of a bit is $T = 1/R$ seconds and the duration of a signal element is $T_s = LT$ seconds. If T_c is greater than or equal to T_s, the spreading modulation is referred to as slow-frequency-hop spread spectrum; otherwise it is known as fast-frequency-hop spread spectrum.[4] To summarize,

Slow-frequency-hop spread spectrum	$T_c \geq T_s$
Fast-frequency-hop spread spectrum	$T_c < T_s$

Figure 9.4 shows an example of slow FHSS, using the MFSK example from Figure 5.9. Here we have $M = 4$, which means that four different frequencies are used to encode the data input 2 bits at a time. Each signal element is a discrete frequency tone, and the total MFSK bandwidth is $W_d = Mf_d$. We use an FHSS scheme with $k = 2$. That is, there are $4 = 2^k$ different channels, each of width W_d. The total FHSS bandwidth is $W_s = 2^k W_d$. Each 2 bits of the PN sequence is used to select one of the four channels. That channel is held for a duration of two signal elements, or four bits ($T_c = 2T_s = 4T$).

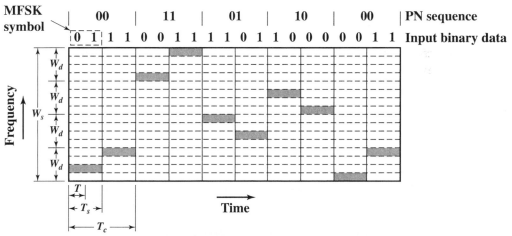

Figure 9.4   Slow-Frequency-Hop Spread Spectrum Using MFSK ($M = 4, k = 2$)

---

[4] Some authors use a somewhat different definition (e.g., [PICK82]) of multiple hops per bit for fast frequency hop, multiple bits per hop for slow frequency hop, and one hop per bit if neither fast nor slow. The more common definition, which we use, relates hops to signal elements rather than bits.

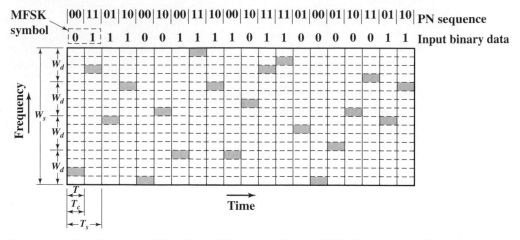

Figure 9.5 Fast-Frequency-Hop Spread Spectrum Using MFSK ($M = 4, k = 2$)

Figure 9.5 shows an example of fast FHSS, using the same MFSK example. Again, $M = 4$ and $k = 2$. In this case, however, each signal element is represented by two frequency tones. Again, $W_d = Mf_d$ and $W_s = 2^k W_d$. In this example $T_s = 2T_c = 2T$. In general, fast FHSS provides improved performance compared to slow FHSS in the face of noise or jamming. For example, if three or more frequencies (chips) are used for each signal element, the receiver can decide which signal element was sent on the basis of a majority of the chips being correct.

FHSS Performance Considerations

Typically, a large number of frequencies is used in FHSS so that W_s is much larger than W_d. One benefit of this is that a large value of k results in a system that is quite resistant to jamming. For example, suppose we have an MFSK transmitter with bandwidth W_d and noise jammer of the same bandwidth and fixed power S_j on the signal carrier frequency. Then we have a ratio of signal energy per bit to noise power density per Hertz of

$$\frac{E_b}{N_j} = \frac{E_b W_d}{S_j}$$

If frequency hopping is used, the jammer must jam all 2^k frequencies. With a fixed power, this reduces the jamming power in any one frequency band to $S_j/2^k$. The gain in signal-to-noise ratio, or processing gain, is

$$G_P = 2^k = \frac{W_s}{W_d} \tag{9.3}$$

9.3 DIRECT SEQUENCE SPREAD SPECTRUM

With direct sequence spread spectrum (DSSS), each bit in the original signal is represented by multiple bits in the transmitted signal, using a spreading code. The spreading code spreads the signal across a wider frequency band in direct proportion

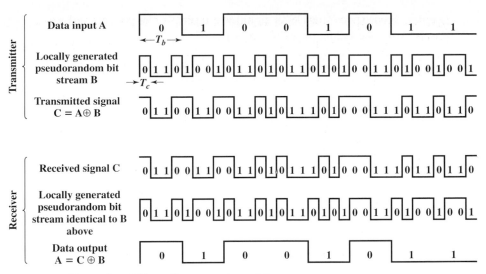

Figure 9.6 Example of Direct Sequence Spread Spectrum

to the number of bits used. Therefore, a 10-bit spreading code spreads the signal across a frequency band that is 10 times greater than a 1-bit spreading code.

One technique with direct sequence spread spectrum is to combine the digital information stream with the spreading code bit stream using an exclusive-OR (XOR). The XOR obeys the following rules:

$$0 \oplus 0 = 0 \qquad 0 \oplus 1 = 1 \qquad 1 \oplus 0 = 1 \qquad 1 \oplus 1 = 0$$

Figure 9.6 shows an example. Note that an information bit of one inverts the spreading code bits in the combination, while an information bit of zero causes the spreading code bits to be transmitted without inversion. The combination bit stream has the data rate of the original spreading code sequence, so it has a wider bandwidth than the information stream. In this example, the spreading code bit stream is clocked at four times the information rate.

DSSS Using BPSK

To see how this technique works out in practice, assume that a BPSK modulation scheme is to be used. Rather than represent binary data with 1 and 0, it is more convenient for our purposes to use +1 and −1 to represent the two binary digits. In that case, a BPSK signal can be represented as was shown in Equation (5.6):

$$s_d(t) = A\, d(t)\, \cos(2\pi f_c t) \tag{9.4}$$

where

A = amplitude of signal
f_c = carrier frequency
$d(t)$ = the discrete function that takes on the value of +1 for one bit time if the corresponding bit in the bit stream is 1 and the value of −1 for one bit time if the corresponding bit in the bit stream is 0

To produce the DSSS signal, we multiply the preceding by $c(t)$, which is the PN sequence taking on values of $+1$ and -1:

$$s(t) = A\, d(t)c(t) \cos(2\pi f_c t) \tag{9.5}$$

At the receiver, the incoming signal is multiplied again by $c(t)$. But $c(t) \times c(t) = 1$ and therefore the original signal is recovered:

$$s(t)c(t) = A\, d(t)c(t)c(t) \cos(2\pi f_c t) = s_d(t)$$

Equation (9.5) can be interpreted in two ways, leading to two different implementations. The first interpretation is to first multiply $d(t)$ and $c(t)$ together and then perform the BPSK modulation. That is the interpretation we have been discussing. Alternatively, we can first perform the BPSK modulation on the data stream $d(t)$ to generate the data signal $s_d(t)$. This signal can then be multiplied by $c(t)$.

An implementation using the second interpretation is shown in Figure 9.7. Figure 9.8 is an example of this approach.

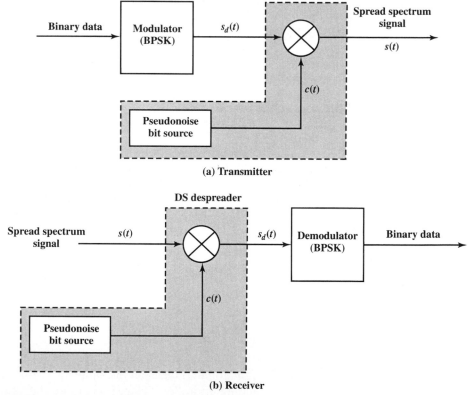

(a) Transmitter

(b) Receiver

Figure 9.7 Direct Sequence Spread Spectrum System

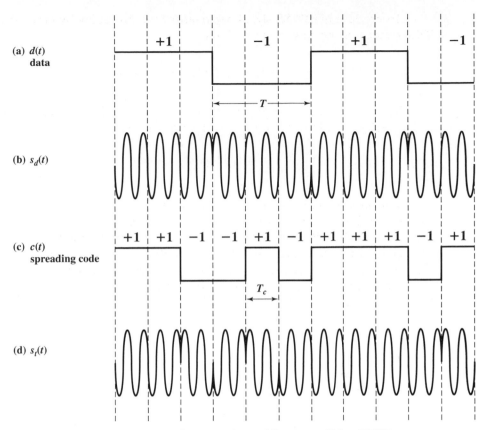

Figure 9.8 Example of Direct Sequence Spread Spectrum Using BPSK

DSSS Performance Considerations

The spectrum spreading achieved by the direct sequence technique is easily determined (Figure 9.9). In our example, the information signal has a bit width of T, which is equivalent to a data rate of $1/T$. In that case, the spectrum of the signal, depending on the encoding technique, is roughly $2/T$. Similarly, the spectrum of the PN signal is $2/T_c$. Figure 9.9c shows the resulting spectrum spreading. The amount of spreading that is achieved is a direct result of the data rate of the PN stream.

As with FHSS, we can get some insight into the performance of DSSS by looking at its effectiveness against jamming. Let us assume a simple jamming signal at the center frequency of the DSSS system. The jamming signal has the form

$$s_j(t) = \sqrt{2S_j}\cos(2\pi f_c t)$$

and the received signal is

$$s_r(t) = s(t) + s_j(t) + n(t)$$

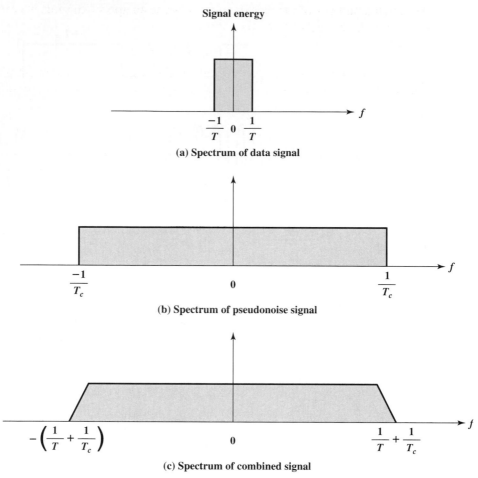

Figure 9.9 Approximate Spectrum of Direct Sequence Spread Spectrum Signal

where

$$s(t) = \text{transmitted signal}$$
$$s_j(t) = \text{jamming signal}$$
$$n(t) = \text{additive white noise}$$
$$S_j = \text{jammer signal power}$$

The despreader at the receiver multiplies $s_r(t)$ by $c(t)$, so the signal component due to the jamming signal is

$$y_j(t) = \sqrt{2S_j}c(t)\cos(2\pi f_c t)$$

This is simply a BPSK modulation of the carrier tone. Thus, the carrier power S_j is spread over a bandwidth of approximately $2/T_c$. However, the BPSK demodulator (Figure 9.7) following the DSSS despreader includes a bandpass filter matched to the BPSK data, with bandwidth of $2/T$. Thus, most of the jamming power is filtered.

Although a number of factors come into play, as an approximation, we can say that the jamming power passed by the filter is

$$S_{jF} = S_j(2/T)/(2/T_c) = S_j(T_c/T)$$

The jamming power has been reduced by a factor of (T_c/T) through the use of spread spectrum. The inverse of this factor is the gain in signal-to-noise ratio:

$$G_p = \frac{T}{T_c} = \frac{R_c}{R} \approx \frac{W_s}{W_d} \qquad (9.6)$$

where R_c is the spreading bit rate, R is the data rate, W_d is the signal bandwidth, and W_s is the spread spectrum signal bandwidth. The result is similar to the result for FHSS [Equation (9.3)].

9.4 CODE DIVISION MULTIPLE ACCESS

Basic Principles

CDMA is a multiplexing technique used with spread spectrum. The scheme works in the following manner. We start with a data signal with rate D, which we call the bit data rate. We break each bit into k *chips* according to a fixed pattern that is specific to each user, called the user's code. The new channel has a chip data rate of kD chips per second. As an illustration we consider a simple example[5] with $k = 6$. It is simplest to characterize a code as a sequence of 1s and -1s. Figure 9.10 shows the codes for three users, A, B, and C, each of which is communicating with the same base station receiver, R. Thus, the code for user A is $c = \langle 1, -1, -1, 1, -1, 1 \rangle$. Similarly, user B has code $c_B = \langle 1, 1, -1, -1, 1, 1 \rangle$, and user C has $c_C = \langle 1, 1, -1, 1, 1, -1 \rangle$.

We now consider the case of user A communicating with the base station. The base station is assumed to know A's code. For simplicity, we assume that communication is already synchronized so that the base station knows when to look for codes. If A wants to send a 1 bit, A transmits its code as a chip pattern $\langle 1, -1, -1, 1, -1, 1 \rangle$. If a 0 bit is to be sent, A transmits the complement (1s and -1s reversed) of its code, $\langle -1, 1, 1, -1, 1, -1 \rangle$. At the base station the receiver decodes the chip patterns. In our simple version, if the receiver R receives a chip pattern $d = \langle d1, d2, d3, d4, d5, d6 \rangle$, and the receiver is seeking to communicate with a user u so that it has at hand u's code, $\langle c1, c2, c3, c4, c5, c6 \rangle$, the receiver performs electronically the following decoding function:

$$S_u(d) = d1 \times c1 + d2 \times c2 + d3 \times c3 + d4 \times c4 + d5 \times c5 + d6 \times c6$$

The subscript u on S simply indicates that u is the user that we are interested in. Let's suppose the user u is actually A and see what happens. If A sends a 1 bit, then d is $\langle 1, -1, -1, 1, -1, 1 \rangle$ and the preceding computation using S_A becomes

$$S_A(1, -1, -1, 1, -1, 1) = 1 \times 1 + (-1) \times (-1) + (-1) \times (-1) + 1 \times 1$$
$$+ (-1) \times (-1) + 1 \times 1 = 6$$

---

[5] This example was provided by Professor Richard Van Slyke of the Polytechnic University of Brooklyn.

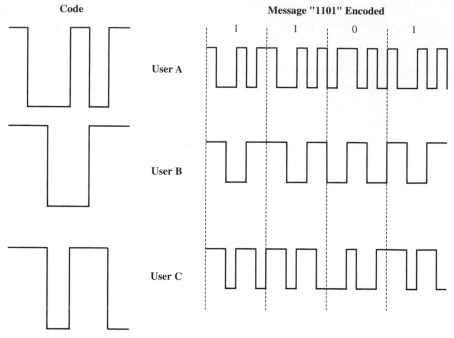

Figure 9.10 CDMA Example

If A sends a 0 bit that corresponds to $d = \langle -1, 1, 1, -1, 1, -1 \rangle$, we get

$$S_A(-1, 1, 1, -1, 1, -1) = -1 \times 1 + 1 \times (-1) + 1 \times (-1) + (-1) \times 1$$
$$+ 1 \times (-1) + (-1) \times 1 = -6$$

Please note that it is always the case that $-6 \le S_A(d) \le 6$ no matter what sequence of -1s and 1s that d is, and that the only d's resulting in the extreme values of 6 and -6 are A's code and its complement, respectively. So if S_A produces a $+6$, we say that we have received a 1 bit from A; if S_A produces a -6, we say that we have received a 0 bit from user A; otherwise, we assume that someone else is sending information or there is an error. So why go through all this? The reason becomes clear if we see what happens if user B is sending and we try to receive it with S_A, that is, we are decoding with the wrong code, A's. If B sends a 1 bit, then $d = \langle 1, 1, -1, -1, 1, 1 \rangle$. Then

$$S_A(1, 1, -1, -1, 1, 1) = 1 \times 1 + 1 \times (-1) + (-1) \times (-1)$$
$$+ (-1) \times 1 + 1 \times (-1) + 1 \times 1 = 0$$

Thus, the unwanted signal (from B) does not show up at all. You can easily verify that if B had sent a 0 bit, the decoder would produce a value of 0 for S_A again. This means that if the decoder is linear and if A and B transmit signals s_A and s_B, respectively, at the same time, then $S_A(s_A + s_B) = S_A(s_A) + S_A(s_B) = S_A(s_A)$ since the decoder ignores B when it is using A's code. The codes of A and B that have the property that $S_A(c_B) = S_B(c_A) = 0$ are called *orthogonal*. Such codes are very nice to have but there are not all that many of them. More common is the case when $S_X(c_Y)$ is small in absolute value when $X \neq Y$. Then it is easy to distinguish between the two cases when $X = Y$ and when $X \neq Y$. In our example $S_A(c_C) = S_C(c_A) = 0$, but $S_B(c_C) = S_C(c_B) = 2$. In the latter case the C signal would make a small contribution to the decoded signal instead of 0. Using the decoder, S_u, the receiver can sort out transmission from u even when there may be other users broadcasting in the same cell.

Table 9.1 summarizes the example from the preceding discussion.

Table 9.1   CDMA Example

(a) User's codes

User A	1	−1	−1	1	−1	1
User B	1	1	−1	−1	1	1
User C	1	1	−1	1	1	−1

(b) Transmission from A

Transmit (data bit = 1)	1	−1	−1	1	−1	1	
Receiver codeword	1	−1	−1	1	−1	1	
Multiplication	1	1	1	1	1	1	= 6

Transmit (data bit = 0)	−1	1	1	−1	1	−1	
Receiver codeword	1	−1	−1	1	−1	1	
Multiplication	−1	−1	−1	−1	−1	−1	= −6

(c) Transmission from B, receiver attempts to recover A's transmission

Transmit (data bit = 1)	1	1	−1	−1	1	1	
Receiver codeword	1	−1	−1	1	−1	1	
Multiplication	1	−1	1	−1	−1	1	= 0

(d) Transmission from C, receiver attempts to recover B's transmission

Transmit (data bit = 1)	1	1	−1	1	1	−1	
Receiver codeword	1	1	−1	−1	1	1	
Multiplication	1	1	1	−1	1	−1	= 2

(e) Transmission from B and C, receiver attempts to recover B's transmission

B (data bit = 1)	1	1	−1	−1	1	1	
C (data bit = 1)	1	1	−1	1	1	−1	
Combined signal	2	2	−2	0	2	0	
Receiver codeword	1	1	−1	−1	1	1	
Multiplication	2	2	2	0	2	0	= 8

In practice, the CDMA receiver can filter out the contribution from unwanted users or they appear as low-level noise. However, if there are many users competing for the channel with the user the receiver is trying to listen to, or if the signal power of one or more competing signals is too high, perhaps because it is very near the receiver (the "near/far" problem), the system breaks down.

CDMA for Direct Sequence Spread Spectrum

Let us now look at CDMA from the viewpoint of a DSSS system using BPSK. Figure 9.11 depicts a configuration in which there are n users, each transmitting using a different, orthogonal, PN sequence (compare Figure 9.7). For each user, the data stream to be transmitted, $d_i(t)$, is BPSK modulated to produce a signal with a bandwidth of W_s and then multiplied by the spreading code for that user, $c_i(t)$. All of the signals, plus noise, are received at the receiver's antenna. Suppose that the receiver is attempting to recover the data of user 1. The incoming signal is multiplied by the spreading code of user 1 and then demodulated. The effect of this is to narrow the bandwidth of that portion of the incoming signal corresponding to user 1 to the original bandwidth of the unspread signal, which is proportional to the data rate. Because the remainder of the incoming signal is orthogonal to the spreading code of user 1, that remainder still has the bandwidth W_s. Thus the unwanted signal energy remains spread over a large bandwidth and the wanted signal is concentrated in a narrow bandwidth. The bandpass filter at the demodulator can therefore recover the desired signal.

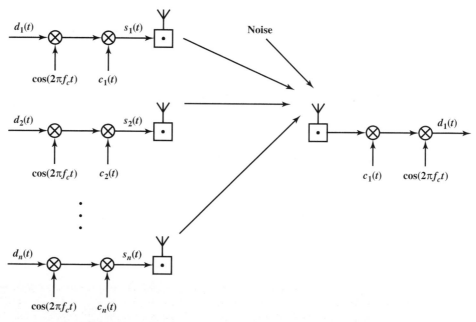

Figure 9.11   CDMA in a DSSS Environment

9.5 RECOMMENDED READING

Both [PETE95] and [DIXO94] provide comprehensive treatment of spread spectrum. [TANT98] contains reprints of many important papers in the field, including [PICK82], which provides an excellent introduction to spread spectrum.

DIXO94   Dixon, R. *Spread Spectrum Systems with Commercial Applications.* New York: Wiley, 1994.

PETE95   Peterson, R.; Ziemer, R.; and Borth, D. *Introduction to Spread Spectrum Communications.* Englewood Cliffs, NJ: Prentice Hall, 1995.

PICK82   Pickholtz, R.; Schilling, D.; and Milstein, L. "Theory of Spread Spectrum Communications—A Tutorial." IEEE Transactions on Communications, May 1982. Reprinted in [TANT98].

TANT98   Tantaratana, S, and Ahmed, K., eds. *Wireless Applications of Spread Spectrum Systems: Selected Readings.* Piscataway, NJ: IEEE Press, 1998.

9.6 KEY TERMS, REVIEW QUESTIONS, AND PROBLEMS

Key Terms

chip code division multiple access (CDMA) direct sequence spread spectrum (DSSS)	fast FHSS frequency-hopping spread spectrum (FHSS) orthogonal pseudonoise (PN)	slow FHSS spread spectrum spreading code spreading sequence

Review Questions

9.1 What is the relationship between the bandwidth of a signal before and after it has been encoded using spread spectrum?

9.2 List three benefits of spread spectrum.

9.3 What is frequency-hopping spread spectrum?

9.4 Explain the difference between slow FHSS and fast FHSS.

9.5 What is direct sequence spread spectrum?

9.6 What is the relationship between the bit rate of a signal before and after it has been encoded using DSSS?

9.7 What is CDMA?

Problems

9.1 Assume we wish to transmit a 56-kbps data stream using spread spectrum.
   a. Find the channel bandwidth required when SNR = 0.1, 0.01, and 0.001.
   b. In an ordinary (not spread spectrum) system, a reasonable goal for bandwidth efficiency might be 1 bps/Hz. That is, to transmit a data stream of 56 kbps, a bandwidth

of 56 kHz is used. In this case, what is the minimum SNR that can be endured for transmission without appreciable errors? Compare to the spread spectrum case. *Hint:* Review the discussion of channel capacity in Section 3.4.

9.2 An FHSS system employs a total bandwidth of $W_s = 400$ MHz and an individual channel bandwidth of 100 Hz. What is the minimum number of PN bits required for each frequency hop?

9.3 An FHSS system using MFSK with $M = 4$ employs 1000 different frequencies. What is the processing gain?

9.4 The following table illustrates the operation of an FHSS system for one complete period of the PN sequence.

Time	0	1	2	3	4	5	6	7	8	9	10	11
Input data	0	1	1	1	1	1	1	0	0	0	1	0
Frequency	f_1		f_3		f_{27}		f_{26}		f_8		f_{10}	
PN sequence	001				110				011			

Time	12	13	14	15	16	17	18	19
Input data	0	1	1	1	1	0	1	0
Frequency	f_1		f_3		f_2		f_2	
PN sequence	001				001			

a. What is the period of the PN sequence?
b. The system makes use of a form of FSK. What form of FSK is it?
c. What is the number of bits per symbol?
d. What is the number of FSK frequencies?
e. What is the length of a PN sequence per hop?
f. Is this a slow or fast FH system?
g. What is the total number of possible hops?
h. Show the variation of the dehopped frequency with time.

9.5 The following table illustrates the operation of a FHSS system using the same PN sequence as Problem 4.

Time	0	1	2	3	4	5	6	7	8	9	10	11
Input data	0	1	1	1	1	1	1	0	0	0	1	0
Frequency	f_1	f_{21}	f_{11}	f_3	f_3	f_3	f_{22}	f_{10}	f_0	f_0	f_2	f_{22}
PN sequence	001	110	011	001	001	001	110	011	001	001	001	110

Time	12	13	14	15	16	17	18	19
Input data	0	1	1	1	1	0	1	0
Frequency	f_9	f_1	f_3	f_3	f_{22}	f_{10}	f_2	f_2
PN sequence	011	001	001	001	110	011	001	001

  a. What is the period of the PN sequence?
  b. The system makes use of a form of FSK. What form of FSK is it?
  c. What is the number of bits per symbol?
  d. What is the number of FSK frequencies?
  e. What is the length of a PN sequence per hop?
  f. Is this a slow or fast FH system?
  g. What is the total number of possible hops?
  h. Show the variation of the dehopped frequency with time.

9.6 Consider an MFSK scheme with $f_c = 250\,kHz$, $f_d = 25\,kHz$, and $M = 8(L = 3\,bits)$.
  a. Make a frequency assignment for each of the eight possible 3-bit data combinations.
  b. We wish to apply FHSS to this MFSK scheme with $k = 2$; that is, the system will hop among four different carrier frequencies. Expand the results of part (a) to show the $4 \times 8 = 32$ frequency assignments.

9.7 Figure 9.12, based on one in [BELL00], depicts a simplified scheme for CDMA encoding and decoding. There are seven logical channels, all using DSSS with a spreading code of 7 bits. Assume that all sources are synchronized. If all seven sources transmit a data bit, in the form of a 7-bit sequence, the signals from all sources combine at the receiver so that two positive or two negative values reinforce and a positive and negative value cancel. To decode a given channel, the receiver multiplies the incoming composite signal by the spreading code for that channel, sums the result, and assigns binary 1 for a positive value and binary 0 for a negative value.
  a. What are the spreading codes for the seven channels?
  b. Determine the receiver output measurement for channel 1 and the bit value assigned.
  c. Repeat part (b) for channel 2.

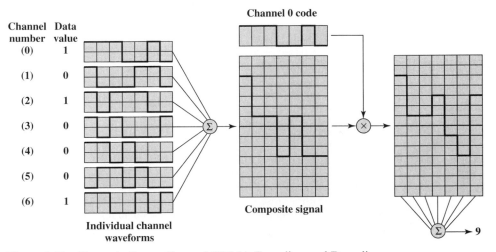

Figure 9.12   Example Seven-Channel CDMA Encoding and Decoding

9.8 By far, the most widely used technique for pseudorandom number generation is the linear congruential method. The algorithm is parameterized with four numbers, as follows:

$$m \quad \text{the modulus} \quad m > 0$$
$$a \quad \text{the multiplier} \quad 0 \le a < m$$
$$c \quad \text{the increment} \quad 0 \le c < m$$
$$X_0 \quad \text{the starting value, or seed} \quad 0 \le X_0 < M$$

The sequence of pseudorandom numbers $\{X_n\}$ is obtained via the following iterative equation:

$$X_{n+1} = (aX_n + c) \bmod m$$

If m, a, c, and X_0 are integers, then this technique will produce a sequence of integers with each integer in the range $0 \leq X_n < m$. An essential characteristic of a pseudo-random number generator is that the generated sequence should appear random. Although the sequence is not random, because it is generated deterministically, there is a variety of statistical tests that can be used to assess the degree to which a sequence exhibits randomness. Another desirable characteristic is that the function should be a full-period generating function. That is, the function should generate all the numbers between 0 and m before repeating.

With the linear congruential algorithm, a choice of parameters that provides a full period does not necessarily provide a good randomization. For example, consider the two generators:

$$X_{n+1} = (6X_n) \bmod 13$$
$$X_{n+1} = (7X_n) \bmod 13$$

Write out the two sequences to show that both are full period. Which one appears more random to you?

9.9   We would like m to be very large so that there is the potential for producing a long series of distinct random numbers. A common criterion is that m be nearly equal to the maximum representable nonnegative integer for a given computer. Thus, a value of m near to or equal to 2^{31} is typically chosen. Many experts recommend a value of $2^{31} - 1$. You may wonder why one should not simply use 2^{31}, because this latter number can be represented with no additional bits, and the mod operation should be easier to perform. In general, the modulus $2^k - 1$ is preferable to 2^k. Why is this so?

9.10   In any use of pseudorandom numbers, whether for encryption, simulation, or statistical design, it is dangerous to trust blindly the random number generator that happens to be available in your computer's system library. [PARK88] found that many contemporary textbooks and programming packages make use of flawed algorithms for pseudorandom number generation. This exercise will enable you to test your system.

The test is based on a theorem attributed to Ernesto Cesaro (see [KNUT98] for a proof), which states that the probability is equal to $\dfrac{6}{\pi^2}$ that the greatest common divisor of two randomly chosen integers is 1. Use this theorem in a program to determine statistically the value of π. The main program should call three subprograms: the random number generator from the system library to generate the random integers; a subprogram to calculate the greatest common divisor of two integers using Euclid's algorithm; and a subprogram that calculates square roots. If these latter two programs are not available, you will have to write them as well. The main program should loop through a large number of random numbers to give an estimate of the aforementioned probability. From this, it is a simple matter to solve for your estimate of π.

If the result is close to 3.14, congratulations! If not, then the result is probably low, usually a value of around 2.7. Why would such an inferior result be obtained?

PART THREE

Wide Area Networks

ISSUES FOR PART THREE

Part Two dealt with the transfer of data between devices that are directly connected, generally by a point-to-point link. Often, however, this arrangement is impractical, and a data communication network is required to transmit data between devices, either because the devices are very far apart or because there are many devices to be interconnected. In general terms, communications networks can be categorized as wide area networks (WANs) and local area networks (LANs). Part Three focuses on WANs, while Part Four covers LANs.

Two perspectives on the material in this part are of particular significance as they relate to the treatment of internetworking in Part Five. First, the constituent networks of the Internet and other internetworks are LANs and WANs. Thus, a full understanding of the technology and architecture of internetworks includes an understanding of the underlying networks. Second, and perhaps more important, many of the technologies developed for switched data WANs (including packet-switching, frame relay, and ATM networks) carry over into the design of internetworks. This is especially true in the cases of routing and congestion control.

ROAD MAP FOR PART THREE

Chapter 10 Circuit Switching and Packet Switching

Our treatment of the technology and architecture of circuit-switching networks begins with the internal operation of a single switch. This is in contrast to packet-switching networks, which are best explained by the collective behavior of the set of switches that make up a network. Thus, Chapter 10 begins by examining digital switching concepts, including space- and time division switching. Then the concepts of a multinode circuit-switching network are discussed; here we are primarily concerned with the topic of signaling.

The remainder of Chapter 10 introduces packet-switching technology. The chapter covers the basic principles of packet switching and analyzes datagram and virtual circuit approaches. The chapter also covers frame relay networks.

Chapter 11 ATM and Frame Relay

Chapter 11 focuses on the transmission technology that is the foundation of broadband ISDN: asynchronous transfer mode (ATM). ATM is also finding widespread application beyond its use as part of broadband ISDN. ATM is in essence a packet switching technology, but it is far more streamlined and efficient than traditional packet switching and is designed to support very high data rates. This chapter begins with a description of the ATM protocol and format. Then the physical layer issues relating to the transmission of ATM cells and the ATM Adaptation Layer (AAL) are discussed.

Chapter 12 Routing in Switched Networks

One significant technical issue associated with switched networks is routing. Because the source and destination nodes are not directly connected, the network must route each packet, from node to node, through the network. Chapter 12 provides a brief overview of routing issues for circuit-switching networks and then concentrates on routing in packet-switching networks.

Chapter 13 Congestion Control in Data Networks

A critical design issue for switching data networks is congestion control. The chapter begins with an explanation of the nature of congestion in data networks and both the importance and difficulty of controlling congestion. Chapter 13 provides a general discussion of congestion control in traditional packet-switching networks and also examines frame relay congestion control. The focus of the remainder of the chapter is on congestion and traffic control for ATM networks. This is one of the most complex aspects of ATM and is the subject of intensive ongoing research. This chapter surveys those techniques that have been accepted as having broad utility in ATM environments.

Chapter 14 Cellular Wireless Networks

Chapter 14 begins with a discussion of the important design issues related to cellular wireless networks. Next, the chapter covers the traditional mobile telephony service, now know as first-generation analog. Chapter 14 then examines second-generation digital cellular networks. Finally, an overview of third-generation networks is provided.

CHAPTER 10

CIRCUIT SWITCHING AND PACKET SWITCHING

KEY POINTS

- Circuit switching is used in public telephone networks and is the basis for private networks built on leased lines and using on-site circuit switches. Circuit switching was developed to handle voice traffic but can also handle digital data, although this latter use is often inefficient.

- With circuit switching, a dedicated path is established between two stations for communication. Switching and transmission resources within the network are reserved for the exclusive use of the circuit for the duration of the connection. The connection is transparent: Once it is established, it appears to attached devices as if there were a direct connection.

- Several important aspects of circuit-switching networks have changed dramatically in the wake of the increasing complexity and digitization of public telecommunications networks. Simple hierarchical routing schemes have been replaced with more flexible and powerful nonhierarchical schemes. This reflects a corresponding change in the underlying architecture, which leads to increased efficiency and resilience. Simple inchannel control signaling methods have been replaced with more complex and higher-speed common channel signaling.

- Packet switching was designed to provide a more efficient facility than circuit switching for bursty data traffic. With packet switching, a station transmits data in small blocks, called packets. Each packet contains some portion of the user data plus control information needed for proper functioning of the network.

- A key distinguishing element of packet-switching networks is whether the internal operation is datagram or virtual circuit. With internal virtual circuits, a route is defined between two endpoints and all packets for that virtual circuit follow the same route. With internal datagrams, each packet is treated independently, and packets intended for the same destination may follow different routes.

- X.25 is the standard protocol for the interface between an end system and a packet-switching network.

- Frame relay is a form of packet switching that provides a streamlined interface compared to X.25, with improved performance.

Part Two described how information can be encoded and transmitted over a communications link. We now turn to the broader discussion of networks, which can be used to interconnect many devices. The chapter begins with a general discussion of switched communications networks. The remainder of the chapter focuses on wide area networks and, in particular, on traditional approaches to wide area network design: circuit switching and packet switching.

Since the invention of the telephone, circuit switching has been the dominant technology for voice communications, and it has remained so well into the digital era. This chapter looks at the key characteristics of a circuit-switching network.

Around 1970, research began on a new form of architecture for long-distance digital data communications: packet switching. Although the technology of packet switching has evolved substantially since that time, it is remarkable that (1) the basic technology of packet switching is fundamentally the same today as it was in the early 1970s networks, and (2) packet switching remains one of the few effective technologies for long-distance data communications.

This chapter provides an overview of packet-switching technology. We will see, in this chapter and later in this part, that many of the advantages of packet switching (flexibility, resource sharing, robustness, responsiveness) come with a cost. The packet-switching network is a distributed collection of packet-switching nodes. Ideally, all packet-switching nodes would always know the state of the entire network. Unfortunately, because the nodes are distributed, there is a time delay between a change in status in one portion of the network and knowledge of that change elsewhere. Furthermore, there is overhead involved in communicating status information. As a result, a packet-switching network can never perform "perfectly," and elaborate algorithms are used to cope with the time delay and overhead penalties of network operation. These same issues will appear again when we discuss internetworking in Part Five.

Finally, this chapter provides an overview of a popular form of packet switching known as frame relay.

10.1 SWITCHED COMMUNICATIONS NETWORKS

For transmission of data[1] beyond a local area, communication is typically achieved by transmitting data from source to destination through a network of intermediate switching nodes; this switched network design is sometimes used to implement LANs as well. The switching nodes are not concerned with the content of the data; rather, their purpose is to provide a switching facility that will move the data from node to node until they reach their destination. Figure 10.1 illustrates a simple network. The end devices that wish to communicate may be referred to as *stations*. The stations may be computers, terminals, telephones, or other communicating devices. We shall refer to the switching devices whose purpose is to provide communication as *nodes*. The nodes are connected to one another in some topology by transmission links. Each station attaches to a node, and the collection of nodes is referred to as a *communications network*.

The types of networks that are discussed in this and the next three chapters are referred to as *switched communication networks*. Data entering the network from a station are routed to the destination by being switched from node to node. For example, in Figure 10.1, data from station A intended for station F are sent to node 4. They may then be routed via nodes 5 and 6 or nodes 7 and 6 to the destination. Several observations are in order:

1. Some nodes connect only to other nodes (e.g., 5 and 7). Their sole task is the internal (to the network) switching of data. Other nodes have one or more stations attached as well; in addition to their switching functions, such nodes accept data from and deliver data to the attached stations.

---

[1] We use this term here in a very general sense, to include voice, image, and video, as well as ordinary data (e.g., numerical, text).

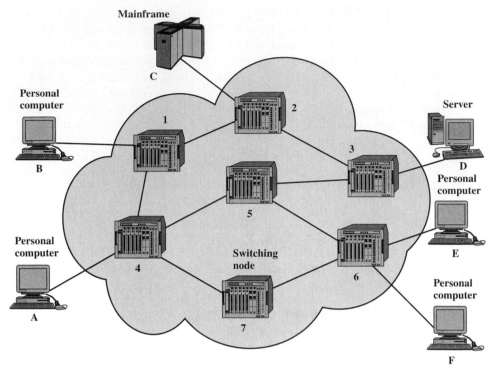

Figure 10.1 Simple Switching Network

2. Node-node links are usually multiplexed, using either frequency division multiplexing (FDM) or time division multiplexing (TDM).

3. Usually, the network is not fully connected; that is, there is not a direct link between every possible pair of nodes. However, it is always desirable to have more than one possible path through the network for each pair of stations. This enhances the reliability of the network.

Two quite different technologies are used in wide area switched networks: circuit switching and packet switching. These two technologies differ in the way the nodes switch information from one link to another on the way from source to destination.

10.2 CIRCUIT-SWITCHING NETWORKS

Communication via circuit switching implies that there is a dedicated communication path between two stations. That path is a connected sequence of links between network nodes. On each physical link, a logical channel is dedicated to the connection. Communication via circuit switching involves three phases, which can be explained with reference to Figure 10.1.

1. **Circuit establishment.** Before any signals can be transmitted, an end-to-end (station-to-station) circuit must be established. For example, station A sends a request to node 4 requesting a connection to station E. Typically, the link from A to 4 is a dedicated line, so that part of the connection already exists. Node 4 must find the next leg in a route leading to node 6. Based on routing information and measures of availability and perhaps cost, node 4 selects the link to node 5, allocates a free channel (using FDM or TDM) on that link and sends a message requesting connection to E. So far, a dedicated path has been established from A through 4 to 5. Because a number of stations may attach to 4, it must be able to establish internal paths from multiple stations to multiple nodes. The remainder of the process proceeds similarly. Node 5 dedicates a channel to node 6 and internally ties that channel to the channel from node 4. Node 6 completes the connection to E. In completing the connection, a test is made to determine if E is busy or is prepared to accept the connection.

2. **Data transfer.** Information can now be transmitted from A through the network to E. The data may be analog or digital, depending on the nature of the network. As the carriers evolve to fully integrated digital networks, the use of digital (binary) transmission for both voice and data is becoming the dominant method. The path is A-4 link, internal switching through 4, 4-5 channel, internal switching through 5, 5-6 channel, internal switching through 6, 6-E link. Generally, the connection is full duplex.

3. **Circuit disconnect.** After some period of data transfer, the connection is terminated, usually by the action of one of the two stations. Signals must be propagated to nodes 4, 5, and 6 to deallocate the dedicated resources.

Note that the connection path is established before data transmission begins. Thus, channel capacity must be reserved between each pair of nodes in the path, and each node must have available internal switching capacity to handle the requested connection. The switches must have the intelligence to make these allocations and to devise a route through the network.

Circuit switching can be rather inefficient. Channel capacity is dedicated for the duration of a connection, even if no data are being transferred. For a voice connection, utilization may be rather high, but it still does not approach 100%. For a terminal-to-computer connection, the capacity may be idle during most of the time of the connection. In terms of performance, there is a delay prior to signal transfer for call establishment. However, once the circuit is established, the network is effectively transparent to the users. Information is transmitted at a fixed data rate with no delay other than the propagation delay through the transmission links. The delay at each node is negligible.

Circuit switching was developed to handle voice traffic but is now also used for data traffic. The best-known example of a circuit-switching network is the public telephone network (Figure 10.2). This is actually a collection of national networks interconnected to form the international service. Although originally designed and implemented to service analog telephone subscribers, it handles substantial data traffic via modem and is gradually being converted to a digital network. Another well-known application of circuit switching is the private branch exchange (PBX), used to interconnect telephones within a building or office. Circuit switching is also

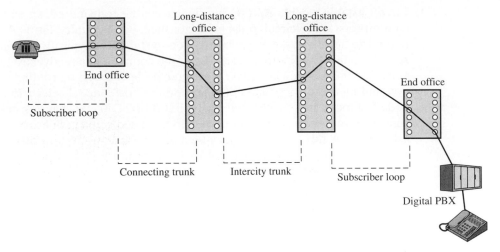

Figure 10.2 Example Connection over a Public Circuit-Switching Network

used in private networks. Typically, such a network is set up by a corporation or other large organization to interconnect its various sites. Such a network usually consists of PBX systems at each site interconnected by dedicated, leased lines obtained from one of the carriers, such as AT&T. A final common example of the application of circuit switching is the data switch. The data switch is similar to the PBX but is designed to interconnect digital data processing devices, such as terminals and computers.

A public telecommunications network can be described using four generic architectural components:

- **Subscribers:** The devices that attach to the network. It is still the case that most subscriber devices to public telecommunications networks are telephones, but the percentage of data traffic increases year by year.
- **Subscriber line:** The link between the subscriber and the network, also referred to as the *subscriber loop* or *local loop*. Almost all local loop connections use twisted-pair wire. The length of a local loop is typically in a range from a few kilometers to a few tens of kilometers.
- **Exchanges:** The switching centers in the network. A switching center that directly supports subscribers is known as an end office. Typically, an end office will support many thousands of subscribers in a localized area. There are over 19,000 end offices in the United States, so it is clearly impractical for each end office to have a direct link to each of the other end offices; this would require on the order of 2×10^8 links. Rather, intermediate switching nodes are used.
- **Trunks:** The branches between exchanges. Trunks carry multiple voice-frequency circuits using either FDM or synchronous TDM. Earlier, these were referred to as carrier systems.

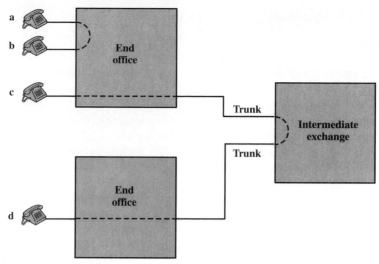

Figure 10.3 Circuit Establishment

Subscribers connect directly to an end office, which switches traffic between subscribers and between a subscriber and other exchanges. The other exchanges are responsible for routing and switching traffic between end offices. This distinction is shown in Figure 10.3. To connect two subscribers attached to the same end office, a circuit is set up between them in the same fashion as described before. If two subscribers connect to different end offices, a circuit between them consists of a chain of circuits through one or more intermediate offices. In the figure, a connection is established between lines a and b by simply setting up the connection through the end office. The connection between c and d is more complex. In c's end office, a connection is established between line c and one channel on a TDM trunk to the intermediate switch. In the intermediate switch, that channel is connected to a channel on a TDM trunk to d's end office. In that end office, the channel is connected to line d.

Circuit-switching technology has been driven by those applications that handle voice traffic. One of the key requirements for voice traffic is that there must be virtually no transmission delay and certainly no variation in delay. A constant signal transmission rate must be maintained, because transmission and reception occur at the same signal rate. These requirements are necessary to allow normal human conversation. Further, the quality of the received signal must be sufficiently high to provide, at a minimum, intelligibility.

Circuit switching achieved its widespread, dominant position because it is well suited to the analog transmission of voice signals. In today's digital world, its inefficiencies are more apparent. However, despite the inefficiency, circuit switching will remain an attractive choice for both local area and wide area networking. One of its key strengths is that it is transparent. Once a circuit is established, it appears as a direct connection to the two attached stations; no special networking logic is needed at the station.

10.3 CIRCUIT-SWITCHING CONCEPTS

The technology of circuit switching is best approached by examining the operation of a single circuit-switching node. A network built around a single circuit-switching node consists of a collection of stations attached to a central switching unit. The central switch establishes a dedicated path between any two devices that wish to communicate. Figure 10.4 depicts the major elements of such a one-node network. The dotted lines inside the switch symbolize the connections that are currently active.

The heart of a modern system is a **digital switch**. The function of the digital switch is to provide a transparent signal path between any pair of attached devices. The path is transparent in that it appears to the attached pair of devices that there is a direct connection between them. Typically, the connection must allow full-duplex transmission.

The **network interface** element represents the functions and hardware needed to connect digital devices, such as data processing devices and digital telephones, to the network. Analog telephones can also be attached if the network interface contains

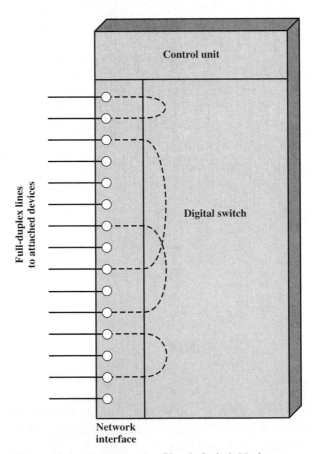

Figure 10.4 Elements of a Circuit-Switch Node

the logic for converting to digital signals. Trunks to other digital switches carry TDM signals and provide the links for constructing multiple-node networks.

The **control unit** performs three general tasks. First, it establishes connections. This is generally done on demand, that is, at the request of an attached device. To establish the connection, the control unit must handle and acknowledge the request, determine if the intended destination is free, and construct a path through the switch. Second, the control unit must maintain the connection. Because the digital switch uses time division principles, this may require ongoing manipulation of the switching elements. However, the bits of the communication are transferred transparently (from the point of view of the attached devices). Third, the control unit must tear down the connection, either in response to a request from one of the parties or for its own reasons.

An important characteristic of a circuit-switching device is whether it is blocking or nonblocking. Blocking occurs when the network is unable to connect two stations because all possible paths between them are already in use. A blocking network is one in which such blocking is possible. Hence a nonblocking network permits all stations to be connected (in pairs) at once and grants all possible connection requests as long as the called party is free. When a network is supporting only voice traffic, a blocking configuration is generally acceptable, because it is expected that most phone calls are of short duration and that therefore only a fraction of the telephones will be engaged at any time. However, when data processing devices are involved, these assumptions may be invalid. For example, for a data entry application, a terminal may be continuously connected to a computer for hours at a time. Hence, for data applications, there is a requirement for a nonblocking or "nearly nonblocking" (very low probability of blocking) configuration.

We turn now to an examination of the switching techniques internal to a single circuit-switching node.

Space Division Switching

Space division switching was originally developed for the analog environment and has been carried over into the digital realm. The fundamental principles are the same, whether the switch is used to carry analog or digital signals. As its name implies, a space division switch is one in which the signal paths are physically separate from one another (divided in space). Each connection requires the establishment of a physical path through the switch that is dedicated solely to the transfer of signals between the two endpoints. The basic building block of the switch is a metallic crosspoint or semiconductor gate that can be enabled and disabled by a control unit.

Figure 10.5 shows a simple crossbar matrix with 10 full-duplex I/O lines. The matrix has 10 inputs and 10 outputs; each station attaches to the matrix via one input and one output line. Interconnection is possible between any two lines by enabling the appropriate crosspoint. Note that a total of 100 crosspoints is required. The crossbar switch has a number of limitations:

- The number of crosspoints grows with the square of the number of attached stations. This is costly for a large switch.
- The loss of a crosspoint prevents connection between the two devices whose lines intersect at that crosspoint.

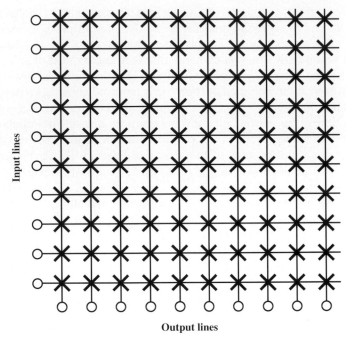

Input lines

Output lines

Figure 10.5 Space Division Switch

- The crosspoints are inefficiently utilized; even when all of the attached devices are active, only a small fraction of the crosspoints are engaged.

To overcome these limitations, multiple-stage switches are employed. Figure 10.6 is an example of a three-stage switch. This type of arrangement has two advantages over a single-stage crossbar matrix:

- The number of crosspoints is reduced, increasing crossbar utilization. In this example, the total number of crosspoints for 10 stations is reduced from 100 to 48.
- There is more than one path through the network to connect two endpoints, increasing reliability.

Of course, a multistage network requires a more complex control scheme. To establish a path in a single-stage network, it is only necessary to enable a single gate. In a multistage network, a free path through the stages must be determined and the appropriate gates enabled.

A consideration with a multistage space division switch is that it may be blocking. It should be clear from Figure 10.5 that a single-stage crossbar matrix is nonblocking; that is, a path is always available to connect an input to an output. That this may not be the case with a multiple-stage switch can be seen in Figure 10.6. The heavier lines indicate the lines that are already in use. In this state, input line 10, for example, cannot be connected to output line 3, 4, or 5, even though all of these output lines are available. A multiple-stage switch can be made non-

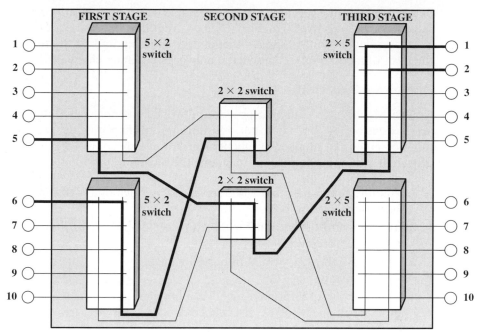

Figure 10.6   Three-Stage Space Division Switch

blocking by increasing the number or size of the intermediate switches, but of course this increases the cost.

Time Division Switching

The technology of switching has a long history, most of it covering an era when analog signal switching predominated. With the advent of digitized voice and synchronous time division multiplexing techniques, both voice and data can be transmitted via digital signals. This has led to a fundamental change in the design and technology of switching systems. Instead of relatively dumb space division systems, modern digital systems rely on intelligent control of space- and time division elements.

Virtually all modern circuit switches use digital time division techniques for establishing and maintaining "circuits." Time division switching involves the partitioning of a lower-speed bit stream into pieces that share a higher-speed stream with other bit streams. The individual pieces, or slots, are manipulated by control logic to route data from input to output. There are a number of variations on this basic concept, which are beyond the scope of this book.

10.4 CONTROL SIGNALING

In a circuit-switching network, control signals are the means by which the network is managed and by which calls are established, maintained, and terminated. Both call management and overall network management require that information be exchanged between subscriber and switch, among switches, and between switch and network management center. For a large public telecommunications network, a relatively complex control signaling scheme is required. In this section, we provide a brief overview of control signal functionality and then look at the technique that is the basis of modern integrated digital networks, common channel signaling.

Signaling Functions

Control signals affect many aspects of network behavior, including both network services visible to the subscriber and internal mechanisms. As networks become more complex, the number of functions performed by control signaling necessarily grows. The following functions are among the most important:

1. Audible communication with the subscriber, including dial tone, ringing tone, busy signal, and so on.
2. Transmission of the number dialed to switching offices that will attempt to complete a connection.
3. Transmission of information between switches indicating that a call cannot be completed.
4. Transmission of information between switches indicating that a call has ended and that the path can be disconnected.
5. A signal to make a telephone ring.
6. Transmission of information used for billing purposes.
7. Transmission of information giving the status of equipment or trunks in the network. This information may be used for routing and maintenance purposes.
8. Transmission of information used in diagnosing and isolating system failures.
9. Control of special equipment such as satellite channel equipment.

As an example of the use of control signaling, consider a typical telephone connection sequence from one line to another in the same central office:

1. Prior to the call, both telephones are not in use (on-hook). The call begins when one subscriber lifts the receiver (off-hook), which is automatically signaled to the end office switch.
2. The switch responds with an audible dial tone, signaling the subscriber that the number may be dialed.
3. The caller dials the number, which is communicated as a called address to the switch.
4. If the called subscriber is not busy, the switch alerts that subscriber to an incoming call by sending a ringing signal, which causes the telephone to ring.
5. Feedback is provided to the calling subscriber by the switch:
   a. If the called subscriber is not busy, the switch returns an audible ringing tone to the caller while the ringing signal is being sent to the called subscriber.
   b. If the called subscriber is busy, the switch sends an audible busy signal to the caller.
   c. If the call cannot be completed through the switch, the switch sends an audible "reorder" message to the caller.

6. The called party accepts the call by lifting the receiver (off-hook), which is automatically signaled to the switch.

7. The switch terminates the ringing signal and the audible ringing tone and establishes a connection between the two subscribers.

8. The connection is released when either subscriber hangs up.

When the called subscriber is attached to a different switch than the calling subscriber, the following switch-to-switch trunk signaling functions are required:

1. The originating switch seizes an idle interswitch trunk, sends an off-hook indication on the trunk, and requests a digit register at the far end, so that the address may be communicated.

2. The terminating switch sends an off-hook followed by an on-hook signal, known as a "wink." This indicates a register-ready status.

3. The originating switch sends the address digits to the terminating switch.

This example gives some idea of the functions that are performed using control signals. The functions performed by control signals can be roughly grouped into the categories of supervisory, address, call information, and network management.

The term **supervisory** is generally used to refer to control functions that have a binary character (true/false; on/off), such as request for service, answer, alerting, and return to idle. They deal with the availability of the called subscriber and of the needed network resources. Supervisory control signals are used to determine if a needed resource is available and, if so, to seize it. They are also used to communicate the status of requested resources.

Address signals identify a subscriber. Initially, an address signal is generated by a calling subscriber when dialing a telephone number. The resulting address may be propagated through the network to support the routing function and to locate and ring the called subscriber's phone.

The term **call information** refers to those signals that provide information to the subscriber about the status of a call. This is in contrast to internal control signals between switches used in call establishment and termination. Such internal signals are analog or digital electrical messages. In contrast, call information signals are audible tones that can be heard by the caller or an operator with the proper phone set.

Supervisory, address, and call information control signals are directly involved in the establishment and termination of a call. In contrast, **network management** signals are used for the maintenance, troubleshooting, and overall operation of the network. Such signals may be in the form of messages, such as a list of preplanned routes being sent to a station to update its routing tables. These signals cover a broad scope and it is this category that will expand most with the increasing complexity of switched networks.

Location of Signaling

Control signaling needs to be considered in two contexts: signaling between a subscriber and the network, and signaling within the network. Typically, signaling operates differently within these two contexts.

The signaling between a telephone or other subscriber device and the switching office to which it attaches is, to a large extent, determined by the characteristics of the subscriber device and the needs of the human user. Signals within the network are entirely computer-to-computer. The internal signaling is concerned not only with the management of subscriber calls but with the management of the network itself. Thus, for internal signaling, a more complex repertoire of commands, responses, and set of parameters is needed.

Because two different signaling techniques are used, the local switching office to which the subscriber is attached must provide a mapping between the relatively less complex signaling technique used by the subscriber and the more complex technique used within the network.

Common Channel Signaling

Traditional control signaling in circuit-switching networks has been on a per-trunk or inchannel basis. With **inchannel signaling**, the same channel is used to carry control signals as is used to carry the call to which the control signals relate. Such signaling begins at the originating subscriber and follows the same path as the call itself. This has the merit that no additional transmission facilities are needed for signaling; the facilities for voice transmission are shared with control signaling.

Two forms of inchannel signaling are in use: inband and out-of-band. **Inband signaling** uses not only the same physical path as the call it serves, but it also uses the same frequency band as the voice signals that are carried. This form of signaling has several advantages. Because the control signals have the same electromagnetic properties as the voice signals, they can go anywhere that the voice signals go. Thus, there are no limits on the use of inband signaling anywhere in the network, including places where analog-to-digital or digital-to-analog conversion takes place. In addition, it is impossible to set up a call on a faulty speech path, because the control signals that are used to set up that path would have to follow the same path.

Out-of-band signaling takes advantage of the fact that voice signals do not use the full 4-kHz bandwidth allotted to them. A separate narrow signaling band within the 4 kHz is used to send control signals. The major advantage of this approach is that the control signals can be sent whether or not voice signals are on the line, thus allowing continuous supervision and control of a call. However, an out-of-band scheme needs extra electronics to handle the signaling band, and the signaling rates are slower because the signal has been confined to a narrow bandwidth.

As public telecommunications networks become more complex and provide a richer set of services, the drawbacks of inchannel signaling become more apparent. The information transfer rate is quite limited with inchannel signaling. With inband signals, the voice channel being used is only available for control signals when there are no voice signals on the circuit. With out-of-band signals, a very narrow bandwidth is available. With such limits, it is difficult to accommodate, in a timely fashion, any but the simplest form of control messages. However, to take advantage of the potential services and to cope with the increasing complexity of evolving network technology, a richer and more powerful control signal repertoire is needed.

A second drawback of inchannel signaling is the amount of delay from the time a subscriber enters an address (dials a number) and the connection is established. The requirement to reduce this delay is becoming more important as the

Table 10.1 Signaling Techniques for Circuit-Switched Networks

	Description	Comment
Inchannel		
Inband	Transmits control signals in the same band of frequencies used by the voice signals.	The simplest technique. It is necessary for call information signals and may be used for other control signals. Inband can be used over any type of subscriber line interface.
Out of band	Transmits control signals using the same facilities as the voice signal but a different part of the frequency band.	Unlike inband, out-of-band signaling provides continuous supervision for the duration of a connection.
Common Channel	Transmits control signals over signaling channels that are dedicated to control signals and are common to a number of voice channels.	Reduces call setup time compared with inchannel methods. It is also more adaptable to evolving functional needs.

network is used in new ways. For example, computer-controlled calls, such as with transaction processing, use relatively short messages; therefore, the call setup time represents an appreciable part of the total transaction time.

Both of these problems can be addressed with **common channel signaling**, in which control signals are carried over paths completely independent of the voice channels (Table 10.1). One independent control signal path can carry the signals for a number of subscriber channels, and hence is a common control channel for these subscriber channels.

The principle of common channel signaling is illustrated and contrasted with inchannel signaling in Figure 10.7. As can be seen, the signal path for common channel

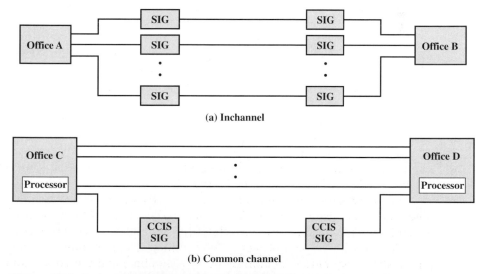

(a) Inchannel

(b) Common channel

Figure 10.7 Inchannel and Common Channel Signaling

signaling is physically separate from the path for voice or other subscriber signals. The common channel can be configured with the bandwidth required to carry control signals for a rich variety of functions. Thus, both the signaling protocol and the network architecture to support that protocol are more complex than inchannel signaling. However, the continuing drop in computer hardware costs makes common channel signaling increasingly attractive. The control signals are messages that are passed between switches and between a switch and the network management center. Thus, the control signaling portion of the network is, in effect, a distributed computer network carrying short messages.

Two modes of operation are used in common channel signaling (Figure 10.8). In the **associated mode**, the common channel closely tracks, along its entire length, the interswitch trunk groups that are served between endpoints. The control signals are on different channels from the subscriber signals, and inside the switch, the control signals are routed directly to a control signal processor. A more complex, but

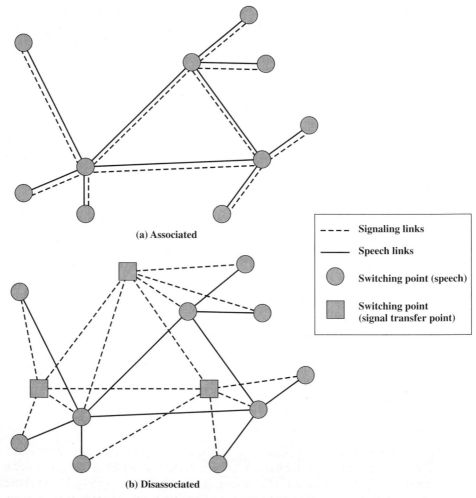

(a) Associated

- - - -	**Signaling links**
——	**Speech links**
●	**Switching point (speech)**
■	**Switching point (signal transfer point)**

(b) Disassociated

Figure 10.8 Common Channel Signaling Modes [FREE96]

more powerful, mode is the **disassociated mode**. With this mode, the network is augmented by additional nodes, known as signal transfer points. There is now no close or simple assignment of control channels to trunk groups. In effect, there are now two separate networks, with links between them so that the control portion of the network can exercise control over the switching nodes that are servicing the subscriber calls. Network management is more easily exerted in the disassociated mode because control channels can be assigned to tasks in a more flexible manner. The disassociated mode is the mode used in ISDN.

With inchannel signaling, control signals from one switch are originated by a control processor and switched onto the outgoing channel. On the receiving end, the control signals must be switched from the voice channel into the control processor. With common channel signaling, the control signals are transferred directly from one control processor to another, without being tied to a voice signal. This is a simpler procedure, and one that is less susceptible to accidental or intentional interference between subscriber and control signals. This is one of the main motivations for common channel signaling. Another key motivation for common channel signaling is that call setup time is reduced. Consider the sequence of events for call setup with inchannel signaling when more than one switch is involved. A control signal will be sent from one switch to the next in the intended path. At each switch, the control signal cannot be transferred through the switch to the next leg of the route until the associated circuit is established through that switch. With common channel signaling, forwarding of control information can overlap the circuit-setup process.

With disassociated signaling, a further advantage emerges: One or more central control points can be established. All control information can be routed to a network control center, where requests are processed and from which control signals are sent to switches that handle subscriber traffic. In this way, requests can be processed with a more global view of network conditions.

Of course, there are disadvantages to common channel signaling. These primarily have to do with the complexity of the technique. However, the dropping cost of digital hardware and the increasingly digital nature of telecommunication networks make common channel signaling the appropriate technology.

All of the discussion in this section has dealt with the use of common channel signaling inside the network, that is, to control switches. Even in a network that is completely controlled by common channel signaling, inchannel signaling is needed for at least some of the communication with the subscriber. For example, dial tone, ringback, and busy signals must be inchannel to reach the user. In a simple telephone network, the subscriber does not have access to the common channel signaling portion of the network and does not employ the common channel signaling protocol. However, in more sophisticated digital networks, including ISDN, a common channel signaling protocol is employed between subscriber and network and is mapped to the internal signaling protocol.

Signaling System Number 7

Common channel signaling is more flexible and powerful than inchannel signaling and is well suited to support the requirements of integrated digital networks. The most widely used scheme is Signaling System Number 7 (SS7). SS7 is designed to be an open-ended common channel signaling standard that can be used over a variety of digital circuit-switching networks. Furthermore, SS7 is specifically designed to be used in ISDNs. SS7 is the mechanism that provides the internal control and network intelligence essential to an ISDN.

The overall purpose of SS7 is to provide an internationally standardized, general-purpose common channel signaling system with the following primary characteristics:

- Optimized for use in digital telecommunication networks in conjunction with digital stored program-control exchanges, utilizing 64-kbps digital channels
- Designed to meet present and future information transfer requirements for call control, remote control, management, and maintenance
- Designed to be a reliable means for the transfer of information in the correct sequence without loss or duplication
- Suitable for operation over analog channels and at speeds below 64 kbps
- Suitable for use on point-to-point terrestrial and satellite links

The scope of SS7 is immense, because it must cover all aspects of control signaling for complex digital networks, including the reliable routing and delivery of control messages and the application-oriented content of those messages. In this section, we provide a brief overview.

With SS7, control messages are routed through the network to perform call management (setup, maintenance, termination) and network management functions. These messages are short blocks or packets that must be routed through the network. Thus, although the network being controlled is a circuit-switching network, the control signaling is implemented using packet-switching technology. In effect, a packet-switching network is overlaid on a circuit-switching network to operate and control the circuit-switching network.

SS7 defines the functions that are performed in the packet-switching network but does not dictate any particular hardware implementation. For example, all of the SS7 functions could be implemented in the circuit-switching nodes as additional functions; this approach is the associated signaling mode depicted in Figure 10.8a. Alternatively, separate switching points that carry only the control packets and are not used for carrying circuits can be used, as depicted in Figure 10.8b. Even in this case, the circuit-switching nodes would need to implement portions of SS7 so that they could receive control signals.

Signaling Network Elements

SS7 defines three functional entities: signaling points, signal transfer points, and signaling links. A **signaling point** (SP) is any point in the signaling network capable of handling SS7 control messages. It may be an endpoint for control messages and incapable of processing messages not directly addressed to itself. The circuit-switching nodes of the network, for example, could be endpoints. Another example is a network control center. A **signal transfer point** (STP) is a signaling point that is capable of routing control messages; that is, a message received on one signaling link is transferred to another link. An STP could be a pure routing node or could also include the functions of an endpoint. Finally, a signaling link is a data link that connects signaling points.

Figure 10.9 highlights the distinction between the packet-switching signaling function and the circuit-switching information transfer function, in the case of a disassociated signaling architecture. We can consider that there are two planes of operation. The **control plane** is responsible for establishing and managing connections. These connections are requested by the user. The user-network dialogue is between the user and the local exchange. For this purpose, the local exchange acts as a signaling point, because it must convert between the dialogue with the user and the control messages inside the network that actually perform user-requested actions (SS7). Internal to the network, SS7 is used to establish and maintain a connection; this process may involve one or more signaling points and signal transfer points.

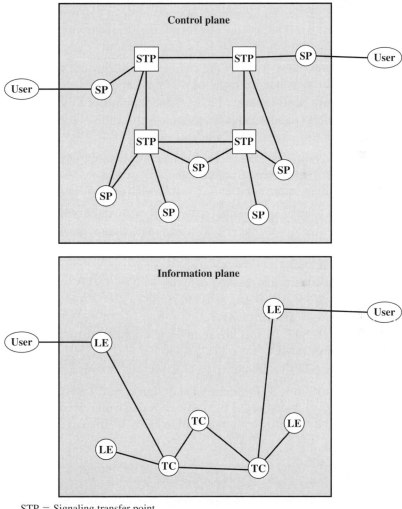

STP = Signaling transfer point
SP = Signaling point
TC = Transit center
LE = Local exchange

Figure 10.9   SS7 Signaling and Information Transfer Points

Once a connection is set up, information is transferred from one user to another, end-to-end, in the **information plane**. A circuit is set up from the local exchange of one user to that of another, perhaps being routed through one or more other circuit-switching nodes, referred to as transit centers. All of these nodes (local exchanges, transit centers) are also signaling points, because they must be able to send and receive SS7 messages to establish and manage the connection.

Signaling Network Structures

A complex network will typically have both signaling points (SP) and signal transfer points (STP). A signaling network that includes both SP and STP nodes could be considered as having a hierarchical structure in which the SPs constitute the lower level and the STPs represent the higher level. The latter may further be divided into several STP levels. Figure 10.9 is an example of a network with a single STP level.

Several parameters could influence the decisions concerning design of the network and the number of levels to be implemented:

- **STP capacities:** Includes the number of signaling links that can be handled by the STP, the signaling message transfer time, and the message throughput capacity
- **Network performance:** Includes the number of SPs and the signaling delays
- **Availability and reliability:** Measures the ability of the network to provide service in the face of STP failures

When considering the network constraints in terms of performance, one STP level seems preferable. However, considerations of reliability and availability may dictate a solution with more than one level. The following guidelines are suggested by ITU-T:

- In a hierarchical signaling network with a single STP level
  - Each SP that is not an STP at the same time is connected to at least two STPs.
  - The meshing of STPs is as complete as possible (full mesh: every STP has a direct link to every other STP).
- In a hierarchical signaling network with two STP levels
  - Each SP that is not an STP at the same time is connected to at least two STPs of the lower level.
  - Each STP in the lower level is connected to at least two STPs of the upper level.
  - The STPs in the upper level are fully meshed.

The two-level STP hierarchical design would be typically designed such that the lower level is dedicated to traffic in a particular geographic region of the network, and the higher level handles interregion traffic.

10.5 SOFTSWITCH ARCHITECTURE

The latest trend in the development of circuit-switching technology is generally referred to as the softswitch. In essence, a softswitch is a general-purpose computer running specialized software that turns it into a smart phone switch. Softswitches cost significantly less than tradition circuit switches and can provide more functionality.

In particular, in addition to handling the traditional circuit-switching functions, a softswitch can convert a stream of digitized voice bits into packets. This opens up a number of options for transmission, including the increasingly popular voice over IP (Internet Protocol) approach.

In any telephone network switch, the most complex element is the software that controls call processing. This software performs call routing and implements call-processing logic for hundreds of custom calling features. Typically, this software runs on a proprietary processor that is integrated with the physical circuit-switching hardware. A more flexible approach is to physically separate the call processing function from the hardware switching function. In softswitch terminology, the physical switching function is perform by a **media gateway** (MG) and the call processing logic resides is a **media gateway controller** (MGC).

Figure 10.10 contrasts the architecture of a traditional telephone network circuit switch with the softswitch architecture. In the latter case, the MG and MGC are distinct entities and may be provided by different vendors. To facilitate interoperability, a standard has been issued for a media gateway control protocol between the MG and MGC (RFC 3015).

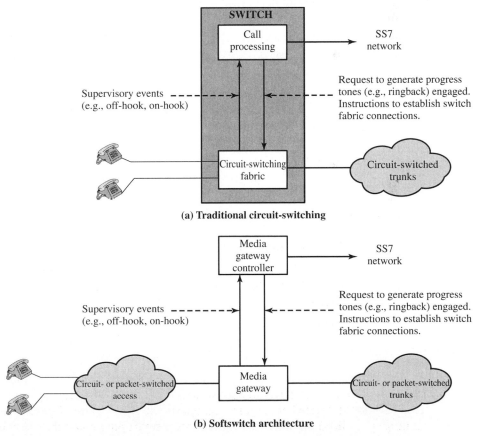

(a) Traditional circuit-switching

(b) Softswitch architecture

Figure 10.10   Comparison between Traditional Circuit Switching and Softswitch

10.6 PACKET-SWITCHING PRINCIPLES

The long-haul circuit-switching telecommunications network was originally designed to handle voice traffic, and the majority of traffic on these networks continues to be voice. A key characteristic of circuit-switching networks is that resources within the network are dedicated to a particular call. For voice connections, the resulting circuit will enjoy a high percentage of utilization because, most of the time, one party or the other is talking. However, as the circuit-switching network began to be used increasingly for data connections, two shortcomings became apparent:

- In a typical user/host data connection (e.g., personal computer user logged on to a database server), much of the time the line is idle. Thus, with data connections, a circuit-switching approach is inefficient.
- In a circuit-switching network, the connection provides for transmission at a constant data rate. Thus, each of the two devices that are connected must transmit and receive at the same data rate as the other. This limits the utility of the network in interconnecting a variety of host computers and workstations.

To understand how packet switching addresses these problems, let us briefly summarize packet-switching operation. Data are transmitted in short packets. A typical upper bound on packet length is 1000 octets (bytes). If a source has a longer message to send, the message is broken up into a series of packets (Figure 10.11). Each packet contains a portion (or all for a short message) of the user's data plus some control information. The control information, at a minimum, includes the information that the network requires to be able to route the packet through the network and deliver it to the intended destination. At each node en route, the packet is received, stored briefly, and passed on to the next node.

Let us return to Figure 10.1, but now assume that it depicts a simple packet-switching network. Consider a packet to be sent from station A to station E. The packet includes control information that indicates that the intended destination is E. The packet is sent from A to node 4. Node 4 stores the packet, determines the next leg of the route (say 5), and queues the packet to go out on that link (the 4-5 link). When the link is available, the packet is transmitted to node 5, which forwards

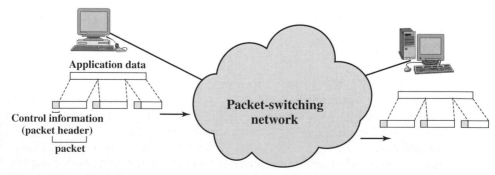

Figure 10.11   The Use of Packets

the packet to node 6, and finally to E. This approach has a number of advantages over circuit switching:

- Line efficiency is greater, because a single node-to-node link can be dynamically shared by many packets over time. The packets are queued up and transmitted as rapidly as possible over the link. By contrast, with circuit switching, time on a node-to-node link is preallocated using synchronous time division multiplexing. Much of the time, such a link may be idle because a portion of its time is dedicated to a connection that is idle.

- A packet-switching network can perform data-rate conversion. Two stations of different data rates can exchange packets because each connects to its node at its proper data rate.

- When traffic becomes heavy on a circuit-switching network, some calls are blocked; that is, the network refuses to accept additional connection requests until the load on the network decreases. On a packet-switching network, packets are still accepted, but delivery delay increases.

- Priorities can be used. Thus, if a node has a number of packets queued for transmission, it can transmit the higher-priority packets first. These packets will therefore experience less delay than lower-priority packets.

Switching Technique

If a station has a message to send through a packet-switching network that is of length greater than the maximum packet size, it breaks the message up into packets and sends these packets, one at a time, to the network. A question arises as to how the network will handle this stream of packets as it attempts to route them through the network and deliver them to the intended destination. Two approaches are used in contemporary networks: datagram and virtual circuit.

In the **datagram** approach, each packet is treated independently, with no reference to packets that have gone before. This approach is illustrated in Figure 10.12. Each node chooses the next node on a packet's path, taking into account information received from neighboring nodes on traffic, line failures, and so on. So the packets, each with the same destination address, do not all follow the same route (c), and they may arrive out of sequence at the exit point. In this example, the exit node restores the packets to their original order before delivering them to the destination. In some datagram networks, it is up to the destination rather than the exit node to do the reordering. Also, it is possible for a packet to be destroyed in the network. For example, if a packet-switching node crashes momentarily, all of its queued packets may be lost. Again, it is up to either the exit node or the destination to detect the loss of a packet and decide how to recover it. In this technique, each packet, treated independently, is referred to as a datagram.

In the **virtual circuit** approach, a preplanned route is established before any packets are sent. Once the route is established, all the packets between a pair of communicating parties follow this same route through the network. This is illustrated in Figure 10.13. Because the route is fixed for the duration of the logical connection, it is somewhat similar to a circuit in a circuit-switching network and is referred to as a virtual circuit. Each packet contains a virtual circuit identifier as well as data.

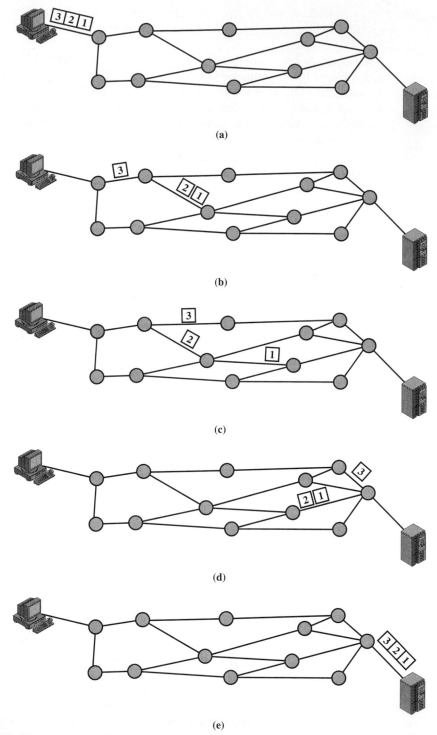

Figure 10.12 Packet Switching: Datagram Approach

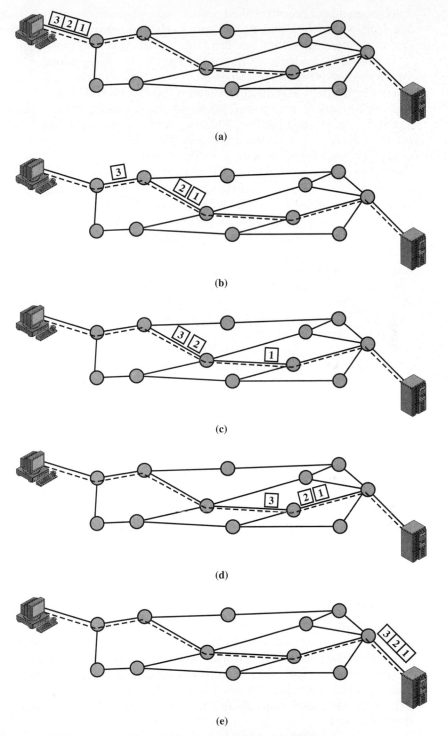

Figure 10.13 Packet Switching: Virtual Circuit Approach

Each node on the preestablished route knows where to direct such packets; no routing decisions are required. At any time, each station can have more than one virtual circuit to any other station and can have virtual circuits to more than one station.

So the main characteristic of the virtual circuit technique is that a route between stations is set up prior to data transfer. Note that this does not mean that this is a dedicated path, as in circuit switching. A packet is still buffered at each node, and queued for output over a line, while other packets on other virtual circuits may share the use of the line. The difference from the datagram approach is that, with virtual circuits, the node need not make a routing decision for each packet. It is made only once for all packets using that virtual circuit.

If two stations wish to exchange data over an extended period of time, there are certain advantages to virtual circuits. First, the network may provide services related to the virtual circuit, including sequencing and error control. Sequencing refers to the fact that, because all packets follow the same route, they arrive in the original order. Error control is a service that assures not only that packets arrive in proper sequence, but that all packets arrive correctly. For example, if a packet in a sequence from node 4 to node 6 fails to arrive at node 6, or arrives with an error, node 6 can request a retransmission of that packet from node 4. Another advantage is that packets should transit the network more rapidly with a virtual circuit; it is not necessary to make a routing decision for each packet at each node.

One advantage of the datagram approach is that the call setup phase is avoided. Thus, if a station wishes to send only one or a few packets, datagram delivery will be quicker. Another advantage of the datagram service is that, because it is more primitive, it is more flexible. For example, if congestion develops in one part of the network, incoming datagrams can be routed away from the congestion. With the use of virtual circuits, packets follow a predefined route, and thus it is more difficult for the network to adapt to congestion. A third advantage is that datagram delivery is inherently more reliable. With the use of virtual circuits, if a node fails, all virtual circuits that pass through that node are lost. With datagram delivery, if a node fails, subsequent packets may find an alternate route that bypasses that node. A datagram-style of operation is common in internetworks, discussed in Part Five.

Packet Size

There is a significant relationship between packet size and transmission time, as shown in Figure 10.14. In this example, it is assumed that there is a virtual circuit from station X through nodes a and b to station Y. The message to be sent comprises 40 octets, and each packet contains 3 octets of control information, which is placed at the beginning of each packet and is referred to as a header. If the entire message is sent as a single packet of 43 octets (3 octets of header plus 40 octets of data), then the packet is first transmitted from station X to node a (Figure 10.14a). When the entire packet is received, it can then be transmitted from a to b. When the entire packet is received at node b, it is then transferred to station Y. Ignoring switching time, total transmission time is 129 octet-times (43 octets × 3 packet transmissions).

Suppose now that we break the message up into two packets, each containing 20 octets of the message and, of course, 3 octets each of header, or control information.

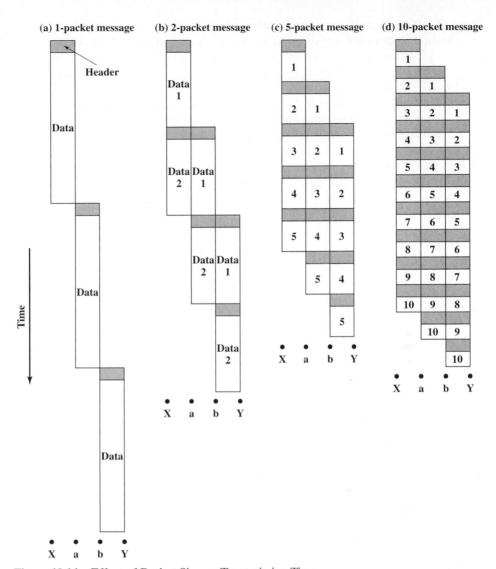

Figure 10.14   Effect of Packet Size on Transmission Time

In this case, node a can begin transmitting the first packet as soon as it has arrived from X, without waiting for the second packet. Because of this overlap in transmission, the total transmission time drops to 92 octet-times. By breaking the message up into five packets, each intermediate node can begin transmission even sooner and the savings in time is greater, with a total of 77 octet-times for transmission. However, this process of using more and smaller packets eventually results in increased, rather than reduced, delay as illustrated in Figure 10.14d. This is because each packet contains a fixed amount of header, and more packets mean more of these headers. Furthermore, the example does not show the processing and queuing delays at each node. These delays are also greater when more packets are handled for a single message. However, we shall see in the next chapter that an extremely small packet size (53 octets) can result in an efficient network design.

Comparison of Circuit Switching and Packet Switching

Having looked at the internal operation of packet switching, we can now return to a comparison of this technique with circuit switching. We first look at the important issue of performance and then examine other characteristics.

Performance

A simple comparison of circuit switching and the two forms of packet switching is provided in Figure 10.15. The figure depicts the transmission of a message across four nodes, from a source station attached to node 1 to a destination station attached to node 4. In this figure, we are concerned with three types of delay:

- **Propagation delay:** The time it takes a signal to propagate from one node to the next. This time is generally negligible. The speed of electromagnetic signals through a wire medium, for example, is typically 2×10^8 m/s.
- **Transmission time:** The time it takes for a transmitter to send out a block of data. For example, it takes 1 s to transmit a 10,000-bit block of data onto a 10-kbps line.

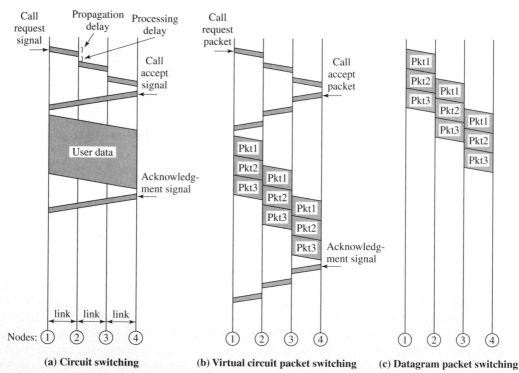

Figure 10.15   Event Timing for Circuit Switching and Packet Switching

- **Node delay:** The time it takes for a node to perform the necessary processing as it switches data.

For circuit switching, there is a certain amount of delay before the message can be sent. First, a Call Request signal is sent through the network, to set up a connection to the destination. If the destination station is not busy, a Call Accepted signal returns. Note that a processing delay is incurred at each node during the call request; this time is spent at each node setting up the route of the connection. On the return, this processing is not needed because the connection is already set up. After the connection is set up, the message is sent as a single block, with no noticeable delay at the switching nodes.

Virtual circuit packet switching appears quite similar to circuit switching. A virtual circuit is requested using a Call Request packet, which incurs a delay at each node. The virtual circuit is accepted with a Call Accept packet. In contrast to the circuit-switching case, the call acceptance also experiences node delays, even though the virtual circuit route is now established. The reason is that this packet is queued at each node and must wait its turn for transmission. Once the virtual circuit is established, the message is transmitted in packets. It should be clear that this phase of the operation can be no faster than circuit switching, for comparable networks. This is because circuit switching is an essentially transparent process, providing a constant data rate across the network. Packet switching involves some delay at each node in the path. Worse, this delay is variable and will increase with increased load.

Datagram packet switching does not require a call setup. Thus, for short messages, it will be faster than virtual circuit packet switching and perhaps circuit switching. However, because each individual datagram is routed independently, the processing for each datagram at each node may be longer than for virtual circuit packets. Thus, for long messages, the virtual circuit technique may be superior.

Figure 10.15 is intended only to suggest what the relative performance of the techniques might be; actual performance depends on a host of factors, including the size of the network, its topology, the pattern of load, and the characteristics of typical exchanges.

Other Characteristics

Besides performance, there are a number of other characteristics that may be considered in comparing the techniques we have been discussing. Table 10.2 summarizes the most important of these. Most of these characteristics have already been discussed. A few additional comments follow.

As was mentioned, circuit switching is essentially a transparent service. Once a connection is established, a constant data rate is provided to the connected stations. This is not the case with packet switching, which typically introduces variable delay, so that data arrive in a choppy manner. Indeed, with datagram packet switching, data may arrive in a different order than they were transmitted.

An additional consequence of transparency is that there is no overhead required to accommodate circuit switching. Once a connection is established, the analog or digital data are passed through, as is, from source to destination. For packet switching, analog data must be converted to digital before transmission; in addition, each packet includes overhead bits, such as the destination address.

Table 10.2 Comparison of Communication Switching Techniques

Circuit Switching	Datagram Packet Switching	Virtual Circuit Packet Switching
Dedicated transmission path	No dedicated path	No dedicated path
Continuous transmission of data	Transmission of packets	Transmission of packets
Fast enough for interactive	Fast enough for interactive	Fast enough for interactive
Messages are not stored	Packets may be stored until delivered	Packets stored until delivered
The path is established for entire conversation	Route established for each packet	Route established for entire conversation
Call setup delay; negligible transmission delay	Packet transmission delay	Call setup delay; packet transmission delay
Busy signal if called party busy	Sender may be notified if packet not delivered	Sender notified of connection denial
Overload may block call setup; no delay for established calls	Overload increases packet delay	Overload may block call setup; increases packet delay
Electromechanical or computerized switching nodes	Small switching nodes	Small switching nodes
User responsible for message loss protection	Network may be responsible for individual packets	Network may be responsible for packet sequences
Usually no speed or code conversion	Speed and code conversion	Speed and code conversion
Fixed bandwidth	Dynamic use of bandwidth	Dynamic use of bandwidth
No overhead bits after call setup	Overhead bits in each packet	Overhead bits in each packet

10.7 X.25

One technical aspect of packet-switching networks remains to be examined: the interface between attached devices and the network. We have seen that a circuit-switching network provides a transparent communications path for attached devices that makes it appear that the two communicating stations have a direct link. However, in the case of packet-switching networks, the attached stations must organize their data into packets for transmission. This requires a certain level of cooperation between the network and the attached stations. This cooperation is embodied in an interface standard. The almost universally used standard for this purpose is X.25.

X.25 is an ITU-T standard that specifies an interface between a host system and a packet-switching network. The functionality of X.25 is specified on three levels:

- Physical level
- Link level
- Packet level

The physical level deals with the physical interface between an attached station (computer, terminal) and the link that attaches that station to the packet-switching node. It makes use of the physical-level specification in a standard known as X.21, but in many cases other standards, such as EIA-232, are substituted. The link level provides for the reliable transfer of data across the physical link, by transmitting the data as a sequence of frames. The link level standard is referred to as LAPB (Link Access Protocol–Balanced). LAPB is a subset of HDLC, which was described in Chapter 7.

The packet level provides a virtual circuit service. This service enables any subscriber to the network to set up logical connections, called virtual circuits, to other subscribers. An example is shown in Figure 10.16 (compare Figure 10.1). In this example, station A has a virtual circuit connection to C; station B has two virtual circuits established, one to C and one to D; and stations E and F each have a virtual circuit connection to D.

In this context, the term *virtual circuit* refers to the logical connection between two stations through the network; this is perhaps best termed an external virtual circuit. Earlier, we used the term *virtual circuit* to refer to a specific preplanned route through the network between two stations; this could be called an internal virtual circuit. Typically, there is a one-to-one relationship between external and internal virtual circuits. However, it is also possible to employ X.25 with a datagram-style network.

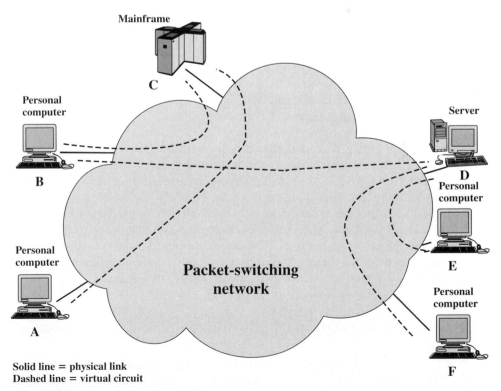

Solid line = physical link
Dashed line = virtual circuit

Figure 10.16   The Use of Virtual Circuits

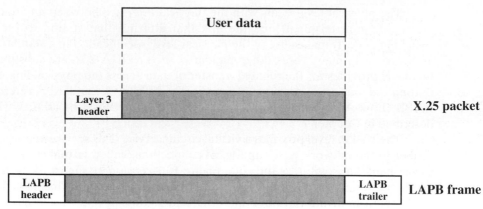

Figure 10.17 User Data and X.25 Protocol Control Information

What is important for an external virtual circuit is that there is a logical relationship, or logical channel, established between two stations, and all of the data associated with that logical channel are considered as part of a single stream of data between the two stations. For example, in Figure 10.16, station D keeps track of data packets arriving from three different workstations (B, E, F) on the basis of the virtual circuit number associated with each incoming packet.

Figure 10.17 illustrates the relationship among the levels of X.25. User data are passed down to X.25 level 3, which appends control information as a header, creating a packet. This control information serves several purposes, including

1. Identifying by number a particular virtual circuit with which this data is to be associated
2. Providing sequence numbers that can be used for flow and error control on a virtual circuit basis

The entire X.25 packet is then passed down to the LAPB entity, which appends control information at the front and back of the packet, forming a LAPB frame (see Figure 7.7). Again, the control information in the frame is needed for the operation of the LAPB protocol.

The operation of the X.25 packet level is similar to that of HDLC as described in Chapter 7. Each X.25 data packet includes send and receive sequence numbers. The send sequence number, P(S), is used to number sequentially all outgoing data packets on a particular virtual circuit. The receive sequence number, P(R), is an acknowledgment of packets received on that virtual circuit.

10.8 FRAME RELAY

Frame relay is designed to provide a more efficient transmission scheme than X.25. The standards for frame relay matured earlier than those for ATM, and commercial products also arrived earlier. Accordingly, there is a large installed base of frame relay products. Interest has since shifted to ATM for high-speed data networking, but because of the remaining popularity of frame relay, we provide a survey in this section.

Background

The traditional approach to packet switching makes use of X.25, which not only determines the user-network interface but also influences the internal design of the network. The following are several key features of the X.25 approach:

- Call control packets, used for setting up and clearing virtual circuits, are carried on the same channel and same virtual circuit as data packets. In effect, inband signaling is used.
- Multiplexing of virtual circuits takes place at layer 3.
- Both layer 2 and layer 3 include flow control and error control mechanisms.

The X.25 approach results in considerable overhead. At each hop through the network, the data link control protocol involves the exchange of a data frame and an acknowledgment frame. Furthermore, at each intermediate node, state tables must be maintained for each virtual circuit to deal with the call management and flow control/error control aspects of the X.25 protocol. All of this overhead may be justified when there is a significant probability of error on any of the links in the network. This approach may not be the most appropriate for modern digital communication facilities. Today's networks employ reliable digital transmission technology over high-quality, reliable transmission links, many of which are optical fiber. In addition, with the use of optical fiber and digital transmission, high data rates can be achieved. In this environment, the overhead of X.25 is not only unnecessary but degrades the effective utilization of the available high data rates.

Frame relaying is designed to eliminate much of the overhead that X.25 imposes on end user systems and on the packet-switching network. The key differences between frame relaying and a conventional X.25 packet-switching service are as follows:

- Call control signaling is carried on a separate logical connection from user data. Thus, intermediate nodes need not maintain state tables or process messages relating to call control on an individual per-connection basis.
- Multiplexing and switching of logical connections takes place at layer 2 instead of layer 3, eliminating one entire layer of processing.
- There is no hop-by-hop flow control and error control. End-to-end flow control and error control are the responsibility of a higher layer, if they are employed at all.

Thus, with frame relay, a single user data frame is sent from source to destination, and an acknowledgment, generated at a higher layer, is carried back in a frame. There are no hop-by-hop exchanges of data frames and acknowledgments.

Let us consider the advantages and disadvantages of this approach. The principal potential disadvantage of frame relaying, compared to X.25, is that we have lost the ability to do link-by-link flow and error control. (Although frame relay does not provide end-to-end flow and error control, this is easily provided at a higher layer.) In X.25, multiple virtual circuits are carried on a single physical link, and LAPB is available at the link level for providing reliable transmission from the source to the packet-switching network and from the packet-switching network to the destination. In addition, at each hop through the network, the link control protocol can be used for reliability. With the use of frame relaying, this hop-by-hop link control is lost. However, with the increasing reliability of transmission and switching facilities, this is not a major disadvantage.

The advantage of frame relaying is that we have streamlined the communications process. The protocol functionality required at the user-network interface is reduced, as is the internal network processing. As a result, lower delay and higher throughput can be expected. Studies indicate an improvement in throughput using frame relay, compared to X.25, of an order of magnitude or more [HARB92]. The ITU-T Recommendation I.233 indicates that frame relay is to be used at access speeds up to 2 Mbps. However, frame relay service at even higher data rates are now available.

Frame Relay Protocol Architecture

Figure 10.18 depicts the protocol architecture to support the frame mode bearer service. We need to consider two separate planes of operation: a control (C) plane, which is involved in the establishment and termination of logical connections, and a user (U) plane, which is responsible for the transfer of user data between subscribers. Thus, C-plane protocols are between a subscriber and the network, while U-plane protocols provide end-to-end functionality.

Control Plane

The control plane for frame mode bearer services is similar to that for common channel signaling for circuit-switching services, in that a separate logical channel is used for control information. At the data link layer, LAPD (Q.921) is used to

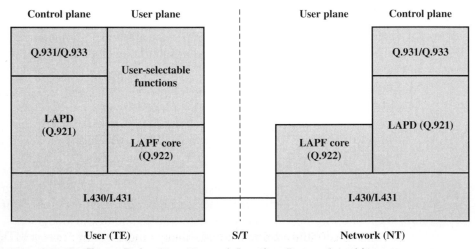

Figure 10.18   Frame Relay User-Network Interface Protocol Architecture

provide a reliable data link control service, with error control and flow control, between user (TE) and network (NT) over the D channel. This data link service is used for the exchange of Q.933 control signaling messages.

User Plane

For the actual transfer of information between end users, the user-plane protocol is LAPF (Link Access Procedure for Frame Mode Bearer Services), which is defined in Q.922. Only the core functions of LAPF are used for frame relay:

- Frame delimiting, alignment, and transparency
- Frame multiplexing/demultiplexing using the address field
- Inspection of the frame to ensure that it consists of an integral number of octets prior to zero bit insertion or following zero bit extraction
- Inspection of the frame to ensure that it is neither too long nor too short
- Detection of transmission errors
- Congestion control functions

The last function listed is new to LAPF. The remaining functions listed are also functions of LAPD.

The core functions of LAPF in the user plane constitute a sublayer of the data link layer. This provides the bare service of transferring data link frames from one subscriber to another, with no flow control or error control. Above this, the user may choose to select additional data link or network-layer end-to-end functions. These are not part of the frame relay service. Based on the core functions, a network offers frame relaying as a connection-oriented link layer service with the following properties:

- Preservation of the order of frame transfer from one edge of the network to the other
- A small probability of frame loss

User Data Transfer

The operation of frame relay for user data transfer is best explained by considering the frame format, illustrated in Figure 10.19a. This is the format defined for the minimum-function LAPF protocol (known as LAPF core protocol). The format is similar to that of LAPD and LAPB with one obvious omission: There is no Control field. This has the following implications:

- There is only one frame type, used for carrying user data. There are no control frames.
- It is not possible to use inband signaling; a logical connection can only carry user data.

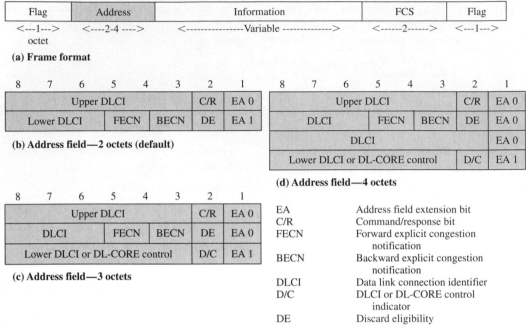

Figure 10.19   LAPF-Core Formats

• It is not possible to perform flow control and error control, because there are no sequence numbers.

The Flag and Frame Check Sequence (FCS) fields function as in HDLC. The information field carries higher-layer data. If the user selects to implement additional data link control functions end-to-end, then a data link frame can be carried in this field. Specifically, a common selection will be to use the full LAPF protocol (known as LAPF control protocol), to perform functions above the LAPF core functions. Note that the protocol implemented in this fashion is strictly between the end subscribers and is transparent to the frame relay network.

The Address field has a default length of 2 octets and may be extended to 3 or 4 octets. It carries a data link connection identifier (DLCI) of 10, 16, or 23 bits. The DLCI serves the same function as the virtual circuit number in X.25: It allows multiple logical frame relay connections to be multiplexed over a single channel. As in X.25, the connection identifier has only local significance: Each end of the logical connection assigns its own DLCI from the pool of locally unused numbers, and the network must map from one to the other. The alternative, using the same DLCI on both ends, would require some sort of global management of DLCI values.

The length of the Address field, and hence of the DLCI, is determined by the Address field extension (EA) bits. The C/R bit is application specific and not used by the standard frame relay protocol. The remaining bits in the address field have to do with congestion control and are discussed in Chapter 13.

10.9 RECOMMENDED READING AND WEB SITES

As befits its age, circuit switching has inspired a voluminous literature. Two good books on the subject are [BELL00] and [FREE96]. Discussions of control signaling can be found in [BOSS98] and [FREE98]. [STAL99] covers SS7 in more detail. For greater depth, [BLAC97] and [RUSS95] are good. [BHAT97] also provides a detailed technical treatment, with emphasis on practical implementation issues.

The literature on packet switching is enormous. Books with good treatments of this subject include [SPOH02], [BERT92], and [SPRA91].

A more in-depth treatment of frame relay can be found in [STAL99]. An excellent book-length treatment is [BUCK00].

BELL00   Bellamy, J. *Digital Telephony.* New York: Wiley, 2000.

BERT92   Bertsekas, D., and Gallager, R. *Data Networks.* Englewood Cliffs, NJ: Prentice Hall, 1992.

BHAT97   Bhatnagar, P. *Engineering Networks for Synchronization, CCS 7 and ISDN.* New York: IEEE Press, 1997.

BLAC97   Black, U. *ISDN and SS7: Architectures for Digital Signaling Networks.* Upper Saddle River, NJ: Prentice Hall, 1997.

BOSS98   Bosse, J. *Signaling in Telecommunication Networks.* New York: Wiley, 1998.

BUCK00   Buckwalter, J. *Frame Relay: Technology and Practice.* Reading, MA: Addison-Wesley, 2000.

FREE96   Freeman, R. *Telecommunication System Engineering.* New York: Wiley, 1996.

FREE98   Freeman, R. *Telecommunications Transmission Handbook.* New York: Wiley, 1998.

RUSS95   Russell, R. *Signaling System #7.* New York: McGraw-Hill, 1995.

SPOH02   Spohn, D. *Data Network Design.* New York: McGraw-Hill, 2002.

SPRA91   Spragins, J.; Hammond, J.; and Pawlikowski, K. *Telecommunications Protocols and Design.* Reading, MA.: Addison-Wesley, 1991.

STAL99   Stallings, W. *ISDN and Broadband ISDN, with Frame Relay and ATM.* Upper Saddle River, NJ: Prentice Hall, 1999.

Recommended Web Sites:

- **International Softswitch Consortium:** News, technical information, and vendor information on softswitch technology and products.
- **Media Gateway Control Working Group:** Chartered by IETF to develop the media gateway control protocol and related standards.
- **Frame Relay Forum:** An association of corporate members comprised of vendors, carriers, users, and consultants committed to the implementation of frame relay in accordance with national and international standards. Site includes list of technical and implementation documents for sale.
- **Frame Relay Resource Center:** Good source of information on frame relay.

10.10 KEY TERMS, REVIEW QUESTIONS, AND PROBLEMS

Key Terms

associated mode	frame relay	Signaling System Number 7
circuit switching	inchannel signaling	(SS7)
circuit-switching network	LAPB	softswitch
common channel signaling	LAPF	space division switching
control signaling	local loop	subscriber
crossbar matrix	media gateway	subscriber line
datagram	controller	subscriber loop
digital switch	out-of-band signaling	time division switching
disassociated mode	packet switching	trunk
exchange	signal transfer point	virtual circuit
inband signaling	signaling point	X.25

Review Questions

10.1 Why is it useful to have more than one possible path through a network for each pair of stations?

10.2 What are the four generic architectural components of a public communications network? Define each term.

10.3 What is the principal application that has driven the design of circuit-switching networks?

10.4 What is the difference between inchannel and common channel signaling?

10.5 What are the advantages of packet switching compared to circuit switching?

10.6 Explain the difference between datagram and virtual circuit operation.

10.7 What is the significance of packet size in a packet-switching network?

10.8 What types of delay are significant in assessing the performance of a packet-switching network?

10.9 How does frame relay differ from X.25?

10.10 What are the relative advantages and disadvantages of frame relay compared to X.25?

Problems

10.1 Consider a simple telephone network consisting of two end offices and one intermediate switch with a 1-MHz full-duplex trunk between each end office and the intermediate switch. Assume a 4-kHz channel for each voice call. The average telephone is used to make four calls per 8-hour workday, with a mean call duration of six minutes. Ten percent of the calls are long distance. What is the maximum number of telephones an end office can support?

10.2 Would it be possible to provide a circuit-switching rather than a packet-switching implementation of SS7? What would be the relative merits of such an approach?

10.3 Explain the flaw in the following reasoning: Packet switching requires control and address bits to be added to each packet. This introduces considerable overhead in packet switching. In circuit switching, a transparent circuit is established. No extra bits are needed. Therefore, there is no overhead in circuit switching. Because there is no overhead in circuit switching, line utilization must be more efficient than in packet switching.

10.4 Define the following parameters for a switching network:

N = number of hops between two given end systems
L = message length in bits
B = data rate, in bits per second (bps), on all links
P = fixed packet size, in bits
H = overhead (header) bits per packet
S = call setup time (circuit switching or virtual circuit) in seconds
D = propagation delay per hop in seconds

  a. For $N = 4$, $L = 3200$, $B = 9600$, $P = 1024$, $H = 16$, $S = 0.2$, $D = 0.001$, compute the end-to-end delay for circuit switching, virtual circuit packet switching, and datagram packet switching. Assume that there are no acknowledgments. Ignore processing delay at the nodes.
  b. Derive general expressions for the three techniques of part (a), taken two at a time (three expressions in all), showing the conditions under which the delays are equal.

10.5 What value of P, as a function of N, L, and H, results in minimum end-to-end delay on a datagram network? Assume that L is much larger than P, and D is zero.

10.6 Assuming no malfunction in any of the stations or nodes of a network, is it possible for a packet to be delivered to the wrong destination?

10.7 Flow-control mechanisms are used at both levels 2 and 3 of X.25. Are both necessary, or is this redundant? Explain.

10.8 There is no error-detection mechanism (frame check sequence) in X.25. Isn't this needed to assure that all of the packets are delivered properly?

10.9 In X.25, why is the virtual circuit number used by one station of two communicating stations different from the virtual circuit number used by the other station? After all, it is the same full-duplex virtual circuit.

10.10 Q.933 recommends a procedure for negotiating the sliding-window flow control window, which may take on a value from 1 to 127. The negotiation makes use of a variable k that is calculated from the following parameters:

L_d = data frame size in octets
R_u = throughput bits/sec
T_{td} = end-to-end transit delay in sec
k = window size (maximum number of outstanding I frames)

The procedure is described as follows:

> The window size should be negotiated as follows. The originating user should calculate k using the above formula, substituting maximum end-to-end transit delay and outgoing maximum frame size for T_{td} and L_d, respectively. The SETUP message shall include the link layer protocol parameters, the link layer core parameters, and the end-to-end transit delay information elements. The destination user should calculate its own k using the above formula, substituting cumulative end-to-end transit delay and its own outgoing maximum frame size for T_{td} and L_d, respectively. The CONNECT message shall include the link layer core parameters and the end-to-end transit delay information element so that the originating user can adjust its k based on the information conveyed in these information elements. The originating user should calculate k using the above formula, substituting cumulative end-to-end transit delay and Incoming maximum frame size for T_{td} and L_d, respectively.

SETUP and CONNECT are messages exchanged on a control channel during the setup of a frame relay connection. Suggest a formula for calculating k from the other variables and justify the formula.

CHAPTER 11

ASYNCHRONOUS TRANSFER MODE

KEY POINTS

- ATM is a streamlined packet transfer interface. ATM makes use of fixed-size packets, called cells. The use of a fixed size and fixed format results in an efficient scheme for transmission over high-speed networks.

- Some form of transmission structure must be used to transport ATM cells. One option is the use of a continuous stream of cells, with no multiplex frame structure imposed at the interface. Synchronization is on a cell-by-cell basis. The second option is to place the cells in a synchronous time division multiplex envelope. In this case, the bit stream at the interface has an external frame based on the Synchronous Digital Hierarchy (SDH).

- ATM provides both real-time and non-real-time services. An ATM-based network can support a wide range of traffic, include synchronous TDM streams such as T1, using the constant bit rate (CBR) service, compressed voice and video using the real-time variable bit rate (rt-VBR) service, traffic with specific quality-of-service requirements, using the non-real-time VBR (nrt-VBR) service, and IP-based traffic using the available bit rate (ABR), unspecified bit rate (UBR), and guaranteed frame rate (GFR) services.

- The use of ATM creates the need for an adaptation layer to support information transfer protocols not based on ATM. The ATM adaptation layer (AAL) packages information from the AAL user into 48-octet packages to fit into the ATM cell. This may involve aggregating bits from a bit stream or segmenting a frame into smaller pieces.

Asynchronous transfer mode (ATM), also known as cell relay, takes advantage of the reliability and fidelity of modern digital facilities to provide faster packet switching than X.25. ATM was developed as part of the work on broadband ISDN but has found application in non-ISDN environments where very high data rates are required.

We begin with a discussion of the details of the ATM scheme. Then we examine the important concept of the ATM adaptation layer (AAL).

11.1 PROTOCOL ARCHITECTURE

Asynchronous transfer mode is in some ways similar to packet switching using X.25 and to frame relay. Like packet switching and frame relay, ATM involves the transfer of data in discrete chunks. Also, like packet switching and frame relay, ATM allows multiple logical connections to be multiplexed over a single physical interface. In the case of ATM, the information flow on each logical connection is organized into fixed-size packets, called **cells**.

ATM is a streamlined protocol with minimal error- and flow control capabilities. This reduces the overhead of processing ATM cells and reduces the number of overhead bits required with each cell, thus enabling ATM to operate at high data rates. Further, the use of fixed-size cells simplifies the processing required at each ATM node, again supporting the use of ATM at high data rates.

The standards issued for ATM by ITU-T are based on the protocol architecture shown in Figure 11.1, which illustrates the basic architecture for an interface

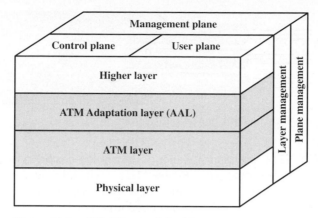

Figure 11.1   ATM Protocol Architecture

between user and network. The physical layer involves the specification of a transmission medium and a signal encoding scheme. The data rates specified at the physical layer range from 25.6 Mbps to 622.08 Mbps. Other data rates, both higher and lower, are possible.

Two layers of the protocol architecture relate to ATM functions. There is an ATM layer common to all services that provides packet transfer capabilities, and an ATM adaptation layer (AAL) that is service dependent. The ATM layer defines the transmission of data in fixed-size cells and defines the use of logical connections. The use of ATM creates the need for an adaptation layer to support information transfer protocols not based on ATM. The AAL maps higher-layer information into ATM cells to be transported over an ATM network, then collects information from ATM cells for delivery to higher layers.

The protocol reference model involves three separate planes:

- **User plane:** Provides for user information transfer, along with associated controls (e.g., flow control, error control)
- **Control plane:** Performs call control and connection control functions
- **Management plane:** Includes plane management, which performs management functions related to a system as a whole and provides coordination between all the planes, and layer management, which performs management functions relating to resources and parameters residing in its protocol entities

11.2 ATM LOGICAL CONNECTIONS

Logical connections in ATM are referred to as virtual channel connections (VCCs). A VCC is analogous to a virtual circuit in X.25; it is the basic unit of switching in an ATM network. A VCC is set up between two end users through the network and a variable-rate, full-duplex flow of fixed-size cells is exchanged over the connection. VCCs are also used for user-network exchange (control signaling) and network-network exchange (network management and routing).

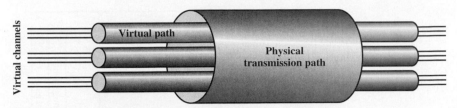

Figure 11.2 ATM Connection Relationships

For ATM, a second sublayer of processing has been introduced that deals with the concept of virtual path (Figure 11.2). A virtual path connection (VPC) is a bundle of VCCs that have the same endpoints. Thus, all of the cells flowing over all of the VCCs in a single VPC are switched together.

The virtual path concept was developed in response to a trend in high-speed networking in which the control cost of the network is becoming an increasingly higher proportion of the overall network cost. The virtual path technique helps contain the control cost by grouping connections sharing common paths through the network into a single unit. Network management actions can then be applied to a small number of groups of connections instead of a large number of individual connections.

Several advantages can be listed for the use of virtual paths:

- **Simplified network architecture:** Network transport functions can be separated into those related to an individual logical connection (virtual channel) and those related to a group of logical connections (virtual path).
- **Increased network performance and reliability:** The network deals with fewer, aggregated entities.
- **Reduced processing and short connection setup time:** Much of the work is done when the virtual path is set up. By reserving capacity on a virtual path connection in anticipation of later call arrivals, new virtual channel connections can be established by executing simple control functions at the endpoints of the virtual path connection; no call processing is required at transit nodes. Thus, the addition of new virtual channels to an existing virtual path involves minimal processing.
- **Enhanced network services:** The virtual path is used internal to the network but is also visible to the end user. Thus, the user may define closed user groups or closed networks of virtual channel bundles.

Figure 11.3 suggests in a general way the call establishment process using virtual channels and virtual paths. The process of setting up a virtual path connection is decoupled from the process of setting up an individual virtual channel connection:

- The virtual path control mechanisms include calculating routes, allocating capacity, and storing connection state information.
- To set up a virtual channel, there must first be a virtual path connection to the required destination node with sufficient available capacity to support the virtual channel, with the appropriate quality of service. A virtual channel is set up by storing the required state information (virtual channel/virtual path mapping).

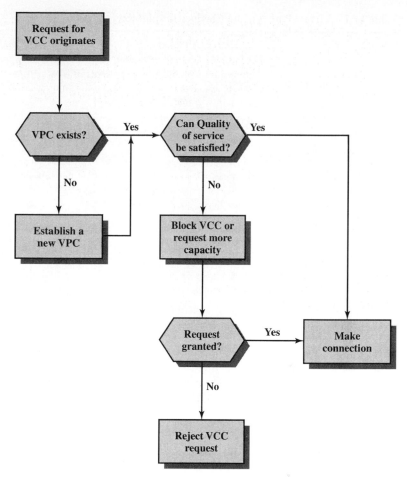

Figure 11.3 Call Establishment Using Virtual Paths

The terminology of virtual paths and virtual channels used in the standard is a bit confusing and is summarized in Table 11.1. Whereas most of the network-layer protocols that we deal with in this book relate only to the user-network interface, the concepts of virtual path and virtual channel are defined in the ITU-T Recommendations with reference to both the user-network interface and the internal network operation.

Virtual Channel Connection Uses

The endpoints of a VCC may be end users, network entities, or an end user and a network entity. In all cases, cell sequence integrity is preserved within a VCC: That is, cells are delivered in the same order in which they are sent. Let us consider examples of the three uses of a VCC:

Table 11.1 Virtual Path/Virtual Channel Terminology

Virtual Channel (VC)	A generic term used to describe unidirectional transport of ATM cells associated by a common unique identifier value.
Virtual Channel Link	A means of unidirectional transport of ATM cells between a point where a VCI value is assigned and the point where that value is translated or terminated.
Virtual Channel Identifier (VCI)	A unique numerical tag that identifies a particular VC link for a given VPC.
Virtual Channel Connection (VCC)	A concatenation of VC links that extends between two points where ATM service users access the ATM layer. VCCs are provided for the purpose of user-user, user-network, or network-network information transfer. Cell sequence integrity is preserved for cells belonging to the same VCC.
Virtual Path	A generic term used to describe unidirectional transport of ATM cells belonging to virtual channels that are associated by a common unique identifier value.
Virtual Path Link	A group of VC links, identified by a common value of VPI, between a point where a VPI value is assigned and the point where that value is translated or terminated.
Virtual Path Identifier (VPI)	Identifies a particular VP link.
Virtual Path Connection (VPC)	A concatenation of VP links that extends between the point where the VCI values are assigned and the point where those values are translated or removed (i.e., extending the length of a bundle of VC links that share the same VPI). VPCs are provided for the purpose of user-user, user-network, or network-network information transfer.

- **Between end users:** Can be used to carry end-to-end user data; can also be used to carry control signaling between end users, as explained later. A VPC between end users provides them with an overall capacity; the VCC organization of the VPC is up to the two end users, provided the set of VCCs does not exceed the VPC capacity.
- **Between an end user and a network entity:** Used for user-to-network control signaling, as discussed subsequently. A user-to-network VPC can be used to aggregate traffic from an end user to a network exchange or network server.
- **Between two network entities:** Used for network traffic management and routing functions. A network-to-network VPC can be used to define a common route for the exchange of network management information.

Virtual Path/Virtual Channel Characteristics

ITU-T Recommendation I.150 lists the following as characteristics of virtual channel connections:

- **Quality of service:** A user of a VCC is provided with a quality of service specified by parameters such as cell loss ratio (ratio of cells lost to cells transmitted) and cell delay variation.

- **Switched and semipermanent virtual channel connections:** A switched VCC is an on-demand connection, which requires call control signaling for setup and tearing down. A semipermanent VCC is one that is of long duration and is set up by configuration or network management action.
- **Cell sequence integrity:** The sequence of transmitted cells within a VCC is preserved.
- **Traffic parameter negotiation and usage monitoring:** Traffic parameters can be negotiated between a user and the network for each VCC. The input of cells to the VCC is monitored by the network to ensure that the negotiated parameters are not violated.

The types of traffic parameters that can be negotiated include average rate, peak rate, burstiness, and peak duration. The network may need a number of strategies to deal with congestion and to manage existing and requested VCCs. At the crudest level, the network may simply deny new requests for VCCs to prevent congestion. Additionally, cells may be discarded if negotiated parameters are violated or if congestion becomes severe. In an extreme situation, existing connections might be terminated.

I.150 also lists characteristics of VPCs. The first four characteristics listed are identical to those for VCCs. That is, quality of service; switched and semipermanent VPCs; cell sequence integrity; and traffic parameter negotiation and usage monitoring are all also characteristics of a VPC. There are a number of reasons for this duplication. First, this provides some flexibility in how the network service manages the requirements placed upon it. Second, the network must be concerned with the overall requirements for a VPC, and within a VPC may negotiate the establishment of virtual channels with given characteristics. Finally, once a VPC is set up, it is possible for the end users to negotiate the creation of new VCCs. The VPC characteristics impose a discipline on the choices that the end users may make.

In addition, a fifth characteristic is listed for VPCs:

- **Virtual channel identifier restriction within a VPC:** One or more virtual channel identifiers, or numbers, may not be available to the user of the VPC but may be reserved for network use. Examples include VCCs used for network management.

Control Signaling

In ATM, a mechanism is needed for the establishment and release of VPCs and VCCs. The exchange of information involved in this process is referred to as control signaling and takes place on separate connections from those that are being managed.

For VCCs, I.150 specifies four methods for providing an establishment/release facility. One or a combination of these methods will be used in any particular network:

1. **Semipermanent VCCs** may be used for user-to-user exchange. In this case, no control signaling is required.

2. If there is no preestablished call control signaling channel, then one must be set up. For that purpose, a control signaling exchange must take place between the user and the network on some channel. Hence we need a permanent channel, probably of low data rate, that can be used to set up VCCs that can be used for call control. Such a channel is called a **meta-signaling channel**, as the channel is used to set up signaling channels.

3. The meta-signaling channel can be used to set up a VCC between the user and the network for call control signaling. This **user-to-network signaling virtual channel** can then be used to set up VCCs to carry user data.

4. The meta-signaling channel can also be used to set up a **user-to-user signaling virtual channel**. Such a channel must be set up within a preestablished VPC. It can then be used to allow the two end users, without network intervention, to establish and release user-to-user VCCs to carry user data.

For VPCs, three methods are defined in I.150:

1. A VPC can be established on a **semipermanent** basis by prior agreement. In this case, no control signaling is required.

2. VPC establishment/release may be **customer controlled**. In this case, the customer uses a signaling VCC to request the VPC from the network.

3. VPC establishment/release may be **network controlled**. In this case, the network establishes a VPC for its own convenience. The path may be network-to-network, user-to-network, or user-to-user.

11.3 ATM CELLS

The asynchronous transfer mode makes use of fixed-size cells, consisting of a 5-octet header and a 48-octet information field. There are several advantages to the use of small, fixed-size cells. First, the use of small cells may reduce queuing delay for a high-priority cell, because it waits less if it arrives slightly behind a lower-priority cell that has gained access to a resource (e.g., the transmitter). Second, it appears that fixed-size cells can be switched more efficiently, which is important for the very high data rates of ATM [PARE88]. With fixed-size cells, it is easier to implement the switching mechanism in hardware.

Header Format

Figure 11.4a shows the cell header format at the user–network interface. Figure 11.4b shows the cell header format internal to the network.

The **generic flow control** (GFC) field does not appear in the cell header internal to the network, but only at the user-network interface. Hence, it can be used for control of cell flow only at the local user-network interface. The field could be used to assist the customer in controlling the flow of traffic for different qualities of service. In any case, the GFC mechanism is used to alleviate short-term overload conditions in the network.

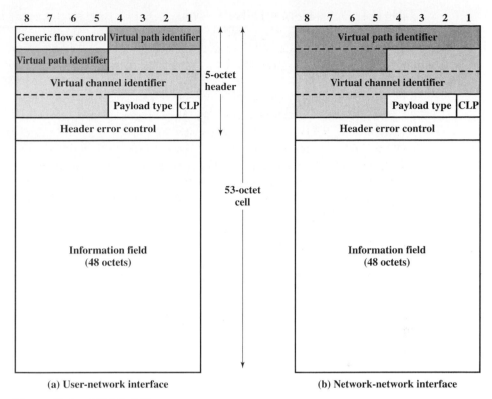

Figure 11.4 ATM Cell Format

I.150 lists as a requirement for the GFC mechanism that all terminals be able to get access to their assured capacities. This includes all constant-bit-rate (CBR) terminals as well as the variable-bit-rate (VBR) terminals that have an element of guaranteed capacity (CBR and VBR are explained in Section 11.5). The current GFC mechanism is described in a subsequent subsection.

The **virtual path identifier** (VPI) constitutes a routing field for the network. It is 8 bits at the user-network interface and 12 bits at the network-network interface. The latter allows support for an expanded number of VPCs internal to the network, to include those supporting subscribers and those required for network management. The **virtual channel identifier** (VCI) is used for routing to and from the end user.

The **payload type** (PT) field indicates the type of information in the information field. Table 11.2 shows the interpretation of the PT bits. A value of 0 in the first bit indicates user information (that is, information from the next higher layer). In this case, the second bit indicates whether congestion has been experienced; the third bit, known as the service data unit (SDU)[1] type bit, is a one-bit field that can

---

[1] This is the term used in ATM Forum documents. In ITU-T documents, this bit is referred to as the ATM-user-to-ATM-user (AAU) indication bit. The meaning is the same.

Table 11.2 Payload Type (PT) Field Coding

PT Coding	Interpretation		
0 0 0	User data cell,	congestion not experienced,	SDU type = 0
0 0 1	User data cell,	congestion not experienced,	SDU type = 1
0 1 0	User data cell,	congestion experienced,	SDU type = 0
0 1 1	User data cell,	congestion experienced,	SDU type = 1
1 0 0	OAM segment associated cell		
1 0 1	OAM end-to-end associated cell		
1 1 0	Resource management cell		
1 1 1	Reserved for future function		

SDU = Service data unit
OAM = Operations, administration, and maintenance

be used to discriminate two types of ATM SDUs associated with a connection. The term *SDU* refers to the 48-octet payload of the cell. A value of 1 in the first bit of the payload type field indicates that this cell carries network management or maintenance information. This indication allows the insertion of network-management cells onto a user's VCC without impacting the user's data. Thus, the PT field can provide inband control information.

The **cell loss priority** (CLP) bit is used to provide guidance to the network in the event of congestion. A value of 0 indicates a cell of relatively higher priority, which should not be discarded unless no other alternative is available. A value of 1 indicates that this cell is subject to discard within the network. The user might employ this field so that extra cells (beyond the negotiated rate) may be inserted into the network, with a CLP of 1, and delivered to the destination if the network is not congested. The network may set this field to 1 for any data cell that is in violation of an agreement concerning traffic parameters between the user and the network. In this case, the switch that does the setting realizes that the cell exceeds the agreed traffic parameters but that the switch is capable of handling the cell. At a later point in the network, if congestion is encountered, this cell has been marked for discard in preference to cells that fall within agreed traffic limits.

The **header error control** field is used for both error control and synchronization, as explained subsequently.

Generic Flow Control

I.150 specifies the use of the GFC field to control traffic flow at the user-network interface (UNI) in order to alleviate short-term overload conditions. The actual flow control mechanism is defined in I.361. GFC flow control is part of a proposed controlled cell transfer (CCT) capability intended to meet the requirements of non-ATM LANs connected to a wide area ATM network [LUIN97]. In particular, CCT is intended to provide good service for high-volume bursty traffic with variable-length messages. In the remainder of this subsection, we examine the GFC mechanism, as so far standardized.

When the equipment at the UNI is configured to support the GFC mechanism, two sets of procedures are used: uncontrolled transmission and controlled transmission. In essence, every connection is identified as either subject to flow control or not. Of those subject to flow control, there may be one group of controlled connections (Group A) that is the default, or controlled traffic may be classified into two groups of controlled connections (Group A and Group B); these are known, respectively, as the 1-queue and 2-queue models. Flow control is exercised in the direction from the subscriber to the network by the network side.

First, we consider the operation of the GFC mechanism when there is only one group of controlled connections. The controlled equipment, called terminal equipment (TE), initializes two variables: TRANSMIT is a flag initialized to SET (1), and GO_CNTR, which is a credit counter, is initialized to 0. A third variable, GO_VALUE, is either initialized to 1 or set to some larger value at configuration time. The rules for transmission by the controlled device are as follows:

1. If TRANSMIT = 1, cells on uncontrolled connections may be sent at any time. If TRANSMIT = 0, no cells may be sent on either controlled or uncontrolled connections.
2. If a HALT signal is received from the controlling equipment, TRANSMIT is set to 0 and remains at zero until a NO_HALT signal is received, at which time TRANSMIT is set to 1.
3. If TRANSMIT = 1 and there is no cell to transmit on any uncontrolled connections, then
   - If GO_CNTR > 0, then the TE may send a cell on a controlled connection. The TE marks that cell as a cell on a controlled connection and decrements GO_CNTR.
   - If GO_CNTR = 0, then the TE may not send a cell on a controlled connection.
4. The TE sets GO_CNTR to GO_VALUE upon receiving a SET signal; a null signal has no effect on GO_CNTR.

The HALT signal is used logically to limit the effective ATM data rate and should be cyclic. For example, to reduce the data rate over a link by half, the HALT command is issued by the controlling equipment so as to be in effect 50% of the time. This is done in a predictable, regular pattern over the lifetime of the physical connection.

For the 2-queue model, there are two counters, each with a current counter value and an initialization value: GO_CNTR_A, GO_VALUE_A, GO_CNTR_B, and GO_VALUE_B. This enables the NT2 to control two separate groups of connections.

Table 11.3 summarizes the rules for setting GFC bits.

Header Error Control

Each ATM cell includes an 8-bit header error control field (HEC) that is calculated based on the remaining 32 bits of the header. The polynomial used to generate the code is $X^8 + X^2 + X + 1$. In most existing protocols that include an error control field, such as HDLC, the data that serve as input to the error code calculation are in

Table 11.3 Generic Flow Control (GFC) Field Coding

	Uncontrolled	Controlling → controlled		Controlled → controlling	
		1-queue model	**2-queue model**	**1-queue model**	**2-queue model**
First bit	0	HALT(0)/ NO_HALT(1)	HALT(0)/ NO_HALT(1)	0	0
Second bit	0	SET(1)/ NULL(0)	SET(1)/ NULL(0) for Group A	Cell belongs to controlled(1)/ uncontrolled(0)	Cell belongs to Group A(1)/ or not (0)
Third bit	0	0	SET(1)/ NULL(0) for Group B	0	Cell belongs to Group B(1)/ or not (0)
Fourth bit	0	0	0	Equipment is uncontrolled(0)/ controlled(1)	Equipment is uncontrolled(0)/ controlled(1)

general much longer than the size of the resulting error code. This allows for error detection. In the case of ATM, the input to the calculation is only 32 bits, compared to 8 bits for the code. The fact that the input is relatively short allows the code to be used not only for error detection but, in some cases, for actual error correction. This is because there is sufficient redundancy in the code to recover from certain error patterns.

Figure 11.5 depicts the operation of the HEC algorithm at the receiver. At initialization, the receiver's error correction algorithm is in the default mode for single-bit error correction. As each cell is received, the HEC calculation and comparison is performed. As long as no errors are detected, the receiver remains in error correction mode. When an error is detected, the receiver will correct the error if it is a single-bit error or will detect that a multibit error has occurred. In either case, the receiver now moves to detection mode. In this mode, no attempt is made to correct errors. The reason for this change is a recognition that a noise burst or other event might cause a sequence of errors, a condition for which the HEC is insufficient for error correction. The receiver remains in detection mode as long as errored

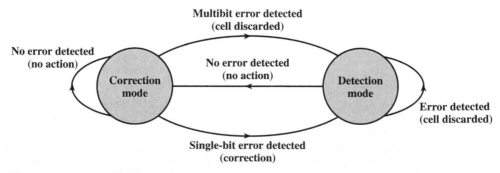

Figure 11.5 HEC Operation at Receiver

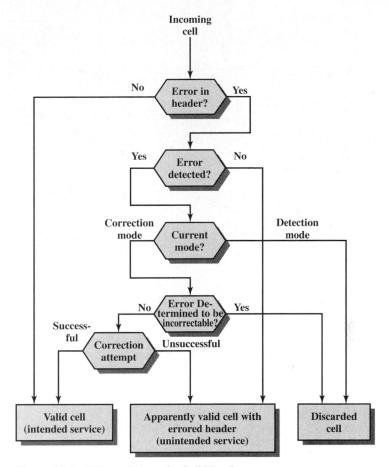

Figure 11.6 Effect of Error in Cell Header

cells are received. When a header is examined and found not to be in error, the receiver switches back to correction mode. The flowchart of Figure 11.6 shows the consequence of errors in the cell header.

The error-protection function provides both recovery from single-bit header errors and a low probability of the delivery of cells with errored headers under bursty error conditions. The error characteristics of fiber-based transmission systems appear to be a mix of single-bit errors and relatively large burst errors. For some transmission systems, the error-correction capability, which is more time-consuming, might not be invoked.

Figure 11.7, based on one in ITU-T I.432, indicates how random bit errors impact the probability of occurrence of discarded cells and valid cells with errored headers, when HEC is employed.

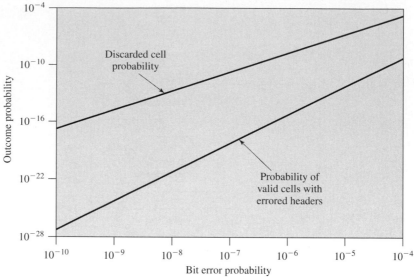

Figure 11.7 Impact of Random Bit Errors on HEC Performance

11.4 TRANSMISSION OF ATM CELLS

I.432 specifies that ATM cells may be transmitted at one of several data rates: 622.08 Mbps, 155.52 Mbps, 51.84 Mbps, or 25.6 Mbps. We need to specify the transmission structure that will be used to carry this payload. Two approaches are defined in I.432: a cell-based physical layer and an SDH-based physical layer.[2] We examine each of these approaches in turn.

Cell–Based Physical Layer

For the cell-based physical layer, no framing is imposed. The interface structure consists of a continuous stream of 53-octet cells. Because there is no external frame imposed in the cell-based approach, some form of synchronization is needed. Synchronization is achieved on the basis of the header error control (HEC) field in the cell header. The procedure is as follows (Figure 11.8):

1. In the HUNT state, a cell delineation algorithm is performed bit by bit to determine if the HEC coding law is observed (i.e., match between received HEC and calculated HEC). Once a match is achieved, it is assumed that one header has been found, and the method enters the PRESYNC state.

2. In the PRESYNC state, a cell structure is now assumed. The cell delineation algorithm is performed cell by cell until the encoding law has been confirmed consecutively δ times.

---

[2] The SDH-based approach is not defined for 25.6 Mbps.

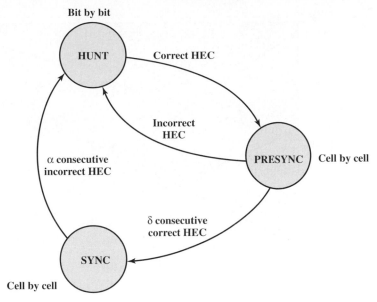

Figure 11.8 Cell Delineation State Diagram

3. In the SYNC state, the HEC is used for error detection and correction (see Figure 11.5). Cell delineation is assumed to be lost if the HEC coding law is recognized consecutively as incorrect α times.

The values of α and δ are design parameters. Greater values of δ result in longer delays in establishing synchronization but in greater robustness against false delineation. Greater values of α result in longer delays in recognizing a misalignment but in greater robustness against false misalignment. Figures 11.9 and 11.10, based on I.432, show the impact of random bit errors on cell delineation performance for various values of α and δ. The first figure shows the average amount of time that the receiver will maintain synchronization in the face of errors, with α as a parameter. The second figure shows the average amount of time to acquire synchronization as a function of error rate, with δ as a parameter.

The advantage of using a cell-based transmission scheme is the simplified interface that results when both transmission and transfer mode functions are based on a common structure.

SDH–Based Physical Layer

The SDH-based physical layer imposes a structure on the ATM cell stream. In this section, we look at the I.432 specification for 155.52 Mbps; similar structures are used at other data rates. For the SDH-based physical layer, framing is imposed using the STM-1 (STS-3) frame. Figure 11.11 shows the payload portion of an STM-1 frame (see Figure 8.11). This payload may be offset from the beginning of the frame, as indicated by the pointer in the section overhead of the frame. As can be seen, the

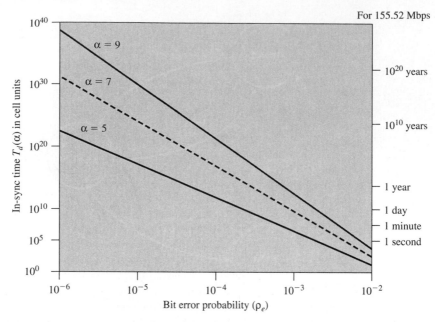

Figure 11.9 Impact of Random Bit Errors on Cell-Delineation Performance

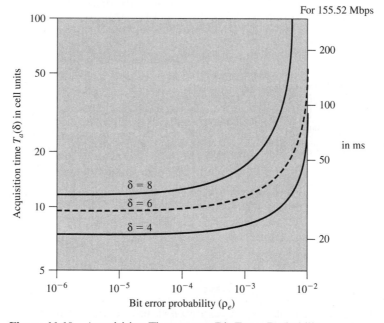

Figure 11.10 Acquisition Time versus Bit Error Probability

payload consists of a 9-octet path overhead portion and the remainder, which contains ATM cells. Because the payload capacity (2340 octets) is not an integer multiple of the cell length (53 octets), a cell may cross a payload boundary.

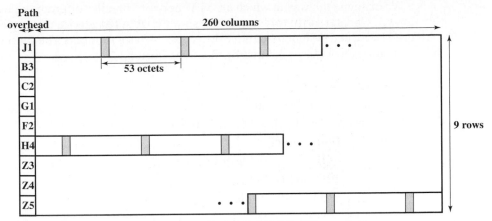

Figure 11.11 STM-1 Payload for SDH-Based ATM Cell Transmission

The H4 octet in the path overhead is set at the sending side to indicate the next occurrence of a cell boundary. That is, the value in the H4 field indicates the number of octets to the first cell boundary following the H4 octet. The permissible range of values is 0 to 52.

The advantages of the SDH-based approach include the following:

- It can be used to carry either ATM-based or STM-based (synchronous transfer mode) payloads, making it possible to initially deploy a high-capacity fiber-based transmission infrastructure for a variety of circuit-switched and dedicated applications and then readily migrate to the support of ATM.
- Some specific connections can be circuit-switched using an SDH channel. For example, a connection carrying constant-bit-rate video traffic can be mapped into its own exclusive payload envelope of the STM-1 signal, which can be circuit switched. This may be more efficient than ATM switching.
- Using SDH synchronous multiplexing techniques, several ATM streams can be combined to build interfaces with higher bit rates than those supported by the ATM layer at a particular site. For example, four separate ATM streams, each with a bit rate of 155 Mbps (STM-1), can be combined to build a 622-Mbps (STM-4) interface. This arrangement may be more cost effective than one using a single 622-Mbps ATM stream.

11.5 ATM SERVICE CATEGORIES

An ATM network is designed to be able to transfer many different types of traffic simultaneously, including real-time flows such as voice, video, and bursty TCP flows. Although each such traffic flow is handled as a stream of 53-octet cells traveling through a virtual channel, the way in which each data flow is handled within the network depends on the characteristics of the traffic flow and the requirements of the application. For example, real-time video traffic must be delivered within minimum variation in delay.

We examine the way in which an ATM network handles different types of traffic flows in Chapter 14. In this section, we summarize ATM service categories, which are used by an end system to identify the type of service required. The following service categories have been defined by the ATM Forum:

- **Real-Time Service**
  - Constant bit rate (CBR)
  - Real-time variable bit rate (rt-VBR)
- **Non-Real-Time Service**
  - Non-real-time variable bit rate (nrt-VBR)
  - Available bit rate (ABR)
  - Unspecified bit rate (UBR)
  - Guaranteed frame rate (GFR)

Real-Time Services

The most important distinction among applications concerns the amount of delay and the variability of delay, referred to as jitter, that the application can tolerate. Real-time applications typically involve a flow of information to a user that is intended to reproduce that flow at a source. For example, a user expects a flow of audio or video information to be presented in a continuous, smooth fashion. A lack of continuity or excessive loss results in significant loss of quality. Applications that involve interaction between people have tight constraints on delay. Typically, any delay above a few hundred milliseconds becomes noticeable and annoying. Accordingly, the demands in the ATM network for switching and delivery of real-time data are high.

Constant Bit Rate (CBR)

The CBR service is perhaps the simplest service to define. It is used by applications that require a fixed data rate that is continuously available during the connection lifetime and a relatively tight upper bound on transfer delay. CBR is commonly used for uncompressed audio and video information. Example of CBR applications include:

- Videoconferencing
- Interactive audio (e.g., telephony)
- Audio/video distribution (e.g., television, distance learning, pay-per-view)
- Audio/video retrieval (e.g., video-on-demand, audio library)

Real-Time Variable Bit Rate (rt-VBR)

The rt-VBR category is intended for time-sensitive applications; that is, those requiring tightly constrained delay and delay variation. The principal difference between applications appropriate for rt-VBR and those appropriate for CBR is that rt-VBR applications transmit at a rate that varies with time. Equivalently, an rt-VBR source can be characterized as somewhat bursty. For example, the standard approach to video compression results in a sequence of image frames of varying sizes.

Because real-time video requires a uniform frame transmission rate, the actual data rate varies.

The rt-VBR service allows the network more flexibility than CBR. The network is able to statistically multiplex a number of connections over the same dedicated capacity and still provide the required service to each connection.

Non–Real–Time Services

Non-real-time services are intended for applications that have bursty traffic characteristics and do not have tight constraints on delay and delay variation. Accordingly, the network has greater flexibility in handling such traffic flows and can make greater use of statistical multiplexing to increase network efficiency.

Non-Real-Time Variable Bit Rate (nrt-VBR)

For some non-real-time applications, it is possible to characterize the expected traffic flow so that the network can provide substantially improved quality of service (QoS) in the areas of loss and delay. Such applications can use the nrt-VBR service. With this service, the end system specifies a peak cell rate, a sustainable or average cell rate, and a measure of how bursty or clumped the cells may be. With this information, the network can allocate resources to provide relatively low delay and minimal cell loss.

The nrt-VBR service can be used for data transfers that have critical response-time requirements. Examples include airline reservations, banking transactions, and process monitoring.

Unspecified Bit Rate (UBR)

At any given time, a certain amount of the capacity of an ATM network is consumed in carrying CBR and the two types of VBR traffic. Additional capacity is available for one or both of the following reasons: (1) Not all of the total resources have been committed to CBR and VBR traffic, and (2) the bursty nature of VBR traffic means that at some times less than the committed capacity is being used. All of this unused capacity could be made available for the UBR service. This service is suitable for applications that can tolerate variable delays and some cell losses, which is typically true of TCP-based traffic. With UBR, cells are forwarded on a first-in-first-out (FIFO) basis using the capacity not consumed by other services; both delays and variable losses are possible. No initial commitment is made to a UBR source and no feedback concerning congestion is provided; this is referred to as a **best-effort service**. Examples of UBR applications include

- Text/data/image transfer, messaging, distribution, retrieval
- Remote terminal (e.g., telecommuting)

Available Bit Rate (ABR)

Bursty applications that use a reliable end-to-end protocol such as TCP can detect congestion in a network by means of increased round-trip delays and packet discarding. This is discussed in Chapter 17. However, TCP has no mechanism for

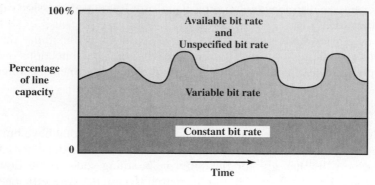

Figure 11.12   ATM Bit Rate Services

causing the resources within the network to be shared fairly among many TCP connections. Further, TCP does not minimize congestion as efficiently as is possible
using explicit information from congested nodes within the network.

To improve the service provided to bursty sources that would otherwise use
UBR, the ABR service has been defined. An application using ABR specifies a
peak cell rate (PCR) that it will use and a minimum cell rate (MCR) that it requires.
The network allocates resources so that all ABR applications receive at least their
MCR capacity. Any unused capacity is then shared in a fair and controlled fashion
among all ABR sources. The ABR mechanism uses explicit feedback to sources to
assure that capacity is fairly allocated. Any capacity not used by ABR sources
remains available for UBR traffic.

An example of an application using ABR is LAN interconnection. In this case,
the end systems attached to the ATM network are routers.

Figure 11.12 suggests how a network allocates resources during a steady-state
period of time (no additions or deletions of virtual channels).

Guaranteed Frame Rate (GFR)

The most recent addition to the set of ATM service categories is GFR, which is
designed specifically to support IP backbone subnetworks. GFR provides better
service than UBR for frame-based traffic, including IP and Ethernet. A major goal
of GFR is to optimize the handling of frame-based traffic that passes from a LAN
through a router onto an ATM backbone network. Such ATM networks are increasingly being used in large enterprise, carrier, and Internet service provider networks
to consolidate and extend IP services over the wide area. While ABR is also an
ATM service meant to provide a greater measure of guaranteed packet performance over ATM backbones, ABR is relatively difficult to implement between
routers over an ATM network. With the increased emphasis on using ATM to support IP-based traffic, especially traffic that originates on Ethernet LANs, GFR may
offer the most attractive alternative for providing ATM service.

One of the techniques used by GFR to provide improved performance compared to UBR is to require that network elements be aware of frame or packet
boundaries. Thus, when congestion requires the discard of cells, network elements
must discard all of the cells that comprise a single frame. GFR also allows a user to

reserve capacity for each GFR VC. The user is guaranteed that this minimum capacity will be supported. Additional frames may be transmitted if the network is not congested.

11.6 ATM ADAPTATION LAYER

The use of ATM creates the need for an adaptation layer to support information transfer protocols not based on ATM. Two examples are PCM (pulse code modulation) voice and the Internet Protocol (IP). PCM voice is an application that produces a stream of bits from a voice signal. To employ this application over ATM, it is necessary to assemble PCM bits into cells for transmission and to read them out on reception in such a way as to produce a smooth, constant flow of bits to the receiver. In a mixed environment, in which IP-based networks interconnect with ATM networks, a convenient way of integrating the two is to map IP packets into ATM cells; this will usually mean segmenting one IP packet into a number of cells on transmission and reassembling the frame from cells on reception. By allowing the use of IP over ATM, all of the existing IP infrastructure can be used over an ATM network.

AAL Services

ITU-T I.362 lists the following general examples of services provided by AAL:

- Handling of transmission errors
- Segmentation and reassembly, to enable larger blocks of data to be carried in the information field of ATM cells
- Handling of lost and misinserted cell conditions
- Flow control and timing control

To minimize the number of different AAL protocols that must be specified to meet a variety of needs, ITU-T defined four classes of service that cover a broad range of requirements. The classification was based on whether a timing relationship must be maintained between source and destination, whether the application requires a constant bit rate, and whether the transfer is connection oriented or connectionless. The classification system is no longer found in ITU-T documents, but the concept has guided the development of AAL protocols. In essence, the AAL layer provides mechanisms for mapping a wide variety of applications onto the ATM layer and provides protocols that are built on top of the traffic management capabilities of the ATM layer. Accordingly, the design of the AAL protocols must relate to the service categories discussed in Section 11.5.

Table 11.4, based on a table in [MCDY99], relates the four AAL protocols to the service categories defined by the ATM Forum. The entries in the table suggest the types of applications that AAL and ATM together can support. They include the following:

- **Circuit emulation:** Refers to the support of synchronous TDM transmission structures, such as T1, over an ATM network.

Table 11.4 AAL Protocols and Services

	CBR	rt-VBR	nrt-VBR	ABR	UBR
AAL1	Circuit emulation, ISDN, voice over ATM				
AAL 2		VBR voice and video			
AAL 3/4			General data services		
AAL 5	LAN emulation	Voice on demand, LANE emulation	Frame relay, ATM, LANE emulation	LANE emulation	IP over ATM

- **VBR voice and video:** These are real-time applications that are transmitted in compressed format. One effect of the compression is that a variable bit rate can support the application, which requires a continuous bit-stream delivery to the destination.
- **General data services:** These include messaging and transaction services that do not require real-time support.
- **IP over ATM:** Transmission of IP packets in ATM cells.
- **Multiprotocol encapsulation over ATM (MPOA):** Support of a variety of protocols other than IP (e.g., IPX, AppleTalk, DECNET) over ATM.
- **LAN emulation (LANE):** Support of LAN-to-LAN traffic across ATM networks, with emulation of the LAN broadcast capability (a transmission from one station reaches many other stations). LANE is designed to allow an easy transition from a LAN environment to an ATM environment.

AAL Protocols

The AAL layer is organized in two logical sublayers: the convergence sublayer (CS) and the segmentation and reassembly sublayer (SAR). The convergence sublayer provides the functions needed to support specific applications using AAL. Each AAL user attaches to AAL at a service access point (SAP), which is simply the address of the application. This sublayer is thus service dependent.

The SAR sublayer is responsible for packaging information received from CS into cells for transmission and unpacking the information at the other end. As we have seen, at the ATM layer, each cell consists of a 5-octet header and a 48-octet information field. Thus, SAR must pack any SAR headers and trailers plus CS information into 48-octet blocks.

Figure 11.13 indicates the general protocol architecture for ATM and AAL. Typically, a higher-layer block of data is encapsulated in a single protocol data unit (PDU) consisting of the higher-layer data and possibly a header and trailer containing protocol information at the CS level. This CS PDU is then passed down to the SAR layer and segmented into a number of blocks. Each of these blocks is encapsu-

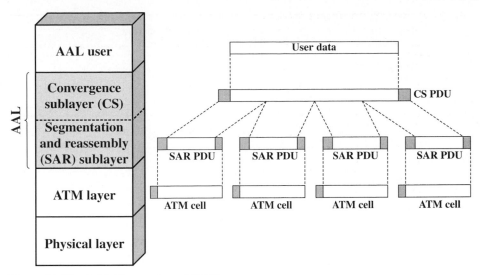

Figure 11.13   AAL Protocols and PDUs

lated in a single 48-octet SAR PDU, which may include a header and a trailer in addition to the block of data passed down from CS. Finally, each SAR PDU forms the payload of a single ATM cell.

Initially, ITU-T defined four protocol types, named type 1 through type 4. Actually, each protocol type consists of two protocols, one at the CS sublayer and one at the SAR sublayer. More recently, types 3 and 4 were merged into a type 3/4, and a new type, type 5, was defined. In each case, a block of data from a higher layer is encapsulated into a protocol data unit (PDU) at the CS sublayer. In fact, this sublayer is referred to as the common part convergence sublayer (CPCS), leaving open the possibility that additional, specialized functions may be performed at the CS level. The CPCS PDU is then passed to the SAR sublayer, where it is broken up into payload blocks. Each payload block can fit into a SAR PDU, which has a total length of 48 octets. Each 48-octet SAR PDU fits into a single ATM cell.

Figure 11.14 shows the formats of the protocol data units (PDUs) at the SAR level for type 1 and type 5.

AAL Type 1

For type 1 operation, we are dealing with a constant-bit-rate source. In this case, the only responsibility of the SAR protocol is to pack the bits into cells for transmission and unpack them at reception. Each block is accompanied by a **sequence number** (SN) so that errored PDUs can be tracked. The 4-bit SN field consists of a convergence sublayer indication (CSI) bit and a 3-bit sequence count (SC). On transmission, the CS sublayer provides the SAR sublayer with a CSI value to place in the SN field. On reception, the SAR sublayer passes this value up to the CS sublayer. The CSI bit is used to communicate information in the following fashion: The 3-bit sequence count defines a frame structure consisting of 8 consecutive ATM cells, numbered 0 through 7. The CSI values in cells 1, 3, 5, and 7 are interpreted as a 4-bit timing value. This value is used to provide a measure of the frequency

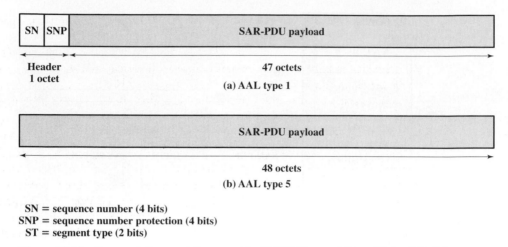

SN = sequence number (4 bits)
SNP = sequence number protection (4 bits)
ST = segment type (2 bits)

Figure 11.14 Segmentation and Reassembly (SAR) Protocol Data Units (PDUs)

difference between the network's reference clock and the transmitter's clock. In even-numbered cells, the CSI can be used to support the blocking of information from a higher layer. If the CSI bit is set to one in an even-numbered cell $(0, 2, 4, 6)$, then the first octet of the SAR PDU payload is a pointer that indicates the start of the next structured block within the payload of this cell and the next cell. That is, two cells (0-1, 2-3, 4-5, 6-7) are treated as containing a one-octet pointer and a 93-octet payload, and the pointer indicates where in that 93-octet payload is the first octet of the next block of data. The offset value 93 is used to indicate that the end of the 93-octet payload coincides with the end of a structured block. The dummy offset value 127 is used when no structure boundary is being indicated.

The 3-bit SC field, as we have just seen, provides an 8-cell frame structure. It also provides a means of detecting lost/misordered cells.

The **sequence number protection** (SNP) field is an error code for error detection and possibly correction on the sequence number field. It consists of a 3-bit cyclic redundancy check (CRC), calculated over the 4-bit SN field, and a parity bit. The parity bit is set so that the parity of the 8-bit SAR header is even.

No CS PDU has been defined for type 1. The functions of the CS sublayer for type 1 primarily have to do with clocking and synchronization, and a separate CS header is not needed.

AAL Type 2 and 3/4

The remainder of the protocol types (2, 3/4, and 5) deal with variable-bit-rate information. Type 2 is intended for analog applications, such as video and audio, that require timing information but do not require a constant bit rate. An initial specification for the type 2 protocols (SAR and CS) has been withdrawn, and the current version of I.363 simply lists the services and functions to be provided.

The initial specifications of AAL type 3 and AAL type 4 were very similar in terms of PDU format and functionality. Accordingly, it was decided within ITU-T to combine the two into a single protocol specification at the SAR and CS sublayers, known as type 3/4.

The types of service provided by AAL type 3/4 can be characterized along two dimensions:

1. The service may be connectionless or connection oriented. In the former case, each block of data presented to the SAR layer (SAR service data unit, or SAR SDU) is treated independently. In the latter case, it is possible to define multiple SAR logical connections over a single ATM connection.

2. The service may be message mode or streaming mode. Message-mode service transfers framed data. Thus, any of the OSI-related protocols and applications would fit into this category. In particular, LAPD or frame relay would be message mode. A single block of data from the layer above AAL is transferred in one or more cells. Streaming-mode service supports the transfer of low-speed continuous data with low delay requirements. The data are presented to AAL in fixed-size blocks that may be as small as one octet. One block is transferred per cell.

The type 3/4 AAL provides its data transfer service by accepting blocks of data from the next higher layer and transmitting each to a destination AAL user. Since the ATM layer limits data transfer to a cell payload of 48 octets, the AAL layer must provide, at minimum, a segmentation and reassembly function.

The approach taken by type 3/4 AAL is as follows. A block of data from a higher layer, such as a PDU, is encapsulated into a PDU at the CPCS sublayer. The CPCS PDU is then passed to the SAR sublayer, where it is broken up into 44-octet payload blocks. Each payload block can fit into a SAR PDU, which includes a header and a trailer for a total length of 48 octets. Each 48-octet SAR PDU fits into a single ATM cell.

A distinctive feature of AAL 3/4 is that it can multiplex different streams of data on the same virtual ATM connection (VCI/VPI). For the connection-oriented service, each logical connection between AAL users is assigned a unique 10-bit MID value. Thus, the cell traffic from up to 2^{10} different AAL connections can be multiplexed and interleaved over a single ATM connection. For the connectionless service, the MID field can be used to communicate a unique identifier associated with each connectionless user and, again, traffic from multiple AAL users may be multiplexed.

AAL Type 5

AAL 5 was introduced to provide a streamlined transport facility for higher-layer protocols that are connection oriented. If it is assumed that the higher layer takes care of connection management and that the ATM layer produces minimal errors, then most of the fields in the type 3/4 SAR and CPCS PDUs are not necessary. For example, with connection-oriented service, the MID field is not necessary: The VCI/VPI is available for cell-by-cell multiplexing, and the higher layer supports message-by-message multiplexing.

Type 5 was introduced to

- Reduce protocol processing overhead
- Reduce transmission overhead
- Ensure adaptability to existing transport protocols

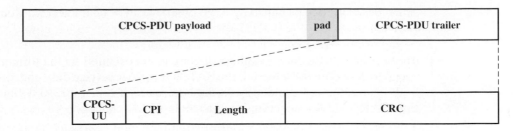

CPCS-UU = CPCS user-to-user indication (1 octet)
CPI   = common part indicator (1 octet)
Length   = length of CPCS-PDU payload (2 octets)
CRC   = cyclic redundancy check (4 octets)

Figure 11.15 AAL 5 PDU

Figures 11.14b and 11.15 show the SAR PDU and CPCS PDU formats for type 5. To understand the operation of type 5, let us begin with the CPCS level. The CPCS PDU includes a trailer with the following fields:

- **CPCS User-to-User Indication (1 octet):** Used to transfer user-to-user information transparently.

- **Common Part Indicator (1 octet):** Indicates the interpretation of the remaining fields in the CPCS PDU trailer. Currently, only one interpretation is defined.

- **Length (2 octets):** Length of the CPCS PDU payload field.

- **Cyclic Redundancy Check (4 octets):** Used to detect bit errors in the CPCS PDU.

A 32-bit CRC protects the entire CPCS PDU, whereas for AAL type 3/4, a 10-bit CRC is provided for each SAR PDU. The type 5 CRC provides strong protection against bit errors. In addition, [WANG92] shows that the 32-bit CRC provides robust detection of cell misordering, a fault condition that might be possible under network failure conditions.

The payload from the next higher layer is padded out so that the entire CPCS PDU is a multiple of 48 octets. The SAR PDU consists simply of 48 octets of payload carrying a portion of the CPCS PDU. The lack of protocol overhead has several implications:

- Because there is no sequence number, the receiver must assume that all SAR PDUs arrive in the proper order for reassembly. The CRC field in the CPCS PDU is intended to verify that.

- The lack of MID field means that it is not possible to interleave cells from different CPCS PDUs. Therefore, each successive SAR PDU carries a portion of the current CPCS PDU or the first block of the next CPCS PDU. To distinguish between these two cases, the ATM SDU type bit in the payload type field of the ATM cell header is used (Figure 11.4). A CPCS PDU consists of zero or more consecutive SAR PDUs with the SDU type bit set to 0 followed immediately by an SAR PDU with the SDU type bit set to 1.

- The lack of an LI field means that there is no way for the SAR entity to distinguish between CPCS PDU octets and filler in the last SAR PDU. Therefore, there is no way for the SAR entity to find the CPCS PDU trailer in the last SAR PDU. To avoid this situation, it is required that the CPCS PDU payload be padded out so that the last bit of the CPCS-trailer occurs as the last bit of the final SAR PDU.

Figure 11.16 shows an example of AAL 5 transmission. The CPCS PDU, including padding and trailer, is divided into 48-octet blocks. Each block is transmitted in a single ATM cell.

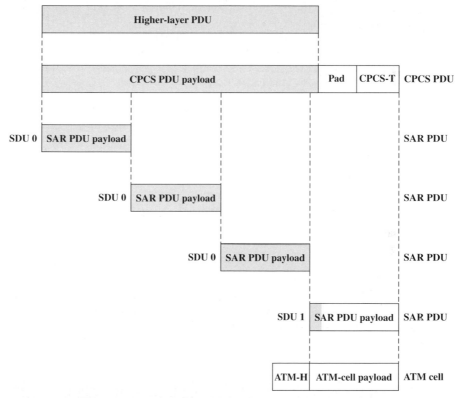

CPCS	= common part convergence sublayer
SAR	= segmentation and reassembly
PDU	= protocol data unit
CPCS-T	= CPCS trailer
ATM-H	= ATM header
SDU	= service data unit type bit

Figure 11.16 Example of AAL 5 Transmission

11.7 RECOMMENDED READING AND WEB SITES

[MCDY99] and [BLAC99] provide good coverage of ATM. The virtual path/virtual channel approach of ATM is examined in [SATO90], [SATO91], and [BURG91].

[GARR96] provides a rationale for the ATM service categories and discusses the traffic management implications of each. [ARMI93] and [SUZU94] discuss AAL and compare types 3/4 and 5.

ARMI93 Armitage, G., and Adams, K. "Packet Reassembly During Cell Loss." *IEEE Network*, September 1995.

BLAC99 Black, U. *ATM Volume I: Foundation for Broadband Networks*. Upper Saddle River, NJ: Prentice Hall, 1992.

BURG91 Burg, J., and Dorman, D. "Broadband ISDN Resource Management: The Role of Virtual Paths." *IEEE Communications Magazine*, September 1991.

GARR96 Garrett, M. "A Service Architecture for ATM: From Applications to Scheduling." *IEEE Network*, May/June 1996.

MCDY99 McDysan, D., and Spohn, D. *ATM: Theory and Application*. New York: McGraw-Hill, 1999.

SATO90 Sato, K.; Ohta, S.; and Tokizawa, I. "Broad-band ATM Network Architecture Based on Virtual Paths." *IEEE Transactions on Communications*, August 1990.

SATO91 Sato, K.; Ueda, H.; and Yoshikai, M. "The Role of Virtual Path Crossconnection." *IEEE LTS*, August 1991.

SUZU94 Suzuki, T. "ATM Adaptation Layer Protocol." *IEEE Communications Magazine*, April 1995.

Recommended Web Sites:

- **ATM Hot Links:** Excellent collection of white papers and links maintained by the University of Minnesota
- **ATM Forum:** Contains technical specifications, white papers, and online copies of the Forum's publication, *53 Bytes*
- **Cell Relay Retreat:** Contains archives of the cell-relay mailing list, links to numerous ATM-related documents, and links to many ATM-related Web sites

11.8 KEY TERMS, REVIEW QUESTIONS, AND PROBLEMS

Key Terms

asynchronous transfer mode (ATM)	guaranteed frame rate (GFR)	service data unit (SDU)
ATM adaptation layer (AAL)	header error control (HEC)	unspecified bit rate (UBR)
available bit rate (ABR)	non-real-time variable bit rate (nrt-VBR)	variable bit rate (VBR)
cell loss priority (CLP)	payload type	virtual channel
constant bit rate (CBR)	real-time variable bit rate (rt-VBR)	virtual path
generic flow control (GFC)		

Review Questions

11.1   How does ATM differ from frame relay?

11.2   What are the relative advantages and disadvantages of ATM compared to frame relay?

11.3   What is the difference between a virtual channel and a virtual path?

11.4   What are the advantages of the use of virtual paths?

11.5   What are the characteristics of a virtual channel connection?

11.6   What are the characteristics of a virtual path connection?

11.7   List and briefly explain the fields in an ATM cell.

11.8   Briefly explain two methods for transmitting ATM cells.

11.9   List and briefly define the ATM service categories.

11.10   What services are provided by AAL?

Problems

11.1   List all 16 possible values of the GFC field and the interpretation of each value (some values are illegal).

11.2   One key design decision for ATM was whether to use fixed or variable length cells. Let us consider this decision from the point of view of efficiency. We can define transmission efficiency as

$$N = \frac{\text{Number of information octets}}{\text{Number of information octets } + \text{ Number of overhead octets}}$$

  a.   Consider the use of fixed-length packets. In this case the overhead consists of the header octets. Define

  L = Data field size of the cell in octets
  H = Header size of the cell in octets
  X = Number of information octets to be transmitted as a single message

  Derive an expression for N. *Hint:* The expression will need to use the operator $\lceil \cdot \rceil$, where $\lceil Y \rceil$ = the smallest integer greater than or equal to Y.

  b.   If cells have variable length, then overhead is determined by the header, plus the flags to delimit the cells or an additional length field in the header. Let Hv = additional overhead octets required to enable the use of variable-length cells. Derive an expression for N in terms of X, H, and Hv.

  c.   Let $L = 48$, $H = 5$, and $Hv = 2$. Plot N versus message size for fixed- and variable-length cells. Comment on the results.

11.3   Another key design decision for ATM is the size of the data field for fixed-size cells. Let us consider this decision from the point of view of efficiency and delay.

  a.   Assume that an extended transmission takes place, so that all cells are completely filled. Derive an expression for the efficiency N as a function of H and L.

  b.   Packetization delay is the delay introduced into a transmission stream by the need to buffer bits until an entire packet is filled before transmission. Derive an expression for this delay as a function of L and the data rate R of the source.

  c.   Common data rates for voice coding are 32 kbps and 64 kbps. Plot packetization delay as a function of L for these two data rates; use a left-hand y-axis with a maximum value of 2 ms. On the same graph, plot transmission efficiency as a function of L; use a right-hand y-axis with a maximum value of 100%. Comment on the results.

11.4 Consider compressed video transmission in an ATM network. Suppose standard ATM cells must be transmitted through 5 switches. The data rate is 43 Mbps.
   a. What is the transmission time for one cell through one switch?
   b. Each switch may be transmitting a cell from other traffic all of which we assume to have lower (non-preemptive for the cell) priority. If the switch is busy transmitting a cell, our cell has to wait until the other cell completes transmission. If the switch is free, our cell is transmitted immediately. What is the maximum time from when a typical video cell arrives at the first switch (and possibly waits) until it is finished being transmitted by the fifth and last one? Assume that you can ignore propagation time, switching time, and everything else but the transmission time and the time spent waiting for another cell to clear a switch.
   c. Now suppose we know that each switch is utilized 60% of the time with the other low priority traffic. By this we mean that with probability 0.6, when we look at a switch it is busy. Suppose that if there is a cell being transmitted by a switch, the average delay spent waiting for a cell to finish transmission is one-half a cell transmission time. What is the average time from the input of the first switch to clearing the fifth?
   d. However, the measure of most interest is not delay but jitter, which is the variability in the delay. Use parts (b) and (c) to calculate the maximum and average variability, respectively, in the delay.
   In all cases assume that the various random events are independent of one another; for example, we ignore the burstiness typical of such traffic.

11.5 Suppose that AAL 3/4 is being used and that the receiver is in an idle state (no incoming cells). Then a block of user data is transmitted as a sequence of SAR PDUs.
   a. Suppose that the BOM SAR PDU is lost. What happens at the receiving end?
   b. Suppose that one of the COM SAR PDUs is lost. What happens at the receiving end?
   c. Suppose that 16 consecutive COM SAR PDUs are lost. What happens at the receiving end?
   d. Suppose that a multiple of 16 consecutive COM SAR PDUs are lost. What happens at the receiving end?

11.6 Again using AAL 3/4, suppose that the receiver is in an idle state and that two blocks of user data are transmitted as two separate sequences of SAR PDUs.
   a. Suppose that the EOM SAR PDU of the first sequence is lost. What happens at the receiving end?
   b. Suppose that the EOM SAR PDU of the first sequence and the BOM SAR PDU of the second sequence are both lost. What happens at the receiving end?

11.7 Suppose that AAL 5 is being used and that the receiver is in an idle state (no incoming cells). Then a block of user data is transmitted as a sequence of SAR PDUs.
   a. Suppose that a single bit error in one of the SAR PDUs occurs. What happens at the receiving end?
   b. Suppose that one of the cells with SDU type bit = 0 is lost. What happens at the receiving end?
   c. Suppose that one of the cells with SDU type bit = 1 is lost. What happens at the receiving end?

CHAPTER 12

ROUTING IN SWITCHED NETWORKS

KEY POINTS

- Routing in circuit-switching networks has traditionally involved a static routing strategy with the use of alternate paths to respond to increased load. Modern routing strategies provide more adaptive and flexible approaches.
- The routing function of a packet-switching network attempts to find the least-cost route through the network, with cost based on number of hops, expected delay, or other metrics. Adaptive routing algorithms typically rely on the exchange of information about traffic conditions among nodes.

A key design issue in switched networks, including circuit-switching, packet-switching, frame relay, and ATM networks, and with internets, is that of routing. In general terms, the routing function seeks to design routes through the network for individual pairs of communicating end nodes such that the network is used efficiently.

This chapter begins with a brief overview of issues involved in routing in circuit-switching networks. Next, we look at the routing function in packet-switching networks and then examine least-cost algorithms that are a central part of routing in packet-switching networks. These latter two topics cover issues that are relevant to routing in internets.

12.1 ROUTING IN CIRCUIT-SWITCHING NETWORKS

In a large circuit-switching network, such as the AT&T long-distance telephone network, many of the circuit connections will require a path through more than one switch. When a call is placed, the network must devise a route through the network from calling subscriber to called subscriber that passes through some number of switches and trunks. There are two main requirements for the network's architecture that bear on the routing strategy: efficiency and resilience. First, it is desirable to minimize the amount of equipment (switches and trunks) in the network, subject to the ability to handle the expected load. The load requirement is usually expressed in terms of a busy-hour traffic load. This is simply the average load expected over the course of the busiest hour of use during the course of a day. From a functional point of view, it is necessary to handle that amount of load. From a cost point of view, we would like to handle that load with minimum equipment. Another requirement is resilience. Although the network may be sized for the busy hour load, it is possible for the traffic to surge temporarily above that level (for example, during a major storm). It will also be the case that, from time to time, switches and trunks will fail and be temporarily unavailable (unfortunately, maybe during the same storm). We would like the network to provide a reasonable level of service under such conditions.

The key design issue that determines the nature of the tradeoff between efficiency and resilience is the routing strategy. Traditionally, the routing function in public telecommunications networks has been quite simple. In essence, the switches of a network were organized into a tree structure, or hierarchy. A path was constructed by starting at the calling subscriber, tracing up the tree to the first common node, and then tracing down the tree to the called subscriber. To add some resilience to the network, additional high-usage trunks were added that cut across the tree structure to connect exchanges with high volumes of traffic between them. In general, this is a static approach. The addition of high-usage trunks provides redundancy and extra capacity, but limitations remain both in terms of efficiency and resilience. Because this routing scheme is not able to adapt to changing conditions, the network must be designed to meet some typical heavy demand. As an example of the problems raised by this approach, the busy hours for east-west traffic and north-south traffic do not coincide and place different demands on the system. It is difficult to analyze the effects of these variables, which leads to oversizing and therefore inefficiency. In terms of resilience, the fixed hierarchical structure with supplemental trunks may respond poorly to failures. Typically in such designs the result of a failure is a major local congestion near the site of the failure.

To cope with the growing demands on public telecommunications networks, virtually all providers have moved away from the static hierarchical approach to a dynamic approach. A dynamic routing approach is one in which routing decisions are influenced by current traffic conditions. Typically, the circuit-switching nodes have a peer relationship with each other rather than a hierarchical one. All nodes are capable of performing the same functions. In such an architecture, routing is both more complex and more flexible. It is more complex because the architecture does not provide a "natural" path or set of paths based on hierarchical structure. But it is also more flexible, because more alternative routes are available.

As an example, we look at a form of routing in circuit-switching networks known as **alternate routing**. The essence of alternate routing schemes is that the possible routes to be used between two end offices are predefined. It is the responsibility of the originating switch to select the appropriate route for each call. Each switch is given a set of preplanned routes for each destination, in order of preference. If a direct trunk connection exists between two switches, this is usually the preferred choice. If this trunk is unavailable, then the second choice is to be tried, and so on. The routing sequences (sequence in which the routes in the set are tried) reflect an analysis based on historical traffic patterns and are designed to optimize the use of network resources.

If there is only one routing sequence defined for each source-destination pair, the scheme is known as a fixed alternate routing scheme. More commonly, a dynamic alternate routing scheme is used. In the latter case, a different set of preplanned routes is used for different time periods, to take advantage of the differing traffic patterns in different time zones and at different times of day. Thus, the routing decision is based both on current traffic status (a route is rejected if busy) and historical traffic patterns (which determines the sequence of routes to be considered).

A simple example is shown in Figure 12.1. The originating switch, X, has four possible routes to the destination switch, Y. The direct route a will always be tried first. If this trunk is unavailable (busy, out of service), the other routes will be tried in a particular order, depending on the time period. For example, during weekday mornings, route b is tried next.

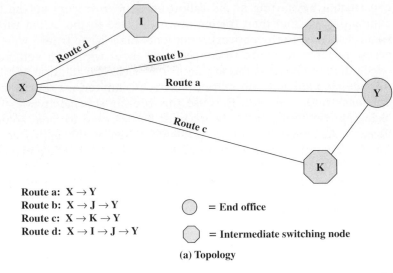

Route a: X → Y
Route b: X → J → Y
Route c: X → K → Y
Route d: X → I → J → Y

⬡ = End office

⬢ = Intermediate switching node

(a) Topology

Time Period	First route	Second route	Third route	Fourth and final route
Morning	a	b	c	d
Afternoon	a	d	b	c
Evening	a	d	c	b
Weekend	a	c	b	d

(b) Routing table

Figure 12.1   Alternate Routes from End Office X to End Office Y

12.2 ROUTING IN PACKET-SWITCHING NETWORKS

One of the most complex and crucial aspects of packet-switching network design is routing. This section begins with a survey of key characteristic that can be used to classify routing strategies. Then some specific routing strategies are discussed.

The principles described in this section are also applicable to internetwork routing, discussed in Part Five.

Characteristics

The primary function of a packet-switching network is to accept packets from a source station and deliver them to a destination station. To accomplish this, a path or route through the network must be determined; generally, more than one route is possible. Thus, a routing function must be performed. The requirements for this function include

- Correctness
- Simplicity

- Fairness
- Optimality

- Robustness
- Efficiency
- Stability

The first two items on the list, correctness and simplicity, are self-explanatory. Robustness has to do with the ability of the network to deliver packets via some route in the face of localized failures and overloads. Ideally, the network can react to such contingencies without the loss of packets or the breaking of virtual circuits. The designer who seeks robustness must cope with the competing requirement for stability. Techniques that react to changing conditions have an unfortunate tendency to either react too slowly to events or to experience unstable swings from one extreme to another. For example, the network may react to congestion in one area by shifting most of the load to a second area. Now the second area is overloaded and the first is underutilized, causing a second shift. During these shifts, packets may travel in loops through the network.

A tradeoff also exists between fairness and optimality. Some performance criteria may give higher priority to the exchange of packets between nearby stations compared to an exchange between distant stations. This policy may maximize average throughput but will appear unfair to the station that primarily needs to communicate with distant stations.

Finally, any routing technique involves some processing overhead at each node and often a transmission overhead as well, both of which impair network efficiency. The penalty of such overhead needs to be less than the benefit accrued based on some reasonable metric, such as increased robustness or fairness.

With these requirements in mind, we are in a position to assess the various design elements that contribute to a routing strategy. Table 12.1 lists these elements. Some of these categories overlap or are dependent on one another. Nevertheless, an examination of this list serves to clarify and organize routing concepts.

Table 12.1 Elements of Routing Techniques for Packet-Switching Networks

Performance Criteria	Network Information Source
Number of hops	None
Cost	Local
Delay	Adjacent node
Throughput	Nodes along route
	All nodes
Decision Time	
Packet (datagram)	**Network Information Update Timing**
Session (virtual circuit)	Continuous
	Periodic
Decision Place	Major load change
Each node (distributed)	Topology change
Central node (centralized)	
Originating node (source)	

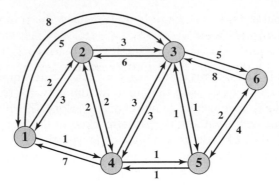

Figure 12.2 Example Packet-Switching Network

Performance Criteria

The selection of a route is generally based on some performance criterion. The simplest criterion is to choose the minimum-hop route (one that passes through the least number of nodes) through the network.[1] This is an easily measured criterion and should minimize the consumption of network resources. A generalization of the minimum-hop criterion is least-cost routing. In this case, a cost is associated with each link, and, for any pair of attached stations, the route through the network that accumulates the least cost is sought. For example, Figure 12.2 illustrates a network in which the two arrowed lines between a pair of nodes represent a link between these nodes, and the corresponding numbers represent the current link cost in each direction. The shortest path (fewest hops) from node 1 to node 6 is 1-3-6 (cost = 5 + 5 = 10), but the least-cost path is 1-4-5-6 (cost = 1 + 1 + 2 = 4). Costs are assigned to links to support one or more design objectives. For example, the cost could be inversely related to the data rate (i.e., the higher the data rate on a link, the lower the assigned cost of the link) or the current queuing delay on the link. In the first case, the least-cost route should provide the highest throughput. In the second case, the least-cost route should minimize delay.

In either the minimum-hop or least-cost approach, the algorithm for determining the optimum route for any pair of stations is relatively straightforward, and the processing time would be about the same for either computation. Because the least-cost criterion is more flexible, this is more common than the minimum-hop criterion.

Several least-cost routing algorithms are in common use. These are described in Section 12.3.

Decision Time and Place

Routing decisions are made on the basis of some performance criterion. Two key characteristics of the decision are the time and place that the decision is made.

---

[1] The term *hop* is used somewhat loosely in the literature. The more common definition, which we use, is that the number of hops along a path from a given source to a given destination is the number of network nodes (packet-switching nodes, ATM switches, routers, etc.) that a packet encounters along that path. Sometimes the number of hops is equated to the number of links, or graph edges, traversed. This latter definition produces a value one greater than the definition we use.

Decision time is determined by whether the routing decision is made on a packet or virtual circuit basis. When the internal operation of the network is datagram, a routing decision is made individually for each packet. For internal virtual circuit operation, a routing decision is made at the time the virtual circuit is established. In the simplest case, all subsequent packets using that virtual circuit follow the same route. In more sophisticated network designs, the network may dynamically change the route assigned to a particular virtual circuit in response to changing conditions (e.g., overload or failure of a portion of the network).

The term *decision place* refers to which node or nodes in the network are responsible for the routing decision. Most common is distributed routing, in which each node has the responsibility of selecting an output link for routing packets as they arrive. For centralized routing, the decision is made by some designated node, such as a network control center. The danger of this latter approach is that the loss of the network control center may block operation of the network. The distributed approach is perhaps more complex but is also more robust. A third alternative, used in some networks, is source routing. In this case, the routing decision is actually made by the source station rather than by a network node, and is then communicated to the network. This allows the user to dictate a route through the network that meets criteria local to that user.

The decision time and decision place are independent design variables. For example, in Figure 12.2, suppose that the decision place is each node and that the values depicted are the costs at a given instant in time: the costs may change. If a packet is to be delivered from node 1 to node 6, it might follow the route 1-4-5-6, with each leg of the route determined locally by the transmitting node. Now let the values change such that 1-4-5-6 is no longer the optimum route. In a datagram network, the next packet may follow a different route, again determined by each node along the way. In a virtual circuit network, each node will remember the routing decision that was made when the virtual circuit was established, and simply pass on the packets without making a new decision.

Network Information Source and Update Timing

Most routing strategies require that decisions be based on knowledge of the topology of the network, traffic load, and link cost. Surprisingly, some strategies use no such information and yet manage to get packets through; flooding and some random strategies (discussed later) are in this category.

With distributed routing, in which the routing decision is made by each node, the individual node may make use of only local information, such as the cost of each outgoing link. Each node might also collect information from adjacent (directly connected) nodes, such as the amount of congestion experienced at that node. Finally, there are algorithms in common use that allow the node to gain information from all nodes on any potential route of interest. In the case of centralized routing, the central node typically makes use of information obtained from all nodes.

A related concept is that of information update timing, which is a function of both the information source and the routing strategy. Clearly, if no information is used (as in flooding), there is no information to update. If only local information is used, the update is essentially continuous. That is, an individual node always knows its local conditions. For all other information source categories (adjacent nodes, all nodes), update timing depends on the routing strategy. For a fixed strategy, the information is never updated. For an adaptive strategy, information is updated from time to time to enable the routing decision to adapt to changing conditions.

As you might expect, the more information available, and the more frequently it is updated, the more likely the network is to make good routing decisions. On the other hand, the transmission of that information consumes network resources.

Routing Strategies

A large number of routing strategies have evolved for dealing with the routing requirements of packet-switching networks. Many of these strategies are also applied to internetwork routing, which we cover in Part Five. In this section, we survey four key strategies: fixed, flooding, random, and adaptive.

Fixed Routing

For fixed routing, a single, permanent route is configured for each source-destination pair of nodes in the network. Either of the least-cost routing algorithms described in Section 12.3 could be used. The routes are fixed, or at least only change when there is a change in the topology of the network. Thus, the link costs used in designing routes cannot be based on any dynamic variable such as traffic. They could, however, be based on expected traffic or capacity.

Figure 12.3 suggests how fixed routing might be implemented. A central routing matrix is created, to be stored perhaps at a network control center. The matrix shows, for each source-destination pair of nodes, the identity of the next node on the route.

Note that it is not necessary to store the complete route for each possible pair of nodes. Rather, it is sufficient to know, for each pair of nodes, the identity of the first node on the route. To see this, suppose that the least-cost route from X to Y begins with the X-A link. Call the remainder of the route R_1; this is the part from A to Y. Define R_2 as the least-cost route from A to Y. Now, if the cost of R_1 is greater than that of R_2, then the X-Y route can be improved by using R_2 instead. If the cost of R_1 is less than R_2, then R_2 is not the least-cost route from A to Y. Therefore, $R_1 = R_2$. Thus, at each point along a route, it is only necessary to know the identity of the next node, not the entire route. In our example, the route from node 1 to node 6 begins by going through node 4. Again consulting the matrix, the route from node 4 to node 6 goes through node 5. Finally, the route from node 5 to node 6 is a direct link to node 6. Thus, the complete route from node 1 to node 6 is 1-4-5-6.

From this overall matrix, routing tables can be developed and stored at each node. From the reasoning in the preceding paragraph, it follows that each node need only store a single column of the routing directory. The node's directory shows the next node to take for each destination.

With fixed routing, there is no difference between routing for datagrams and virtual circuits. All packets from a given source to a given destination follow the same route. The advantage of fixed routing is its simplicity, and it should work well in a reliable network with a stable load. Its disadvantage is its lack of flexibility. It does not react to network congestion or failures.

A refinement to fixed routing that would accommodate link and node outages would be to supply the nodes with an alternate next node for each destination. For example, the alternate next nodes in the node 1 directory might be 4, 3, 2, 3, 3.

CENTRAL ROUTING DIRECTORY

From Node

To Node	1	2	3	4	5	6
1	—	1	5	2	4	5
2	2	—	5	2	4	5
3	4	3	—	5	3	5
4	4	4	5	—	4	5
5	4	4	5	5	—	5
6	4	4	5	5	6	—

Node 1 Directory

Destination	Next Node
2	2
3	4
4	4
5	4
6	4

Node 2 Directory

Destination	Next Node
1	1
3	3
4	4
5	4
6	4

Node 3 Directory

Destination	Next Node
1	5
2	5
4	5
5	5
6	5

Node 4 Directory

Destination	Next Node
1	2
2	2
3	5
5	5
6	5

Node 5 Directory

Destination	Next Node
1	4
2	4
3	3
4	4
6	6

Node 6 Directory

Destination	Next Node
1	5
2	5
3	5
4	5
5	5

Figure 12.3 Fixed Routing (using Figure 12.2)

Flooding

Another simple routing technique is flooding. This technique requires no network information whatsoever and works as follows. A packet is sent by a source node to every one of its neighbors. At each node, an incoming packet is retransmitted on all outgoing links except for the link on which it arrived. For example, if node 1 in Figure 12.2 has a packet to send to node 6, it sends a copy of that packet (with a destination address of 6), to nodes 2, 3, and 4. Node 2 will send a copy to nodes 3 and 4. Node 4 will send a copy to nodes 2, 3, and 5. And so it goes. Eventually, a number of copies of the packet will arrive at node 6. The packet must have some unique identifier (e.g., source node and sequence number, or virtual circuit number and sequence number) so that node 6 knows to discard all but the first copy.

Unless something is done to stop the incessant retransmission of packets, the number of packets in circulation just from a single source packet grows without bound. One way to prevent this is for each node to remember the identity of those packets it has already retransmitted. When duplicate copies of the packet arrive, they are discarded. A simpler technique is to include a hop count field with each packet. The count can originally be set to some maximum value, such as the diameter (length of the longest minimum-hop path through the network)[2] of the network. Each time a node passes on a packet, it decrements the count by one. When the count reaches zero, the packet is discarded.

An example of the latter tactic is shown in Figure 12.4. A packet is to be sent from node 1 to node 6 and is assigned a hop count of 3. On the first hop, three copies of the packet are created. For the second hop of all these copies, a total of nine copies are created. One of these copies reaches node 6, which recognizes that it is the intended destination and does not retransmit. However, the other nodes generate a total of 22 new copies for their third and final hop. Note that if a node is not keeping track of the packet identifier, it may generate multiple copies at this third

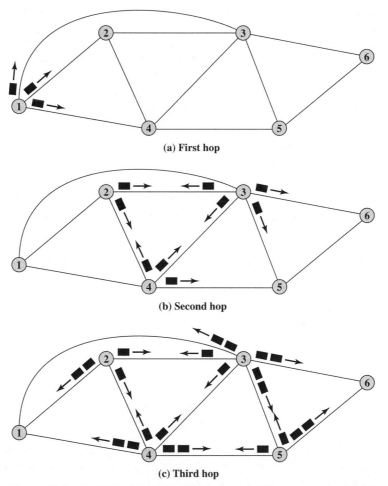

(a) First hop

(b) Second hop

(c) Third hop

Figure 12.4 Flooding Example (Hop Count = 3)

---

[2] For each pair of end systems attached to the network, there is a minimum-hop path. The length of the longest such minimum-hop path is the diameter of the network.

stage. All packets received from the third hop are discarded. In all, node 6 has received four additional copies of the packet.

The flooding technique has three remarkable properties:

- All possible routes between source and destination are tried. Thus, no matter what link or node outages have occurred, a packet will always get through if at least one path between source and destination exists.
- Because all routes are tried, at least one copy of the packet to arrive at the destination will have used a minimum-hop route.
- All nodes that are directly or indirectly connected to the source node are visited.

Because of the first property, the flooding technique is highly robust and could be used to send emergency messages. An example application is a military network that is subject to extensive damage. Because of the second property, flooding might be used initially to set up the route for a virtual circuit. The third property suggests that flooding can be useful for the dissemination of important information to all nodes; we will see that it is used in some schemes to disseminate routing information.

The principal disadvantage of flooding is the high traffic load that it generates, which is directly proportional to the connectivity of the network.

Random Routing

Random routing has the simplicity and robustness of flooding with far less traffic load. With random routing, a node selects only one outgoing path for retransmission of an incoming packet. The outgoing link is chosen at random, excluding the link on which the packet arrived. If all links are equally likely to be chosen, then a node may simply utilize outgoing links in a round-robin fashion.

A refinement of this technique is to assign a probability to each outgoing link and to select the link based on that probability. The probability could be based on data rate, in which case we have

$$P_i = \frac{R_i}{\sum_j R_i}$$

where

$$P_i = \text{probability of selecting link } i$$
$$R_i = \text{data rate on link } i$$

The sum is taken over all candidate outgoing links. This scheme should provide good traffic distribution. Note that the probabilities could also be based on fixed link costs.

Like flooding, random routing requires the use of no network information. Because the route taken is random, the actual route will typically not be the least-cost route nor the minimum-hop route. Thus, the network must carry a higher than optimum traffic load, although not nearly as high as for flooding.

Adaptive Routing

In virtually all packet-switching networks, some sort of adaptive routing technique is used. That is, the routing decisions that are made change as conditions on the network change. The principal conditions that influence routing decisions are

- **Failure:** When a node or trunk fails, it can no longer be used as part of a route.
- **Congestion:** When a particular portion of the network is heavily congested, it is desirable to route packets around rather than through the area of congestion.

For adaptive routing to be possible, information about the state of the network must be exchanged among the nodes. There are several drawbacks associated with the use of adaptive routing, compared to fixed routing:

- The routing decision is more complex; therefore, the processing burden on network nodes increases.
- In most cases, adaptive strategies depend on status information that is collected at one place but used at another. There is a tradeoff here between the quality of the information and the amount of overhead. The more information that is exchanged, and the more frequently it is exchanged, the better will be the routing decisions that each node makes. On the other hand, this information is itself a load on the constituent networks, causing a performance degradation.
- An adaptive strategy may react too quickly, causing congestion-producing oscillation, or too slowly, being irrelevant.

Despite these real dangers, adaptive routing strategies are by far the most prevalent, for two reasons:

- An adaptive routing strategy can improve performance, as seen by the network user.
- An adaptive routing strategy can aid in congestion control, which is discussed in Chapter 13. Because an adaptive routing strategy tends to balance loads, it can delay the onset of severe congestion.

These benefits may or may not be realized, depending on the soundness of the design and the nature of the load. By and large, adaptive routing is an extraordinarily complex task to perform properly. As demonstration of this, most major packet-switching networks, such as ARPANET and its successors, and many commercial networks, have endured at least one major overhaul of their routing strategy.

A convenient way to classify adaptive routing strategies is on the basis of information source: local, adjacent nodes, all nodes. An example of an adaptive routing strategy that relies only on local information is one in which a node routes each packet to the outgoing link with the shortest queue length, Q. This would have the effect of balancing the load on outgoing links. However, some outgoing links may not be headed in the correct general direction. We can improve matters by also taking into account preferred direction, much as with random routing. In this case, each link emanating from the node would have a bias B_i, for each destination i. For each

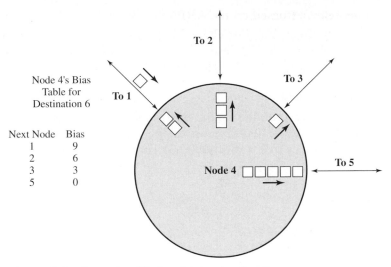

Node 4's Bias
Table for
Destination 6

Next Node	Bias
1	9
2	6
3	3
5	0

Figure 12.5   Example of Isolated Adaptive Routing

incoming packet headed for node i, the node would choose the outgoing link that minimizes $Q + B_i$. Thus a node would tend to send packets in the right direction, with a concession made to current traffic delays.

As an example, Figure 12.5 show the status of node 4 of Figure 12.2 at a certain point in time. Node 4 has links to four other nodes. A fair number of packets have been arriving and a backlog has built up, with a queue of packets waiting for each of the outgoing links. A packet arrives from node 1 destined for node 6. To which outgoing link should the packet be routed? Based on current queue lengths and the values of bias (B_6) for each outgoing link, the minimum value of $Q + B_6$ is 4, on the link to node 3. Thus, node 4 routes the packet through node 3.

Adaptive schemes based only on local information are rarely used because they do not exploit easily available information. Strategies based on information from adjacent nodes or all nodes are commonly found. Both take advantage of information that each node has about delays and outages that it experiences. Such adaptive strategies can be either distributed or centralized. In the distributed case, each node exchanges delay information with other nodes. Based on incoming information, a node tries to estimate the delay situation throughout the network, and applies a least-cost routing algorithm. In the centralized case, each node reports its link delay status to a central node, which designs routes based on this incoming information and sends the routing information back to the nodes.

Examples

In this section, we look at several examples of routing strategies. All of these were initially developed for ARPANET, which is a packet-switching network that was the foundation of the present-day Internet. It is instructive to examine these strategies for several reasons. First, these strategies and similar ones are also used in other packet-switching networks, including a number of networks on the Internet. Second, routing schemes based on the ARPANET work have also been used for internetwork routing in the Internet and in private internetworks. And finally, the ARPANET routing scheme evolved in a way that illuminates some of the key design issues related to routing algorithms.

First Generation

The original routing algorithm, designed in 1969, was a distributed adaptive algorithm using estimated delay as the performance criterion and a version of the Bellman-Ford algorithm (Section 12.3). For this algorithm, each node maintains two vectors:

$$D_i = \begin{bmatrix} d_{i1} \\ \vdots \\ d_{iN} \end{bmatrix} \qquad S_i = \begin{bmatrix} s_{i1} \\ \vdots \\ s_{iN} \end{bmatrix}$$

where

D_i = delay vector for node i

d_{ij} = current estimate of minimum delay from node i to node j ($d_{ii} = 0$)

N = number of nodes in the network

S_i = successor node vector for node i

s_{ij} = the next node in the current minimum-delay route from i to j

Periodically (every 128 ms), each node exchanges its delay vector with all of its neighbors. On the basis of all incoming delay vectors, a node k updates both of its vectors as follows:

$$d_{kj} = \min_{i \in A} [d_{ij} + l_{ki}]$$

$s_{kj} = i$ using i that minimizes the preceding expression

where

A = set of neighbor nodes for k

l_{ki} = current estimate of delay from k to i

Figure 12.6 provides an example of the original ARPANET algorithm, using the network of Figure 12.7. This is the same network as that of Figure 12.2, with some of the link costs having different values (and assuming the same cost in both directions). Figure 12.6a shows the routing table for node 1 at an instant in time that reflects the link costs of Figure 12.7. For each destination, a delay is specified, and the next node on the route that produces that delay. At some point, the link costs change to those of Figure 12.2. Assume that node 1's neighbors (nodes 2, 3, and 4) learn of the change before node 1. Each of these nodes updates its delay vector and sends a copy to all of its neighbors, including node 1 (Figure 12.6b). Node 1 discards its current routing table and builds a new one, based solely on the incoming delay vector and its own estimate of link delay to each of its neighbors. The result is shown in Figure 12.6c.

Desti-nation	Delay	Next node
1	0	—
2	2	2
3	5	3
4	1	4
5	6	3
6	8	3
	D_1	S_1

D_2	D_3	D_4
3	7	5
0	4	2
3	0	2
2	2	0
3	1	1
5	3	3

Desti-nation	Delay	Next node
1	0	—
2	2	2
3	3	4
4	1	4
5	2	4
6	4	4

$$l_{1,2} = 2$$
$$l_{1,3} = 5$$
$$l_{1,4} = 1$$

(a) Node 1's routing table before update   **(b) Delay vectors sent to node 1 from neighbor nodes**   **(c) Node 1's routing table after update and link costs used in update**

Figure 12.6   Original ARPANET Routing Algorithm

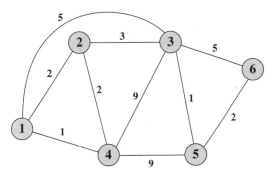

Figure 12.7   Network for Example of Figure 12.6a

The estimated link delay is simply the queue length for that link. Thus, in building a new routing table, the node will tend to favor outgoing links with shorter queues. This tends to balance the load on outgoing links. However, because queue lengths vary rapidly with time, the distributed perception of the shortest route could change while a packet is en route. This could lead to a thrashing situation in which a packet continues to seek out areas of low congestion rather than aiming at the destination.

Second Generation

After some years of experience and several minor modifications, the original routing algorithm was replaced by a quite different one in 1979 [MCQU80]. The major shortcomings of the old algorithm were as follows:

- The algorithm did not consider line speed, merely queue length. Thus, higher-capacity links were not given the favored status they deserved.

- Queue length is, in any case, an artificial measure of delay, because some variable amount of processing time elapses between the arrival of a packet at a node and its placement in an outbound queue.

- The algorithm was not very accurate. In particular, it responded slowly to congestion and delay increases.

The new algorithm is also a distributed adaptive one, using delay as the performance criterion, but the differences are significant. Rather than using queue length as a surrogate for delay, the delay is measured directly. At a node, each incoming packet is timestamped with an arrival time. A departure time is recorded when the packet is transmitted. If a positive acknowledgment is returned, the delay for that packet is recorded as the departure time minus the arrival time plus transmission time and propagation delay. The node must therefore know link data rate and propagation time. If a negative acknowledgment comes back, the departure time is updated and the node tries again, until a measure of successful transmission delay is obtained.

Every 10 seconds, the node computes the average delay on each outgoing link. If there are any significant changes in delay, the information is sent to all other nodes using flooding. Each node maintains an estimate of delay on every network link. When new information arrives, it recomputes its routing table using Dijkstra's algorithm (Section 12.3).

Third Generation

Experience with this new strategy indicated that it was more responsive and stable than the old one. The overhead induced by flooding was moderate because each node does this at most once every 10 seconds. However, as the load on the network grew, a shortcoming in the new strategy began to appear, and the strategy was revised in 1987 [KHAN89].

The problem with the second strategy is the assumption that the measured packet delay on a link is a good predictor of the link delay encountered after all nodes reroute their traffic based on this reported delay. Thus, it is an effective routing mechanism only if there is some correlation between the reported values and those actually experienced after re-routing. This correlation tends to be rather high under light and moderate traffic loads. However, under heavy loads, there is little correlation. Therefore, immediately after all nodes have made routing updates, the routing tables are obsolete!

As an example, consider a network that consists of two regions with only two links, A and B, connecting the two regions (Figure 12.8). Each route between two nodes in different regions must pass through one of these links. Assume that a situation develops in which most of the traffic is on link A. This will cause the link delay on A to be significant, and at the next opportunity, this delay value will be reported to all other nodes. These updates will arrive at all nodes at about the same time, and all will update their routing tables immediately. It is likely that this new delay value for link A will be high enough to make link B the preferred choice for most, if not all, interregion routes. Because all nodes adjust their routes at the same time, most

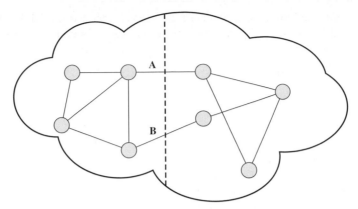

Figure 12.8 Packet-Switching Network Subject to Oscillations

or all interregion traffic shifts at the same time to link B. Now the link delay value on B will become high, and there will be a subsequent shift to link A. This oscillation will continue until the traffic volume subsides.

There are a number of reasons why this oscillation is undesirable:

- A significant portion of available capacity is unused at just the time when it is needed most: under heavy traffic load.
- The overutilization of some links can lead to the spread of congestion within the network (this will be seen in the discussion of congestion in Chapter 13).
- The large swings in measured delay values result in the need for more frequent routing update messages. This increases the load on the network at just the time when the network is already stressed.

The ARPANET designers concluded that the essence of the problem was that every node was trying to obtain the best route for all destinations, and that these efforts conflicted. It was concluded that under heavy loads, the goal of routing should be to give the average route a good path instead of attempting to give all routes the best path.

The designers decided that it was unnecessary to change the overall routing algorithm. Rather, it was sufficient to change the function that calculates link costs. This was done in such a way as to damp routing oscillations and reduce routing overhead. The calculation begins with measuring the average delay over the last 10 seconds. This value is then transformed with the following steps:

1. Using a simple single-server queuing model, the measured delay is transformed into an estimate of link utilization. From queuing theory, utilization can be expressed as a function of delay as follows:

$$\rho = \frac{2(T_s - T)}{T_s - 2T}$$

where

$$\rho = \text{link utilization}$$
$$T = \text{measured delay}$$
$$T_s = \text{service time}$$

The service time was set at the network-wide average packet size (600 bits) divided by the data rate of the link.

2. The result is then smoothed by averaging it with the previous estimate of utilization:

$$U(n + 1) = 0.5 \times \rho(n + 1) + 0.5 \times U(n)$$

where

$$U(n) = \text{average utilization calculated at sampling time } n$$
$$\rho(n) = \text{link utilization measured at sampling time } n$$

Averaging increases the period of routing oscillations, thus reducing routing overhead.

3. The link cost is then set as a function of average utilization that is designed to provide a reasonable estimate of cost while avoiding oscillation. Figure 12.9 indicates the way in which the estimate of utilization is converted into a cost value. The final cost value is, in effect, a transformed value of delay.

In Figure 12.9, delay is normalized to the value achieved on an idle line, which is just propagation delay plus transmission time. One curve on the figure indicates the way in which the actual delay rises as a function of utilization; the increase in delay is due to queuing delay at the node. For the revised algorithm, the cost value is

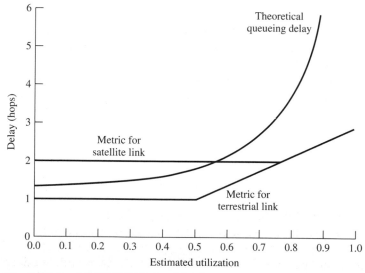

Figure 12.9   ARPANET Delay Metrics

kept at the minimum value until a given level of utilization is reached. This feature has the effect of reducing routing overhead at low traffic levels. Above a certain level of utilization, the cost level is allowed to rise to a maximum value that is equal to three times the minimum value. The effect of this maximum value is to dictate that traffic should not be routed around a heavily utilized line by more than two additional hops.

Note that the minimum threshold is set higher for satellite links. This encourages the use of terrestrial links under conditions of light traffic, because the terrestrial links have much lower propagation delay. Note also that the actual delay curve is much steeper than the transformation curves at high utilization levels. It is this steep rise in link cost that causes all of the traffic on a link to be shed, which in turn causes routing oscillations.

In summary, the revised cost function is keyed to utilization rather than delay. The function acts similar to a delay-based metric under light loads and to a capacity-based metric under heavy loads.

12.3 LEAST-COST ALGORITHMS

Virtually all packet-switching networks and all internets base their routing decision on some form of least-cost criterion. If the criterion is to minimize the number of hops, each link has a value of 1. More typically, the link value is inversely proportional to the link capacity, proportional to the current load on the link, or some combination. In any case, these link or hop costs are used as input to a least-cost routing algorithm, which can be simply stated as follows:

> Given a network of nodes connected by bidirectional links, where each link has a cost associated with it in each direction, define the cost of a path between two nodes as the sum of the costs of the links traversed. For each pair of nodes, find a path with the least cost.

Note that the cost of a link may differ in its two directions. This would be true, for example, if the cost of a link equaled the length of the queue of packets awaiting transmission from each of the two nodes on the link.

Most least-cost routing algorithms in use in packet-switching networks and internets are variations of one of two common algorithms, known as Dijkstra's algorithm and the Bellman-Ford algorithm. This section provides a summary of these two algorithms.

Dijkstra's Algorithm

Dijkstra's algorithm [DIJK59] can be stated as: Find the shortest paths from a given source node to all other nodes, by developing the paths in order of increasing path length. The algorithm proceeds in stages. By the kth stage, the shortest paths to the k nodes closest to (least cost away from) the source node have been determined; these nodes are in a set T. At stage $(k + 1)$, the node not in T that has the shortest path from the source node is added to T. As each node is added to T, its path from the source is defined. The algorithm can be formally described as follows. Define

N = set of nodes in the network

s = source node

T = set of nodes so far incorporated by the algorithm

$w(i, j)$ = link cost from node i to node j; $w(i, i) = 0$; $w(i, j) = \infty$ if the two nodes are not directly connected; $w(i, j) \geq 0$ if the two nodes are directly connected

$L(n)$ = cost of the least-cost path from node s to node n that is currently known to the algorithm; at termination, this is the cost of the least-cost path in the graph from s to n

The algorithm has three steps; steps 2 and 3 are repeated until $T = N$. That is, steps 2 and 3 are repeated until final paths have been assigned to all nodes in the network:

1. **[Initialization]**

$T = \{s\}$ i.e., the set of nodes so far incorporated consists of only the source node

$L(n) = w(s, n)$ for $n \neq s$ i.e., the initial path costs to neighboring nodes are simply the link costs

2. **[Get Next Node]** Find the neighboring node not in T that has the least-cost path from node s and incorporate that node into T. Also incorporate the edge that is incident on that node and a node in T that contributes to the path. This can be expressed as

$$\text{Find } x \notin T \text{ such that } L(x) = \min_{j \notin T} L(j)$$

Add x to T; add to T the edge that is incident on x and that contributes the least cost component to $L(x)$, that is, the last hop in the path.

3. **[Update Least-Cost Paths]**

$$L(n) = \min[L(n), L(x) + w(x, n)] \quad \text{for all } n \notin T$$

If the latter term is the minimum, the path from s to n is now the path from s to x concatenated with the edge from x to n.

The algorithm terminates when all nodes have been added to T. At termination, the value $L(x)$ associated with each node x is the cost (length) of the least-cost path from s to x. In addition, T defines the least-cost path from s to each other node.

One iteration of steps 2 and 3 adds one new node to T and defines the least-cost path from s to that node. That path passes only through nodes that are in T. To see this, consider the following line of reasoning. After k iterations, there are k nodes

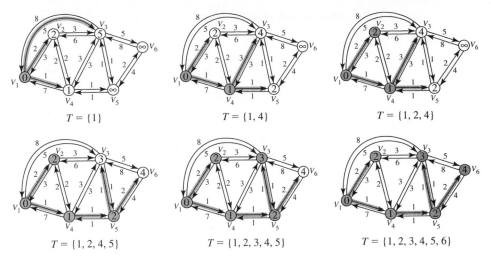

Figure 12.10 Dijkstra's Algorithm Applied to Graph of Figure 12.2

in T, and the least-cost path from s to each of these nodes has been defined. Now consider all possible paths from s to nodes not in T. Among those paths, there is one of least cost that passes exclusively through nodes in T (see Problem 12.4), ending with a direct link from some node in T to a node not in T. This node is added to T and the associated path is defined as the least-cost path for that node.

Table 12.2a and Figure 12.10 show the result of applying this algorithm to the graph of Figure 12.2, using $s = 1$. The shaded edges define the spanning tree for the graph. The values in each circle are the current estimates of $L(x)$ for each node x. A node is shaded when it is added to T. Note that at each step the path to each node plus the total cost of that path is generated. After the final iteration, the least-cost path to each node and the cost of that path have been developed. The same procedure can be used with node 2 as source node, and so on.

Bellman-Ford Algorithm

The Bellman-Ford algorithm [FORD62] can be stated as follows: Find the shortest paths from a given source node subject to the constraint that the paths contain at most one link, then find the shortest paths with a constraint of paths of at most two links, and so on. This algorithm also proceeds in stages. The algorithm can be formally described as follows. Define

s = source node

$w(i, j)$ = link cost from node i to node j; $w(i, i) = 0$; $w(i, j) = \infty$ if the two nodes are not directly connected; $w(i, j) \geq 0$ if the two nodes are directly connected

h = maximum number of links in a path at the current stage of the algorithm

$L_h(n)$ = cost of the least-cost path from node s to node n under the constraint of no more than h links

Table 12.2   Example of Least-Cost Routing Algorithms (using Figure 12.2)

(a) Dijkstra'a Algorithm ($s = 1$)

Iteration	T	L(2)	Path	L(3)	Path	L(4)	Path	L(5)	Path	L(6)	Path
1	{1}	2	1-2	5	1-3	1	1-4	∞	—	∞	—
2	{1, 4}	2	1-2	4	1-4-3	1	1-4	2	1-4-5	∞	—
3	{1, 2, 4}	2	1-2	4	1-4-3	1	1-4	2	1-4-5	∞	—
4	{1, 2, 4, 5}	2	1-2	3	1-4-5-3	1	1-4	2	1-4-5	4	1-4-5-6
5	{1, 2, 3, 4, 5}	2	1-2	3	1-4-5-3	1	1-4	2	1-4-5	4	1-4-5-6
6	{1, 2, 3, 4, 5, 6}	2	1-2	3	1-4-5-3	1	1-4	2	1-4-5	4	1-4-5-6

(b) Bellman-Ford Algorithm ($s = 1$)

h	$L_h(2)$	Path	$L_h(3)$	Path	$L_h(4)$	Path	$L_h(5)$	Path	$L_h(6)$	Path
0	∞	—	∞	—	∞	—	∞	—	∞	—
1	2	1-2	5	1-3	1	1-4	∞	—	∞	—
2	2	1-2	4	1-4-3	1	1-4	2	1-4-5	10	1-3-6
3	2	1-2	3	1-4-5-3	1	1-4	2	1-4-5	4	1-4-5-6
4	2	1-2	3	1-4-5-3	1	1-4	2	1-4-5	4	1-4-5-6

1. **[Initialization]**

$$L_0(n) = \infty, \quad \text{for all } n \neq s$$
$$L_h(s) = 0, \quad \text{for all } h$$

2. **[Update]**

For each successive $h \geq 0$:
    For each $n \neq s$, compute

$$L_{h+1}(n) = \min_{j} [L_h(j) + w(j, n)]$$

Connect n with the predecessor node j that achieves the minimum, and eliminate any connection of n with a different predecessor node formed during an earlier iteration. The path from s to n terminates with the link from j to n.

For the iteration of step 2 with $h = K$, and for each destination node n, the algorithm compares potential paths from s to n of length $K + 1$ with the path that existed at the end of the previous iteration. If the previous, shorter, path has less cost, then that path is retained. Otherwise a new path with length $K + 1$ is defined from s to n; this path consists of a path of length K from s to some node j, plus a direct hop from node j to node n. In this case, the path from s to j that is used is the K-hop path for j defined in the previous iteration (see Problem 12.5).

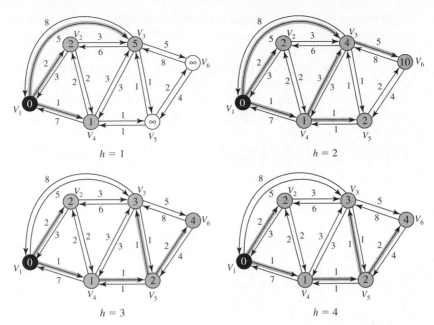

Figure 12.11 Bellman-Ford Algorithm Applied to Graph of Figure 10.6

Table 12.2b and Figure 12.11 show the result of applying this algorithm to Figure 12.2, using $s = 1$. At each step, the least-cost paths with a maximum number of links equal to h are found. After the final iteration, the least-cost path to each node and the cost of that path have been developed. The same procedure can be used with node 2 as source node, and so on. Note that the results agree with those obtained using Dijkstra's algorithm.

Comparison

One interesting comparison can be made between these two algorithms, having to do with what information needs to be gathered. Consider first the Bellman-Ford algorithm. In step 2, the calculation for node n involves knowledge of the link cost to all neighboring nodes to node n [i.e., $w(j, n)$] plus the total path cost to each of those neighboring nodes from a particular source node s [i.e., $L_h(j)$]. Each node can maintain a set of costs and associated paths for every other node in the network and exchange this information with its direct neighbors from time to time. Each node can therefore use the expression in step 2 of the Bellman-Ford algorithm, based only on information from its neighbors and knowledge of its link costs, to update its costs and paths. On the other hand, consider Dijkstra's algorithm. Step 3 appears to require that each node must have complete topological information about the network. That is, each node must know the link costs of all links in the network. Thus, for this algorithm, information must be exchanged with all other nodes.

In general, evaluation of the relative merits of the two algorithms should consider the processing time of the algorithms and the amount of information that must be collected from other nodes in the network or internet. The evaluation will depend on the implementation approach and the specific implementation.

A final point: Both algorithms are known to converge under static conditions of topology, and link costs and will converge to the same solution. If the link costs change over time, the algorithm will attempt to catch up with these changes. However, if the link cost depends on traffic, which in turn depends on the routes chosen, then a feedback condition exists, and instabilities may result.

12.4 RECOMMENDED READING

[GIRA90] provides good coverage of routing in circuit-switching networks. [CORM01] contains a detailed analysis of the least-cost algorithms discussed in this chapter. [BERT92] also discusses these algorithms in detail.

BERT92	Bertsekas, D. and Gallager, R. *Data Networks*. Upper Saddle River, NJ: Prentice Hall, 1992.
CORM01	Cormen, T., et al., *Introduction to Algorithms*. Cambridge, MA: MIT Press, 2001.
GIRA90	Girard, A. *Routing and Dimensioning in Circuit-switching Networks*. Reading, MA: Addison-Wesley, 1990.

12.5 KEY TERMS, REVIEW QUESTIONS, AND PROBLEMS

Key Terms

adaptive routing alternate routing Bellman-Ford algorithm	Dijkstra's algorithm fixed routing flooding	least-cost algorithms random routing

Review Questions

12.1 What is the busy-hour traffic load?

12.2 What is the major tradeoff in the design of a routing strategy for a circuit-switching network?

12.3 Distinguish between static and alternate routing in a circuit-switching network.

12.4 What are the key requirements for a routing function for a packet-switching network?

12.5 What is fixed routing?

12.6 What is flooding?

12.7 What are the advantages and disadvantages of adaptive routing?

12.8 What is a least-cost algorithm?

12.9 What is the essential difference between Dijkstra's algorithm and the Bellman-Ford algorithm?

Problems

12.1 Consider a packet-switching network of N nodes, connected by the following topologies:

a. Star: one central node with no attached station; all other nodes attach to the central node.

b. Loop: each node connects to two other nodes to form a closed loop.

c. Fully connected: each node is directly connected to all other nodes.

For each case, give the average number of hops between stations.

12.2 Consider a binary tree topology for a packet-switching network. The root node connects to two other nodes. All intermediate nodes connect to one node in the direction toward the root, and two in the direction away from the root. At the bottom are nodes with just one link back toward the root. If there are $2^N - 1$ nodes, derive an expression for the mean number of hops per packet for large N, assuming that trips between all node pairs are equally likely. *Hint:* You will find the following equalities useful:

$$\sum_{i=1}^{\infty} X^i = \frac{X}{1 - X}; \quad \sum_{i=1}^{\infty} iX^i = \frac{X}{(1 - X)^2}$$

12.3 Dijkstra's algorithm, for finding the least-cost path from a specified node *s* to a specified node *t*, can be expressed in the following program:

```
for n := 1 to N do
    begin
        L[n] := ∞; final[n] := false; {all nodes are
        temporarily labeled with ∞}
        pred[n] := 1
    end;
L[s] := 0; final[s] := true;        {node s is permanently la-
                                     beled with 0}
recent := s;                         {the most recent node to be
                                     permanently labeled is s}

path := true;
{initialization over }

while final[t] = false do
begin
    for n := 1 to N do   {find new label}
        if (w[recent, n] < ∞) AND (NOT final[n]) then
        {for every immediate successor of recent that is not
        permanently labeled, do }
            begin {update temporary labels}
                newlabel := L[recent] + w[recent,n];
                if newlabel <L[n] then
                    begin L[n] := newlabel; pred[n] := recent end
                    {re-label n if there is a shorter path via
                    node recent and make
                        recent the predecessor of n on the
                        shortest path from s}
            end;
    temp := ∞;
    for x := 1 to N do {find node with smallest temporary
    label}
        if (NOT final[x]) AND (L[x] < temp) then
            begin y := x; temp :=L[x] end;
    if temp < ∞ then {there is a path} then
        begin final[y] := true; recent := y end
        {y, the next closest node to s gets permanently
        labeled}
    else begin path := false; final[t] := true end
end
```

In this program, each node is assigned a temporary label initially. As a final path to a node is determined, it is assigned a permanent label equal to the cost of the path from s. Write a similar program for the Bellman-Ford algorithm. *Hint:* The Bellman-Ford algorithm is often called a label-correcting method, in contrast to Dijkstra's label-setting method.

12.4 In the discussion of Dijkstra's algorithm in Section 12.3, it is asserted that at each iteration, a new node is added to T and that the least-cost path for that new node passes only through nodes already in T. Demonstrate that this is true. *Hint:* Begin at the beginning. Show that the first node added to T must have a direct link to the source node. Then show that the second node to T must either have a direct link to the source node or a direct link to the first node added to T, and so on. Remember that all link costs are assumed nonnegative.

12.5 In the discussion of the Bellman-Ford algorithm, it is asserted that at the iteration for which $h = K$, if any path of length $K + 1$ is defined, the first K hops of that path form a path defined in the previous iteration. Demonstrate that this is true.

12.6 In step 3 of Dijkstra's algorithm, the least-cost path values are only updated for nodes not yet in T. Is it possible that a lower-cost path could be found to a node already in T? If so, demonstrate by example. If not, provide reasoning as to why not.

12.7 Using Dijkstra's algorithm, generate a least-cost route to all other nodes for nodes 2 through 6 of Figure 12.2. Display the results as in Table 12.2a.

12.8 Repeat Problem 12.7 using the Bellman-Ford algorithm.

12.9 Apply Dijkstra's routing algorithm to the networks in Figure 12.12. Provide a table similar to Table 12.2a and a figure similar to Figure 12.10.

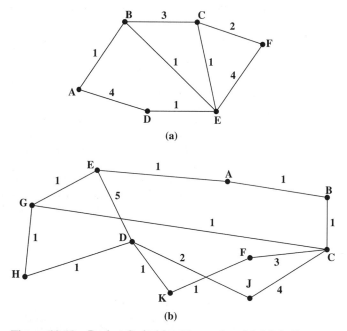

Figure 12.12   Packet-Switching Networks with Link Costs

12.10 Repeat Problem 12.9 using the Bellman-Ford algorithm.

12.11 Will Dijkstra's algorithm and the Bellman-Ford algorithm always yield the same solutions? Why or why not?

12.12 Both Dijkstra's algorithm and the Bellman-Ford algorithm find the least-cost paths from one node to all other nodes. The Floyd-Warshall algorithm finds the least-cost paths between all pairs of nodes together. Define

$$N = \text{set of nodes in the network}$$
$$w(i, j) = \text{link cost from node } i \text{ to node } j; w(i,i) = 0; w(i, j) = \infty \text{ if the two nodes are not directly connected}$$
$$L_n(i, j) = \text{cost of the least-cost path from node } i \text{ to node } j \text{ with the constraint that only nodes } 1, 2, \ldots, n \quad \text{can be used as intermediate nodes on paths}$$

The algorithm has the following steps:
1. Initialize:

$$L_0(i, j) = w(i, j), \quad \text{for all } i, j, i \quad j$$

2. For $n = 0, 1, \ldots, N - 1$

$$L_{n+1}(i, j) = \min[L_n(i, j), L_n(i, n + 1) + L_n(n + 1, j)] \quad \text{for all } i, \quad j$$

Explain the algorithm in words. Use induction to demonstrate that the algorithm works.

12.13 In Figure 12.4, node 1 sends a packet to node 6 using flooding. Counting the transmission of one packet across one link as a load of one, what is the total load generated if
   a. Each node discards duplicate incoming packets?
   b. A hop count field is used and is initially set to 5, and no duplicate is discarded?

12.14 It was shown that flooding can be used to determine the minimum-hop route. Can it be used to determine the minimum delay route?

12.15 With random routing, only one copy of the packet is in existence at a time. Nevertheless, it would be wise to utilize a hop count field. Why?

12.16 Another adaptive routing scheme is known as backward learning. As a packet is routed through the network, it carries not only the destination address, but the source address plus a running hop count that is incremented for each hop. Each node builds a routing table that gives the next node and hop count for each destination. How is the packet information used to build the table? What are the advantages and disadvantages of this technique?

12.17 Build a centralized routing directory for the networks of Figure 12.12.

12.18 Consider a system using flooding with a hop counter. Suppose that the hop counter is originally set to the "diameter" of the network. When the hop count reaches zero, the packet is discarded except at its destination. Does this always ensure that a packet will reach its destination if there exists at least one operable path? Why or why not?

CHAPTER 13

CONGESTION IN DATA NETWORKS

KEY POINTS

- Congestion occurs when the number of packets being transmitted through a network begins to approach the packet-handling capacity of the network. The objective of congestion control is to maintain the number of packets within the network below the level at which performance falls off dramatically.
- The lack of flow control mechanisms built into the ATM and frame relay protocols makes congestion control difficult. A variety of techniques have been developed to cope with congestion and to give different quality-of-service guarantees to different types of traffic.
- ATM networks establish a traffic contract with each user that specifies the characteristics of the expected traffic and the type of service that the network will provide. The network implements congestion control techniques in such a way as to protect the network from congestion while meeting the traffic contracts.
- An ATM network monitors the cell flow from each incoming source and may discard or label for potential discard cells that exceed the agreed traffic contract. In addition, the network may shape the traffic coming from users by temporarily buffering cells to smooth out traffic flows.

A key design issue that must be confronted both with data networks, such as packet-switching, frame relay, and ATM networks, and also with internets, is that of congestion control. The phenomenon of congestion is a complex one, as is the subject of congestion control. In very general terms, congestion occurs when the number of packets[1] being transmitted through a network begins to approach the packet-handling capacity of the network. The objective of congestion control is to maintain the number of packets within the network below the level at which performance falls off dramatically.

To understand the issues involved in congestion control, we need to look at some results from queuing theory. In essence, a data network or internet is a network of queues. At each node (data network switch, internet router), there is a queue of packets for each outgoing channel. If the rate at which packets arrive and queue up exceeds the rate at which packets can be transmitted, the queue size grows without bound and the delay experienced by a packet goes to infinity. Even if the packet arrival rate is less than the packet transmission rate, queue length will grow dramatically as the arrival rate approaches the transmission rate. As a rule of thumb, when the line for which packets are queuing becomes more than 80% utilized, the queue length grows at an alarming rate. This growth in queue length means that the delay experienced by a packet at each node increases. Further, since the size of any queue is finite, as queue length grows, eventually the queue must overflow.

This chapter focuses on congestion control in switched data networks, including packet-switching, frame relay, and ATM networks. The principles examined here are also applicable to internetworks. In Part Five, we look at additional congestion control mechanisms in our discussion of internetwork operation and TCP congestion control.

---

[1] In this chapter we use the term *packet* in a broad sense, to include packets in a packet-switching network, frames in a frame relay network, cells in an ATM network, or IP datagrams in an internet.

13.1 EFFECTS OF CONGESTION

Consider the queuing situation at a single packet switch or router, such as is illustrated in Figure 13.1. Any given node has a number of I/O ports[2] attached to it: one or more to other nodes, and zero or more to end systems. On each port, packets arrive and depart. We can consider that there are two buffers, or queues, at each port, one to accept arriving packets, and one to hold packets that are waiting to depart. In practice, there might be two fixed-size buffers associated with each port, or there might be a pool of memory available for all buffering activities. In the latter case, we can think of each port having two variable-size buffers associated with it, subject to the constraint that the sum of all buffer sizes is a constant.

In any case, as packets arrive, they are stored in the input buffer of the corresponding port. The node examines each incoming packet, makes a routing decision, and then moves the packet to the appropriate output buffer. Packets queued for output are transmitted as rapidly as possible; this is, in effect, statistical time division

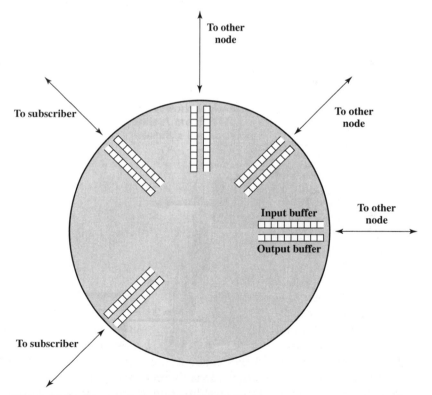

Figure 13.1   Input and Output Queues at Node

---

[2] In the case of a switch of a packet-switching, frame relay, or ATM network, each I/O port connects to a transmission link that connects to another node or end system. In the case of a router of an internet, each I/O port connects to either a direct link to another node or to a subnetwork.

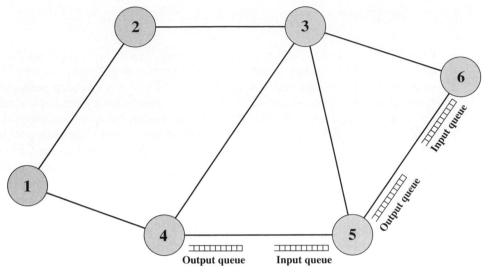

Figure 13.2 Interaction of Queues in a Data Network

multiplexing. If packets arrive too fast for the node to process them (make routing decisions) or faster than packets can be cleared from the outgoing buffers, then eventually packets will arrive for which no memory is available.

When such a saturation point is reached, one of two general strategies can be adopted. The first such strategy is to discard any incoming packet for which there is no available buffer space. The alternative is for the node that is experiencing these problems to exercise some sort of flow control over its neighbors so that the traffic flow remains manageable. But, as Figure 13.2 illustrates, each of a node's neighbors is also managing a number of queues. If node 6 restrains the flow of packets from node 5, this causes the output buffer in node 5 for the port to node 6 to fill up. Thus, congestion at one point in the network can quickly propagate throughout a region or the entire network. While flow control is indeed a powerful tool, we need to use it in such a way as to manage the traffic on the entire network.

Ideal Performance

Figure 13.3 suggests the ideal goal for network utilization. The top graph plots the steady-state total throughput (number of packets delivered to destination end systems) through the network as a function of the offered load (number of packets transmitted by source end systems), both normalized to the maximum theoretical throughput of the network. For example, if a network consists of a single node with two full-duplex 1-Mbps links, then the theoretical capacity of the network is 2 Mbps, consisting of a 1-Mbps flow in each direction. In the ideal case, the throughput of the network increases to accommodate load up to an offered load equal to the full capacity of the network; then normalized throughput remains at 1.0 at higher input loads. Note, however, what happens to the end-to-end delay experienced by the average packet even with this assumption of ideal performance. At negligible load, there is some small constant amount of delay that consists of the propagation delay

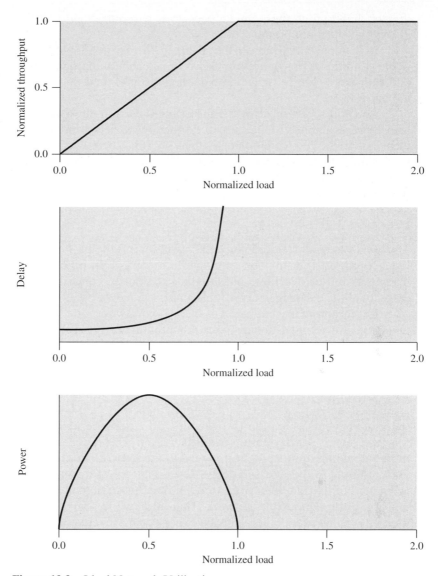

Figure 13.3   Ideal Network Utilization

through the network from source to destination plus processing delay at each node. As the load on the network increases, queuing delays at each node are added to this fixed amount of delay. When the load exceeds the network capacity, delays increase without bound.

Here is a simple intuitive explanation of why delay must go to infinity. Suppose that each node in the network is equipped with buffers of infinite size and suppose that the input load exceeds network capacity. Under ideal conditions, the network will continue to sustain a normalized throughput of 1.0. Therefore, the rate of packets leaving the network is 1.0. Because the rate of packets entering the network is greater than 1.0, internal queue sizes grow. In the steady state, with input greater than output, these queue sizes grow without bound and therefore queuing delays grow without bound.

It is important to grasp the meaning of Figure 13.3 before looking at real-world conditions. This figure represents the ideal, but unattainable, goal of all traffic and congestion control schemes. No scheme can exceed the performance depicted in Figure 13.3.

You will sometimes see the term *power* used in network performance literature. Power is defined as the ratio of throughput to delay, and this is depicted for the ideal case in the bottom graph of Figure 13.3. It has been shown that, typically, a network configuration and congestion control scheme that results in higher throughput also results in higher delay [JAIN91], and that power is a concise metric that can be used to compare different schemes.

Practical Performance

The ideal case reflected in Figure 13.3 assumes infinite buffers and no overhead related to packet transmission or congestion control. In practice, buffers are finite, leading to buffer overflow, and attempts to control congestion consume network capacity in the exchange of control signals.

Let us consider what happens in a network with finite buffers if no attempt is made to control congestion or to restrain input from end systems. The details will, of course, differ depending on network configuration and on the statistics of the presented traffic. However, the graphs in Figure 13.4 depict the devastating outcome in general terms.

At light loads, throughput and hence network utilization increases as the offered load increases. As the load continues to increase, a point is reached (point A in the plot) beyond which the throughput of the network increases at a rate slower than the rate at which offered load is increased. This is due to network entry into a moderate congestion state. In this region, the network continues to cope with the load, although with increased delays. The departure of throughput from the ideal is accounted for by a number of factors. For one thing, the load is unlikely to be spread uniformly throughout the network. Therefore, while some nodes may experience moderate congestion, others may be experiencing severe congestion and may need to discard traffic. In addition, as the load increases, the network will attempt to balance the load by routing packets through areas of lower congestion. For the routing function to work, an increased number of routing messages must be exchanged between nodes to alert each other to areas of congestion; this overhead reduces the capacity available for data packets.

As the load on the network continues to increase, the queue lengths of the various nodes continue to grow. Eventually, a point is reached (point B in the plot) beyond which throughput actually drops with increased offered load. The reason for this is that the buffers at each node are of finite size. When the buffers at a node become full, the node must discard packets. Thus, the sources must retransmit the discarded packets in addition to new packets. This only exacerbates the situation: As more and more packets are retransmitted, the load on the system grows, and more buffers become saturated. While the system is trying desperately to clear the backlog, users are pumping old and new packets into the system. Even successfully delivered packets may be retransmitted because it takes too long, at a higher layer

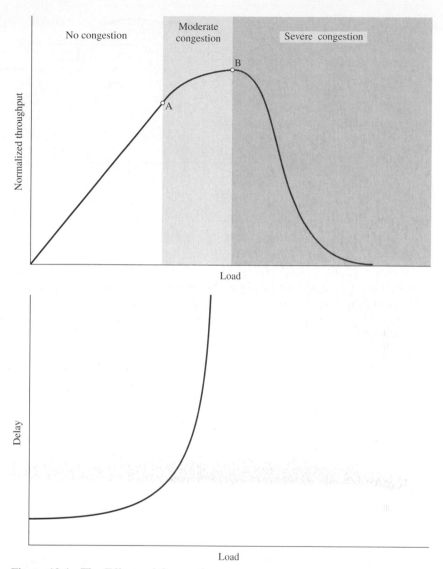

Figure 13.4   The Effects of Congestion

(e.g., transport layer), to acknowledge them: The sender assumes the packet did not get through and retransmits. Under these circumstances, the effective capacity of the system declines to zero.

13.2 CONGESTION CONTROL

In this book, we discuss various techniques for controlling congestion in packet-switching, frame relay, and ATM networks, and in IP-based internets. To give context to this discussion, Figure 13.5 provides a general depiction of important congestion control techniques.

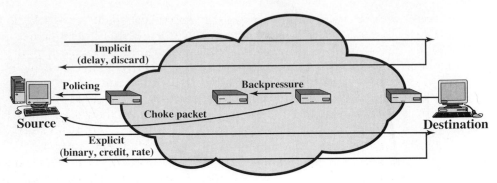

Figure 13.5   Mechanisms for Congestion Control

Backpressure

We have already made reference to backpressure as a technique for congestion control. This technique produces an effect similar to backpressure in fluids flowing down a pipe. When the end of a pipe is closed (or restricted), the fluid pressure backs up the pipe to the point of origin, where the flow is stopped (or slowed).

Backpressure can be exerted on the basis of links or logical connections (e.g., virtual circuits). Referring again to Figure 13.2, if node 6 becomes congested (buffers fill up), then node 6 can slow down or halt the flow of all packets from node 5 (or node 3, or both nodes 5 and 3). If this restriction persists, node 5 will need to slow down or halt traffic on its incoming links. This flow restriction propagates backward (against the flow of data traffic) to sources, which are restricted in the flow of new packets into the network.

Backpressure can be selectively applied to logical connections, so that the flow from one node to the next is only restricted or halted on some connections, generally the ones with the most traffic. In this case, the restriction propagates back along the connection to the source.

Backpressure is of limited utility. It can be used in a connection-oriented network that allows hop-by-hop (from one node to the next) flow control. X.25-based packet-switching networks typically provide this feature. However, neither frame relay nor ATM has any capability for restricting flow on a hop-by-hop basis. In the case of IP-based internets, there have traditionally been no built-in facilities for regulating the flow of data from one router to the next along a path through the internet. Recently, some flow-based schemes have been developed; this topic is introduced in Part Five.

Choke Packet

A choke packet is a control packet generated at a congested node and transmitted back to a source node to restrict traffic flow. An example of a choke packet is the ICMP (Internet Control Message Protocol) Source Quench packet. Either a router or a destination end system may send this message to a source end system, requesting that it reduce the rate at which it is sending traffic to the internet destination. On receipt of a source quench message, the source host should cut back the rate at which it is sending traffic to the specified destination until it no longer receives source quench messages. The source quench message can be used by a router or host that must discard IP datagrams because of a full buffer. In that case, the router or host will issue a source quench message for every datagram that it discards. In addition, a system may anticipate congestion and issue source quench messages when its buffers approach capacity. In that case, the datagram referred to in the source quench message may well be delivered. Thus, receipt of a source quench message does not imply delivery or nondelivery of the corresponding datagram.

The choke package is a relatively crude technique for controlling congestion. More sophisticated forms of explicit congestion signaling are discussed subsequently.

Implicit Congestion Signaling

When network congestion occurs, two things may happen: (1) The transmission delay for an individual packet from source to destination increases, so that it is noticeably longer than the fixed propagation delay; and (2) packets are discarded. If a source is able to detect increased delays and packet discards, then it has implicit evidence of network congestion. If all sources can detect congestion and, in response, reduce flow on the basis of congestion, then the network congestion will be relieved. Thus, congestion control on the basis of implicit signaling is the responsibility of end systems and does not require action on the part of network nodes.

Implicit signaling is an effective congestion control technique in connectionless, or datagram, configurations, such as datagram packet-switching networks and IP-based internets. In such cases, there are no logical connections through the internet on which flow can be regulated. However, between the two end systems, logical connections can be established at the TCP level. TCP includes mechanisms for acknowledging receipt of TCP segments and for regulating the flow of data between source and destination on a TCP connection. TCP congestion control techniques based on the ability to detect increased delay and segment loss are discussed in Chapter 20.

Implicit signaling can also be used in connection-oriented networks. For example, in frame relay networks, the LAPF control protocol, which is end to end, includes facilities similar to those of TCP for flow and error control. LAPF control is capable of detecting lost frames and adjusting the flow of data accordingly.

Explicit Congestion Signaling

It is desirable to use as much of the available capacity in a network as possible but still react to congestion in a controlled and fair manner. This is the purpose of explicit congestion avoidance techniques. In general terms, for explicit congestion avoidance, the network alerts end systems to growing congestion within the network and the end systems take steps to reduce the offered load to the network.

Typically, explicit congestion control techniques operate over connection-oriented networks and control the flow of packets over individual connections. Explicit congestion signaling approaches can work in one of two directions:

- **Backward:** Notifies the source that congestion avoidance procedures should be initiated where applicable for traffic in the opposite direction of the received notification. It indicates that the packets that the user transmits on this logical connection may encounter congested resources. Backward information is transmitted either by altering bits in a header of a data packet headed for the source to be controlled or by transmitting separate control packets to the source.

- **Forward:** Notifies the user that congestion avoidance procedures should be initiated where applicable for traffic in the same direction as the received notification. It indicates that this packet, on this logical connection, has encountered congested resources. Again, this information may be transmitted either as altered bits in data packets or in separate control packets. In some schemes, when a forward signal is received by an end system, it echoes the signal back along the logical connection to the source. In other schemes, the end system is expected to exercise flow control upon the source end system at a higher layer (e.g., TCP).

We can divide explicit congestion signaling approaches into three general categories:

- **Binary:** A bit is set in a data packet as it is forwarded by the congested node. When a source receives a binary indication of congestion on a logical connection, it may reduce its traffic flow.

- **Credit based:** These schemes are based on providing an explicit credit to a source over a logical connection. The credit indicates how many octets or how many packets the source may transmit. When the credit is exhausted, the source must await additional credit before sending additional data. Credit-based schemes are common for end-to-end flow control, in which a destination system uses credit to prevent the source from overflowing the destination buffers, but credit-based schemes have also been considered for congestion control.

- **Rate based:** These schemes are based on providing an explicit data rate limit to the source over a logical connection. The source may transmit data at a rate up to the set limit. To control congestion, any node along the path of the connection can reduce the data rate limit in a control message to the source.

13.3 TRAFFIC MANAGEMENT

There are a number of issues related to congestion control that might be included under the general category of traffic management. In its simplest form, congestion control is concerned with efficient use of a network at high load. The various mechanisms discussed in the previous section can be applied as the situation arises, without regard to the particular source or destination affected. When a node is saturated and must discard packets, it can apply some simple rule, such as discard the most recent arrival. However, other considerations can be used to refine the application of congestion control techniques and discard policy. We briefly introduce several of those areas here.

Fairness

As congestion develops, flows of packets between sources and destinations will experience increased delays and, with high congestion, packet losses. In the absence of other requirements, we would like to assure that the various flows suffer from congestion equally. Simply to discard on a last-in-first-discarded basis may not be fair. As an example of a technique that might promote fairness, a node can maintain a separate queue for each logical connection or for each source-destination pair. If all of the queue buffers are of equal length, then the queues with the highest traffic load will suffer discards more often, allowing lower-traffic connections a fair share of the capacity.

Quality of Service

We might wish to treat different traffic flows differently. For example, as [JAIN92] points out, some applications, such as voice and video, are delay sensitive but loss insensitive. Others, such as file transfer and electronic mail, are delay insensitive but loss sensitive. Still others, such as interactive graphics or interactive computing applications, are delay sensitive and loss sensitive. Also, different traffic flows have different priorities; for example, network management traffic, particularly during times of congestion or failure, is more important than application traffic.

It is particularly important during periods of congestion that traffic flows with different requirements be treated differently and provided a different quality of service (QoS). For example, a node might transmit higher-priority packets ahead of lower-priority packets in the same queue. Or a node might maintain different queues for different QoS levels and give preferential treatment to the higher levels.

Reservations

One way to avoid congestion and also to provide assured service to applications is to use a reservation scheme. Such a scheme is an integral part of ATM networks. When a logical connection is established, the network and the user enter into a traffic contract, which specifies a data rate and other characteristics of the traffic flow. The network agrees to give a defined QoS so long as the traffic flow is within contract parameters; excess traffic is either discarded or handled on a best-effort basis, subject to discard. If the current outstanding reservations are such that the network resources are inadequate to meet the new reservation, then the new reservation is denied. A similar type of scheme has now been developed for IP-based internets (RSVP, which is discussed in Chapter 19).

One aspect of a reservation scheme is traffic policing (Figure 13.5). A node in the network, typically the node to which the end system attaches, monitors the traffic flow and compares it to the traffic contract. Excess traffic is either discarded or marked to indicate that it is liable to discard or delay.

13.4 CONGESTION CONTROL IN PACKET-SWITCHING NETWORKS

A number of control mechanisms for congestion control in packet-switching networks have been suggested and tried. The following are examples:

1. Send a control packet from a congested node to some or all source nodes. This choke packet will have the effect of stopping or slowing the rate of transmission from sources and hence limit the total number of packets in the network. This approach requires additional traffic on the network during a period of congestion.

2. Rely on routing information. Routing algorithms, such as ARPANET's, provide link delay information to other nodes, which influences routing decisions. This information could also be used to influence the rate at which new packets are produced. Because these delays are being influenced by the routing decision, they may vary too rapidly to be used effectively for congestion control.

3. Make use of an end-to-end probe packet. Such a packet could be timestamped to measure the delay between two particular endpoints. This has the disadvantage of adding overhead to the network.

4. Allow packet-switching nodes to add congestion information to packets as they go by. There are two possible approaches here. A node could add such information to packets going in the direction opposite of the congestion. This information quickly reaches the source node, which can reduce the flow of packets into the network. Alternatively, a node could add such information to packets going in the same direction as the congestion. The destination either asks the source to adjust the load or returns the signal back to the source in the packets (or acknowledgments) going in the reverse direction.

13.5 FRAME RELAY CONGESTION CONTROL

I.370 defines the objectives for frame relay congestion control to be the following:

- Minimize frame discard.
- Maintain, with high probability and minimum variance, an agreed quality of service.
- Minimize the possibility that one end user can monopolize network resources at the expense of other end users.
- Be simple to implement, and place little overhead on either end user or network.
- Create minimal additional network traffic.
- Distribute network resources fairly among end users.
- Limit spread of congestion to other networks and elements within the network.
- Operate effectively regardless of the traffic flow in either direction between end users.

- Have minimum interaction or impact on other systems in the frame-relaying network.
- Minimize the variance in quality of service delivered to individual frame relay connections during congestion (e.g., individual logical connections should not experience sudden degradation when congestion approaches or has occurred).

Congestion control is difficult for a frame relay network because of the limited tools available to the frame handlers (frame-switching nodes). The frame relay protocol has been streamlined to maximize throughput and efficiency. A consequence of this is that a frame handler cannot control the flow of frames coming from a subscriber or an adjacent frame handler using the typical sliding-window flow control protocol, such as is found in HDLC.

Congestion control is the joint responsibility of the network and the end users. The network (i.e., the collection of frame handlers) is in the best position to monitor the degree of congestion, while the end users are in the best position to control congestion by limiting the flow of traffic.

Table 13.1 lists the congestion control techniques defined in the various ITU-T and ANSI documents. **Discard strategy** deals with the most fundamental response to congestion: When congestion becomes severe enough, the network is forced to discard frames. We would like to do this in a way that is fair to all users.

Congestion avoidance procedures are used at the onset of congestion to minimize the effect on the network. Thus, these procedures would be initiated at or prior to point A in Figure 13.4, to prevent congestion from progressing to point B. Near point A, there would be little evidence available to end users that congestion is increasing. Thus, there must be some **explicit signaling** mechanism from the network that will trigger the congestion avoidance.

Congestion recovery procedures are used to prevent network collapse in the face of severe congestion. These procedures are typically initiated when the network has begun to drop frames due to congestion. Such dropped frames will be reported

Table 13.1 Frame Relay Congestion Control Techniques

Technique	Type	Function	Key Elements
Discard control	Discard strategy	Provides guidance to network concerning which frames to discard	DE bit
Backward explicit Congestion Notification	Congestion avoidance	Provides guidance to end systems about congestion in network	BECN bit or CLLM message
Forward explicit Congestion Notification	Congestion avoidance	Provides guidance to end systems about congestion in network	FECN bit
Implicit congestion notification	Congestion recovery	End system infers congestion from frame loss	Sequence numbers in higher-layer PDU

by some higher layer of software (e.g., LAPF control protocol or TCP) and serve as an **implicit signaling** mechanism. Congestion recovery procedures operate around point B and within the region of severe congestion, as shown in Figure 13.4.

ITU-T and ANSI consider congestion avoidance with explicit signaling and congestion recovery with implicit signaling to be complementary forms of congestion control in the frame-relaying bearer service.

Traffic Rate Management

As a last resort, a frame-relaying network must discard frames to cope with congestion. There is no getting around this fact. Because each frame handler in the network has finite memory available for queuing frames (Figure 13.2), it is possible for a queue to overflow, necessitating the discard of either the most recently arrived frame or some other frame.

The simplest way to cope with congestion is for the frame-relaying network to discard frames arbitrarily, with no regard to the source of a particular frame. In that case, because there is no reward for restraint, the best strategy for any individual end system is to transmit frames as rapidly as possible. This, of course, exacerbates the congestion problem.

To provide for a fairer allocation of resources, the frame relay bearer service includes the concept of a committed information rate (CIR). This is a rate, in bits per second, that the network agrees to support for a particular frame-mode connection. Any data transmitted in excess of the CIR are vulnerable to discard in the event of congestion. Despite the use of the term *committed*, there is no guarantee that even the CIR will be met. In cases of extreme congestion, the network may be forced to provide a service at less than the CIR for a given connection. However, when it comes time to discard frames, the network will choose to discard frames on connections that are exceeding their CIR before discarding frames that are within their CIR.

In theory, each frame-relaying node should manage its affairs so that the aggregate of CIRs of all the connections of all the end systems attached to the node does not exceed the capacity of the node. In addition, the aggregate of the CIRs should not exceed the physical data rate across the user-network interface, known as the access rate. The limitation imposed by access rate can be expressed as follows:

$$\sum_i \text{CIR}_{i,j} \le \text{AccessRate}_j \tag{13.1}$$

where

$$\text{CIR}_{i,j} = \text{Committed information rate for connection } i \text{ on channel } j$$
$$\text{AccessRate}_j = \text{Data rate of user access channel } j; \text{ a channel is a fixed-data-rate TDM channel between the user and the network}$$

Considerations of node capacity may result in the selection of lower values for some of the CIRs.

For permanent frame relay connections, the CIR for each connection must be established at the time the connection is agreed between user and network. For switched connections, the CIR parameter is negotiated; this is done in the setup phase of the call control protocol.

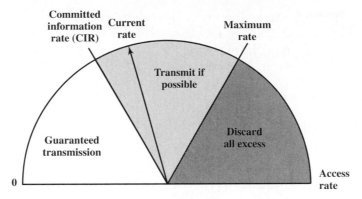

Figure 13.6   Operation of the CIR

The CIR provides a way of discriminating among frames in determining which frames to discard in the face of congestion. Discrimination is indicated by means of the discard eligibility (DE) bit in the LAPF frame (Figure 10.19). The frame handler to which the user's station attaches performs a metering function (Figure 13.6). If the user is sending data at less than the CIR, the incoming frame handler does not alter the DE bit. If the rate exceeds the CIR, the incoming frame handler will set the DE bit on the excess frames and then forward them; such frames may get through or may be discarded if congestion is encountered. Finally, a maximum rate is defined, such that any frames above the maximum are discarded at the entry frame handler.

The CIR, by itself, does not provide much flexibility in dealing with traffic rates. In practice, a frame handler measures traffic over each logical connection for a time interval specific to that connection and then makes a decision based on the amount of data received during that interval. Two additional parameters, assigned on permanent connections and negotiated on switched connections, are needed:

- **Committed burst size (B_c):** The maximum amount data that the network agrees to transfer, under normal conditions, over a measurement interval T. These data may or may not be contiguous (i.e., they may appear in one frame or in several frames).
- **Excess burst size (B_e):** The maximum amount of data in excess of B_c that the network will attempt to transfer, under normal conditions, over a measurement interval T. These data are uncommitted in the sense that the network does not commit to delivery under normal conditions. Put another way, the data that represent B_e are delivered with lower probability than the data within B_c.

The quantities B_c and CIR are related. Because B_c is the amount of committed data that may be transmitted by the user over a time T, and CIR is the rate at which committed data may be transmitted, we must have

$$T = \frac{B_c}{\text{CIR}} \qquad (13.2)$$

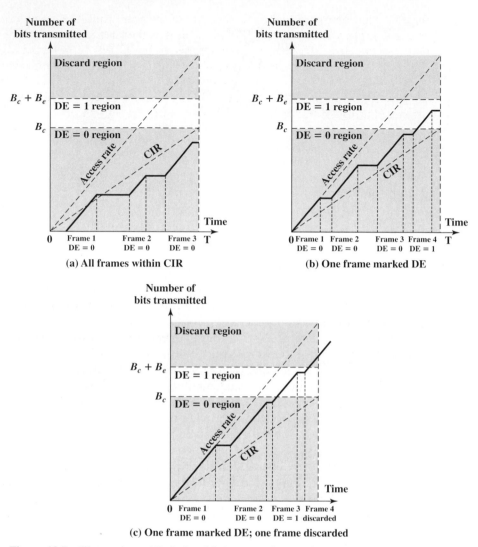

Figure 13.7 Illustration of Relationships among Congestion Parameters

Figure 13.7, based on a figure in ITU-T Recommendation I.370, illustrates the relationship among these parameters. On each graph, the solid line plots the cumulative number of information bits transferred over a given connection since time $T = 0$. The dashed line labeled Access Rate represents the data rate over the channel containing this connection. The dashed line labeled CIR represents the committed information rate over the measurement interval T. Note that when a frame is being transmitted, the solid line is parallel to the Access Rate line; when a frame is transmitted on a channel, that channel is dedicated to the transmission of that frame. When no frame is being transmitted, the solid line is horizontal.

Figure 13.7a shows an example in which three frames are transmitted within the measurement interval and the total number of bits in the three frames is less than B_c. Note that during the transmission of the first frame, the actual transmission rate temporarily exceeds the CIR. This is of no consequence because the frame handler is only concerned with the cumulative number of bits transmitted over the entire interval. In Figure 13.7b, the last frame transmitted during the interval causes the cumulative number of bits transmitted to exceed B_c. Accordingly, the DE bit of that frame is set by the frame handler. In Figure 13.7c, the third frame exceeds B_c and so is labeled for potential discard. The fourth frame exceeds $B_c + B_e$ and is discarded.

Congestion Avoidance with Explicit Signaling

It is desirable to use as much of the available capacity in a frame relay network as possible but still react to congestion in a controlled and fair manner. This is the purpose of explicit congestion avoidance techniques. In general terms, for explicit congestion avoidance, the network alerts end systems to growing congestion within the network and the end systems take steps to reduce the offered load to the network.

As the standards for explicit congestion avoidance were being developed, two general strategies were considered [BERG91]. One group believed that congestion always occurred slowly and almost always in the network egress nodes. Another group had seen cases in which congestion grew very quickly in the internal nodes and required quick decisive action to prevent network congestion. We will see that these two approaches are reflected in the forward and backward explicit congestion avoidance techniques, respectively.

For explicit signaling, two bits in the address field of each frame are provided. Either bit may be set by any frame handler that detects congestion. If a frame handler receives a frame in which one or both of these bits are set, it must not clear the bits before forwarding the frame. Thus, the bits constitute signals from the network to the end user. The two bits are as follows:

- **Backward explicit congestion notification (BECN):** Notifies the user that congestion avoidance procedures should be initiated where applicable for traffic in the opposite direction of the received frame. It indicates that the frames that the user transmits on this logical connection may encounter congested resources.
- **Forward explicit congestion notification (FECN):** Notifies the user that congestion avoidance procedures should be initiated where applicable for traffic in the same direction as the received frame. It indicates that this frame, on this logical connection, has encountered congested resources.

Let us consider how these bits are used by the network and the user. First, for the **network response**, it is necessary for each frame handler to monitor its queuing behavior. If queue lengths begin to grow to a dangerous level, then either FECN or BECN bits or a combination should be set to try to reduce the flow of frames through that frame handler. The choice of FECN or BECN may be determined by whether the end users on a given logical connection are prepared to respond to one or the other of these bits. This may be determined at configuration time. In any case, the frame handler has some choice as to which logical connections should be alerted to congestion. If congestion is becoming quite serious, all logical connections through a frame handler might be notified. In the early stages of congestion, the frame handler might just notify users for those connections that are generating the most traffic.

The **user response** is determined by the receipt of BECN or FECN signals. The simplest procedure is the response to a BECN signal: The user simply reduces the rate at which frames are transmitted until the signal ceases. The response to an FECN is more complex, as it requires the user to notify its peer user of this connection to restrict its flow of frames. The core functions used in the frame relay protocol do not support this notification; therefore, it must be done at a higher layer, such as the transport layer. The flow control could also be accomplished by the LAPF control protocol or some other link control protocol implemented above the frame relay sublayer. The LAPF control protocol is particularly useful because it includes an enhancement to LAPD that permits the user to adjust window size.

13.6 ATM TRAFFIC MANAGEMENT

Because of their high speed and small cell size, ATM networks present difficulties in effectively controlling congestion not found in other types of data networks. The complexity of the problem is compounded by the limited number of overhead bits available for exerting control over the flow of user cells. This area is currently the subject of intense research, and approaches to traffic and congestion control are still evolving. ITU-T has defined a restricted initial set of traffic and congestion control capabilities aiming at simple mechanisms and realistic network efficiency; these are specified in I.371. The ATM Forum has published a somewhat more advanced version of this set in its Traffic Management Specification 4.0 [ATM96]. This section focuses on the ATM Forum specifications.

We begin with an overview of the congestion problem and the framework adopted by ITU-T and the ATM Forum. We then discuss some of the specific techniques that have been developed for traffic management and congestion control.

Requirements for ATM Traffic and Congestion Control

Both the types of traffic patterns imposed on ATM networks and the transmission characteristics of those networks differ markedly from those of other switching networks. Most packet-switching and frame relay networks carry non-real-time data traffic. Typically, the traffic on individual virtual circuits or frame relay connections is bursty in nature, and the receiving system expects to receive incoming traffic on each connection in a bursty fashion. As a result,

- The network does not need to replicate the exact timing pattern of incoming traffic at the exit node.
- Therefore, simple statistical multiplexing can be used to accommodate multiple logical connections over the physical interface between user and network. The average data rate required by each connection is less than the burst rate for that connection, and the user-network interface (UNI) need only be

designed for a capacity somewhat greater than the sum of the average data rates for all connections.

A number of tools are available for control of congestion in packet-switched and frame relay networks, some of which are discussed elsewhere in this chapter. These types of congestion control schemes are inadequate for ATM networks. [GERS91] cites the following reasons:

- The majority of traffic is not amenable to flow control. For example, voice and video traffic sources cannot stop generating cells even when the network is congested.
- Feedback is slow due to the drastically reduced cell transmission time compared to propagation delays across the network.
- ATM networks typically support a wide range of applications requiring capacity ranging from a few kbps to several hundred Mbps. Relatively simple-minded congestion control schemes generally end up penalizing one end or the other of that spectrum.
- Applications on ATM networks may generate very different traffic patterns (e.g., constant bit rate versus variable bit rate sources). Again, it is difficult for conventional congestion control techniques to handle fairly such variety.
- Different applications on ATM networks require different network services (e.g., delay-sensitive service for voice and video, and loss-sensitive service for data).
- The very high speeds in switching and transmission make ATM networks more volatile in terms of congestion and traffic control. A scheme that relies heavily on reacting to changing conditions will produce extreme and wasteful fluctuations in routing policy and flow control.

Two key performance issues that relate to the preceding points are latency/speed effects and cell delay variation, topics to which we now turn.

Latency/Speed Effects

Consider the transfer of ATM cells over a network at a data rate of 150 Mbps. At that rate, it takes $(53 \times 8 \text{ bits})/(150 \times 10^6 \text{ bps}) \approx 2.8 \times 10^{-6}$ seconds to insert a single cell onto the network. The time it takes to transfer the cell from the source to the destination user will depend on the number of intermediate ATM switches, the switching time at each switch, and the propagation time along all links in the path from source to destination. For simplicity, ignore ATM switching delays and assume propagation at two-thirds the speed of light. Then, if source and destination are on opposite coasts of the United States, the round-trip propagation delay is about 48×10^{-3} seconds.

With these conditions in place, suppose that source A is performing a long file transfer to destination B and that implicit congestion control is being used (i.e., there are no explicit congestion notifications; the source deduces the presence of congestion by the loss of data). If the network drops a cell due to congestion, B can return a reject message to A, which must then retransmit the dropped cell and possibly all subsequent cells. But by the time the notification gets back to A, it has transmitted an additional N cells, where

$$N = \frac{48 \times 10^{-3}\, \text{seconds}}{2.8 \times 10^{-6}\, \text{seconds/cell}} = 1.7 \times 10^4\, \text{cells} = 7.2 \times 10^6\, \text{bits}$$

Over 7 megabits have been transmitted before A can react to the congestion indication.

This calculation helps to explain why the techniques that are satisfactory for more traditional networks break down when dealing with ATM WANs.

Cell Delay Variation

For an ATM network, voice and video signals can be digitized and transmitted as a stream of cells. A key requirement, especially for voice, is that the delay across the network be short. Generally, this will be the case for ATM networks. As we have discussed, ATM is designed to minimize the processing and transmission overhead internal to the network so that very fast cell switching and routing is possible.

There is another important requirement that to some extent conflicts with the preceding requirement, namely that the rate of delivery of cells to the destination user must be constant. It is inevitable that there will be some variability in the rate of delivery of cells due both to effects within the network and at the source UNI; we summarize these effects presently. First, let us consider how the destination user might cope with variations in the delay of cells as they transit from source user to destination user.

A general procedure for achieving a constant bit rate (CBR) is illustrated in Figure 13.8. Let $D(i)$ represent the end-to-end delay experienced by the ith cell. The destination system does not know the exact amount of this delay: There is no time-stamp information associated with each cell and, even if there were, it is impossible

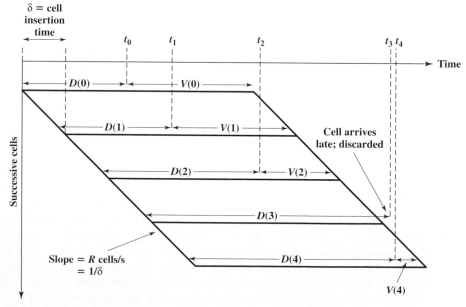

Figure 13.8   Time Reassembly of CBR Cells

to keep source and destination clocks perfectly synchronized. When the first cell on a connection arrives at time t_0, the target user delays the cell an additional amount $V(0)$ prior to delivery to the application. $V(0)$ is an estimate of the amount of cell delay variation that this application can tolerate and that is likely to be produced by the network.

Subsequent cells are delayed so that they are delivered to the user at a constant rate of R cells per second. The time between delivery of cells to the target application (time between the start of delivery of one cell and the start of delivery of the next cell) is therefore $\delta = 1/R$. To achieve a constant rate, the next cell is delayed a variable amount $V(1)$ to satisfy

$$t_1 + V(1) = t_0 + V(0) + \delta$$

So

$$V(1) = V(0) - [t_1 - (t_0 + \delta)]$$

In general,

$$V(i) = V(0) - [t_i - (t_0 + i \times \delta)]$$

which can also be expressed as

$$V(i) = V(i - 1) - [t_i - (t_{i-1} + \delta)]$$

If the computed value of $V(i)$ is negative, then that cell is discarded. The result is that data are delivered to the higher layer at a constant bit rate, with occasional gaps due to dropped cells.

The amount of the initial delay $V(0)$ which is also the average delay applied to all incoming cells, is a function of the anticipated cell delay variation. To minimize this delay, a subscriber will therefore request a minimal cell delay variation from the network provider. This leads to a tradeoff: Cell delay variation can be reduced by increasing the data rate at the UNI relative to the load and by increasing resources within the network.

Network Contribution to Cell Delay Variation

One component of cell delay variation is due to events within the network. For packet-switching networks, packet delay variation can be considerable due to queuing effects at each of the intermediate switching nodes and the processing time required to analyze packet headers and perform routing. To a much lesser extent, this is also true of frame delay variation in frame relay networks. In the case of ATM networks, cell delay variations due to network effects are likely to be even less than for frame relay. The principal reasons for this are the following:

- The ATM protocol is designed to minimize processing overhead at intermediate switching nodes. The cells are fixed size with fixed header formats, and there is no flow control or error control processing required.

- To accommodate the high speeds of ATM networks, ATM switches have had to be designed to provide extremely high throughput. Thus, the processing time for an individual cell at a node is negligible.

The only factor that could lead to noticeable cell delay variation within the network is congestion. If the network begins to become congested, either cells must be discarded or there will be a buildup of queuing delays at affected switches. Thus, it is important that the total load accepted by the network at any time not be such as to cause congestion.

Cell Delay Variation at the UNI

Even if an application generates data for transmission at a constant bit rate, cell delay variation can occur at the source due to the processing that takes place at the three layers of the ATM model.

Figure 13.9 illustrates the potential causes of cell delay variation. In this example, ATM connections A and B support user data rates of X and Y Mbps, respectively $(X > Y)$. At the AAL level, data are segmented into 48-octet blocks. Note that on a time diagram, the blocks appear to be of different sizes for the two connections; specifically, the time required to generate a 48-octet block of data, in microseconds, is

$$\text{Connection A: } \frac{48 \times 8}{X}$$

$$\text{Connection B: } \frac{48 \times 8}{Y}$$

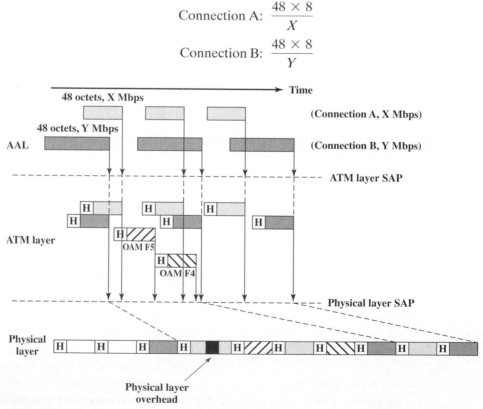

Figure 13.9   Origins of Cell Delay Variation (I.371)

The ATM layer encapsulates each segment into a 53-octet cell. These cells must be interleaved and delivered to the physical layer to be transmitted at the data rate of the physical link. Delay is introduced into this interleaving process: If two cells from different connections arrive at the ATM layer at overlapping times, one of the cells must be delayed by the amount of the overlap. In addition, the ATM layer is generating OAM (operation and maintenance) cells that must also be interleaved with user cells.

At the physical layer, there is opportunity for the introduction of further cell delays. For example, if cells are transmitted in SDH (synchronous digital hierarchy) frames, overhead bits for those frames will be inserted onto the physical link, delaying bits from the ATM layer.

None of the delays just listed can be predicted in any detail, and none follow any repetitive pattern. Accordingly, there is a random element to the time interval between reception of data at the ATM layer from the AAL and the transmission of that data in a cell across the UNI.

Traffic and Congestion Control Framework

I.371 lists the following objectives of ATM layer traffic and congestion control:

- ATM layer traffic and congestion control should support a set of ATM layer QoS (Quality of Service) classes sufficient for all foreseeable network services; the specification of these QoS classes should be consistent with network performance parameters currently under study.
- ATM layer traffic and congestion control should not rely on AAL protocols that are network service specific, nor on higher-layer protocols that are application specific. Protocol layers above the ATM layer may make use of information provided by the ATM layer to improve the utility those protocols can derive from the network.
- The design of an optimum set of ATM layer traffic controls and congestion controls should minimize network and end-system complexity while maximizing network utilization.

To meet these objectives, ITU-T and the ATM Forum have defined a collection of traffic and congestion control functions that operate across a spectrum of timing intervals. Table 13.2 lists these functions with respect to the response times within which they operate. Four levels of timing are considered:

- **Cell insertion time:** Functions at this level react immediately to cells as they are transmitted.
- **Round-trip propagation time:** At this level, the network responds within the lifetime of a cell in the network and may provide feedback indications to the source.
- **Connection duration:** At this level, the network determines whether a new connection at a given QoS can be accommodated and what performance levels will be agreed to.
- **Long term:** These are controls that affect more than one ATM connection and are established for long-term use.

Table 13.2 Traffic Control and Congestion Control Functions

Response Time	Traffic Control Functions	Congestion Control Functions
Long Term	• Resource management using virtual paths	
Connection Duration	• Connection admission control (CAC)	
Round-Trip Propagation Time	• Fast resource management	• Explicit forward congestion indication (EFCI) • ABR flow control
Cell Insertion Time	• Usage parameter control (UPC) • Priority control • Traffic shaping	• Selective cell discard

The essence of the traffic control strategy is based on (1) determining whether a given new ATM connection can be accommodated and (2) agreeing with the subscriber on the performance parameters that will be supported. In effect, the subscriber and the network enter into a traffic contract: The network agrees to support traffic at a certain level of performance on this connection, and the subscriber agrees not to exceed traffic parameter limits. Traffic control functions are concerned with establishing these traffic parameters and enforcing them. Thus, they are concerned with congestion avoidance. If traffic control fails in certain instances, then congestion may occur. At this point, congestion control functions are invoked to respond to and recover from the congestion.

Traffic Management and Congestion Control Techniques

The ITU-T and the ATM Forum have defined a range of traffic management functions to maintain the quality of service (QoS) of ATM connections. ATM traffic management function refers to the set of actions taken by the network to avoid congestion conditions or to minimize congestion effects. In this subsection, we highlight the following techniques:

- Resource management using virtual paths
- Connection admission control
- Usage parameter control
- Selective cell discard
- Traffic shaping

Resource Management Using Virtual Paths

The essential concept behind network resource management is to allocate network resources in such a way as to separate traffic flows according to service characteristics. So far, the only specific traffic control function based on network resource management defined by the ATM Forum deals with the use of virtual paths.

As discussed in Chapter 11, a virtual path connection (VPC) provides a convenient means of grouping similar virtual channel connections (VCCs). The network provides aggregate capacity and performance characteristics on the virtual path, and these are shared by the virtual connections. There are three cases to consider:

- **User-to-user application:** The VPC extends between a pair of UNIs. In this case the network has no knowledge of the QoS of the individual VCCs within a VPC. It is the user's responsibility to assure that the aggregate demand from the VCCs can be accommodated by the VPC.

- **User-to-network application:** The VPC extends between a UNI and a network node. In this case, the network is aware of the QoS of the VCCs within the VPC and has to accommodate them.

- **Network-to-network application:** The VPC extends between two network nodes. Again, in this case, the network is aware of the QoS of the VCCs within the VPC and has to accommodate them.

The QoS parameters that are of primary concern for network resource management are cell loss ratio, cell transfer delay, and cell delay variation, all of which are affected by the amount of resources devoted to the VPC by the network. If a VCC extends through multiple VPCs, then the performance on that VCC depends on the performances of the consecutive VPCs, and on how the connection is handled at any node that performs VCC-related functions. Such a node may be a switch, concentrator, or other network equipment. The performance of each VPC depends on the capacity of that VPC and the traffic characteristics of the VCCs contained within the VPC. The performance of each VCC-related function depends on the switching/processing speed at the node and on the relative priority with which various cells are handled.

Figure 13.10 gives an example. VCCs 1 and 2 experience a performance that depends on VPCs b and c and on how these VCCs are handled by the intermediate nodes. This may differ from the performance experienced by VCCs 3, 4, and 5.

There are a number of alternatives for the way in which VCCs are grouped and the type of performance they experience. If all of the VCCs within a VPC are handled similarly, then they should experience similar expected network performance, in terms of cell loss ratio, cell transfer delay, and cell delay variation. Alternatively, when different VCCs within the same VPC require different QoS, the VPC performance objective agreed to by network and subscriber should be set suitably for the most demanding VCC requirement.

In either case, with multiple VCCs within the same VPC, the network has two general options for allocating capacity to the VPC:

- **Aggregate peak demand:** The network may set the capacity (data rate) of the VPC equal to the total of the peak data rates of all of the VCCs within the VPC. The advantage of this approach is that each VCC can be given a QoS that accommodates its peak demand. The disadvantage is that most of the time, the VPC capacity will not be fully utilized and therefore the network will have underutilized resources.

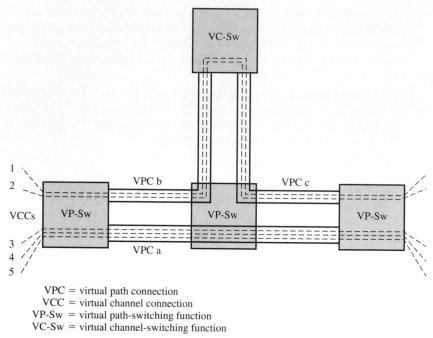

VPC = virtual path connection
VCC = virtual channel connection
VP-Sw = virtual path-switching function
VC-Sw = virtual channel-switching function

Figure 13.10 Configuration of VCCs and VPCs

- **Statistical multiplexing:** If the network sets the capacity of the VPC to be greater than or equal to the average data rates of all the VCCs but less than the aggregate peak demand, then a statistical multiplexing service is supplied. With statistical multiplexing, VCCs experience greater cell delay variation and greater cell transfer delay. Depending on the size of buffers used to queue cells for transmission, VCCs may also experience greater cell loss ratio. This approach has the advantage of more efficient utilization of capacity and is attractive if the VCCs can tolerate the lower QoS.

When statistical multiplexing is used, it is preferable to group VCCs into VPCs on the basis of similar traffic characteristics and similar QoS requirements. If dissimilar VCCs share the same VPC and statistical multiplexing is used, it is difficult to provide fair access to both high-demand and low-demand traffic streams.

Connection Admission Control

Connection admission control is the first line of defense for the network in protecting itself from excessive loads. In essence, when a user requests a new VPC or VCC, the user must specify (implicitly or explicitly) the traffic characteristics in both directions for that connection. The user selects traffic characteristics by selecting a QoS from among the QoS classes that the network provides. The network accepts the connection only if it can commit the resources necessary to support that traffic level while at the same time maintaining the agreed QoS of existing connections. By accepting the connection, the network forms a *traffic contract* with the user. Once the connection is accepted, the network continues to provide the agreed QoS as long as the user complies with the traffic contract.

The traffic contract may consist of the four parameters defined in Table 13.3: peak cell rate (PCR), cell delay variation (CDV), sustainable cell rate (SCR), and burst tolerance. Only the first two parameters are relevant for a constant-bit-rate (CBR) source; all four parameters may be used for variable-bit-rate (VBR) sources.

As the name suggests, the peak cell rate is the maximum rate at which cells are generated by the source on this connection. However, we need to take into account the cell delay variation. Although a source may be generating cells at a constant peak rate, cell delay variations introduced by various factors (see Figure 13.9) will affect the timing, causing cells to clump up and gaps to occur. Thus, a source may temporarily exceed the peak cell rate due to clumping. For the network to properly allocate resources to this connection, it must know not only the peak cell rate but also the CDV.

The exact relationship between peak cell rate and CDV depends on the operational definitions of these two terms. The standards provide these definitions in terms of a cell rate algorithm. Because this algorithm can be used for usage parameter control, we defer a discussion until the next subsection.

The PCR and CDV must be specified for every connection. As an option for variable-bit-rate sources, the user may also specify a sustainable cell rate and burst tolerance. These parameters are analogous to PCR and CDV, respectively, but apply

Table 13.3   Traffic Parameters Used in Defining VCC/VPC Quality of Service

Parameter	Description	Traffic Type
Peak Cell Rate (PCR)	An upper bound on the traffic that can be submitted on an ATM connection.	CBR, VBR
Cell Delay Variation (CDV)	An upper bound on the variability in the pattern of cell arrivals observed at a single measurement point with reference to the peak cell rate.	CBR, VBR
Sustainable Cell Rate (SCR)	An upper bound on the average rate of an ATM connection, calculated over the duration of the connection.	VBR
Burst Tolerance	An upper bound on the variability in the pattern of cell arrivals observed at a single measurement point with reference to the sustainable cell rate.	VBR

CBR = constant bit rate
VBR = variable bit rate

Table 13.4 Procedures Used to Set Values of Traffic Contract Parameters

	Explicitly Specified Parameters		Implicitly Specified Parameters
	Parameter values set at connection-setup time	Parameter values specified at subscription time	Parameter values set using default rules
	Requested by user/NMS	Assigned by network operator	
SVC	Signaling	By subscription	Network-operator default rules
PVC	NMS	By subscription	Network-operator default rules

SVC = switched virtual connection
PVC = permanent virtual connection
NMS = network management system

to an average rate of cell generation rather than a peak rate. The user can describe the future flow of cells in greater detail by using the SCR and burst tolerance as well as the PCR and CDV. With this additional information, the network may be able to utilize the network resources more efficiently. For example, if a number of VCCs are statistically multiplexed over a VPC, knowledge of both average and peak cell rates enables the network to allocate buffers of sufficient size to handle the traffic efficiently without cell loss.

For a given connection (VPC or VCC) the four traffic parameters may be specified in several ways, as illustrated in Table 13.4. Parameter values may be implicitly defined by default rules set by the network operator. In this case, all connections are assigned the same values, or all connections of a given class are assigned the same values for that class. The network operator may also associate parameter values with a given subscriber and assign these at the time of subscription. Finally, parameter values tailored to a particular connection may be assigned at connection time. In the case of a permanent virtual connection, these values are assigned by the network when the connection is set up. For a switched virtual connection, the parameters are negotiated between the user and the network via a signaling protocol.

Another aspect of quality of service that may be requested or assigned for a connection is cell loss priority. A user may request two levels of cell loss priority for an ATM connection; the priority of an individual cell is indicated by the user through the CLP bit in the cell header (Figure 11.4). When two priority levels are used, the traffic parameters for both cell flows must be specified. Typically, this is done by specifying a set of traffic parameters for high-priority traffic (CLP = 0) and a set of traffic parameters for all traffic (CLP = 0 or 1). Based on this breakdown, the network may be able to allocate resources more efficiently.

Usage Parameter Control

Once a connection has been accepted by the connection admission control function, the usage parameter control (UPC) function of the network monitors the connection to determine whether the traffic conforms to the traffic contract. The main purpose of usage parameter control is to protect network resources from an overload on one connection that would adversely affect the QoS on other connections by detecting violations of assigned parameters and taking appropriate actions.

Usage parameter control can be done at both the virtual path and virtual channel levels. Of these, the more important is VPC-level control, because network resources are, in general, initially allocated on the basis of virtual paths, with the virtual path capacity shared among the member virtual channels.

There are two separate functions encompassed by usage parameter control:

- Control of peak cell rate and the associated cell delay variation (CDV)
- Control of sustainable cell rate and the associated burst tolerance

Let us first consider the peak cell rate and the associated cell delay variation. In simple terms, a traffic flow is compliant if the peak rate of cell transmission does not exceed the agreed peak cell rate, subject to the possibility of cell delay variation within the agreed bound. I.371 defines an algorithm, the peak cell rate algorithm, that monitors compliance. The algorithm operates on the basis of two parameters: a peak cell rate R and a CDV tolerance limit of τ. Then $T = 1/R$ is the interarrival time between cells if there were no CDV. With CDV, T is the average interarrival time at the peak rate. The algorithm has been defined to monitor the rate at which cells arrive and to assure that the interarrival time is not too short to cause the flow to exceed the peak cell rate by an amount greater than the tolerance limit.

The same algorithm, with different parameters, can be used to monitor the sustainable cell rate and the associated burst tolerance. In this case, the parameters are the sustainable cell rate R_s and a burst tolerance τ_s.

The cell rate algorithm is rather complex; details can be found in [STAL99b]. The algorithm simply defines a way to monitor compliance with the traffic contract. To perform usage parameter control, the network must act on the results of the algorithm. The simplest strategy is that compliant cells are passed along and noncompliant cells are discarded at the point of the UPC function.

At the network's option, cell tagging may also be used for noncompliant cells. In this case, a noncompliant cell may be tagged with CLP = 1 (low priority) and passed. Such cells are then subject to discard at a later point in the network, should congestion be encountered.

If the user has negotiated two levels of cell loss priority for a network, then the situation is more complex. Recall that the user may negotiate a traffic contract for high priority traffic (CLP = 0) and a separate contract for aggregate traffic (CLP 0 or 1) The following rules apply:

1. A cell with CLP = 0 that conforms to the traffic contract for CLP = 0 passes.
2. A cell with CLP = 0 that is noncompliant for (CLP = 0) traffic but compliant for (CLP 0 or 1) traffic is tagged and passed.
3. A cell with CLP = 0 that is noncompliant for (CLP = 0) traffic and noncompliant for (CLP 0 or 1) traffic is discarded.

4. A cell with CLP = 1 that is compliant for (CLP = 0 or 1) traffic is passed.

5. A cell with CLP = 1 that is noncompliant for (CLP 0 or 1) traffic is discarded.

Selective Cell Discard

Selective cell discard comes into play when the network, at some point beyond the UPC function, discards (CLP = 1) cells. The objective is to discard lower-priority cells during congestion to protect the performance for higher-priority cells. Note that the network has no way to discriminate between cells that were labeled as lower priority by the source and cells that were tagged by the UPC function.

Traffic Shaping

The UPC algorithm is referred to as a form of **traffic policing**. Traffic policing occurs when a flow of data is regulated so that cells (or frames or packets) that exceed a certain performance level are discarded or tagged. It may be desirable to supplement a traffic-policing policy with a **traffic-shaping** policy. Traffic shaping is used to smooth out a traffic flow and reduce cell clumping. This can result in a fairer allocation of resources and a reduced average delay time.

A simple approach to traffic shaping is to use a form of the UPC algorithm known as token bucket. In contrast to the UPC algorithm, which simply monitors the traffic and tags or discards noncompliant cells, a traffic-shaping token bucket controls the flow of compliant cells.

Figure 13.11 illustrates the basic principle of the token bucket. A token generator produces tokens at a rate of ρ tokens per second and places these in the token bucket, which has a maximum capacity of β tokens. Cells arriving from the source are placed in a buffer with a maximum capacity of K cells. To transmit a cell through the server, one token must be removed from the bucket. If the token bucket is empty, the cell is queued waiting for the next token. The result of this scheme is that if there is a backlog of cells and an empty bucket, then cells are emitted at a smooth flow of ρ cells per second with no cell delay variation until the backlog is cleared. Thus, the token bucket smoothes out bursts of cells.

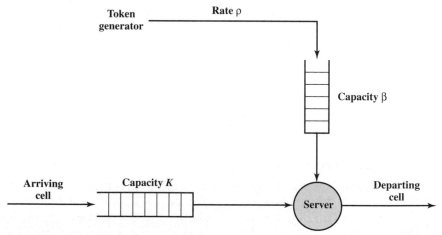

Figure 13.11   Token Bucket for Traffic Shaping

13.7 ATM-GFR TRAFFIC MANAGEMENT

GFR (guaranteed frame rate) provides a service that is as simple as UBR (unspecified bit rate) from the end system's point of view while placing a relatively modest requirement on the ATM network elements in terms of processing complexity and overhead. In essence, with GFR, an end system does no policing or shaping of the traffic it transmits but may transmit at the line rate of the ATM adapter. As with UBR, there is no guarantee of frame delivery. It is up to a higher layer, such as TCP, to react to congestion that results in dropped frames by employing the window management and congestion control techniques discussed in Part Five. Unlike UBR, GFR allows the user to reserve a certain amount of capacity, in terms of a cell rate, for each GFR VC. This reservation assures that user's application that it may transmit at a minimum rate without losses. If the network is not congested, the user will be able to transmit at a higher rate.

A distinctive characteristic of GFR is that it requires the network to recognize frames as well as cells. When congestion occurs, the network discards entire frames rather than individual cells. Further, GFR requires that all of the cells of a frame have the same CLP bit setting. The CLP = 1 AAL 5 frames are treated as lower-priority frames that are to be transmitted on a best-effort basis. The minimum guaranteed capacity applies to the CLP = 0 frames.

The GFR traffic contract consists of the following parameters:

- Peak cell rate (PCR)
- Minimum cell rate (MCR)
- Maximum burst size (MBS)
- Maximum frame size (MFS)
- Cell delay variation tolerance (CDVT)

Mechanisms for Supporting Rate Guarantees

There are three basic approaches that can be used by the network to provide per-VC guarantees for GFR and to enable a number of users to efficiently use and fairly share the available network capacity [GOYA98]:

- Tagging and policing
- Buffer management
- Scheduling

These approaches can be combined in various ways in an ATM network elements to yield a number of possible GFR implementations. Figure 13.12 illustrates their use.

Tagging and Policing

Tagging is used to discriminate between frames that conform to the GFR traffic contract and those that do not. The network element doing the conformance checking sets CLP = 1 on all cells of each frame that does not conform. Because tagged cells are assumed to be in violation of the traffic contract, they are given a lower quality of service than untagged cells by subsequent mechanisms, such as

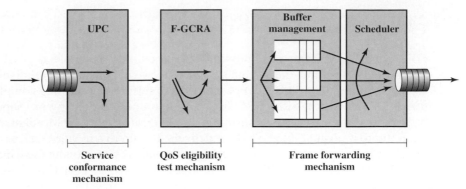

Figure 13.12 The Fundamental Components of a GFR Mechamism [ANDR99]

buffer management and scheduling. Tagging can be done by the network, especially the network element at the ingress to the ATM network. But tagging may also be done by the source end system to indicate less important frames.

The network, at either the ingress network element or at other ATM switching elements, may also choose to discard cells of nonconforming frames (i.e., cells with CLP = 1). Cell discard is considered a policing function.

Buffer Management

Buffer management mechanisms have to do with the way in which cells are treated that have been buffered at a network switch or that arrive at a network switch and must be buffered prior to forwarding. When a congestion condition exists, as reflected by high buffer occupancy, a network element will discard tagged cells in preference to untagged cells. In particular, a network element may discard a tagged cell that is already in a buffer to make room for an incoming untagged cell. To provide fair and efficient use of buffer resources, a network element may perform per-VC buffering, dedicating a certain amount of buffer space to individual VCs. Then, on the basis of the traffic contracts for each VC and the buffer occupancy per VC, the network element can make decisions concerning cell discard. That is, cell discard can be based on queue-specific occupancy thresholds.

Scheduling

A scheduling function, at minimum, can give preferential treatment to untagged cells over tagged cells. A network can also maintain separate queues for each VC and make per-VC scheduling decisions. Thus, within each queue, a first-come, first-served discipline can be used, perhaps modified to give higher priority for scheduling to CLP = 0 frames. Scheduling among the queues enables the network element to control the outgoing rate of individual VCs and thus ensure that individual VCs receive a fair allocation of capacity while meeting traffic contract requirements for minimum cell rate for each VC.

GFR Conformance Definition

The first function indicated in Figure 13.12 is a UPC function. UPC monitors each active VC to ensure that the traffic on each connection conforms to the traffic contract, and tags or discards nonconforming cells.

A frame is conforming if all of its cells are conforming, and is nonconforming if one or more cells are nonconforming. Three conditions must be met for a cell to be conforming:

1. The rate of cells must be within the cell rate contract.
2. All cells of a frame must have the same CLP value. Thus, the CLP bit of the current cell must have the same value as the CLP bit of the first cell of the frame.
3. The frame containing this cell must satisfy the MFS parameter. This condition can be met by performing the following test on each cell: The cell either is the last cell of the frame or the number of cells in the frame up to and including this cell is less than MFS.

QoS Eligibility Test Mechanism

The first two boxes in Figure 13.12 show what amounts to a two-stage filtering process. First, frames are tested for conformance to the traffic contract. Frames that do not conform may be discarded immediately. If a nonconforming frame is not discarded, its cells are tagged (CLP = 1), making them vulnerable to discard later on in the network. This first stage is therefore looking at an upper bound on traffic and penalizing cells that push the traffic flow above the upper bound.

The second stage of filtering determines which frames are eligible for QoS guarantees under the GFR contract for a given VC. This stage is looking at a lower bound on traffic; over a given period of time, those frames that constitute a traffic flow below the defined threshold are designated as eligible for QoS handling.

Therefore, the frames transmitted on a GFR VC fall into three categories:

- **Nonconforming frame:** Cells of this frame will be tagged or discarded.
- **Conforming but ineligible frames:** Cells will receive a best-effort service.
- **Conforming and eligible frames:** Cells will receive a guarantee of delivery.

To determine eligibility, a form of the cell rate algorithm referred to in Section 13.6 is used. A network may discard or tag any cells that are not eligible. However, TM 4.1 states that it is expected that an implementation will attempt to deliver conforming but ineligible traffic in on the basis of available resources, with each GFR connection being provided at each link with a fair share of the local residual bandwidth. The specification does not attempt to define a criterion by which to determine if a given implementation meets the aforementioned expectation.

13.8 RECOMMENDED READING

[YANG95] is a comprehensive survey of congestion control techniques. [JAIN90] and [JAIN92] provide excellent discussions of the requirements for congestion control, the various approaches that can be taken, and performance considerations. An excellent discussion of data network performance issues is provided by [KLEI93]. While somewhat dated, the definitive reference on flow control is [GERL80].

[GARR96] provides a rationale for the ATM service categories and discusses the traffic management implications of each. [MCDY99] contains a thorough discussion of ATM traffic control for CBR and VBR. Two excellent treatments of ATM traffic characteristics and performance are [GIRO99] and [SCHW96].

[ANDR99] provides a clear, detailed description of GFR. Another useful description is [BONA01].

Interesting examinations of frame relay congestion control issues are found in [CHEN89] and [DOSH88]. Good treatments are also found in [BUCK00], [GORA99], and [BLAC98].

ANDR99   Andrikopoulos, I.; Liakopoulous, A.; Pavlou, G.; and Sun, Z. "Providing Rate Guarantees for Internet Application Traffic Across ATM Networks." *IEEE Communications Surveys*, Third Quarter 1999. http://www.comsoc.org/pubs/surveys.

BLAC98   Black, U. *Frame Relay Networks.* New York: McGraw-Hill, 1998.

BONA01   Bonaventure, O., and Nelissen, J. "Guaranteed Frame Rate: A Better Service for TCP/IP in ATM Networks." *IEEE Network*, January/February 2001.

BUCK00   Buckwalter, J. *Frame Relay: Technology and Practice.* Reading, MA: Addison-Wesley, 2000.

CHEN89   Chen, K.; Ho, K.; and Saksena, V. "Analysis and Design of a Highly Reliable Transport Architecture for ISDN Frame-Relay Networks." *IEEE Journal on Selected Areas in Communications,* October 1989.

DOSH88   Doshi, B., and Nguyen, H. "Congestion Control in ISDN Frame-Relay Networks." *AT&T Technical Journal*, November/December 1988.

GARR96   Garrett, M. "A Service Architecture for ATM: From Applications to Scheduling." *IEEE Network*, May/June 1996.

GERL80   Gerla, M., and Kleinrock, L. "Flow Control: A Comparative Survey." *IEEE Transactions on Communications*, April 1980.

GIRO99   Giroux, N., and Ganti, S. *Quality of Service in ATM Networks.* Upper Saddle River, NJ: Prentice Hall, 1999.

GORA99   Goralski, W. *Frame Relay for High-Speed Networks.* New York: Wiley, 1999.

JAIN90   Jain, R. "Congestion Control in Computer Networks: Issues and Trends." *IEEE Network Magazine*, May 1990.

JAIN92   Jain, R. "Myths About Congestion Management in High-Speed Networks." *Internetworking: Research and Experience*, Volume 3, 1992.

KLEI93   Kleinrock, L. "On the Modeling and Analysis of Computer Networks." *Proceedings of the IEEE*, August 1993.

MCDY99   McDysan, D., and Spohn, D. *ATM: Theory and Application.* New York: McGraw-Hill, 1999.

SCHW96   Schwartz, M. *Broadband Integrated Networks.* Upper Saddle River, NJ: Prentice Hall PTR, 1996.

YANG95   Yang, C., and Reddy, A. "A Taxonomy for Congestion Control Algorithms in Packet Switching Networks." *IEEE Network*, July/August 1995.

13.9 KEY TERMS, REVIEW QUESTIONS, AND PROBLEMS

Key Terms

backpressure	congestion control	reservations
cell delay variation	explicit congestion signaling	traffic management
choke packet	implicit congestion signaling	
congestion	quality of service (QoS)	

Review Questions

13.1 When a node experiences saturation with respect to incoming packets, what general strategies may be used?

13.2 Why is it that when the load exceeds the network capacity, delay tends to infinity?

13.3 Give a brief explanation of each of the congestion control techniques illustrated in Figure 13.5.

13.4 What is the difference between backward and forward explicit congestion signaling?

13.5 Briefly explain the three general approaches to explicit congestion signaling.

13.6 Explain the concept of committed information rate (CIR) in frame relay networks.

13.7 What is the significance of cell delay variation in an ATM network?

13.8 What functions are included in ATM usage parameter control?

13.9 What is the difference between traffic policing and traffic shaping?

Problems

13.1 A proposed congestion control technique is known as isarithmic control. In this method, the total number of frames in transit is fixed by inserting a fixed number of permits into the network. These permits circulate at random through the frame relay network. Whenever a frame handler wants to relay a frame just given to it by an attached user, it must first capture and destroy a permit. When the frame is delivered to the destination user by the frame handler to which it attaches, that frame handler reissues the permit. List three potential problems with this technique.

13.2 In the discussion of latency/speed effects in Section 13.5, an example was given in which over 7 megabits were transmitted before the source could react. But isn't a sliding-window flow control technique, such as described for HDLC, designed to cope with long propagation delays?

13.3 Consider the frame relay network depicted in Figure 13.13. C is the capacity of a link in frames per second. Node A presents a constant load of 0.8 frames per second destined for A'. Node B presents a load λ destined for B'. Node S has a common pool

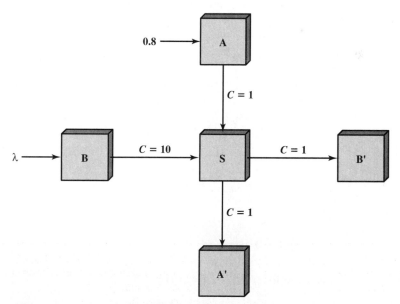

Figure 13.13 Network of Nodes

of buffers that it uses for traffic both to A′ and B′. When the buffer is full, frames are discarded and are later retransmitted by the source user. S has a throughput capacity of 2. Plot the total throughput (i.e., the sum of A-A′ and B-B′ delivered traffic) as a function of λ. What fraction of the throughput is A-A′ traffic for $\lambda > 1$?

13.4 Compare sustainable cell rate and burst tolerance, as used in ATM networks, with committed information rate and excess burst size, as used in frame relay networks. Do the respective terms represent the same concepts?

13.5 For a frame relay network to be able to detect and then signal congestion, it is necessary for each frame handler to monitor its queuing behavior. If queue lengths begin to grow to a dangerous level, then either forward or backward explicit notification or a combination should be set to try to reduce the flow of frames through that frame handler. The frame handler has some choice as to which logical connections should be alerted to congestion. If congestion is becoming quite serious, all logical connections through a frame handler might be notified. In the early stages of congestion, the frame handler might just notify users for those connections that are generating the most traffic.

In one of the frame relay specifications, an algorithm for monitoring queue lengths is suggested; this is shown in Figure 13.14. A cycle begins when the outgoing circuit goes from idle (queue empty) to busy (nonzero queue size, including the current frame). If a threshold value is exceeded, then the circuit is in a state of incipient congestion, and the congestion avoidance bits should be set on some or all logical connections that use that circuit. Describe the algorithm in words and explain its advantages.

The algorithm makes use of the following variables:

t = current time
t_i = time of ith arrival or departure event
q_i = number of frames in the system after the event
T_0 = time at the beginning of the previous cycle
T_1 = time at the beginning of the current cycle

The algorithm consists of three components:

1. Update: Beginning with $q_0 := 0$
   If the ith event is an arrival event, $q_i := q_{i-1} + 1$
   If the ith event is a departure event, $q_i := q_{i-1} - 1$

2.
$$A_{i-1} = \sum_{\substack{i \\ t_i \in [T_0, T_1)}} q_{i-1}(t_i - t_{i-1})$$

$$A_i = \sum_{\substack{i \\ t_i \in [T_1, t)}} q_{i-1}(t_i - t_{i-1})$$

3.
$$L = \frac{A_i + A_{i-1}}{t - T_0}$$

Figure 13.14 A Frame Relay Algorithm

CHAPTER 14

CELLULAR WIRELESS NETWORKS

KEY POINTS

- The essence of a cellular network is the use of multiple low-power transmitters. The area to be covered is divided into cells in a hexagonal tile pattern that provide full coverage of the area.

- A major technical problem for cellular networks is fading, which refers to the time variation of received signal power caused by changes in the transmission medium or path(s).

- First generation cellular networks were analog, making use of frequency division multiplexing.

- Second generation cellular networks are digital. One technique in widespread use is based on code division multiple access (CDMA).

- The objective of the third-generation (3G) of wireless communication is to provide fairly high speed wireless communications to support multimedia, data, and video in addition to voice.

Of all the tremendous advances in data communications and telecommunications, perhaps the most revolutionary is the development of cellular networks. Cellular technology is the foundation of mobile wireless communications and supports users in locations that are not easily served by wired networks. Cellular technology is the underlying technology for mobile telephones, personal communications systems, wireless Internet and wireless Web applications, and much more.

We begin this chapter with a look at the basic principles used in all cellular networks. Then we look at specific cellular technologies and standards, which are conveniently grouped into three generations. The first generation is analog based and, while still widely used, is passing from the scene. The dominant technology today is the digital second-generation systems. Finally, third-generation high-speed digital systems have begun to emerge.

14.1 PRINCIPLES OF CELLULAR NETWORKS

Cellular radio is a technique that was developed to increase the capacity available for mobile radio telephone service. Prior to the introduction of cellular radio, mobile radio telephone service was only provided by a high-power transmitter/receiver. A typical system would support about 25 channels with an effective radius of about 80 km. The way to increase the capacity of the system is to use lower-power systems with shorter radius and to use numerous transmitters/receivers. We begin this section with a look at the organization of cellular systems and then examine some of the details of their implementation.

Cellular Network Organization

The essence of a cellular network is the use of multiple low-power transmitters, on the order of 100 W or less. Because the range of such a transmitter is small, an area can be divided into cells, each one served by its own antenna. Each cell is allocated a band of frequencies and is served by a **base station**, consisting of transmitter,

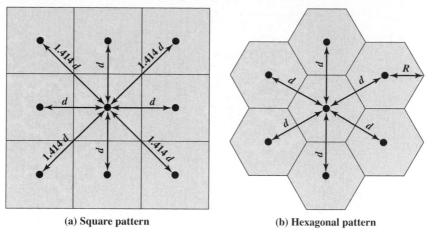

(a) Square pattern   (b) Hexagonal pattern

Figure 14.1 Cellular Geometries

receiver, and control unit. Adjacent cells are assigned different frequencies to avoid interference or crosstalk. However, cells sufficiently distant from each other can use the same frequency band.

The first design decision to make is the shape of cells to cover an area. A matrix of square cells would be the simplest layout to define (Figure 14.1a). However, this geometry is not ideal. If the width of a square cell is d, then a cell has four neighbors at a distance d and four neighbors at a distance $\sqrt{2}d$. As a mobile user within a cell moves toward the cell's boundaries, it is best if all of the adjacent antennas are equidistant. This simplifies the task of determining when to switch the user to an adjacent antenna and which antenna to choose. A hexagonal pattern provides for equidistant antennas (Figure 14.1b). The radius of a hexagon is defined to be the radius of the circle that circumscribes it (equivalently, the distance from the center to each vertex; also equal to the length of a side of a hexagon). For a cell radius R, the distance between the cell center and each adjacent cell center is $d = \sqrt{3}R$.

In practice, a precise hexagonal pattern is not used. Variations from the ideal are due to topographical limitations, local signal propagation conditions, and practical limitation on siting antennas.

With a wireless cellular system, you are limited in how often you can use the same frequency for different communications because the signals, not being constrained, can interfere with one another even if geographically separated. Systems supporting a large number of communications simultaneously need mechanisms to conserve spectrum.

Frequency Reuse

In a cellular system, each cell has a base transceiver. The transmission power is carefully controlled (to the extent that it is possible in the highly variable mobile communication environment) to allow communication within the cell using a given frequency while limiting the power at that frequency that escapes the cell into adjacent ones. The objective is to use the same frequency in other nearby cells, thus allowing the frequency to be used for multiple simultaneous conversations. Generally, 10 to 50 frequencies are assigned to each cell, depending on the traffic expected.

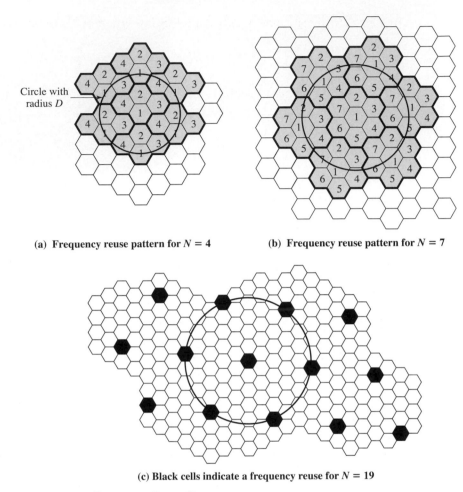

(a) Frequency reuse pattern for $N = 4$ (b) Frequency reuse pattern for $N = 7$

(c) Black cells indicate a frequency reuse for $N = 19$

Figure 14.2 Frequency Reuse Patterns

The essential issue is to determine how many cells must intervene between two cells using the same frequency so that the two cells do not interfere with each other. Various patterns of frequency reuse are possible. Figure 14.2 shows some examples. If the pattern consists of N cells and each cell is assigned the same number of frequencies, each cell can have K/N frequencies, where K is the total number of frequencies allotted to the system. For AMPS (Section 14.2), $K = 395$, and $N = 7$ is the smallest pattern that can provide sufficient isolation between two uses of the same frequency. This implies that there can be at most 57 frequencies per cell on average.

In characterizing frequency reuse, the following parameters are commonly used:

D = minimum distance between centers of cells that use the same band of frequencies (called cochannels)

R = radius of a cell

d = distance between centers of adjacent cells $\left(d = \sqrt{3}R\right)$

N = number of cells in a repetitious pattern (each cell in the pattern uses a unique band of frequencies), termed the **reuse factor**

In a hexagonal cell pattern, only the following values of N are possible:

$$N = I^2 + J^2 + (I \times J), \quad I, J = 0, 1, 2, 3, \ldots$$

Hence, possible values of N are $1, 3, 4, 7, 9, 12, 13, 16, 19, 21$, and so on. The following relationship holds:

$$\frac{D}{R} = \sqrt{3N}$$

This can also be expressed as $D/d = \sqrt{N}$.

Increasing Capacity

In time, as more customers use the system, traffic may build up so that there are not enough frequencies assigned to a cell to handle its calls. A number of approaches have been used to cope with this situation, including the following:

- **Adding new channels:** Typically, when a system is set up in a region, not all of the channels are used, and growth and expansion can be managed in an orderly fashion by adding new channels.
- **Frequency borrowing:** In the simplest case, frequencies are taken from adjacent cells by congested cells. The frequencies can also be assigned to cells dynamically.
- **Cell splitting:** In practice, the distribution of traffic and topographic features is not uniform, and this presents opportunities for capacity increase. Cells in areas of high usage can be split into smaller cells. Generally, the original cells are about 6.5 to 13 km in size. The smaller cells can themselves be split; however, 1.5-km cells are close to the practical minimum size as a general solution (but see the subsequent discussion of microcells). To use a smaller cell, the power level used must be reduced to keep the signal within the cell. Also, as the mobile units move, they pass from cell to cell, which requires transferring the call from one base transceiver to another. This process is called a *handoff*. As the cells get smaller, these handoffs become much more frequent. Figure 14.3 indicates schematically how cells can be divided to provide more capacity. A radius reduction by a factor of F reduces the coverage area and increases the required number of base stations by a factor of F^2.
- **Cell sectoring:** With cell sectoring, a cell is divided into a number of wedge-shaped sectors, each with its own set of channels, typically 3 or 6 sectors per cell. Each sector is assigned a separate subset of the cell's channels, and directional antennas at the base station are used to focus on each sector.
- **Microcells:** As cells become smaller, antennas move from the tops of tall buildings or hills, to the tops of small buildings or the sides of large buildings, and finally to lamp posts, where they form microcells. Each decrease in cell size is accompanied by a reduction in the radiated power levels from the base stations and the mobile units. Microcells are useful in city streets in congested areas, along highways, and inside large public buildings.

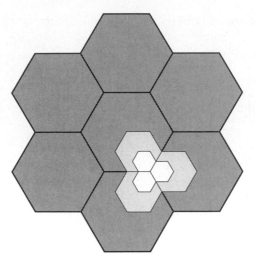

Figure 14.3   Cell Splitting

Table 14.1   Typical Parameters for Macrocells and Microcells [ANDE95]

	Macrocell	**Microcell**
Cell radius	1 to 20 km	0.1 to 1 km
Transmission power	1 to 10 W	0.1 to 1 W
Average delay spread	0.1 to 10 μs	10 to 100 ns
Maximum bit rate	0.3 Mbps	1 Mbps

Table 14.1 suggests typical parameters for traditional cells, called macrocells, and microcells with current technology. The average delay spread refers to multipath delay spread (i.e., the same signal follows different paths and there is a time delay between the earliest and latest arrival of the signal at the receiver). As indicated, the use of smaller cells enables the use of lower power and provides superior propagation conditions.

Example [HAAS00].   Assume a system of 32 cells with a cell radius of 1.6 km, a total of 32 cells, a total frequency bandwidth that supports 336 traffic channels, and a reuse factor of $N = 7$. If there are 32 total cells, what geographic area is covered, how many channels are there per cell, and what is the total number of concurrent calls that can be handled? Repeat for a cell radius of 0.8 km and 128 cells.

Figure 14.4a shows an approximately square pattern. The area of a hexagon of radius R is $1.5R^2\sqrt{3}$. A hexagon of radius 1.6 km has an area of 6.65 km^2, and the total area covered is $6.65 \times 32 = 213$ km^2. For $N = 7$, the number of channels per cell is $336/7 = 48$, for a total channel capacity of $48 \times 32 = 1536$ channels. For the layout of Figure 14.4b, the area covered is $1.66 \times 128 = 213$ km^2. The number of channels per cell is $336/7 = 48$, for a total channel capacity of $48 \times 128 = 6144$ channels.

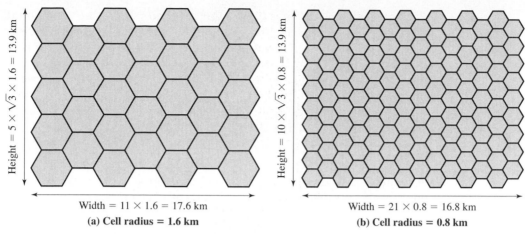

Height = $5 \times \sqrt{3} \times 1.6 = 13.9$ km

Width = $11 \times 1.6 = 17.6$ km

(a) Cell radius = 1.6 km

Height = $10 \times \sqrt{3} \times 0.8 = 13.9$ km

Width = $21 \times 0.8 = 16.8$ km

(b) Cell radius = 0.8 km

Figure 14.4 Frequency Reuse Example

Operation of Cellular Systems

Figure 14.5 shows the principal elements of a cellular system. In the approximate center of each cell is a base station (BS). The BS includes an antenna, a controller, and a number of transceivers, for communicating on the channels assigned to that cell. The controller is used to handle the call process between the mobile unit and the rest of the network. At any time, a number of mobile user units may be active and moving about within a cell, communicating with the BS. Each BS is connected to a mobile telecommunications switching office (MTSO), with one MTSO serving multiple BSs. Typically, the link between an MTSO and a BS is by a wire line, although a wireless link is also possible. The MTSO connects calls between mobile units. The MTSO is also connected to the public telephone or telecommunications network and can make a connection between a fixed subscriber to the public network and a mobile subscriber to the cellular network. The MTSO assigns the voice channel to each call, performs handoffs, and monitors the call for billing information.

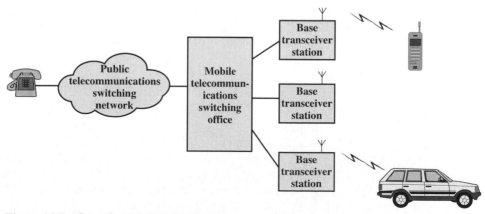

Figure 14.5 Overview of Cellular System

The use of a cellular system is fully automated and requires no action on the part of the user other than placing or answering a call. Two types of channels are available between the mobile unit and the base station (BS): control channels and traffic channels. **Control channels** are used to exchange information having to do with setting up and maintaining calls and with establishing a relationship between a mobile unit and the nearest BS. **Traffic channels** carry a voice or data connection between users. Figure 14.6 illustrates the steps in a typical call between two mobile users within an area controlled by a single MTSO:

- **Mobile unit initialization:** When the mobile unit is turned on, it scans and selects the strongest setup control channel used for this system (Figure 14.6a). Cells with different frequency bands repetitively broadcast on different setup channels. The receiver selects the strongest setup channel and monitors that channel. The effect of this procedure is that the mobile unit has automatically selected the BS antenna of the cell within which it will operate.[1] Then a handshake takes place between the mobile unit and the MTSO controlling this cell, through the BS in this cell. The handshake is used to identify the user and register its location. As long as the mobile unit is on, this scanning procedure is repeated periodically to account for the motion of the unit. If the unit enters a new cell, then a new BS is selected. In addition, the mobile unit is monitoring for pages, discussed subsequently.

- **Mobile-originated call:** A mobile unit originates a call by sending the number of the called unit on the preselected setup channel (Figure 14.6b). The receiver at the mobile unit first checks that the setup channel is idle by examining information in the forward (from the BS) channel. When an idle is detected, the mobile may transmit on the corresponding reverse (to BS) channel. The BS sends the request to the MTSO.

- **Paging:** The MTSO then attempts to complete the connection to the called unit. The MTSO sends a paging message to certain BSs depending on the called mobile number (Figure 14.6c). Each BS transmits the paging signal on its own assigned setup channel.

- **Call accepted:** The called mobile unit recognizes its number on the setup channel being monitored and responds to that BS, which sends the response to the MTSO. The MTSO sets up a circuit between the calling and called BSs. At the same time, the MTSO selects an available traffic channel within each BS's cell and notifies each BS, which in turn notifies its mobile unit (Figure 14.6d). The two mobile units tune to their respective assigned channels.

- **Ongoing call:** While the connection is maintained, the two mobile units exchange voice or data signals, going through their respective BSs and the MTSO (Figure 14.6e).

- **Handoff:** If a mobile unit moves out of range of one cell and into the range of another during a connection, the traffic channel has to change to one assigned to the BS in the new cell (Figure 14.6f). The system makes this change without either interrupting the call or alerting the user.

---

[1] Usually, but not always, the antenna and therefore the base station selected is the closest one to the mobile unit. However, because of propagation anomalies, this is not always the case.

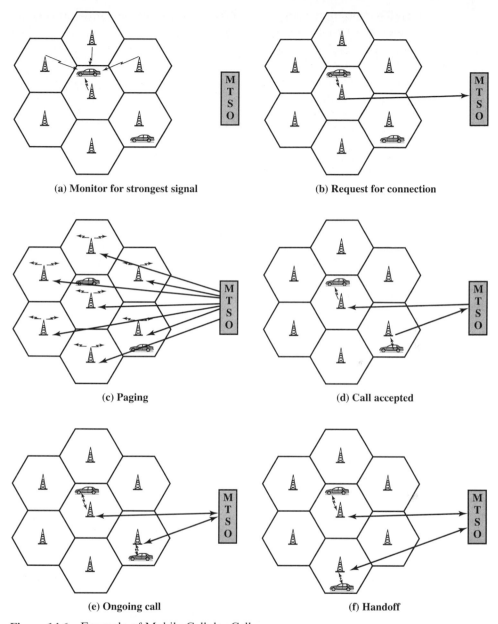

(a) Monitor for strongest signal

(b) Request for connection

(c) Paging

(d) Call accepted

(e) Ongoing call

(f) Handoff

Figure 14.6 Example of Mobile Cellular Call

Other functions performed by the system but not illustrated in Figure 14.6 include the following:

- **Call blocking:** During the mobile-initiated call stage, if all the traffic channels assigned to the nearest BS are busy, then the mobile unit makes a preconfigured number of repeated attempts. After a certain number of failed tries, a busy tone is returned to the user.

- **Call termination:** When one of the two users hangs up, the MTSO is informed and the traffic channels at the two BSs are released.

- **Call drop:** During a connection, because of interference or weak signal spots in certain areas, if the BS cannot maintain the minimum required signal strength for a certain period of time, the traffic channel to the user is dropped and the MTSO is informed.

- **Calls to/from fixed and remote mobile subscriber:** The MTSO connects to the public switched telephone network. Thus, the MTSO can set up a connection between a mobile user in its area and a fixed subscriber via the telephone network. Further, the MTSO can connect to a remote MTSO via the telephone network or via dedicated lines and set up a connection between a mobile user in its area and a remote mobile user.

Mobile Radio Propagation Effects

Mobile radio communication introduces complexities not found in wire communication or in fixed wireless communication. Two general areas of concern are signal strength and signal propagation effects.

- **Signal strength:** The strength of the signal between the base station and the mobile unit must be strong enough to maintain signal quality at the receiver but not so strong as to create too much cochannel interference with channels in another cell using the same frequency band. Several complicating factors exist. Human-made noise varies considerably, resulting in a variable noise level. For example, automobile ignition noise in the cellular frequency range is greater in the city than in a suburban area. Other signal sources vary from place to place. The signal strength varies as a function of distance from the BS to a point within its cell. Moreover, the signal strength varies dynamically as the mobile unit moves.

- **Fading:** Even if signal strength is within an effective range, signal propagation effects may disrupt the signal and cause errors. Fading is discussed subsequently in this section.

In designing a cellular layout, the communications engineer must take account of these various propagation effects, the desired maximum transmit power level at the base station and the mobile units, the typical height of the mobile unit antenna, and the available height of the BS antenna. These factors will determine the size of the individual cell. Unfortunately, as just described, the propagation effects are dynamic and difficult to predict. The best that can be done is to come up with a model based on empirical data and to apply that model to a given environment to develop guidelines for cell size. One of the most widely used models was developed by Okumura et al. [OKUM68] and subsequently refined by Hata [HATA80]. The original was a detailed analysis of the Tokyo area and produced path loss information for an urban environment. Hata's model is an empirical formulation that takes into account a variety of environments and conditions. For an urban environment, predicted path loss is

$$L_{dB} = 69.55 + 26.16 \log f_c - 13.82 \log h_t - A(h_r) + (44.9 - 6.55 \log h_t) \log d \quad (14.1)$$

where

f_c = carrier frequency in MHz from 150 to 1500 MHz
h_t = height of transmitting antenna (base station) in m, from 30 to 300 m
h_r = height of receiving antenna (mobile station) in m, from 1 to 10 m
d = propagation distance between antennas in km, from 1 to 20 km
$A(h_r)$ = correction factor for mobile antenna height

For a small- or medium-sized city, the correction factor is given by

$$A(h_r) = (1.1 \log f_c - 0.7)h_r - (1.56 \log f_c - 0.8) \text{ dB}$$

And for a large city it is given by

$$A(h_r) = 8.29[\log(1.54 h_r)]^2 - 1.1 \text{ dB} \quad \text{for } f_c \leq 300 \text{ MHz}$$
$$A(h_r) = 3.2[\log(11.75 h_r)]^2 - 4.97 \text{ dB} \quad \text{for } f_c \geq 300 \text{ MHz}$$

To estimate the path loss in a suburban area, the formula for urban path loss in Equation (14.1) is modified as

$$L_{dB}(\text{suburban}) = L_{dB}(\text{urban}) - 2[\log(f_c/28)]^2 - 5.4$$

And for the path loss in open areas, the formula is modified as

$$L_{dB}(\text{open}) = L_{dB}(\text{urban}) - 4.78(\log f_c)^2 - 18.733(\log f_c) - 40.98$$

The Okumura/Hata model is considered to be among the best in terms of accuracy in path loss prediction and provides a practical means of estimating path loss in a wide variety of situations [FREE97, RAPP97].

Example [FREE97]. Let $f_c = 900$ MHz, $h_t = 40$ m, $h_r = 5$ m, and $d = 10$ km. Estimate the path loss for a medium-size city.

$$A(h_r) = (1.1 \log 900 - 0.7)5 - (1.56 \log 900 - 0.8) \text{ dB}$$
$$= 12.75 - 3.8 = 8.95 \text{ dB}$$

$$L_{dB} = 69.55 + 26.16 \log 900 - 13.82 \log 40 - 8.95$$
$$+ (44.9 - 6.55 \log 40) \log 10$$
$$= 69.55 + 77.28 - 22.14 - 8.95 + 34.4 = 150.14 \text{ dB}$$

Fading in the Mobile Environment

Perhaps the most challenging technical problem facing communications systems engineers is fading in a mobile environment. The term *fading* refers to the time variation of received signal power caused by changes in the transmission medium or path(s). In a fixed environment, fading is affected by changes in atmospheric conditions, such as rainfall. But in a mobile environment, where one of the two antennas is moving relative to the other, the relative location of various obstacles changes over time, creating complex transmission effects.

Multipath Propagation

Three propagation mechanisms, illustrated in Figure 14.7, play a role. **Reflection** occurs when an electromagnetic signal encounters a surface that is large relative to the wavelength of the signal. For example, suppose a ground-reflected wave near the mobile unit is received. Because the ground-reflected wave has a 180° phase shift after reflection, the ground wave and the line of sight (LOS) wave may tend to cancel, resulting in high signal loss.[2] Further, because the mobile antenna is

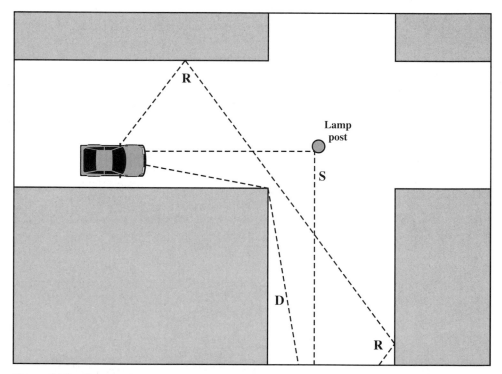

Figure 14.7 Sketch of Three Important Propagation Mechanisms: Reflection (R), Scattering (S), Diffraction (D) [ANDE95]

---

[2] On the other hand, the reflected signal has a longer path, which creates a phase shift due to delay relative to the unreflected signal. When this delay is equivalent to half a wavelength, the two signals are back in phase.

lower than most human-made structures in the area, multipath interference occurs. These reflected waves may interfere constructively or destructively at the receiver.

Diffraction occurs at the edge of an impenetrable body that is large compared to the wavelength of the radio wave. When a radio wave encounters such an edge, waves propagate in different directions with the edge as the source. Thus, signals can be received even when there is no unobstructed LOS from the transmitter.

If the size of an obstacle is on the order of the wavelength of the signal or less, **scattering** occurs. An incoming signal is scattered into several weaker outgoing signals. At typical cellular microwave frequencies, there are numerous objects, such as lamp posts and traffic signs, that can cause scattering. Thus, scattering effects are difficult to predict.

These three propagation effects influence system performance in various ways depending on local conditions and as the mobile unit moves within a cell. If a mobile unit has a clear LOS to the transmitter, then diffraction and scattering are generally minor effects, although reflection may have a significant impact. If there is no clear LOS, such as in an urban area at street level, then diffraction and scattering are the primary means of signal reception.

The Effects of Multipath Propagation

As just noted, one unwanted effect of multipath propagation is that multiple copies of a signal may arrive at different phases. If these phases add destructively, the signal level relative to noise declines, making signal detection at the receiver more difficult.

A second phenomenon, of particular importance for digital transmission, is intersymbol interference (ISI). Consider that we are sending a narrow pulse at a given frequency across a link between a fixed antenna and a mobile unit. Figure 14.8 shows what the channel may deliver to the receiver if the impulse is sent at two different times. The upper line shows two pulses at the time of transmission. The lower line shows the resulting pulses at the receiver. In each case the first received pulse is the desired LOS signal. The magnitude of that pulse may change because of changes

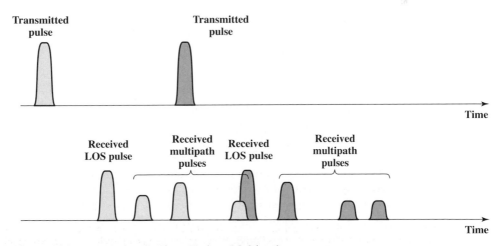

Figure 14.8   Two Pulses in Time-Variant Multipath

in atmospheric attenuation. Further, as the mobile unit moves farther away from the fixed antenna, the amount of LOS attenuation increases. But in addition to this primary pulse, there may be multiple secondary pulses due to reflection, diffraction, and scattering. Now suppose that this pulse encodes one or more bits of data. In that case, one or more delayed copies of a pulse may arrive at the same time as the primary pulse for a subsequent bit. These delayed pulses act as a form of noise to the subsequent primary pulse, making recovery of the bit information more difficult.

As the mobile antenna moves, the location of various obstacles changes; hence the number, magnitude, and timing of the secondary pulses change. This makes it difficult to design signal processing techniques that will filter out multipath effects so that the intended signal is recovered with fidelity.

Types of Fading

Fading effects in a mobile environment can be classified as either fast or slow. Referring to Figure 14.7, as the mobile unit moves down a street in an urban environment, rapid variations in signal strength occur over distances of about one-half a wavelength. At a frequency of 900 MHz, which is typical for mobile cellular applications, a wavelength is 0.33 m. Changes of amplitude can be as much as 20 or 30 dB over a short distance. This type of rapidly changing fading phenomenon, known as **fast fading**, affects not only mobile phones in automobiles, but even a mobile phone user walking down an urban street.

As the mobile user covers distances well in excess of a wavelength, the urban environment changes, as the user passes buildings of different heights, vacant lots, intersections, and so forth. Over these longer distances, there is a change in the average received power level about which the rapid fluctuations occur. This is referred to as **slow fading**.

Fading effects can also be classified as flat or selective. **Flat fading**, or nonselective fading, is that type of fading in which all frequency components of the received signal fluctuate in the same proportions simultaneously. **Selective fading** affects unequally the different spectral components of a radio signal. The term *selective fading* is usually significant only relative to the bandwidth of the overall communications channel. If attenuation occurs over a portion of the bandwidth of the signal, the fading is considered to be selective; nonselective fading implies that the signal bandwidth of interest is narrower than, and completely covered by, the spectrum affected by the fading.

Error Compensation Mechanisms

The efforts to compensate for the errors and distortions introduced by multipath fading fall into three general categories: forward error correction, adaptive equalization, and diversity techniques. In the typical mobile wireless environment, techniques from all three categories are combined to combat the error rates encountered.

Forward error correction is applicable in digital transmission applications: those in which the transmitted signal carries digital data or digitized voice or video data. Typically in mobile wireless applications, the ratio of total bits sent to data bits sent is between 2 and 3. This may seem an extravagant amount of overhead, in that the capacity of the system is cut to one-half or one-third of its potential, but the mobile wireless environment is so difficult that such levels of redundancy are necessary. Chapter 6 discusses forward error correction.

Adaptive equalization can be applied to transmissions that carry analog information (e.g., analog voice or video) or digital information (e.g., digital data, digitized voice or video) and is used to combat intersymbol interference. The process of equalization involves some method of gathering the dispersed symbol energy back together into its original time interval. Equalization is a broad topic; techniques include the use of so-called lumped analog circuits as well as sophisticated digital signal processing algorithms.

Diversity is based on the fact that individual channels experience independent fading events. We can therefore compensate for error effects by providing multiple logical channels in some sense between transmitter and receiver and sending part of the signal over each channel. This technique does not eliminate errors but it does reduce the error rate, since we have spread the transmission out to avoid being subjected to the highest error rate that might occur. The other techniques (equalization, forward error correction) can then cope with the reduced error rate.

Some diversity techniques involve the physical transmission path and are referred to as **space diversity**. For example, multiple nearby antennas may be used to receive the message, with the signals combined in some fashion to reconstruct the most likely transmitted signal. Another example is the use of collocated multiple directional antennas, each oriented to a different reception angle with the incoming signals again combined to reconstitute the transmitted signal.

More commonly, the term *diversity* refers to frequency diversity or time diversity techniques. With **frequency diversity**, the signal is spread out over a larger frequency bandwidth or carried on multiple frequency carriers. The most important example of this approach is spread spectrum, which is examined in Chapter 9.

14.2 FIRST-GENERATION ANALOG

The original cellular telephone networks provided analog traffic channels; these are now referred to as first-generation systems. Since the early 1980s the most common first-generation system in North America has been the **Advanced Mobile Phone Service (AMPS)** developed by AT&T. This approach is also common in South America, Australia, and China. Although gradually being replaced by second-generation systems, AMPS is still in common use. In this section, we provide an overview of AMPS.

Spectral Allocation

In North America, two 25-MHz bands are allocated to AMPS (Table 14.2), one for transmission from the base station to the mobile unit (869–894 MHz), the other for transmission from the mobile to the base station (824–849 MHz). Each of these bands is split in two to encourage competition (i.e., so that in each market two operators can be accommodated). An operator is allocated only 12.5 MHz in each direction for its system. The channels are spaced 30 kHz apart, which allows a total of 416 channels per operator. Twenty-one channels are allocated for control, leaving 395 to carry calls. The control channels are data channels operating at 10 kbps. The conversation

Table 14.2 AMPS Parameters

Base station transmission band	869 to 894 MHz
Mobile unit transmission band	824 to 849 MHz
Spacing between forward and reverse channels	45 MHz
Channel bandwidth	30 kHz
Number of full-duplex voice channels	790
Number of full-duplex control channels	42
Mobile unit maximum power	3 watts
Cell size, radius	2 to 20 km
Modulation, voice channel	FM, 12-kHz peak deviation
Modulation, control channel	FSK, 8-kHz peak deviation
Data transmission rate	10 kbps
Error control coding	BCH (48, 36, 5) and (40, 28, 5)

channels carry the conversations in analog using frequency modulation. Control information is also sent on the conversation channels in bursts as data. This number of channels is inadequate for most major markets, so some way must be found either to use less bandwidth per conversation or to reuse frequencies. Both approaches have been taken in the various approaches to mobile telephony. For AMPS, frequency reuse is exploited.

Operation

Each AMPS-capable cellular telephone includes a *numeric assignment module* (NAM) in read-only memory. The NAM contains the telephone number of the phone, which is assigned by the service provider, and the serial number of the phone, which is assigned by the manufacturer. When the phone is turned on, it transmits its serial number and phone number to the MTSO (Figure 14.5); the MTSO maintains a database with information about mobile units that have been reported stolen and uses serial numbers to lock out stolen units. The MTSO uses the phone number for billing purposes. If the phone is used in a remote city, the service is still billed to the user's local service provider.

When a call is placed, the following sequence of events occurs [COUC01]:

1. The subscriber initiates a call by keying in the telephone number of the called party and presses the send key.
2. The MTSO verifies that the telephone number is valid and that the user is authorized to place the call; some service providers require the user to enter a PIN (personal identification number) as well as the called number to counter theft.
3. The MTSO issues a message to the user's cell phone indicating which traffic channels to use for sending and receiving.
4. The MTSO sends out a ringing signal to the called party. All of these operations (steps 2 through 4) occur within 10 s of initiating the call.

5. When the called party answers, the MTSO establishes a circuit between the two parties and initiates billing information.

6. When one party hangs up, the MTSO releases the circuit, frees the radio channels, and completes the billing information.

AMPS Control Channels

Each AMPS service includes 21 full-duplex 30-kHz control channels, consisting of 21 reverse control channels (RCCs) from subscriber to base station, and 21 forward channels base station to subscriber. These channels transmit digital data using FSK. In both channels, data are transmitted in frames.

Control information can be transmitted over a voice channel during a conversation. The mobile unit or the base station can insert a burst of data by turning off the voice FM transmission for about 100 ms and replacing it with an FSK-encoded message. These messages are used to exchange urgent messages, such as change power level and handoff.

14.3 SECOND-GENERATION CDMA

This section begins with an overview and then looks in detail at one type of second-generation cellular system.

First- and Second-Generation Cellular Systems

First-generation cellular networks, such as AMPS, quickly became highly popular, threatening to swamp available capacity. Second-generation systems have been developed to provide higher quality signals, higher data rates for support of digital services, and greater capacity. [BLAC99b] lists the following as the key differences between the two generations:

- **Digital traffic channels:** The most notable difference between the two generations is that first-generation systems are almost purely analog, whereas second-generation systems are digital. In particular, the first-generation systems are designed to support voice channels using FM; digital traffic is supported only by the use of a modem that converts the digital data into analog form. Second-generation systems provide digital traffic channels. These readily support digital data; voice traffic is first encoded in digital form before transmitting. Of course, for second-generation systems, the user traffic (data or digitized voice) must be converted to an analog signal for transmission between the mobile unit and the base station (e.g., see Figure 5.15).

- **Encryption:** Because all of the user traffic, as well as control traffic, is digitized in second-generation systems, it is a relatively simple matter to encrypt all of the traffic to prevent eavesdropping. All second-generation systems provide this capability, whereas first-generation systems send user traffic in the clear, providing no security.

- **Error detection and correction:** The digital traffic stream of second-generation systems also lends itself to the use of error detection and correction techniques, such as those discussed in Chapter 6. The result can be very clear voice reception.

- **Channel access:** In first-generation systems, each cell supports a number of channels. At any given time a channel is allocated to only one user. Second-generation systems also provide multiple channels per cell, but each channel is dynamically shared by a number of users using time division multiple access (TDMA) or code division multiple access (CDMA). We look at CDMA-based systems in this section.

Beginning around 1990, a number of different second-generation systems have been deployed. A good example is the IS-95 scheme using CDMA.

Code Division Multiple Access

CDMA for cellular systems can be described as follows. As with FDMA, each cell is allocated a frequency bandwidth, which is split into two parts, half for reverse (mobile unit to base station) and half for forward (base station to mobile unit). For full duplex communication, a mobile unit uses both reverse and forward channels. Transmission is in the form of direct-sequence spread spectrum (DS-SS), which uses a chipping code to increase the data rate of the transmission, resulting in an increased signal bandwidth. Multiple access is provided by assigning orthogonal chipping codes to multiple users, so that the receiver can recover the transmission of an individual unit from multiple transmissions.

CDMA has a number of advantages for a cellular network:

- **Frequency diversity:** Because the transmission is spread out over a larger bandwidth, frequency-dependent transmission impairments, such as noise bursts and selective fading, have less effect on the signal.
- **Multipath resistance:** In addition to the ability of DS-SS to overcome multipath fading by frequency diversity, the chipping codes used for CDMA not only exhibit low cross correlation but also low autocorrelation. Therefore, a version of the signal that is delayed by more than one chip interval does not interfere with the dominant signal as much as in other multipath environments.
- **Privacy:** Because spread spectrum is obtained by the use of noiselike signals, where each user has a unique code, privacy is inherent.
- **Graceful degradation:** With FDMA or TDMA, a fixed number of users can access the system simultaneously. However, with CDMA, as more users access the system simultaneously, the noise level and hence the error rate increases; only gradually does the system degrade to the point of an unacceptable error rate.

Two drawbacks of CDMA cellular should also be mentioned:

- **Self-jamming:** Unless all of the mobile users are perfectly synchronized, the arriving transmissions from multiple users will not be perfectly aligned on chip boundaries. Thus the spreading sequences of the different users are not orthogonal and there is some level of cross correlation. This is distinct from either TDMA or FDMA, in which for reasonable time or frequency guardbands, respectively, the received signals are orthogonal or nearly so.

- **Near-far problem:** Signals closer to the receiver are received with less attenuation than signals farther away. Given the lack of complete orthogonality, the transmissions from the more remote mobile units may be more difficult to recover.

Mobile Wireless CDMA Design Considerations

Before turning to the specific example of IS-95, it will be useful to consider some general design elements of a CDMA cellular system.

RAKE Receiver

In a multipath environment, which is common in cellular systems, if the multiple versions of a signal arrive more than one chip interval apart from each other, the receiver can recover the signal by correlating the chip sequence with the dominant incoming signal. The remaining signals are treated as noise. However, even better performance can be achieved if the receiver attempts to recover the signals from multiple paths and then combine them, with suitable delays. This principle is used in the RAKE receiver.

Figure 14.9 illustrates the principle of the RAKE receiver. The original binary signal to be transmitted is spread by the exclusive-OR (XOR) operation with the

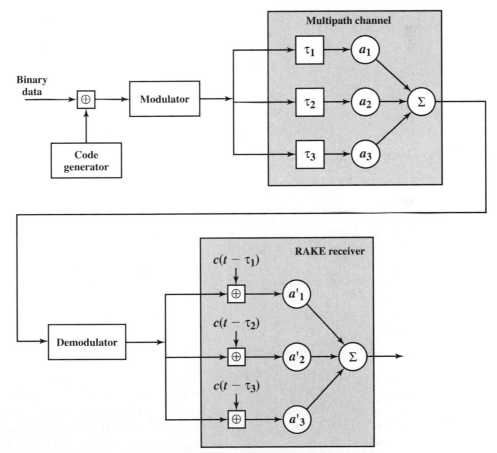

Figure 14.9   Principle of RAKE Receiver [PRAS98]

transmitter's chipping code. The spread sequence is then modulated for transmission over the wireless channel. Because of multipath effects, the channel generates multiple copies of the signal, each with a different amount of time delay (τ_1, τ_2, etc.), and each with different attenuation factors (a_1, a_2, etc.). At the receiver, the combined signal is demodulated. The demodulated chip stream is then fed into multiple correlators, each delayed by a different amount. These signals are then combined using weighting factors estimated from the channel.

IS-95

The most widely used second-generation CDMA scheme is IS-95, which is primarily deployed in North America. The transmission structures on the forward and reverse links differ and are described separately.

IS-95 Forward Link

Table 14.3 lists forward link channel parameters. The forward link consists of up to 64 logical CDMA channels each occupying the same 1228-kHz bandwidth (Figure 14.10a). The forward link supports four types of channels:

- **Pilot (channel 0):** A continuous signal on a single channel. This channel allows the mobile unit to acquire timing information, provides phase reference for the demodulation process, and provides a means for signal strength comparison for the purpose of handoff determination. The pilot channel consists of all zeros.

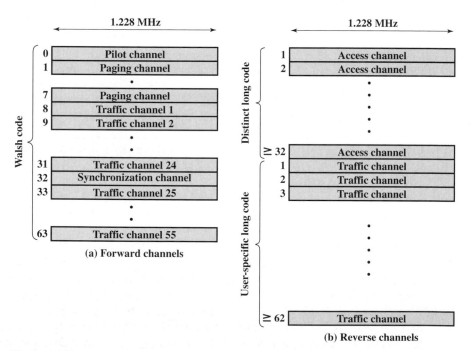

Figure 14.10   IS-95 Channel Structure

Table 14.3   IS-95 Forward Link Channel Parameters

Channel	Sync	Paging		Traffic Rate Set 1				Traffic Rate Set 2			
Data rate (bps)	1200	4800	9600	1200	2400	4800	9600	1800	3600	7200	14400
Code repetition	2	2	1	8	4	2	1	8	4	2	1
Modulation symbol rate (sps)	4800	19,200	19,200	19,200	19,200	19,200	19,200	19,200	19,200	19,200	19,200
PN chips/ modulation symbol	256	64	64	64	64	64	64	64	64	64	64
PN chips/bit	1024	256	128	1024	512	256	128	682.67	341.33	170.67	85.33

- **Synchronization (channel 32):** A 1200-bps channel used by the mobile station to obtain identification information about the cellular system (system time, long code state, protocol revision, etc.).

- **Paging (channels 1 to 7):** Contain messages for one or more mobile stations.

- **Traffic (channels 8 to 31 and 33 to 63):** The forward channel supports 55 traffic channels. The original specification supported data rates of up to 9600 bps. A subsequent revision added a second set of rates up to 14,400 bps.

Note that all of these channels use the same bandwidth. The chipping code is used to distinguish among the different channels. For the forward channel, the chipping codes are the 64 orthogonal 64-bit codes derived from a 64×64 matrix known as the Walsh matrix (discussed in [STAL02]).

Figure 14.11 shows the processing steps for transmission on a forward traffic channel using rate set 1. For voice traffic, the speech is encoded at a data rate of 8550 bps. After additional bits are added for error detection, the rate is 9600 bps. The full channel capacity is not used when the user is not speaking. During quiet periods the data rate is lowered to as low as 1200 bps. The 2400-bps rate is used to transmit transients in the background noise, and the 4800-bps rate is used to mix digitized speech and signaling data.

The data or digitized speech is transmitted in 20-ms blocks with forward error correction provided by a convolutional encoder with rate 1/2, thus doubling the effective data rate to a maximum of 19.2 kbps. For lower data rates, the encoder output bits (called code symbols) are replicated to yield the 19.2-kbps rate. The data are then interleaved in blocks to reduce the effects of errors by spreading them out.

Following the interleaver, the data bits are scrambled. The purpose of this is to serve as a privacy mask and to prevent the sending of repetitive patterns, which in turn reduces the probability of users sending at peak power at the same time. The scrambling is accomplished by means of a long code that is generated as a pseudo-random number from a 42-bit-long shift register. The shift register is initialized with the user's electronic serial number. The output of the long code generator is at a rate of 1.2288 Mbps, which is 64 times the rate of 19.2 kbps, so only one bit in 64 is selected (by the decimator function). The resulting stream is XORed with the output of the block interleaver.

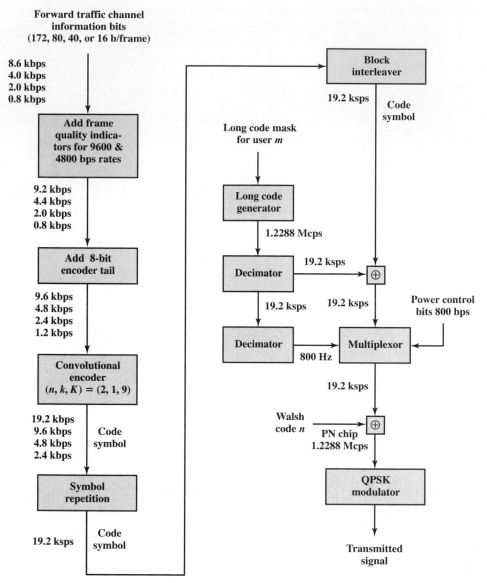

Figure 14.11   IS-95 Forward Link Transmission

The next step in the processing inserts power control information in the traffic channel, to control the power output of the antenna. The power control function of the base station robs the traffic channel of bits at a rate of 800 bps. These are inserted by stealing code bits. The 800-bps channel carries information directing the mobile unit to increment, decrement, or keep stable its current output level. This power control stream is multiplexed into the 19.2 kbps by replacing some of the code bits, using the long code generator to encode the bits.

The next step in the process is the DS-SS function, which spreads the 19.2 kbps to a rate of 1.2288 Mbps using one row of the 64 × 64 Walsh matrix. One row of the matrix is assigned to a mobile station during call setup. If a 0 bit is presented to the XOR function, then the 64 bits of the assigned row are sent. If a 1 is presented, then the bitwise XOR of the row is sent. Thus, the final bit rate is 1.2288 Mbps. This digital bit stream is then modulated onto the carrier using a QPSK modulation scheme. Recall from Chapter 5 that QPSK involves creating two bits streams that are separately modulated (see Figure 5.11). In the IS-95 scheme, the data are split into I and Q (in-phase and quadrature) channels and the data in each channel are XORed with a unique short code. The short codes are generated as pseudorandom numbers from a 15-bit-long shift register.

IS-95 Reverse Link

Table 14.4 lists reverse link channel parameters. The reverse link consists of up to 94 logical CDMA channels each occupying the same 1228-kHz bandwidth (Figure 14.10b). The reverse link supports up to 32 access channels and up to 62 traffic channels.

The traffic channels in the reverse link are mobile unique. Each station has a unique long code mask based on its electronic serial number. The long code mask is a 42-bit number, so there are $2^{42} - 1$ different masks. The access channel is used by a mobile to initiate a call, to respond to a paging channel message from the base station, and for a location update.

Figure 14.12 shows the processing steps for transmission on a reverse traffic channel using rate set 1. The first few steps are the same as for the forward channel. For the reverse channel, the convolutional encoder has a rate of 1/3, thus tripling the effective data rate to a maximum of 28.8 kbps. The data are then block interleaved.

Table 14.4   IS-95 Reverse Link Channel Parameters

Channel	Access	Traffic Rate Set 1				Traffic Rate Set 2			
Data rate (bps)	4800	1200	2400	4800	9600	1800	3600	7200	14400
Code rate	1/3	1/3	1/3	1/3	1/3	1/2	1/2	1/2	1/2
Symbol rate before repetition (sps)	14,400	3600	7200	14,400	28,800	3600	7200	14,400	28,800
Symbol repetition	2	8	4	2	1	8	4	2	1
Symbol rate after repetition (sps)	28,800	28,800	28,800	28,800	28,800	28,800	28,800	28,800	28,800
Transmit duty cycle	1	1/8	1/4	1/2	1	1/8	1/4	1/2	1
Code symbols/ modulation symbol	6	6	6	6	6	6	6	6	6
PN chips/modulation symbol	256	256	256	256	256	256	256	256	256
PN chips/bit	256	128	128	128	128	256/3	256/3	256/3	256/3

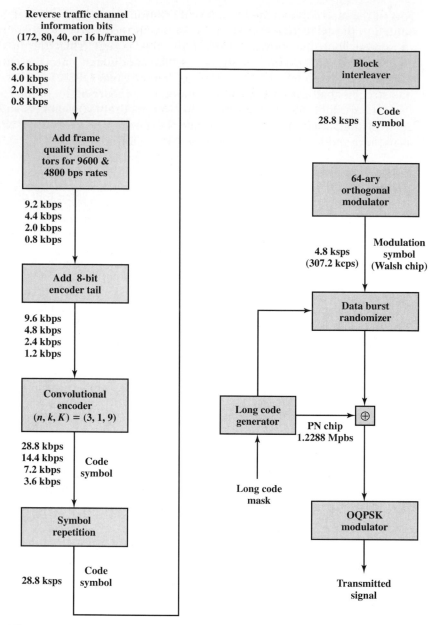

Figure 14.12   IS-95 Reverse Link Transmission

The next step is a spreading of the data using the Walsh matrix. The way in which the matrix is used, and its purpose, are different from that of the forward channel. In the reverse channel, the data coming out of the block interleaver are grouped in units of 6 bits. Each 6-bit unit serves as an index to select a row of the 64×64 Walsh matrix ($2^6 = 64$), and that row is substituted for the input. Thus the data rate is expanded by a factor of 64/6 to 307.2 kbps. The purpose of this encoding is to improve reception at the base station. Because the 64 possible codings are orthogonal, the block coding enhances the decision-making algorithm at the receiver and is also computationally efficient (see [PETE95] for details). We can view this Walsh modulation as a form of block error-correcting code with $(n, k) = (64, 6)$ and $d_{min} = 32$. In fact, all distances are 32.

The data burst randomizer is implemented to help reduce interference from other mobile stations (see [BLAC99b] for a discussion). The operation involves using the long code mask to smooth the data out over each 20-ms frame.

The next step in the process is the DS-SS function. In the case of the reverse channel, the long code unique to the mobile is XORed with the output of the randomizer to produce the 1.2288-Mbps final data stream. This digital bit stream is then modulated onto the carrier using an orthogonal QPSK modulation scheme. This differs from the forward channel in the use of a delay element in the modulator (Figure 5.11) to produce orthogonality. The reason the modulators are different is that in the forward channel, the spreading codes are orthogonal, all coming from the Walsh matrix, whereas in the reverse channel, orthogonality of the spreading codes is not guaranteed.

14.4 THIRD-GENERATION SYSTEMS

The objective of the third generation (3G) of wireless communication is to provide fairly high-speed wireless communications to support multimedia, data, and video in addition to voice. The ITU's International Mobile Telecommunications for the year 2000 (IMT-2000) initiative has defined the ITU's view of third-generation capabilities as follows:

- Voice quality comparable to the public switched telephone network
- 144 kbps data rate available to users in high-speed motor vehicles over large areas
- 384 kbps available to pedestrians standing or moving slowly over small areas
- Support (to be phased in) for 2.048 Mbps for office use
- Symmetrical and asymmetrical data transmission rates
- Support for both packet-switched and circuit-switched data services
- An adaptive interface to the Internet to reflect efficiently the common asymmetry between inbound and outbound traffic
- More efficient use of the available spectrum in general
- Support for a wide variety of mobile equipment
- Flexibility to allow the introduction of new services and technologies

More generally, one of the driving forces of modern communication technology is the trend toward universal personal telecommunications and universal communications access. The first concept refers to the ability of a person to identify himself or herself easily and use conveniently any communication system in an entire country, over a continent, or even globally, in terms of a single account. The second refers to the capability of using one's terminal in a wide variety of environments to connect to information services (e.g., to have a portable terminal that will work in the office, on the street, and on airplanes equally well). This revolution in personal computing will obviously involve wireless communication in a fundamental way.

Personal communications services (PCSs) and personal communication networks (PCNs) are names attached to these concepts of global wireless communications, and they also form objectives for third-generation wireless.

Generally, the technology planned is digital, using time division multiple access or code division multiple access to provide efficient use of the spectrum and high capacity.

PCS handsets are designed to be low power and relatively small and light. Efforts are being made internationally to allow the same terminals to be used worldwide.

Alternative Interfaces

Figure 14.13 shows the alternative schemes that have been adopted as part of IMT-2000. The specification covers a set of radio interfaces for optimized performance in different radio environments. A major reason for the inclusion of five alternatives was to enable a smooth evolution from existing first- and second-generation systems.

The five alternatives reflect the evolution from the second generation. Two of the specifications grow out of the work at the European Telecommunications Standards Institute (ETSI) to develop a UMTS (universal mobile telecommunications system) as Europe's 3G wireless standard. UMTS includes two standards. One of these is known as wideband CDMA, or W-CDMA. This scheme fully exploits CDMA technology to provide high data rates with efficient use of bandwidth. Table 14.5 shows some of the key parameters of W-CDMA. The other European

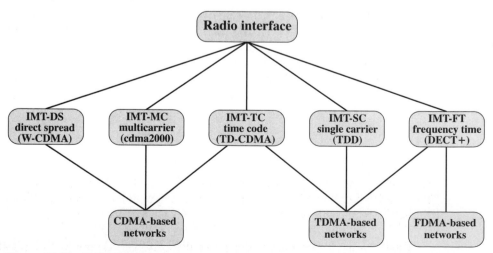

Figure 14.13   IMT-2000 Terrestrial Radio Interfaces

Table 14.5   W-CDMA Parameters

Channel bandwidth	5 MHz
Forward RF channel structure	Direct spread
Chip rate	3.84 Mcps
Frame length	10 ms
Number of slots/frame	15
Spreading modulation	Balanced QPSK (forward) Dual channel QPSK (reverse) Complex spreading circuit
Data modulation	QPSK (forward) BPSK (reverse)
Coherent detection	Pilot symbols
Reverse channel multiplexing	Control and pilot channel time multiplexed. I and Q multiplexing for data and control channels
Multirate	Various spreading and multicode
Spreading factors	4 to 256
Power control	Open and fast closed loop (1.6 kHz)
Spreading (forward)	Variable length orthogonal sequences for channel separation. Gold sequences 2^{18} for cell and user separation
Spreading (reverse)	Same as forward, different time shifts in I and Q channels

effort under UMTS is known as IMT-TC, or TD-CDMA. This approach is a combination of W-CDMA and TDMA technology. IMT-TC is intended to provide an upgrade path for the TDMA-based GSM systems.

Another CDMA-based system, known as cdma2000, has a North American origin. This scheme is similar to, but incompatible with, W-CDMA, in part because the standards use different chip rates. Also, cdma2000 uses a technique known as multicarrier, not used with W-CDMA.

Two other interface specifications are shown in Figure 14.13. IMT-SC is primarily designed for TDMA-only networks. IMT-FC can be used by both TDMA and FDMA carriers to provide some 3G services; it is an outgrowth of the Digital European Cordless Telecommunications (DECT) standard.

CDMA Design Considerations

The dominant technology for 3G systems is CDMA. Although three different CDMA schemes have been adopted, they share some common design issues. [OJAN98] lists the following:

- **Bandwidth:** An important design goal for all 3G systems is to limit channel usage to 5 MHz. There are several reasons for this goal. On the one hand, a bandwidth of 5 MHz or more improves the receiver's ability to resolve multi-path when compared to narrower bandwidths. On the other hand, available spectrum is limited by competing needs, and 5 MHz is a reasonable upper limit on what can be allocated for 3G. Finally, 5 MHz is adequate for supporting data rates of 144 and 384 kHz, the main targets for 3G services.

- **Chip rate:** Given the bandwidth, the chip rate depends on desired data rate, the need for error control, and bandwidth limitations. A chip rate of 3 Mcps or more is reasonable given these design parameters.

- **Multirate:** The term *multirate* refers to the provision of multiple fixed-data-rate logical channels to a given user, in which different data rates are provided on different logical channels. Further, the traffic on each logical channel can be switched independently through the wireless and fixed networks to different destinations. The advantage of multirate is that the system can flexibly support multiple simultaneous applications from a given user and can efficiently use available capacity by only providing the capacity required for each service. Multirate can be achieved with a TDMA scheme within a single CDMA channel, in which a different number of slots per frame are assigned to achieve different data rates. All the subchannels at a given data rate would be protected by error correction and interleaving techniques (Figure 14.14a). An alternative is to use multiple CDMA codes, with separate coding and interleaving, and map them to separate CDMA channels (Figure 14.14b).

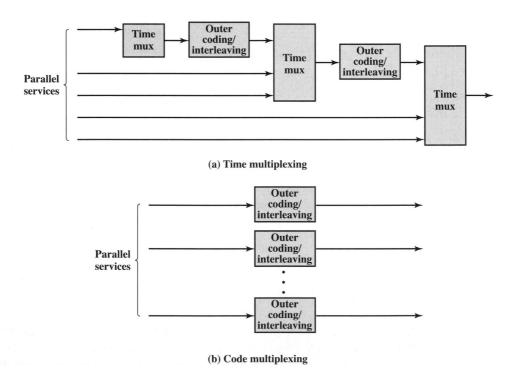

(a) Time multiplexing

(b) Code multiplexing

Figure 14.14 Time and Code Multiplexing Principles [OJAN98]

14.5 RECOMMENDED READING AND WEB SITES

[BERT94] and [ANDE95] are instructive surveys of cellular wireless propagation effects. [BLAC99] is one of the best technical treatments of second-generation cellular systems.

[TANT98] contains reprints of numerous important papers dealing with CDMA in cellular networks. [DINA98] provides an overview of both PN and orthogonal spreading codes for cellular CDMA networks.

[OJAN98] provides an overview of key technical design considerations for 3G systems. Another useful survey is [ZENG00]. [PRAS00] is a much more detailed analysis.

ANDE95   Anderson, J.; Rappaport, T.; and Yoshida, S. "Propagation Measurements and Models for Wireless Communications Channels." *IEEE Communications Magazine*, January 1995.

BERT94   Bertoni, H.; Honcharenko, W.; Maciel, L.; and Xia, H. "UHF Propagation Prediction for Wireless Personal Communications." *Proceedings of the IEEE*, September 1994.

BLAC99   Black, U. *Second-Generation Mobile and Wireless Networks*. Upper Saddle River, NJ: Prentice Hall, 1999.

DINA98   Dinan, E., and Jabbari, B. "Spreading Codes for Direct Sequence CDMA and Wideband CDMA Cellular Networks." *IEEE Communications Magazine*, September 1998.

OJAN98   Ojanpera, T., and Prasad, G. "An Overview of Air Interface Multiple Access for IMT-2000/UMTS." *IEEE Communications Magazine*, September 1998.

PRAS00   Prasad, R.; Mohr, W.; and Konhauser, W., eds. *Third-Generation Mobile Communication Systems*. Boston: Artech House, 2000.

TANT98   Tantaratana, S., and Ahmed, K., eds. *Wireless Applications of Spread Spectrum Systems: Selected Readings*. Piscataway, NJ: IEEE Press, 1998.

ZENG00   Zeng, M.; Annamalai, A.; and Bhargava, V. "Harmonization of Global Third-Generation Mobile Systems. *IEEE Communications Magazine*, December 2000.

Recommended Web Sites:

- **Cellular Telecommunications and Internet Association:** An industry consortium that provides information on successful applications of wireless technology.
- **CDMA Development Group:** Information and links for IS-95 and CDMA generally.
- **3G Americas:** A trade group of Western Hemisphere companies supporting a variety of second- and third-generation schemes. Includes industry news, white papers, and other technical information.

14.6 KEY TERMS, REVIEW QUESTIONS, AND PROBLEMS

Key Terms

adaptive equalization	fast fading	reuse factor
Advanced Mobile Phone Service (AMPS)	flat fading	reverse channel
	first-generation (1G) network	scattering
base station	forward channel	second-generation (2G)
cellular network	frequency diversity	network
code division multiple access (CDMA)	frequency reuse	selective fading
	handoff	slow fading
diffraction	mobile radio	space diversity
diversity	power control	third-generation (3G) network
fading	reflection	

Review Questions

14.1 What geometric shape is used in cellular system design?

14.2 What is the principle of frequency reuse in the context of a cellular network?

14.3 List five ways of increasing the capacity of a cellular system.

14.4 Explain the paging function of a cellular system.

14.5 What is fading?

14.6 What is the difference between diffraction and scattering?

14.7 What is the difference between fast and slow fading?

14.8 What is the difference between flat and selective fading?

14.9 What are the key differences between first- and second-generation cellular systems?

14.10 What are the advantages of using CDMA for a cellular network?

14.11 What are the disadvantages of using CDMA for a cellular network?

14.12 What are some key characteristics that distinguish third-generation cellular systems from second-generation cellular systems?

Problems

14.1 Consider four different cellular systems that share the following characteristics. The frequency bands are 825 to 845 MHz for mobile unit transmission and 870 to 890 MHz for base station transmission. A duplex circuit consists of one 30-kHz channel in each direction. The systems are distinguished by the reuse factor, which is 4, 7, 12, and 19, respectively.

    a. Suppose that in each of the systems, the cluster of cells (4, 7, 12, 19) is duplicated 16 times. Find the number of simultaneous communications that can be supported by each system.

    b. Find the number of simultaneous communications that can be supported by a single cell in each system.

    c. What is the area covered, in cells, by each system?

    d. Suppose the cell size is the same in all four systems and a fixed area of 100 cells is covered by each system. Find the number of simultaneous communications that can be supported by each system.

14.2 Describe a sequence of events similar to that of Figure 14.6 for

    a. a call from a mobile unit to a fixed subscriber

    b. a call from a fixed subscriber to a mobile unit

14.3   An analog cellular system has a total of 33 MHz of bandwidth and uses two 25-kHz simplex (one-way) channels to provide full duplex voice and control channels.
  a.   What is the number of channels available per cell for a frequency reuse factor of (1) 4 cells, (2) 7 cells, and (3) 12 cells?
  b.   Assume that 1 MHz is dedicated to control channels but that only one control channel is needed per cell. Determine a reasonable distribution of control channels and voice channels in each cell for the three frequency reuse factors of part (a).

14.4   A cellular system uses FDMA with a spectrum allocation of 12.5 MHz in each direction, a guard band at the edge of the allocated spectrum of 10 kHz, and a channel bandwidth of 30 kHz. What is the number of available channels?

14.5   For a cellular system, FDMA spectral efficiency is defined as $\eta_a = \dfrac{B_c N_T}{B_w}$, where

  B_c = channel bandwidth
  B_w = total bandwidth in one direction
  N_T = total number of voice channels in the covered area

What is an upper bound on η_a?

PART FOUR Local Area Networks

ISSUES FOR PART FOUR

The trend in local area networks (LANs) involves the use of shared transmission media or shared switching capacity to achieve high data rates over relatively short distances. Several key issues present themselves. One is the choice of transmission medium. Whereas coaxial cable was commonly used in traditional LANs, contemporary LAN installations emphasize the use of twisted pair or optical fiber. In the case of twisted pair, efficient encoding schemes are needed to enable high data rates over the medium. Wireless LANs have also assumed increased importance. Another design issue is that of access control.

ROAD MAP FOR PART FOUR

Chapter 15 LAN Technology

The essential technology underlying all forms of LANs comprises topology, transmission medium, and medium access control technique. Chapter 15 examines the first two of these elements. Four topologies are in common use: bus, tree, ring, and star. The most common transmission media for local networking are twisted pair (unshielded and shielded), coaxial cable (baseband and broadband), optical fiber, and wireless (microwave and infrared). These topologies and transmission media are discussed, with the exception of wireless, which is covered in Chapter 17.

The increasing deployment of LANs has led to an increased need to interconnect LANs with each other and with WANs. Chapter 15 also discusses a key device used in interconnecting LANs: the bridge.

Chapter 16 LAN Systems

Chapter 16 looks in detail at the topologies, transmission media, and MAC protocols of the most important LAN systems in current use; all of these have been defined in standards documents. The most important of these is Ethernet, which has been deployed in versions at 10 Mbps, 100 Mbps, 1 Gbps, and 10 Gbps. Then the chapter looks at the IEEE 802.5 token ring LANs. Finally, the chapter examines Fibre Channel.

Chapter 17 Wireless LAN Technology

Wireless LANs use one of three transmission techniques: spread spectrum, narrowband microwave, and infrared. Chapter 17 provides an overview of wireless LAN technology and applications. The most significant set of standards defining wireless LANs are those defined by the IEEE 802.11 committee. Chapter 17 also examines this set of standards in depth.

CHAPTER **15**

LOCAL AREA NETWORK OVERVIEW

KEY POINTS

- A LAN consists of a shared transmission medium and a set of hardware and software for interfacing devices to the medium and regulating the orderly access to the medium.
- The topologies that have been used for LANs are ring, bus, tree, and star. A ring LAN consists of a closed loop of repeaters that allow data to circulate around the ring. A repeater may also function as a device attachment point. Transmission is generally in the form of frames. The bus and tree topologies are passive sections of cable to which stations are attached. A transmission of a frame by any one station can be heard by any other station. A star LAN includes a central node to which stations are attached.
- A set of standards has been defined for LANs that specifies a range of data rates and encompasses a variety of topologies and transmission media.
- In most cases, an organization will have multiple LANs that need to be interconnected. The simplest approach to meeting this requirement is the bridge.
- Hubs and switches form the basic building blocks of most LANs.

We turn now to a discussion of **local area networks** (LANs). Whereas wide area networks may be public or private, LANs usually are owned by the organization that is using the network to interconnect equipment. LANs have much greater capacity than wide area networks, to carry what is generally a greater internal communications load.

In this chapter we look at the underlying technology and protocol architecture of LANs. Chapter 16 is devoted to a discussion of specific LAN systems.

15.1 BACKGROUND

The variety of applications for LANs is wide. To provide some insight into the types of requirements that LANs are intended to meet, this section provides a brief discussion of some of the most important general application areas for these networks.

Personal Computer LANs

A common LAN configuration is one that supports personal computers. With the relatively low cost of such systems, individual managers within organizations often independently procure personal computers for departmental applications, such as spreadsheet and project management tools, and Internet access.

But a collection of department-level processors will not meet all of an organization's needs; central processing facilities are still required. Some programs, such as econometric forecasting models, are too big to run on a small computer. Corporate-wide data files, such as accounting and payroll, require a centralized facility but should be accessible to a number of users. In addition, there are other kinds of files that, although specialized, must be shared by a number of users. Further, there are sound reasons for connecting individual intelligent workstations not only to a central facility but to each other as well. Members of a project or organization team need to share work and information. By far the most efficient way to do so is digitally.

Certain expensive resources, such as a disk or a laser printer, can be shared by all users of the departmental LAN. In addition, the network can tie into larger corporate network facilities. For example, the corporation may have a building-wide LAN and a wide area private network. A communications server can provide controlled access to these resources.

LANs for the support of personal computers and workstations have become nearly universal in organizations of all sizes. Even those sites that still depend heavily on the mainframe have transferred much of the processing load to networks of personal computers. Perhaps the prime example of the way in which personal computers are being used is to implement client/server applications.

For personal computer networks, a key requirement is low cost. In particular, the cost of attachment to the network must be significantly less than the cost of the attached device. Thus, for the ordinary personal computer, an attachment cost in the hundreds of dollars is desirable. For more expensive, high-performance workstations, higher attachment costs can be tolerated. In any case, this suggests that the data rate of the network may be limited; in general, the higher the data rate, the higher the cost.

Backend Networks and Storage Area Networks

Backend networks are used to interconnect large systems such as mainframes, supercomputers, and mass storage devices. The key requirement here is for bulk data transfer among a limited number of devices in a small area. High reliability is generally also a requirement. Typical characteristics include the following:

- **High data rate:** To satisfy the high-volume demand, data rates of 100 Mbps or more are required.
- **High-speed interface:** Data transfer operations between a large host system and a mass storage device are typically performed through high-speed parallel I/O interfaces, rather than slower communications interfaces. Thus, the physical link between station and network must be high speed.
- **Distributed access:** Some sort of distributed medium access control (MAC) technique is needed to enable a number of devices to share the medium with efficient and reliable access.
- **Limited distance:** Typically, a backend network will be employed in a computer room or a small number of contiguous rooms.
- **Limited number of devices:** The number of expensive mainframes and mass storage devices found in the computer room generally numbers in the tens of devices.

Typically, backend networks are found at sites of large companies or research installations with large data processing budgets. Because of the scale involved, a small difference in productivity can mean millions of dollars.

Consider a site that uses a dedicated mainframe computer. This implies a fairly large application or set of applications. As the load at the site grows, the existing mainframe may be replaced by a more powerful one, perhaps a multiprocessor system. At some sites, a single-system replacement will not be able to keep up; equipment performance growth rates will be exceeded by demand growth rates. The facility will eventually require multiple independent computers. Again, there are compelling reasons for interconnecting these systems. The cost of system interrupt is high, so it should be possible, easily and quickly, to shift applications to backup systems. It must be possible to test new procedures and applications without degrading the production system. Large bulk storage files must be accessible from more than one computer. Load leveling should be possible to maximize utilization and performance.

It can be seen that some key requirements for backend networks differ from those for personal computer LANs. High data rates are required to keep up with the work, which typically involves the transfer of large blocks of data. The equipment for achieving high speeds is expensive. Fortunately, given the much higher cost of the attached devices, such costs are reasonable.

A concept related to that of the backend network is the **storage area network** (SAN). A SAN is a separate network to handle storage needs. The SAN detaches storage tasks from specific servers and creates a shared storage facility across a high-speed network. The collection of networked storage devices can include hard disks, tape libraries, and CD arrays. Most SANs use Fibre Channel, which is described in Chapter 16. Figure 15.1 contrasts the SAN with the traditional server-based means of supporting shared storage. In a typical large LAN installation, a number of servers and perhaps mainframes each has its own dedicated storage devices. If a client needs access to a particular storage device, it must go through the server that controls that device. In a SAN, no server sits between the storage devices and the network; instead, the storage devices and servers are linked directly to the network. The SAN arrangement improves client-to-storage access efficiency, as well as direct storage-to-storage communications for backup and replication functions.

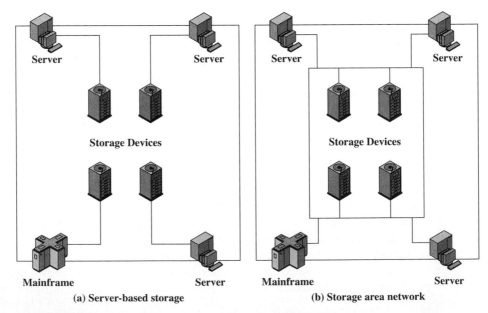

(a) Server-based storage   (b) Storage area network

Figure 15.1   The Use of Storage Area Networks [HURW98]

High-Speed Office Networks

Traditionally, the office environment has included a variety of devices with low- to medium-speed data transfer requirements. However, applications in today's office environment would overwhelm the limited speeds (up to 10 Mbps) of traditional LAN. Desktop image processors have increased network data flow by an unprecedented amount. Examples of these applications include fax machines, document image processors, and graphics programs on personal computers and workstations. Consider that a typical page with 200 picture elements, or pels[1] (black or white points), per inch resolution (which is adequate but not high resolution) generates 3,740,000 bits (8.5 inches $\times$ 11 inches $\times$ 40,000 pels per square inch). Even with compression techniques, this will generate a tremendous load. In addition, disk technology and price/performance have evolved so that desktop storage capacities multiple gigabytes are common. These new demands require LANs with high speed that can support the larger numbers and greater geographic extent of office systems as compared to backend systems.

Backbone LANs

The increasing use of distributed processing applications and personal computers has led to a need for a flexible strategy for local networking. Support of premises-wide data communications requires a networking service that is capable of spanning the distances involved and that interconnects equipment in a single (perhaps large) building or a cluster of buildings. Although it is possible to develop a single LAN to interconnect all the data processing equipment of a premises, this is probably not a practical alternative in most cases. There are several drawbacks to a single-LAN strategy:

- **Reliability:** With a single LAN, a service interruption, even of short duration, could result in a major disruption for users.
- **Capacity:** A single LAN could be saturated as the number of devices attached to the network grows over time.
- **Cost:** A single LAN technology is not optimized for the diverse requirements of interconnection and communication. The presence of large numbers of low-cost microcomputers dictates that network support for these devices be provided at low cost. LANs that support very-low-cost attachment will not be suitable for meeting the overall requirement.

A more attractive alternative is to employ lower-cost, lower-capacity LANs within buildings or departments and to interconnect these networks with a higher-capacity LAN. This latter network is referred to as a backbone LAN. If confined to a single building or cluster of buildings, a high-capacity LAN can perform the backbone function.

---

[1] A *picture element*, or *pel*, is the smallest discrete scanning-line sample of a facsimile system, which contains only black-white information (no gray scales). A *pixel* is a picture element that contains gray-scale information.

15.2 TOPOLOGIES AND TRANSMISSION MEDIA

The key elements of a LAN are

- Topology
- Transmission medium
- Layout
- Medium access control

Together, these elements determine not only the cost and capacity of the LAN, but also the type of data that may be transmitted, the speed and efficiency of communications, and even the kinds of applications that can be supported.

This section provides a survey of the major technologies in the first two of these categories. It will be seen that there is an interdependence among the choices in different categories. Accordingly, a discussion of pros and cons relative to specific applications is best done by looking at preferred combinations. This, in turn, is best done in the context of standards, which is a subject of a later section.

Topologies

In the context of a communication network, the term *topology* refers to the way in which the end points, or stations, attached to the network are interconnected. The common topologies for LANs are bus, tree, ring, and star (Figure 15.2). The bus is a special case of the tree, with only one trunk and no branches.

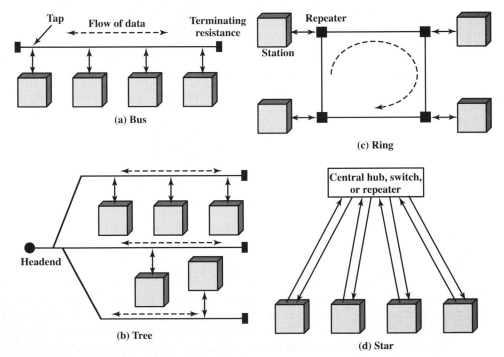

Figure 15.2   Local Area Network Topologies

Bus and Tree Topologies

Both bus and tree topologies are characterized by the use of a multipoint medium. For the **bus**, all stations attach, through appropriate hardware interfacing known as a tap, directly to a linear transmission medium, or bus. Full-duplex operation between the station and the tap allows data to be transmitted onto the bus and received from the bus. A transmission from any station propagates the length of the medium in both directions and can be received by all other stations. At each end of the bus is a terminator, which absorbs any signal, removing it from the bus.

The **tree topology** is a generalization of the bus topology. The transmission medium is a branching cable with no closed loops. The tree layout begins at a point known as the *headend*. One or more cables start at the headend, and each of these may have branches. The branches in turn may have additional branches to allow quite complex layouts. Again, a transmission from any station propagates throughout the medium and can be received by all other stations.

Two problems present themselves in this arrangement. First, because a transmission from any one station can be received by all other stations, there needs to be some way of indicating for whom the transmission is intended. Second, a mechanism is needed to regulate transmission. To see the reason for this, consider that if two stations on the bus attempt to transmit at the same time, their signals will overlap and become garbled. Or consider that one station decides to transmit continuously for a long period of time.

To solve these problems, stations transmit data in small blocks, known as frames. Each frame consists of a portion of the data that a station wishes to transmit, plus a frame header that contains control information. Each station on the bus is assigned a unique address, or identifier, and the destination address for a frame is included in its header.

Figure 15.3 illustrates the scheme. In this example, station C wishes to transmit a frame of data to A. The frame header includes A's address. As the frame propagates along the bus, it passes B. B observes the address and ignores the frame. A, on the other hand, sees that the frame is addressed to itself and therefore copies the data from the frame as it goes by.

So the frame structure solves the first problem mentioned previously: It provides a mechanism for indicating the intended recipient of data. It also provides the basic tool for solving the second problem, the regulation of access. In particular, the stations take turns sending frames in some cooperative fashion. This involves putting additional control information into the frame header, as discussed later.

With the bus or tree, no special action needs to be taken to remove frames from the medium. When a signal reaches the end of the medium, it is absorbed by the terminator.

Ring Topology

In the **ring** topology, the network consists of a set of *repeaters* joined by point-to-point links in a closed loop. The repeater is a comparatively simple device, capable of receiving data on one link and transmitting them, bit by bit, on the other link as fast as they are received. The links are unidirectional; that is, data are transmitted in one direction only, so that data circulate around the ring in one direction (clockwise or counterclockwise).

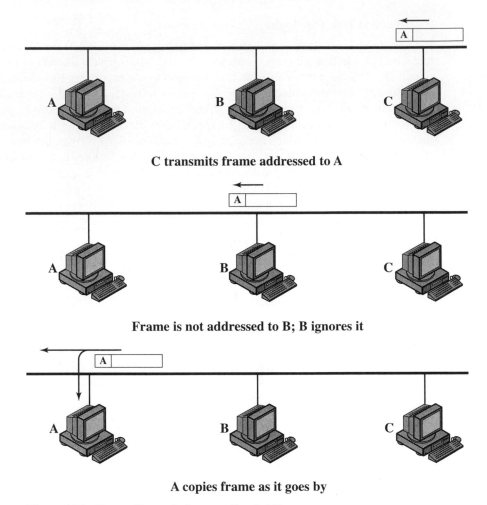

C transmits frame addressed to A

Frame is not addressed to B; B ignores it

A copies frame as it goes by

Figure 15.3 Frame Transmission on a Bus LAN

Each station attaches to the network at a repeater and can transmit data onto the network through the repeater. As with the bus and tree, data are transmitted in frames. As a frame circulates past all the other stations, the destination station recognizes its address and copies the frame into a local buffer as it goes by. The frame continues to circulate until it returns to the source station, where it is removed (Figure 15.4). Because multiple stations share the ring, medium access control is needed to determine at what time each station may insert frames.

Star Topology

In the **star** LAN topology, each station is directly connected to a common central node. Typically, each station attaches to a central node via two point-to-point links, one for transmission and one for reception.

In general, there are two alternatives for the operation of the central node. One approach is for the central node to operate in a broadcast fashion. A transmission

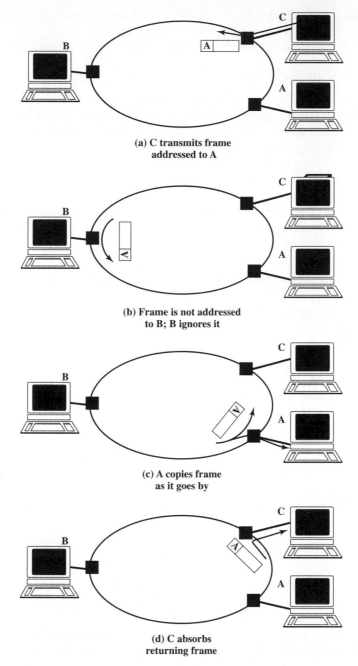

(a) C transmits frame
addressed to A

(b) Frame is not addressed
to B; B ignores it

(c) A copies frame
as it goes by

(d) C absorbs
returning frame

Figure 15.4   Frame Transmission on a Ring LAN

of a frame from one station to the node is retransmitted on all of the outgoing links. In this case, although the arrangement is physically a star, it is logically a bus: A transmission from any station is received by all other stations, and only one station at a time may successfully transmit. In this case, the central element is referred to as a **hub**. Another approach is for the central node to act as a frame-switching device. An incoming frame is buffered in the node and then retransmitted on an outgoing link to the destination station. These approaches are explored in Section 15.5.

Choice of Topology

The choice of topology depends on a variety of factors, including reliability, expandability, and performance. This choice is part of the overall task of designing a LAN and thus cannot be made in isolation, independent of the choice of transmission medium, wiring layout, and access control technique. A few general remarks can be made at this point. There are four alternative media that can be used for a bus LAN:

- **Twisted pair:** In the early days of LAN development, voice-grade twisted pair was used to provide an inexpensive, easily installed bus LAN. A number of systems operating at 1 Mbps were implemented. Scaling twisted pair up to higher data rates in a shared-medium bus configuration is not practical, so this approach was dropped long ago.
- **Baseband coaxial cable:** A baseband coaxial cable is one that makes use of digital signaling. The original Ethernet scheme makes use of baseband coaxial cable.
- **Broadband coaxial cable:** Broadband coaxial cable is the type of cable used in cable television systems. Analog signaling is used at radio and television frequencies. This type of system is more expensive and more difficult to install and maintain than baseband coaxial cable. This approach never achieved popularity and such LANs are no longer made.
- **Optical fiber:** There has been considerable research relating to this alternative over the years, but the expense of the optical fiber taps and the availability of better alternatives have resulted in the demise of this option as well.

Thus, for a bus topology, only baseband coaxial cable has achieved widespread use, primarily for Ethernet systems. Compared to a star-topology twisted pair or optical fiber installation, the bus topology using baseband coaxial cable is difficult to work with. Even simple changes may require access to the coaxial cable, movement of taps, and rerouting of cable segments. Accordingly, few if any new installations are being attempted. Despite its limitations, there is a considerable installed base of baseband coaxial cable bus LANs.

Very-high-speed links over considerable distances can be used for the ring topology. Hence, the ring has the potential of providing the best throughput of any topology. One disadvantage of the ring is that a single link or repeater failure could disable the entire network.

The star topology takes advantage of the natural layout of wiring in a building. It is generally best for short distances and can support a small number of devices at high data rates.

Choice of Transmission Medium

The choice of transmission medium is determined by a number of factors. It is, we shall see, constrained by the topology of the LAN. Other factors come into play, including the following:

- **Capacity:** to support the expected network traffic
- **Reliability:** to meet requirements for availability
- **Types of data supported:** tailored to the application
- **Environmental scope:** to provide service over the range of environments required

The choice is part of the overall task of designing a local network, which is addressed in Chapter 16. Here we can make a few general observations.

Voice-grade unshielded twisted pair (UTP) is an inexpensive, well-understood medium; this is the Category 3 UTP referred to in Chapter 4. Typically, office buildings are wired to meet the anticipated telephone system demand plus a healthy margin; thus, there are no cable installation costs in the use of Category 3 UTP. However, the data rate that can be supported is generally quite limited, with the exception of very small LAN. Category 3 UTP is likely to be the most cost-effective for a single-building, low-traffic LAN installation.

Shielded twisted pair and baseband coaxial cable are more expensive than Category 3 UTP but provide greater capacity. Broadband cable is even more expensive but provides even greater capacity. However, in recent years, the trend has been toward the use of high-performance UTP, especially Category 5 UTP. Category 5 UTP supports high data rates for a small number of devices, but larger installations can be supported by the use of the star topology and the interconnection of the switching elements in multiple star-topology configurations. We discuss this point in Chapter 16.

Optical fiber has a number of attractive features, such as electromagnetic isolation, high capacity, and small size, which have attracted a great deal of interest. As yet the market penetration of fiber LANs is low; this is primarily due to the high cost of fiber components and the lack of skilled personnel to install and maintain fiber systems. This situation is beginning to change rapidly as more products using fiber are introduced.

15.3 LAN PROTOCOL ARCHITECTURE

The architecture of a LAN is best described in terms of a layering of protocols that organize the basic functions of a LAN. This section opens with a description of the standardized protocol architecture for LANs, which encompasses physical, medium access control (MAC), and logical link control (LLC) layers. The physical layer encompasses topology and transmission medium and is covered in Section 15.2. This section provides an overview of the MAC and LLC layers.

IEEE 802 Reference Model

Protocols defined specifically for LAN and MAN transmission address issues relating to the transmission of blocks of data over the network. In OSI terms, higher-layer protocols (layer 3 or 4 and above) are independent of network architecture and are applicable to LANs, MANs, and WANs. Thus, a discussion of LAN protocols is concerned principally with lower layers of the OSI model.

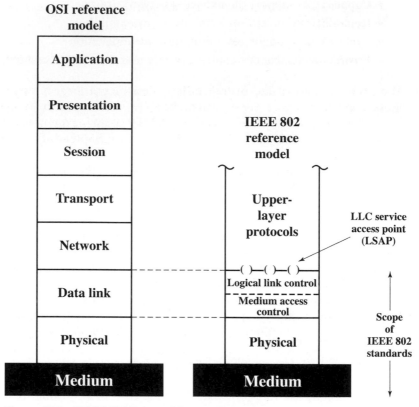

Figure 15.5 IEEE 802 Protocol Layers Compared to OSI Model

Figure 15.5 relates the LAN protocols to the OSI architecture (Figure 2.6). This architecture was developed by the IEEE 802 committee and has been adopted by all organizations working on the specification of LAN standards. It is generally referred to as the IEEE 802 reference model.

Working from the bottom up, the lowest layer of the IEEE 802 reference model corresponds to the **physical layer** of the OSI model and includes such functions as

- Encoding/decoding of signals
- Preamble generation/removal (for synchronization)
- Bit transmission/reception

In addition, the physical layer of the 802 model includes a specification of the transmission medium and the topology. Generally, this is considered "below" the lowest layer of the OSI model. However, the choice of transmission medium and topology is critical in LAN design, and so a specification of the medium is included.

Above the physical layer are the functions associated with providing service to LAN users. These include the following:

- On transmission, assemble data into a frame with address and error-detection fields.

- On reception, disassemble frame, and perform address recognition and error detection.
- Govern access to the LAN transmission medium.
- Provide an interface to higher layers and perform flow and error control.

These are functions typically associated with OSI layer 2. The set of functions in the last bullet item are grouped into a **logical link control (LLC)** layer. The functions in the first three bullet items are treated as a separate layer, called **medium access control (MAC)**. The separation is done for the following reasons:

- The logic required to manage access to a shared-access medium is not found in traditional layer 2 data link control.
- For the same LLC, several MAC options may be provided.

Figure 15.6 illustrates the relationship between the levels of the architecture (compare Figure 2.14). Higher-level data are passed down to LLC, which appends control information as a header, creating an *LLC protocol data unit (PDU)*. This control information is used in the operation of the LLC protocol. The entire LLC PDU is then passed down to the MAC layer, which appends control information at the front and back of the packet, forming a *MAC frame*. Again, the control information in the frame is needed for the operation of the MAC protocol. For context, the figure also shows the use of TCP/IP and an application layer above the LAN protocols.

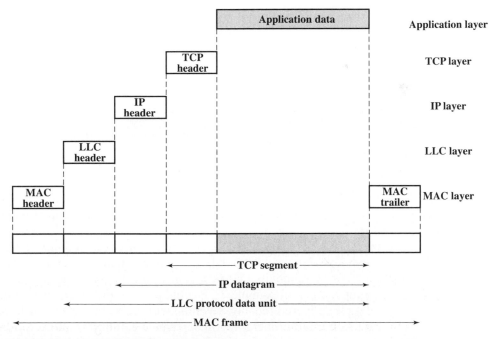

Figure 15.6 LAN Protocols in Context

Logical Link Control

The LLC layer for LANs is similar in many respects to other link layers in common use. Like all link layers, LLC is concerned with the transmission of a link-level PDU between two stations, without the necessity of an intermediate switching node. LLC has two characteristics not shared by most other link control protocols:

1. It must support the multiaccess, shared-medium nature of the link (this differs from a multidrop line in that there is no primary node).
2. It is relieved of some details of link access by the MAC layer.

Addressing in LLC involves specifying the source and destination LLC users. Typically, a user is a higher-layer protocol or a network management function in the station. These LLC user addresses are referred to as service access points (SAPs), in keeping with OSI terminology for the user of a protocol layer.

We look first at the services that LLC provides to a higher-level user, and then at the LLC protocol.

LLC Services

LLC specifies the mechanisms for addressing stations across the medium and for controlling the exchange of data between two users. The operation and format of this standard is based on HDLC. Three services are provided as alternatives for attached devices using LLC:

- **Unacknowledged connectionless service:** This service is a datagram-style service. It is a very simple service that does not involve any of the flow- and error-control mechanisms. Thus, the delivery of data is not guaranteed. However, in most devices, there will be some higher layer of software that deals with reliability issues.
- **Connection-mode service:** This service is similar to that offered by HDLC. A logical connection is set up between two users exchanging data, and flow control and error control are provided.
- **Acknowledged connectionless service:** This is a cross between the previous two services. It provides that datagrams are to be acknowledged, but no prior logical connection is set up.

Typically, a vendor will provide these services as options that the customer can select when purchasing the equipment. Alternatively, the customer can purchase equipment that provides two or all three services and select a specific service based on application.

The **unacknowledged connectionless service** requires minimum logic and is useful in two contexts. First, it will often be the case that higher layers of software will provide the necessary reliability and flow-control mechanism, and it is efficient to avoid duplicating them. For example, TCP could provide the mechanisms needed to ensure that data is delivered reliably. Second, there are instances in which the overhead of connection establishment and maintenance is unjustified or even counterproductive (for example, data collection activities that involve the periodic sampling of data sources, such as sensors and automatic self-test reports from security equipment or network components). In a monitoring application, the loss of an occasional data unit would not cause distress, as the next report should arrive shortly. Thus, in most cases, the unacknowledged connectionless service is the preferred option.

The **connection-mode service** could be used in very simple devices, such as terminal controllers, that have little software operating above this level. In these cases, it would provide the flow control and reliability mechanisms normally implemented at higher layers of the communications software.

The **acknowledged connectionless service** is useful in several contexts. With the connection-mode service, the logical link control software must maintain some sort of table for each active connection, to keep track of the status of that connection. If the user needs guaranteed delivery but there are a large number of destinations for data, then the connection-mode service may be impractical because of the large number of tables required. An example is a process control or automated factory environment where a central site may need to communicate with a large number of processors and programmable controllers. Another use of this is the handling of important and time-critical alarm or emergency control signals in a factory. Because of their importance, an acknowledgment is needed so that the sender can be assured that the signal got through. Because of the urgency of the signal, the user might not want to take the time first to establish a logical connection and then send the data.

LLC Protocol

The basic LLC protocol is modeled after HDLC and has similar functions and formats. The differences between the two protocols can be summarized as follows:

- LLC makes use of the asynchronous balanced mode of operation of HDLC, to support connection-mode LLC service; this is referred to as type 2 operation. The other HDLC modes are not employed.
- LLC supports an unacknowledged connectionless service using the unnumbered information PDU; this is known as type 1 operation.
- LLC supports an acknowledged connectionless service by using two new unnumbered PDUs; this is known as type 3 operation.
- LLC permits multiplexing by the use of LLC service access points (LSAPs).

All three LLC protocols employ the same PDU format (Figure 15.7), which consists of four fields. The DSAP (destination service access point) and SSAP (source service access point) fields each contain a 7-bit address, which specify the destination and source users of LLC. One bit of the DSAP indicates whether the DSAP is an individual or group address. One bit of the SSAP indicates whether the PDU is a command or response PDU. The format of the LLC control field is identical to that of HDLC (Figure 7.7), using extended (7-bit) sequence numbers.

For **type 1 operation**, which supports the unacknowledged connectionless service, the unnumbered information (UI) PDU is used to transfer user data. There is no acknowledgment, flow control, or error control. However, there is error detection and discard at the MAC level.

Two other PDUs are used to support management functions associated with all three types of operation. Both PDUs are used in the following fashion. An LLC

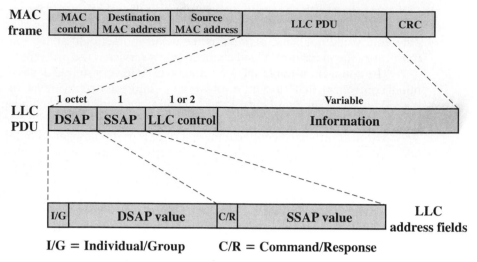

I/G = Individual/Group   C/R = Command/Response

Figure 15.7 LLC PDU in a Generic MAC Frame Format

entity may issue a command (C/R bit = 0) XID or TEST. The receiving LLC entity issues a corresponding XID or TEST in response. The XID PDU is used to exchange two types of information: types of operation supported and window size. The TEST PDU is used to conduct a loopback test of the transmission path between two LLC entities. Upon receipt of a TEST command PDU, the addressed LLC entity issues a TEST response PDU as soon as possible.

With **type 2 operation**, a data link connection is established between two LLC SAPs prior to data exchange. Connection establishment is attempted by the type 2 protocol in response to a request from a user. The LLC entity issues a SABME PDU[2] to request a logical connection with the other LLC entity. If the connection is accepted by the LLC user designated by the DSAP, then the destination LLC entity returns an unnumbered acknowledgment (UA) PDU. The connection is henceforth uniquely identified by the pair of user SAPs. If the destination LLC user rejects the connection request, its LLC entity returns a disconnected mode (DM) PDU.

Once the connection is established, data are exchanged using information PDUs, as in HDLC. The information PDUs include send and receive sequence numbers, for sequencing and flow control. The supervisory PDUs are used, as in HDLC, for flow control and error control. Either LLC entity can terminate a logical LLC connection by issuing a disconnect (DISC) PDU.

With **type 3 operation**, each transmitted PDU is acknowledged. A new (not found in HDLC) unnumbered PDU, the Acknowledged Connectionless (AC) Information PDU, is defined. User data are sent in AC command PDUs and must be acknowledged using an AC response PDU. To guard against lost PDUs, a 1-bit sequence number is used. The sender alternates the use of 0 and 1 in its AC command

---

[2] This stands for Set Asynchronous Balanced Mode Extended. It is used in HDLC to choose ABM and to select extended sequence numbers of seven bits. Both ABM and 7-bit sequence numbers are mandatory in type 2 operation.

PDU, and the receiver responds with an AC PDU with the opposite number of the corresponding command. Only one PDU in each direction may be outstanding at any time.

Medium Access Control

All LANs and MANs consist of collections of devices that must share the network's transmission capacity. Some means of controlling access to the transmission medium is needed to provide for an orderly and efficient use of that capacity. This is the function of a medium access control (MAC) protocol.

The key parameters in any medium access control technique are where and how. *Where* refers to whether control is exercised in a centralized or distributed fashion. In a centralized scheme, a controller is designated that has the authority to grant access to the network. A station wishing to transmit must wait until it receives permission from the controller. In a decentralized network, the stations collectively perform a medium access control function to determine dynamically the order in which stations transmit. A centralized scheme has certain advantages, including the following:

- It may afford greater control over access for providing such things as priorities, overrides, and guaranteed capacity.
- It enables the use of relatively simple access logic at each station.
- It avoids problems of distributed coordination among peer entities.

The principal disadvantages of centralized schemes are as follows:

- It creates a single point of failure; that is, there is a point in the network that, if it fails, causes the entire network to fail.
- It may act as a bottleneck, reducing performance.

The pros and cons of distributed schemes are mirror images of the points just made.

The second parameter, *how*, is constrained by the topology and is a tradeoff among competing factors, including cost, performance, and complexity. In general, we can categorize access control techniques as being either synchronous or asynchronous. With synchronous techniques, a specific capacity is dedicated to a connection. This is the same approach used in circuit switching, frequency division multiplexing (FDM), and synchronous time division multiplexing (TDM). Such techniques are generally not optimal in LANs and MANs because the needs of the stations are unpredictable. It is preferable to be able to allocate capacity in an asynchronous (dynamic) fashion, more or less in response to immediate demand. The asynchronous approach can be further subdivided into three categories: round robin, reservation, and contention.

Round Robin

With round robin, each station in turn is given the opportunity to transmit. During that opportunity, the station may decline to transmit or may transmit subject to a specified upper bound, usually expressed as a maximum amount of data transmitted or time for this opportunity. In any case, the station, when it is finished, relinquishes its turn, and the right to transmit passes to the next station in logical sequence. Control of sequence may be centralized or distributed. Polling is an example of a centralized technique.

When many stations have data to transmit over an extended period of time, round-robin techniques can be very efficient. If only a few stations have data to transmit over an extended period of time, then there is a considerable overhead in passing the turn from station to station, because most of the stations will not transmit but simply pass their turns. Under such circumstances other techniques may be preferable, largely depending on whether the data traffic has a stream or bursty characteristic. Stream traffic is characterized by lengthy and fairly continuous transmissions; examples are voice communication, telemetry, and bulk file transfer. Bursty traffic is characterized by short, sporadic transmissions; interactive terminal-host traffic fits this description.

Reservation

For stream traffic, reservation techniques are well suited. In general, for these techniques, time on the medium is divided into slots, much as with synchronous TDM. A station wishing to transmit reserves future slots for an extended or even an indefinite period. Again, reservations may be made in a centralized or distributed fashion.

Contention

For bursty traffic, contention techniques are usually appropriate. With these techniques, no control is exercised to determine whose turn it is; all stations contend for time in a way that can be, as we shall see, rather rough and tumble. These techniques are of necessity distributed in nature. Their principal advantage is that they are simple to implement and, under light to moderate load, efficient. For some of these techniques, however, performance tends to collapse under heavy load.

Although both centralized and distributed reservation techniques have been implemented in some LAN products, round-robin and contention techniques are the most common.

MAC Frame Format

The MAC layer receives a block of data from the LLC layer and is responsible for performing functions related to medium access and for transmitting the data. As with other protocol layers, MAC implements these functions making use of a protocol data unit at its layer. In this case, the PDU is referred to as a MAC frame.

The exact format of the MAC frame differs somewhat for the various MAC protocols in use. In general, all of the MAC frames have a format similar to that of Figure 15.7. The fields of this frame are as follows:

- **MAC control:** This field contains any protocol control information needed for the functioning of the MAC protocol. For example, a priority level could be indicated here.

- **Destination MAC address:** The destination physical attachment point on the LAN for this frame.
- **Source MAC address:** The source physical attachment point on the LAN for this frame.
- **LLC:** The LLC data from the next higher layer.
- **CRC:** The cyclic redundancy check field (also known as the frame check sequence, FCS, field). This is an error-detecting code, as we have seen in HDLC and other data link control protocols (Chapter 7).

In most data link control protocols, the data link protocol entity is responsible not only for detecting errors using the CRC, but for recovering from those errors by retransmitting damaged frames. In the LAN protocol architecture, these two functions are split between the MAC and LLC layers. The MAC layer is responsible for detecting errors and discarding any frames that are in error. The LLC layer optionally keeps track of which frames have been successfully received and retransmits unsuccessful frames.

15.4 BRIDGES

In virtually all cases, there is a need to expand beyond the confines of a single LAN, to provide interconnection to other LANs and to wide area networks. Two general approaches are used for this purpose: bridges and routers. The bridge is the simpler of the two devices and provides a means of interconnecting similar LANs. The router is a more general-purpose device, capable of interconnecting a variety of LANs and WANs. We explore bridges in this section and look at routers in Part Five.

The bridge is designed for use between local area networks (LANs) that use identical protocols for the physical and link layers (e.g., all conforming to IEEE 802.3). Because the devices all use the same protocols, the amount of processing required at the bridge is minimal. More sophisticated bridges are capable of mapping from one MAC format to another (e.g., to interconnect an Ethernet and a token ring LAN).

Because the bridge is used in a situation in which all the LANs have the same characteristics, the reader may ask, why not simply have one large LAN? Depending on circumstance, there are several reasons for the use of multiple LANs connected by bridges:

- **Reliability:** The danger in connecting all data processing devices in an organization to one network is that a fault on the network may disable communication for all devices. By using bridges, the network can be partitioned into self-contained units.
- **Performance:** In general, performance on a LAN declines with an increase in the number of devices or the length of the wire. A number of smaller LANs will often give improved performance if devices can be clustered so that intranetwork traffic significantly exceeds internetwork traffic.

- **Security:** The establishment of multiple LANs may improve security of communications. It is desirable to keep different types of traffic (e.g., accounting, personnel, strategic planning) that have different security needs on physically separate media. At the same time, the different types of users with different levels of security need to communicate through controlled and monitored mechanisms.
- **Geography:** Clearly, two separate LANs are needed to support devices clustered in two geographically distant locations. Even in the case of two buildings separated by a highway, it may be far easier to use a microwave bridge link than to attempt to string coaxial cable between the two buildings.

Functions of a Bridge

Figure 15.8 illustrates the action of a bridge connecting two LANs, A and B, using the same MAC protocol. In this example, a single bridge attaches to both LANs; frequently, the bridge function is performed by two "half-bridges," one on each LAN. The functions of the bridge are few and simple:

- Read all frames transmitted on A and accept those addressed to any station on B.
- Using the medium access control protocol for B, retransmit each frame on B.
- Do the same for B-to-A traffic.

Several design aspects of a bridge are worth highlighting:

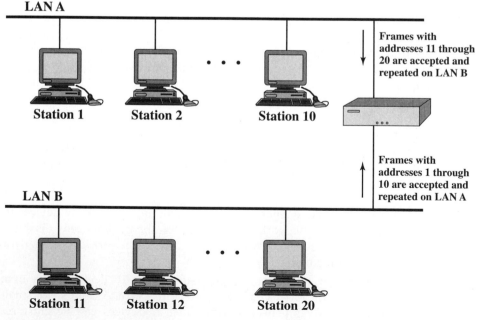

Figure 15.8 Bridge Operation

- The bridge makes no modification to the content or format of the frames it receives, nor does it encapsulate them with an additional header. Each frame to be transferred is simply copied from one LAN and repeated with exactly the same bit pattern as the other LAN. Because the two LANs use the same LAN protocols, it is permissible to do this.
- The bridge should contain enough buffer space to meet peak demands. Over a short period of time, frames may arrive faster than they can be retransmitted.
- The bridge must contain addressing and routing intelligence. At a minimum, the bridge must know which addresses are on each network to know which frames to pass. Further, there may be more than two LANs interconnected by a number of bridges. In that case, a frame may have to be routed through several bridges in its journey from source to destination.
- A bridge may connect more than two LANs.

In summary, the bridge provides an extension to the LAN that requires no modification to the communications software in the stations attached to the LANs. It appears to all stations on the two (or more) LANs that there is a single LAN on which each station has a unique address. The station uses that unique address and need not explicitly discriminate between stations on the same LAN and stations on other LANs; the bridge takes care of that.

Bridge Protocol Architecture

The IEEE 802.1D specification defines the protocol architecture for MAC bridges. Within the 802 architecture, the endpoint or station address is designated at the MAC level. Thus, it is at the MAC level that a bridge can function. Figure 15.9 shows the simplest case, which consists of two LANs connected by a single bridge. The LANs employ the same MAC and LLC protocols. The bridge operates as previously described. A MAC frame whose destination is not on the immediate LAN is captured by the bridge, buffered briefly, and then transmitted on the other LAN. As far as the LLC layer is concerned, there is a dialogue between peer LLC entities in the

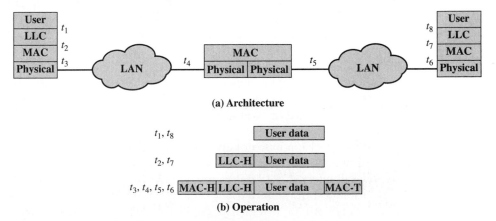

Figure 15.9 Connection of Two LANs by a Bridge

two endpoint stations. The bridge need not contain an LLC layer because it is merely serving to relay the MAC frames.

Figure 15.9b indicates the way in which data are encapsulated using a bridge. Data are provided by some user to LLC. The LLC entity appends a header and passes the resulting data unit to the MAC entity, which appends a header and a trailer to form a MAC frame. On the basis of the destination MAC address in the frame, it is captured by the bridge. The bridge does not strip off the MAC fields; its function is to relay the MAC frame intact to the destination LAN. Thus, the frame is deposited on the destination LAN and captured by the destination station.

The concept of a MAC relay bridge is not limited to the use of a single bridge to connect two nearby LANs. If the LANs are some distance apart, then they can be connected by two bridges that are in turn connected by a communications facility. The intervening communications facility can be a network, such as a wide area packet-switching network, or a point-to-point link. In such cases, when a bridge captures a MAC frame, it must encapsulate the frame in the appropriate packaging and transmit it over the communications facility to a target bridge. The target bridge strips off these extra fields and transmits the original, unmodified MAC frame to the destination station.

Fixed Routing

There is a trend within many organizations to an increasing number of LANs interconnected by bridges. As the number of LANs grows, it becomes important to provide alternate paths between LANs via bridges for load balancing and reconfiguration in response to failure. Thus, many organizations will find that static, preconfigured routing tables are inadequate and that some sort of dynamic routing is needed.

Consider the configuration of Figure 15.10. Suppose that station 1 transmits a frame on LAN A intended for station 6. The frame will be read by bridges 101, 102, and 107. For each bridge, the addressed station is not on a LAN to which the bridge is attached. Therefore, each bridge must make a decision whether or not to retransmit the frame on its other LAN, in order to move it closer to its intended destination. In this case, bridge 102 should repeat the frame on LAN C, whereas bridges 101 and 107 should refrain from retransmitting the frame. Once the frame has been transmitted on LAN C, it will be picked up by both bridges 105 and 106. Again, each must decide whether or not to forward the frame. In this case, bridge 105 should retransmit the frame on LAN F, where it will be received by the destination, station 6.

Thus we see that, in the general case, the bridge must be equipped with a routing capability. When a bridge receives a frame, it must decide whether or not to forward it. If the bridge is attached to two or more networks, then it must decide whether or not to forward the frame and, if so, on which LAN the frame should be transmitted.

The routing decision may not always be a simple one. Figure 15.10 also shows that there are two routes between LAN A and LAN E. Such redundancy provides for higher overall internet availability and creates the possibility for load balancing. In this case, if station 1 transmits a frame on LAN A intended for station 5 on LAN E, then either bridge 101 or bridge 107 could forward the frame. It would appear preferable for bridge 107 to forward the frame, since it will involve only one hop,

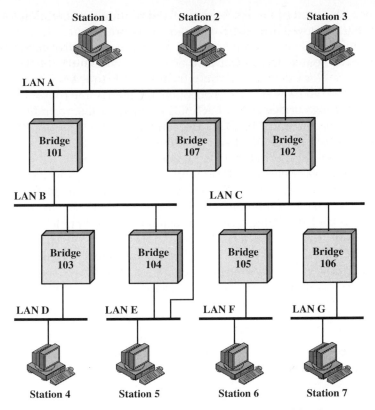

Figure 15.10 Configuration of Bridges and LANs, with Alternate
Routes

whereas if the frame travels through bridge 101, it must suffer two hops. Another
consideration is that there may be changes in the configuration. For example, bridge
107 may fail, in which case subsequent frames from station 1 to station 5 should go
through bridge 101. So we can say that the routing capability must take into account
the topology of the internet configuration and may need to be dynamically altered.

A variety of routing strategies have been proposed and implemented in recent
years. The simplest and most common strategy is **fixed routing**. This strategy is suitable for small internets and for internets that are relatively stable. In addition, two
groups within the IEEE 802 committee have developed specifications for routing
strategies. The IEEE 802.1 group has issued a standard for routing based on the use
of a **spanning tree** algorithm. The token ring committee, IEEE 802.5, has issued its
own specification, referred to as **source routing**. In the remainder of this section, we
look at fixed routing and the spanning tree algorithm, which is the most commonly
used bridge routing algorithm.

For fixed routing, a route is selected for each source-destination pair of LANs
in the configuration. If alternate routes are available between two LANs, then typically the route with the least number of hops is selected. The routes are fixed, or at
least only change when there is a change in the topology of the internet.

The strategy for developing a fixed routing configuration for bridges is similar to that employed in a packet-switching network (Figure 12.3). A central routing matrix is created, to be stored perhaps at a network control center. The matrix shows, for each source-destination pair of LANs, the identity of the first bridge on the route. So, for example, the route from LAN E to LAN F begins by going through bridge 107 to LAN A. Again consulting the matrix, the route from LAN A to LAN F goes through bridge 102 to LAN C. Finally, the route from LAN C to LAN F is directly through bridge 105. Thus the complete route from LAN E to LAN F is bridge 107, LAN A, bridge 102, LAN C, bridge 105.

From this overall matrix, routing tables can be developed and stored at each bridge. Each bridge needs one table for each LAN to which it attaches. The information for each table is derived from a single row of the matrix. For example, bridge 105 has two tables, one for frames arriving from LAN C and one for frames arriving from LAN F. The table shows, for each possible destination MAC address, the identity of the LAN to which the bridge should forward the frame.

Once the directories have been established, routing is a simple matter. A bridge copies each incoming frame on each of its LANs. If the destination MAC address corresponds to an entry in its routing table, the frame is retransmitted on the appropriate LAN.

The fixed routing strategy is widely used in commercially available products. It requires that a network manager manually load the data into the routing tables. It has the advantage of simplicity and minimal processing requirements. However, in a complex internet, in which bridges may be dynamically added and in which failures must be allowed for, this strategy is too limited.

The Spanning Tree Approach

The spanning tree approach is a mechanism in which bridges automatically develop a routing table and update that table in response to changing topology. The algorithm consists of three mechanisms: frame forwarding, address learning, and loop resolution.

Frame Forwarding

In this scheme, a bridge maintains a **forwarding database** for each port attached to a LAN. The database indicates the station addresses for which frames should be forwarded through that port. We can interpret this in the following fashion. For each port, a list of stations is maintained. A station is on the list if it is on the "same side" of the bridge as the port. For example, for bridge 102 of Figure 15.10, stations on LANs C, F, and G are on the same side of the bridge as the LAN C port, and stations on LANs A, B, D, and E are on the same side of the bridge as the LAN A port. When a frame is received on any port, the bridge must decide whether that frame is to be forwarded through the bridge and out through one of the bridge's other ports. Suppose that a bridge receives a MAC frame on port x. The following rules are applied:

1. Search the forwarding database to determine if the MAC address is listed for any port except port x.

2. If the destination MAC address is not found, forward frame out all ports except the one from which is was received. This is part of the learning process described subsequently.

3. If the destination address is in the forwarding database for some port y, then determine whether port y is in a blocking or forwarding state. For reasons explained later, a port may sometimes be blocked, which prevents it from receiving or transmitting frames.

4. If port y is not blocked, transmit the frame through port y onto the LAN to which that port attaches.

Address Learning

The preceding scheme assumes that the bridge is already equipped with a forwarding database that indicates the direction, from the bridge, of each destination station. This information can be preloaded into the bridge, as in fixed routing. However, an effective automatic mechanism for learning the direction of each station is desirable. A simple scheme for acquiring this information is based on the use of the source address field in each MAC frame.

The strategy is this. When a frame arrives on a particular port, it clearly has come from the direction of the incoming LAN. The source address field of the frame indicates the source station. Thus, a bridge can update its forwarding database for that port on the basis of the source address field of each incoming frame. To allow for changes in topology, each element in the database is equipped with a timer. When a new element is added to the database, its timer is set. If the timer expires, then the element is eliminated from the database, since the corresponding direction information may no longer be valid. Each time a frame is received, its source address is checked against the database. If the element is already in the database, the entry is updated (the direction may have changed) and the timer is reset. If the element is not in the database, a new entry is created, with its own timer.

Spanning Tree Algorithm

The address learning mechanism described previously is effective if the topology of the internet is a tree; that is, if there are no alternate routes in the network. The existence of alternate routes means that there is a closed loop. For example in Figure 15.10, the following is a closed loop: LAN A, bridge 101, LAN B, bridge 104, LAN E, bridge 107, LAN A.

To see the problem created by a closed loop, consider Figure 15.11. At time t_0, station A transmits a frame addressed to station B. The frame is captured by both bridges. Each bridge updates its database to indicate that station A is in the direction of LAN X, and retransmits the frame on LAN Y. Say that bridge α retransmits at time t_1 and bridge β a short time later t_2. Thus B will receive two copies of the frame. Furthermore, each bridge will receive the other's transmission on LAN Y. Note that each transmission is a frame with a source address of A and a destination address of B. Thus each bridge will update its database to indicate that station A is in the direction of LAN Y. Neither bridge is now capable of forwarding a frame addressed to station A.

To overcome this problem, a simple result from graph theory is used: For any connected graph, consisting of nodes and edges connecting pairs of nodes, there is a

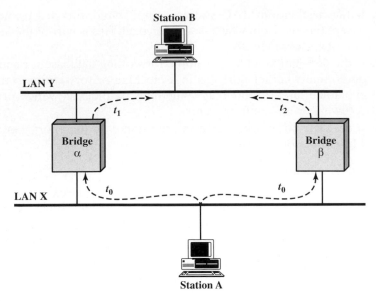

Figure 15.11   Loop of Bridges

spanning tree of edges that maintains the connectivity of the graph but contains no closed loops. In terms of internets, each LAN corresponds to a graph node, and each bridge corresponds to a graph edge. Thus, in Figure 15.10, the removal of one (and only one) of bridges 107, 101, and 104, results in a spanning tree. What is desired is to develop a simple algorithm by which the bridges of the internet can exchange sufficient information to automatically (without user intervention) derive a spanning tree. The algorithm must be dynamic. That is, when a topology change occurs, the bridges must be able to discover this fact and automatically derive a new spanning tree.

The spanning tree algorithm developed by IEEE 802.1, as the name suggests, is able to develop such a spanning tree. All that is required is that each bridge be assigned a unique identifier and that costs be assigned to each bridge port. In the absence of any special considerations, all costs could be set equal; this produces a minimum-hop tree. The algorithm involves a brief exchange of messages among all of the bridges to discover the minimum-cost spanning tree. Whenever there is a change in topology, the bridges automatically recalculate the spanning tree.

15.5 LAYER 2 AND LAYER 3 SWITCHES

In recent years, there has been a proliferation of types of devices for interconnecting LANs that goes beyond the bridges discussed in Section 15.4 and the routers discussed in Part Five. These devices can conveniently be grouped into the categories of layer 2 switches and layer 3 switches. We begin with a discussion of hubs and then explore these two concepts.

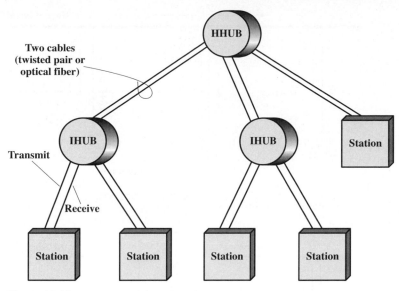

Figure 15.12 Two-Level Star Topology

Hubs

Earlier, we used the term *hub* in reference to a star-topology LAN. The hub is the active central element of the star layout. Each station is connected to the hub by two lines (transmit and receive). The hub acts as a repeater: When a single station transmits, the hub repeats the signal on the outgoing line to each station. Ordinarily, the line consists of two unshielded twisted pairs. Because of the high data rate and the poor transmission qualities of unshielded twisted pair, the length of a line is limited to about 100 m. As an alternative, an optical fiber link may be used. In this case, the maximum length is about 500 m.

Note that although this scheme is physically a star, it is logically a bus: A transmission from any one station is received by all other stations, and if two stations transmit at the same time, there will be a collision.

Multiple levels of hubs can be cascaded in a hierarchical configuration. Figure 15.12 illustrates a two-level configuration. There is one **header hub** (HHUB) and one or more **intermediate hubs** (IHUB). Each hub may have a mixture of stations and other hubs attached to it from below. This layout fits well with building wiring practices. Typically, there is a wiring closet on each floor of an office building, and a hub can be placed in each one. Each hub could service the stations on its floor.

Layer 2 Switches

In recent years, a new device, the layer 2 switch, has replaced the hub in popularity, particularly for high-speed LANs. The layer 2 switch is also sometimes referred to as a switching hub.

To clarify the distinction between hubs and switches, Figure 15.13a shows a typical bus layout of a traditional 10-Mbps LAN. A bus is installed that is laid out so that all the devices to be attached are in reasonable proximity to a point on the bus.

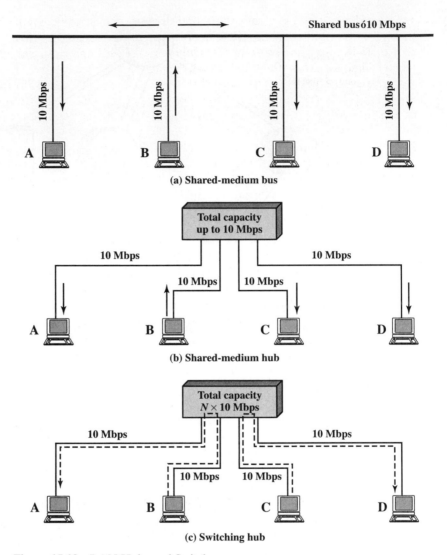

Figure 15.13   LAN Hubs and Switches

In the figure, station B is transmitting. This transmission goes from B, across the lead from B to the bus, along the bus in both directions, and along the access lines of each of the other attached stations. In this configuration, all the stations must share the total capacity of the bus, which is 10 Mbps.

A hub, often in a building wiring closet, uses a star wiring arrangement to attach stations to the hub. In this arrangement, a transmission from any one station is received by the hub and retransmitted on all of the outgoing lines. Therefore, to avoid collision, only one station can transmit at a time. Again, the total capacity of the LAN is 10 Mbps. The hub has several advantages over the simple bus arrangement. It exploits standard building wiring practices in the layout of cable. In addition, the hub can be configured to recognize a malfunctioning station that is jamming the network and to cut that station out of the network. Figure 15.13b illustrates the operation of a hub. Here again, station B is transmitting. This transmission goes from B, across the transmit line from B to the hub, and from the hub along the receive lines of each of the other attached stations.

We can achieve greater performance with a layer 2 switch. In this case, the central hub acts as a switch, much as a packet switch or circuit switch. With a layer 2 switch, an incoming frame from a particular station is switched to the appropriate output line to be delivered to the intended destination. At the same time, other unused lines can be used for switching other traffic. Figure 15.13c shows an example in which B is transmitting a frame to A and at the same time C is transmitting a frame to D. So, in this example, the current throughput on the LAN is 20 Mbps, although each individual device is limited to 10 Mbps. The layer 2 switch has several attractive features:

1. No change is required to the software or hardware of the attached devices to convert a bus LAN or a hub LAN to a switched LAN. In the case of an Ethernet LAN, each attached device continues to use the Ethernet medium access control protocol to access the LAN. From the point of view of the attached devices, nothing has changed in the access logic.
2. Each attached device has a dedicated capacity equal to that of the entire original LAN, assuming that the layer 2 switch has sufficient capacity to keep up with all attached devices. For example, in Figure 15.13c, if the layer 2 switch can sustain a throughput of 20 Mbps, each attached device appears to have a dedicated capacity for either input or output of 10 Mbps.
3. The layer 2 switch scales easily. Additional devices can be attached to the layer 2 switch by increasing the capacity of the layer 2 switch correspondingly.

Two types of layer 2 switches are available as commercial products:

- **Store-and-forward switch:** The layer 2 switch accepts a frame on an input line, buffers it briefly, and then routes it to the appropriate output line.
- **Cut-through switch:** The layer 2 switch takes advantage of the fact that the destination address appears at the beginning of the MAC (medium access control) frame. The layer 2 switch begins repeating the incoming frame onto the appropriate output line as soon as the layer 2 switch recognizes the destination address.

The cut-through switch yields the highest possible throughput but at some risk of propagating bad frames, because the switch is not able to check the CRC prior to retransmission. The store-and-forward switch involves a delay between sender and receiver but boosts the overall integrity of the network.

A layer 2 switch can be viewed as a full-duplex version of the hub. It can also incorporate logic that allows it to function as a multiport bridge. [BREY99] lists the following differences between layer 2 switches and bridges:

- Bridge frame handling is done in software. A layer 2 switch performs the address recognition and frame forwarding functions in hardware.

- A bridge can typically only analyze and forward one frame at a time, whereas a layer 2 switch has multiple parallel data paths and can handle multiple frames at a time.
- A bridge uses store-and-forward operation. With a layer 2 switch, it is possible to have cut-through instead of store-and-forward operation.

Because a layer 2 switch has higher performance and can incorporate the functions of a bridge, the bridge has suffered commercially. New installations typically include layer 2 switches with bridge functionality rather than bridges.

Layer 3 Switches

Layer 2 switches provide increased performance to meet the needs of high-volume traffic generated by personal computers, workstations, and servers. However, as the number of devices in a building or complex of buildings grows, layer 2 switches reveal some inadequacies. Two problems in particular present themselves: broadcast overload and the lack of multiple links.

A set of devices and LANs connected by layer 2 switches is considered to have a flat address space. The term *flat* means that all users share a common MAC broadcast address. Thus, if any device issues a MAC frame with a broadcast address, that frame is to be delivered to all devices attached to the overall network connected by layer 2 switches and/or bridges. In a large network, frequent transmission of broadcast frames can create tremendous overhead. Worse, a malfunctioning device can create a *broadcast storm*, in which numerous broadcast frame clog the network and crowd out legitimate traffic.

A second performance-related problem with the use of bridges and/or layer 2 switches is that the current standards for bridge protocols dictate that there be no closed loops in the network. That is, there can only be one path between any two devices. Thus, it is impossible, in a standards-based implementation, to provide multiple paths through multiple switches between devices. This restriction limits both performance and reliability.

To overcome these problems, it seems logical to break up a large local network into a number of **subnetworks** connected by routers. A MAC broadcast frame is then limited to only the devices and switches contained in a single subnetwork. Furthermore, IP-based routers employ sophisticated routing algorithms that allow the use of multiple paths between subnetworks going through different routers.

However, the problem with using routers to overcome some of the inadequacies of bridges and layer 2 switches is that routers typically do all of the IP-level processing involved in the forwarding of IP traffic in software. High-speed LANs and high-performance layer 2 switches may pump millions of packets per second, whereas a software-based router may only be able to handle well under a million packets per second. To accommodate such a load, a number of vendors have developed layer 3 switches, which implement the packet-forwarding logic of the router in hardware.

There are a number of different layer 3 schemes on the market, but fundamentally they fall into two categories: packet by packet and flow based. The packet-by-packet switch operates in the identical fashion as a traditional router. Because the forwarding logic is in hardware, the packet-by-packet switch can achieve an order of magnitude increase in performance compared to the software-based router. A flow-based switch tries to enhance performance by identifying flows of IP packets that have the same source and destination. This can be done by observing ongoing traffic or by using a special flow label in the packet header (allowed in IPv6 but not IPv4). Once a flow is identified, a predefined route can be established through the network to speed up the forwarding process. Again, huge performance increases over a pure software-based router are achieved.

Figure 15.14 is a typical example of the approach taken to local networking in an organization with a large number of PCs and workstations (thousands to tens of thousands). Desktop systems have links of 10 Mbps to 100 Mbps into a LAN controlled by a layer 2 switch. Wireless LAN connectivity is also likely to be available for mobile users. Layer 3 switches are at the local network's core, forming a local backbone. Typically, these switches are interconnected at 1 Gbps and connect to

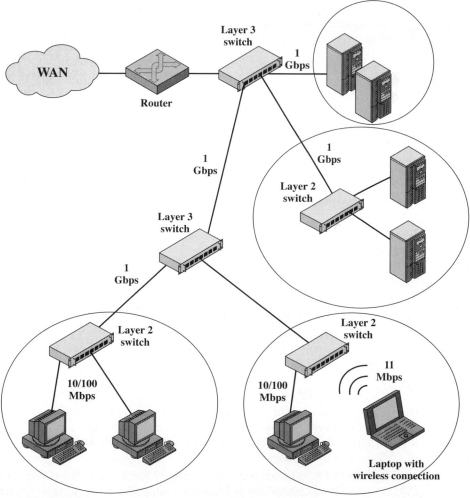

Figure 15.14   Typical Premises Network Configuration

layer 2 switches at from 100 Mbps to 1 Gbps. Servers connect directly to layer 2 or layer 3 switches at 1 Gbps or possibly 100 Mbps. A lower-cost software-based router provides WAN connection. The circles in the figure identify separate LAN subnetworks; a MAC broadcast frame is limited to its own subnetwork.

15.6 RECOMMENDED READING AND WEB SITE

The material in this chapter is covered in much more depth in [STAL00]. [METZ99] is an excellent treatment of layer 2 and layer 3 switches, with a detailed discussion of products and case studies. Another comprehensive account is [SEIF00].

METZ99   Metzler, J., and DeNoia, L. *Layer 2 Switching*. Upper Saddle River, NJ: Prentice Hall, 1999.

SEIF00   Seifert, R. *The Switch Book*. New York: Wiley, 2000.

STAL00   Stallings, W. *Local and Metropolitan Area Networks, 6th ed.* Upper Saddle River, NJ: Prentice Hall, 2000.

Recommended Web Site:

- **IEEE 802 LAN/MAN Standards Committee:** Status and documents for all of the working groups

15.7 KEY TERMS, REVIEW QUESTIONS, AND PROBLEMS

Key Terms

bridge	local area network (LAN)	star topology
bus topology	logical link control	tree topology
hub	medium access control (MAC)	switch
layer 2 switch	ring topology	storage area networks (SAN)
layer 3 switch	spanning tree	

Review Questions

15.1   How do the key requirements for computer room networks differ from those for personal computer local networks?

15.2   What are the differences among backend LANs, SANs, and backbone LANs?

15.3   What is network topology?

15.4   List four common LAN topologies and briefly describe their methods of operation.

15.5   What is the purpose of the IEEE 802 committee?

15.6   Why are there multiple LAN standards?

15.7   List and briefly define the services provided by LLC.

15.8   List and briefly define the types of operation provided by the LLC protocol.

15.9   List some basic functions performed at the MAC layer.

15.10 What functions are performed by a bridge?

15.11 What is a spanning tree?

15.12 What is the difference between a hub and a layer 2 switch?

15.13 What is the difference between a store-and forward switch and a cut-through switch?

Problems

15.1   Instead of LLC, could HDLC be used as a data link control protocol for a LAN? If not, what is lacking?

15.2   An asynchronous device, such as a teletype, transmits characters one at a time with unpredictable delays between characters. What problems, if any, do you foresee if such a device is connected to a LAN and allowed to transmit at will (subject to gaining access to the medium)? How might such problems be resolved?

15.3   Consider the transfer of a file containing one million 8-bit characters from one station to another. What is the total elapsed time and effective throughput for the following cases:

   a. A circuit-switched, star-topology local network. Call setup time is negligible and the data rate on the medium is 64 kbps.

   b. A bus topology local network with two stations a distance D apart, a data rate of B bps, and a frame size of P with 80 bits of overhead per frame. Each frame is acknowledged with an 88-bit frame before the next is sent. The propagation speed on the bus is 200 m/µs. Solve for

   (1) $D = 1$ km, $B = 1$ Mbps, $P = 256$ bits
   (2) $D = 1$ km, $B = 10$ Mbps, $P = 256$ bits
   (3) $D = 10$ km, $B = 1$ Mbps, $P = 256$ bits
   (4) $D = 1$ km, $B = 50$ Mbps, $P = 10,000$ bits

   c. A ring topology local network with a total circular length of $2D$, with the two stations a distance D apart. Acknowledgment is achieved by allowing a frame to circulate past the destination station, back to the source station, with an acknowledgment bit set by the destination. There are N repeaters on the ring, each of which introduces a delay of one bit time. Repeat the calculation for each of b1 through b4 for $N = 10; 100; 1000$.

15.4   Consider a baseband bus with a number of equally spaced stations with a data rate of 10 Mbps and a bus length of 1 km.

   a. What is the mean time to send a frame of 1000 bits to another station, measured from the beginning of transmission to the end of reception? Assume a propagation speed of 200 m/µs.

   b. If two stations begin to transmit at exactly the same time, their packets will interfere with each other. If each transmitting station monitors the bus during transmission, how long before it notices an interference, in second? In bit times?

15.5   Repeat Problem 15.4 for a data rate of 100 Mbps.

15.6   At a propagation speed of 200 m/µs, what is the effective length added to a ring by a bit delay at each repeater?

   a. At 1 Mbps

   b. At 40 Mbps

15.7   A tree topology is to be provided that spans two buildings. If permission can be obtained to string cable between the two buildings, one continuous tree layout will be used. Otherwise, each building will have an independent tree topology network and a point-to-point link will connect a special communications station on one network with a communications station on the other network. What functions must the communications stations perform? Repeat for ring and star.

15.8 System A consists of a single ring with 300 stations, one per repeater. System B consists of three 100-station rings linked by a bridge. If the probability of a link failure is P_1, a repeater failure is P_r, and a bridge failure is P_b, derive an expression for parts (a) through (d):

    a. Probability of failure of system A

    b. Probability of complete failure of system B

    c. Probability that a particular station will find the network unavailable, for systems A and B

    d. Probability that any two stations, selected at random, will be unable to communicate, for systems A and B

    e. Compute values for parts (a) through (d) for $P_1 = P_b = P_r = 10^{-2}$

15.9 Draw figures similar to Figure 15.9 for a configuration in which

    a. Two LANs are connected via two bridges that are connected by a point-to-point link.

    b. Two LANs are connected via two bridges that are connected by an X.25 packet-switching network.

15.10 For the configuration of Figure 15.10, show the central routing matrix and the routing tables at each bridge.

CHAPTER 16

HIGH-SPEED LANS

KEY POINTS

- The IEEE 802.3 standard, known as Ethernet, now encompasses data rates of 10 Mbps, 100 Mbps, 1 Gbps, and 10 Gbps. For the lower data rates, the CSMA/CD MAC protocol is used. For the 1 Gbps and 10 Gbps options, a switched technique is used.
- The IEEE 802.5 token ring standard offers data rates from 4 Mbps to 1 Gbps.
- Fibre Channel is a switched network of nodes designed to provide high-speed linkages for such applications as storage area networks.

Recent years have seen rapid changes in the technology, design, and commercial applications for local area networks (LANs). A major feature of this evolution is the introduction of a variety of new schemes for high-speed local networking. To keep pace with the changing local networking needs of business, a number of approaches to high speed LAN design have become commercial products. The most important of these are as follows:

- **Fast Ethernet and Gigabit Ethernet:** The extension of 10-Mbps CSMA/CD (carrier sense multiple access with collision detection) to higher speeds is a logical strategy, because it tends to preserve the investment in existing systems.
- **Fibre Channel:** This standard provides a low-cost, easily scalable approach to achieving very high data rates in local areas.
- **High-speed wireless LANs:** Wireless LAN technology and standards have at last come of age, and high-speed standards and products are being introduced.

Table 16.1 lists some of the characteristics of these approaches. The remainder of this chapter fills in some of the details on Ethernet and Fibre Channel and also looks at token ring. Chapter 17 covers wireless LANs.

16.1 THE EMERGENCE OF HIGH-SPEED LANS

Personal computers and microcomputer workstations began to achieve widespread acceptance in business computing in the early 1980s and have now achieved virtually the status of the telephone: an essential tool for office workers.

Table 16.1 Characteristics of Some High-Speed LANs

	Fast Ethernet	Gigabit Ethernet	Fibre Channel	Wireless LAN
Data rate	100 Mbps	1 Gbps, 10 Gbps	100 Mbps–3.2 Gbps	1 Mbps–54 Mbps
Transmission media	UTP, STP, optical fiber	UTP, shielded cable, optical fiber	Optical fiber, coaxial cable, STP	2.4-GHz, 5-GHz microwave
Access method	CSMA/CD	Switched	Switched	CSMA/Polling
Supporting standard	IEEE 802.3	IEEE 802.3	Fibre Channel Association	IEEE 802.11

Until relatively recently, office LANs provided basic connectivity services— connecting personal computers and terminals to mainframes and midrange systems that ran corporate applications, and providing workgroup connectivity at the departmental or divisional level. In both cases, traffic patterns were relatively light, with an emphasis on file transfer and electronic mail. The LANs that were available for this type of workload, primarily Ethernet and token ring, are well suited to this environment.

In recent years, two significant trends have altered the role of the personal computer and therefore the requirements on the LAN:

- The speed and computing power of personal computers has continued to enjoy explosive growth. Today's more powerful platforms support graphics-intensive applications and ever more elaborate graphical user interfaces to the operating system.

- MIS organizations have recognized the LAN as a viable and indeed essential computing platform, resulting in the focus on network computing. This trend began with client/server computing, which has become a dominant architecture in the business environment and the more recent intranetwork trend. Both of these approaches involve the frequent transfer of potentially large volumes of data in a transaction-oriented environment.

The effect of these trends has been to increase the volume of data to be handled over LANs and, because applications are more interactive, to reduce the acceptable delay on data transfers. The earlier generation of 10-Mbps Ethernets and 16-Mbps token rings are simply not up to the job of supporting these requirements.

The following are examples of requirements that call for higher-speed LANs:

- **Centralized server farms:** In many applications, there is a need for user, or client, systems to be able to draw huge amounts of data from multiple centralized servers, called server farms. An example is a color publishing operation, in which servers typically contain tens of gigabytes of image data that must be downloaded to imaging workstations. As the performance of the servers themselves has increased, the bottleneck has shifted to the network. Switched Ethernet alone would not solve this problem because of the limit of 10 Mbps on a single link to the client.

- **Power workgroups:** These groups typically consist of a small number of cooperating users who need to draw massive data files across the network. Examples are a software development group that runs tests on a new software version, or a computer-aided design (CAD) company that regularly runs simulations of new designs. In such cases, large amounts of data are distributed to several workstations, processed, and updated at very high speed for multiple iterations.

- **High-speed local backbone:** As processing demand grows, LANs proliferate at a site, and high-speed interconnection is necessary.

16.2 ETHERNET

The most widely used high-speed LANs today are based on Ethernet and were developed by the IEEE 802.3 standards committee. As with other LAN standards, there is both a medium access control layer and a physical layer, which are considered in turn in what follows.

IEEE 802.3 Medium Access Control

It is easier to understand the operation of CSMA/CD if we look first at some earlier schemes from which CSMA/CD evolved.

Precursors

CSMA/CD and its precursors can be termed random access, or contention, techniques. They are random access in the sense that there is no predictable or scheduled time for any station to transmit; station transmissions are ordered randomly. They exhibit contention in the sense that stations contend for time on the shared medium.

The earliest of these techniques, known as ALOHA, was developed for packet radio networks. However, it is applicable to any shared transmission medium. ALOHA, or pure ALOHA as it is sometimes called, specifies that a station may transmit a frame at any time. The station then listens for an amount of time equal to the maximum possible round-trip propagation delay on the network (twice the time it takes to send a frame between the two most widely separated stations) plus a small fixed time increment. If the station hears an acknowledgment during that time, fine; otherwise, it resends the frame. If the station fails to receive an acknowledgment after repeated transmissions, it gives up. A receiving station determines the correctness of an incoming frame by examining a frame check sequence field, as in HDLC. If the frame is valid and if the destination address in the frame header matches the receiver's address, the station immediately sends an acknowledgment. The frame may be invalid due to noise on the channel or because another station transmitted a frame at about the same time. In the latter case, the two frames may interfere with each other at the receiver so that neither gets through; this is known as a **collision**. If a received frame is determined to be invalid, the receiving station simply ignores the frame.

ALOHA is as simple as can be, and pays a penalty for it. Because the number of collisions rises rapidly with increased load, the maximum utilization of the channel is only about 18%.

To improve efficiency, a modification of ALOHA, known as slotted ALOHA, was developed. In this scheme, time on the channel is organized into uniform slots whose size equals the frame transmission time. Some central clock or other technique is needed to synchronize all stations. Transmission is permitted to begin only at a slot boundary. Thus, frames that do overlap will do so totally. This increases the maximum utilization of the system to about 37%.

Both ALOHA and slotted ALOHA exhibit poor utilization. Both fail to take advantage of one of the key properties of both packet radio networks and LANs, which is that propagation delay between stations may be very small compared to frame transmission time. Consider the following observations. If the station-to-station propagation time is large compared to the frame transmission time, then, after a station launches a frame, it will be a long time before other stations know about it. During that time, one of the other stations may transmit a frame; the two frames may interfere with each other and neither gets through. Indeed, if the distances are great enough, many stations may begin transmitting, one after the other, and none of their frames get through unscathed. Suppose, however, that the propagation time is small compared to frame transmission time. In that case, when a station launches a frame, all the other stations know it almost immediately. So, if they had any sense, they would not try transmitting until the first station was done. Collisions would be rare because they would occur only when two stations began to transmit almost simultaneously. Another way to look at it is that a short propagation delay provides the stations with better feedback about the state of the network; this information can be used to improve efficiency.

The foregoing observations led to the development of carrier sense multiple access (CSMA). With CSMA, a station wishing to transmit first listens to the medium to determine if another transmission is in progress (carrier sense). If the medium is in use, the station must wait. If the medium is idle, the station may transmit. It may happen that two or more stations attempt to transmit at about the same time. If this happens, there will be a collision; the data from both transmissions will be garbled and not received successfully. To account for this, a station waits a reasonable amount of time after transmitting for an acknowledgment, taking into account the maximum round-trip propagation delay and the fact that the acknowledging station must also contend for the channel to respond. If there is no acknowledgment, the station assumes that a collision has occurred and retransmits.

One can see how this strategy would be effective for networks in which the average frame transmission time is much longer than the propagation time. Collisions can occur only when more than one user begins transmitting with a short time (the period of the propagation delay). If a station begins to transmit a frame and there are no collisions during the time it takes for the leading edge of the packet to propagate to the farthest station, then there will be no collision for this frame because all other stations are now aware of the transmission.

The maximum utilization achievable using CSMA can far exceed that of ALOHA or slotted ALOHA. The maximum utilization depends on the length of the frame and on the propagation time; the longer the frames or the shorter the propagation time, the higher the utilization.

With CSMA, an algorithm is needed to specify what a station should do if the medium is found busy. Three approaches are depicted in Figure 16.1. One algorithm is **nonpersistent CSMA**. A station wishing to transmit listens to the medium and obeys the following rules:

1. If the medium is idle, transmit; otherwise, go to step 2.
2. If the medium is busy, wait an amount of time drawn from a probability distribution (the retransmission delay) and repeat step 1.

The use of random delays reduces the probability of collisions. To see this, consider that two stations become ready to transmit at about the same time while another transmission is in progress; if both stations delay the same amount of time

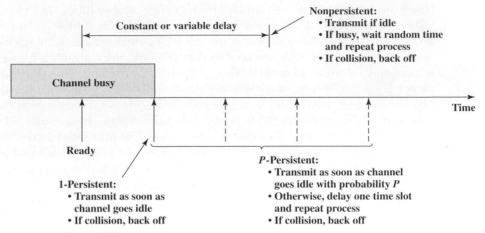

Figure 16.1 CSMA Persistence and Backoff

before trying again, they will both attempt to transmit at about the same time. A problem with nonpersistent CSMA is that capacity is wasted because the medium will generally remain idle following the end of a transmission even if there are one or more stations waiting to transmit.

To avoid idle channel time, the **1-persistent protocol** can be used. A station wishing to transmit listens to the medium and obeys the following rules:

1. If the medium is idle, transmit; otherwise, go to step 2.
2. If the medium is busy, continue to listen until the channel is sensed idle; then transmit immediately.

Whereas nonpersistent stations are deferential, 1-persistent stations are selfish. If two or more stations are waiting to transmit, a collision is guaranteed. Things get sorted out only after the collision.

A compromise that attempts to reduce collisions, like nonpersistent, and reduce idle time, like 1-persistent, is ***p*-persistent**. The rules are as follows:

1. If the medium is idle, transmit with probability p, and delay one time unit with probability $(1 - p)$. The time unit is typically equal to the maximum propagation delay.
2. If the medium is busy, continue to listen until the channel is idle and repeat step 1.
3. If transmission is delayed one time unit, repeat step 1.

The question arises as to what is an effective value of p. The main problem to avoid is one of instability under heavy load. Consider the case in which n stations have frames to send while a transmission is taking place. At the end of the transmission, the expected number of stations that will attempt to transmit is equal to the number of stations ready to transmit times the probability of transmitting, or np. If np is greater than 1, on average multiple stations will attempt to transmit and there will be a collision. What is more, as soon as all these stations realize that their transmission suffered a collision, they will be back again, almost guaranteeing more collisions. Worse yet, these retries will compete with new transmissions from other stations, further increasing the probability of collision. Eventually, all stations will be trying to send, causing continuous collisions, with throughput dropping to zero. To avoid this catastrophe, np must be less than one for the expected peaks of n; therefore, if a heavy load is expected to occur with some regularity, p must be small. However, as p is made smaller, stations must wait longer to attempt transmission. At low loads, this can result in very long delays. For example, if only a single station desires to transmit, the expected number of iterations of step 1 is $1/p$ (see Problem 16.2). Thus, if $p = 0.1$, at low load, a station will wait an average of 9 time units before transmitting on an idle line.

Description of CSMA/CD

CSMA, although more efficient than ALOHA or slotted ALOHA, still has one glaring inefficiency. When two frames collide, the medium remains unusable for the duration of transmission of both damaged frames. For long frames, compared to propagation time, the amount of wasted capacity can be considerable. This waste can be reduced if a station continues to listen to the medium while transmitting. This leads to the following rules for CSMA/CD:

1. If the medium is idle, transmit; otherwise, go to step 2.
2. If the medium is busy, continue to listen until the channel is idle, then transmit immediately.
3. If a collision is detected during transmission, transmit a brief jamming signal to assure that all stations know that there has been a collision and then cease transmission.
4. After transmitting the jamming signal, wait a random amount of time, referred to as the **backoff**, then attempt to transmit again (repeat from step 1).

Figure 16.2 illustrates the technique for a baseband bus. At time t_0, station A begins transmitting a packet addressed to D. At t_1, both B and C are ready to transmit. B senses a transmission and so defers. C, however, is still unaware of A's transmission (because the leading edge of A's transmission has not yet arrived at C) and begins its own transmission. When A's transmission reaches C, at t_2, C detects the collision and ceases transmission. The effect of the collision propagates back to A, where it is detected some time later, t_3, at which time A ceases transmission.

With CSMA/CD, the amount of wasted capacity is reduced to the time it takes to detect a collision. Question: how long does that take? Let us consider the case of a baseband bus and consider two stations as far apart as possible. For example, in Figure 16.2, suppose that station A begins a transmission and that just before that transmission reaches D, D is ready to transmit. Because D is not yet aware of A's transmission, it begins to transmit. A collision occurs almost immediately and is recognized by D. However, the collision must propagate all the way back to A before A is aware of the collision. By this line of reasoning, we conclude that the amount of time that it takes to detect a collision is no greater than twice the end-to-end propagation delay.

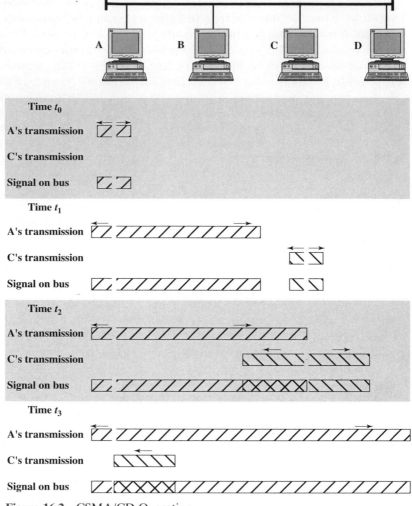

Figure 16.2 CSMA/CD Operation

An important rule followed in most CSMA/CD systems, including the IEEE standard, is that frames should be long enough to allow collision detection prior to the end of transmission. If shorter frames are used, then collision detection does not occur, and CSMA/CD exhibits the same performance as the less efficient CSMA protocol.

For a CSMA/CD LAN, the question arises as to which persistence algorithm to use. You may be surprised to learn that the algorithm used in the IEEE 802.3 standard is 1-persistent. Recall that both nonpersistent and p-persistent have performance problems. In the nonpersistent case, capacity is wasted because the medium will generally remain idle following the end of a transmission even if there are stations waiting to send. In the p-persistent case, p must be set low enough to avoid instability, with the result of sometimes atrocious delays under light load. The 1-persistent algorithm, which means, after all, that $p = 1$, would seem to be even more unstable than *p*-persistent due to the greed of the stations. What saves the day is that the wasted time due to collisions is mercifully short (if the frames are long relative to propagation delay), and with random backoff, the two stations involved in a collision are unlikely to collide on their next tries. To ensure that backoff maintains stability, IEEE 802.3 and Ethernet use a technique known as **binary exponential backoff**. A station will attempt to transmit repeatedly in the face of repeated collisions. For the first 10 retransmission attempts, the mean value of the random delay is doubled. This mean value then remains the same for 6 additional attempts. After 16 unsuccessful attempts, the station gives up and reports an error. Thus, as congestion increases, stations back off by larger and larger amounts to reduce the probability of collision.

The beauty of the 1-persistent algorithm with binary exponential backoff is that it is efficient over a wide range of loads. At low loads, 1-persistence guarantees that a station can seize the channel as soon as it goes idle, in contrast to the non- and *p*-persistent schemes. At high loads, it is at least as stable as the other techniques. However, one unfortunate effect of the backoff algorithm is that it has a last-in, first-out effect; stations with no or few collisions will have a chance to transmit before stations that have waited longer.

For baseband bus, a collision should produce substantially higher voltage swings than those produced by a single transmitter. Accordingly, the IEEE standard dictates that the transmitter will detect a collision if the signal on the cable at the transmitter tap point exceeds the maximum that could be produced by the transmitter alone. Because a transmitted signal attenuates as it propagates, there is a potential problem: If two stations far apart are transmitting, each station will receive a greatly attenuated signal from the other. The signal strength could be so small that when it is added to the transmitted signal at the transmitter tap point, the combined signal does not exceed the CD threshold. For this reason, among others, the IEEE standard restricts the maximum length of coaxial cable to 500 m for 10BASE5 and 200 m for 10BASE2.

A much simpler collision detection scheme is possible with the twisted-pair star-topology approach (Figure 15.12). In this case, collision detection is based on logic rather than sensing voltage magnitudes. For any hub, if there is activity (signal) on more than one input, a collision is assumed. A special signal called the collision presence signal is generated. This signal is generated and sent out as long as activity is sensed on any of the input lines. This signal is interpreted by every node as an occurrence of a collision.

MAC Frame

Figure 16.3 depicts the frame format for the 802.3 protocol. It consists of the following fields:

- **Preamble:** A 7-octet pattern of alternating 0s and 1s used by the receiver to establish bit synchronization.
- **Start Frame Delimiter (SFD):** The sequence 10101011, which indicates the actual start of the frame and enables the receiver to locate the first bit of the rest of the frame.

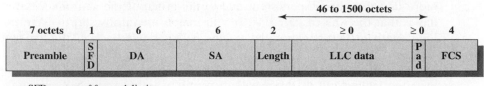

SFD = start of frame delimiter
DA = destination address
SA = source address
FCS = frame check sequence

Figure 16.3 IEEE 802.3 Frame Format

- **Destination Address (DA):** Specifies the station(s) for which the frame is intended. It may be a unique physical address, a group address, or a global address.
- **Source Address (SA):** Specifies the station that sent the frame.
- **Length/Type:** Length of LLC data field in octets, or Ethernet Type field, depending on whether the frame conforms to the IEEE 802.3 standard or the earlier Ethernet specification. In either case, the maximum frame size, excluding the Preamble and SFD, is 1518 octets.
- **LLC Data:** Data unit supplied by LLC.
- **Pad:** Octets added to ensure that the frame is long enough for proper CD operation.
- **Frame Check Sequence (FCS):** A 32-bit cyclic redundancy check, based on all fields except preamble, SFD, and FCS.

IEEE 802.3 10–Mbps Specifications (Ethernet)

The IEEE 802.3 committee has been the most active in defining alternative physical configurations. This is both good and bad. On the good side, the standard has been responsive to evolving technology. On the bad side, the customer, not to mention the potential vendor, is faced with a bewildering array of options. However, the committee has been at pains to ensure that the various options can be easily integrated into a configuration that satisfies a variety of needs. Thus, the user that has a complex set of requirements may find the flexibility and variety of the 802.3 standard to be an asset.

To distinguish the various implementations that are available, the committee has developed a concise notation:

⟨data rate in Mbps⟩⟨signaling method⟩⟨maximum segment length in hundreds of meters⟩

The defined alternatives are as follows:[1]

---

[1] There is also a 1BASE-T alternative that defines a 1-Mbps twisted-pair system using a star topology; this is considered obsolete. There is also a 10BROAD36 option, specifying a 1-Mbps broadband bus; this option is rarely used.

- **10BASE5:** Specifies the use of 50-ohm coaxial cable and Manchester digital signaling.[2] The maximum length of a cable segment is set at 500 meters. The length of the network can be extended by the use of repeaters. A repeater is transparent to the MAC level; as it does no buffering, it does not isolate one segment from another. So, for example, if two stations on different segments attempt to transmit at the same time, their transmissions will collide. To avoid looping, only one path of segments and repeaters is allowed between any two stations. The standard allows a maximum of four repeaters in the path between any two stations, extending the effective length of the medium to 2.5 kilometers.

- **10BASE2:** Similar to 10BASE5, but uses a thinner cable, which supports fewer taps over a shorter distance than the 10BASE5 cable. This is a lower-cost alternative to 10BASE5.

- **10BASE-T:** Uses unshielded twisted pair in a star-shaped topology. Because of the high data rate and the poor transmission qualities of unshielded twisted pair, the length of a link is limited to 100 meters. As an alternative, an optical fiber link may be used. In this case, the maximum length is 500 m.

- **10BASE-F:** Contains three specifications: a passive-star topology for interconnecting stations and repeaters with up to 1 km per segment; a point-to-point link that can be used to connect stations or repeaters at up to 2 km; a point-to-point link that can be used to connect repeaters at up to 2 km.

Note that 10BASE-T and 10-BASE-F do not quite follow the notation: "T" stands for twisted pair and "F" stands for optical fiber. Table 16.2 summarizes the remaining options. All of the alternatives listed in the table specify a data rate of 10 Mbps. In addition to these alternatives, there are versions that operate at 100 Mbps, 1 Gbps and 10 Gbps; these are covered later in this section.

Table 16.2 IEEE 802.3 10-Mbps Physical Layer Medium Alternatives

	10BASE5	10BASE2	10BASE-T	10BASE-FP
Transmission medium	Coaxial cable (50 ohm)	Coaxial cable (50 ohm)	Unshielded twisted pair	850-nm optical fiber pair
Signaling technique	Baseband (Manchester)	Baseband (Manchester)	Baseband (Manchester)	Manchester/on-off
Topology	Bus	Bus	Star	Star
Maximum segment length (m)	500	185	100	500
Nodes per segment	100	30	—	33
Cable diameter (mm)	10	5	0.4 to 0.6	62.5/125 μm

---

[2] See Section 5.1.

IEEE 802.3 100–Mbps Specifications (Fast Ethernet)

Fast Ethernet refers to a set of specifications developed by the IEEE 802.3 committee to provide a low-cost, Ethernet-compatible LAN operating at 100 Mbps. The blanket designation for these standards is 100BASE-T. The committee defined a number of alternatives to be used with different transmission media.

Figure 16.4 shows the terminology used in labeling the specifications and indicates the media used. All of the 100BASE-T options use the IEEE 802.3 MAC protocol and frame format. 100BASE-X refers to a set of options that use the physical medium specifications originally defined for Fiber Distributed Data Interface (FDDI; covered in the next section). All of the 100BASE-X schemes use two physical links between nodes; one for transmission and one for reception. 100BASE-TX makes use of shielded twisted pair (STP) or high-quality (Category 5) unshielded twisted pair (UTP). 100BASE-FX uses optical fiber.

In many buildings, any of the 100BASE-X options requires the installation of new cable. For such cases, 100BASE-T4 defines a lower-cost alternative that can use Category 3, voice-grade UTP in addition to the higher-quality Category 5 UTP.[3] To achieve the 100-Mbps data rate over lower-quality cable, 100BASE-T4 dictates the use of four twisted-pair lines between nodes, with the data transmission making use of three pairs in one direction at a time.

For all of the 100BASE-T options, the topology is similar to that of 10BASE-T, namely a star-wire topology.

Table 16.3 summarizes key characteristics of the 100BASE-T options.

100BASE-X

For all of the transmission media specified under 100BASE-X, a unidirectional data rate of 100 Mbps is achieved transmitting over a single link (single twisted pair, single optical fiber). For all of these media, an efficient and effective signal

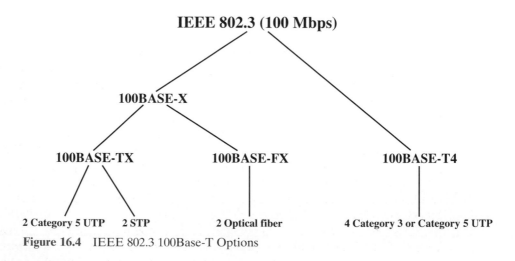

Figure 16.4 IEEE 802.3 100Base-T Options

---

[3] See Chapter 4 for a discussion of Category 3 and Category 5 cable.

Table 16.3 IEEE 802.3 100BASE-T Physical Layer Medium Alternatives

	100BASE-TX	100BASE-FX	100BASE-T4
Transmission medium	2 pair, STP	2 pair, Category 5 UTP	2 optical fibers	4 pair, Category 3, 4, or 5 UTP
Signaling technique	MLT-3	MLT-3	4B5B, NRZI	8B6T, NRZ
Data rate	100 Mbps	100 Mbps	100 Mbps	100 Mbps
Maximum segment length	100 m	100 m	100 m	100 m
Network span	200 m	200 m	400 m	200 m

encoding scheme is required. The one chosen was originally defined for FDDI and can be referred to as 4B/5B-NRZI. This scheme is further modified for each option. See Appendix 16A for a description.

The 100BASE-X designation includes two physical medium specifications, one for twisted pair, known as 100BASE-TX, and one for optical fiber, known as 100-BASE-FX.

100BASE-TX makes use of two pairs of twisted-pair cable, one pair used for transmission and one for reception. Both STP and Category 5 UTP are allowed. The MTL-3 signaling scheme is used (described in Appendix 16A).

100BASE-FX makes use of two optical fiber cables, one for transmission and one for reception. With 100BASE-FX, a means is needed to convert the 4B/5B-NRZI code group stream into optical signals. The technique used is known as intensity modulation. A binary 1 is represented by a burst or pulse of light; a binary 0 is represented by either the absence of a light pulse or a light pulse at very low intensity.

100BASE-T4

100BASE-T4 is designed to produce a 100-Mbps data rate over lower-quality Category 3 cable, thus taking advantage of the large installed base of Category 3 cable in office buildings. The specification also indicates that the use of Category 5 cable is optional. 100BASE-T4 does not transmit a continuous signal between packets, which makes it useful in battery-powered applications.

For 100BASE-T4 using voice-grade Category 3 cable, it is not reasonable to expect to achieve 100 Mbps on a single twisted pair. Instead, 100BASE-T4 specifies that the data stream to be transmitted is split up into three separate data streams, each with an effective data rate of $33\frac{1}{3}$ Mbps. Four twisted pairs are used. Data are transmitted using three pairs and received using three pairs. Thus, two of the pairs must be configured for bidirectional transmission.

As with 100BASE-X, a simple NRZ encoding scheme is not used for 100BASE-T4. This would require a signaling rate of 33 Mbps on each twisted pair and does not provide synchronization. Instead, a ternary signaling scheme known as 8B6T is used (described in Appendix 16A).

Full-Duplex Operation

A traditional Ethernet is half duplex: A station can either transmit or receive a frame, but it cannot do both simultaneously. With full-duplex operation, a station can transmit and receive simultaneously. If a 100-Mbps Ethernet ran in full-duplex mode, the theoretical transfer rate becomes 200 Mbps.

Several changes are needed to operate in full-duplex mode. The attached stations must have full-duplex rather than half-duplex adapter cards. The central point in the star wire cannot be a simple multiport repeater but rather must be a switching hub. In this case each station constitutes a separate collision domain. In fact, there are no collisions and the CSMA/CD algorithm is no longer needed. However, the same 802.3 MAC frame format is used and the attached stations can continue to execute the CSMA/CD algorithm, even though no collisions can ever be detected.

Mixed Configuration

One of the strengths of the Fast Ethernet approach is that it readily supports a mixture of existing 10-Mbps LANs and newer 100-Mbps LANs. For example, the 100-Mbps technology can be used as a backbone LAN to support a number of 10-Mbps hubs. Many of the stations attach to 10-Mbps hubs using the 10BASE-T standard. These hubs are in turn connected to switching hubs that conform to 100BASE-T and that can support both 10-Mbps and 100-Mbps links. Additional high-capacity workstations and servers attach directly to these 10/100 switches. These mixed-capacity switches are in turn connected to 100-Mbps hubs using 100-Mbps links. The 100-Mbps hubs provide a building backbone and are also connected to a router that provides connection to an outside WAN.

Gigabit Ethernet

In late 1995, the IEEE 802.3 committee formed a High-Speed Study Group to investigate means for conveying packets in Ethernet format at speeds in the gigabits per second range. A set of 1000-Mbps standards have now been issued.

The strategy for Gigabit Ethernet is the same as that for Fast Ethernet. While defining a new medium and transmission specification, Gigabit Ethernet retains the CSMA/CD protocol and Ethernet format of its 10-Mbps and 100-Mbps predecessors. It is compatible with 100BASE-T and 10BASE-T, preserving a smooth migration path. As more organizations move to 100BASE-T, putting huge traffic loads on backbone networks, demand for Gigabit Ethernet has intensified.

Figure 16.5 shows a typical application of Gigabit Ethernet. A 1-Gbps switching hub provides backbone connectivity for central servers and high-speed workgroup hubs. Each workgroup hub supports both 1-Gbps links, to connect to the backbone hub and to support high-performance workgroup servers, and 100-Mbps links, to support high-performance workstations, servers, and 100-Mbps hubs.

Media Access Layer

The 1000-Mbps specification calls for the same CSMA/CD frame format and MAC protocol as used in the 10-Mbps and 100-Mbps version of IEEE 802.3. For

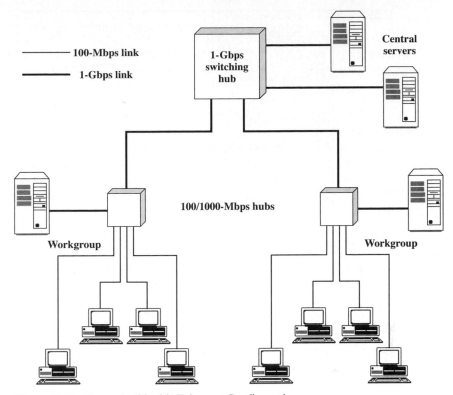

Figure 16.5   Example Gigabit Ethernet Configuration

shared-medium hub operation (Figure 15.13b), there are two enhancements to the basic CSMA/CD scheme:

- **Carrier extension:** Carrier extension appends a set of special symbols to the end of short MAC frames so that the resulting block is at least 4096 bit-times in duration, up from the minimum 512 bit-times imposed at 10 and 100 Mbps. This is so that the frame length of a transmission is longer than the propagation time at 1 Gbps.
- **Frame bursting:** This feature allows for multiple short frames to be transmitted consecutively, up to a limit, without relinquishing control for CSMA/CD between frames. Frame bursting avoids the overhead of carrier extension when a single station has a number of small frames ready to send.

With a switching hub (Figure 15.13c), which provides dedicated access to the medium, the carrier extension and frame bursting features are not needed. This is because data transmission and reception at a station can occur simultaneously without interference and with no contention for a shared medium.

Physical Layer

The current 1-Gbps specification for IEEE 802.3 includes the following physical layer alternatives (Figure 16.6):

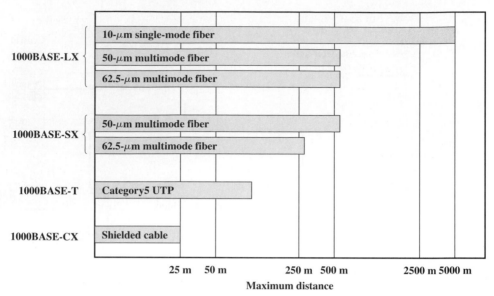

Figure 16.6 Gigabit Ethernet Medium Options (Log Scale)

- **1000BASE-SX:** This short-wavelength option supports duplex links of up to 275 m using 62.5-μm multimode or up to 550 m using 50-μm multimode fiber. Wavelengths are in the range of 770 to 860 nm.
- **1000BASE-LX:** This long-wavelength option supports duplex links of up to 550 m of 62.5-μm or 50-μm multimode fiber or 5 km of 10-μm single-mode fiber. Wavelengths are in the range of 1270 to 1355 nm.
- **1000BASE-CX:** This option supports 1-Gbps links among devices located within a single room or equipment rack, using copper jumpers (specialized shielded twisted-pair cable that spans no more than 25 m). Each link is composed of a separate shielded twisted pair running in each direction.
- **1000BASE-T:** This option makes use of four pairs of Category 5 unshielded twisted pair to support devices over a range of up to 100 m.

The signal encoding scheme used for the first three Gigabit Ethernet options just listed is 8B/10B, which is described in Appendix 16A. The signal encoding scheme used for 1000BASE-T is 4D-PAM5, a relatively complicated scheme whose description is beyond our scope.

10–Gbps Ethernet

With gigabit products still fairly new, attention has turned in the past several years to a 10-Gbps Ethernet capability. The principle driving requirement for 10 Gigabit Ethernet is the increase in Internet and intranet traffic. A number of factors contribute to the explosive growth in both Internet and intranet traffic:

- An increase in the number of network connections

- An increase in the connection speed of each end-station (e.g., 10 Mpbs users moving to 100 Mpbs, analog 56-kbps users moving to DSL and cable modems)
- An increase in the deployment of bandwidth-intensive applications such as high-quality video
- An increase in Web hosting and application hosting traffic

Initially network managers will use 10-Gbps Ethernet to provide high-speed, local backbone interconnection between large-capacity switches. As the demand for bandwidth increases, 10-Gbps Ethernet will be deployed throughout the entire network and will include server farm, backbone, and campuswide connectivity. This technology enables Internet service providers (ISPs) and network service providers (NSPs) to create very high-speed links at a very low cost, between co-located, carrier-class switches and routers.

The technology also allows the construction of metropolitan area networks (MANs) and WANs that connect geographically dispersed LANs between campuses or points of presence (PoPs). Thus, Ethernet begins to compete with ATM and other wide area transmission and networking technologies. In most cases where the customer requirement is data and TCP/IP transport, 10-Gbps Ethernet provides substantial value over ATM transport for both network end users and service providers:

- No expensive, bandwidth-consuming conversion between Ethernet packets and ATM cells is required; the network is Ethernet, end to end.
- The combination of IP and Ethernet offers quality of service and traffic policing capabilities that approach those provided by ATM, so that advanced traffic engineering technologies are available to users and providers.
- A wide variety of standard optical interfaces (wavelengths and link distances) have been specified for 10 Gigabit Ethernet, optimizing its operation and cost for LAN, MAN, or WAN applications.

The goal for maximum link distances cover a range of applications: from 300 m to 40 km. The links operate in full-duplex mode only, using a variety of optical fiber physical media.

Four physical layer options are defined for 10-Gbps Ethernet (Figure 16.7):

- **10GBASE-S (short):** Designed for 850 nm transmission on multimode fiber. This medium can achieve distances up to 300 m.
- **10GBASE-L (long):** Designed for 1310 nm transmission on single-mode fiber. This medium can achieve distances up to 10 km.
- **10GBASE-E (extended):** Designed for 1550 nm transmission on single-mode fiber. This medium can achieve distances up to 40 km.
- **10GBASE-LX4:** Designed for 1310 nm transmission on single-mode or multimode fiber. This medium can achieve distances up to 10 km. This medium uses wavelength-division multiplexing (WDM) to multiplex the bit stream across four light waves.

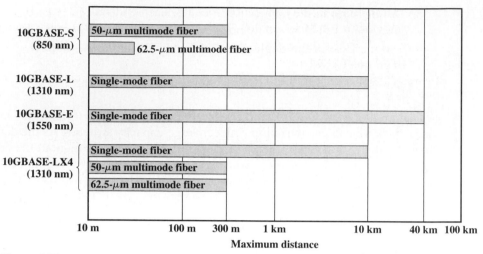

Figure 16.7 10-Gbps Ethernet Data Rate and Distance Options (Log Scale)

16.3 TOKEN RING

The IEEE 802.5 **token ring** standard is an outgrowth of IBM's commercial token ring LAN product. Because of IBM's presence in the corporate marketplace, token ring LANs have gained broad acceptance. However, token ring has never achieved the popularity of Ethernet-type systems. Currently, there is a large installed base of token ring products, but the token ring market share is likely to decline rapidly over the next few years.

We begin with a brief overview of ring LAN operation and then look at the IEEE 802.5 standard.

Ring Operation

A ring consists of a number of repeaters, each connected to two others by unidirectional transmission links to form a single closed path. Data are transferred sequentially, bit by bit, around the ring from one repeater to the next. Each repeater regenerates and retransmits each bit.

For a ring to operate as a communication network, three functions are required: data insertion, data reception, and data removal. These functions are provided by the repeaters. Each repeater, in addition to serving as an active element on the ring, serves as a device attachment point. Data insertion is accomplished by the repeater. Data are transmitted in packets, each of which contains a destination address field. As a packet circulates past a repeater, the address field is copied. If the attached station recognizes the address, the remainder of the packet is copied.

Repeaters perform the data insertion and reception functions in a manner not unlike that of taps, which serve as device attachment points on a bus or tree. Data removal, however, is more difficult on a ring. For a bus or tree, signals inserted onto the line propagate to the endpoints and are absorbed by terminators. Hence, shortly after transmission ceases, the bus or tree is clean of data. However, because the ring is a closed loop, a packet will circulate indefinitely unless it is removed. A packet may by removed by the addressed repeater. Alternatively, each packet could be removed by the transmitting repeater after it has made one trip around the loop. This latter approach is more desirable because (1) it permits automatic acknowledgment and (2) it permits multicast addressing: one packet sent simultaneously to multiple stations.

A variety of strategies can be used for determining how and when packets are inserted onto the ring. These strategies are, in effect, medium access control protocols. The most common method is token ring.

The repeater, then, can be seen to have two main purposes: (1) to contribute to the proper functioning of the ring by passing on all the data that come its way, and (2) to provide an access point for attached stations to send and receive data. Corresponding to these two purposes are two states (Figure 16.8): the listen state and the transmit state.

In the listen state, each received bit is retransmitted with a small delay, required to allow the repeater to perform required functions. Ideally, the delay should be on the order of one bit time (the time it takes for a repeater to transmit one complete bit onto the outgoing line). These functions are as follows:

- Scan passing bit stream for pertinent patterns. Chief among these is the address or addresses of attached stations. Another pattern, used in the token control strategy explained later, indicates permission to transmit. Note that to perform the scanning function, the repeater must have some knowledge of packet format.
- Copy each incoming bit and send it to the attached station while continuing to retransmit each bit. This will be done for each bit of each packet addressed to this station.
- Modify a bit as it passes by. In certain control strategies, bits may be modified to, for example, indicate that the packet has been copied. This would serve as an acknowledgment.

When a repeater's station has data to send and when the repeater, based on the control strategy, has permission to send, the repeater enters the transmit state. In

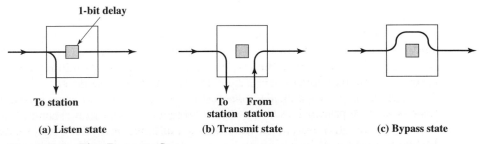

1-bit delay

To station

To   From
station station

(a) Listen state   (b) Transmit state   (c) Bypass state

Figure 16.8 Ring Repeater States

this state, the repeater receives bits from the station and retransmits them on its outgoing link. During the period of transmission, bits may appear on the incoming ring link. There are two possibilities, and they are treated differently:

- The bits could be from the same packet that the repeater is still in the process of sending. This will occur if the "bit length" of the ring is shorter than the packet. In this case, the repeater passes the bits back to the station, which can check them as a form of acknowledgment.
- For some control strategies, more than one packet could be on the ring at the same time. If the repeater, while transmitting, receives bits from a packet it did not originate, it must buffer them to be transmitted later.

These two states, listen and transmit, are sufficient for proper ring operation. A third state, the bypass state, is also useful. In this state, a bypass relay can be activated, so that signals propagate past the repeater with no delay other than medium propagation. The bypass relay affords two benefits: (1) It provides a partial solution to the reliability problem, discussed later, and (2) it improves performance by eliminating repeater delay for those stations that are not active on the network.

Medium Access Control

The token ring technique is based on the use of a small frame, called a token, that circulates when all stations are idle. A station wishing to transmit must wait until it detects a token passing by. It then seizes the token by changing one bit in the token, which transforms it from a token to a start-of-frame sequence for a data frame. The station then appends and transmits the remainder of the fields needed to construct a data frame.

When a station seizes a token and begins to transmit a data frame, there is no token on the ring, so other stations wishing to transmit must wait. The frame on the ring will make a round trip and be absorbed by the transmitting station. In the default operation, the transmitting station will insert a new token on the ring when both of the following conditions have been met:

- The station has completed transmission of its frame.
- The leading edge of the transmitted frame has returned (after a complete circulation of the ring) to the station.

If the bit length of the ring is less than the frame length, the first condition implies the second. If not, a station could release a free token after it has finished transmitting but before it begins to receive its own transmission; the second condition is not strictly necessary and is relaxed for the configuration option known as early token release. The advantage of imposing the second condition is that it ensures that only one data frame at a time may be on the ring and only one station at a time may be transmitting, simplifying error recovery procedures.

Once the new token has been inserted on the ring, the next station downstream with data to send will be able to seize the token and transmit. Figure 16.9 illustrates the technique. In the example, A sends a frame to C, which receives it and then, once it has also received a token, sends its own frames to A and D.

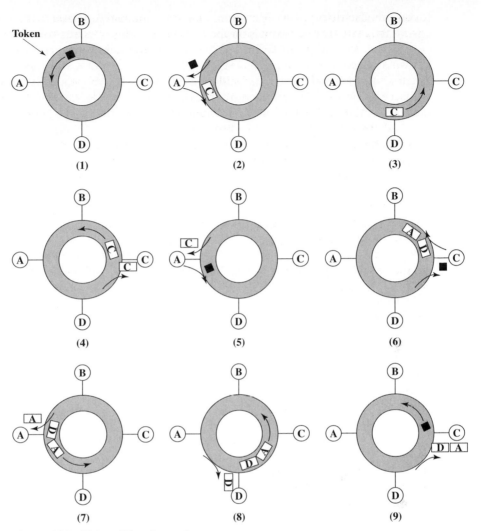

Figure 16.9 Token Ring Operation

Note that under lightly loaded conditions, there is some inefficiency with token ring because a station must wait for the token to come around before transmitting. However, under heavy loads, which is when it matters, the ring functions in a round-robin fashion, which is both efficient and fair. To see this, consider the configuration in Figure 16.9. After station A transmits, it releases a token. The first station with an opportunity to transmit is D. If D transmits, it then releases a token and C has the next opportunity, and so on.

The principal advantage of token ring is the flexible control over access that it provides. In the simple scheme just described, the access is fair. Token passing can also easily provide for priority and guaranteed bandwidth services.

The principal disadvantage of token ring is the requirement for token maintenance. Loss of the token prevents further utilization of the ring. Duplication of the token can also disrupt ring operation. One station must be selected as a monitor to ensure that exactly one token is on the ring and to reinsert a free token if necessary.

The 1997 update to IEEE 802.5 introduced a new access control technique known as **dedicated token ring** (DTR). DTR makes use of a star-topology layout. The token-passing algorithm can still be used so that the ring capacity is still shared and access control is determined by the token. However, it is also possible to have the central hub function as a layer 2 switch, so that the connection between each station and the switch functions as a full-duplex point-to-point link. The DTR specification defines the use of stations and concentrators in this switched mode. The DTR concentrator acts as a frame-level relay rather than a bit-level repeater, so that each link from concentrator to station is a dedicated link with immediate access possible; token passing is not used.

IEEE 802.5 Transmission Medium Options

The 802.5 standard offers a variety of data rates and transmission media, as shown in Table 16.4. The standard imposes a maximum frame size of 4550 octets at 4 Mpbs and 18,200 octets for 16 Mpbs, 100 Mpbs, and 1 Gbps. This compares with a maximum frame size of 1518 octets for IEEE 802.3 LANs. At 4 Mpbs and 16 Mpbs, either the traditional token-passing access control or the switched DTR technique can be used. At 100 Mpbs, the DTR technique is mandatory.

The 802.5 committee completed work on a 1-Gbps version of token ring in 2001. As with the 100-Mbps version, the gigabit version adopts the 802.3 physical layer specification.

16.4 FIBRE CHANNEL

As the speed and memory capacity of personal computers, workstations, and servers have grown, and as applications have become ever more complex with greater reliance on graphics and video, the requirement for greater speed in delivering data to

Table 16.4 IEEE 802.5 Physical Layer Medium Alternatives

Data rate (Mbps)	4	16	100	100	1000
Transmission medium	UTP or STP or fiber	UTP or STP or fiber	UTP or STP	Fiber	Fiber
Signaling technique	Differential Manchester	Differential Manchester	MLT-3	4B5B, NRZI	8B/10B
Maximum frame size (octets)	4550	18,200	18,200	18,200	18,200
Access control	TP or DTR	TP or DTR	DTR	DTR	DTR

UTP = unshielded twisted pair
STP = shielded twisted pair
 TP = token passing access control
DTR = dedicated token ring

the processor has grown. This requirement affects two methods of data communications with the processor: I/O channel and network communications.

An I/O channel is a direct point-to-point or multipoint communications link, predominantly hardware based and designed for high speed over very short distances. The I/O channel transfers data between a buffer at the source device and a buffer at the destination device, moving only the user contents from one device to another, without regard to the format or meaning of the data. The logic associated with the channel typically provides the minimum control necessary to manage the transfer plus hardware error detection. I/O channels typically manage transfers between processors and peripheral devices, such as disks, graphics equipment, CD-ROMs, and video I/O devices.

A network is a collection of interconnected access points with a software protocol structure that enables communication. The network typically allows many different types of data transfer, using software to implement the networking protocols and to provide flow control, error detection, and error recovery. As we have discussed in this book, networks typically manage transfers between end systems over local, metropolitan, or wide area distances.

Fibre Channel is designed to combine the best features of both technologies—the simplicity and speed of channel communications with the flexibility and interconnectivity that characterize protocol-based network communications. This fusion of approaches allows system designers to combine traditional peripheral connection, host-to-host internetworking, loosely coupled processor clustering, and multimedia applications in a single multiprotocol interface. The types of channel-oriented facilities incorporated into the Fibre Channel protocol architecture include the following:

- Data-type qualifiers for routing frame payload into particular interface buffers
- Link-level constructs associated with individual I/O operations
- Protocol interface specifications to allow support of existing I/O channel architectures, such as the Small Computer System Interface (SCSI)

The types of network-oriented facilities incorporated into the Fibre Channel protocol architecture include the following:

- Full multiplexing of traffic between multiple destinations
- Peer-to-peer connectivity between any pair of ports on a Fibre Channel network
- Capabilities for internetworking to other connection technologies

Depending on the needs of the application, either channel or networking approaches can be used for any data transfer. The Fibre Channel Industry Association, which is the industry consortium promoting Fibre Channel, lists the following ambitious requirements that Fibre Channel is intended to satisfy [FCIA01]:

- Full-duplex links with two fibers per link
- Performance from 100 Mpbs to 800 Mpbs on a single line (full-duplex 200 Mpbs to 1600 Mpbs per link)

- Support for distances up to 10 km
- Small connectors
- High-capacity utilization with distance insensitivity
- Greater connectivity than existing multidrop channels
- Broad availability (i.e., standard components)
- Support for multiple cost/performance levels, from small systems to super-computers
- Ability to carry multiple existing interface command sets for existing channel and network protocols

The solution was to develop a simple generic transport mechanism based on point-to-point links and a switching network. This underlying infrastructure supports a simple encoding and framing scheme that in turn supports a variety of channel and network protocols.

Fibre Channel Elements

The key elements of a Fibre Channel network are the end systems, called **nodes**, and the network itself, which consists of one or more switching elements. The collection of switching elements is referred to as a **fabric**. These elements are interconnected by point-to-point links between ports on the individual nodes and switches. Communication consists of the transmission of frames across the point-to-point links.

Each node includes one or more ports, called N_ports, for interconnection. Similarly, each fabric-switching element includes multiple ports, called F_ports. Interconnection is by means of bidirectional links between ports. Any node can communicate with any other node connected to the same fabric using the services of the fabric. All routing of frames between N_ports is done by the fabric. Frames may be buffered within the fabric, making it possible for different nodes to connect to the fabric at different data rates.

A fabric can be implemented as a single fabric element with attached nodes (a simple star arrangement) or as a more general network of fabric elements, as shown in Figure 16.10. In either case, the fabric is responsible for buffering and for routing frames between source and destination nodes.

The Fibre Channel network is quite different from the IEEE 802 LANs. Fibre Channel is more like a traditional circuit-switching or packet-switching network, in contrast to the typical shared-medium LAN. Thus, Fibre Channel need not be concerned with medium access control issues. Because it is based on a switching network, the Fibre Channel scales easily in terms of N_ports, data rate, and distance covered. This approach provides great flexibility. Fibre Channel can readily accommodate new transmission media and data rates by adding new switches and F_ports to an existing fabric. Thus, an existing investment is not lost with an upgrade to new technologies and equipment. Further, the layered protocol architecture accommodates existing I/O interface and networking protocols, preserving the preexisting investment.

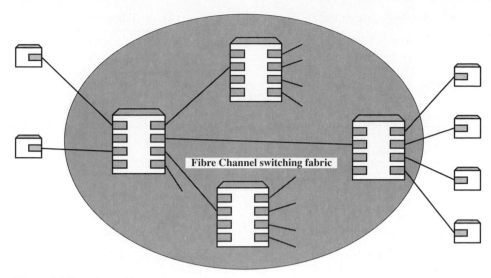

Figure 16.10   Fibre Channel Network

Fibre Channel Protocol Architecture

The Fibre Channel standard is organized into five levels. Each level defines a function or set of related functions. The standard does not dictate a correspondence between levels and actual implementations, with a specific interface between adjacent levels. Rather, the standard refers to the level as a "document artifice" used to group related functions. The layers are as follows:

- **FC-0 Physical Media:** Includes optical fiber for long-distance applications, coaxial cable for high speeds over short distances, and shielded twisted pair for lower speeds over short distances
- **FC-1 Transmission Protocol:** Defines the signal encoding scheme
- **FC-2 Framing Protocol:** Deals with defining topologies, frame format, flow and error control, and grouping of frames into logical entities called sequences and exchanges
- **FC-3 Common Services:** Includes multicasting
- **FC-4 Mapping:** Defines the mapping of various channel and network protocols to Fibre Channel, including IEEE 802, ATM, IP, and the Small Computer System Interface (SCSI)

Fibre Channel Physical Media and Topologies

One of the major strengths of the Fibre Channel standard is that it provides a range of options for the physical medium, the data rate on that medium, and the topology of the network (Table 16.5).

Transmission Media

The transmission media options that are available under Fibre Channel include shielded twisted pair, video coaxial cable, and optical fiber. Standardized data

Table 16.5   Maximum Distance for Fibre Channel Media Types

	800 Mbps	400 Mbps	200 Mbps	100 Mbps
Single mode fiber	10 km	10 km	10 km	—
50-μm multimode fiber	0.5 km	1 km	2 km	—
62.5-μm multimode fiber	175 m	1 km	1 km	—
Video coaxial cable	50 m	71 m	100 m	100 m
Miniature coaxial cable	14 m	19 m	28 m	42 m
Shielded twisted pair	28 m	46 m	57 m	80 m

rates range from 100 Mpbs to 3.2 Gbps. Point-to-point link distances range from 33 m to 10 km.

Topologies

The most general topology supported by Fibre Channel is referred to as a fabric or switched topology. This is an arbitrary topology that includes at least one switch to interconnect a number of end systems. The fabric topology may also consist of a number of switches forming a switched network, with some or all of these switches also supporting end nodes.

Routing in the fabric topology is transparent to the nodes. Each port in the configuration has a unique address. When data from a node are transmitted into the fabric, the edge switch to which the node is attached uses the destination port address in the incoming data frame to determine the destination port location. The switch then either delivers the frame to another node attached to the same switch or transfers the frame to an adjacent switch to begin routing the frame to a remote destination.

The fabric topology provides scalability of capacity: As additional ports are added, the aggregate capacity of the network increases, thus minimizing congestion and contention and increasing throughput. The fabric is protocol independent and largely distance insensitive. The technology of the switch itself and of the transmission links connecting the switch to nodes may be changed without affecting the overall configuration. Another advantage of the fabric topology is that the burden on nodes is minimized. An individual Fibre Channel node (end system) is only responsible for managing a simple point-to-point connection between itself and the fabric; the fabric is responsible for routing between ports and error detection.

In addition to the fabric topology, the Fibre Channel standard defines two other topologies. With the point-to-point topology there are only two ports, and these are directly connected, with no intervening fabric switches. In this case there is no routing. The arbitrated loop topology is a simple, low-cost topology for connecting up

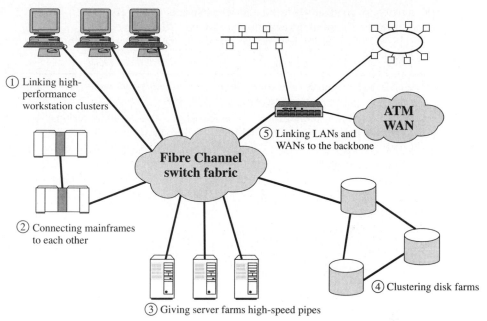

Figure 16.11 Five Applications of Fibre Channel

to 126 nodes in a loop. The arbitrated loop operates in a manner roughly equivalent to the token ring protocols that we have seen.

Topologies, transmission media, and data rates may be combined to provide an optimized configuration for a given site. Figure 16.11 is an example that illustrates the principal applications of Fiber Channel.

Prospects for Fibre Channel

Fibre Channel is backed by an industry interest group known as the Fibre Channel Association, and a variety of interface cards for different applications are available. Fibre Channel has been most widely accepted as an improved peripheral device interconnect, providing services that can eventually replace such schemes as SCSI. It is a technically attractive solution to general high-speed LAN requirements but must compete with Ethernet and ATM LANs. Cost and performance issues should dominate the manager's consideration of these competing technologies.

16.5 RECOMMENDED READING AND WEB SITES

[STAL00] covers in greater detail all of the LAN systems discussed in this chapter.

[SPUR00] provides a concise but thorough overview of all of the 10-Mbps through 1-Gbps 802.3 systems, including configuration guidelines for a single segment of each media type, as well as guidelines for building multisegment Ethernets using a variety of media types. Two excellent treatments of both 100-Mbps and Gigabit Ethernet are [SEIF98] and

[KADA98]. A good survey article on Gigabit Ethernet is [FRAZ99]. [10GE02] is a white paper providing a useful introduction to 10-Gbps Ethernet.

[SACH96] is a good survey of Fibre Channel. A short but worthwhile treatment is [FCIA01].

10GE02	10 Gigabit Ethernet Alliance. *10 Gigabit Ethernet—Technology Overview.* White paper, April 2002.
FCIA01	Fibre Channel Industry Association. *Fibre Channel Storage Area Networks.* San Francisco: Fibre Channel Industry Association, 2001.
FRAZ99	Frazier, H., and Johnson, H. "Gigabit Ethernet: From 100 to 1,000 Mpbs." *IEEE Internet Computing*, January/February 1999.
KADA98	Kadambi, J.; Crayford, I.; and Kalkunte, M. *Gigabit Ethernet.* Upper Saddle River, NJ: Prentice Hall, 1998.
SACH96	Sachs. M., and Varma, A. "Fibre Channel and Related Standards." *IEEE Communications Magazine*, August 1996.
SEIF98	Seifert, R. *Gigabit Ethernet.* Reading, MA: Addison-Wesley, 1998.
SPUR00	Spurgeon, C. *Ethernet: The Definitive Guide.* Cambridge, MA: O'Reilly and Associates, 2000.
STAL00	Stallings, W. *Local and Metropolitan Area Networks, Sixth Edition.* Upper Saddle River, NJ: Prentice Hall, 2000.

Useful Web Sites:

- **Interoperability Lab:** University of New Hampshire site for equipment testing for high-speed LANs
- **Charles Spurgeon's Ethernet Web Site:** Provides extensive information about Ethernet, including links and documents
- **10 Gigabit Ethernet Alliance:** This group promotes the 10-Gbps Ethernet standard
- **Fibre Channel Industry Association:** Includes tutorials, white papers, links to vendors, and descriptions of Fibre Channel applications
- **Storage Network Industry Association:** An industry forum of developers, integrators, and IT professionals who evolve and promote storage networking technology and solutions

16.6 KEY TERMS, REVIEW QUESTIONS, AND PROBLEMS

Key Terms

1-persistent CSMA	with collision detection	full-duplex operation
ALOHA	(CSMA/CD)	nonpersistent CSMA
binary exponential backoff	collision	*p*-persistent CSMA
carrier sense multiple access	dedicated token ring (DTR)	repeater
(CSMA)	Ethernet	slotted ALOHA
carrier sense multiple access	Fibre Channel	token ring

Review Questions

16.1 What is a server farm?

16.2 Explain the three persistence protocols that can be used with CSMA.

16.3 What is CSMA/CD?

16.4 Explain binary exponential backoff.

16.5 What are the transmission medium options for Fast Ethernet?

16.6 How does Fast Ethernet differ from 10BASE-T, other than the data rate?

16.7 In the context of Ethernet, what is full-duplex operation?

16.8 What functions are performed by a token ring repeater?

16.9 What is the difference between traditional token ring MAC and dedicated token ring?

16.10 List the levels of Fibre Channel and the functions of each level.

16.11 What are the topology options for Fibre Channel?

16.12 Under heavy loads, how do the behavior of CSMA/CD and token ring differ?

Problems

16.1 A disadvantage of the contention approach for LANs, such as CSMA/CD, is the capacity wasted due to multiple stations attempting to access the channel at the same time. Suppose that time is divided into discrete slots, with each of N stations attempting to transmit with probability p during each slot. What fraction of slots are wasted due to multiple simultaneous transmission attempts?

16.2 For p-persistent CSMA, consider the following situation. A station is ready to transmit and is listening to the current transmission. No other station is ready to transmit, and there will be no other transmission for an indefinite period. If the time unit used in the protocol is T, show that the average number of iterations of step 1 of the protocol is $1/p$ and that therefore the expected time that the station will have to wait after the current transmission is $T\left(\dfrac{1}{p} - 1\right)$. *Hint:* Use the equality $\displaystyle\sum_{i=1}^{\infty} iX^{i-1} = \dfrac{1}{(1 - X)^2}$.

16.3 The binary exponential backoff algorithm is defined by IEEE 802 as follows:

The delay is an integral multiple of slot time. The number of slot times to delay before the nth retransmission attempt is chosen as a uniformly distributed random integer r in the range $0 \leq r < 2^K$, where $K = \min(n, 10)$.

Slot time is, roughly, twice the round-trip propagation delay. Assume that two stations always have a frame to send. After a collision, what is the mean number of retransmission attempts before one station successfully retransmits? What is the answer if three stations always have frames to send?

16.4 Describe the signal pattern produced on the medium by the Manchester-encoded preamble of the IEEE 802.3 MAC frame.

16.5 For a token ring LAN, suppose that the destination station removes the data frame and immediately sends a short acknowledgment frame to the sender rather than letting the original frame return to sender. How will this affect performance?

16.6 Another medium access control technique for rings is the slotted ring. A number of fixed-length slots circulate continuously on the ring. Each slot contains a leading bit to designate the slot as empty or full. A station wishing to transmit waits until an empty slot arrives, marks the slot full, and inserts a frame of data as the slot goes by. The full slot makes a complete round trip, to be marked empty again by the station that marked it full. In what sense are the slotted ring and token ring protocols the complement (dual) of each other?

16.7 Consider a slotted ring of length 10 km with a data rate of 10 Mpbs and 500 repeaters, each of which introduces a 1-bit delay. Each slot contains room for one source address byte, one destination address byte, two data bytes, and five control bits for a total length of 37 bits. How many slots are on the ring?

16.8 With 8B6T coding, the effective data rate on a single channel is 33 Mpbs with a signaling rate of 25 Mbaud. If a pure ternary scheme were used, what is the effective data rate for a signaling rate of 25 Mbaud?

16.9 With 8B6T coding, the DC algorithm sometimes negates all of the ternary symbols in a code group. How does the receiver recognize this condition? How does the receiver discriminate between a negated code group and one that has not been negated? For example, the code group for data byte 00 is $+-00+-$ and the code group for data byte 38 is the negation of that, namely, $-+00-+$.

16.10 Draw the MLT decoder state diagram that corresponds to the encoder state diagram of Figure 16.12.

16.11 For the bit stream 0101110, sketch the waveforms for NRZ-L, NRZI, Manchester, and Differential Manchester, and MLT-3.

APPENDIX 16A   DIGITAL SIGNAL ENCODING FOR LANS

In Chapter 5, we looked at some of the common techniques for encoding digital data for transmission, including Manchester and differential Manchester, which are used in some of the LAN standards. In this appendix, we examine some additional encoding schemes referred to in this chapter.

4B/5B-NRZI

This scheme, which is actually a combination of two encoding algorithms, is used both for 100BASE-X and FDDI. To understand the significance of this choice, first consider the simple alternative of a NRZ (nonreturn to zero) coding scheme. With NRZ, one signal state represents binary one and one signal state represents binary zero. The disadvantage of this approach is its lack of synchronization. Because transitions on the medium are unpredictable, there is no way for the receiver to synchronize its clock to the transmitter. A solution to this problem is to encode the binary data to guarantee the presence of transitions. For example, the data could first be encoded using Manchester encoding. The disadvantage of this approach is that the efficiency is only 50%. That is, because there can be as many as two transitions per bit time, a signaling rate of 200 million signal elements per second (200 Mbaud) is needed to achieve a data rate of 100 Mpbs. This represents an unnecessary cost and technical burden.

Greater efficiency can be achieved using the 4B/5B code. In this scheme, encoding is done 4 bits at a time; each 4 bits of data are encoded into a symbol with five *code bits,* such that each code bit contains a single signal element; the block of five code bits is called a *code group*. In effect, each set of 4 bits is encoded as 5 bits. The efficiency is thus raised to 80%: 100 Mpbs is achieved with 125 Mbaud.

To ensure synchronization, there is a second stage of encoding: Each code bit of the 4B/5B stream is treated as a binary value and encoded using nonreturn to zero inverted (NRZI) (see Figure 5.2). In this code, a binary 1 is represented with a transition at the beginning of the bit interval and a binary 0 is represented with no transition at the beginning of the bit interval; there are no other transitions. The advantage of NRZI is that it employs differential encoding. Recall from Chapter 5 that in differential encoding, the signal is decoded by comparing the polarity of adjacent signal elements rather than the absolute value of a signal element. A benefit of this scheme is that it is generally more reliable to detect a transition in the presence of noise and distortion than to compare a value to a threshold.

Now we are in a position to describe the 4B/5B code and to understand the selections that were made. Table 16.6 shows the symbol encoding. Each 5-bit code group pattern is shown, together with its NRZI realization. Because we are encoding 4 bits with a 5-bit pattern, only 16 of the 32 possible patterns are needed for data encoding. The codes selected to represent the 16 4-bit data blocks are such that a transition is present at least twice for each 5-code group code. No more than three zeros in a row are allowed across one or more code groups.

The encoding scheme can be summarized as follows:

1. A simple NRZ encoding is rejected because it does not provide synchronization; a string of 1s or 0s will have no transitions.
2. The data to be transmitted must first be encoded to assure transitions. The 4B/5B code is chosen over Manchester because it is more efficient.
3. The 4B/5B code is further encoded using NRZI so that the resulting differential signal will improve reception reliability.
4. The specific 5-bit patterns for the encoding of the 16 4-bit data patterns are chosen to guarantee no more than three zeros in a row to provide for adequate synchronization.

Those code groups not used to represent data are either declared invalid or assigned special meaning as control symbols. These assignments are listed in Table 16.6. The nondata symbols fall into the following categories:

- **Idle:** The idle code group is transmitted between data transmission sequences. It consists of a constant flow of binary ones, which in NRZI comes out as a continuous alternation between the two signal levels. This continuous fill pattern establishes and maintains synchronization and is used in the CSMA/CD protocol to indicate that the shared medium is idle.
- **Start of stream delimiter:** Used to delineate the starting boundary of a data transmission sequence; consists of two different code groups.
- **End of stream delimiter:** Used to terminate normal data transmission sequences; consists of two different code groups.
- **Transmit error:** This code group is interpreted as a signaling error. The normal use of this indicator is for repeaters to propagate received errors.

MLT-3

Although 4B/5B-NRZI is effective over optical fiber, it is not suitable as is for use over twisted pair. The reason is that the signal energy is concentrated in such a way as to produce undesirable radiated emissions from the wire. MLT-3, which is used on both 100BASE-TX and the twisted pair version of FDDI, is designed to overcome this problem.

Table 16.6 4B/5B Code Groups

Data Input (4 bits)	Code Group (5 bits)	NRZI Pattern	Interpretation
0000	11110		Data 0
0001	01001		Data 1
0010	10100		Data 2
0011	10101		Data 3
0100	01010		Data 4
0101	01011		Data 5
0110	01110		Data 6
0111	01111		Data 7
1000	10010		Data 8
1001	10011		Data 9
1010	10110		Data A
1011	10111		Data B
1100	11010		Data C
1101	11011		Data D
1110	11100		Data E

(continues on next page)

Table 16.6 *(continued)*

Data Input (4 bits)	Code Group (5 bits)	NRZI Pattern	Interpretation
1111	11101		Data F
	11111		Idle
	11000		Start of stream delimiter, part 1
	10001		Start of stream delimiter, part 2
	01101		End of stream delimiter, part 1
	00111		End of stream delimiter, part 2
	00100		Transmit error
	other		Invalid codes

The following steps are involved:

1. **NRZI to NRZ conversion.** The 4B/5B NRZI signal of the basic 100BASE-X is converted back to NRZ.
2. **Scrambling.** The bit stream is scrambled to produce a more uniform spectrum distribution for the next stage.
3. **Encoder.** The scrambled bit stream is encoded using a scheme known as MLT-3.
4. **Driver.** The resulting encoding is transmitted.

The effect of the MLT-3 scheme is to concentrate most of the energy in the transmitted signal below 30 MHz, which reduces radiated emissions. This in turn reduces problems due to interference.

The MLT-3 encoding produces an output that has a transition for every binary one and that uses three levels: a positive voltage ($+V$), a negative voltage ($-V$), and no voltage (0). The encoding rules are best explained with reference to the encoder state diagram shown in Figure 16.12:

1. If the next input bit is zero, then the next output value is the same as the preceding value.

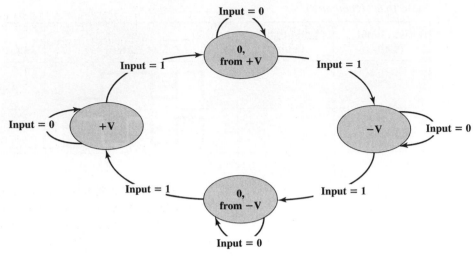

Figure 16.12 MLT-3 Encoder State Diagram

2. If the next input bit is one, then the next output value involves a transition:
   a. If the preceding output value was either +V or −V, then the next output value is 0.
   b. If the preceding output value was 0, then the next output value is nonzero, and that output is of the opposite sign to the last nonzero output.

   Figure 16.13 provides an example. Every time there is an input of 1, there is a transition. The occurrences of +V and −V alternate.

8B6T

The 8B6T encoding algorithm uses ternary signaling. With ternary signaling, each signal element can take on one of three values (positive voltage, negative voltage, zero voltage). A pure ternary code is one in which the full information-carrying capacity of the ternary signal is exploited. However, pure ternary is not attractive for the same reasons that a pure binary (NRZ) code is rejected: the lack of synchronization. However, there are schemes referred to as *block-coding methods* that approach the efficiency of ternary and overcome this disadvantage. A new block-coding scheme known as 8B6T is used for 100BASE-T4.

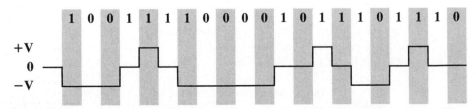

Figure 16.13 Example of MLT-3 Encoding

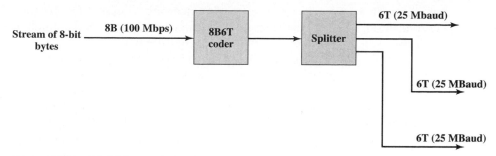

Figure 16.14 8B6T Transmission Scheme

With 8B6T the data to be transmitted are handled in 8-bit blocks. Each block of 8 bits is mapped into a code group of 6 ternary symbols. The stream of code groups is then transmitted in round-robin fashion across the three output channels (Figure 16.14). Thus the ternary transmission rate on each output channel is

$$\frac{6}{8} \times 33\frac{1}{3} = 25 \text{ Mbaud}$$

Table 16.7 shows a portion of the 8B6T code table; the full table maps all possible 8-bit patterns into a unique code group of 6 ternary symbols. The mapping was

Table 16.7 Portion of 8B6T Code Table

Data Octet	6T Code Group	Data Octet	6T Code Group	Data Octet	6T Code Group	Data Octet	6T Code Group
00	+-00+-	10	+0+--0	20	00-++-	30	+-00-+
01	0+-+-0	11	++0-0-	21	--+00+	31	0+---+0
02	+-0+-0	12	+0+-0-	22	++-0+-	32	+-0-+0
03	-0++-0	13	0++-0-	23	++-0-+	33	-0+--+0
04	-0+0+-	14	0++--0	24	00+0-+	34	-0+0-+
05	0+--0+	15	++00--	25	00+0+-	35	0+-+0-
06	+-0-0+	16	+0+0--	26	00-00+	36	+-0+0-
07	-0+-0+	17	0++0--	27	--++--+-	37	-0++0-
08	-+00+-	18	0+-0+-	28	-0-++0	38	-+00-+
09	0-++-0	19	0+-0-+	29	--0+0+	39	0-+-+0
0A	-+0+-0	1A	0+-++-	2A	-0-+0+	3A	-+0-+0
0B	+0-+-0	1B	0+-00+	2B	0--+0+	3B	+0--+0
0C	+0-0+-	1C	0-+00+	2C	0--++0	3C	+0-0-+
0D	0-+-0+	1D	0-+++-	2D	--00++	3D	0-++0-
0E	-+0-0+	1E	0-+0-+	2E	-0-0++	3E	-+0+0-
0F	+0--0+	1F	0-+0+-	2F	0--0++	3F	+0-+0-

chosen with two requirements in mind: synchronization and DC balance. For synchronization, the codes were chosen so to maximize the average number of transitions per code group. The second requirement is to maintain DC balance, so that the average voltage on the line is zero. For this purpose all of the selected code groups either have an equal number of positive and negative symbols or an excess of one positive symbol. To maintain balance, a DC balancing algorithm is used. In essence, this algorithm monitors the cumulative weight of the of all code groups transmitted on a single pair. Each code group has a weight of 0 or 1. To maintain balance, the algorithm may negate a transmitted code group (change all + symbols to − symbols and all − symbols to + symbols), so that the cumulative weight at the conclusion of each code group is always either 0 or 1.

8B/10B

The encoding scheme used for Fibre Channel and Gigabit Ethernet is 8B/10B, in which each 8 bits of data is converted into 10 bits for transmission. This scheme has a similar philosophy to the 4B/5B scheme used for FDDI, as discussed earlier. The 8B/10B scheme was developed and patented by IBM for use in its 200-megabaud ESCON interconnect system [WIDM83]. The 8B/10B scheme is more powerful than 4B/5B in terms of transmission characteristics and error detection capability.

The developers of this code list the following advantages:

- It can be implemented with relatively simple and reliable transceivers at low cost.
- It is well balanced, with minimal deviation from the occurrence of an equal number of 1 and 0 bits across any sequence.
- It provides good transition density for easier clock recovery.
- It provides useful error-detection capability.

The 8B/10B code is an example of the more general mBnB code, in which m binary source bits are mapped into n binary bits for transmission. Redundancy is built into the code to provide the desired transmission features by making $n > m$.

The 8B/10B code actually combines two other codes, a 5B/6B code and a 3B/4B code. The use of these two codes is simply an artifact that simplifies the definition of the mapping and the implementation; the mapping could have been defined directly as an 8B/10B code. In any case, a mapping is defined that maps each of the possible 8-bit source blocks into a 10-bit code block. There is also a function called *disparity control*. In essence, this function keeps track of the excess of zeros over ones or ones over zeros. An excess in either direction is referred to as a disparity. If there is a disparity, and if the current code block would add to that disparity, then the disparity control block complements the 10-bit code block. This has the effect of either eliminating the disparity or at least moving it in the opposite direction of the current disparity.

APPENDIX 16B   PERFORMANCE ISSUES

The choice of a LAN or MAN architecture is based on many factors, but one of the most important is performance. Of particular concern is the behavior (throughput, response time) of the network under heavy load. In this appendix, we provide an introduction to this topic. A more detailed discussion can be found in [STAL00].

The Effect of Propagation Delay and Transmission Rate

In Chapter 7, we introduced the parameter a, defined as

$$a = \frac{\text{Propagation time}}{\text{Transmission time}}$$

In that context, we were concerned with a point-to-point link, with a given propagation time between the two endpoints and a transmission time for either a fixed or average frame size. It was shown that a could be expressed as

$$a = \frac{\text{Length of data link in bits}}{\text{Length of frame in bits}}$$

This parameter is also important in the context of LANs and MANs, and in fact determines an upper bound on utilization. Consider a perfectly efficient access mechanism that allows only one transmission at a time. As soon as one transmission is over, another station begins transmitting. Furthermore, the transmission is pure data; no overhead bits. What is the maximum possible utilization of the network? It can be expressed as the ratio of total throughput of the network to its data rate:

$$U = \frac{\text{Throughput}}{\text{Data Rate}} \tag{16.1}$$

Now define, as in Chapter 7:

$$R = \text{data rate of the channel}$$
$$d = \text{maximum distance between any two stations}$$
$$V = \text{velocity of signal propagation}$$
$$L = \text{average or fixed frame length}$$

The throughput is just the number of bits transmitted per unit time. A frame contains L bits, and the amount of time devoted to that frame is the actual transmission time (L/R) plus the propagation delay (d/V). Thus

$$\text{Throughput} = \frac{L}{d/V + L/R} \tag{16.2}$$

But by our preceding definition of a,

$$a = \frac{d/V}{L/R} = \frac{Rd}{LV} \tag{16.3}$$

Substituting (16.2) and (16.3) into (16.1),

$$U = \frac{1}{1 + a} \tag{16.4}$$

Note that this differs from Equation (7.4) in Appendix 7A. This is because the latter assumed a half-duplex protocol (no piggybacked acknowledgments).

So utilization varies with a. This can be grasped intuitively by studying Figure 16.15, which shows a baseband bus with two stations as far apart as possible (worst case) that take turns sending frames. If we normalize time such that frame transmission time = 1, then the propagation time = a. For $a < 1$, the sequence of events is as follows:

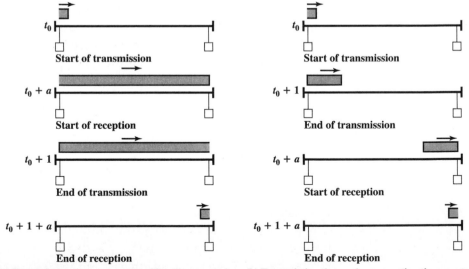

(a) Transmission time = 1; propagation time = $a < 1$ (b) Transmission time = 1; propagation time = $a > 1$

Figure 16.15   The Effect of a on Utilization for Baseband Bus

1. A station begins transmitting at t_0.
2. Reception begins at $t_0 + a$.
3. Transmission is completed at $t_0 + 1$.
4. Reception ends at $t_0 + 1 + a$.
5. The other station begins transmitting.

For $a > 1$, events 2 and 3 are interchanged. In both cases, the total time for one "turn" is $1 + a$, but the transmission time is only 1, for a utilization of $1/(1 + a)$.

The same effect can be seen to apply to a ring network in Figure 16.16. Here we assume that one station transmits and then waits to receive its own transmission before any other station transmits. The identical sequence of events just outlined applies.

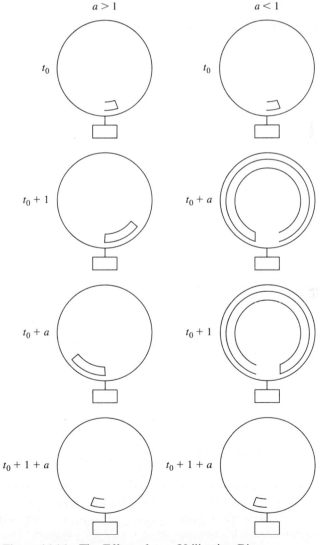

Figure 16.16   The Effect of a on Utilization Ring

Table 16.8 Representative Values of a

Data Rate (Mbps)	Frame Size (bits)	Network Length (km)	a	$1/(1 + a)$
1	100	1	0.05	0.95
1	1,000	10	0.05	0.95
1	100	10	0.5	0.67
10	100	1	0.5	0.67
10	1,000	1	0.05	0.95
10	1,000	10	0.5	0.67
10	10,000	10	0.05	0.95
100	35,000	200	2.8	0.26
100	1,000	50	25	0.04

Typical values of a range from about 0.01 to 0.1 for LANs and 0.1 to well over 1.0 for MANs. Table 16.8 gives some representative values for a bus topology. As can be seen, for larger and/or higher-speed networks, utilization suffers. For this reason, the restriction of only one frame at a time is lifted for LANs such as FDDI.

Finally, the preceding analysis assumes a "perfect" protocol, for which a new frame can be transmitted as soon as an old frame is received. In practice, the MAC protocol adds overhead that makes utilization worse. This is demonstrated in the next subsection for token passing and CSMA/CD.

Simple Performance Models of Token Passing and CSMA/CD

The purpose of this section is to give the reader some insight into the relative performance of the most important LAN protocols: CSMA/CD, token bus, and token ring, by developing two simple performance models. It is hoped that this exercise will aid in understanding the results of more rigorous analyses.

For these models we assume a local network with N active stations and a maximum normalized propagation delay of a. To simplify the analysis, we assume that each station is always prepared to transmit a frame. This allows us to develop an expression for maximum achievable utilization (U). Although this should not be construed to be the sole figure of merit for a local network, it is the single most analyzed figure of merit and does permit useful performance comparisons.

First, let us consider token ring. Time on the ring will alternate between data frame transmission and token passing. Refer to a single instance of a data frame followed by a token as a cycle and define

$$C = \text{average time for one cycle}$$
$$T_1 = \text{average time to transmit a data frame}$$
$$T_2 = \text{average time to pass a token}$$

It should be clear that the average cycle rate is just $1/C = 1/(T_1 + T_2)$. Intuitively,

$$U = \frac{T_1}{T_1 + T_2} \tag{16.5}$$

That is, the throughput, normalized to system capacity, is just the fraction of time that is spent transmitting data.

Refer now to Figure 16.16; time is normalized such that frame transmission time equals 1 and propagation time equals a. Note that the propagation time must include repeater delays. For the case of $a < 1$, a station transmits a frame at time t_0, receives the leading edge of its own frame at $t_0 + a$, and completes transmission at $t_0 + 1$. The station then emits a token, which takes an average time a/N to reach the next station. Thus one cycle takes $1 + a/N$ and the transmission time is 1. So $U = 1/(1 + a/N)$.

For $a > 1$ the reasoning is slightly different. A station transmits at t_0, completes transmission at $t_0 + 1$, and receives the leading edge of its frame at $t_0 + a$. At that point, it is free to emit a token, which takes an average time a/N to reach the next station. The cycle time is therefore $a + a/N$ and $U = 1/(a(1 + 1/N))$.

Summarizing,

$$\textbf{Token ring:} \quad U = \begin{cases} \dfrac{1}{1 + a/N} & a < 1 \\[2ex] \dfrac{1}{a(1 + 1/N)} & a > 1 \end{cases} \tag{16.6}$$

For CSMA/CD, consider time on the medium to be organized into slots whose length is twice the end-to-end propagation delay. This is a convenient way to view the activity on the medium; the slot time is the maximum time, from the start of transmission, required to detect a collision. Again, assume that there are N active stations. Clearly, if each station always has a frame to transmit and does so, there will be nothing but collisions on the line. So we assume that each station restrains itself to transmitting during an available slot with probability P.

Time on the medium consists of two types of intervals. First is a transmission interval, which lasts $1/2a$ slots. Second is a contention interval, which is a sequence of slots with either a collision or no transmission in each slot. The throughput is just the proportion of time spent in transmission intervals [similar to the reasoning for Equation (16.5)].

To determine the average length of a contention interval, we begin by computing A, the probability that exactly one station attempts a transmission in a slot and therefore acquires the medium. This is just the binomial probability that any one station attempts to transmit and the others do not:

$$A = \binom{N}{1} P^1 (1 - P)^{N-1}$$
$$= NP(1 - P)^{N-1}$$

This function takes on a maximum over P when $P = 1/N$:

$$A = (1 - 1/N)^{N-1}$$

We are interested in the maximum because we want to calculate the maximum throughput of the medium. It should be clear that the maximum throughput will be achieved if we maximize the probability of successful seizure of the medium. Therefore, the following rule should be enforced: During periods of heavy usage, a station should restrain its offered load to $1/N$. (This assumes that each station knows the value of N. To derive an expression for maximum possible throughput, we live with this assumption.) On the other hand, during periods of light usage, maximum utilization cannot be achieved because the load is too low; this region is not of interest here.

Now we can estimate the mean length of a contention interval, w, in slots:

$$E[w] = \sum_{i=1}^{\infty} i \times \Pr \begin{bmatrix} i \text{ slots in a row with a collision or no} \\ \text{transmission followed by a slot with one} \\ \text{transmission} \end{bmatrix}$$

$$= \sum_{i=1}^{\infty} i(1 - A)^i A$$

The summation converges to

$$E[w] = \frac{1 - A}{A}$$

We can now determine the maximum utilization, which is just the length of a transmission interval as a proportion of a cycle consisting of a transmission and a contention interval:

CSMA/CD: $$U = \frac{1/2a}{1/2a + (1 - A)/A} = \frac{1}{1 + 2a(1 - A)/A} \qquad (16.7)$$

Figure 16.17 shows normalized throughput as a function of a for various values of N and for both token passing and CSMA/CD. For both protocols, throughput declines as a increases. This is to be expected. But the dramatic difference between the

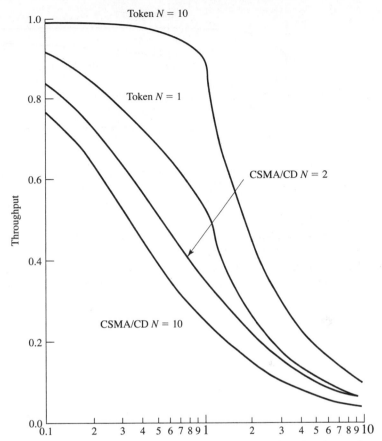

Figure 16.17   Throughput as a Function of *a* for Token Passing and CSMA/CD

two protocols is seen in Figure 16.18, which shows throughput as a function of *N*. Token-passing performance actually improves as a function of *N*, because less time is spent in token passing. Conversely, the performance of CSMA/CD decreases because of the increased likelihood of collision or no transmission.

It is interesting to note the asymptotic value of *U* as *N* increases. For token ring,

$$\textbf{Token ring:} \qquad \lim_{N \to \infty} U = \begin{cases} 1 & a < 1 \\ \frac{1}{a} & a > 1 \end{cases} \tag{16.8}$$

For CSMA/CD, we need to know that $\lim (1 - 1/N)^{N-1} = 1/e$. Then we have

$$\textbf{CSMA/CD:} \qquad \lim_{N \to \infty} U = \frac{1}{1 + 3.44a} \tag{16.9}$$

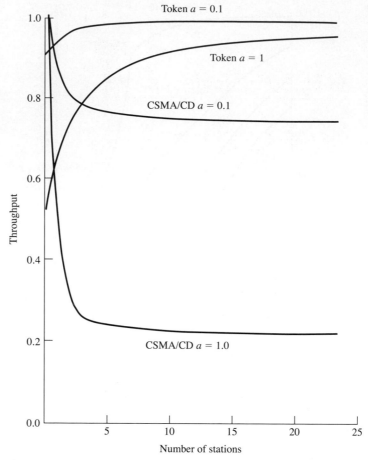

Figure 16.18 Throughput as a Function of *N* for Token Passing for CSMA/CD

CHAPTER **17**

WIRELESS LANS

KEY POINTS

- The principal technologies used for wireless LANs are infrared, spread spectrum, and narrowband microwave.
- The IEEE 802.11 standard defines a set of services and physical layer options for wireless LANs.
- The IEEE 802.11 services include managing associations, delivering data, and security.
- The IEEE 802.11 physical layer includes infrared and spread spectrum and covers a range of data rates.

In just the past few years, wireless LANs have come to occupy a significant niche in the local area network market. Increasingly, organizations are finding that wireless LANs are an indispensable adjunct to traditional wired LANs, to satisfy requirements for mobility, relocation, ad hoc networking, and coverage of locations difficult to wire.

This chapter provides a survey of wireless LANs. We begin with an overview that looks at the motivations for using wireless LANs and summarizes the various approaches in current use. The next section examines the three principal types of wireless LANs, classified according to transmission technology: infrared, spread spectrum, and narrowband microwave.

The most prominent specification for wireless LANs was developed by the IEEE 802.11 working group. The remainder of the chapter focuses on this standard.

17.1 OVERVIEW

As the name suggests, a wireless LAN is one that makes use of a wireless transmission medium. Until relatively recently, wireless LANs were little used. The reasons for this included high prices, low data rates, occupational safety concerns, and licensing requirements. As these problems have been addressed, the popularity of wireless LANs has grown rapidly.

In this section, we survey the key wireless LAN application areas and then look at the requirements for and advantages of wireless LANs.

Wireless LAN Applications

[PAHL95] lists four application areas for wireless LANs: LAN extension, cross-building interconnect, nomadic access, and ad hoc networks. Let us consider each of these in turn.

LAN Extension

Early wireless LAN products, introduced in the late 1980s, were marketed as substitutes for traditional wired LANs. A wireless LAN saves the cost of the installation of LAN cabling and eases the task of relocation and other modifications to network structure. However, this motivation for wireless LANs was overtaken by events. First, as awareness of the need for LANs became greater, architects designed new buildings to include extensive prewiring for data applications. Second, with advances in data transmission technology, there is an increasing reliance on twisted pair cabling for LANs and, in particular, Category 3 and Category 5 unshielded twisted pair. Most older buildings are already wired with an abundance of Category 3 cable, and many newer buildings are prewired with Category 5. Thus, the use of a wireless LAN to replace wired LANs has not happened to any great extent.

However, in a number of environments, there is a role for the wireless LAN as an alternative to a wired LAN. Examples include buildings with large open areas, such as manufacturing plants, stock exchange trading floors, and warehouses; historical buildings with insufficient twisted pair and where drilling holes for new wiring is prohibited; and small offices where installation and maintenance of wired LANs is not economical. In all of these cases, a wireless LAN provides an effective and more attractive alternative. In most of these cases, an organization will also have a wired LAN to support servers and some stationary workstations. For example, a manufacturing facility typically has an office area that is separate from the factory floor but that must be linked to it for networking purposes. Therefore, typically, a wireless LAN will be linked into a wired LAN on the same premises. Thus, this application area is referred to as LAN extension.

Figure 17.1 indicates a simple wireless LAN configuration that is typical of many environments. There is a backbone wired LAN, such as Ethernet, that supports servers, workstations, and one or more bridges or routers to link with other

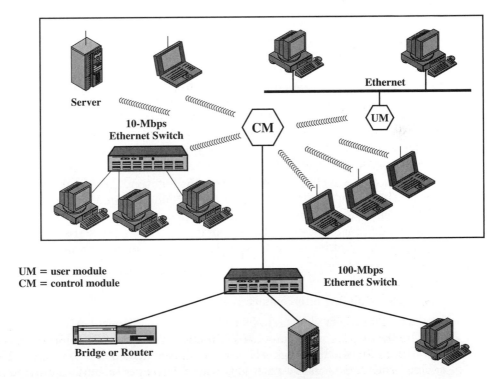

Figure 17.1 Example Single-Cell Wireless LAN Configuration

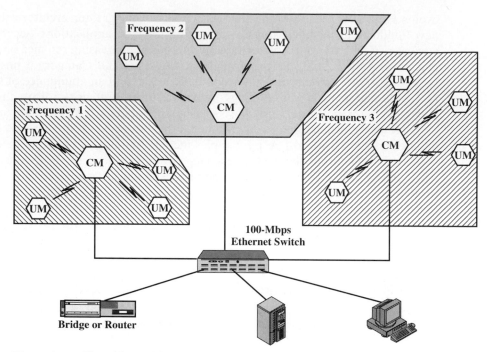

Figure 17.2 Example Multiple-Cell Wireless LAN Configuration

networks. In addition, there is a control module (CM) that acts as an interface to a wireless LAN. The control module includes either bridge or router functionality to link the wireless LAN to the backbone. It includes some sort of access control logic, such as a polling or token-passing scheme, to regulate the access from the end systems. Note that some of the end systems are standalone devices, such as a workstation or a server. Hubs or other user modules (UMs) that control a number of stations off a wired LAN may also be part of the wireless LAN configuration.

The configuration of Figure 17.1 can be referred to as a single-cell wireless LAN; all of the wireless end systems are within range of a single control module. Another common configuration, suggested by Figure 17.2, is a multiple-cell wireless LAN. In this case, there are multiple control modules interconnected by a wired LAN. Each control module supports a number of wireless end systems within its transmission range. For example, with an infrared LAN, transmission is limited to a single room; therefore, one cell is needed for each room in an office building that requires wireless support.

Cross-Building Interconnect

Another use of wireless LAN technology is to connect LANs in nearby buildings, be they wired or wireless LANs. In this case, a point-to-point wireless link is used between two buildings. The devices so connected are typically bridges or routers. This single point-to-point link is not a LAN per se, but it is usual to include this application under the heading of wireless LAN.

Nomadic Access

Nomadic access provides a wireless link between a LAN hub and a mobile data terminal equipped with an antenna, such as a laptop computer or notepad computer. One example of the utility of such a connection is to enable an employee returning from a trip to transfer data from a personal portable computer to a server in the office. Nomadic access is also useful in an extended environment such as a campus or a business operating out of a cluster of buildings. In both of these cases, users may move around with their portable computers and may wish access to the servers on a wired LAN from various locations.

Ad Hoc Networking

An ad hoc network is a peer-to-peer network (no centralized server) set up temporarily to meet some immediate need. For example, a group of employees, each with a laptop or palmtop computer, may convene in a conference room for a business or classroom meeting. The employees link their computers in a temporary network just for the duration of the meeting.

Figure 17.3 suggests the differences between a wireless LAN that supports LAN extension and nomadic access requirements and an ad hoc wireless LAN. In the former case, the wireless LAN forms a stationary infrastructure consisting of one or more cells with a control module for each cell. Within a cell, there may be a number of stationary end systems. Nomadic stations can move from one cell to another. In contrast, there is no infrastructure for an ad hoc network. Rather, a peer collection of stations within range of each other may dynamically configure themselves into a temporary network.

Wireless LAN Requirements

A wireless LAN must meet the same sort of requirements typical of any LAN, including high capacity, ability to cover short distances, full connectivity among attached stations, and broadcast capability. In addition, there are a number of requirements specific to the wireless LAN environment. The following are among the most important requirements for wireless LANs:

- **Throughput:** The medium access control protocol should make as efficient use as possible of the wireless medium to maximize capacity.
- **Number of nodes:** Wireless LANs may need to support hundreds of nodes across multiple cells.
- **Connection to backbone LAN:** In most cases, interconnection with stations on a wired backbone LAN is required. For infrastructure wireless LANs, this is easily accomplished through the use of control modules that connect to both types of LANs. There may also need to be accommodation for mobile users and ad hoc wireless networks.
- **Service area:** A typical coverage area for a wireless LAN has a diameter of 100 to 300 m.
- **Battery power consumption:** Mobile workers use battery-powered workstations that need to have a long battery life when used with wireless adapters. This suggests that a MAC protocol that requires mobile nodes to monitor

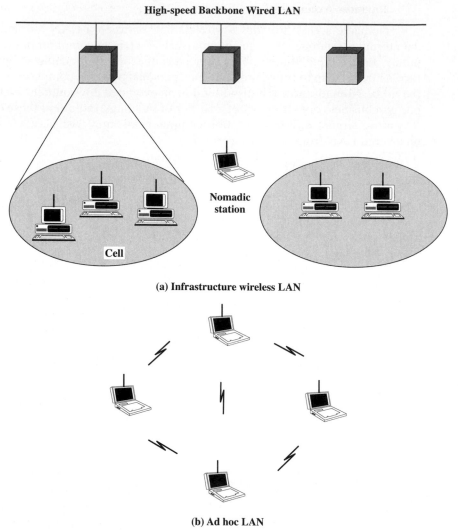

(a) Infrastructure wireless LAN

(b) Ad hoc LAN

Figure 17.3 Wireless LAN Configurations

access points constantly or engage in frequent handshakes with a base station is inappropriate. Typical wireless LAN implementations have features to reduce power consumption while not using the network, such as a sleep mode.

- **Transmission robustness and security:** Unless properly designed, a wireless LAN may be interference prone and easily eavesdropped. The design of a wireless LAN must permit reliable transmission even in a noisy environment and should provide some level of security from eavesdropping.

- **Collocated network operation:** As wireless LANs become more popular, it is quite likely for two or more wireless LANs to operate in the same area or in some area where interference between the LANs is possible. Such interference may thwart the normal operation of a MAC algorithm and may allow unauthorized access to a particular LAN.

- **License-free operation:** Users would prefer to buy and operate wireless LAN products without having to secure a license for the frequency band used by the LAN.
- **Handoff/roaming:** The MAC protocol used in the wireless LAN should enable mobile stations to move from one cell to another.
- **Dynamic configuration:** The MAC addressing and network management aspects of the LAN should permit dynamic and automated addition, deletion, and relocation of end systems without disruption to other users.

17.2 WIRELESS LAN TECHNOLOGY

Wireless LANs are generally categorized according to the transmission technique that is used. All current wireless LAN products fall into one of the following categories:

- **Infrared (IR) LANs:** An individual cell of an IR LAN is limited to a single room, because infrared light does not penetrate opaque walls.
- **Spread spectrum LANs:** This type of LAN makes use of spread spectrum transmission technology. In most cases, these LANs operate in the ISM (industrial, scientific, and medical) bands so that no Federal Communications Commission (FCC) licensing is required for their use in the United States.
- **Narrowband microwave:** These LANs operate at microwave frequencies but do not use spread spectrum. Some of these products operate at frequencies that require FCC licensing, while others use one of the unlicensed ISM bands.

Table 17.1 summarizes some of the key characteristics of these three technologies; the details are explored in the next three subsections.

Infrared LANs

Optical wireless communication in the infrared portion of the spectrum is commonplace in most homes, where it is used for a variety of remote control devices. More recently, attention has turned to the use of infrared technology to construct wireless LANs. In this section, we begin with a comparison of the characteristics of infrared LANs with those of radio LANs and then look at some of the details of infrared LANs.

Strengths and Weaknesses

The two competing transmission media for wireless LANs are microwave radio, using either spread spectrum or narrowband transmission, and infrared. Infrared offers a number of significant advantages over the microwave radio approaches. First, the spectrum for infrared is virtually unlimited, which presents the possibility of achieving extremely high data rates. The infrared spectrum is unregulated worldwide, which is not true of some portions of the microwave spectrum.

In addition, infrared shares some properties of visible light that make it attractive for certain types of LAN configurations. Infrared light is diffusely reflected by light-colored objects; thus it is possible to use ceiling reflection to achieve coverage of an entire room. Infrared light does not penetrate walls or other opaque objects.

Table 17.1   Comparison of Wireless LAN Technologies

	Infrared		Spread Spectrum		Radio
	Diffused Infrared	**Directed Beam Infrared**	**Frequency Hopping**	**Direct Sequence**	**Narrowband Microwave**
Data Rate (Mbps)	1 to 4	1 to 10	1 to 3	2 to 50	10 to 20
Mobility	Stationary/mobile	Stationary with LOS	Mobile	Stationary/mobile	
Range (m)	15 to 60	25	30 to 100	30 to 250	10 to 40
Detectability	Negligible		Little		Some
Wavelength/frequency	λ: 800 to 900 nm		902 to 928 MHz 2.4 to 2.4835 GHz 5.725 to 5.85 GHz		902 to 928 MHz 5.2 to 5.775 GHz 18.825 to 19.205 GHz
Modulation technique	ASK		FSK	QPSK	FS/QPSK
Radiated power	—		<1W		25 mW
Access method	CSMA	Token ring, CSMA	CSMA		Reservation ALOHA, CSMA
License required	No		No		Yes unless ISM

This has two advantages: First, infrared communications can be more easily secured against eavesdropping than microwave; and second, a separate infrared installation can be operated in every room in a building without interference, enabling the construction of very large infrared LANs.

Another strength of infrared is that the equipment is relatively inexpensive and simple. Infrared data transmission typically uses intensity modulation, so that IR receivers need to detect only the amplitude of optical signals, whereas most microwave receivers must detect frequency or phase.

The infrared medium also exhibits some drawbacks. Many indoor environments experience rather intense infrared background radiation, from sunlight and indoor lighting. This ambient radiation appears as noise in an infrared receiver, requiring the use of transmitters of higher power than would otherwise be required and also limiting the range. However, increases in transmitter power are limited by concerns of eye safety and excessive power consumption.

Transmission Techniques

There are three alternative transmission techniques commonly used for IR data transmission: the transmitted signal can be focused and aimed (as in a remote TV control); it can be radiated omnidirectionally; or it can be reflected from a light-colored ceiling.

Directed-beam IR can be used to create point-to-point links. In this mode, the range depends on the emitted power and on the degree of focusing. A focused IR data link can have a range of kilometers. Such ranges are not needed for constructing indoor wireless LANs. However, an IR link can be used for cross-building interconnect between bridges or routers located in buildings within a line of sight of each other.

One indoor use of point-to-point IR links is to set up a token ring LAN. A set of IR transceivers can be positioned so that data circulate around them in a ring configuration. Each transceiver supports a workstation or a hub of stations, with the hub providing a bridging function.

An **omnidirectional configuration** involves a single base station that is within line of sight of all other stations on the LAN. Typically, this station is mounted on the ceiling. The base station acts as a multiport repeater. The ceiling transmitter broadcasts an omnidirectional signal that can be received by all of the other IR transceivers in the area. These other transceivers transmit a directional beam aimed at the ceiling base unit.

In a **diffused** configuration, all of the IR transmitters are focused and aimed at a point on a diffusely reflecting ceiling. IR radiation striking the ceiling is reradiated omnidirectionally and picked up by all of the receivers in the area.

Spread Spectrum LANs

Currently, the most popular type of wireless LAN uses spread spectrum techniques.

Configuration

Except for quite small offices, a spread spectrum wireless LAN makes use of a multiple-cell arrangement, as was illustrated in Figure 17.2. Adjacent cells make use of different center frequencies within the same band to avoid interference.

Within a given cell, the topology can be either hub or peer to peer. The hub topology is indicated in Figure 17.2. In a hub topology, the hub is typically mounted on the ceiling and connected to a backbone wired LAN to provide connectivity to stations attached to the wired LAN and to stations that are part of wireless LANs in other cells. The hub may also control access, as in the IEEE 802.11 point coordination function. The hub may also control access by acting as a multiport repeater with similar functionality to the multiport repeaters of 10 Mbps and 100 Mbps Ethernet. In this case, all stations in the cell transmit only to the hub and receive only from the hub. Alternatively, and regardless of access control mechanism, each station may broadcast using an omnidirectional antenna so that all other stations in the cell may receive; this corresponds to a logical bus configuration.

One other potential function of a hub is automatic handoff of mobile stations. At any time, a number of stations are dynamically assigned to a given hub based on proximity. When the hub senses a weakening signal, it can automatically hand off to the nearest adjacent hub.

A peer-to-peer topology is one in which there is no hub. A MAC algorithm such as CSMA is used to control access. This topology is appropriate for ad hoc LANs.

Transmission Issues

A desirable, though not necessary, characteristic of a wireless LAN is that it be usable without having to go through a licensing procedure. The licensing regulations differ from one country to another, which complicates this objective. Within the United States, the FCC has authorized two unlicensed applications within the ISM band: spread spectrum systems, which can operate at up to 1 watt, and very low power systems, which can operate at up to 0.5 watts. Since this band was opened up by the FCC, its use for spread spectrum wireless LANs has become popular.

In the United States, three microwave bands have been set aside for unlicensed spread spectrum use: 902–928 MHz (915-MHz band), 2.4–2.4835 GHz (2.4-GHz band), and 5.725–5.825 GHz (5.8-GHz band). Of these, the 2.4 GHz is also used in this manner in Europe and Japan. The higher the frequency, the higher the potential bandwidth, so the three bands are of increasing order of attractiveness from a capacity point of view. In addition, the potential for interference must be considered. There are a number of devices that operate at around 900 MHz, including cordless telephones, wireless microphones, and amateur radio. There are fewer devices operating at 2.4 GHz; one notable example is the microwave oven, which tends to have greater leakage of radiation with increasing age. At present there is little competition at the 5.8-GHz band; however, the higher the frequency band, in general the more expensive the equipment.

Narrowband Microwave LANs

The term *narrowband microwave* refers to the use of a microwave radio frequency band for signal transmission, with a relatively narrow bandwidth—just wide enough to accommodate the signal. Until recently, all narrowband microwave LAN products have used a licensed microwave band. More recently, at least one vendor has produced a LAN product in the ISM band.

Licensed Narrowband RF

Microwave radio frequencies usable for voice, data, and video transmission are licensed and coordinated within specific geographic areas to avoid potential interference between systems. Within the United States, licensing is controlled by the FCC. Each geographic area has a radius of 28 km and can contain five licenses, with each license covering two frequencies. Motorola holds 600 licenses (1200 frequencies) in the 18-GHz range that cover all metropolitan areas with populations of 30,000 or more.

A narrowband scheme typically makes use of the cell configuration illustrated in Figure 17.2. Adjacent cells use nonoverlapping frequency bands within the overall 18-GHz band. In the United States, because Motorola controls the frequency band, it can assure that independent LANs in nearby geographical locations do not interfere with one another. To provide security from eavesdropping, all transmissions are encrypted.

One advantage of the licensed narrowband LAN is that it guarantees interference-free communication. Unlike unlicensed spectrum, such as ISM, licensed spectrum gives the license holder a legal right to an interference-free data communications channel. Users of an ISM-band LAN are at risk of interference disrupting their communications, for which they may not have a legal remedy.

Unlicensed Narrowband RF

In 1995, RadioLAN became the first vendor to introduce a narrowband wireless LAN using the unlicensed ISM spectrum. This spectrum can be used for narrowband transmission at low power (0.5 watts or less). The RadioLAN product operates at 10 Mbps in the 5.8-GHz band. The product has a range of 50 m in a semiopen office and 100 m in an open office.

The RadioLAN product makes use of a peer-to-peer configuration with an interesting feature. As a substitute for a stationary hub, the RadioLAN product automatically elects one node as the dynamic master, based on parameters such as location, interference, and signal strength. The identity of the master can change automatically as conditions change. The LAN also includes a dynamic relay function, which allows each station to act as a repeater to move data between stations that are out of range of each other.

17.3 IEEE 802.11 ARCHITECTURE AND SERVICES

In 1990 the IEEE 802.11 was formed with a charter to develop a MAC protocol and physical medium specification for wireless LANs. Table 17.2 briefly defines key terms used in the IEEE 802.11 standard.

IEEE 802.11 Architecture

Figure 17.4 illustrates the model developed by the 802.11 working group. The smallest building block of a wireless LAN is a basic service set (BSS), which consists of some number of stations executing the same MAC protocol and competing for access to the same shared wireless medium. A BSS may be isolated or it may connect to a backbone distribution system (DS) through an access point (AP). The access

Table 17.2 IEEE 802.11 Terminology

Access point (AP)	Any entity that has station functionality and provides access to the distribution system via the wireless medium for associated stations
Basic service set (BSS)	A set of stations controlled by a single coordination function
Coordination function	The logical function that determines when a station operating within a BSS is permitted to transmit and may be able to receive PDUs
Distribution system x (DS)	A system used to interconnect a set of BSSs and integrated LANs to create an ESS
Extended service set (ESS)	A set of one or more interconnected BSSs and integrated LANs that appear as a single BSS to the LLC layer at any station associated with one of these BSSs
MAC protocol data unit (MPDU)	The unit of data exchanged between two peer MAC entities using the services of the physical layer
MAC service data unit (MSDU)	Information that is delivered as a unit between MAC users
Station	Any device that contains an IEEE 802.11 conformant MAC and physical layer

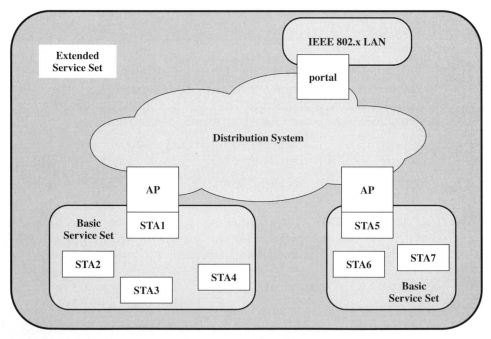

STA = station
AP = access point

Figure 17.4 IEEE 802.11 Architecture

point functions as a bridge. The MAC protocol may be fully distributed or controlled by a central coordination function housed in the access point. The BSS generally corresponds to what is referred to as a cell in the literature. The DS can be a switch, a wired network, or a wireless network.

The simplest configuration is shown in Figure 17.4, in which each station belongs to a single BSS; that is, each station is within wireless range only of other stations within the same BSS. It is also possible for two BSSs to overlap geographically, so that a single station could participate in more than one BSS. Further, the association between a station and a BSS is dynamic. Stations may turn off, come within range, and go out of range.

An extended service set (ESS) consists of two or more basic service sets interconnected by a distribution system. Typically, the distribution system is a wired backbone LAN but can be any communications network. The extended service set appears as a single logical LAN to the logical link control (LLC) level.

Figure 17.4 indicates that an AP is implemented as part of a station; the AP is the logic within a station that provides access to the DS by providing DS services in addition to acting as a station. To integrate the IEEE 802.11 architecture with a traditional wired LAN, a portal is used. The portal logic is implemented in a device, such as a bridge or router, that is part of the wired LAN and that is attached to the DS.

IEEE 802.11 Services

IEEE 802.11 defines nine services that need to be provided by the wireless LAN to provide functionality equivalent to that which is inherent to wired LANs. Table 17.3 lists the services and indicates two ways of categorizing them.

1. The service provider can be either the station or the DS. Station services are implemented in every 802.11 station, including AP stations. Distribution services are provided between BSSs; these services may be implemented in an AP or in another special-purpose device attached to the distribution system.

Table 17.3 IEEE 802.11 Services

Service	Provider	Used to support
Association	Distribution system	MSDU delivery
Authentication	Station	LAN access and security
Deauthentication	Station	LAN access and security
Dissassociation	Distribution system	MSDU delivery
Distribution	Distribution system	MSDU delivery
Integration	Distribution system	MSDU delivery
MSDU delivery	Station	MSDU delivery
Privacy	Station	LAN access and security
Reassocation	Distribution system	MSDU delivery

2. Three of the services are used to control IEEE 802.11 LAN access and confidentiality. Six of the services are used to support delivery of MAC service data units (MSDUs) between stations. The MSDU is a block of data passed down from the MAC user to the MAC layer; typically this is a LLC PDU. If the MSDU is too large to be transmitted in a single MAC frame, it may be fragmented and transmitted in a series of MAC frames. Fragmentation is discussed in Section 17.4.

Following the IEEE 802.11 document, we next discuss the services in an order designed to clarify the operation of an IEEE 802.11 ESS network. **MSDU delivery**, which is the basic service, has already been mentioned.

Distribution of Messages within a DS

The two services involved with the distribution of messages within a DS are distribution and integration. **Distribution** is the primary service used by stations to exchange MAC frames when the frame must traverse the DS to get from a station in one BSS to a station in another BSS. For example, suppose a frame is to be sent from station 2 (STA 2) to STA 7 in Figure 17.4. The frame is sent from STA 2 to STA 1, which is the AP for this BSS. The AP gives the frame to the DS, which has the job of directing the frame to the AP associated with STA 5 in the target BSS. STA 5 receives the frame and forwards it to STA 7. How the message is transported through the DS is beyond the scope of the IEEE 802.11 standard.

If the two stations that are communicating are within the same BSS, then the distribution service logically goes through the single AP of that BSS.

The **integration** service enables transfer of data between a station on an IEEE 802.11 LAN and a station on an integrated IEEE 802.x LAN. The term *integrated* refers to a wired LAN that is physically connected to the DS and whose stations may be logically connected to an IEEE 802.11 LAN via the integration service. The integration service takes care of any address translation and media conversion logic required for the exchange of data.

Association-Related Services

The primary purpose of the MAC layer is to transfer MSDUs between MAC entities; this purpose is fulfilled by the distribution service. For that service to function, it requires information about stations within the ESS that is provided by the association-related services. Before the distribution service can deliver data to or accept data from a station, that station must be *associated*. Before looking at the concept of association, we need to describe the concept of mobility. The standard defines three transition types of based on mobility:

- **No transition:** A station of this type is either stationary or moves only within the direct communication range of the communicating stations of a single BSS.
- **BSS transition:** This is defined as a station movement from one BSS to another BSS within the same ESS. In this case, delivery of data to the station requires that the addressing capability be able to recognize the new location of the station.

- **ESS transition:** This is defined as a station movement from a BSS in one ESS to a BSS within another ESS. This case is supported only in the sense that the station can move. Maintenance of upper-layer connections supported by 802.11 cannot be guaranteed. In fact, disruption of service is likely to occur.

To deliver a message within a DS, the distribution service needs to know where the destination station is located. Specifically, the DS needs to know the identity of the AP to which the message should be delivered in order for that message to reach the destination station. To meet this requirement, a station must maintain an association with the AP within its current BSS. Three services relate to this requirement:

- **Association:** Establishes an initial association between a station and an AP. Before a station can transmit or receive frames on a wireless LAN, its identity and address must be known. For this purpose, a station must establish an association with an AP within a particular BSS. The AP can then communicate this information to other APs within the ESS to facilitate routing and delivery of addressed frames.
- **Reassociation:** Enables an established association to be transferred from one AP to another, allowing a mobile station to move from one BSS to another.
- **Disassociation:** A notification from either a station or an AP that an existing association is terminated. A station should give this notification before leaving an ESS or shutting down. However, the MAC management facility protects itself against stations that disappear without notification.

Access and Privacy Services

There are two characteristics of a wired LAN that are not inherent in a wireless LAN:

1. In order to transmit over a wired LAN, a station must be physically connected to the LAN. On the other hand, with a wireless LAN, any station within radio range of the other devices on the LAN can transmit. In a sense, there is a form of authentication with a wired LAN, in that it requires some positive and presumably observable action to connect a station to a wired LAN.
2. Similarly, in order to receive a transmission from a station that is part of a wired LAN, the receiving station must also be attached to the wired LAN. On the other hand, with a wireless LAN, any station within radio range can receive. Thus, a wired LAN provides a degree of privacy, limiting reception of data to stations connected to the LAN.

IEEE 802.11 defines three services that provide a wireless LAN with these two features:

- **Authentication:** Used to establish the identity of stations to each other. In a wired LAN, it is generally assumed that access to a physical connection conveys authority to connect to the LAN. This is not a valid assumption for a wireless LAN, in which connectivity is achieved simply by having an attached antenna that is properly tuned. The authentication service is used by stations to establish their identity with stations they wish to communicate with. IEEE 802.11 supports several authentication schemes and allows for expansion of the functionality of these schemes. The standard does not mandate any particular authentication scheme, which could range from relatively unsecure handshaking to public-key encryption schemes. However, IEEE 802.11 requires mutually acceptable, successful authentication before a station can establish an association with an AP.

- **Deauthentication:** This service is invoked whenever an existing authentication is to be terminated.
- **Privacy:** Used to prevent the contents of messages from being read by other than the intended recipient. The standard provides for the optional use of encryption to assure privacy.

17.4 IEEE 802.11 MEDIUM ACCESS CONTROL

The IEEE 802.11 MAC layer covers three functional areas: reliable data delivery, access control, and security. In this section we examine reliable data delivery and access control; the security area is beyond our scope.

Reliable Data Delivery

As with any wireless network, a wireless LAN using the IEEE 802.11 physical and MAC layers is subject to considerable unreliability. Noise, interference, and other propagation effects result in the loss of a significant number of frames. Even with error-correction codes, a number of MAC frames may not successfully be received. This situation can be dealt with by reliability mechanisms at a higher layer, such as TCP. However, timers used for retransmission at higher layers are typically on the order of seconds. It is therefore more efficient to deal with errors at the MAC level. For this purpose, IEEE 802.11 includes a frame exchange protocol. When a station receives a data frame from another station, it returns an Acknowledgment (ACK) frame to the source station. This exchange is treated as an atomic unit, not to be interrupted by a transmission from any other station. If the source does not receive an ACK within a short period of time, either because its data frame was damaged or because the returning ACK was damaged, the source retransmits the frame.

Thus, the basic data transfer mechanism in IEEE 802.11 involves an exchange of two frames. To further enhance reliability, a four-frame exchange may be used. In this scheme, a source first issues a Request to Send (RTS) frame to the destination. The destination then responds with a Clear to Send (CTS). After receiving the CTS, the source transmits the data frame, and the destination responds with an ACK. The RTS alerts all stations that are within reception range of the source that an exchange is under way; these stations refrain from transmission in order to avoid a collision between two frames transmitted at the same time. Similarly, the CTS alerts all stations that are within reception range of the destination that an exchange is under way. The RTS/CTS portion of the exchange is a required function of the MAC but may be disabled.

Access Control

The 802.11 working group considered two types of proposals for a MAC algorithm: distributed access protocols, which, like Ethernet, distribute the decision to transmit over all the nodes using a carrier-sense mechanism; and centralized access protocols, which involve regulation of transmission by a centralized decision maker. A distributed access protocol makes sense for an ad hoc network of peer workstations and may also be attractive in other wireless LAN configurations that consist primarily of bursty traffic. A centralized access protocol is natural for configurations in which a number of wireless stations are interconnected with each other and some sort of base station that attaches to a backbone wired LAN; it is especially useful if some of the data is time sensitive or high priority.

The end result for 802.11 is a MAC algorithm called DFWMAC (distributed foundation wireless MAC) that provides a distributed access control mechanism with an optional centralized control built on top of that. Figure 17.5 illustrates the architecture. The lower sublayer of the MAC layer is the distributed coordination function (DCF). DCF uses a contention algorithm to provide access to all traffic. Ordinary asynchronous traffic directly uses DCF. The point coordination function (PCF) is a centralized MAC algorithm used to provide contention-free service. PCF is built on top of DCF and exploits features of DCF to assure access for its users. Let us consider these two sublayers in turn.

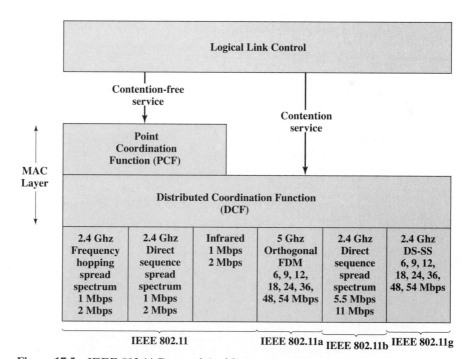

Figure 17.5   IEEE 802.11 Protocol Architecture

Distributed Coordination Function

The DCF sublayer makes use of a simple CSMA (carrier sense multiple access) algorithm. If a station has a MAC frame to transmit, it listens to the medium. If the medium is idle, the station may transmit; otherwise the station must wait until the current transmission is complete before transmitting. The DCF does not include a collision detection function (i.e., CSMA/CD) because collision detection is not practical on a wireless network. The dynamic range of the signals on the medium is very large, so that a transmitting station cannot effectively distinguish incoming weak signals from noise and the effects of its own transmission.

To ensure the smooth and fair functioning of this algorithm, DCF includes a set of delays that amounts to a priority scheme. Let us start by considering a single delay known as an interframe space (IFS). In fact, there are three different IFS values, but the algorithm is best explained by initially ignoring this detail. Using an IFS, the rules for CSMA access are as follows (Figure 17.6):

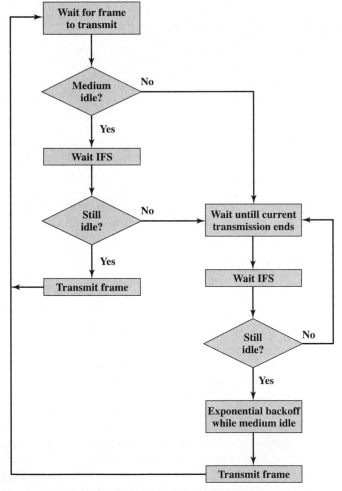

Figure 17.6 IEEE 802.11 Medium Access Control Logic

1. A station with a frame to transmit senses the medium. If the medium is idle, it waits to see if the medium remains idle for a time equal to IFS. If so, the station may transmit immediately.

2. If the medium is busy (either because the station initially finds the medium busy or because the medium becomes busy during the IFS idle time), the station defers transmission and continues to monitor the medium until the current transmission is over.

3. Once the current transmission is over, the station delays another IFS. If the medium remains idle for this period, then the station backs off a random amount of time and again senses the medium. If the medium is still idle, the station may transmit. During the backoff time, if the medium becomes busy, the backoff timer is halted and resumes when the medium becomes idle.

To ensure that backoff maintains stability, binary exponential backoff, described in Chapter 16, is used. Binary exponential backoff provides a means of handling a heavy load. Repeated failed attempts to transmit result in longer and longer backoff times, which helps to smooth out the load. Without such a backoff, the following situation could occur: Two or more stations attempt to transmit at the same time, causing a collision. These stations then immediately attempt to retransmit, causing a new collision.

The preceding scheme is refined for DCF to provide priority-based access by the simple expedient of using three values for IFS:

- **SIFS (short IFS):** The shortest IFS, used for all immediate response actions, as explained in the following discussion
- **PIFS (point coordination function IFS):** A midlength IFS, used by the centralized controller in the PCF scheme when issuing polls
- **DIFS (distributed coordination function IFS):** The longest IFS, used as a minimum delay for asynchronous frames contending for access

Figure 17.7a illustrates the use of these time values. Consider first the SIFS. Any station using SIFS to determine transmission opportunity has, in effect, the highest priority, because it will always gain access in preference to a station waiting an amount of time equal to PIFS or DIFS. The SIFS is used in the following circumstances:

- **Acknowledgment (ACK):** When a station receives a frame addressed only to itself (not multicast or broadcast), it responds with an ACK frame after waiting only for an SIFS gap. This has two desirable effects. First, because collision detection is not used, the likelihood of collisions is greater than with CSMA/CD, and the MAC-level ACK provides for efficient collision recovery. Second, the SIFS can be used to provide efficient delivery of an LLC protocol data unit (PDU) that requires multiple MAC frames. In this case, the following scenario occurs. A station with a multiframe LLC PDU to transmit sends out the MAC frames one at a time. Each frame is acknowledged after SIFS by the recipient. When the source receives an ACK, it immediately (after SIFS)

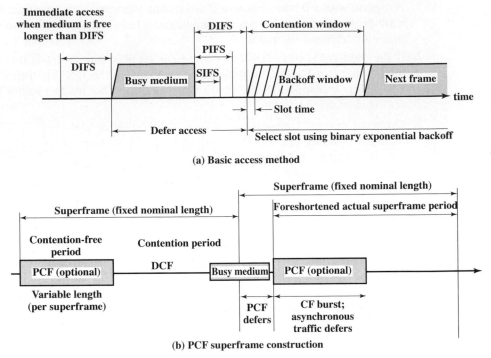

Figure 17.7 IEEE 802.11 MAC Timing

sends the next frame in the sequence. The result is that once a station has contended for the channel, it will maintain control of the channel until it has sent all of the fragments of an LLC PDU.

- **Clear to Send (CTS):** A station can ensure that its data frame will get through by first issuing a small Request to Send (RTS) frame. The station to which this frame is addressed should immediately respond with a CTS frame if it is ready to receive. All other stations receive the RTS and defer using the medium.
- **Poll response:** This is explained in the following discussion of PCF.

The next longest IFS interval is the PIFS. This is used by the centralized controller in issuing polls and takes precedence over normal contention traffic. However, those frames transmitted using SIFS have precedence over a PCF poll.

Finally, the DIFS interval is used for all ordinary asynchronous traffic.

Point Coordination Function

PCF is an alternative access method implemented on top of the DCF. The operation consists of polling by the centralized polling master (point coordinator). The point coordinator makes use of PIFS when issuing polls. Because PIFS is smaller than DIFS, the point coordinator can seize the medium and lock out all asynchronous traffic while it issues polls and receives responses.

As an extreme, consider the following possible scenario. A wireless network is configured so that a number of stations with time-sensitive traffic are controlled by the point coordinator while remaining traffic contends for access using CSMA. The point coordinator could issue polls in a round-robin fashion to all stations configured for polling. When a poll is issued, the polled station may respond using SIFS. If the point coordinator receives a response, it issues another poll using PIFS. If no response is received during the expected turnaround time, the coordinator issues a poll.

If the discipline of the preceding paragraph were implemented, the point coordinator would lock out all asynchronous traffic by repeatedly issuing polls. To prevent this, an interval known as the superframe is defined. During the first part of this interval, the point coordinator issues polls in a round-robin fashion to all stations configured for polling. The point coordinator then idles for the remainder of the superframe, allowing a contention period for asynchronous access.

Figure 17.7b illustrates the use of the superframe. At the beginning of a superframe, the point coordinator may optionally seize control and issue polls for a given period of time. This interval varies because of the variable frame size issued by responding stations. The remainder of the superframe is available for contention-based access. At the end of the superframe interval, the point coordinator contends for access to the medium using PIFS. If the medium is idle, the point coordinator gains immediate access and a full superframe period follows. However, the medium may be busy at the end of a superframe. In this case, the point coordinator must wait until the medium is idle to gain access; this results in a foreshortened superframe period for the next cycle.

MAC Frame

Figure 17.8 shows the 802.11 frame format. This general format is used for all data and control frames, but not all fields are used in all contexts. The fields are as follows:

- **Frame Control:** Indicates the type of frame (control, management, or data) and provides control information. Control information includes whether the frame is to or from a DS, fragmentation information, and privacy information.
- **Duration/Connection ID:** If used as a duration field, indicates the time (in microseconds) the channel will be allocated for successful transmission of a MAC frame. In some control frames, this field contains an association, or connection, identifier.
- **Addresses:** The number and meaning of the address fields depend on context. Address types include source, destination, transmitting station, and receiving station.

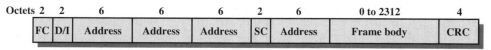

Octets 2	2	6	6	6	2	6	0 to 2312	4
FC	D/I	Address	Address	Address	SC	Address	Frame body	CRC

FC = Frame control
D/I = Duration/Connection ID
SC = Sequence control

Figure 17.8   IEEE 802.11 MAC Frame Format

- **Sequence Control:** Contains a 4-bit fragment number subfield, used for fragmentation and reassembly, and a 12-bit sequence number used to number frames sent between a given transmitter and receiver.
- **Frame Body:** Contains an MSDU or a fragment of an MSDU. The MSDU is a LLC protocol data unit or MAC control information.
- **Frame Check Sequence:** A 32-bit cyclic redundancy check.

We now look at the three MAC frame types.

Control Frames

Control frames assist in the reliable delivery of data frames. There are six control frame subtypes:

- **Power Save-Poll (PS-Poll):** This frame is sent by any station to the station that includes the AP (access point). Its purpose is to request that the AP transmit a frame that has been buffered for this station while the station was in power-saving mode.
- **Request to Send (RTS):** This is the first frame in the four-way frame exchange discussed under the subsection on reliable data delivery at the beginning of Section 17.3. The station sending this message is alerting a potential destination, and all other stations within reception range, that it intends to send a data frame to that destination.
- **Clear to Send (CTS):** This is the second frame in the four-way exchange. It is sent by the destination station to the source station to grant permission to send a data frame.
- **Acknowledgment:** Provides an acknowledgment from the destination to the source that the immediately preceding data, management, or PS-Poll frame was received correctly.
- **Contention-Free (CF)-End:** Announces the end of a contention-free period that is part of the point coordination function.
- **CF-End + CF-Ack:** Acknowledges the CF-end. This frame ends the contention-free period and releases stations from the restrictions associated with that period.

Data Frames

There are eight data frame subtypes, organized into two groups. The first four subtypes define frames that carry upper-level data from the source station to the destination station. The four data-carrying frames are as follows:

- **Data:** This is the simplest data frame. It may be used in both a contention period and a contention-free period.
- **Data + CF-Ack:** May only be sent during a contention-free period. In addition to carrying data, this frame acknowledges previously received data.
- **Data + CF-Poll:** Used by a point coordinator to deliver data to a mobile station and to request that the mobile station send a data frame that it may have buffered.

- **Data + CF-Ack + CF-Poll:** Combines the functions of the Data + CF-Ack and Data + CF-Poll into a single frame.

The remaining four subtypes of data frames do not in fact carry any user data. The Null Function data frame carries no data, polls, or acknowledgments. It is used only to carry the power management bit in the frame control field to the AP, to indicate that the station is changing to a low-power operating state. The remaining three frames (CF-Ack, CF-Poll, CF-Ack + CF-Poll) have the same functionality as the corresponding data frame subtypes in the preceding list (Data + CF-Ack, Data + CF-Poll, Data + CF-Ack + CF-Poll) but without the data.

Management Frames

Management frames are used to manage communications between stations and APs. Functions covered include management of associations (request, response, reassociation, dissociation, and authentication).

17.5 IEEE 802.11 PHYSICAL LAYER

The physical layer for IEEE 802.11 has been issued in four stages; the first part was issued in 1997, two additional parts in 1999, and the most recent in 2002. The first part, simply called IEEE 802.11, includes the MAC layer and three physical layer specifications, two in the 2.4-GHz band and one in the infrared, all operating at 1 and 2 Mbps. IEEE 802.11a operates in the 5-GHz band at data rates up to 54 Mbps. IEEE 802.11b operates in the 2.4-Ghz band at 5.5 and 11 Mbps. IEEE 802.g extends IEEE 802.11b to higher data rates. We look at each of these in turn.

Original IEEE 802.11 Physical Layer

Three physical media are defined in the original 802.11 standard:

- Direct-sequence spread spectrum operating in the 2.4 GHz ISM band, at data rates of 1 Mbps and 2 Mbps
- Frequency-hopping spread spectrum operating in the 2.4 GHz ISM band, at data rates of 1 Mbps and 2 Mbps
- Infrared at 1 Mbps and 2 Mbps operating at a wavelength between 850 and 950 nm

Direct-Sequence Spread Spectrum

Up to seven channels, each with a data rate of 1 Mbps or 2 Mbps, can be used in the DS-SS system. The number of channels available depends on the bandwidth allocated by the various national regulatory agencies. This ranges from 13 in most European countries to just one available channel in Japan. Each channel has a bandwidth of 5 MHz. The encoding scheme that is used is DBPSK for the 1-Mbps rate and DQPSK for the 2-Mbps rate.

Frequency-Hopping Spread Spectrum

Recall from Chapter 7 that an FH-SS system makes use of multiple channels, with the signal hopping from one channel to another based on a pseudonoise sequence. In the case of the IEEE 802.11 scheme, 1-MHz channels are used. The number of channels available ranges from 23 in Japan to 70 in the United States.

The details of the hopping scheme are adjustable. For example, the minimum hop rate for the United States is 2.5 hops per second. The minimum hop distance in frequency is 6 MHz in North America and most of Europe and 5 MHz in Japan.

For modulation, the FH-SS scheme uses two-level Gaussian FSK for the 1-Mbps system. The bits zero and one are encoded as deviations from the current carrier frequency. For 2 Mbps, a four-level GFSK scheme is used, in which four different deviations from the center frequency define the four 2-bit combinations.

Infrared

The IEEE 802.11 infrared scheme is omnidirectional rather than point to point. A range of up to 20 m is possible. The modulation scheme for the 1-Mbps data rate is known as 16-PPM (pulse position modulation). In this scheme, each group of 4 data bits is mapped into one of the 16-PPM symbols; each symbol is a string of 16 bits. Each 16-bit string consists of fifteen 0s and one binary 1. For the 2-Mbps data rate, each group of 2 data bits is mapped into one of four 4-bit sequences. Each sequence consists of three 0s and one binary 1. The actual transmission uses an intensity modulation scheme, in which the presence of a signal corresponds to a binary 1 and the absence of a signal corresponds to binary 0.

IEEE 802.11a

The IEEE 802.11a specification makes use of the 5-GHz band. Unlike the 2.4-GHz specifications, IEEE 802.11 does not use a spread spectrum scheme but rather uses orthogonal frequency division multiplexing (OFDM). OFDM, also called multicarrier modulation, uses multiple carrier signals at different frequencies, sending some of the bits on each channel. This is similar to FDM. However, in the case of OFDM, all of the subchannels are dedicated to a single data source.

The possible data rates for IEEE 802.11a are 6, 9, 12, 18, 24, 36, 48, and 54 Mbps. The system uses up to 52 subcarriers that are modulated using BPSK, QPSK, 16-QAM, or 64-QAM, depending on the rate required. Subcarrier frequency spacing is 0.3125 MHz. A convolutional code at a rate of 1/2, 2/3, or 3/4, provides forward error correction.

IEEE 802.11b

IEEE 802.11b is an extension of the IEEE 802.11 DS-SS scheme, providing data rates of 5.5 and 11 Mbps. The chipping rate is 11 MHz, which is the same as the original DS-SS scheme, thus providing the same occupied bandwidth. To achieve a higher data rate in the same bandwidth at the same chipping rate, a modulation scheme known as complementary code keying (CCK) is used.

The CCK modulation scheme is quite complex and is not examined in detail here. Figure 17.9 provides an overview of the scheme for the 11-Mbps rate. Input data are treated in blocks of 8 bits at a rate of 1.375 MHz (8 bits/symbol $\times$ 1.375 MHz =

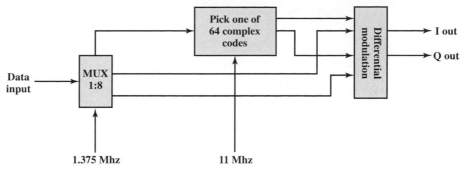

Figure 17.9 11-Mbps CCK Modulation Scheme

11 Mbps). Six of these bits are mapped into one of 64 code sequences. The output of the mapping, plus the two additional bits, forms the input to a QPSK modulator.

IEEE 802.11g

IEEE 802.11g is a higher-speed extension to IEEE 802.11b. This scheme combines a variety of physical layer encoding techniques used in 802.11a and 802.11b to provide service at a variety of data rates.

17.6 RECOMMENDED READING AND WEB SITES

[PAHL95] and [BANT94] are detailed survey articles on wireless LANs. [KAHN97] provides good coverage of infrared LANs.

[OHAR99] is an excellent technical treatment of IEEE 802.11. Another good treatment is [LARO02]. [GEIE99] also provides detailed coverage of the IEEE 802.11 standards, and numerous case studies. [CROW97] is a good survey article on the 802.11 standards. Neither of the last two references covers IEEE 802.11a and IEEE 802.11b. [GEIE01] has a good discussion of IEEE 802.11a. [SHOE02] provides an overview of IEEE 802.11b.

BANT94   Bantz, D., and Bauchot, F. "Wireless LAN Design Alternatives." *IEEE Network*, March/April 1994.

CROW97   Crow, B., et al., "IEEE 802.11 Wireless Local Area Networks." *IEEE Communications Magazine*, September 1997.

GEIE99   Geier, J. *Wireless LANs*. New York: Macmillan Technical Publishing, 1999.

GEIE01   Geier, J. "Enabling Fast Wireless Networks with OFDM." *Communications System Design*, February 2001. (www.csdmag.com)

KAHN97   Kahn, J., and Barry, J. "Wireless Infrared Communications." *Proceedings of the IEEE*, February 1997.

LARO02   LaRocca, J., and LaRocca, R. *802.11 Demystified*. New York: McGraw-Hill, 2002.

OHAR99   Ohara, B., and Petrick, A. *IEEE 802.11 Handbook: A Designer's Companion*. New York: IEEE Press, 1999.

PAHL95   Pahlavan, K.; Probert, T.; and Chase, M. "Trends in Local Wireless Networks." *IEEE Communications Magazine*, March 1995.

SHOE02   Shoemake, M. "IEEE 802.11g Jells as Applications Mount." *Communications System Design*, April 2002. www.commsdesign.com.

Recommended Web Sites:

- **Wireless LAN Alliance:** Gives an introduction to the technology, including a discussion of implementation considerations and case studies from users. Links to related sites.
- **The IEEE 802.11 Wireless LAN Working Group:** Contains working group documents plus discussion archives.
- **Wi–Fi Alliance:** An industry group promoting the interoperability of 802.11 products with each other and with Ethernet.

17.7 KEY TERMS AND REVIEW QUESTIONS

Key Terms

access point (AP)	distributed coordination	nomadic access
ad hoc networking	function (DCF)	point coordination
Barker sequence	distribution system (DS)	function (PCF)
basic service set (BSS)	extended service set (ESS)	spread spectrum LAN
complementary code	infrared LAN	wireless LAN
keying (CCK)	LAN extension	
coordination function	narrowband microwave LAN	

Review Questions

17.1 List and briefly define four application areas for wireless LANs.

17.2 List and briefly define key requirements for wireless LANs.

17.3 What is the difference between a single-cell and a multiple-cell wireless LAN?

17.4 What are some key advantages of infrared LANs?

17.5 What are some key disadvantages of infrared LANs?

17.6 List and briefly define three transmission techniques for infrared LANs.

17.7 What is the difference between an access point and a portal?

17.8 Is a distribution system a wireless network?

17.9 List and briefly define IEEE 802.11 services.

17.10 How is the concept of an association related to that of mobility?

Networking Protocols

We have dealt, so far, with the technologies and techniques used to exchange data between two devices. Part Two dealt with the case in which the two devices share a transmission link. Parts Three and Four were concerned with the case in which a communication network provides a shared transmission capacity for multiple attached end systems.

In a distributed data processing system, much more is needed. The data processing systems (workstations, PCs, servers, mainframes) must implement a set of functions that will allow them to perform some task cooperatively. This set of functions is organized into a communications architecture and involves a layered set of protocols, including internetwork, transport, and application-layer protocols.

Before proceeding with Part Five, the reader is advised to revisit Chapter 2, which introduces the concept of a protocol architecture and discusses the key elements of a protocol.

Chapter 18 Internetwork Protocols

With the proliferation of networks, internetworking facilities have become essential components of network design. Chapter 18 begins with an examination of the requirements for an internetworking facility and the various design approaches that can be taken to satisfy those requirements. The remainder of the chapter deals with the use of routers for internetworking. The Internet Protocol (IP) and the new IPv6 are examined.

Chapter 19 Internetwork Operation

Chapter 19 begins with a discussion of multicasting across an internet. Then issues of routing and quality of service are explored.

The traffic that the Internet and these private internetworks must carry continues to grow and change. The demand generated by traditional data-based applications, such as electronic mail, Usenet news, file transfer, and remote logon, is sufficient to challenge these systems. But the driving factors are the heavy use of the World Wide Web, which demands real-time response, and the increasing use of voice, image, and even video over internetwork architectures.

These internetwork schemes are essentially datagram packet-switching technology with routers functioning as the switches. This technology was not designed to handle voice and video and is straining to meet the demands placed on it. While some foresee the replacement of this conglomeration of Ethernet-based LANs, packet-based WANs, and IP-datagram-based routers with a seamless ATM transport service from desktop to backbone, that day is far off. Meanwhile, the internetworking and routing functions of these networks must be engineered to meet the load.

Chapter 19 looks at some of the tools and techniques designed to meet the new demand, beginning with a discussion of routing schemes, which can help smooth out load surges. The remainder of the chapter looks at recent efforts to provide a given level of Quality of Service (QoS) to various applications. The most important elements of this new approach are integrated services and differentiated services.

Chapter 20 Transport Protocols

The transport protocol is the keystone of the whole concept of a computer communications architecture. It can also be one of the most complex of protocols. Chapter 20 examines in detail transport protocol mechanisms and then discusses two important examples, TCP and UDP. The bulk of the chapter is devoted to an analysis of the complex set of TCP mechanisms and of TCP congestion control schemes.

Chapter 21 Network Security

Network security has become increasingly important with the growth in the number and importance of networks. Chapter 21 provides a survey of security techniques and services. The chapter begins with a look at encryption techniques for ensuring confidentiality, which include the use of conventional and public-key encryption. Then the area of authentication and digital signatures is explored. The two most important encryption algorithms, AES and RSA, are examined, as well as SHA-1, a one-way hash function important in a number of security applications. Chapter 21 also discusses SSL and the set of IP security standards.

Chapter 22 Distributed Applications

The purpose of a communications architecture is to support distributed applications. Chapter 22 examines three of the most important of these applications; in each case, general principles are discussed, followed by a specific example. The applications discussed are electronic mail, Web exchanges, and network management. The corresponding examples are SMTP and MIME; http; and SNMP.

CHAPTER **18**

INTERNET PROTOCOLS

KEY POINTS

- Key functions typically performed by a protocol include encapsulation, fragmentation and reassembly, connection control, ordered delivery, flow control, error control, addressing, and multiplexing.

- An internet consists of multiple separate networks that are interconnected by routers. Data are transmitted in packets from a source system to a destination across a path involving multiple networks and routers. Typically, a connectionless or datagram operation is used. A router accepts datagrams and relays them on toward their destination and is responsible for determining the route, much the same way as packet-switching nodes operate.

- The most widely used protocol for internetworking is the Internet Protocol (IP). IP attaches a header to upper-layer (e.g., TCP) data to form an IP datagram. The header includes source and destination addresses, information used for fragmentation and reassembly, a time-to-live field, a type of service field, and a checksum.

- A next-generation IP, known as IPv6, has been defined. IPv6 provides longer address fields and more functionality than the current IP.

The purpose of this chapter is to examine the Internet Protocol, which is the foundation on which all of the internet-based protocols and on which internetworking is based. First, it will be useful to review the basic functions of networking protocols. This review serves to summarize some of the material introduced previously and to set the stage for the study of internet-based protocols in Part Five. We then move to a discussion of internetworking. The remainder of the chapter is devoted to the two standard internet protocols: IPv4 and IPv6.

Refer to Figure 2.15 to see the position within the TCP/IP suite of the protocols discussed in this chapter.

18.1 BASIC PROTOCOL FUNCTIONS

Before turning to a discussion of internet protocols, let us consider a rather small set of functions that form the basis of all protocols. Not all protocols have all functions; this would involve a significant duplication of effort. There are, nevertheless, many instances of the same type of function being present in protocols at different levels.

We can group protocol functions into the following categories:

- Encapsulation
- Fragmentation and reassembly
- Connection control
- Ordered delivery
- Flow control
- Error control

- Addressing
- Multiplexing
- Transmission services

Encapsulation

For virtually all protocols, data are transferred in blocks, called protocol data units (PDUs). Each PDU contains not only data but also control information. Indeed, some PDUs consist solely of control information and no data. The control information falls into three general categories:

- **Address:** The address of the sender and/or receiver may be indicated.
- **Error-detecting code:** Some sort of frame check sequence is often included for error detection.
- **Protocol control:** Additional information is included to implement the protocol functions listed in the remainder of this section.

The addition of control information to data is referred to as **encapsulation**. Data are accepted or generated by an entity and encapsulated into a PDU containing that data plus control information. Numerous examples of PDUs appear in the preceding chapters [e.g., TFTP (Figure 2.17), HDLC (Figure 7.7), frame relay (Figure 10.19), ATM (Figure 11.4), AAL5 (Figure 11.15), LLC (Figure 15.7), IEEE 802.3 (Figure 16.3), IEEE 802.11 (Figure 17.8)].

Fragmentation and Reassembly[1]

A protocol is concerned with exchanging streams of data between two entities. Usually, the transfer can be characterized as consisting of a sequence of PDUs of some bounded size. At the application level, we refer to a logical unit of data transfer as a message. Whether the application entity sends data in messages or in a continuous stream, lower-level protocols may need to break the data up into blocks of some smaller bounded size. This process is called fragmentation.

There are a number of motivations for fragmentation, depending on the context. The following are among the typical reasons for fragmentation:

- The communications network may only accept blocks of data up to a certain size. For example, an ATM network is limited to blocks of 53 octets; Ethernet imposes a maximum size of 1526 octets.
- Error control may be more efficient with a smaller PDU size. With smaller PDUs, fewer bits need to be retransmitted when a PDU suffers an error.
- More equitable access to shared transmission facilities, with shorter delay, can be provided. For example, without a maximum block size, one station could monopolize a multipoint medium.

---

[1] The term *segmentation* is used in OSI-related documents, but in protocol specifications related to the TCP/IP protocol suite, the term *fragmentation* is used. The meaning is the same.

- A smaller PDU size may mean that receiving entities can allocate smaller buffers.
- An entity may require that data transfer comes to some sort of "closure" from time to time, for checkpoint and restart/recovery operations.

There are several disadvantages to fragmentation that argue for making PDUs as large as possible:

- As just explained, each PDU contains a certain amount of control information. Hence the smaller the block, the greater the percentage of overhead.
- PDU arrival may generate an interrupt that must be serviced. Smaller blocks result in more interrupts.
- More time is spent processing smaller, more numerous PDUs.

All of these factors must be taken into account by the protocol designer in determining minimum and maximum PDU size.

The counterpart of fragmentation is reassembly. Eventually, the segmented data must be reassembled into messages appropriate to the application level. If PDUs arrive out of order, the task is complicated.

The process of fragmentation is illustrated in Figure 2.4.

Connection Control

An entity may transmit data to another entity in such a way that each PDU is treated independently of all prior PDUs. This is known as connectionless data transfer; an example is the use of the datagram, described in Chapter 10. While this mode is useful, an equally important technique is connection-oriented data transfer, of which the virtual circuit, also described in Chapter 10, is an example.

Connection-oriented data transfer is to be preferred (even required) if stations anticipate a lengthy exchange of data and/or certain details of their protocol must be worked out dynamically. A logical association, or connection, is established between the entities. Three phases occur (Figure 18.1):

- Connection establishment
- Data transfer
- Connection termination

With more sophisticated protocols, there may also be connection interrupt and recovery phases to cope with errors and other sorts of interruptions.

During the connection establishment phase, two entities agree to exchange data. Typically, one station will issue a connection request (in connectionless fashion) to the other. A central authority may or may not be involved. In simpler protocols, the receiving entity either accepts or rejects the request and, in the former case, the connection is considered to be established. In more complex proposals, this phase includes a negotiation concerning the syntax, semantics, and timing of the protocol. Both entities must, of course, be using the same protocol. But the protocol may allow certain optional features and these must be agreed upon by means of negotiation. For example, the protocol may specify a PDU size of up to 8000 octets; one station may wish to restrict this to 1000 octets.

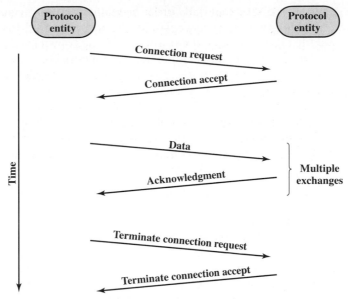

Figure 18.1 The Phases of a Connection-Oriented Data Transfer

Following connection establishment, the data transfer phase is entered. During this phase both data and control information (e.g., flow control, error control) are exchanged. Figure 18.1 shows a situation in which all of the data flow in one direction, with acknowledgments returned in the other direction. More typically, data and acknowledgments flow in both directions. Finally, one side or the other wishes to terminate the connection and does so by sending a termination request. Alternatively, a central authority might forcibly terminate a connection.

A key characteristic of many connection-oriented data transfer protocols is that sequencing is used (e.g., HDLC, IEEE 802.11). Each side sequentially numbers the PDUs that it sends to the other side. Because each side remembers that it is engaged in a logical connection, it can keep track of both outgoing numbers, which it generates, and incoming numbers, which are generated by the other side. Indeed, one can essentially define a connection-oriented data transfer as one in which both sides number PDUs and keep track of both incoming and outgoing numbers. Sequencing supports three main functions: ordered deliver, flow control, and error control.

Sequencing is not found in all connection-oriented protocols. Examples include frame relay and ATM. However, all connection-oriented protocols include in the PDU format some way of identifying the connection, which may be a unique connection identifier or a combination of source and destination addresses.

Ordered Delivery

If two communicating entities are in different hosts[2] connected by a network, there is a risk that PDUs will not arrive in the order in which they were sent, because they may traverse different paths through the network. In connection-oriented protocols,

---

[2] The term *host* refers to any end system attached to a network, such as a PC, workstation, or server.

it is generally required that PDU order be maintained. For example, if a file is transferred between two systems, we would like to be assured that the records of the received file are in the same order as those of the transmitted file, and not shuffled. If each PDU is given a unique number, and numbers are assigned sequentially, then it is a logically simple task for the receiving entity to reorder received PDUs on the basis of sequence number. A problem with this scheme is that, with a finite sequence number field, sequence numbers repeat (modulo some maximum number). Evidently, the maximum sequence number must be greater than the maximum number of PDUs that could be outstanding at any time. In fact, the maximum number may need to be twice the maximum number of PDUs that could be outstanding (e.g., selective-repeat ARQ; see Chapter 7).

Flow Control

Flow control is a function performed by a receiving entity to limit the amount or rate of data that is sent by a transmitting entity.

The simplest form of flow control is a stop-and-wait procedure, in which each PDU must be acknowledged before the next can be sent. More efficient protocols involve some form of credit provided to the transmitter, which is the amount of data that can be sent without an acknowledgment. The HDLC sliding-window technique is an example of this mechanism (Chapter 7).

Flow control is a good example of a function that must be implemented in several protocols. Consider again Figure 2.3. The network will need to exercise flow control over X via the network access protocol, to enforce network traffic control. At the same time, Y's network access module has only limited buffer space and needs to exercise flow control over X's network access module via the transport protocol. Finally, even though Y's network access module can control its data flow, Y's application may be vulnerable to overflow. For example, the application could be hung up waiting for disk access. Thus, flow control is also needed over the application-oriented protocol.

Error Control

Error control techniques are needed to guard against loss or damage of data and control information. Typically, error control is implemented as two separate functions: error detection and retransmission. To achieve error detection, the sender inserts an error-detecting code in the transmitted PDU, which is a function of the other bits in the PDU. The receiver checks the value of the code on the incoming PDU. If an error is detected the receiver discards the PDU. Upon failing to receive an acknowledgment to the PDU in a reasonable time, the sender retransmits the PDU. Some protocols also employ an error-correction code, which enables the receiver not only to detect errors but, in some cases, to correct them.

As with flow control, error control is a function that must be performed at various layers of protocol. Consider again Figure 2.3. The network access protocol should include error control to assure that data are successfully exchanged between station and network. However, a packet of data may be lost inside the network, and the transport protocol should be able to recover from this loss.

Addressing

The concept of addressing in a communications architecture is a complex one and covers a number of issues, including

- Addressing level
- Addressing scope
- Connection identifiers
- Addressing mode

During the discussion, we illustrate the concepts using Figure 18.2, which repeats Figure 2.13 and which shows a configuration using the TCP/IP architecture. The concepts are essentially the same for the OSI architecture or any other communications architecture.

Addressing level refers to the level in the communications architecture at which an entity is named. Typically, a unique address is associated with each end system (e.g., workstation or server) and each intermediate system (e.g., router) in a configuration. Such an address is, in general, a network-level address. In the case of the TCP/IP architecture, this is referred to as an IP address, or simply an internet address. In the case of the OSI architecture, this is referred to as a network service access point (NSAP). The network-level address is used to route a PDU through a network or networks to a system indicated by a network-level address in the PDU.

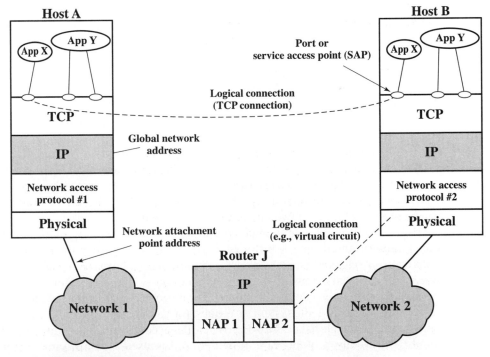

Figure 18.2 TCP/IP Concepts

Once data arrive at a destination system, they must be routed to some process or application in the system. Typically, a system will support multiple applications and an application may support multiple users. Each application and, perhaps, each concurrent user of an application, is assigned a unique identifier, referred to as a port in the TCP/IP architecture and as a service access point (SAP) in the OSI architecture. For example, a host system might support both an electronic mail application and a file transfer application. At minimum each application would have a port number or SAP that is unique within that system. Further, the file transfer application might support multiple simultaneous transfers, in which case, each transfer is dynamically assigned a unique port number or SAP.

Figure 18.2 illustrates two levels of addressing within a system. This is typically the case for the TCP/IP architecture. However, there can be addressing at each level of an architecture. For example, a unique SAP can be assigned to each level of the OSI architecture.

Another issue that relates to the address of an end system or intermediate system is **addressing scope**. The internet address or NSAP address referred to previously is a global address. The key characteristics of a global address are as follows:

- **Global nonambiguity:** A global address identifies a unique system. Synonyms are permitted. That is, a system may have more than one global address.
- **Global applicability:** It is possible at any global address to identify any other global address, in any system, by means of the global address of the other system.

Because a global address is unique and globally applicable, it enables an internet to route data from any system attached to any network to any other system attached to any other network.

Figure 18.2 illustrates that another level of addressing may be required. Each network must maintain a unique address for each device interface on the network. Examples are a MAC address on an IEEE 802 network and an ATM host address. This address enables the network to route data units (e.g., MAC frames, ATM cells) through the network and deliver them to the intended attached system. We can refer to such an address as a *network attachment point address*.

The issue of addressing scope is generally only relevant for network-level addresses. A port or SAP above the network level is unique within a given system but need not be globally unique. For example, in Figure 18.2, there can be a port 1 in system A and a port 1 in system B. The full designation of these two ports could be expressed as A.1 and B.1, which are unique designations.

The concept of **connection identifiers** comes into play when we consider connection-oriented data transfer (e.g., virtual circuit) rather than connectionless data transfer (e.g., datagram). For connectionless data transfer, a global identifier is used with each data transmission. For connection-oriented transfer, it is sometimes desirable to use only a connection identifier during the data transfer phase. The scenario is this: Entity 1 on system A requests a connection to entity 2 on system B, perhaps using the global address B.2. When B.2 accepts the connection, a connection identifier (usually a number) is provided and is used by both entities for future transmissions. The use of a connection identifier has several advantages:

- **Reduced overhead:** Connection identifiers are generally shorter than global identifiers. For example, in the frame relay protocol (discussed in Chapter 10), connection request packets contain both source and destination address fields. After a logical connection, called a data link connection, is established, data frames contain a data link connection identifier (DLCI) of 10, 16, or 23 bits.

- **Routing:** In setting up a connection, a fixed route may be defined. The connection identifier serves to identify the route to intermediate systems, such as packet-switching nodes, for handling future PDUs.

- **Multiplexing:** We address this function in more general terms later. Here we note that an entity may wish to enjoy more than one connection simultaneously. Thus, incoming PDUs must be identified by connection identifier.

- **Use of state information:** Once a connection is established, the end systems can maintain state information relating to the connection. This enables such functions as flow control and error control using sequence numbers. We see examples of this with HDLC (Chapter 7) and IEEE 802.11 (Chapter 17).

Figure 18.2 shows several examples of connections. The logical connection between router J and host B is at the network level. For example, if network 2 is a frame relay network, then this logical connection would be a data link connection. At a higher level, many transport-level protocols, such as TCP, support logical connections between users of the transport service. Thus, TCP can maintain a connection between two ports on different systems.

Another addressing concept is that of **addressing mode**. Most commonly, an address refers to a single system or port; in this case it is referred to as an individual or **unicast** address. It is also possible for an address to refer to more than one entity or port. Such an address identifies multiple simultaneous recipients for data. For example, a user might wish to send a memo to a number of individuals. The network control center may wish to notify all users that the network is going down. An address for multiple recipients may be **broadcast**, intended for all entities within a domain, or **multicast**, intended for a specific subset of entities. Table 18.1 illustrates the possibilities.

Table 18.1 Addressing Modes

Destination	Network Address	System Address	Port/SAP Address
Unicast	Individual	Individual	Individual
Multicast	Individual	Individual	Group
	Individual	All	Group
	All	All	Group
Broadcast	Individual	Individual	All
	Individual	All	All
	All	All	All

Multiplexing

Related to the concept of addressing is that of multiplexing. One form of multiplexing is supported by means of multiple connections into a single system. For example, with frame relay, there can be multiple data link connections terminating in a single end system; we can say that these data link connections are multiplexed over the single physical interface between the end system and the network. Multiplexing can also be accomplished via port names, which also permit multiple simultaneous connections. For example, there can be multiple TCP connections terminating in a given system, each connection supporting a different pair of ports.

Multiplexing is used in another context as well, namely the mapping of connections from one level to another. Consider again Figure 18.2. Network 1 might provide a connection-oriented service. For each process-to-process connection established at the next higher level, a data link connection could be created at the network access level. This is a one-to-one relationship, but need not be so. Multiplexing can be used in one of two directions. Upward multiplexing, or inward multiplexing, occurs when multiple higher-level connections are multiplexed on, or share, a single lower-level connection. This may be needed to make more efficient use of the lower-level service or to provide several higher-level connections in an environment where only a single lower-level connection exists. Downward multiplexing, or splitting, means that a single higher-level connection is built on top of multiple lower-level connections, the traffic on the higher connection being divided among the various lower connections. This technique may be used to provide reliability, performance, or efficiency.

Transmission Services

A protocol may provide a variety of additional services to the entities that use it. We mention here three common examples:

- **Priority:** Certain messages, such as control messages, may need to get through to the destination entity with minimum delay. An example would be a terminate-connection request. Thus, priority could be assigned on a message basis. Additionally, priority could be assigned on a connection basis.
- **Quality of service:** Certain classes of data may require a minimum throughput or a maximum delay threshold.
- **Security:** Security mechanisms, restricting access, may be invoked.

All of these services depend on the underlying transmission system and any intervening lower-level entities. If it is possible for these services to be provided from below, the protocol can be used by the two entities to exercise those services.

18.2 PRINCIPLES OF INTERNETWORKING

Packet-switching and packet-broadcasting networks grew out of a need to allow the computer user to have access to resources beyond that available in a single system. In a similar fashion, the resources of a single network are often inadequate to meet users' needs. Because the networks that might be of interest exhibit so many differences, it is impractical to consider merging them into a single network. Rather, what is needed is the ability to interconnect various networks so that any two stations on any of the constituent networks can communicate.

Table 18.2 lists some commonly used terms relating to the interconnection of networks, or internetworking. An interconnected set of networks, from a user's point of view, may appear simply as a larger network. However, if each of the constituent networks retains its identity and special mechanisms are needed for communicating across multiple networks, then the entire configuration is often referred to as an **internet**.

Each constituent network in an internet supports communication among the devices attached to that network; these devices are referred to as **end systems** (ESs). In addition, networks are connected by devices referred to in the ISO documents as **intermediate systems** (ISs). ISs provide a communications path and perform the necessary relaying and routing functions so that data can be exchanged between devices attached to different networks in the internet.

Table 18.2   Internetworking Terms

Communication Network
    A facility that provides a data transfer service among devices attached to the network.

Internet
    A collection of communication networks interconnected by bridges and/or routers.

Intranet
    An internet used by a single organization that provides the key Internet applications, especially the World Wide Web. An intranet operates within the organization for internal purposes and can exist as an isolated, self-contained internet, or may have links to the Internet.

Subnetwork
    Refers to a constituent network of an internet. This avoids ambiguity because the entire internet, from a user's point of view, is a single network.

End System (ES)
    A device attached to one of the networks of an internet that is used to support end-user applications or services.

Intermediate System (IS)
    A device used to connect two networks and permit communication between end systems attached to different networks.

Bridge
    An IS used to connect two LANs that use similar LAN protocols. The bridge acts as an address filter, picking up packets from one LAN that are intended for a destination on another LAN and passing those packets on. The bridge does not modify the contents of the packets and does not add anything to the packet. The bridge operates at layer 2 of the OSI model.

Router
    An IS used to connect two networks that may or may not be similar. The router employs an internet protocol present in each router and each end system of the network. The router operates at layer 3 of the OSI model.

Two types of ISs of particular interest are bridges and routers. The differences between them have to do with the types of protocols used for the internetworking logic. In essence, a **bridge** operates at layer 2 of the open systems interconnection (OSI) seven-layer architecture and acts as a relay of frames between similar networks; bridges are discussed in Chapter 15. A **router** operates at layer 3 of the OSI architecture and routes packets between potentially different networks. Both the bridge and the router assume that the same upper-layer protocols are in use.

We begin our examination of internetworking with a discussion of the basic principles of internetworking. We then examine the most important architectural approach to internetworking: the connectionless router. Then we describe the most widely used internetworking protocol, called simply the Internet Protocol (IP). Next, we look at the newest standardized internetworking protocol, known as IPv6.

Requirements

The overall requirements for an internetworking facility are as follows:

1. Provide a link between networks. At minimum, a physical and link control connection is needed.
2. Provide for the routing and delivery of data between processes on different networks.
3. Provide an accounting service that keeps track of the use of the various networks and routers and maintains status information.
4. Provide the services just listed in such a way as not to require modifications to the networking architecture of any of the constituent networks. This means that the internetworking facility must accommodate a number of differences among networks. These include the following:
   - **Different addressing schemes:** The networks may use different endpoint names and addresses and directory maintenance schemes. Some form of global network addressing must be provided, as well as a directory service.
   - **Different maximum packet size:** Packets from one network may have to be broken up into smaller pieces for another. This process is referred to as fragmentation.
   - **Different network access mechanisms:** The network access mechanism between station and network may be different for stations on different networks.
   - **Different timeouts:** Typically, a connection-oriented transport service will await an acknowledgment until a timeout expires, at which time it will retransmit its block of data. In general, longer times are required for successful delivery across multiple networks. Internetwork timing procedures must allow successful transmission that avoids unnecessary retransmissions.
   - **Error recovery:** Network procedures may provide anything from no error recovery up to reliable end-to-end (within the network) service. The internetwork service should not depend on nor be interfered with by the nature of the individual network's error recovery capability.

- **Status reporting:** Different networks report status and performance differently. Yet it must be possible for the internetworking facility to provide such information on internetworking activity to interested and authorized processes.
- **Routing techniques:** Intranetwork routing may depend on fault detection and congestion control techniques peculiar to each network. The internetworking facility must be able to coordinate these to route data adaptively between stations on different networks.
- **User access control:** Each network will have its own user access control technique (authorization for use of the network). These must be invoked by the internetwork facility as needed. Further, a separate internetwork access control technique may be required.
- **Connection, connectionless:** Individual networks may provide connection-oriented (e.g., virtual circuit) or connectionless (datagram) service. It may be desirable for the internetwork service not to depend on the nature of the connection service of the individual networks.

Some of these requirements are met by the Internet Protocol (IP). Others require additional control and application software, as we shall see in this chapter and the next.

Architectural Approaches

A key characteristic of an internet architecture is whether the mode of operation is connection oriented or connectionless.

Connection-Oriented Operation

In connection-oriented operation, it is assumed that each network provides a connection-oriented form of service. That is, it is possible to establish a logical network connection (e.g., virtual circuit) between any two end systems (ESs) attached to the same network. The connection is set up first, and then data are exchanged. With this in mind, we can summarize the connection-oriented approach as follows:

1. ISs are used to connect two or more networks; each IS appears as an ES to each of the networks to which it is attached.
2. When ES A wishes to exchange data with ES B, a logical connection is set up between them. This logical connection consists of the concatenation of a sequence of logical connections across networks. The sequence is such that it forms a path from ES A to ES B.
3. The individual network logical connections are spliced together by ISs. Any traffic arriving at an IS on one logical connection is retransmitted on a second logical connection and vice versa.

It is not always the case that the constituent networks of an internet provide a connection-oriented service. For example, an IEEE 802 LAN provides a service defined by the logical link control (LLC). Two of the options with LLC provide only connectionless service. So, in effect, these networks have a datagram style of transmission. Therefore, in this case, the network service must be enhanced. An example of how this would be done is for the ISs to implement X.25 on top of LLC across the LAN.

A connection-oriented IS performs the following key functions:

- **Relaying:** Data units arriving from one network via the network layer protocol are relayed (retransmitted) on another network. Traffic is over logical connections that are spliced together at the ISs.
- **Routing:** When an end-to-end logical connection, consisting of a sequence of logical connections, is to be set up, each IS in the sequence must make a routing decision that determines the next hop in the sequence.

Thus, at layer 3, a relaying operation is performed. It is assumed that all of the end systems share common protocols at layer 4 (transport) and above for successful end-to-end communication.

An example of the connection-oriented approach is the X.75 standard, used to interconnect X.25 packet-switching networks. In practice, the connection-oriented approach is not commonly used. The connectionless approach, using IP, is dominant.

Connectionless Operation

Whereas connection-oriented operation corresponds to the virtual circuit mechanism of a packet-switching network (Figure 10.13), connectionless-mode operation corresponds to the datagram mechanism of a packet-switching network (Figure 10.12). Each network protocol data unit is treated independently and routed from source ES to destination ES through a series of routers and networks. For each data unit transmitted by A, A makes a decision as to which router should receive the data unit. The data unit hops across the internet from one router to the next until it reaches the destination network. At each router, a routing decision is made (independently for each data unit) concerning the next hop. Thus, different data units may travel different routes between source and destination ES.

All ESs and all routers share a common network-layer protocol known generically as the internet protocol. An Internet Protocol (IP) was initially developed for the DARPA internet project and published as RFC 791 and has become an Internet Standard. Below this internet protocol, a protocol is needed to access a particular network. Thus, there are typically two protocols operating in each ES and router at the network layer: an upper sublayer that provides the internetworking function, and a lower sublayer that provides network access.

18.3 CONNECTIONLESS INTERNETWORKING

In this section, we examine the essential functions of an internetwork protocol. For convenience, we refer specifically to the Internet Standard IP, but the narrative in this section applies to any connectionless Internet Protocol, such as IPv6.

Operation of a Connectionless Internetworking Scheme

IP provides a connectionless, or datagram, service between end systems. There are a number of advantages to this approach:

- A connectionless internet facility is flexible. It can deal with a variety of networks, some of which are themselves connectionless. In essence, IP requires very little from the constituent networks.

- A connectionless internet service can be made highly robust. This is basically the same argument made for a datagram network service versus a virtual circuit service. For a further discussion, the reader is referred to Section 10.6.

- A connectionless internet service is best for connectionless transport protocols, because it does not impose unnecessary overhead.

Figure 18.3 depicts a typical example using IP, in which two LANs are interconnected by a frame relay WAN. The figure depicts the operation of the Internet Protocol for data exchange between host A on one LAN (network 1) and host B on another LAN (network 2) through the WAN. The figure shows the protocol architecture and format of the data unit at each stage. The end systems and routers must all share a common internet protocol. In addition, the end systems must share the same protocols above IP. The intermediate routers need only implement up through IP.

The IP at A receives blocks of data to be sent to B from the higher layers of software in A. IP attaches a header (at time t_1) specifying, among other things, the global internet address of B. That address is logically in two parts: network identifier and end system identifier. The combination of IP header and upper-level data is called an internet protocol data unit (PDU), or simply a datagram (see Figure 2.14). The datagram is then encapsulated with the LAN protocol (LLC header at t_2; MAC header and trailer at t_3) and sent to the router, which strips off the LAN fields to read the IP header (t_6). The router then encapsulates the datagram with the frame relay protocol fields (t_8) and transmits it across the WAN to another router. This router strips off the frame relay fields and recovers the datagram, which it then wraps in LAN fields appropriate to LAN 2 and sends it to B.

Let us now look at this example in more detail. End system A has a datagram to transmit to end system B; the datagram includes the internet address of B. The IP module in A recognizes that the destination (B) is on another network. So the first step is to send the data to a router, in this case router X. To do this, IP passes the datagram down to the next lower layer (in this case LLC) with instructions to send it to router X. LLC in turn passes this information down to the MAC layer, which inserts the MAC-level address of router X into the MAC header. Thus, the block of data transmitted onto LAN 1 includes data from a layer or layers above TCP, plus a TCP header, an IP header, an LLC header, and a MAC header and trailer (time t_3 in Figure 18.3).

Next, the packet travels through network 1 to router X. The router removes MAC and LLC fields and analyzes the IP header to determine the ultimate destination of the data, in this case B. The router must now make a routing decision. There are three possibilities:

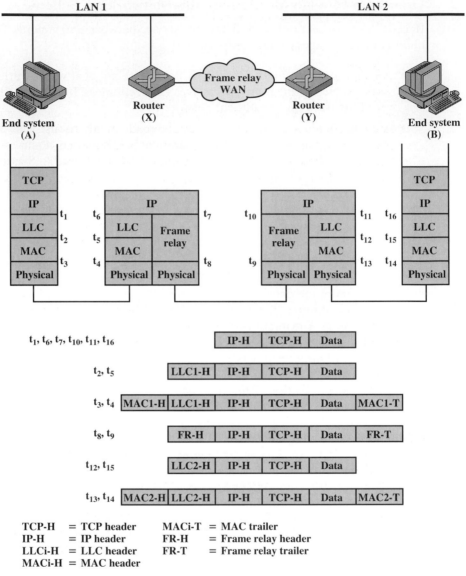

Figure 18.3 Internet Protocol Operation

1. The destination station B is connected directly to one of the networks to which the router is attached. If so, the router sends the datagram directly to the destination.
2. To reach the destination, one or more additional routers must be traversed. If so, a routing decision must be made: To which router should the datagram be sent? In both cases 1 and 2, the IP module in the router sends the datagram down to the next lower layer with the destination network address. Please note that we are speaking here of a lower-layer address that refers to this network.

3. The router does not know the destination address. In this case, the router returns an error message to the source of the datagram.

In this example, the data must pass through router Y before reaching the destination. So router X constructs a new frame by appending a frame relay header and trailer to the IP data unit. The frame relay header indicates a logical connection to router Y, when this frame arrives at router Y, the frame header and trailer are stripped off. The router determines that this IP data unit is destined for B, which is connected directly to a network to which this router is attached. The router therefore creates a frame with a layer-2 destination address of B and sends it out onto LAN 2. The data finally arrive at B, where the LAN and IP headers can be stripped off.

At each router, before the data can be forwarded, the router may need to fragment the data unit to accommodate a smaller maximum packet size limitation on the outgoing network. The data unit is split into two or more fragments, each of which becomes an independent IP data unit. Each new data unit is wrapped in a lower-layer packet and queued for transmission. The router may also limit the length of its queue for each network to which it attaches so as to avoid having a slow network penalize a faster one. Once the queue limit is reached, additional data units are simply dropped.

The process just described continues through as many routers as it takes for the data unit to reach its destination. As with a router, the destination end system recovers the IP data unit from its network wrapping. If fragmentation has occurred, the IP module in the destination end system buffers the incoming data until the entire original data field can be reassembled. This block of data is then passed to a higher layer in the end system.

This service offered by IP is an unreliable one. That is, IP does not guarantee that all data will be delivered or that the data that are delivered will arrive in the proper order. It is the responsibility of the next higher layer (e.g., TCP) to recover from any errors that occur. This approach provides for a great deal of flexibility.

With the internet protocol approach, each unit of data is passed from router to router in an attempt to get from source to destination. Because delivery is not guaranteed, there is no particular reliability requirement on any of the networks. Thus, the protocol will work with any combination of network types. Because the sequence of delivery is not guaranteed, successive data units can follow different paths through the internet. This allows the protocol to react to both congestion and failure in the internet by changing routes.

Design Issues

With that brief sketch of the operation of an IP-controlled internet, we can now go back and examine some design issues in greater detail:

- Routing
- Datagram lifetime
- Fragmentation and reassembly
- Error control
- Flow control

In IP, datagram fragments are reassembled at the destination end system. The IP fragmentation technique uses the following information in the IP header:

- Data Unit Identifier (ID)
- Data Length
- Offset
- More Flag

The *ID* is a means of uniquely identifying an end-system-originated datagram. In IP, it consists of the source and destination addresses, a number that corresponds to the protocol layer that generated the data (e.g., TCP), and an identification supplied by that protocol layer. The *Data Length* is the length of the user data field in octets, and the *Offset* is the position of a fragment of user data in the data field of the original datagram, in multiples of 64 bits.

The source end system creates a datagram with a *Data Length* equal to the entire length of the data field, with *Offset* = 0, and a *More Flag* set to 0 (false). To fragment a long datagram into two pieces, an IP module in a router performs the following tasks:

1. Create two new datagrams and copy the header fields of the incoming datagram into both.
2. Divide the incoming user data field into two approximately equal portions along a 64-bit boundary, placing one portion in each new datagram. The first portion must be a multiple of 64 bits (8 octets).
3. Set the *Data Length* of the first new datagram to the length of the inserted data, and set *More Flag* to 1 (true). The *Offset* field is unchanged.
4. Set the *Data Length* of the second new datagram to the length of the inserted data, and add the length of the first data portion divided by 8 to the *Offset* field. The *More Flag* remains the same.

Figure 18.5 gives an example. The procedure is easily generalized to an *n*-way split.

To reassemble a datagram, there must be sufficient buffer space at the reassembly point. As fragments with the same ID arrive, their data fields are inserted in the proper position in the buffer until the entire data field is reassembled, which is achieved when a contiguous set of data exists starting with an *Offset* of zero and ending with data from a fragment with a false *More Flag*.

One eventuality that must be dealt with is that one or more of the fragments may not get through: The IP service does not guarantee delivery. Some method is needed to decide when to abandon a reassembly effort to free up buffer space. Two approaches are commonly used. First, assign a reassembly lifetime to the first fragment to arrive. This is a local, real-time clock assigned by the reassembly function and decremented while the fragments of the original datagram are being buffered. If the time expires prior to complete reassembly, the received fragments are discarded. A second approach is to make use of the datagram lifetime, which is part of the header of each incoming fragment. The lifetime field continues to be decremented by the reassembly function; as with the first approach, if the lifetime expires prior to complete reassembly, the received fragments are discarded.

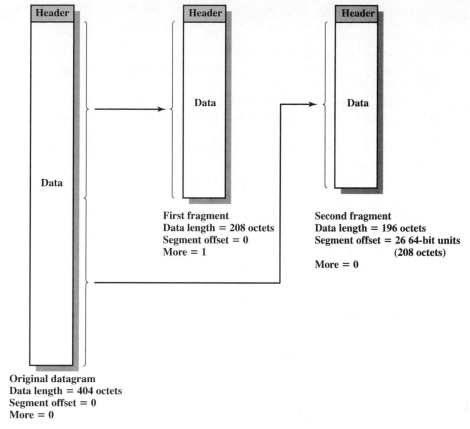

First fragment
Data length = 208 octets
Segment offset = 0
More = 1

Second fragment
Data length = 196 octets
Segment offset = 26 64-bit units
                   (208 octets)

More = 0

Original datagram
Data length = 404 octets
Segment offset = 0
More = 0

Figure 18.5 Fragmentation Example

Error Control

The internetwork facility does not guarantee successful delivery of every datagram. When a datagram is discarded by a router, the router should attempt to return some information to the source, if possible. The source internet protocol entity may use this information to modify its transmission strategy and may notify higher layers. To report that a specific datagram has been discarded, some means of datagram identification is needed.

Datagrams may be discarded for a number of reasons, including lifetime expiration, congestion, and FCS error. In the latter case, notification is not possible because the source address field may have been damaged.

Flow Control

Internet flow control allows routers and/or receiving stations to limit the rate at which they receive data. For the connectionless type of service we are describing, flow control mechanisms are limited. The best approach would seem to be to send flow control packets, requesting reduced data flow, to other routers and source stations. We will see one example of this with ICMP, discussed in the next section.

18.4 INTERNET PROTOCOL

In this section, we look at version 4 of IP, officially defined in RFC 791. Although it is intended that IPv4 will ultimately be replaced by IPv6, it is currently the standard IP used in TCP/IP networks.

The Internet Protocol (IP) is part of the TCP/IP suite and is the most widely used internetworking protocol. As with any protocol standard, IP is specified in two parts:

- The interface with a higher layer (e.g., TCP), specifying the services that IP provides
- The actual protocol format and mechanisms

In this section, we examine first IP services and then the protocol. This is followed by a discussion of IP address formats. Finally, the Internet Control Message Protocol (ICMP), which is an integral part of IP, is described.

IP Services

The services to be provided across adjacent protocol layers (e.g., between IP and TCP) are expressed in terms of primitives and parameters. A primitive specifies the function to be performed, and the parameters are used to pass data and control information. The actual form of a primitive is implementation dependent. An example is a subroutine call.

IP provides two service primitives at the interface to the next higher layer. The Send primitive is used to request transmission of a data unit. The Deliver primitive is used by IP to notify a user of the arrival of a data unit. The parameters associated with the two primitives are as follows:

- **Source address:** Internetwork address of sending IP entity.
- **Destination address:** Internetwork address of destination IP entity.
- **Protocol:** Recipient protocol entity (an IP user, such as TCP).
- **Type of service indicators:** Used to specify the treatment of the data unit in its transmission through component networks.
- **Identification:** Used in combination with the source and destination addresses and user protocol to identify the data unit uniquely. This parameter is needed for reassembly and error reporting.
- **Don't fragment identifier:** Indicates whether IP can fragment data to accomplish delivery.
- **Time to live:** Measured in seconds.
- **Data length:** Length of data being transmitted.
- **Option data:** Options requested by the IP user.
- **Data:** User data to be transmitted.

The *identification, don't fragment identifier*, and *time to live* parameters are present in the Send primitive but not in the Deliver primitive. These three parameters provide instructions to IP that are not of concern to the recipient IP user.

The options parameter allows for future extensibility and for inclusion of parameters that are usually not invoked. The currently defined options are as follows:

- **Security:** Allows a security label to be attached to a datagram.
- **Source routing:** A sequenced list of router addresses that specifies the route to be followed. Routing may be strict (only identified routers may be visited) or loose (other intermediate routers may be visited).
- **Route recording:** A field is allocated to record the sequence of routers visited by the datagram.
- **Stream identification:** Names reserved resources used for stream service. This service provides special handling for volatile periodic traffic (e.g., voice).
- **Timestamping:** The source IP entity and some or all intermediate routers add a timestamp (precision to milliseconds) to the data unit as it goes by.

Internet Protocol

The protocol between IP entities is best described with reference to the IP datagram format, shown in Figure 18.6. The fields are as follows:

- **Version (4 bits):** Indicates version number, to allow evolution of the protocol; the value is 4.
- **Internet Header Length (IHL) (4 bits):** Length of header in 32-bit words. The minimum value is five, for a minimum header length of 20 octets.
- **Type of Service (8 bits):** Specifies reliability, precedence, delay, and throughput parameters. This field is rarely used; its interpretation has now been superseded. The first six bits of the TOS field are now referred to as the DS (differentiated services) field, discussed in Chapter 19. The remaining 2 bits are reserved for an ECN (explicit congestion notification) field, currently in the process of standardization. The ECN field will provide for explicit signaling of congestion in a manner similar to that discussed for frame relay (Section 13.5).

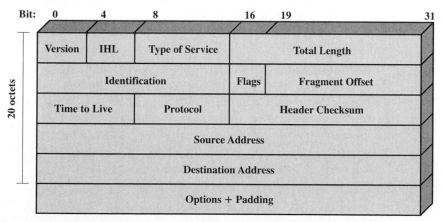

Figure 18.6   IPv4 Header

- **Total Length (16 bits):** Total datagram length, in octets.
- **Identification (16 bits):** A sequence number that, together with the source address, destination address, and user protocol, is intended to identify a datagram uniquely. Thus, this number should be unique for the datagram's source address, destination address, and user protocol for the time during which the datagram will remain in the internet.
- **Flags (3 bits):** Only two of the bits are currently defined. The More bit is used for fragmentation and reassembly, as previously explained. The Don't Fragment bit prohibits fragmentation when set. This bit may be useful if it is known that the destination does not have the capability to reassemble fragments. However, if this bit is set, the datagram will be discarded if it exceeds the maximum size of an en route network. Therefore, if the bit is set, it may be advisable to use source routing to avoid networks with small maximum packet size.
- **Fragment Offset (13 bits):** Indicates where in the original datagram this fragment belongs, measured in 64-bit units. This implies that fragments other than the last fragment must contain a data field that is a multiple of 64 bits in length.
- **Time to Live (8 bits):** Specifies how long, in seconds, a datagram is allowed to remain in the internet. Every router that processes a datagram must decrease the TTL by at least one, so the TTL is somewhat similar to a hop count.
- **Protocol (8 bits):** Indicates the next higher level protocol that is to receive the data field at the destination; thus, this field identifies the type of the next header in the packet after the IP header.
- **Header Checksum (16 bits):** An error-detecting code applied to the header only. Because some header fields may change during transit (e.g., time to live, fragmentation-related fields), this is reverified and recomputed at each router. The checksum is formed by taking the ones complement of the 16-bit ones complement addition of all 16-bit words in the header. For purposes of computation, the checksum field is itself initialized to a value of zero.[3]
- **Source Address (32 bits):** Coded to allow a variable allocation of bits to specify the network and the end system attached to the specified network, as discussed subsequently.
- **Destination Address (32 bits):** Same characteristics as source address.
- **Options (variable):** Encodes the options requested by the sending user.
- **Padding (variable):** Used to ensure that the datagram header is a multiple of 32 bits in length.
- **Data (variable):** The data field must be an integer multiple of 8 bits in length. The maximum length of the datagram (data field plus header) is 65,535 octets.

It should be clear how the IP services specified in the Send and Deliver primitives map into the fields of the IP datagram.

---

[3] A discussion of this checksum is contained in a supporting document at this book's Web site.

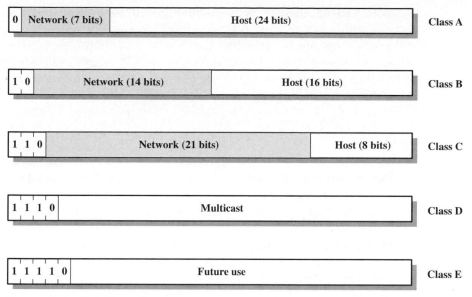

Figure 18.7 IP Address Formats

IP Addresses

The source and destination address fields in the IP header each contain a 32-bit global internet address, generally consisting of a network identifier and a host identifier.

Network Classes

The address is coded to allow a variable allocation of bits to specify network and host, as depicted in Figure 18.7. This encoding provides flexibility in assigning addresses to hosts and allows a mix of network sizes on an internet. The three principal network classes are best suited to the following conditions:

- **Class A:** Few networks, each with many hosts
- **Class B:** Medium number of networks, each with a medium number of hosts
- **Class C:** Many networks, each with a few hosts

In a particular environment, it may be best to use addresses all from one class. For example, a corporate internetwork that consist of a large number of departmental local area networks may need to use Class C addresses exclusively. However, the format of the addresses is such that it is possible to mix all three classes of addresses on the same internetwork; this is what is done in the case of the Internet itself. A mixture of classes is appropriate for an internetwork consisting of a few large networks, many small networks, plus some medium-sized networks.

IP addresses are usually written in what is called *dotted decimal notation*, with a decimal number representing each of the octets of the 32-bit address. For example, the IP address 11000000 11100100 00010001 00111001 is written as 192.228.17.57.

Note that all Class A network addresses begin with a binary 0. Network addresses with a first octet of 0 (binary 00000000) and 127 (binary 01111111) are reserved, so there are 126 potential Class A network numbers, which have a first dotted decimal number in the range 1 to 126. Class B network addresses begin with a binary 10, so that the range of the first decimal number in a Class B address is 128 to 191 (binary 10000000 to 10111111). The second octet is also part of the Class B address, so that there are $2^{14} = 16,384$ Class B addresses. For Class C addresses, the first decimal number ranges from 192 to 223 (11000000 to 11011111). The total number of Class C addresses is $2^{21} = 2,097,152$.

Subnets and Subnet Masks

The concept of subnet was introduced to address the following requirement. Consider an internet that includes one or more WANs and a number of sites, each of which has a number of LANs. We would like to allow arbitrary complexity of interconnected LAN structures within an organization, while insulating the overall internet against explosive growth in network numbers and routing complexity. One approach to this problem is to assign a single network number to all of the LANs at a site. From the point of view of the rest of the internet, there is a single network at that site, which simplifies addressing and routing. To allow the routers within the site to function properly, each LAN is assigned a subnet number. The *host* portion of the internet address is partitioned into a subnet number and a host number to accommodate this new level of addressing.

Within the subnetted network, the local routers must route on the basis of an extended network number consisting of the *network* portion of the IP address and the subnet number. The bit positions containing this extended network number are indicated by the address mask. The use of the address mask allows the host to determine whether an outgoing datagram is destined for a host on the same LAN (send directly) or another LAN (send datagram to router). It is assumed that some other means (e.g., manual configuration) are used to create address masks and make them known to the local routers.

Table 18.3a shows the calculations involved in the use of a subnet mask. Note that the effect of the subnet mask is to erase the portion of the host field that refers to an actual host on a subnet. What remains is the network number and the subnet number. Figure 18.8 shows an example of the use of subnetting. The figure shows a local complex consisting of three LANs and two routers. To the rest of the internet, this complex is a single network with a Class C address of the form 192.228.17.*x*, where the leftmost three octets are the network number and the rightmost octet contains a host number *x*. Both routers R1 and R2 are configured with a subnet mask with the value 255.255.255.224 (see Table 18.3a). For example, if a datagram with the destination address 192.228.17.57 arrives at R1 from either the rest of the internet or from LAN Y, R1 applies the subnet mask to determine that this address refers to subnet 1, which is LAN X, and so forwards the datagram to LAN X. Similarly, if a datagram with that destination address arrives at R2 from LAN Z, R2 applies the mask and then determines from its forwarding database that datagrams destined for subnet 1 should be forwarded to R1. Hosts must also employ a subnet mask to make routing decisions.

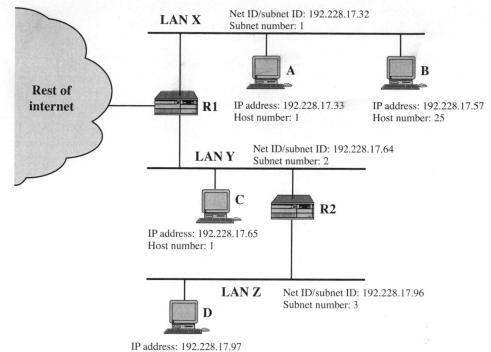

Figure 18.8   Example of Subnetworking

The default subnet mask for a given class of addresses is a null mask (Table 18.3b), which yields the same network and host number as the non-subnetted address.

Internet Control Message Protocol (ICMP)

The IP standard specifies that a compliant implementation must also implement ICMP (RFC 792). ICMP provides a means for transferring messages from routers and other hosts to a host. In essence, ICMP provides feedback about problems in the communication environment. Examples of its use are when a datagram cannot

Table 18.3   IP Addresses and Subnet Masks [STEI95]

(a) Dotted decimal and binary representations of IP address and subnet masks

	Binary Representation	**Dotted Decimal**
IP address	11000000.11100100.00010001.00111001	192.228.17.57
Subnet mask	11111111.11111111.11111111.11100000	255.255.255.224
Bitwise AND of address and mask (resultant network/subnet number)	11000000.11100100.00010001.00100000	192.228.17.32
Subnet number	11000000.11100100.00010001.001	1
Host number	00000000.00000000.00000000.00011001	25

(continues on next page)

Table 18.3 *(continued)*

(b) Default subnet masks

	Binary Representation	Dotted Decimal
Class A default mask	11111111.00000000.00000000.00000000	255.0.0.0
Example Class A mask	11111111.11000000.00000000.00000000	255.192.0.0
Class B default mask	11111111.11111111.00000000.00000000	255.255.0.0
Example Class B mask	11111111.11111111.11111000.00000000	255.255.248.0
Class C default mask	11111111.11111111.11111111.00000000	255. 255. 255.0
Example Class C mask	11111111.11111111.11111111.11111100	255. 255. 255.252

reach its destination, when the router does not have the buffering capacity to forward a datagram, and when the router can direct the station to send traffic on a shorter route. In most cases, an ICMP message is sent in response to a datagram, either by a router along the datagram's path or by the intended destination host.

Although ICMP is, in effect, at the same level as IP in the TCP/IP architecture, it is a user of IP. An ICMP message is constructed and then passed down to IP, which encapsulates the message with an IP header and then transmits the resulting datagram in the usual fashion. Because ICMP messages are transmitted in IP datagrams, their delivery is not guaranteed and their use cannot be considered reliable.

Figure 18.9 shows the format of the various ICMP message types. An ICMP message starts with a 64-bit header consisting of the following:

Type (8 bits): Specifies the type of ICMP message.

Code (8 bits): Used to specify parameters of the message that can be encoded in one or a few bits.

Checksum (16 bits): Checksum of the entire ICMP message. This is the same checksum algorithm used for IP.

Parameters (32 bits): Used to specify more lengthy parameters.

These fields are generally followed by additional information fields that further specify the content of the message.

In those cases in which the ICMP message refers to a prior datagram, the information field includes the entire IP header plus the first 64 bits of the data field of the original datagram. This enables the source host to match the incoming ICMP message with the prior datagram. The reason for including the first 64 bits of the data field is that this will enable the IP module in the host to determine which upper-level protocol or protocols were involved. In particular, the first 64 bits would include a portion of the TCP header or other transport-level header.

The **destination unreachable** message covers a number of contingencies. A router may return this message if it does not know how to reach the destination network. In some networks, an attached router may be able to determine if a particular host is unreachable, and return the message. The destination host itself may return this message if the user protocol or some higher-level service access point is unreachable. This could happen if the corresponding field in the IP header was set

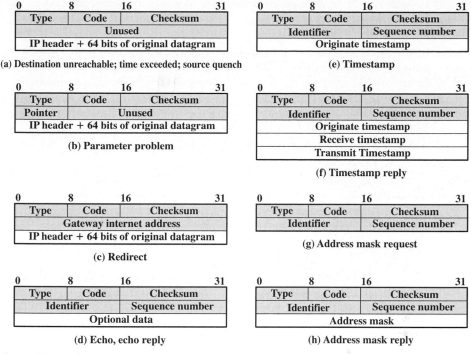

Figure 18.9   ICMP Message Formats

incorrectly. If the datagram specifies a source route that is unusable, a message is returned. Finally, if a router must fragment a datagram but the Don't Fragment flag is set, the datagram is discarded and a message is returned.

A router will return a **time exceeded** message if the lifetime of the datagram expires. A host will send this message if it cannot complete reassembly within a time limit.

A syntactic or semantic error in an IP header will cause a **parameter problem** message to be returned by a router or host. For example, an incorrect argument may be provided with an option. The parameter field contains a pointer to the octet in the original header where the error was detected.

The **source quench** message provides a rudimentary form of flow control. Either a router or a destination host may send this message to a source host, requesting that it reduce the rate at which it is sending traffic to the internet destination. On receipt of a source quench message, the source host should cut back the rate at which it is sending traffic to the specified destination until it no longer receives source quench messages. The source quench message can be used by a router or host that must discard datagrams because of a full buffer. In that case, the router or host will issue a source quench message for every datagram that it discards. In addition, a system may anticipate congestion and issue source quench messages when its buffers approach capacity. In that case, the datagram referred to in the source quench message may well be delivered. Thus, receipt of a source quench message does not imply delivery or nondelivery of the corresponding datagram.

A router sends a **redirect** message to a host on a directly connected router to advise the host of a better route to a particular destination. The following is an example, using Figure 18.8. Router R1 receives a datagram from host C on network Y, to which R1 is attached. R1 checks its routing table and obtains the address for the next router, R2, on the route to the datagram's internet destination network, Z. Because R2 and the host identified by the internet source address of the datagram are on the same network, R1 sends a redirect message to C. The redirect message advises the host to send its traffic for network Z directly to router R2, because this is a shorter path to the destination. The router forwards the original datagram to its internet destination (via R2). The address of R2 is contained in the parameter field of the redirect message.

The **echo** and **echo reply** messages provide a mechanism for testing that communication is possible between entities. The recipient of an echo message is obligated to return the message in an echo reply message. An identifier and sequence number are associated with the echo message to be matched in the echo reply message. The identifier might be used like a service access point to identify a particular session, and the sequence number might be incremented on each echo request sent.

The **timestamp** and **timestamp reply** messages provide a mechanism for sampling the delay characteristics of the internet. The sender of a timestamp message may include an identifier and sequence number in the parameters field and include the time that the message is sent (originate timestamp). The receiver records the time it received the message and the time that it transmits the reply message in the timestamp reply message. If the timestamp message is sent using strict source routing, then the delay characteristics of a particular route can be measured.

The **address mask request** and **address mask reply** messages are useful in an environment that includes subnets. The address mask request and reply messages allow a host to learn the address mask for the LAN to which it connects. The host broadcasts an address mask request message on the LAN. The router on the LAN responds with an address mask reply message that contains the address mask.

18.5 IPv6

The Internet Protocol (IP) has been the foundation of the Internet and virtually all multivendor private internetworks. This protocol is reaching the end of its useful life and a new protocol, known as IPv6 (IP version 6), has been defined to ultimately replace IP.[4]

We first look at the motivation for developing a new version of IP and then examine some of its details.

---

[4] You may think this narrative has skipped a few versions. The currently deployed version of IP is actually IP version 4; previous versions of IP (1 through 3) were successively defined and replaced to reach IPv4. Version 5 is the number assigned to the Stream Protocol, a connection-oriented internet-layer protocol. Hence the use of the label version 6.

IP Next Generation

The driving motivation for the adoption of a new version of IP was the limitation imposed by the 32-bit address field in IPv4. With a 32-bit address field, it is possible in principle to assign 2^{32} different addresses, which is over 4 billion possible addresses. One might think that this number of addresses was more than adequate to meet addressing needs on the Internet. However, in the late 1980s it was perceived that there would be a problem, and this problem began to manifest itself in the early 1990s. Reasons for the inadequacy of 32-bit addresses include the following:

- The two-level structure of the IP address (network number, host number) is convenient but wasteful of the address space. Once a network number is assigned to a network, all of the host-number addresses for that network number are assigned to that network. The address space for that network may be sparsely used, but as far as the effective IP address space is concerned, if a network number is used, then all addresses within the network are used.
- The IP addressing model generally requires that a unique network number be assigned to each IP network whether or not it is actually connected to the Internet.
- Networks are proliferating rapidly. Most organizations boast multiple LANs, not just a single LAN system. Wireless networks have rapidly assumed a major role. The Internet itself has grown explosively for years.
- Growth of TCP/IP usage into new areas will result in a rapid growth in the demand for unique IP addresses. Examples include using TCP/IP to interconnect electronic point-of-sale terminals and for cable television receivers.
- Typically, a single IP address is assigned to each host. A more flexible arrangement is to allow multiple IP addresses per host. This, of course, increases the demand for IP addresses.

So the need for an increased address space dictated that a new version of IP was needed. In addition, IP is a very old protocol, and new requirements in the areas of address configuration, routing flexibility, and traffic support had been defined.

In response to these needs, the Internet Engineering Task Force (IETF) issued a call for proposals for a next-generation IP (IPng) in July of 1992. A number of proposals were received, and by 1994 the final design for IPng emerged. A major milestone was reached with the publication of RFC 1752, "The Recommendation for the IP Next Generation Protocol," issued in January 1995. RFC 1752 outlines the requirements for IPng, specifies the PDU formats, and highlights the IPng approach in the areas of addressing, routing, and security. A number of other Internet documents defined details of the protocol, now officially called IPv6; these include an overall specification of IPv6 (RFC 2460), an RFC dealing with addressing structure of IPv6 (RFC 2373), and numerous others.

IPv6 includes the following enhancements over IPv4:

- **Expanded address space:** IPv6 uses 128-bit addresses instead of the 32-bit addresses of IPv4. This is an increase of address space by a factor of 2^{96}. It has been pointed out [HIND95] that this allows on the order of 6×10^{23} unique addresses per square meter of the surface of the earth. Even if addresses are very inefficiently allocated, this address space seems secure.

- **Improved option mechanism:** IPv6 options are placed in separate optional headers that are located between the IPv6 header and the transport-layer header. Most of these optional headers are not examined or processed by any router on the packet's path. This simplifies and speeds up router processing of IPv6 packets compared to IPv4 datagrams.[5] It also makes it easier to add additional options.
- **Address autoconfiguration:** This capability provides for dynamic assignment of IPv6 addresses.
- **Increased addressing flexibility:** IPv6 includes the concept of an anycast address, for which a packet is delivered to just one of a set of nodes. The scalability of multicast routing is improved by adding a scope field to multicast addresses.
- **Support for resource allocation:** Instead of the type-of-service field in IPv4, IPv6 enables the labeling of packets belong to a particular traffic flow for which the sender requests special handling. This aids in the support of specialized traffic such as real-time video.

All of these features are explored in the remainder of this section, except for the security features, which are discussed in Chapter 21.

IPv6 Structure

An IPv6 protocol data unit (known as a packet) has the following general form:

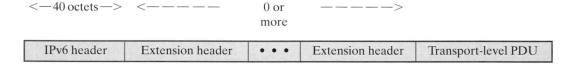

The only header that is required is referred to simply as the IPv6 header. This is of fixed size with a length of 40 octets, compared to 20 octets for the mandatory portion of the IPv4 header (Figure 18.6). The following extension headers have been defined:

- **Hop-by-Hop Options header:** Defines special options that require hop-by-hop processing
- **Routing header:** Provides extended routing, similar to IPv4 source routing
- **Fragment header:** Contains fragmentation and reassembly information
- **Authentication header:** Provides packet integrity and authentication
- **Encapsulating Security Payload header:** Provides privacy
- **Destination Options header:** Contains optional information to be examined by the destination node

---

[5] The protocol data unit for IPv6 is referred to as a packet rather than a datagram, which is the term used for IPv4 PDUs.

The IPv6 standard recommends that, when multiple extension headers are used, the IPv6 headers appear in the following order.

1. IPv6 header: Mandatory, must always appear first
2. Hop-by-Hop Options header
3. Destination Options header: For options to be processed by the first destination that appears in the IPv6 Destination Address field plus subsequent destinations listed in the Routing header
4. Routing header
5. Fragment header
6. Authentication header
7. Encapsulating Security Payload header
8. Destination Options header: For options to be processed only by the final destination of the packet

Figure 18.10 shows an example of an IPv6 packet that includes an instance of each header, except those related to security. Note that the IPv6 header and each

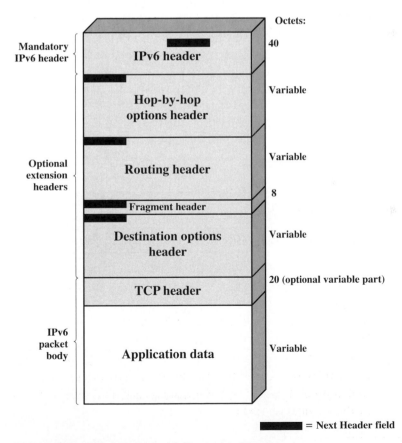

Figure 18.10 IPv6 Packet with Extension Headers (containing a TCP Segment)

extension header include a Next Header field. This field identifies the type of the immediately following header. If the next header is an extension header, then this field contains the type identifier of that header. Otherwise, this field contains the protocol identifier of the upper-layer protocol using IPv6 (typically a transport-level protocol), using the same values as the IPv4 Protocol field. In Figure 18.10, the upper-layer protocol is TCP, so that the upper-layer data carried by the IPv6 packet consist of a TCP header followed by a block of application data.

We first look at the main IPv6 header and then examine each of the extensions in turn.

IPv6 Header

The IPv6 header has a fixed length of 40 octets, consisting of the following fields (Figure 18.11):

- **Version (4 bits):** Internet protocol version number; the value is 6.
- **Traffic Class (8 bits):** Available for use by originating nodes and/or forwarding routers to identify and distinguish between different classes or priorities of IPv6 packets. This field is now used for the 0s and ECN fields, as described for the IPv4 TOS field.
- **Flow Label (20 bits):** May be used by a host to label those packets for which it is requesting special handling by routers within a network; discussed subsequently.
- **Payload Length (16 bits):** Length of the remainder of the IPv6 packet following the header, in octets. In other words, this is the total length of all of the extension headers plus the transport-level PDU.
- **Next Header (8 bits):** Identifies the type of header immediately following the IPv6 header; this will either be an IPv6 extension header or a higher-layer header, such as TCP or UDP.

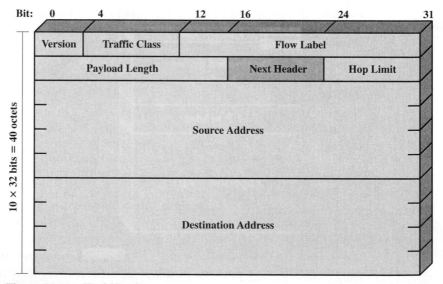

Figure 18.11 IPv6 Header

- **Hop Limit (8 bits):** The remaining number of allowable hops for this packet. The hop limit is set to some desired maximum value by the source and decremented by 1 by each node that forwards the packet. The packet is discarded if Hop Limit is decremented to zero. This is a simplification over the processing required for the time-to-live field of IPv4. The consensus was that the extra effort in accounting for time intervals in IPv4 added no significant value to the protocol. In fact, IPv4 routers, as a general rule, treat the time-to-live field as a hop limit field.
- **Source Address (128 bits):** The address of the originator of the packet.
- **Destination Address (128 bits):** The address of the intended recipient of the packet. This may not in fact be the intended ultimate destination if a Routing header is present, as explained subsequently.

Although the IPv6 header is longer than the mandatory portion of the IPv4 header (40 octets versus 20 octets), it contains fewer fields (8 versus 12). Thus, routers have less processing to do per header, which should speed up routing.

Traffic Class

The 8-bit traffic class field enables a source to identify desired traffic-handling characteristics of each packet relative to other packets from the same source. As with the IPv4 TOS field, the original intent of the traffic class field has been superseded. Now, the first six bits of the traffic class field are now referred to as the DS (differentiated services) field, discussed in Chapter 19. The remaining 2 bits are reserved for an ECN (explicit congestion notification) field, currently in the process of standardization. The ECN field will provide for explicit signaling of congestion in a manner similar to that discussed for frame relay (Section 13.5).

Flow Label

The IPv6 standard defines a flow as a sequence of packets sent from a particular source to a particular (unicast or multicast) destination for which the source desires special handling by the intervening routers. A flow is uniquely identified by the combination of a source address, destination address, and a nonzero 20-bit flow label. Thus, all packets that are to be part of the same flow are assigned the same flow label by the source.

From the source's point of view, a flow typically will be a sequence of packets that are generated from a single application instance at the source and that have the same transfer service requirements. A flow may comprise a single TCP connection or even multiple TCP connections; an example of the latter is a file transfer application, which could have one control connection and multiple data connections. A single application may generate a single flow or multiple flows. An example of the latter is multimedia conferencing, which might have one flow for audio and one for graphic windows, each with different transfer requirements in terms of data rate, delay, and delay variation.

From the router's point of view, a flow is a sequence of packets that share attributes that affect how these packets are handled by the router. These include path, resource allocation, discard requirements, accounting, and security attributes. The router may treat packets from different flows differently in a number of ways, including allocating different buffer sizes, giving different precedence in terms of forwarding, and requesting different quality of service from networks.

There is no special significance to any particular flow label. Instead the special handling to be provided for a packet flow must be declared in some other way. For example, a source might negotiate or request special handling ahead of time from routers by means of a control protocol, or at transmission time by information in one of the extension headers in the packet, such as the Hop-by-Hop Options header. Examples of special handling that might be requested include some sort of non-default quality of service and some form of real-time service.

In principle, all of a user's requirements for a particular flow could be defined in an extension header and included with each packet. If we wish to leave the concept of flow open to include a wide variety of requirements, this design approach could result in very large packet headers. The alternative, adopted for IPv6, is the flow label, in which the flow requirements are defined prior to flow commencement and a unique flow label is assigned to the flow. In this case, the router must save flow requirement information about each flow.

The following rules apply to the flow label:

1. Hosts or routers that do not support the Flow Label field must set the field to zero when originating a packet, pass the field unchanged when forwarding a packet, and ignore the field when receiving a packet.

2. All packets originating from a given source with the same nonzero Flow Label must have the same Destination Address, Source Address, Hop-by-Hop Options header contents (if this header is present), and Routing header contents (if this header is present). The intent is that a router can decide how to route and process the packet by simply looking up the flow label in a table and without examining the rest of the header.

3. The source assigns a flow label to a flow. New flow labels must be chosen (pseudo-) randomly and uniformly in the range 1 to $2^{20} - 1$, subject to the restriction that a source must not reuse a flow label for a new flow within the lifetime of the existing flow. The zero flow label is reserved to indicate that no flow label is being used.

This last point requires some elaboration. The router must maintain information about the characteristics of each active flow that may pass through it, presumably in some sort of table. To forward packets efficiently and rapidly, table lookup must be efficient. One alternative is to have a table with 2^{20} (about one million) entries, one for each possible flow label; this imposes an unnecessary memory burden on the router. Another alternative is to have one entry in the table per active flow, include the flow label with each entry, and require the router to search the entire table each time a packet is encountered. This imposes an unnecessary processing burden on the router. Instead, most router designs are likely to use some sort of hash table approach. With this approach a moderate-sized table is used, and each flow entry is mapped into the table using a hashing function on the flow label. The hashing function might simply be the low-order few bits (say 8 or 10) of the flow label or some simple calculation on the 20 bits of the flow label. In any case, the efficiency of the hash approach typically depends on the flow labels being uniformly distributed over their possible range. Hence requirement number 3 in the preceding list.

IPv6 Addresses

IPv6 addresses are 128 bits in length. Addresses are assigned to individual interfaces on nodes, not to the nodes themselves.[6] A single interface may have multiple unique unicast addresses. Any of the unicast addresses associated with a node's interface may be used to uniquely identify that node.

The combination of long addresses and multiple addresses per interface enables improved routing efficiency over IPv4. In IPv4, addresses generally do not have a structure that assists routing, and therefore a router may need to maintain huge table of routing paths. Longer internet addresses allow for aggregating addresses by hierarchies of network, access provider, geography, corporation, and so on. Such aggregation should make for smaller routing tables and faster table lookups. The allowance for multiple addresses per interface would allow a subscriber that uses multiple access providers across the same interface to have separate addresses aggregated under each provider's address space.

IPv6 allows three types of addresses:

- **Unicast:** An identifier for a single interface. A packet sent to a unicast address is delivered to the interface identified by that address.
- **Anycast:** An identifier for a set of interfaces (typically belonging to different nodes). A packet sent to an anycast address is delivered to one of the interfaces identified by that address (the "nearest" one, according to the routing protocols' measure of distance).
- **Multicast:** An identifier for a set of interfaces (typically belonging to different nodes). A packet sent to a multicast address is delivered to all interfaces identified by that address.

Hop-by-Hop Options Header

The Hop-by-Hop Options header carries optional information that, if present, must be examined by every router along the path. This header consists of the following (Figure 18.12a):

- **Next Header (8 bits):** Identifies the type of header immediately following this header.
- **Header Extension Length (8 bits):** Length of this header in 64-bit units, not including the first 64 bits.
- **Options:** A variable-length field consisting of one or more option definitions. Each definition is in the form of three subfields: Option Type (8 bits), which

---

[6] In IPv6, a *node* is any device that implements IPv6; this includes hosts and routers.

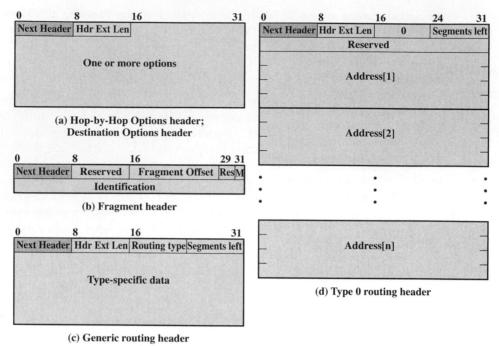

Figure 18.12   IPv6 Extension Headers

identifies the option; Length (8 bits), which specifies the length of the Option Data field in octets; and Option Data, which is a variable-length specification of the option.

It is actually the lowest-order five bits of the Option Type field that are used to specify a particular option. The high-order two bits indicate that action to be taken by a node that does not recognize this option type, as follows:

- 00—skip over this option and continue processing the header.
- 01—discard the packet.
- 10—discard the packet and send an ICMP Parameter Problem message to the packet's Source Address, pointing to the unrecognized Option Type.
- 11—discard the packet and, only if the packet's Destination Address is not a multicast address, send an ICMP Parameter Problem message to the packet's Source Address, pointing to the unrecognized Option Type.

The third highest-order bit specifies whether the Option Data field does not change (0) or may change (1) en route from source to destination. Data that may change must be excluded from authentication calculations, as discussed in Chapter 21.

These conventions for the Option Type field also apply to the Destination Options header.

Four hop-by-hop options have been specified so far:

- **Pad1:** Used to insert one byte of padding into the Options area of the header.
- **PadN:** Used to insert N bytes ($N \geq 2$) of padding into the Options area of the header. The two padding options ensure that the header is a multiple of 8 bytes in length.
- **Jumbo payload:** Used to send IPv6 packets with payloads longer than 65,535 octets. The Option Data field of this option is 32 bits long and gives the length of the packet in octets, excluding the IPv6 header. For such packets, the Payload Length field in the IPv6 header must be set to zero, and there must be no Fragment header. With this option, IPv6 supports packet sizes up to more than 4 billion octets. This facilitates the transmission of large video packets and enables IPv6 to make the best use of available capacity over any transmission medium.
- **Router alert:** Informs the router that the contents of this packet is of interest to the router and to handle any control data accordingly. The absence of this option in an IPv6 datagram informs the router that the packet does not contain information needed by the router and hence can be safely routed without further packet parsing. Hosts originating IPv6 packets are required to include this option in certain circumstances. The purpose of this option is to provide efficient support for protocols such as RSVP (Chapter 19) that generate packets that need to be examined by intermediate routers for purposes of traffic control. Rather than requiring the intermediate routers to look in detail at the extension headers of a packet, this option alerts the router when such attention is required.

Fragment Header

In IPv6, fragmentation may only be performed by source nodes, not by routers along a packet's delivery path. To take full advantage of the internetworking environment, a node must perform a path discovery algorithm that enables it to learn the smallest maximum transmission unit (MTU) supported by any network on the path. With this knowledge, the source node will fragment, as required, for each given destination address. Otherwise the source must limit all packets to 1280 octets, which is the minimum MTU that must be supported by each network.

The fragment header consists of the following (Figure 18.12b):

- **Next Header (8 bits):** Identifies the type of header immediately following this header.
- **Reserved (8 bits):** For future use.
- **Fragment Offset (13 bits):** Indicates where in the original packet the payload of this fragment belongs. It is measured in 64-bit units. This implies that fragments (other than the last fragment) must contain a data field that is a multiple of 64 bits long.

- **Res (2 bits):** Reserved for future use.
- **M Flag (1 bit):** 1 = more fragments; 0 = last fragment.
- **Identification (32 bits):** Intended to uniquely identify the original packet. The identifier must be unique for the packet's source address and destination address for the time during which the packet will remain in the internet. All fragments with the same identifier, source address, and destination address are reassembled to form the original packet.

The fragmentation algorithm is the same as that described in Section 18.3.

Routing Header

The Routing header contains a list of one or more intermediate nodes to be visited on the way to a packet's destination. All routing headers start with a 32-bit block consisting of four 8-bit fields, followed by routing data specific to a given routing type (Figure 18.12c). The four 8-bit fields are as follows:

- **Next Header:** Identifies the type of header immediately following this header.
- **Header Extension Length:** Length of this header in 64-bit units, not including the first 64 bits.
- **Routing Type:** Identifies a particular Routing header variant. If a router does not recognize the Routing Type value, it must discard the packet.
- **Segments Left:** Number of route segments remaining; that is, the number of explicitly listed intermediate nodes still to be visited before reaching the final destination.

The only specific routing header format defined in RFC 2460 is the Type 0 Routing header (Figure 18.12d). When using the Type 0 Routing header, the source node does not place the ultimate destination address in the IPv6 header. Instead, that address is the last address listed in the Routing header (Address[*n*] in Figure 18.12d), and the IPv6 header contains the destination address of the first desired router on the path. The Routing header will not be examined until the packet reaches the node identified in the IPv6 header. At that point, the IPv6 and Routing header contents are updated and the packet is forwarded. The update consists of placing the next address to be visited in the IPv6 header and decrementing the Segments Left field in the Routing header.

Destination Options Header

The Destination Options header carries optional information that, if present, is examined only by the packet's destination node. The format of this header is the same as that of the Hop-by-Hop Options header (Figure 18.12a).

18.6 RECOMMENDED READING AND WEB SITES

[RODR02] provides clear coverage of all of the topics in this chapter. Good coverage of internetworking and IPv4 can be found in [COME01] and [STEV94]. [HUIT98] is a straightforward technical description of the various RFCs that together make up the IPv6 specification; the book provides a discussion of the purpose of various features and of the operation of the protocol. [KESH98] provides an instructive look at present and future router functionality.

COME01   Comer, D. *Internetworking with TCP/IP, Volume I: Principles, Protocols, and Architecture.* Upper Saddle River, NJ: Prentice Hall, 2001.

HUIT98   Huitema, C. *IPv6: The New Internet Protocol.* Upper Saddle River, NJ: Prentice Hall, 1998.

KESH98   Keshav, S., and Sharma, R. "Issues and Trends in Router Design." *IEEE Communications Magazine*, May 1998.

RODR02   Rodriguez, A., et al., *TCP/IP Tutorial and Technical Overview.* Upper Saddle River: NJ: Prentice Hall, 2002.

STEV94   Stevens, W. *TCP/IP Illustrated, Volume 1: The Protocols.* Reading, MA: Addison-Wesley, 1994.

Recommended Web Sites:

- **IPv6:** Information about IPv6 and related topics.
- **IPv6 Information Page:** Includes introductory material, news on recent IPv6 product developments, and related links.
- **IPv6 Forum:** An industry consortium that promotes IPv6-related products. Includes a number of white papers and articles.

18.7 KEY TERMS, REVIEW QUESTIONS, AND PROBLEMS

Key Terms

broadcast	Internet Protocol (IP)	segmentation
datagram lifetime	internetworking	subnet
end system	intranet	subnet mask
fragmentation	IPv4	subnetwork
intermediate system	IPv6	traffic class
Internet	multicast	unicast
Internet Control Message Protocol (ICMP)	reassembly router	

Review Questions

18.1   Give some reasons for using fragmentation and reassembly.

18.2   List the requirements for an internetworking facility.

18.3   What are the pros and cons of limiting reassembly to the endpoint as compared to allowing en route reassembly.

18.4   Explain the function of the three flags in the IPv4 header.

18.5   How is the IPv4 header checksum calculated?

18.6   What is the difference between the traffic class and flow label fields in the IPv6 header?

18.7   Briefly explain the three types of IPv6 addresses.

18.8   What is the purpose of each of the IPv6 header types?

Problems

18.1   In the discussion of IP, it was mentioned that the *identifier, don't fragment identifier*, and *time to live* parameters are present in the Send primitive but not in the Deliver primitive because they are only of concern to IP. For each of these parameters indicate whether it is of concern to the IP entity in the source, the IP entities in any intermediate routers, and the IP entity in the destination end systems. Justify your answer.

18.2   What is the header overhead in the IP protocol?

18.3   Describe some circumstances where it might be desirable to use source routing rather than let the routers make the routing decision.

18.4   Because of fragmentation, an IP datagram can arrive in several pieces, not necessarily in the correct order. The IP entity at the receiving end system must accumulate these fragments until the original datagram is reconstituted.

   a.   Consider that the IP entity creates a buffer for assembling the data field in the original datagram. As assembly proceeds, the buffer will contain blocks of data and "holes" between the data blocks. Describe an algorithm for reassembly based on this concept.

   b.   For the algorithm in part (a), it is necessary to keep track of the holes. Describe a simple mechanism for doing this.

18.5   A 4480-octet datagram is to be transmitted and needs to be fragmented because it will pass through an Ethernet with a maximum payload of 1500 octets. Show the Total Length, More Flag, and Fragment Offset values in each of the resulting fragments.

18.6   The IP checksum needs to be recalculated at routers because of changes to the IP header, such as the lifetime field. It is possible to recalculate the checksum from scratch. Suggest a procedure that involves less calculation. *Hint:* Suppose that the value in octet k is changed by $Z = $ new_value $-$ old_value; consider the effect of this change on the checksum.

18.7   An IP datagram is to be fragmented. Which options in the option field need to be copied into the header of each fragment, and which need only be retained in the first fragment? Justify the handling of each option.

18.8   A transport layer message consisting of 1500 bits of data and 160 bits of header is sent to an internet layer, which appends another 160 bits of header. This is then transmitted through two networks, each of which uses a 24-bit packet header. The destination network has a maximum packet size of 800 bits. How many bits, including headers, are delivered to the network-layer protocol at the destination?

18.9   The architecture suggested by Figure 18.2 is to be used. What functions could be added to the routers to alleviate some of the problems caused by the mismatched local and long-haul networks?

18.10   Should internetworking be concerned with a network's internal routing? Why or why not?

18.11   Compare the individual fields of the IPv4 header with the IPv6 header. Account for the functionality provided by each IPv4 field by showing how the same functionality is provided in IPv6.

18.12   Justify the recommended order in which IPv6 extension headers appear (i.e., why is the Hop-by-Hop Options header first, why is the Routing header before the Fragment header, and so on).

18.13   The IPv6 standard states that if a packet with a nonzero flow label arrives at a router and the router has no information for that flow label, the router should ignore the flow label and forward the packet.

    a. What are the disadvantages of treating this event as an error, discarding the packet, and sending an ICMP message?

    b. Are there situations in which routing the packet as if its flow label were zero will cause the wrong result? Explain.

18.14 The IPv6 flow mechanism assumes that the state associated with a given flow label is stored in routers, so they know how to handle packets that carry that flow label. A design requirement is to flush flow labels that are no longer being used (stale flow label) from routers.

    a. Assume that a source always send a control message to all affected routers deleting a flow label when the source finishes with that flow. In that case, how could a stale flow label persist?

    b. Suggest router and source mechanisms to overcome the problem of stale flow labels.

18.15 The question arises as to which packets generated by a source should carry nonzero IPv6 flow labels. For some applications, the answer is obvious. Small exchanges of data should have a zero flow label because it is not worth creating a flow for a few packets. Real-time flows should have a flow label; such flows are a primary reason flow labels were created. A more difficult issue is what to do with peers sending large amounts of best-effort traffic (e.g., TCP connections). Make a case for assigning a unique flow label to each long-term TCP connection. Make a case for not doing this.

18.16 The original IPv6 specifications combined the Traffic Class and Flow Label fields into a single 28-bit Flow Label field. This allowed flows to redefine the interpretation of different values of priority. Suggest reasons why the final specification includes the Priority field as a distinct field.

18.17 For Type 0 IPv6 routing, specify the algorithm for updating the IPv6 and Routing headers by intermediate nodes.

CHAPTER **19**

INTERNETWORK OPERATION

KEY POINTS

- The act of sending a packet from a source to multiple destinations is referred to as multicasting. Multicasting raises design issues in the areas of addressing and routing.

- Routing protocols in an internet function in a similar fashion to those used in packet-switching networks. An internet routing protocol is used to exchange information about reachability and traffic delays, allowing each router to construct a next-hop routing table for paths through the internet. Typically, relatively simple routing protocols are used between autonomous systems within a larger internet and more complex routing protocols are used within each autonomous system.

- The integrated services architecture is a response to the growing variety and volume of traffic experienced in the Internet and intranets. It provides a framework for the development of protocols such as RSVP to handle multimedia/multicast traffic and provides guidance to router vendors on the development of efficient techniques for handling a varied load.

- The differentiated services architecture is designed to provide a simple, easy-to-implement, low-overhead tool to support a range of network services that are differentiated on the basis of performance. Differentiated services are provided on the basis of a 6-bit label in the IP header, which classifies traffic in terms of the type of service to be given by routers for that traffic.

As the Internet and private internets grow in scale, a host of new demands march steadily into view. Low-volume TELNET conversations are leapfrogged by high-volume client/server applications. To this has been added more recently the tremendous volume of Web traffic, which is increasingly graphics intensive. Now real-time voice and video applications add to the burden.

To cope with these demands, it is not enough to increase internet capacity. Sensible and effective methods for managing the traffic and controlling congestion are needed. Historically, IP-based internets have been able to provide a simple best-effort delivery service to all applications using an internet. But the needs of users have changed. A company may have spent millions of dollars installing an IP-based internet designed to transport data among LANs but now finds that new real-time, multimedia, and multicasting applications are not well supported by such a configuration. The only networking scheme designed from day one to support both traditional TCP and UDP traffic and real-time traffic is ATM. However, reliance on ATM means either constructing a second networking infrastructure for real-time traffic or replacing the existing IP-based configuration with ATM, both of which are costly alternatives.

Thus, there is a strong need to be able to support a variety of traffic with a variety of quality-of-service (QoS) requirements, within the TCP/IP architecture. This chapter looks at the internetwork functions and services designed to meet this need.

The chapter begins with a discussion of multicasting. Then, we explore the issue of internetwork routing algorithms. Next, we look at the Integrated Services Architecture (ISA), which provides a framework for current and future internet services. Finally, we look at the concept of differentiated services.

Refer to Figure 2.15 to see the position within the TCP/IP suite of the protocols discussed in this chapter.

19.1 MULTICASTING

Typically, an IP address refers to an individual host on a particular network. IP also accommodates addresses that refer to a group of hosts on one or more networks. Such addresses are referred to as **multicast addresses**, and the act of sending a packet from a source to the members of a multicast group is referred to as **multicasting**.

Multicasting has a number of practical applications. For example,

- **Multimedia:** A number of users "tune in" to a video or audio transmission from a multimedia source station.
- **Teleconferencing:** A group of workstations form a multicast group such that a transmission from any member is received by all other group members.
- **Database:** All copies of a replicated file or database are updated at the same time.
- **Distributed computation:** Intermediate results are sent to all participants.
- **Real-time workgroup:** Files, graphics, and messages are exchanged among active group members in real time.

Multicasting done within the scope of a single LAN segment is straightforward. IEEE 802 and other LAN protocols include provision for MAC-level multicast addresses. A packet with a multicast address is transmitted on a LAN segment. Those stations that are members of the corresponding multicast group recognize the multicast address and accept the packet. In this case, only a single copy of the packet is ever transmitted. This technique works because of the broadcast nature of a LAN: A transmission from any one station is received by all other stations on the LAN.

In an internet environment, multicasting is a far more difficult undertaking. To see this, consider the configuration of Figure 19.1; a number of LANs are interconnected by routers. Routers connect to each other either over high-speed links or across a wide area network (network N4). A cost is associated with each link or network in each direction, indicated by the value shown leaving the router for that link or network. Suppose that the multicast server on network N1 is transmitting packets to a multicast address that represents the workstations indicated on networks N3, N5, N6. Suppose that the server does not know the location of the members of the multicast group. Then one way to assure that the packet is received by all members of the group is to **broadcast** a copy of each packet to each network in the configuration, over the least-cost route for each network. For example, one packet would be addressed to N3 and would traverse N1, link L3, and N3. Router B is responsible for translating the IP-level multicast address to a MAC-level multicast address before transmitting the MAC frame onto N3. Table 19.1 summarizes the number of packets generated on the various links and networks in order to transmit one packet to a multicast group by this method. In this table, the source is the multicast server on network N1 in Figure 19.1; the multicast address includes the group members on N3, N5, and N6. Each column in the table refers to the path taken from the source host to a destination router attached to a particular destination network. Each row of the table refers to a network or link in the configuration of Figure 19.1. Each entry in

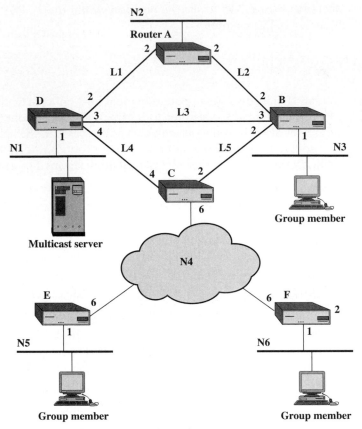

Figure 19.1 Example Configuration

the table gives the number of packets that traverse a given network or link for a given path. A total of 13 copies of the packet are required.

Now suppose the source system knows the location of each member of the multicast group. That is, the source has a table that maps a multicast address into a list of networks that contain members of that multicast group. In that case, the source need only send packets to those networks that contain members of the group. We could refer to this as the **multiple unicast** strategy. Table 19.1 shows that in this case, 11 packets are required.

Both the broadcast and multiple unicast strategies are inefficient because they generate unnecessary copies of the source packet. In a true **multicast** strategy, the following method is used:

1. The least-cost path from the source to each network that includes members of the multicast group is determined. This results in a spanning tree[1] of the configuration. Note that this is not a full spanning tree of the configuration.

---

[1] The concept of spanning tree was introduced in our discussion of bridges in Chapter 15. A spanning tree of a graph consists of all the nodes of the graph plus a subset of the links (edges) of the graph that provides connectivity (a path exists between any two nodes) with no closed loops (there is only one path between any two nodes).

Table 19.1 Traffic Generated by Various Multicasting Strategies

	(a) Broadcast					(b) Multiple Unicast				(c) Multicast
	S→N2	S→N3	S→N5	S→N6	Total	S→N3	S→N5	S→N6	Total	
N1	1	1	1	1	4	1	1	1	3	1
N2										
N3		1			1	1			1	1
N4			1	1	2		1	1	2	2
N5		1			1	1			1	1
N6				1	1			1	1	1
L1	1				1					
L2										
L3		1			1	1			1	1
L4			1	1	2		1	1	2	1
L5										
Total	2	3	4	4	13	3	4	4	11	8

Rather, it is a spanning tree that includes only those networks containing group members.

2. The source transmits a single packet along the spanning tree.
3. The packet is replicated by routers only at branch points of the spanning tree.

Figure 19.2a shows the spanning tree for transmissions from the source to the multicast group, and Figure 19.2b shows this method in action. The source transmits

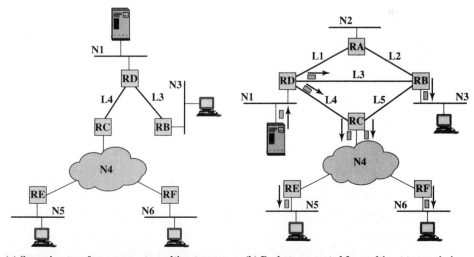

(a) Spanning tree from source to multicast group   (b) Packets generated for multicast transmission

Figure 19.2   Multicast Transmission Example

a single packet over N1 to router D. D makes two copies of the packet, to transmit over links L3 and L4. B receives the packet from L3 and transmits it on N3, where it is read by members of the multicast group on the network. Meanwhile, C receives the packet sent on L4. It must now deliver that packet to both E and F. If network N4 were a broadcast network (e.g., an IEEE 802 LAN), then C would only need to transmit one instance of the packet for both routers to read. If N4 is a packet-switching WAN, then C must make two copies of the packet and address one to E and one to F. Each of these routers, in turn, retransmits the received packet on N5 and N6, respectively. As Table 19.1 shows, the multicast technique requires only eight copies of the packet.

Requirements for Multicasting

In ordinary unicast transmission over an internet, in which each datagram has a unique destination network, the task of each router is to forward the datagram along the shortest path from that router to the destination network. With multicast transmission, the router may be required to forward two or more copies of an incoming datagram. In our example, routers D and C both must forward two copies of a single incoming datagram.

Thus, we might expect that the overall functionality of multicast routing is more complex than unicast routing. The following is a list of required functions:

1. A convention is needed for identifying a multicast address. In IPv4, Class D addresses are reserved for this purpose. These are 32-bit addresses with 1110 as their high-order 4 bits, followed by a 28-bit group identifier. In IPv6, a 128-bit multicast address consists of an 8-bit prefix of all ones, a 4-bit flags field, a 4-bit scope field, and a 112-bit group identifier. The flags field, currently, only indicates whether this address is permanently assigned or not. The scope field indicates the scope of applicability of the address, ranging from a single network to global.

2. Each node (router or source participating in the routing algorithm) must translate between an IP multicast address and a list of networks that contain members of this group. This information allows the node to construct a shortest-path spanning tree to all of the networks containing group members.

3. A router must translate between an IP multicast address and a network multicast address in order to deliver a multicast IP datagram on the destination network. For example, in IEEE 802 networks, a MAC-level address is 48 bits long; if the highest-order bit is 1, then it is a multicast address. Thus, for multicast delivery, a router attached to an IEEE 802 network must translate a 32-bit IPv4 or a 128-bit IPv6 multicast address into a 48-bit IEEE 802 MAC-level multicast address.

4. Although some multicast addresses may be assigned permanently, the more usual case is that multicast addresses are generated dynamically and that individual hosts may join and leave multicast groups dynamically. Thus, a mechanism is needed by which an individual host informs routers attached to the

same network as itself of its inclusion in and exclusion from a multicast group. IGMP, described subsequently, provides this mechanism.

5. Routers must exchange two sorts of information. First, routers need to know which networks include members of a given multicast group. Second, routers need sufficient information to calculate the shortest path to each network containing group members. These requirements imply the need for a multicast routing protocol. A discussion of such protocols is beyond the scope of this book.

6. A routing algorithm is needed to calculate shortest paths to all group members.

7. Each router must determine multicast routing paths on the basis of both source and destination addresses.

The last point is a subtle consequence of the use of multicast addresses. To illustrate the point, consider again Figure 19.1. If the multicast server transmits a unicast packet addressed to a host on network N5, the packet is forwarded by router D to C, which then forwards the packet to E. Similarly, a packet addressed to a host on network N3 is forwarded by D to B. But now suppose that the server transmits a packet with a multicast address that includes hosts on N3, N5, and N6. As we have discussed, D makes two copies of the packet and send one to B and one to C. What will C do when it receives a packet with such a multicast address? C knows that this packet is intended for networks N3, N5, and N6. A simple-minded approach would be for C to calculate the shortest path to each of these three networks. This produces the shortest-path spanning tree shown in Figure 19.3. As a result, C sends two copies of the packet out over N4, one intended for N5 and one intended for N6. But it also sends a copy of the packet to B for delivery on N3. Thus B will receive two copies of the packet, one from D and one from C. This is clearly not what was intended by the host on N1 when it launched the packet.

To avoid unnecessary duplication of packets, each router must route packets on the basis of both source and multicast destination. When C receives a packet intended for the multicast group from a source on N1, it must calculate the spanning tree with N1 as the root (shown in Figure 19.2a) and route on the basis of that spanning tree.

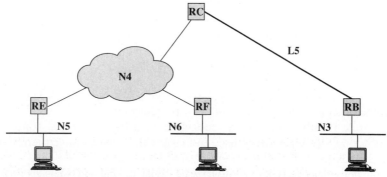

Figure 19.3 Spanning Tree from Router C to Multicast Group

Internet Group Management Protocol (IGMP)

IGMP, defined in RFC 3376, is used by hosts and routers to exchange multicast group membership information over a LAN. IGMP takes advantage of the broadcast nature of a LAN to provide an efficient technique for the exchange of information among multiple hosts and routers. In general, IGMP supports two principle operations:

1. Hosts send messages to routers to subscribe to and unsubscribe from a multicast group defined by a given multicast address.
2. Routers periodically check which multicast groups are of interest to which hosts.

IGMP is currently at version 3. In IGMPv1, hosts could join a multicast group and routers used a timer to unsubscribe group members. IGMPv2 enabled a host to specifically unsubscribe from a group. The first two versions used essentially the following operational model:

- Receivers have to subscribe to multicast groups.
- Sources do not have to subscribe to multicast groups.
- Any host can send traffic to any multicast group.

This paradigm is very general, but it also has some weaknesses:

1. Spamming of multicast groups is easy. Even if there are application level filters to drop unwanted packets, still these packets consume valuable resources in the network and in the receiver that has to process them.
2. Establishment of the multicast distribution trees is problematic. This is mainly because the location of sources is not known.
3. Finding globally unique multicast addresses is difficult. It is always possible that another multicast group uses the same multicast address.

IGMPv3 addresses these weaknesses by

1. Allowing hosts to specify the list of hosts from which they want to receive traffic. Traffic from other hosts is blocked at routers.
2. Allowing hosts to block packets that come from sources that send unwanted traffic.[2]

The remainder of this section discusses IGMPv3.

IGMP Message Format

All IGMP messages are transmitted in IP datagrams. The current version defines two message types: Membership Query and Membership Report.

A **Membership Query** message is sent by a multicast router. There are three subtypes: a **general query**, used to learn which groups have members on an attached

---

[2] The preceding overview of IGMP is based on one by Christo Gkantsidis (cc.gatech.edu/~gantsich/igmpv3.htm).

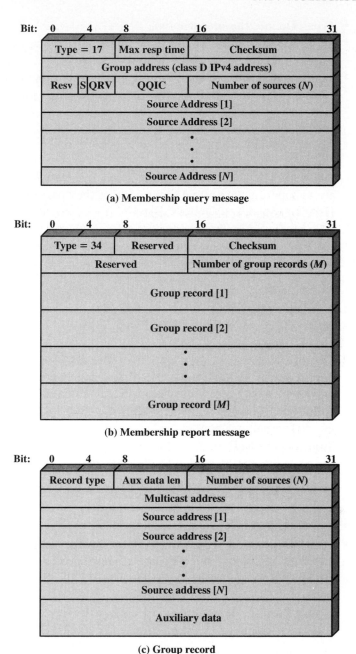

Bit: 0   4   8   16   31

Type = 17	Max resp time	Checksum

Group address (class D IPv4 address)

| Resv | S | QRV | QQIC | Number of sources (*N*) |

Source Address [1]

Source Address [2]

•
•
•

Source Address [*N*]

(a) Membership query message

Bit: 0   4   8   16   31

| Type = 34 | Reserved | Checksum |

| Reserved | Number of group records (*M*) |

Group record [1]

Group record [2]

•
•
•

Group record [*M*]

(b) Membership report message

Bit: 0   4   8   16   31

| Record type | Aux data len | Number of sources (*N*) |

Multicast address

Source address [1]

Source address [2]

•
•
•

Source address [*N*]

Auxiliary data

(c) Group record

Figure 19.4   IGMPv3 Message Formats

network; a **group-specific query**, used to learn if a particular group has any members on an attached network; and a **group-and-source specific query**, used to learn if any attached device desires reception of packets sent to a specified multicast address, from any of a specified list of sources. Figure 19.4a shows the message format, which consists of the following fields:

- **Type:** Defines this message type.
- **Max Response Time:** Specifies the maximum allowed time before sending a responding report in units of 1/10 second.
- **Checksum:** An error-detecting code, calculated as the 16-bit ones complement addition of all the 16-bit words in the message. For purposes of computation, the Checksum field is itself initialized to a value of zero. This is the same checksum algorithm used in IPv4.
- **Group Address:** Zero for a general query message; a valid IP multicast group address when sending a group-specific query or group-and-source-specific query.
- **S Flag:** When set to one, indicates to any receiving multicast routers that they are to suppress the normal timer updates they perform upon hearing a query.
- **QRV (querier's robustness variable):** If nonzero, the QRV field contains the RV value used by the querier (i.e., the sender of the query). Routers adopt the RV value from the most recently received query as their own RV value, unless that most recently received RV was zero, in which case the receivers use the default value or a statically configured value. The RV dictates how many times a host will retransmit a report to assure that it is not missed by any attached multicast routers.
- **QQIC (querier's querier interval code):** Specifies the QI value used by the querier, which is a timer for sending multiple queries. Multicast routers that are not the current querier adopt the QI value from the most recently received query as their own QI value, unless that most recently received QI was zero, in which case the receiving routers use the default QI value.
- **Number of Sources:** Specifies how many source addresses are present in this query. This value is nonzero only for a group-and-source specific query.
- **Source addresses:** If the number of sources is N, then there are N 32-bit unicast addresses appended to the message.

A **Membership Report** message consists of the following fields:

- **Type:** Defines this message type.
- **Checksum:** An error-detecting code, calculated as the 16-bit ones complement addition of all the 16-bit words in the message.
- **Number of Group Records:** Specifies how many group records are present in this report.
- **Group Records:** If the number of sources is M, then there are M 32-bit unicast addresses appended to the message.

A group record includes the following fields:

- **Record Type:** Defines this record type, as described subsequently.
- **Aux Data Length:** Length of the auxiliary data field, in 32-bit words.
- **Number of Sources:** Specifies how many source addresses are present in this record.
- **Multicast Address:** The IP multicast address to which this record pertains.

- **Source Addresses:** If the number of sources is N, then there are N 32-bit unicast addresses appended to the message.
- **Auxiliary Data:** Additional information pertaining to this record. Currently, no auxiliary data values are defined.

IGMP Operation

The objective of each host in using IGMP is to make itself known as a member of a group with a given multicast address to other hosts on the LAN and to all routers on the LAN. IGMPv3 introduces the ability for hosts to signal group membership with filtering capabilities with respect to sources. A host can either signal that it wants to receive traffic from all sources sending to a group except for some specific sources (called EXCLUDE mode) or that it wants to receive traffic only from some specific sources sending to the group (called INCLUDE mode). To join a group, a host sends an IGMP membership report message, in which the group address field is the multicast address of the group. This message is sent in an IP datagram with the same multicast destination address. In other words, the Group Address field of the IGMP message and the Destination Address field of the encapsulating IP header are the same. All hosts that are currently members of this multicast group will receive the message and learn of the new group member. Each router attached to the LAN must listen to all IP multicast addresses in order to hear all reports.

To maintain a valid current list of active group addresses, a multicast router periodically issues an IGMP general query message, sent in an IP datagram with an *all-hosts* multicast address. Each host that still wishes to remain a member of one or more multicast groups must read datagrams with the all-hosts address. When such a host receives the query, it must respond with a report message for each group to which it claims membership.

Note that the multicast router does not need to know the identity of every host in a group. Rather, it needs to know that there is at least one group member still active. Therefore, each host in a group that receives a query sets a timer with a random delay. Any host that hears another host claim membership in the group will cancel its own report. If no other report is heard and the timer expires, a host sends a report. With this scheme, only one member of each group should provide a report to the multicast router.

When a host leaves a group, it sends a leave group message to the all-routers static multicast address. This is accomplished by sending a membership report message with the EXCLUDE option and a null list of source addresses; that is, all sources are to be excluded, effectively leaving the group. When a router receives such a message for a group that has group members on the reception interface, it needs to determine if there are any remaining group members. For this purpose, the router uses the group-specific query message.

Group Membership with IPv6

IGMP was defined for operation with IPv4 and makes use of 32-bit addresses. IPv6 internets need this same functionality. Rather than to define a separate version of IGMP for IPv6, its functions have been incorporated into the new version of the

Internet Control Message Protocol (ICMPv6). ICMPv6 includes all of the functionality of ICMPv4 and IGMP. For multicast support, ICMPv6 includes both a group-membership query and a group-membership report message, which are used in the same fashion as in IGMP.

19.2 ROUTING PROTOCOLS

The routers in an internet are responsible for receiving and forwarding packets through the interconnected set of networks. Each router makes routing decision based on knowledge of the topology and traffic/delay conditions of the internet. In a simple internet, a fixed routing scheme is possible. In more complex internets, a degree of dynamic cooperation is needed among the routers. In particular, the router must avoid portions of the network that have failed and should avoid portions of the network that are congested. To make such dynamic routing decisions, routers exchange routing information using a special routing protocol for that purpose. Information is needed about the status of the internet, in terms of which networks can be reached by which routes, and the delay characteristics of various routes.

In considering the routing function, it is important to distinguish two concepts:

- **Routing information:** Information about the topology and delays of the internet
- **Routing algorithm:** The algorithm used to make a routing decision for a particular datagram, based on current routing information

Autonomous Systems

To proceed with our discussion of routing protocols, we need to introduce the concept of an **autonomous system**. An autonomous system (AS) exhibits the following characteristics:

1. An AS is a set of routers and networks managed by a single organization.
2. An AS consists of a group of routers exchanging information via a common routing protocol.
3. Except in times of failure, an AS is connected (in a graph-theoretic sense); that is, there is a path between any pair of nodes.

A shared routing protocol, which we shall refer to as an **interior router protocol** (IRP), passes routing information between routers within an AS. The protocol used within the AS does not need to be implemented outside of the system. This flexibility allows IRPs to be custom tailored to specific applications and requirements.

It may happen, however, that an internet will be constructed of more than one AS. For example, all of the LANs at a site, such as an office complex or campus, could be linked by routers to form an AS. This system might be linked through a wide area network to other ASs. The situation is illustrated in Figure 19.5. In this case, the routing algorithms and information in routing tables used by routers in different ASs may differ. Nevertheless, the routers in one AS need at least a minimal level of information concerning networks outside the system that can be reached.

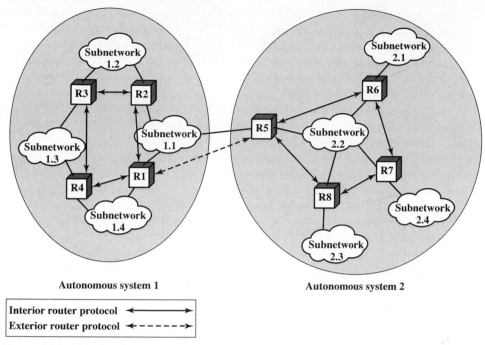

Autonomous system 1   Autonomous system 2

| Interior router protocol | ←————————→ |
| Exterior router protocol | ←— — — — —→ |

Figure 19.5 Application of Exterior and Interior Routing Protocols

We refer to the protocol used to pass routing information between routers in different ASs is referred to as an **exterior router protocol** (ERP).[3]

We can expect that an ERP will need to pass less information than an IRP, for the following reason. If a datagram is to be transferred from a host in one AS to a host in another AS, a router in the first system need only determine the target AS and devise a route to get into that target system. Once the datagram enters the target AS, the routers within that system can cooperate to deliver the datagram; the ERP is not concerned with, and does not know about, the details of the route followed within the target AS.

In the remainder of this section, we look at what are perhaps the most important examples of these two types of routing protocols: BGP and OSPF. But first, it is useful to look at a different way of characterizing routing protocols.

Approaches to Routing

Internet routing protocols employ one of three approaches to gathering and using routing information: distance-vector routing, link-state routing, and path-vector routing.

Distance-vector routing requires that each node (router or host that implements the routing protocol) exchange information with its neighboring nodes. Two

---

[3] In the literature, the terms *interior gateway protocol* (IGP) and *exterior gateway protocol* (EGP) are often used for what are referred to here as IRP and ERP. However, because the terms *IGP* and *EGP* also refer to specific protocols, we avoid their use to define the general concepts.

nodes are said to be neighbors if they are both directly connected to the same network. This approach is that used in the first generation routing algorithm for ARPANET, as described in Section 12.2. For this purpose, each node maintains a vector of link costs for each directly attached network and distance and next-hop vectors for each destination. The relatively simple Routing Information Protocol (RIP) uses this approach.

Distance-vector routing requires the transmission of a considerable amount of information by each router. Each router must send a distance vector to all of its neighbors, and that vector contains the estimated path cost to all networks in the configuration. Furthermore, when there is a significant change in a link cost or when a link is unavailable, it may take a considerable amount of time for this information to propagate through the internet.

Link-state routing is designed to overcome the drawbacks of distance-vector routing. When a router is initialized, it determines the link cost on each of its network interfaces. The router then advertises this set of link costs to all other routers in the internet topology, not just neighboring routers. From then on, the router monitors its link costs. Whenever there is a significant change (a link cost increases or decreases substantially, a new link is created, an existing link becomes unavailable), the router again advertises its set of link costs to all other routers in the configuration.

Because each router receives the link costs of all routers in the configuration, each router can construct the topology of the entire configuration and then calculate the shortest path to each destination network. Having done this, the router can construct its routing table, listing the first hop to each destination. Because the router has a representation of the entire network, it does not use a distributed version of a routing algorithm, as is done in distance-vector routing. Rather, the router can use any routing algorithm to determine the shortest paths. In practice, Dijkstra's algorithm is used. The open shortest path first (OSPF) protocol is an example of a routing protocol that uses link-state routing. The second generation routing algorithm for ARPANET also uses this approach.

Both link-state and distance-vector approaches have been used for interior router protocols. Neither approach is effective for an exterior router protocol.

In a distance-vector routing protocol, each router advertises to its neighbors a vector listing each network it can reach, together with a distance metric associated with the path to that network. Each router builds up a routing database on the basis of these neighbor updates but does not know the identity of intermediate routers and networks on any particular path. There are two problems with this approach for an exterior router protocol:

1. This distance-vector protocol assumes that all routers share a common distance metric with which to judge router preferences. This may not be the case among different ASs. If different routers attach different meanings to a given metric, it may not be possible to create stable, loop-free routes.
2. A given AS may have different priorities from other ASs and may have restrictions that prohibit the use of certain other AS. A distance-vector algorithm gives no information about the ASs that will be visited along a route.

In a link-state routing protocol, each router advertises its link metrics to all other routers. Each router builds up a picture of the complete topology of the configuration and then performs a routing calculation. This approach also has problems if used in an exterior router protocol:

1. Different ASs may use different metrics and have different restrictions. Although the link-state protocol does allow a router to build up a picture of the entire topology, the metrics used may vary from one AS to another, making it impossible to perform a consistent routing algorithm.
2. The flooding of link state information to all routers implementing an exterior router protocol across multiple ASs may be unmanageable.

An alternative, known as **path-vector routing**, is to dispense with routing metrics and simply provide information about which networks can be reached by a given router and the ASs that must be crossed to get there. The approach differs from a distance-vector algorithm in two respects: First, the path-vector approach does not include a distance or cost estimate. Second, each block of routing information lists all of the ASs visited in order to reach the destination network by this route.

Because a path vector lists the ASs that a datagram must traverse if it follows this route, the path information enables a router to perform policy routing. That is, a router may decide to avoid a particular path in order to avoid transiting a particular AS. For example, information that is confidential may be limited to certain kinds of ASs. Or a router may have information about the performance or quality of the portion of the internet that is included in an AS that leads the router to avoid that AS. Examples of performance or quality metrics include link speed, capacity, tendency to become congested, and overall quality of operation. Another criterion that could be used is minimizing the number of transit ASs.

Border Gateway Protocol

The Border Gateway Protocol (BGP) was developed for use in conjunction with internets that employ the TCP/IP suite, although the concepts are applicable to any internet. BGP has become the preferred exterior router protocol for the Internet.

Functions

BGP was designed to allow routers, called gateways in the standard, in different autonomous systems (ASs) to cooperate in the exchange of routing information. The protocol operates in terms of messages, which are sent over TCP connections. The repertoire of messages is summarized in Table 19.2. The current version of BGP is known as BGP-4 (RFC 1771).

Table 19.2   BGP-4 Messages

Open	Used to open a neighbor relationship with another router.
Update	Used to (1) transmit information about a single route and/or (2) list multiple routes to be withdrawn.
Keepalive	Used to (1) acknowledge an Open message and (2) periodically confirm the neighbor relationship.
Notification	Send when an error condition is detected.

Three functional procedures are involved in BGP:

- Neighbor acquisition
- Neighbor reachability
- Network reachability

Two routers are considered to be neighbors if they are attached to the same network. If the two routers are in different autonomous systems, they may wish to exchange routing information. For this purpose, it is necessary first to perform **neighbor acquisition**. In essence, neighbor acquisition occurs when two neighboring routers in different autonomous systems agree to exchange routing information regularly. A formal acquisition procedure is needed because one of the routers may not wish to participate. For example, the router may be overburdened and does not want to be responsible for traffic coming in from outside the system. In the neighbor acquisition process, one router sends a request message to the other, which may either accept or refuse the offer. The protocol does not address the issue of how one router knows the address or even the existence of another router, nor how it decides that it needs to exchange routing information with that particular router. These issues must be dealt with at configuration time or by active intervention of a network manager.

To perform neighbor acquisition, one router sends an Open message to another. If the target router accepts the request, it returns a Keepalive message in response.

Once a neighbor relationship is established, the **neighbor reachability** procedure is used to maintain the relationship. Each partner needs to be assured that the other partner still exists and is still engaged in the neighbor relationship. For this purpose, the two routers periodically issue Keepalive messages to each other.

The final procedure specified by BGP is **network reachability**. Each router maintains a database of the networks that it can reach and the preferred route for reaching each network. Whenever a change is made to this database, the router issues an Update message that is broadcast to all other routers implementing BGP. Because the Update message is broadcast, all BGP routers can build up and maintain their routing information.

BGP Messages

Figure 19.6 illustrates the formats of all of the BGP messages. Each message begins with a 19-octet header containing three fields, as indicated by the shaded portion of each message in the figure:

- **Marker:** Reserved for authentication. The sender may insert a value in this field that would be used as part of an authentication mechanism to enable the recipient to verify the identity of the sender.
- **Length:** Length of message in octets.
- **Type:** Type of message: Open, Update, Notification, Keepalive.

To acquire a neighbor, a router first opens a TCP connection to the neighbor router of interest. It then sends an Open message. This message identifies the AS to which the sender belongs and provides the IP address of the router. It also includes

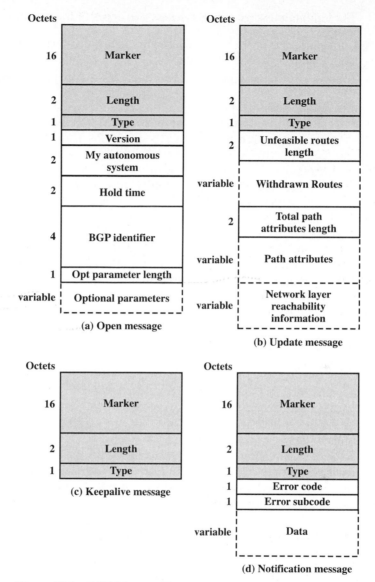

Figure 19.6 BGP Message Formats

a Hold Time parameter, which indicates the number of seconds that the sender proposes for the value of the Hold Timer. If the recipient is prepared to open a neighbor relationship, it calculates a value of Hold Timer that is the minimum of its Hold Time and the Hold Time in the Open message. This calculated value is the maximum number of seconds that may elapse between the receipt of successive Keepalive and/or Update messages by the sender.

The Keepalive message consists simply of the header. Each router issues these messages to each of its peers often enough to prevent the Hold Timer from expiring.

The Update message communicates two types of information:

- Information about a single route through the internet. This information is available to be added to the database of any recipient router.
- A list of routes previously advertised by this router that are being withdrawn.

An Update message may contain one or both types of information. Information about a single route through the network involves three fields: the Network Layer Reachability Information (NLRI) field, the Total Path Attributes Length field, and the Path Attributes field. The NLRI field consists of a list of identifiers of networks that can be reached by this route. Each network is identified by its IP address, which is actually a portion of a full IP address. Recall that an IP address is a 32-bit quantity of the form {network, host}. The left-hand or prefix portion of this quantity identifies a particular network.

The Path Attributes field contains a list of attributes that apply to this particular route. The following are the defined attributes:

- **Origin:** Indicates whether this information was generated by an interior router protocol (e.g., OSPF) or an exterior router protocol (in particular, BGP).
- **AS_Path:** A list of the ASs that are traversed for this route.
- **Next_Hop:** The IP address of the border router that should be used as the next hop to the destinations listed in the NLRI field.
- **Multi_Exit_Disc:** Used to communicate some information about routes internal to an AS. This is described later in this section.
- **Local_Pref:** Used by a router to inform other routers within the same AS of its degree of preference for a particular route. It has no significance to routers in other ASs.
- **Atomic_Aggregate, Aggregator:** These two fields implement the concept of route aggregation. In essence, an internet and its corresponding address space can be organized hierarchically (i.e., as a tree). In this case, network addresses are structured in two or more parts. All of the networks of a given subtree share a common partial internet address. Using this common partial address, the amount of information that must be communicated in NLRI can be significantly reduced.

The AS_Path attribute actually serves two purposes. Because it lists the ASs that a datagram must traverse if it follows this route, the AS_Path information enables a router to implement routing policies. That is, a router may decide to avoid a particular path to avoid transiting a particular AS. For example, information that is confidential may be limited to certain kinds of ASs. Or a router may have information about the performance or quality of the portion of the internet that is included in an AS that leads the router to avoid that AS. Examples of performance or quality metrics include link speed, capacity, tendency to become congested, and overall quality of operation. Another criterion that could be used is minimizing the number of transit ASs.

The reader may wonder about the purpose of the Next_Hop attribute. The requesting router will necessarily want to know which networks are reachable via the responding router, but why provide information about other routers? This is best explained with reference to Figure 19.5. In this example, router R1 in autonomous system 1 and router R5 in autonomous system 2 implement BGP and acquire a neighbor relationship. R1 issues Update messages to R5, indicating which networks it can reach and the distances (network hops) involved. R1 also provides the same information on behalf of R2. That is, R1 tells R5 what networks are reachable via R2. In this example, R2 does not implement BGP. Typically, most of the routers in an autonomous system will not implement BGP. Only a few routers will be assigned responsibility for communicating with routers in other autonomous systems. A final point: R1 is in possession of the necessary information about R2, because R1 and R2 share an interior router protocol (IRP).

The second type of update information is the withdrawal of one or more routes. In this case, the route is identified by the IP address of the destination network.

Finally, the Notification Message is sent when an error condition is detected. The following errors may be reported:

- **Message header error:** Includes authentication and syntax errors.
- **Open message error:** Includes syntax errors and options not recognized in an Open message. This message can also be used to indicate that a proposed Hold Time in an Open message is unacceptable.
- **Update message error:** Includes syntax and validity errors in an Update message.
- **Hold timer expired:** If the sending router has not received successive Keepalive and/or Update and/or Notification messages within the Hold Time period, then this error is communicated and the connection is closed.
- **Finite state machine error:** Includes any procedural error.
- **Cease:** Used by a router to close a connection with another router in the absence of any other error.

BGP Routing Information Exchange

The essence of BGP is the exchange of routing information among participating routers in multiple ASs. This process can be quite complex. In what follows, we provide a simplified overview.

Let us consider router R1 in autonomous system 1 (AS1), in Figure 19.5. To begin, a router that implements BGP will also implement an internal routing protocol such as OSPF. Using OSPF, R1 can exchange routing information with other routers within AS1 and build up a picture of the topology of the networks and routers in AS1 and construct a routing table. Next, R1 can issue an Update message to R5 in AS2. The Update message could include the following:

- **AS_Path:** The identity of AS1
- **Next_Hop:** The IP address of R1
- **NLRI:** A list of all of the networks in AS1

This message informs R5 that all of the networks listed in NLRI are reachable via R1 and that the only autonomous system traversed is AS1.

Suppose now that R5 also has a neighbor relationship with another router in another autonomous system, say R9 in AS3. R5 will forward the information just received from R1 to R9 in a new Update message. This message includes the following:

- **AS_Path:** The list of identifiers {AS2, AS1}
- **Next_Hop:** The IP address of R5
- **NLRI:** A list of all of the networks in AS1

This message informs R9 that all of the networks listed in NLRI are reachable via R5 and that the autonomous systems traversed are AS2 and AS1. R9 must now decide if this is its preferred route to the networks listed. It may have knowledge of an alternate route to some or all of these networks that it prefers for reasons of performance or some other policy metric. If R9 decides that the route provided in R5's update message is preferable, then R9 incorporates that routing information into its routing database and forwards this new routing information to other neighbors. This new message will include an AS_Path field of {AS3, AS2, AS1}.

In this fashion, routing update information is propagated through the larger internet, consisting of a number of interconnected autonomous systems. The AS_Path field is used to assure that such messages do not circulate indefinitely: If an Update message is received by a router in an AS that is included in the AS_Path field, that router will not forward the update information to other routers.

Routers within the same AS, called internal neighbors, may exchange BGP information. In this case, the sending router does not add the identifier of the common AS to the AS_Path field. When a router has selected a preferred route to an external destination, it transmits this route to all of its internal neighbors. Each of these routers then decides if the new route is preferred, in which case the new route is added to its database and a new Update message goes out.

When there are multiple entry points into an AS that are available to a border router in another AS, the Multi_Exit_Disc attribute may be used to choose among them. This attribute contains a number that reflects some internal metric for reaching destinations within an AS. For example, suppose in Figure 19.5 that both R1 and R2 implement BGP and both have a neighbor relationship with R5. Each provides an Update message to R5 for network 1.3 that includes a routing metric used internal to AS1, such as a routing metric associated with the OSPF internal router protocol. R5 could then use these two metrics as the basis for choosing between the two routes.

Open Shortest Path First (OSPF) Protocol

The OSPF protocol (RFC 2328) is now widely used as the interior router protocol in TCP/IP networks. OSPF computes a route through the internet that incurs the least cost based on a user-configurable metric of cost. The user can configure the cost to express a function of delay, data rate, dollar cost, or other factors. OSPF is able to equalize loads over multiple equal-cost paths.

Each router maintains a database that reflects the known topology of the autonomous system of which it is a part. The topology is expressed as a directed graph. The graph consists of

- Vertices, or nodes, of two types:
  1. router
  2. network, which is in turn of two types
     a. transit, if it can carry data that neither originate nor terminate on an end system attached to this network
     b. stub, if it is not a transit network

- Edges of two types:
    1. graph edges that connect two router vertices when the corresponding routers are connected to each other by a direct point-to-point link
    2. graph edges that connect a router vertex to a network vertex when the router is directly connected to the network

Figure 19.7, based on one in RFC 2328, shows an example of an autonomous system, and Figure 19.8 is the resulting directed graph. The mapping is straightforward:

- Two routers joined by a point-to-point link are represented in the graph as being directly connected by a pair of edges, one in each direction (e.g., routers 6 and 10).

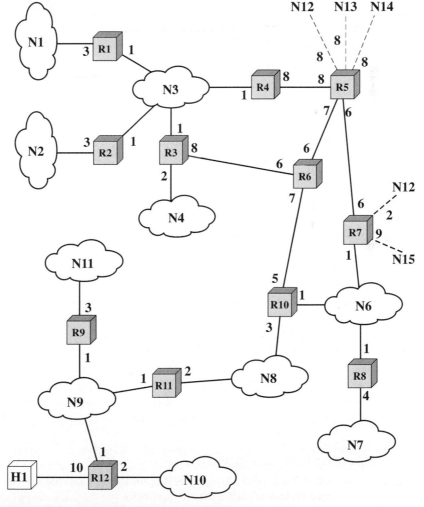

Figure 19.7 A Sample Autonomous System

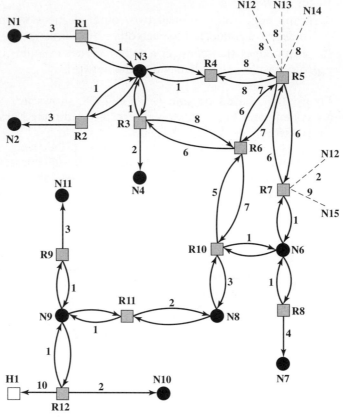

Figure 19.8 Directed Graph of Autonomous System of Figure 19.7

- When multiple routers are attached to a network (such as a LAN or packet-switching network), the directed graph shows all routers bidirectionally connected to the network vertex (e.g., routers 1, 2, 3, and 4 all connect to network 3).
- If a single router is attached to a network, the network will appear in the graph as a stub connection (e.g., network 7).
- An end system, called a host, can be directly connected to a router, in which case it is depicted in the corresponding graph (e.g., host 1).
- If a router is connected to other autonomous systems, then the path cost to each network in the other system must be obtained by some exterior router protocol (ERP). Each such network is represented on the graph by a stub and an edge to the router with the known path cost (e.g., networks 12 through 15).

A cost is associated with the output side of each router interface. This cost is configurable by the system administrator. Arcs on the graph are labeled with the cost of the corresponding router output interface. Arcs having no labeled cost have a cost of 0. Note that arcs leading from networks to routers always have a cost of 0.

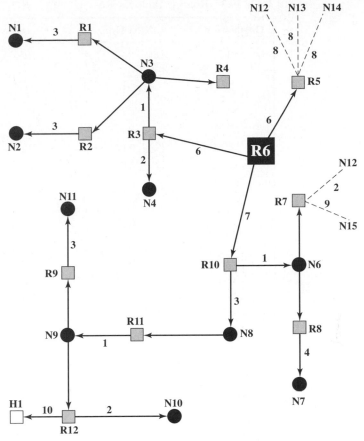

Figure 19.9 The SPF Tree for Router R6

A database corresponding to the directed graph is maintained by each router. It is pieced together from link state messages from other routers in the internet. Using Dijkstra's algorithm (see Section 12.3), a router calculates the least-cost path to all destination networks. The result for router 6 of Figure 19.7 is shown as a tree in Figure 19.9, with R6 as the root of the tree. The tree gives the entire route to any destination network or host. However, only the next hop to the destination is used in the forwarding process. The resulting routing table for router 6 is shown in Table 19.3. The table includes entries for routers advertising external routes (routers 5 and 7). For external networks whose identity is known, entries are also provided.

19.3 INTEGRATED SERVICES ARCHITECTURE

To meet the requirement for QoS-based service, the IETF is developing a suite of standards under the general umbrella of the Integrated Services Architecture (ISA). ISA, intended to provide QoS transport over IP-based internets, is defined in

Table 19.3 Routing Table for R6

Destination	Next Hop	Distance
N1	R3	10
N2	R3	10
N3	R3	7
N4	R3	8
N6	R10	8
N7	R10	12
N8	R10	10
N9	R10	11
N10	R10	13
N11	R10	14
H1	R10	21
R5	R5	6
R7	R10	8
N12	R10	10
N13	R5	14
N14	R5	14
N15	R10	17

overall terms in RFC 1633, while a number of other documents are being developed to fill in the details. Already, a number of vendors have implemented portions of the ISA in routers and end-system software.

This section provides an overview of ISA.

Internet Traffic

Traffic on a network or internet can be divided into two broad categories: elastic and inelastic. A consideration of their differing requirements clarifies the need for an enhanced internet architecture.

Elastic Traffic

Elastic traffic is that which can adjust, over wide ranges, to changes in delay and throughput across an internet and still meet the needs of its applications. This is the traditional type of traffic supported on TCP/IP-based internets and is the type of traffic for which internets were designed. Applications that generate such traffic typically use TCP or UDP as a transport protocol. In the case of UDP, the application will use as much capacity as is available up to the rate that the application generates data. In the case of TCP, the application will use as much capacity as is available up to the maximum rate that the end-to-end receiver can accept data. Also with TCP, traffic on individual connections adjusts to congestion by reducing the rate at which data are presented to the network; this is described in Chapter 20.

Applications that can be classified as elastic include the common applications that operate over TCP or UDP, including file transfer (FTP), electronic mail (SMTP), remote login (TELNET), network management (SNMP), and Web access (HTTP). However, there are differences among the requirements of these applications. For example,

- E-mail is generally quite insensitive to changes in delay.
- When file transfer is done interactively, as it frequently is, the user expects the delay to be proportional to the file size and so is sensitive to changes in throughput.
- With network management, delay is generally not a serious concern. However, if failures in an internet are the cause of congestion, then the need for SNMP messages to get through with minimum delay increases with increased congestion.
- Interactive applications, such as remote logon and Web access, are quite sensitive to delay.

It is important to realize that it is not per-packet delay that is the quantity of interest. As noted in [CLAR95], observation of real delays across the Internet suggest that wide variations in delay do not occur. Because of the congestion control mechanisms in TCP, when congestion develops, delays only increase modestly before the arrival rate from the various TCP connections slow down. Instead, the QoS perceived by the user relates to the total elapsed time to transfer an element of the current application. For an interactive TELNET-based application, the element may be a single keystroke or single line. For a Web access, the element is a Web page, which could be as little as a few kilobytes or could be substantially larger for an image-rich page. For a scientific application, the element could be many megabytes of data.

For very small elements, the total elapsed time is dominated by the delay time across the internet. However, for larger elements, the total elapsed time is dictated by the sliding-window performance of TCP and is therefore dominated by the throughput achieved over the TCP connection. Thus, for large transfers, the transfer time is proportional to the size of the file and the degree to which the source slows due to congestion.

It should be clear that even if we confine our attention to elastic traffic, a QoS-based internet service could be of benefit. Without such a service, routers are dealing evenhandedly with arriving IP packets, with no concern for the type of application and whether a particular packet is part of a large transfer element or a small one. Under such circumstances, and if congestion develops, it is unlikely that resources will be allocated in such a way as to meet the needs of all applications fairly. When inelastic traffic is added to the mix, the results are even more unsatisfactory.

Inelastic Traffic

Inelastic traffic does not easily adapt, if at all, to changes in delay and throughput across an internet. The prime example is real-time traffic. The requirements for inelastic traffic may include the following:

- **Throughput:** A minimum throughput value may be required. Unlike most elastic traffic, which can continue to deliver data with perhaps degraded service, many inelastic applications absolutely require a given minimum throughput.
- **Delay:** An example of a delay-sensitive application is stock trading; someone who consistently receives later service will consistently act later, and with greater disadvantage.
- **Jitter:** The magnitude of delay variation, called jitter, is a critical factor in real-time applications. The larger the allowable delay variation, the longer the real delay in delivering the data and the greater the size of the delay buffer required at receivers. Real-time interactive applications, such as teleconferencing, may require a reasonable upper bound on jitter.
- **Packet loss:** Real-time applications vary in the amount of packet loss, if any, that they can sustain.

These requirements are difficult to meet in an environment with variable queuing delays and congestion losses. Accordingly, inelastic traffic introduces two new requirements into the internet architecture. First, some means is needed to give preferential treatment to applications with more demanding requirements. Applications need to be able to state their requirements, either ahead of time in some sort of service request function, or on the fly, by means of fields in the IP packet header. The former approach provides more flexibility in stating requirements, and it enables the network to anticipate demands and deny new requests if the required resources are unavailable. This approach implies the use of some sort of resource reservation protocol.

A second requirement in supporting inelastic traffic in an internet architecture is that elastic traffic must still be supported. Inelastic applications typically do not back off and reduce demand in the face of congestion, in contrast to TCP-based applications. Therefore, in times of congestion, inelastic traffic will continue to supply a high load, and elastic traffic will be crowded off the internet. A reservation protocol can help control this situation by denying service requests that would leave too few resources available to handle current elastic traffic.

ISA Approach

The purpose of ISA is to enable the provision of QoS support over IP-based internets. The central design issue for ISA is how to share the available capacity in times of congestion.

For an IP-based internet that provides only a best-effort service, the tools for controlling congestion and providing service are limited. In essence, routers have two mechanisms to work with:

- **Routing algorithm:** Most routing protocols in use in internets allow routes to be selected to minimize delay. Routers exchange information to get a picture of the delays throughout the internet. Minimum-delay routing helps to balance loads, thus decreasing local congestion, and helps to reduce delays seen by individual TCP connections.

- **Packet discard:** When a router's buffer overflows, it discards packets. Typically, the most recent packet is discarded. The effect of lost packets on a TCP connection is that the sending TCP entity backs off and reduces its load, thus helping to alleviate internet congestion.

These tools have worked reasonably well. However, as the discussion in the preceding subsection shows, such techniques are inadequate for the variety of traffic now coming to internets.

ISA is an overall architecture within which a number of enhancements to the traditional best-effort mechanisms are being developed. In ISA, each IP packet can be associated with a flow. RFC 1633 defines a flow as a distinguishable stream of related IP packets that results from a single user activity and requires the same QoS. For example, a flow might consist of one transport connection or one video stream distinguishable by the ISA. A flow differs from a TCP connection in two key particulars: A flow is unidirectional, and there can be more than one recipient of a flow (multicast). Typically, an IP packet is identified as a member of a flow on the basis of source and destination IP addresses and port numbers, and protocol type. The flow identifier in the IPv6 header is not necessarily equivalent to an ISA flow, but in future the IPv6 flow identifier could be used in ISA.

ISA makes use of the following functions to manage congestion and provide QoS transport:

- **Admission control:** For QoS transport (other than default best-effort transport), ISA requires that a reservation be made for a new flow. If the routers collectively determine that there are insufficient resources to guarantee the requested QoS, then the flow is not admitted. The protocol RSVP is used to make reservations.
- **Routing algorithm:** The routing decision may be based on a variety of QoS parameters, not just minimum delay. For example, the routing protocol OSPF, discussed in Section 19.2, can select routes based on QoS.
- **Queuing discipline:** A vital element of the ISA is an effective queuing policy that takes into account the differing requirements of different flows.
- **Discard policy:** A discard policy determines which packets to drop when a buffer is full and new packets arrive. A discard policy can be an important element in managing congestion and meeting QoS guarantees.

ISA Components

Figure 19.10 is a general depiction of the implementation architecture for ISA within a router. Below the thick horizontal line are the forwarding functions of the router; these are executed for each packet and therefore must be highly optimized. The remaining functions, above the line, are background functions that create data structures used by the forwarding functions.

The principal background functions are as follows:

- **Reservation protocol:** This protocol is to reserve resources for a new flow at a given level of QoS. It is used among routers and between routers and end systems. The reservation protocol is responsible for maintaining flow-specific

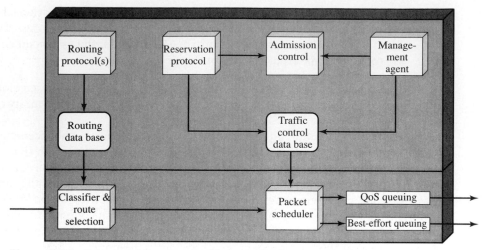

Figure 19.10 Integrated Services Architecture Implemented in Router

state information at the end systems and at the routers along the path of the flow. RSVP is used for this purpose. The reservation protocol updates the traffic control database used by the packet scheduler to determine the service provided for packets of each flow.

- **Admission control:** When a new flow is requested, the reservation protocol invokes the admission control function. This function determines if sufficient resources are available for this flow at the requested QoS. This determination is based on the current level of commitment to other reservations and/or on the current load on the network.

- **Management agent:** A network management agent is able to modify the traffic control database and to direct the admission control module in order to set admission control policies.

- **Routing protocol:** The routing protocol is responsible for maintaining a routing database that gives the next hop to be taken for each destination address and each flow.

These background functions support the main task of the router, which is the forwarding of packets. The two principal functional areas that accomplish forwarding are the following:

- **Classifier and route selection:** For the purposes of forwarding and traffic control, incoming packets must be mapped into classes. A class may correspond to a single flow or to a set of flows with the same QoS requirements. For example, the packets of all video flows or the packets of all flows attributable to a particular organization may be treated identically for purposes of resource allocation and queuing discipline. The selection of class is based on fields in the IP header. Based on the packet's class and its destination IP address, this function determines the next-hop address for this packet.

- **Packet scheduler:** This function manages one or more queues for each output port. It determines the order in which queued packets are transmitted and the selection of packets for discard, if necessary. Decisions are made based on a packet's class, the contents of the traffic control database, and current and past activity on this outgoing port. Part of the packet scheduler's task is that of policing, which is the function of determining whether the packet traffic in a given flow exceeds the requested capacity and, if so, deciding how to treat the excess packets.

ISA Services

ISA service for a flow of packets is defined on two levels. First, a number of general categories of service are provided, each of which provides a certain general type of service guarantees. Second, within each category, the service for a particular flow is specified by the values of certain parameters; together, these values are referred to as a traffic specification (TSpec). Currently, three categories of service are defined:

- Guaranteed
- Controlled load
- Best effort

An application can request a reservation for a flow for a guaranteed or controlled load QoS, with a TSpec that defines the exact amount of service required. If the reservation is accepted, then the TSpec is part of the contract between the data flow and the service. The service agrees to provide the requested QoS as long as the flow's data traffic continues to be described accurately by the TSpec. Packets that are not part of a reserved flow are by default given a best-effort delivery service.

Before looking at the ISA service categories, one general concept should be defined: the token bucket traffic specification. This is a way of characterizing traffic that has three advantages in the context of ISA:

1. Many traffic sources can be defined easily and accurately by a token bucket scheme.
2. The token bucket scheme provides a concise description of the load to be imposed by a flow, enabling the service to determine easily the resource requirement.
3. The token bucket scheme provides the input parameters to a policing function.

A token bucket traffic specification consists of two parameters: a token replenishment rate R and a bucket size B. The token rate R specifies the continually sustainable data rate; that is, over a relatively long period of time, the average data rate to be supported for this flow is R. The bucket size B specifies the amount by which the data rate can exceed R for short periods of time. The exact condition is as follows: During any time period T, the amount of data sent cannot exceed $RT + B$.

Figure 19.11 illustrates this scheme and explains the use of the term *bucket*. The bucket represents a counter that indicates the allowable number of octets of IP data that can be sent at any time. The bucket fills with *octet tokens* at the rate of R (i.e., the counter is incremented R times per second), up to the bucket capacity

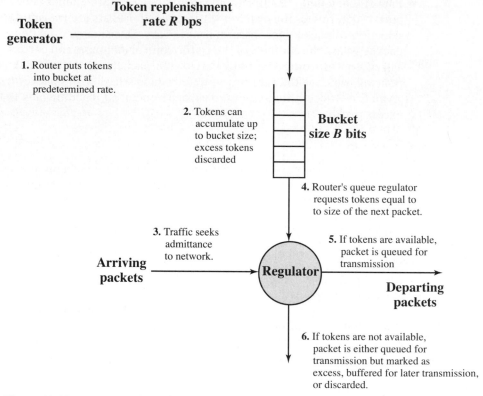

Figure 19.11 Token Bucket Scheme

(up to the maximum counter value). IP packets arrive and are queued for processing. An IP packet may be processed if there are sufficient octet tokens to match the IP data size. If so, the packet is processed and the bucket is drained of the corresponding number of tokens. If a packet arrives and there are insufficient tokens available, then the packet exceeds the TSpec for this flow. The treatment for such packets is not specified in the ISA documents; common actions are relegating the packet to best-effort service, discarding the packet, or marking the packet in such a way that it may be discarded in future.

Over the long run, the rate of IP data allowed by the token bucket is R. However, if there is an idle or relatively slow period, the bucket capacity builds up, so that at most an additional B octets above the stated rate can be accepted. Thus, B is a measure of the degree of burstiness of the data flow that is allowed.

Guaranteed Service

The key elements of the guaranteed service are as follows:

- The service provides assured capacity, or data rate.
- There is a specified upper bound on the queuing delay through the network. This must be added to the propagation delay, or latency, to arrive at the bound on total delay through the network.

- There are no queuing losses. That is, no packets are lost due to buffer overflow; packets may be lost due to failures in the network or changes in routing paths.

With this service, an application provides a characterization of its expected traffic profile, and the service determines the end-to-end delay that it can guarantee.

One category of applications for this service is those that need an upper bound on delay so that a delay buffer can be used for real-time playback of incoming data, and that do not tolerate packet losses because of the degradation in the quality of the output. Another example is applications with hard real-time deadlines.

The guaranteed service is the most demanding service provided by ISA. Because the delay bound is firm, the delay has to be set at a large value to cover rare cases of long queuing delays.

Controlled Load

The key elements of the controlled load service are as follows:

- The service tightly approximates the behavior visible to applications receiving best-effort service under unloaded conditions.
- There is no specified upper bound on the queuing delay through the network. However, the service ensures that a very high percentage of the packets do not experience delays that greatly exceed the minimum transit delay (i.e., the delay due to propagation time plus router processing time with no queuing delays).
- A very high percentage of transmitted packets will be successfully delivered (i.e., almost no queuing loss).

As was mentioned, the risk in an internet that provides QoS for real-time applications is that best-effort traffic is crowded out. This is because best-effort types of applications employ TCP, which will back off in the face of congestion and delays. The controlled load service guarantees that the network will set aside sufficient resources so that an application that receives this service will see a network that responds as if these real-time applications were not present and competing for resources.

The controlled service is useful for applications that have been referred to as adaptive real-time applications [CLAR92]. Such applications do not require an a priori upper bound on the delay through the network. Rather, the receiver measures the jitter experienced by incoming packets and sets the playback point to the minimum delay that still produces a sufficiently low loss rate (e.g., video can be adaptive by dropping a frame or delaying the output stream slightly; voice can be adaptive by adjusting silent periods).

Queuing Discipline

An important component of an ISA implementation is the queuing discipline used at the routers. Routers traditionally have used a first-in-first-out (FIFO) queuing discipline at each output port. A single queue is maintained at each output port. When a new packet arrives and is routed to an output port, it is placed at the end of the queue. As long as the queue is not empty, the router transmits packets from the queue, taking the oldest remaining packet next.

There are several drawbacks to the FIFO queuing discipline:

- No special treatment is given to packets from flows that are of higher priority or are more delay sensitive. If a number of packets from different flows are ready to be forwarded, they are handled strictly in FIFO order.

- If a number of smaller packets are queued behind a long packet, then FIFO queuing results in a larger average delay per packet than if the shorter packets were transmitted before the longer packet. In general, flows of larger packets get better service.

- A greedy TCP connection can crowd out more altruistic connections. If congestion occurs and one TCP connection fails to back off, other connections along the same path segment must back off more than they would otherwise have to do.

To overcome the drawbacks of FIFO queuing, some sort of fair queuing scheme is used, in which a router maintains multiple queues at each output port (Figure 19.12). With simple fair queuing, each incoming packet is placed in the queue for its flow. The queues are serviced in round-robin fashion, taking one packet from each nonempty queue in turn. Empty queues are skipped over. This scheme is fair in that each busy flow gets to send exactly one packet per cycle. Further, this is a form of load balancing among the various flows. There is no advantage in being greedy. A greedy flow finds that its queues become long, increasing its delays, whereas other flows are unaffected by this behavior.

A number of vendors have implemented a refinement of fair queuing known as weighted fair queuing (WFQ). In essence, WFQ takes into account the amount of traffic through each queue and gives busier queues more capacity without completely shutting out less busy queues. In addition WFQ can take into account the amount of service requested by each traffic flow and adjust the queuing discipline accordingly.

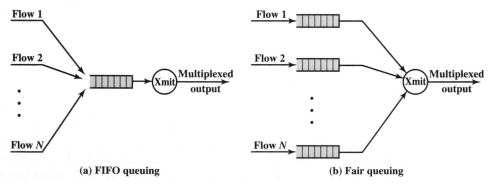

Figure 19.12   FIFO and Fair Queuing

Resource ReSerVation Protocol (RSVP)

RFC 2205 defines RSVP, which provides supporting functionality for ISA. This subsection provides an overview.

A key task, perhaps the key task, of an internetwork is to deliver data from a source to one or more destinations with the desired quality of service (QoS), such as throughput, delay, delay variance, and so on. This task becomes increasingly difficult on any internetwork with increasing number of users, data rate of applications, and use of multicasting. To meet these needs, it is not enough for an internet to react to congestion. Instead a tool is needed to prevent congestion by allowing applications to reserve network resources at a given QoS.

Preventive measures can be useful in both unicast and multicast transmission. For **unicast**, two applications agree on a specific quality of service for a session and expect the internetwork to support that quality of service. If the internetwork is heavily loaded, it may not provide the desired QOS and instead deliver packets at a reduced QOS. In that case, the applications may have preferred to wait before initiating the session or at least to have been alerted to the potential for reduced QOS. A way of dealing with this situation is to have the unicast applications reserve resources in order to meet a given quality of service. Routers along an intended path could then pre-allocate resources (queue space, outgoing capacity) to assure the desired QOS. If a router could not meet the resource reservation because of prior outstanding reservations, then the applications could be informed. The applications may then decide to try again at a reduced QOS reservation or may decide to try later.

Multicast transmission presents a much more compelling case for implementing resource reservation. A multicast transmission can generate a tremendous amount of internetwork traffic if either the application is high-volume (e.g., video) or the group of multicast destinations is large and scattered, or both. What makes the case for multicast resource reservation is that much of the potential load generated by a multicast source may easily be prevented. This is so for two reasons:

1. Some members of an existing multicast group may not require delivery from a particular source over some given period of time. For example, there may be two "channels" (two multicast sources) broadcasting to a particular multicast group at the same time. A multicast destination may wish to "tune in" to only one channel at a time.

2. Some members of a group may only be able to handle a portion of the source transmission. For example, a video source may transmit a video stream that consists of two components: a basic component that provides a reduced picture quality, and an enhanced component. Some receivers may not have the processing power to handle the enhanced component, or may be connected to the internetwork through a subnetwork or link that does not have the capacity for the full signal.

Thus, the use of resource reservation can enable routers to decide ahead of time if they can meet the requirement to deliver a multicast transmission to all designated multicast receivers and to reserve the appropriate resources if possible.

Internet resource reservation differs from the type of resource reservation that may be implemented in a connection-oriented network, such as ATM or frame relay. An internet resource reservation scheme must interact with a dynamic routing strategy that allows the route followed by packets of a given transmission to change. When the route changes, the resource reservations must be changed. To deal with this dynamic situation, the concept of **soft state** is used. A soft state is simply a set of state information at a router that expires unless regularly refreshed from the entity that requested the state. If a route for a given transmission changes, then some soft states will expire and new resource reservations will invoke the appropriate soft states on the new routers along the route. Thus, the end systems requesting resources must periodically renew their requests during the course of an application transmission.

Based on these considerations, the specification lists the following characteristics of RSVP:

- **Unicast and multicast:** RSVP makes reservations for both unicast and multicast transmissions, adapting dynamically to changing group membership as well as to changing routes, and reserving resources based on the individual requirements of multicast members.
- **Simplex:** RSVP makes reservations for unidirectional data flow. Data exchanges between two end systems require separate reservations in the two directions.
- **Receiver-initiated reservation:** The receiver of a data flow initiates and maintains the resource reservation for that flow.
- **Maintaining soft state in the internet:** RSVP maintains a soft state at intermediate routers and leaves the responsibility for maintaining these reservation states to end users.
- **Providing different reservation styles:** These allow RSVP users to specify how reservations for the same multicast group should be aggregated at the intermediate switches. This feature enables a more efficient use of internet resources.
- **Transparent operation through non-RSVP routers:** Because reservations and RSVP are independent of routing protocol, there is no fundamental conflict in a mixed environment in which some routers do not employ RSVP. These routers will simply use a best-effort delivery technique.
- **Support for IPv4 and IPv6:** RSVP can exploit the Type-of-Service field in the IPv4 header and the Flow Label field in the IPv6 header.

19.4 DIFFERENTIATED SERVICES

The Integrated Services Architecture (ISA) and RSVP are intended to support quality of service (QoS) offering in the Internet and in private internets. Although ISA in general and RSVP in particular are useful tools in this regard, these features are relatively complex to deploy. Further, they may not scale well to handle large volumes of traffic because of the amount of control signaling required to coordinate integrated QoS offerings and because of the maintenance of state information required at routers.

As the burden on the Internet grows, and as the variety of applications grow, there is an immediate need to provide differing levels of QoS to different traffic flows. The differentiated services (DS) architecture (RFC 2475) is designed to provide a simple, easy-to-implement, low-overhead tool to support a range of network services that are differentiated on the basis of performance.

Several key characteristics of DS contribute to its efficiency and ease of deployment:

- IP packets are labeled for differing QoS treatment using the existing IPv4 Type of Service octet (Figure 18.6) or IPv6 Traffic Class octet (Figure 18.11). Thus, no change is required to IP.
- A service level agreement (SLA) is established between the service provider (internet domain) and the customer prior to the use of DS. This avoids the need to incorporate DS mechanisms in applications. Thus, existing applications need not be modified to use DS.
- DS provides a built-in aggregation mechanism. All traffic with the same DS octet is treated the same by the network service. For example, multiple voice connections are not handled individually but in the aggregate. This provides for good scaling to larger networks and traffic loads.
- DS is implemented in individual routers by queuing and forwarding packets based on the DS octet. Routers deal with each packet individually and do not have to save state information on packet flows.

Today, DS is the most widely accepted QoS mechanism in enterprise networks.

Although DS is intended to provide a simple service based on relatively simple mechanisms, the set of RFCs related to DS is relatively complex. Table 19.4 summarizes some of the key terms from these specifications.

Services

The DS type of service is provided within a DS domain, which is defined as a contiguous portion of the Internet over which a consistent set of DS policies are administered. Typically, a DS domain would be under the control of one administrative entity. The services provided across a DS domain are defined in a service level agreement (SLA), which is a service contract between a customer and the service provider that specifies the forwarding service that the customer should receive for various classes of packets. A customer may be a user organization or another DS domain. Once the SLA is established, the customer submits packets with the DS octet marked to indicate the packet class. The service provider must assure that the customer gets at least the agreed QoS for each packet class. To provide that QoS, the service provider must configure the appropriate forwarding policies at each router (based on DS octet value) and must measure the performance being provided each class on an ongoing basis.

If a customer submits packets intended for destinations within the DS domain, then the DS domain is expected to provide the agreed service. If the destination is beyond the customer's DS domain, then the DS domain will attempt to forward the packets through other domains, requesting the most appropriate service to match the requested service.

Table 19.4 Terminology for Differentiated Services

Behavior Aggregate	A set of packets with the same DS codepoint crossing a link in a particular direction.
Classifier	Selects packets based on the DS field (BA classifier) or on multiple fields within the packet header (MF classifier).
DS Boundary Node	A DS node that connects one DS domain to a node in another domain.
DS Codepoint	A specified value of the 6-bit DSCP portion of the 8-bit DS field in the IP header.
DS Domain	A contiguous (connected) set of nodes, capable of implementing differentiated services, that operate with a common set of service provisioning policies and per-hop behavior definitions.
DS Interior Node	A DS node that is not a DS boundary node.
DS Node	A node that supports differentiated services. Typically, a DS node is a router. A host system that provides differentiated services for applications in the host is also a DS node.
Dropping	The process of discarding packets based on specified rules; also called policing.
Marking	The process of setting the DS codepoint in a packet. Packets may be marked on initiation and may be re-marked by an en route DS node.
Metering	The process of measuring the temporal properties (e.g., rate) of a packet stream selected by a classifier. The instantaneous state of that process may affect marking, shaping, and dropping functions.
Per-Hop Behavior (PHB)	The externally observable forwarding behavior applied at a node to a behavior aggregate.
Service Level Agreement (SLA)	A service contract between a customer and a service provider that specifies the forwarding service a customer should receive.
Shaping	The process of delaying packets within a packet stream to cause it to conform to some defined traffic profile.
Traffic Conditioning	Control functions performed to enforce rules specified in a TCA, including metering, marking, shaping, and dropping.
Traffic Conditioning Agreement (TCA)	An agreement specifying classifying rules and traffic conditioning rules that are to apply to packets selected by the classifier.

A draft DS framework document lists the following detailed performance parameters that might be included in an SLA:

- Detailed service performance parameters such as expected throughput, drop probability, latency
- Constraints on the ingress and egress points at which the service is provided, indicating the scope of the service
- Traffic profiles that must be adhered to for the requested service to be provided, such as token bucket parameters
- Disposition of traffic submitted in excess of the specified profile

The framework document also gives some examples of services that might be provided:

1. Traffic offered at service level A will be delivered with low latency.
2. Traffic offered at service level B will be delivered with low loss.
3. Ninety percent of in-profile traffic delivered at service level C will experience no more than 50 ms latency.
4. Ninety-five percent of in-profile traffic delivered at service level D will be delivered.
5. Traffic offered at service level E will be allotted twice the bandwidth of traffic delivered at service level F.
6. Traffic with drop precedence X has a higher probability of delivery than traffic with drop precedence Y.

The first two examples are qualitative and are valid only in comparison to other traffic, such as default traffic that gets a best-effort service. The next two examples are quantitative and provide a specific guarantee that can be verified by measurement on the actual service without comparison to any other services offered at the same time. The final two examples are a mixture of quantitative and qualitative.

DS Octet

Packets are labeled for service handling by means of the DS octet, which is placed in the Type of Service field of an IPv4 header or the Traffic Class field of the IPv6 header. RFC 2474 defines the DS octet as having the following format: The leftmost 6 bits form a DS codepoint and the rightmost 2 bits are unused. The DS codepoint is the DS label used to classify packets for differentiated services. Figure 19.13a shows the DS field.

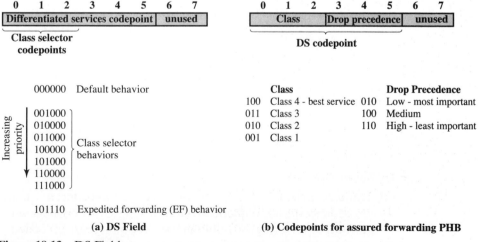

Figure 19.13   DS Field

With a 6-bit codepoint, there are in principle 64 different classes of traffic that could be defined. These 64 codepoints are allocated across three pools of codepoints, as follows:

- Codepoints of the form xxxxx0, where x is either 0 or 1, are reserved for assignment as standards.
- Codepoints of the form xxxx11 are reserved for experimental or local use.
- Codepoints of the form xxxx01 are also reserved for experimental or local use but may be allocated for future standards action as needed.

Within the first pool, several assignments are made in RFC 2474. The codepoint 000000 is the default packet class. The default class is the best-effort forwarding behavior in existing routers. Such packets are forwarded in the order that they are received as soon as link capacity becomes available. If other higher-priority packets in other DS classes are available for transmission, these are given preference over best-effort default packets.

Codepoints of the form xxx000 are reserved to provide backward compatibility with the IPv4 precedence service. To explain this requirement, we need to digress to an explanation of the IPv4 precedence service. The IPv4 type of service (TOS) field includes two subfields: a 3-bit precedence subfield and a 4-bit TOS subfield. These subfields serve complementary functions. The TOS subfield provides guidance to the IP entity (in the source or router) on selecting the next hop for this datagram, and the precedence subfield provides guidance about the relative allocation of router resources for this datagram.

The precedence field is set to indicate the degree of urgency or priority to be associated with a datagram. If a router supports the precedence subfield, there are three approaches to responding:

- **Route selection:** A particular route may be selected if the router has a smaller queue for that route or if the next hop on that route supports network precedence or priority (e.g., a token ring network supports priority).
- **Network service:** If the network on the next hop supports precedence, then that service is invoked.
- **Queuing discipline:** A router may use precedence to affect how queues are handled. For example, a router may give preferential treatment in queues to datagrams with higher precedence.

RFC 1812, Requirements for IP Version 4 Routers, provides recommendations for queuing discipline that fall into two categories:

- **Queue service**
  - **(a)** Routers SHOULD implement precedence-ordered queue service. Precedence-ordered queue service means that when a packet is selected for output on a (logical) link, the packet of highest precedence that has been queued for that link is sent.

(b) Any router MAY implement other policy-based throughput management procedures that result in other than strict precedence ordering, but it MUST be configurable to suppress them (i.e., use strict ordering).

- **Congestion control.** When a router receives a packet beyond its storage capacity, it must discard it or some other packet or packets.

(a) A router MAY discard the packet it has just received; this is the simplest but not the best policy.

(b) Ideally, the router should select a packet from one of the sessions most heavily abusing the link, given that the applicable QoS policy permits this. A recommended policy in datagram environments using FIFO queues is to discard a packet randomly selected from the queue. An equivalent algorithm in routers using fair queues is to discard from the longest queue. A router MAY use these algorithms to determine which packet to discard.

(c) If precedence-ordered queue service is implemented and enabled, the router MUST NOT discard a packet whose IP precedence is higher than that of a packet that is not discarded.

(d) A router MAY protect packets whose IP headers request the maximize reliability TOS, except where doing so would be in violation of the previous rule.

(e) A router MAY protect fragmented IP packets, on the theory that dropping a fragment of a datagram may increase congestion by causing all fragments of the datagram to be retransmitted by the source.

(f) To help prevent routing perturbations or disruption of management functions, the router MAY protect packets used for routing control, link control, or network management from being discarded. Dedicated routers (i.e., routers that are not also general purpose hosts, terminal servers, etc.) can achieve an approximation of this rule by protecting packets whose source or destination is the router itself.

The DS codepoints of the form xxx000 should provide a service that at minimum is equivalent to that of the IPv4 precedence functionality.

DS Configuration and Operation

Figure 19.14 illustrates the type of configuration envisioned in the DS documents. A DS domain consists of a set of contiguous routers; that is, it is possible to get from any router in the domain to any other router in the domain by a path that does not include routers outside the domain. Within a domain, the interpretation of DS codepoints is uniform, so that a uniform, consistent service is provided.

Routers in a DS domain are either boundary nodes or interior nodes. Typically, the interior nodes implement simple mechanisms for handling packets based on their DS codepoint values. This includes queuing discipline to give preferential treatment depending on codepoint value, and packet dropping rules to dictate which packets should be dropped first in the event of buffer saturation. The DS specifications refer to the forwarding treatment provided at a router as per-hop behavior (PHB). This PHB must be available at all routers, and typically PHB is the only part of DS implemented in interior routers.

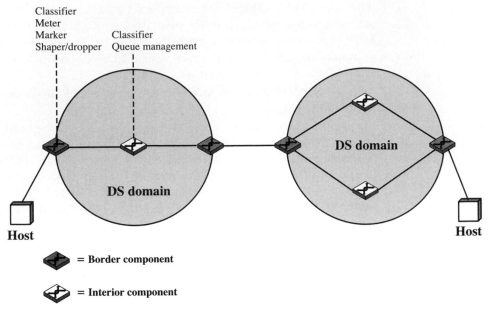

Classifier
Meter
Marker
Shaper/dropper   Classifier
                  Queue management

Figure 19.14   DS Domains

The boundary nodes include PHB mechanisms but more sophisticated traffic conditioning mechanisms are also required to provide the desired service. Thus, interior routers have minimal functionality and minimal overhead in providing the DS service, while most of the complexity is in the boundary nodes. The boundary node function can also be provided by a host system attached to the domain, on behalf of the applications at that host system.

The traffic conditioning function consists of five elements:

- **Classifier:** Separates submitted packets into different classes. This is the foundation of providing differentiated services. A classifier may separate traffic only on the basis of the DS codepoint (behavior aggregate classifier) or based on multiple fields within the packet header or even the packet payload (multifield classifier).

- **Meter:** Measures submitted traffic for conformance to a profile. The meter determines whether a given packet stream class is within or exceeds the service level guaranteed for that class.

- **Marker:** Re-marks packets with a different codepoint as needed. This may be done for packets that exceed the profile; for example, if a given throughput is guaranteed for a particular service class, any packets in that class that exceed the throughput in some defined time interval may be re-marked for best effort handling. Also, re-marking may be required at the boundary between two DS domains. For example, if a given traffic class is to receive the highest supported priority, and this is a value of 3 in one domain and 7 in the next domain, then

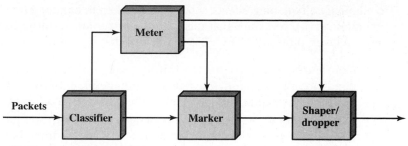

Figure 19.15   DS Traffic Conditioner

packets with a priority 3 value traversing the first domain are remarked as priority 7 when entering the second domain.

- **Shaper:** Delays packets as necessary so that the packet stream in a given class does not exceed the traffic rate specified in the profile for that class.
- **Dropper:** Drops packets when the rate of packets of a given class exceeds that specified in the profile for that class.

Figure 19.15 illustrates the relationship between the elements of traffic conditioning. After a flow is classified, its resource consumption must be measured. The metering function measures the volume of packets over a particular time interval to determine a flow's compliance with the traffic agreement. If the host is bursty, a simple data rate or packet rate may not be sufficient to capture the desired traffic characteristics. A token bucket scheme, such as that illustrated in Figure 19.11, is an example of a way to define a traffic profile to take into account both packet rate and burstiness.

If a traffic flow exceeds some profile, several approaches can be taken. Individual packets in excess of the profile may be re-marked for lower-quality handling and allowed to pass into the DS domain. A traffic shaper may absorb a burst of packets in a buffer and pace the packets over a longer period of time. A dropper may drop packets if the buffer used for pacing becomes saturated.

Per-Hop Behavior

As part of the DS standardization effort, specific types of PHBs need to be defined, which can be associated with specific differentiated services. Currently, two standards-track PHBs have been issued: expedited forwarding PHB (RFC 3246) and assured forwarding PHB (RFC 2597).

Expedited Forwarding PHB

RFC 3246 defines the expedited forwarding (EF) PHB as a mechanism that can be used to support a premium service. A premium service is a low-loss, low-delay, low-jitter, assured bandwidth, end-to-end service through DS domains. In essence, the premium service appears to the endpoints as a point-to-point connection or leased line.

In an internet or packet-switching network, a premium service is difficult to achieve. By its nature, an internet involves queues at each node, or router, where packets are buffered waiting to use a shared output link. It is the queuing behavior at each node that results in loss, delays, and jitter. Thus, unless the internet is grossly oversized to eliminate all queuing effects, care must be taken in handling traffic that is granted premium service to assure that queuing effects do not result in loss, delay, or jitter above a given threshold. RFC 3246 points out that a premium service has two parts:

- Configuring nodes so that the traffic aggregate[4] has a well-defined minimum departure rate. (*Well-defined* means "independent of the dynamic state of the node." In particular, independent of the intensity of other traffic at the node.)
- Conditioning the aggregate (via policing and shaping) so that its arrival rate at any node is always less than that node's configured minimum departure rate.

The EF PHB provides the first of the two capabilities just listed, whereas the second capability is provided by network boundary conditioners. The general concept outlined in RFC 3246 is this: The border nodes control the traffic aggregate to limit its characteristics (rate, burstiness) to some predefined level. Interior nodes must treat the incoming traffic in such a way that queuing effects do not appear. In general terms, the requirement on interior nodes is that the aggregate's maximum arrival rate must be less than the aggregate's minimum departure rate.

RFC 3246 does not mandate a specific queuing policy at the interior nodes to achieve the EF PHB. The RFC notes that a simple priority scheme could achieve the desired effect, with the EF traffic given absolute priority over other traffic. So long as the EF traffic itself did not overwhelm an interior node, this scheme would result in acceptable queuing delays for the EF PHB. However, the risk of a simple priority scheme is that packet flows for other PHB traffic would be disrupted. Thus, some more sophisticated queuing policy might be warranted.

Assured Forwarding PHB

The assured forwarding (AF) PHB is designed to provide a service superior to best-effort but one that does not require the reservation of resources within an internet and does not require the use of detailed discrimination among flows from different users. The concept behind the AF PHB was first introduced in [CLAR98] and is referred to as explicit allocation. The AF PHB is more complex than explicit allocation, but it is useful to first highlight the key elements of the explicit allocation scheme:

1. Users are offered the choice of a number of classes of service for their traffic. Each class describes a different traffic profile in terms of an aggregate data rate and burstiness.
2. Traffic from a user within a given class is monitored at a boundary node. Each packet in a traffic flow is marked *in* or *out* based on whether it does or does not exceed the traffic profile.
3. Inside the network, there is no separation of traffic from different users or even traffic from different classes. Instead, all traffic is treated as a single pool of packets, with the only distinction being whether each packet has been marked *in* or *out*.

---

[4] The term *traffic aggregate* refers to the flow of packets associated with a particular service for a particular user.

4. When congestion occurs, the interior nodes implement a dropping scheme in which *out* packets are dropped before *in* packets.

5. Different users will see different levels of service because they will have different quantities of *in* packets in the service queues.

The advantage of this approach is its simplicity. Very little work is required by the internal nodes. Marking of the traffic at the boundary nodes based on traffic profiles provides different levels of service to different classes.

The AF PHB defined in RFC 2597 expands on the preceding approach in the following ways:

1. Four AF classes are defined, allowing the definition of four distinct traffic profiles. A user may select one or more of these classes to satisfy requirements.

2. Within each class, packets are marked by the customer or by the service provider with one of three drop precedence values. In case of congestion, the drop precedence of a packet determines the relative importance of the packet within the AF class. A congested DS node tries to protect packets with a lower drop precedence value from being lost by preferably discarding packets with a higher drop precedence value.

This approach is still simpler to implement than any sort of resource reservation scheme but provides considerable flexibility. Within an interior DS node, traffic from the four classes can be treated separately, with different amounts of resources (buffer space, data rate) assigned to the four classes. Within each class, packets are handled based on drop precedence. Thus, as RFC 2597 points out, the level of forwarding assurance of an IP packet depends on

- How much forwarding resources has been allocated to the AF class that the packet belongs to
- The current load of the AF class, and, in case of congestion within the class,
- The drop precedence of the packet

RFC 2597 does not mandate any mechanisms at the interior nodes to manage the AF traffic. It does reference the RED algorithm as a possible way of managing congestion.

Figure 19.13b shows the recommended codepoints for AF PHB in the DS field.

19.5 RECOMMENDED READING AND WEB SITES

A number of worthwhile books provide detailed coverage of various routing algorithms: [HUIT00], [BLAC00], and [PERL00]. [MOY98] provides a thorough treatment of OSPF.

Perhaps the clearest and most comprehensive book-length treatment of Internet QoS is [ARMI00]. [XIAO99] provides an overview and overall framework for Internet QoS as well as integrated and differentiated services. [CLAR92] and [CLAR95] provide valuable surveys of the issues involved in internet service allocation for real-time and elastic applications, respectively. [SHEN95] is a masterful analysis of the rationale for a QoS-based internet architecture. [ZHAN95] is a broad survey of queuing disciplines that can be used in an ISA, including an analysis of FQ and WFQ.

[ZHAN93] is a good overview of the philosophy and functionality of RSVP, written by its developers. [WHIT97] is a broad survey of both ISA and RSVP.

[CARP02] and [WEIS98] are instructive surveys of differentiated services, while [KUMA98] looks at differentiated services and supporting router mechanisms that go beyond the current RFCs. For a thorough treatment of DS, see [KILK99].

Two papers that compare IS and DS in terms of services and performance are [BERN00] and [HARJ00].

ARMI00　Armitage, G. *Quality of Service in IP Networks*. Indianapolis, IN: Macmillan Technical Publishing, 2000.

BERN00　Bernet, Y. "The Complementary Roles of RSVP and Differentiated Services in the Full-Service QoS Network." *IEEE Communications Magazine*, February 2000.

BLAC00　Black, U. *IP Routing Protocols: RIP, OSPF, BGP, PNNI & Cisco Routing Protocols.* Upper Saddle River, NJ: Prentice Hall, 2000.

CARP02　Carpenter, B., and Nichols, K. "Differentiated Services in the Internet." *Proceedings of the IEEE*, September 2002.

CLAR92　Clark, D.; Shenker, S.; and Zhang, L. "Supporting Real-Time Applications in an Integrated Services Packet Network: Architecture and Mechanism" *Proceedings, SIGCOMM '92*, August 1992.

CLAR95　Clark, D. *Adding Service Discrimination to the Internet*. MIT Laboratory for Computer Science Technical Report, September 1995. Available at http://ana-www.lcs.mit.edu/anaWeb/papers.html.

HARJ00　Harju, J., and Kivimaki, P. "Cooperation and Comparison of DiffServ and IntServ: Performance Measurements." *Proceedings, 23rd Annual IEEE Conference on Local Computer Networks*, November 2000.

HUIT00　Huitema, C. *Routing in the Internet*. Upper Saddle River, NJ: Prentice Hall, 2000.

KILK99　Kilkki, K. *Differentiated Services for the Internet*. Indianapolis, IN: Macmillan Technical Publishing, 1999.

KUMA98　Kumar, V.; Lakshman, T.; and Stiliadis, D. "Beyond Best Effort: Router Architectures for the Differentiated Services of Tomorrow's Internet." *IEEE Communications Magazine*, May 1998.

MOY98　Moy, J. *OSPF: Anatomy of an Internet Routing Protocol*. Reading, MA: Addison-Wesley, 1998.

PERL00　Perlman, R. *Interconnections: Bridges, Routers, Switches, and Internetworking Protocols*. Reading, MA: Addison-Wesley, 2000.

SHEN95　Shenker, S. "Fundamental Design Issues for the Future Internet." *IEEE Journal on Selected Areas in Communications*, September 1995.

WEIS98　Weiss, W. "QoS with Differentiated Services." *Bell Labs Technical Journal*, October-December 1998.

WHIT97　White, P., and Crowcroft, J. "The Integrated Services in the Internet: State of the Art." *Proceedings of the IEEE*, December 1997.

XIAO99　Xiao, X., and Ni, L. "Internet QoS: A Big Picture." *IEEE Network*, March/April 1999.

ZHAN93　Zhang, L.; Deering, S.; Estrin, D.; Shenker, S.; and Zappala, D. "RSVP: A New Resource ReSerVation Protocol." *IEEE Network*, September 1993.

ZHAN95　Zhang, H. "Service Disciplines for Guaranteed Performance Service in Packet-Switching Networks." *Proceedings of the IEEE*, October 1995.

Recommended Web Sites:

- **RSVP Project:** Home page for RSVP development.
- **RSVP Working Group:** Chartered by IETF to develop standards related to differentiated services. The Web site includes all relevant RFCs and Internet drafts.
- **OSPF working group:** Chartered by IETF to develop OSPF and related standards. The Web site includes all relevant RFCs and Internet drafts.
- **Differentiated services working group:** Chartered by IETF to develop standards related to differentiated services. The Web site includes all relevant RFCs and Internet drafts.
- **Integrated services working group:** Chartered by IETF to develop standards related to integrated services. The Web site includes all relevant RFCs and Internet drafts.

19.6 KEY TERMS, REVIEW QUESTIONS, AND PROBLEMS

Key Terms

autonomous system (AS)	interior router protocol	Open Shortest
Border Gateway Protocol	Internet Group Management	Path First (OSPF)
(BGP)	Protocol	path-vector routing
classifier	jitter	per-hop behavior (PHB)
broadcast address	link-state routing	quality of service (QoS)
Differentiated Services (DS)	marker	queuing discipline
distance-vector routing	meter	Resource ReSerVation
dropper	multicast address	Protocol (RSVP)
elastic traffic	multicasting	shaper
exterior router protocol	neighbor acquisition	unicast address
inelastic traffic	neighbor reachability	
Integrated Services	network reachability	
Architecture (ISA)		

Review Questions

19.1 List some practical applications of multicasting.

19.2 Summarize the differences among unicast, multicast, and broadcast addresses.

19.3 List and briefly explain the functions that are required for multicasting.

19.4 What operations are performed by IGMP?

19.5 What is an autonomous system?

19.6 What is the difference between an interior router protocol and an exterior router protocol?

19.7 Compare the three main approaches to routing.

19.8 List and briefly explain the three main functions of BGP.

19.9 What is the Integrated Services Architecture?

19.10   What is the difference between elastic and inelastic traffic?

19.11   What are the major functions that are part of an ISA?

19.12   List and briefly describe the three categories of service offered by ISA.

19.13   What is the difference between FIFO queuing and WFQ queuing?

19.14   What is the purpose of a DS codepoint?

19.15   List and briefly explain the five main functions of DS traffic conditioning.

19.16   What is meant by per-hop behavior?

Problems

19.1   A connected graph may have more than one spanning tree. Find all spanning trees of this graph:

19.2   In the discussion of Figure 19.1, three alternatives for transmitting a packet to a multicast address were discussed: broadcast, multiple unicast, and true multicast. Yet another alternative is flooding. The source transmits one packet to each neighboring router. Each router, when it receives a packet, retransmits the packet on all outgoing interfaces except the one on which the packet is received. Each packet is labeled with a unique identifier so that a router does not flood the same packet more than once. Fill out a matrix similar to those of Table 19.3 and comment on the results.

19.3   In a manner similar to Figure 19.3, show the spanning tree from router B to the multicast group.

19.4   IGMP specifies that query messages are sent in IP datagrams that have the Time to Live field set to 1. Why?

19.5   When multiple equal-cost routes to a destination exist, OSPF may distribute traffic equally among the routes. This is called *load balancing*. What effect does such load balancing have on a transport layer protocol, such as TCP?

19.6   It is clear that if a router gives preferential treatment to one flow or one class of flows, then that flow or class of flows will receive improved service. It is not as clear that the overall service provided by the internet is improved. This question is intended to illustrate an overall improvement. Consider a network with a single link modeled by an exponential server of rate $T_s = 1$, and consider two classes of flows with Poisson arrival rates of $\lambda 1 = \lambda 1 = 0.25$ and that have utility functions $U_1 = 4 - 2T_{q1}$ and $U_2 = 4 - T_{q2}$, where T_{qi} represents the average queuing delay to class i. Thus, class 1 traffic is more sensitive to delay than class 2. Define the total utility of the network as $V = U_1 + U_2$.

   a.   Assume that the two classes are treated alike and that FIFO queuing is used. What is V?

   b.   Now assume a strict priority service, so that packets from class 1 are always transmitted before packets in class 2. What is V? Comment.

19.7   The token bucket scheme places a limit on the length of time at which traffic can depart at the maximum data rate. Let the token bucket be defined by a bucket size B octets and a token arrival rate of R octets/second, and let the maximum output data rate be M octets/s.

   a.   Derive a formula for S, which is the length of the maximum-rate burst. That is, for how long can a flow transmit at the maximum output rate when governed by a token bucket?

b. What is the value of S for $b = 250$ KB, $r = 2$ MB/s, and $M = 25$ MB/s?

Hint: the formula for S is not so simple as it might appear, because more tokens arrive while the burst is being output.

19.8   In RSVP, because the UDP/TCP port numbers are used for packet classification, each router must be able to examine these fields. This requirement raises problems in the following areas:

a.   IPv6 header processing

b.   IP-level security

Indicate the nature of the problem in each area, and suggest a solution.

CHAPTER **20**

TRANSPORT PROTOCOLS

KEY POINTS

- The transport protocol provides an end-to-end data transfer service that shields upper layer protocols from the details of the intervening network or networks. A transport protocol can be either connection oriented, such as TCP, or connectionless, such as UDP.

- If the underlying network or internetwork service is unreliable, such as with the use of IP, then a reliable connection-oriented transport protocol becomes quite complex. The basic cause of this complexity is the need to deal with the relatively large and variable delays experienced between end systems. These large, variable delays complicate the flow control and error control techniques.

- TCP uses a credit-based flow control technique that is somewhat different from the sliding-window flow control found in X.25 and HDLC. In essence, TCP separates acknowledgments from the management of the size of the sliding window.

- Although the TCP credit-based mechanism was designed for end-to-end flow control, it is also used to assist in internetwork congestion control. When a TCP entity detects the presence of congestion in the Internet, it reduces the flow of data onto the Internet until it detects an easing in congestion.

In a protocol architecture, the transport protocol sits above a network or internetwork layer, which provides network-related services, and just below application and other upper-layer protocols. The transport protocol provides services to transport service (TS) users, such as FTP, SMTP, and TELNET. The local transport entity communicates with some remote transport entity, using the services of some lower layer, such as the Internet Protocol. The general service provided by a transport protocol is the end-to-end transport of data in a way that shields the TS user from the details of the underlying communications systems.

We begin this chapter by examining the protocol mechanisms required to provide these services. We find that most of the complexity relates to reliable connection-oriented services. As might be expected, the less the network service provides, the more the transport protocol must do. The remainder of the chapter looks at two widely used transport protocols: Transmission Control Protocol (TCP) and User Datagram Protocol (UDP).

Refer to Figure 2.15 to see the position within the TCP/IP suite of the protocols discussed in this chapter.

20.1 CONNECTION-ORIENTED TRANSPORT PROTOCOL MECHANISMS

Two basic types of transport service are possible: connection oriented and connectionless or datagram service. A connection-oriented service provides for the establishment, maintenance, and termination of a logical connection between TS users. This has, so far, been the most common type of protocol service available and has a wide variety of applications. The connection-oriented service generally implies that the service is reliable. This section looks at the transport protocol mechanisms need-ed to support the connection-oriented service.

A full-feature connection-oriented transport protocol, such as TCP, is very complex. For purposes of clarity we present the transport protocol mechanisms in an evolutionary fashion. We begin with a network service that makes life easy for the transport protocol, by guaranteeing the delivery of all transport data units in order and defining the required mechanisms. Then we will look at the transport pro-tocol mechanisms required to cope with an unreliable network service. All of this discussion applies in general to transport-level protocols. In Section 20.2, we apply the concepts developed in this section to describe TCP.

Reliable Sequencing Network Service

Let us assume that the network service accepts messages of arbitrary length and, with virtually 100% reliability, delivers them in sequence to the destination. Exam-ples of such networks include the following:

- A highly reliable packet-switching network with an X.25 interface
- A frame relay network using the LAPF control protocol
- An IEEE 802.3 LAN using the connection-oriented LLC service

In all of these cases, the transport protocol is used as an end-to-end protocol between two systems attached to the same network, rather than across an internet.

The assumption of a reliable sequencing networking services allows the use of a quite simple transport protocol. Four issues need to be addressed:

- Addressing
- Multiplexing
- Flow control
- Connection establishment/termination

Addressing

The issue concerned with addressing is simply this: A user of a given transport entity wishes either to establish a connection with or make a data transfer to a user of some other transport entity using the same transport protocol. The target user needs to be specified by all of the following:

- User identification
- Transport entity identification
- Host address
- Network number

The transport protocol must be able to derive the information listed above from the TS user address. Typically, the user address is specified as (Host, Port). The *Port* variable represents a particular TS user at the specified host. Generally, there will be a single transport entity at each host, so a transport entity identification is not needed. If more than one transport entity is present, there is usually only one of each type. In this latter case, the address should include a designation of the type of transport protocol (e.g., TCP, UDP). In the case of a single network, *Host* identifies an attached network device. In the case of an internet, *Host* is a global internet address. In TCP, the combination of port and host is referred to as a **socket**.

Because routing is not a concern of the transport layer, it simply passes the *Host* portion of the address down to the network service. *Port* is included in a transport header, to be used at the destination by the destination transport protocol entity.

One question remains to be addressed: How does the initiating TS user know the address of the destination TS user? Two static and two dynamic strategies suggest themselves:

1. The TS user knows the address it wishes to use ahead of time. This is basically a system configuration function. For example, a process may be running that is only of concern to a limited number of TS users, such as a process that collects statistics on performance. From time to time, a central network management routine connects to the process to obtain the statistics. These processes generally are not, and should not be, well known and accessible to all.

2. Some commonly used services are assigned "well-known addresses." Examples include the server side of FTP, SMTP, and some other standard protocols.

3. A name server is provided. The TS user requests a service by some generic or global name. The request is sent to the name server, which does a directory lookup and returns an address. The transport entity then proceeds with the connection. This service is useful for commonly used applications that change location from time to time. For example, a data entry process may be moved from one host to another on a local network to balance load.

4. In some cases, the target user is to be a process that is spawned at request time. The initiating user can send a process request to a well-known address. The user at that address is a privileged system process that will spawn the new process and return an address. For example, a programmer has developed a private application (e.g., a simulation program) that will execute on a remote server but be invoked from a local workstation. A request can be issued to a remote job-management process that spawns the simulation process.

Multiplexing

Multiplexing was discussed in general terms in Section 18.1. With respect to the interface between the transport protocol and higher-level protocols, the transport protocol performs a multiplexing/demultiplexing function. That is, multiple users employ the same transport protocol and are distinguished by port numbers or service access points.

The transport entity may also perform a multiplexing function with respect to the network services that it uses. Recall that we defined upward multiplexing as the multiplexing of multiple connections on a single lower-level connection, and downward multiplexing as the splitting of a single connection among multiple lower-level connections.

Consider, for example, a transport entity making use of an X.25 service. Why should the transport entity employ upward multiplexing? There are, after all, 4095 virtual circuits available. In the typical case, this is more than enough to handle all active TS users. However, most X.25 networks base part of their charge on virtual circuit connect time, because each virtual circuit consumes some node buffer resources. Thus, if a single virtual circuit provides sufficient throughput for multiple TS users, upward multiplexing is indicated.

On the other hand, downward multiplexing or splitting might be used to improve throughput. For example, each X.25 virtual circuit is restricted to a 3-bit or 7-bit sequence number. A larger sequence space might be needed for high-speed, high-delay networks. Of course, throughput can only be increased so far. If there is a single host-node link over which all virtual circuits are multiplexed, the throughput of a transport connection cannot exceed the data rate of that link.

Flow Control

Whereas flow control is a relatively simple mechanism at the link layer, it is a rather complex mechanism at the transport layer, for two main reasons:

- The transmission delay between transport entities is generally long compared to actual transmission time. This means that there is a considerable delay in the communication of flow control information.
- Because the transport layer operates over a network or internet, the amount of the transmission delay may be highly variable. This makes it difficult to effectively use a timeout mechanism for retransmission of lost data.

In general, there are two reasons why one transport entity would want to restrain the rate of segment[1] transmission over a connection from another transport entity:

- The user of the receiving transport entity cannot keep up with the flow of data.
- The receiving transport entity itself cannot keep up with the flow of segments.

How do such problems manifest themselves? Presumably a transport entity has a certain amount of buffer space. Incoming segments are added to the buffer. Each buffered segment is processed (i.e., the transport header is examined) and the data are sent to the TS user. Either of the two problems just mentioned will cause the buffer to fill up. Thus, the transport entity needs to take steps to stop or slow the flow of segments to prevent buffer overflow. This requirement is difficult to fulfill because of the annoying time gap between sender and receiver. We return to this point subsequently. First, we present four ways of coping with the flow control requirement. The receiving transport entity can

1. Do nothing.
2. Refuse to accept further segments from the network service.
3. Use a fixed sliding-window protocol.
4. Use a credit scheme.

---

[1] Recall from Chapter 2 that the blocks of data (protocol data units) exchanged by TCP entities are referred to as TCP segments.

Alternative 1 means that the segments that overflow the buffer are discarded. The sending transport entity, failing to get an acknowledgment, will retransmit. This is a shame, because the advantage of a reliable network is that one never has to retransmit. Furthermore, the effect of this maneuver is to exacerbate the problem. The sender has increased its output to include new segments plus retransmitted old segments.

The second alternative is a backpressure mechanism that relies on the network service to do the work. When a buffer of a transport entity is full, it refuses additional data from the network service. This triggers flow control procedures within the network that throttle the network service at the sending end. This service, in turn, refuses additional segments from its transport entity. It should be clear that this mechanism is clumsy and coarse grained. For example, if multiple transport connections are multiplexed on a single network connection (virtual circuit), flow control is exercised only on the aggregate of all transport connections.

The third alternative is already familiar to you from our discussions of link layer protocols in Chapter 7. The key ingredients, recall, are as follows:

- The use of sequence numbers on data units
- The use of a window of fixed size
- The use of acknowledgments to advance the window

With a reliable network service, the sliding-window technique would work quite well. For example, consider a protocol with a window size of 7. When the sender receives an acknowledgment to a particular segment, it is automatically authorized to send the succeeding seven segments (of course, some may already have been sent). When the receiver's buffer capacity gets down to seven segments, it can withhold acknowledgment of incoming segments to avoid overflow. The sending transport entity can send at most seven additional segments and then must stop. Because the underlying network service is reliable, the sender will not time out and retransmit. Thus, at some point, a sending transport entity may have a number of segments outstanding for which no acknowledgment has been received. Because we are dealing with a reliable network, the sending transport entity can assume that the segments will get through and that the lack of acknowledgment is a flow control tactic. This tactic would not work well in an unreliable network, because the sending transport entity would not know whether the lack of acknowledgment is due to flow control or a lost segment.

The fourth alternative, a credit scheme, provides the receiver with a greater degree of control over data flow. Although it is not strictly necessary with a reliable network service, a credit scheme should result in a smoother traffic flow. Further, it is a more effective scheme with an unreliable network service, as we shall see.

The credit scheme decouples acknowledgment from flow control. In fixed sliding-window protocols, such as X.25 and HDLC, the two are synonymous. In a credit scheme, a segment may be acknowledged without granting new credit, and vice versa. For the credit scheme, each individual octet of data that is transmitted is considered to have a unique sequence number. In addition to data, each transmitted segment includes in its header three fields related to flow control: sequence number (SN), acknowledgment number (AN), and window (W). When a transport entity sends a segment, it includes the sequence number of the first octet in the segment data field. A transport entity acknowledges an incoming segment with a return segment that includes $(AN = i, W = j)$, with the following interpretation:

- All octets through sequence number $SN = i - 1$ are acknowledged; the next expected octet has sequence number i.
- Permission is granted to send an additional window of $W = j$ octets of data; that is, the j octets corresponding to sequence numbers i through $i + j - 1$.

Figure 20.1 illustrates the mechanism (compare Figure 7.4). For simplicity, we show data flow in one direction only and assume that 200 octets of data are sent in each segment. Initially, through the connection establishment process, the sending and receiving sequence numbers are synchronized and A is granted an initial credit allocation of 1400 octets, beginning with octet number 1001. After sending 600 octets in three segments, A has shrunk its window to a size of 800 octets (numbers 1601 through 2400). After B receives these three segments, 600 octets out of its original 1400 octets of credit are accounted for, and 800 octets of credit are outstanding. Now suppose that, at this point, B is capable of absorbing 1000 octets of incoming data on this connection. Accordingly, B acknowledges receipt of all octets through 1600 and issues a credit of 1000 octets. This means that A can send octets 1601 through 2600 (5 segments). However, by the time that B's message has arrived at A, A has already sent two segments, containing octets 1601 through 2000 (which was permissible under the initial allocation). Thus, A's remaining credit upon receipt of B's credit allocation is only 600 octets (3 segments). As the exchange proceeds, A advances the trailing edge of its window each time that it transmits and advances the leading edge only when it is granted credit.

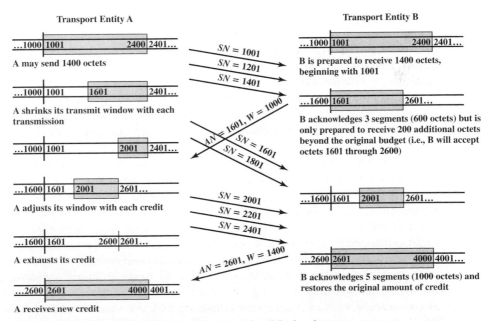

Figure 20.1 Example of TCP Credit Allocation Mechanism

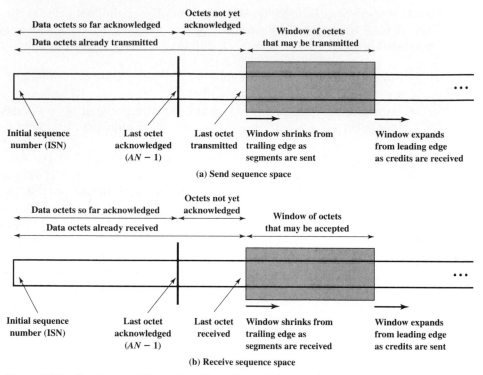

Figure 20.2   Sending and Receiving Flow Control Perspectives

Figure 20.2 shows the view of this mechanism from the sending and receiving sides (compare Figure 7.3). Typically, both sides take both views because data may be exchanged in both directions. Note that the receiver is not required to immediately acknowledge incoming segments but may wait and issue a cumulative acknowledgment for a number of segments.

The receiver needs to adopt some policy concerning the amount of data it permits the sender to transmit. The conservative approach is to only allow new segments up to the limit of available buffer space. If this policy were in effect in Figure 20.1, the first credit message implies that B has 1000 available octets in its buffer, and the second message that B has 1400 available octets.

A conservative flow control scheme may limit the throughput of the transport connection in long-delay situations. The receiver could potentially increase throughput by optimistically granting credit for space it does not have. For example, if a receiver's buffer is full but it anticipates that it can release space for 1000 octets within a round-trip propagation time, it could immediately send a credit of 1000. If the receiver can keep up with the sender, this scheme may increase throughput and can do no harm. If the sender is faster than the receiver, however, some segments may be discarded, necessitating a retransmission. Because retransmissions are not otherwise necessary with a reliable network service (in the absence of internet congestion), an optimistic flow control scheme will complicate the protocol.

Connection Establishment and Termination

Even with a reliable network service, there is a need for connection establishment and termination procedures to support connection-oriented service. Connection establishment serves three main purposes:

- It allows each end to assure that the other exists.
- It allows exchange or negotiation of optional parameters (e.g., maximum segment size, maximum window size, quality of service).
- It triggers allocation of transport entity resources (e.g., buffer space, entry in connection table).

Connection establishment is by mutual agreement and can be accomplished by a simple set of user commands and control segments, as shown in the state diagram of Figure 20.3. To begin, a TS user is in an CLOSED state (i.e., it has no open transport connection). The TS user can signal to the local TCP entity that it will passively wait for a request with a Passive Open command. A server program, such as time-sharing or a file transfer application, might do this. The TS user may change its mind by sending a Close command. After the Passive Open command is issued, the transport entity creates a connection object of some sort (i.e., a table entry) that is in the LISTEN state.

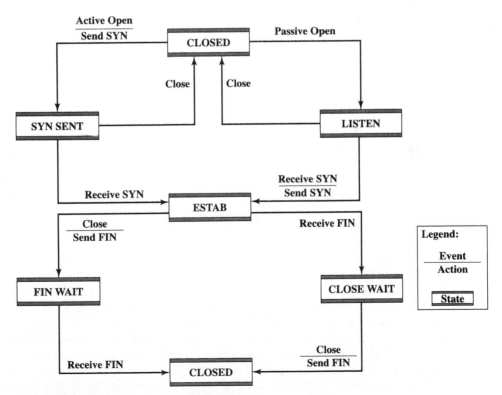

Figure 20.3 Simple Connection State Diagram

From the CLOSED state, a TS user may open a connection by issuing an Active Open command, which instructs the transport entity to attempt connection establishment with a designated remote TS user, which triggers the transport entity to send a SYN (for synchronize) segment. This segment is carried to the receiving transport entity and interpreted as a request for connection to a particular port. If the destination transport entity is in the LISTEN state for that port, then a connection is established by the following actions by the receiving transport entity:

- Signal the local TS user that a connection is open.
- Send a SYN as confirmation to the remote transport entity.
- Put the connection object in an ESTAB (established) state.

When the responding SYN is received by the initiating transport entity, it too can move the connection to an ESTAB state. The connection is prematurely aborted if either TS user issues a Close command.

Figure 20.4 shows the robustness of this protocol. Either side can initiate a connection. Further, if both sides initiate the connection at about the same time, it is established without confusion. This is because the SYN segment functions both as a connection request and a connection acknowledgment.

The reader may ask what happens if a SYN comes in while the requested TS user is idle (not listening). Three courses may be followed:

- The transport entity can reject the request by sending a RST (reset) segment back to the other transport entity.
- The request can be queued until the local TS user issues a matching Open.
- The transport entity can interrupt or otherwise signal the local TS user to notify it of a pending request.

Note that if the third mechanism is used, a Passive Open command is not strictly necessary but may be replaced by an Accept command, which is a signal from the user to the transport entity that it accepts the request for connection.

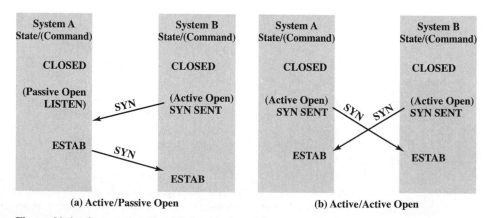

Figure 20.4 Connection Establishment Scenarios

Connection termination is handled similarly. Either side, or both sides, may initiate a close. The connection is closed by mutual agreement. This strategy allows for either abrupt or graceful termination. With abrupt termination, data in transit may be lost; a graceful termination prevents either side from closing the connection until all data have been delivered. To achieve the latter, a connection in the FIN WAIT state must continue to accept data segments until a FIN (finish) segment is received.

Figure 20.3 illustrates the procedure for graceful termination. First, consider the side that initiates the termination procedure:

1. In response to a TS user's Close primitive, a transport entity sends a FIN segment to the other side of the connection, requesting termination.
2. Having sent the FIN, the transport entity places the connection in the FIN WAIT state. In this state, the transport entity must continue to accept data from the other side and deliver that data to its user.
3. When a FIN is received in response, the transport entity informs its user and closes the connection.

From the point of view of the side that does not initiate a termination,

1. When a FIN segment is received, the transport entity informs its user of the termination request and places the connection in the CLOSE WAIT state. In this state, the transport entity must continue to accept data from its user and transmit it in data segments to the other side.
2. When the user issues a Close primitive, the transport entity sends a responding FIN segment to the other side and closes the connection.

This procedure ensures that both sides have received all outstanding data and that both sides agree to connection termination before actual termination.

Unreliable Network Service

A more difficult case for a transport protocol is that of an unreliable network service. Examples of such networks include the following:

- An internetwork using IP
- A frame relay network using only the LAPF core protocol
- An IEEE 802.3 LAN using the unacknowledged connectionless LLC service

The problem is not just that segments are occasionally lost, but that segments may arrive out of sequence due to variable transit delays. As we shall see, elaborate machinery is required to cope with these two interrelated network deficiencies. We shall also see that a discouraging pattern emerges. The combination of unreliability and nonsequencing creates problems with every mechanism we have discussed so far. Generally, the solution to each problem raises new problems. Although there are problems to be overcome for protocols at all levels, it seems that there are more difficulties with a reliable connection-oriented transport protocol than any other sort of protocol.

In the remainder of this section, unless otherwise noted, the mechanisms discussed are those used by TCP. Seven issues need to be addressed:

- Ordered delivery
- Retransmission strategy
- Duplicate detection
- Flow control
- Connection establishment
- Connection termination
- Failure recovery

Ordered Delivery

With an unreliable network service, it is possible that segments, even if they are all delivered, may arrive out of order. The required solution to this problem is to number segments sequentially. We have seen that for data link control protocols, such as HDLC, and for X.25, each data unit (frame, packet) is numbered sequentially with each successive sequence number being one more than the previous sequence number. This scheme is used in some transport protocols, such as the ISO transport protocols. However, TCP uses a somewhat different scheme in which each data octet that is transmitted is implicitly numbered. Thus, the first segment may have a sequence number of 1. If that segment has 200 octets of data, then the second segment would have the sequence number 201, and so on. For simplicity in the discussions of this section, we will continue to assume that each successive segment's sequence number is 200 more than that of the previous segment; that is, each segment contains exactly 200 octets of data.

Retransmission Strategy

Two events necessitate the retransmission of a segment. First, a segment may be damaged in transit but nevertheless arrive at its destination. If a checksum is included with the segment, the receiving transport entity can detect the error and discard the segment. The second contingency is that a segment fails to arrive. In either case, the sending transport entity does not know that the segment transmission was unsuccessful. To cover this contingency, a positive acknowledgment scheme is used: The receiver must acknowledge each successfully received segment by returning a segment containing an acknowledgment number. For efficiency, we do not require one acknowledgment per segment. Rather, a cumulative acknowledgment can be used, as we have seen many times in this book. Thus, the receiver may receive segments numbered 1, 201, and 401, but only send $AN = 601$ back. The sender must interpret $AN = 601$ to mean that the segment with $SN = 401$ and all previous segments have been successfully received.

If a segment does not arrive successfully, no acknowledgment will be issued and a retransmission is in order. To cope with this situation, there must be a timer associated with each segment as it is sent. If the timer expires before the segment is acknowledged, the sender must retransmit.

So the addition of a timer solves that problem. Next problem: At what value should the timer be set? Two strategies suggest themselves. A fixed timer value could be used, based on an understanding of the network's typical behavior. This suffers from an inability to respond to changing network conditions. If the value is too small, there will be many unnecessary retransmissions, wasting network capacity. If the value is too large, the protocol will be sluggish in responding to a lost segment. The timer should be set at a value a bit longer than the round trip time (send segment, receive ACK). Of course, this delay is variable even under constant network load. Worse, the statistics of the delay will vary with changing network conditions.

An adaptive scheme has its own problems. Suppose that the transport entity keeps track of the time taken to acknowledge data segments and sets its retransmission timer based on the average of the observed delays. This value cannot be trusted for three reasons:

- The peer transport entity may not acknowledge a segment immediately. Recall that we gave it the privilege of cumulative acknowledgments.
- If a segment has been retransmitted, the sender cannot know whether the received acknowledgment is a response to the initial transmission or the retransmission.
- Network conditions may change suddenly.

Each of these problems is a cause for some further tweaking of the transport algorithm, but the problem admits of no complete solution. There will always be some uncertainty concerning the best value for the retransmission timer.

Incidentally, the retransmission timer is only one of a number of timers needed for proper functioning of a transport protocol. These are listed in Table 20.1, together with a brief explanation.

Duplicate Detection

If a segment is lost and then retransmitted, no confusion will result. If, however, one or more segments in sequence are successfully delivered, but the corresponding ACK is lost, then the sending transport entity will time out and one or more segments will be retransmitted. If these retransmitted segments arrive successfully, they will be duplicates of previously received segments. Thus, the receiver must be able to recognize duplicates. The fact that each segment carries a sequence number helps, but, nevertheless, duplicate detection and handling is no easy thing. There are two cases:

- A duplicate is received prior to the close of the connection.
- A duplicate is received after the close of the connection.

The second case is discussed in the subsection on connection establishment. We deal with the first case here.

Table 20.1 Transport Protocol Timers

Retransmission timer	Retransmit an unacknowledged segment
Reconnection timer	Minimum time between closing one connection and opening another with the same destination address
Window timer	Maximum time between ACK/CREDIT segments
Retransmit-SYN timer	Time between attempts to open a connection
Persistence timer	Abort connection when no segments are acknowledged
Inactivity timer	Abort connection when no segments are received

Notice that we say "a" duplicate rather than "the" duplicate. From the sender's point of view, the retransmitted segment is the duplicate. However, the retransmitted segment may arrive before the original segment, in which case the receiver views the original segment as the duplicate. In any case, two tactics are needed to cope with a duplicate received prior to the close of a connection:

- The receiver must assume that its acknowledgment was lost and therefore must acknowledge the duplicate. Consequently, the sender must not get confused if it receives multiple acknowledgments to the same segment.
- The sequence number space must be long enough so as not to "cycle" in less than the maximum possible segment lifetime (time it takes segment to transit network).

Figure 20.5 illustrates the reason for the latter requirement. In this example, the sequence space is of length 1600; that is, after $SN = 1600$, the sequence numbers cycle back and begin with $SN = 1$. For simplicity, we assume the receiving transport entity maintains a credit window size of 600. Suppose that A has transmitted data segments with $SN = 1, 201$, and 401. B has received the two segments with $SN = 201$ and 401, but the segment with $SN = 1$ is delayed in transit. Thus, B does not send any acknowledgments. Eventually, A times out and retransmits segment $SN = 1$. When the duplicate segment $SN = 1$ arrives, B acknowledges 1, 201, and 401 with $AN = 601$. Meanwhile, A has timed out again and retransmits $SN = 201$, which B acknowledges with another $AN = 601$. Things now seem to have sorted themselves out and data transfer continues. When the sequence space is exhausted, A cycles back to $SN = 1$ and continues. Alas, the old segment $SN = 1$ makes a belated appearance and is accepted by B before the new segment $SN = 1$ arrives. When the new segment $SN = 1$ does arrive, it is treated as a duplicate and discarded.

It should be clear that the untimely emergence of the old segment would have caused no difficulty if the sequence numbers had not yet wrapped around. The problem is as follows: How big must the sequence space be? This depends on, among other things, whether the network enforces a maximum packet lifetime, and the rate at which segments are being transmitted. Fortunately, each addition of a single bit to the sequence number field doubles the sequence space, so it is rather easy to select a safe size.

Flow Control

The credit allocation flow control mechanism described earlier is quite robust in the face of an unreliable network service and requires little enhancement. As was mentioned, a segment containing $(AN = i, W = j)$ acknowledges all octets through number $i - 1$ and grants credit for an additional j octets beginning with octet i. The credit allocation mechanism is quite flexible. For example, suppose that the last octet of data received by B was octet number $i - 1$ and that the last segment issued by B was $(AN = i, W = j)$. Then

- To increase credit to an amount $k(k > j)$ when no additional data have arrived, B issues $(AN = i, W = k)$.
- To acknowledge an incoming segment containing m octets of data $(m < j)$ without granting additional credit, B issues $(AN = i + m, W = j - m)$.

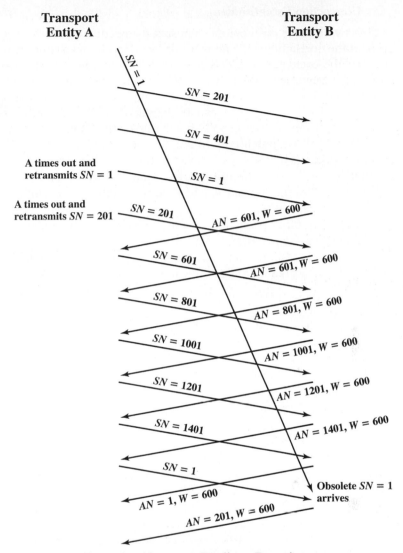

Figure 20.5 Example of Incorrect Duplicate Detection

If an ACK/CREDIT segment is lost, little harm is done. Future acknowledgments will resynchronize the protocol. Further, if no new acknowledgments are forthcoming, the sender times out and retransmits a data segment, which triggers a new acknowledgment. However, it is still possible for deadlock to occur. Consider a situation in which B sends $(AN = i, W = 0)$, temporarily closing the window. Subsequently, B sends $(AN = i, W = j)$, but this segment is lost. A is awaiting the opportunity to send data and B thinks that it has granted that opportunity. To overcome this problem, a window timer can be used. This timer is reset with each outgoing segment (all segments contain the AN and W fields). If the timer ever expires, the protocol entity is required to send a segment, even if it duplicates a previous one. This breaks the deadlock and also assures the other end that the protocol entity is still alive.

Connection Establishment

As with other protocol mechanisms, connection establishment must take into account the unreliability of a network service. Recall that a connection establishment calls for the exchange of SYNs, a procedure sometimes referred to as a two-way handshake. Suppose that A issues a SYN to B. It expects to get a SYN back, confirming the connection. Two things can go wrong: A's SYN can be lost or B's answering SYN can be lost. Both cases can be handled by use of a retransmit-SYN timer (Table 20.1). After A issues a SYN, it will reissue the SYN when the timer expires.

This gives rise, potentially, to duplicate SYNs. If A's initial SYN was lost, there are no duplicates. If B's response was lost, then B may receive two SYNs from A. Further, if B's response was not lost, but simply delayed, A may get two responding SYNs. All of this means that A and B must simply ignore duplicate SYNs once a connection is established.

There are other problems to contend with. Just as a delayed SYN or lost response can give rise to a duplicate SYN, a delayed data segment or lost acknowledgment can give rise to duplicate data segments, as we have seen in Figure 20.5. Such a delayed or duplicated data segment can interfere with data transfer, as illustrated in Figure 20.6. Assume that with each new connection, each transport protocol entity

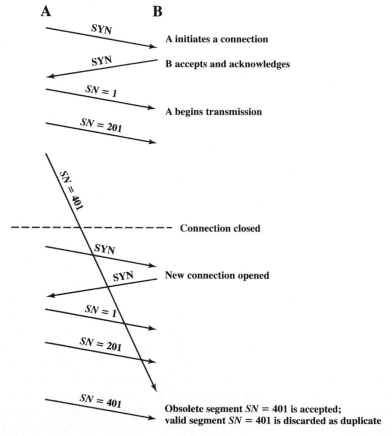

Figure 20.6 The Two-Way Handshake: Problem with Obsolete Data Segment

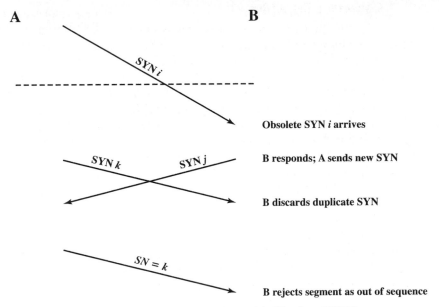

A   **B**

SYN i

Obsolete SYN *i* arrives

SYN k   *SYN j*

B responds; A sends new SYN

B discards duplicate SYN

SN = k

B rejects segment as out of sequence

Figure 20.7   Two-Way Handshake: Problem with Obsolete SYN Segments

begins numbering its data segments with sequence number 1. In the figure, a duplicate copy of segment $SN = 401$ from an old connection arrives during the lifetime of a new connection and is delivered to B before delivery of the legitimate data segment $SN = 401$. One way of attacking this problem is to start each new connection with a different sequence number that is far removed from the last sequence number of the most recent connection. For this purpose, the connection request is of the form SYN i, where i is the sequence number of the first data segment that will be sent on this connection.

Now consider that a duplicate SYN i may survive past the termination of the connection. Figure 20.7 depicts the problem that may arise. An old SYN i arrives at B after the connection is terminated. B assumes that this is a fresh request and responds with SYN j, meaning that B accepts the connection request and will begin transmitting with $SN = j$. Meanwhile, A has decided to open a new connection with B and sends SYN k. B discards this as a duplicate. Now both sides have transmitted and subsequently received a SYN segment, and therefore think that a valid connection exists. However, when A initiates data transfer with a segment numbered k. B rejects the segment as being out of sequence.

The way out of this problem is for each side to acknowledge explicitly the other's SYN and sequence number. The procedure is known as a three-way handshake. The revised connection state diagram, which is the one employed by TCP, is shown in the upper part of Figure 20.8. A new state (SYN RECEIVED) is added. In this state, the transport entity hesitates during connection opening to assure that the SYN segments sent by the two sides have both been acknowledged before the connection is declared established. In addition to the new state, there is a control segment (RST) to reset the other side when a duplicate SYN is detected.

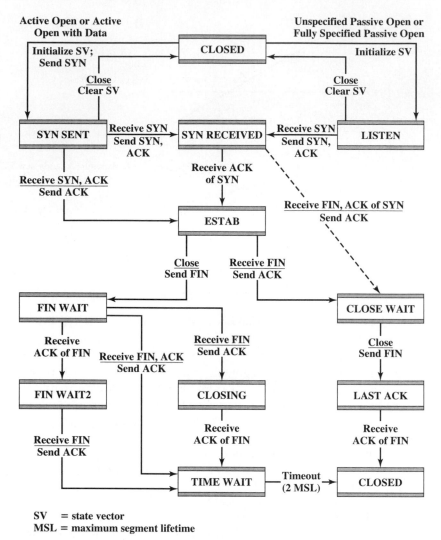

Figure 20.8 TCP Entity State Diagram

Figure 20.9 illustrates typical three-way handshake operations. In Figure 20.9a, transport entity A initiates the connection, with a SYN including the sending sequence number, i. The value i is referred to as the initial sequence number (ISN) and is associated with the SYN; the first data octet to be transmitted will have sequence number $i + 1$. The responding SYN acknowledges the ISN with $(AN = i + 1)$ and includes its ISN. A acknowledges B's SYN/ACK in its first data segment, which begins with sequence number $i + 1$. Figure 20.9b shows a situation in which an old SYN i arrives at B after the close of the relevant connection. B assumes that this is a fresh request and responds with SYN j, $AN = i + 1$. When A

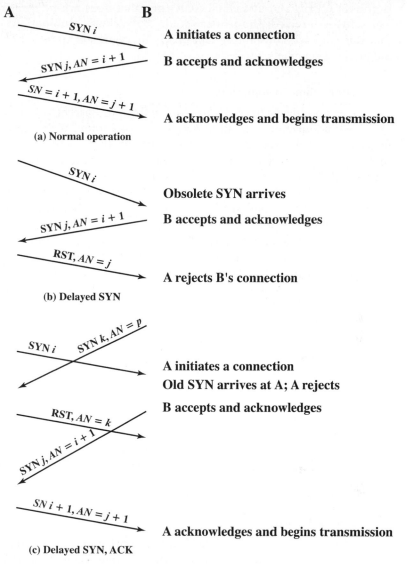

Figure 20.9 Examples of Three-Way Handshake

receives this message, it realizes that it has not requested a connection and there-fore sends an RST, $AN = j$. Note that the $AN = j$ portion of the RST message is essential so that an old duplicate RST does not abort a legitimate connection estab-lishment. Figure 20.9c shows a case in which an old SYN/ACK arrives in the middle of a new connection establishment. Because of the use of sequence numbers in the acknowledgments, this event causes no mischief.

For simplicity, the upper part of Figure 20.8 does not include transitions in which RST is sent. The basic rule is as follows: Send an RST if the connection state is not yet OPEN and an invalid ACK (one that does not reference something that was sent) is received. The reader should try various combinations of events to see that this connection establishment procedure works in spite of any combination of old and lost segments.

Connection Termination

The state diagram of Figure 20.3 defines the use of a simple two-way handshake for connection establishment, which was found to be unsatisfactory in the face of an unreliable network service. Similarly, the two-way handshake defined in that diagram for connection termination is inadequate for an unreliable network service. Misordering of segments could cause the following scenario. A transport entity in the CLOSE WAIT state sends its last data segment, followed by a FIN segment, but the FIN segment arrives at the other side before the last data segment. The receiving transport entity will accept that FIN, close the connection, and lose the last segment of data. To avoid this problem, a sequence number can be associated with the FIN, which can be assigned the next sequence number after the last octet of transmitted data. With this refinement, the receiving transport entity, upon receiving a FIN, will wait if necessary for the late-arriving data before closing the connection.

A more serious problem is the potential loss of segments and the potential presence of obsolete segments. Figure 20.8 shows that the termination procedure adopts a similar solution to that used for connection establishment. Each side must explicitly acknowledge the FIN of the other, using an ACK with the sequence number of the FIN to be acknowledged. For a graceful close, a transport entity requires the following:

- It must send a FIN i and receive $AN = i + 1$.
- It must receive a FIN j and send $AN = j + 1$.
- It must wait an interval equal to twice the maximum expected segment lifetime.

Failure Recovery

When the system upon which a transport entity is running fails and subsequently restarts, the state information of all active connections is lost. The affected connections become *half open* because the side that did not fail does not yet realize the problem.

The still active side of a half-open connection can close the connection using a persistence timer. This timer measures the time the transport machine will continue to await an acknowledgment (or other appropriate reply) of a transmitted segment after the segment has been retransmitted the maximum number of times. When the timer expires, the transport entity assumes that the other transport entity or the intervening network has failed, closes the connection, and signals an abnormal close to the TS user.

In the event that a transport entity fails and quickly restarts, half-open connections can be terminated more quickly by the use of the RST segment. The failed side returns an RST *i* to every segment *i* that it receives. When the RST *i* reaches the other side, it must be checked for validity based on the sequence number *i*, because the RST could be in response to an old segment. If the reset is valid, the transport entity performs an abnormal termination.

These measures clean up the situation at the transport level. The decision as to whether to reopen the connection is up to the TS users. The problem is one of synchronization. At the time of failure, there may have been one or more outstanding segments in either direction. The TS user on the side that did not fail knows how much data it has received, but the other user may not, if state information were lost. Thus, there is the danger that some user data will be lost or duplicated.

20.2 TCP

In this section we look at TCP (RFC 793), first at the service it provides to the TS user and then at the internal protocol details.

TCP Services

TCP is designed to provide reliable communication between pairs of processes (TCP users) across a variety of reliable and unreliable networks and internets. TCP provides two useful facilities for labeling data: push and urgent:

- **Data stream push:** Ordinarily, TCP decides when sufficient data have accumulated to form a segment for transmission. The TCP user can require TCP to transmit all outstanding data up to and including that labeled with a push flag. On the receiving end, TCP will deliver these data to the user in the same manner. A user might request this if it has come to a logical break in the data.

- **Urgent data signaling:** This provides a means of informing the destination TCP user that significant or "urgent" data is in the upcoming data stream. It is up to the destination user to determine appropriate action.

As with IP, the services provided by TCP are defined in terms of primitives and parameters. The services provided by TCP are considerably richer than those provided by IP, and hence the set of primitives and parameters is more complex. Table 20.2 lists TCP service request primitives, which are issued by a TCP user to TCP, and Table 20.3 lists TCP service response primitives, which are issued by TCP to a local TCP user. Table 20.4 provides a brief definition of the parameters involved. The two passive open commands signal the TCP user's willingness to accept a connection request. The active open with data allows the user to begin transmitting data with the opening of the connection.

Table 20.2 TCP Service Request Primitives

Primitive	Parameters	Description
Unspecified Passive Open	source-port, [timeout], [timeout-action], [precedence], [security-range]	Listen for connection attempt at specified security and precedence from any remote destination.
Fully Specified Passive Open	source-port, destination-port, destination-address, [timeout], [timeout-action], [precedence], [security-range]	Listen for connection attempt at specified security and precedence from specified destination.
Active Open	source-port, destination-port, destination-address, [timeout], [timeout-action], [precedence], [security]	Request connection at a particular security and precedence to a specified destination.
Active Open with Data	source-port, destination-port, destination-address, [timeout], [timeout-action], [precedence], [security], data, data-length, PUSH-flag, URGENT-flag	Request connection at a particular security and precedence to a specified destination and transmit data with the request
Send	local-connection-name, data, data-length, PUSH-flag, URGENT-flag, [timeout], [timeout-action]	Transfer data across named connection
Allocate	local-connection-name, data-length	Issue incremental allocation for receive data to TCP
Close	local-connection-name	Close connection gracefully
Abort	local-connection-name	Close connection abruptly
Status	local-connection-name	Query connection status

Note: Square brackets indicate optional parameters.

TCP Header Format

TCP uses only a single type of protocol data unit, called a TCP segment. The header is shown in Figure 20.10. Because one header must serve to perform all protocol mechanisms, it is rather large, with a minimum length of 20 octets. The fields are as follows:

- **Source Port (16 bits):** Source TCP user.
- **Destination Port (16 bits):** Destination TCP user.
- **Sequence Number (32 bits):** Sequence number of the first data octet in this segment except when the SYN flag is set. If SYN is set, it is the initial sequence number (ISN) and the first data octet is ISN + 1.
- **Acknowledgment Number (32 bits):** Contains the sequence number of the next data octet that the TCP entity expects to receive.
- **Data Offset (4 bits):** Number of 32-bit words in the header.

Table 20.3 TCP Service Response Primitives

Primitive	Parameters	Description
Open ID	local-connection-name, source-port, destination-port*, destination-address*	Informs TCP user of connection name assigned to pending connection requested in an Open primitive
Open Failure	local-connection-name	Reports failure of an Active Open request
Open Success	local-connection-name	Reports completion of pending Open request
Deliver	local-connection-name, data, data-length, URGENT-flag	Reports arrival of data
Closing	local-connection-name	Reports that remote TCP user has issued a Close and that all data sent by remote user has been delivered
Terminate	local-connection-name, description	Reports that the connection has been terminated; a description of the reason for termination is provided
Status Response	local-connection-name, source-port, source-address, destination-port, destination-address, connection-state, receive-window, send-window, amount-awaiting-ACK, amount-awaiting-receipt, urgent-state, precedence, security, timeout	Reports current status of connection
Error	local-connection-name, description	Reports service-request or internal error

* = Not used for Unspecified Passive Open.

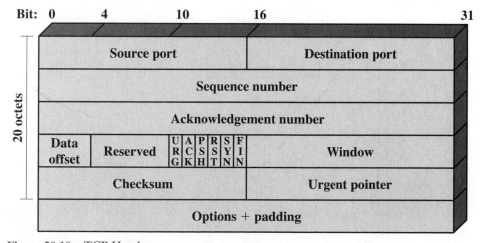

Figure 20.10 TCP Header

Table 20.4 TCP Service Parameters

Source Port	Local TCP user.
Timeout	Longest delay allowed for data delivery before automatic connection termination or error report; user specified.
Timeout-action	Indicates whether the connection is terminated or an error is reported to the TCP user in the event of a timeout.
Precedence	Precedence level for a connection. Takes on values zero (lowest) through seven (highest); same parameter as defined for IP.
Security-range	Allowed ranges in compartment, handling restrictions, transmission control codes, and security levels.
Destination Port	Remote TCP user.
Destination Address	Internet address of remote host.
Security	Security information for a connection, including security level, compartment, handling restrictions, and transmission control code.; same parameter as defined for IP.
Data	Block of data sent by TCP user or delivered to a TCP user.
Data Length	Length of block of data sent or delivered.
PUSH flag	If set, indicates that the associated data are to be provided with the data stream push service.
URGENT flag	If set, indicates that the associated data are to be provided with the urgent data signaling service.
Local Connection Name	Identifier of a connection defined by a (local socket, remote socket) pair; provided by TCP.
Description	Supplementary information in a Terminate or Error primitive.
Source Address	Internet address of the local host.
Connection State	State of referenced connection (CLOSED, ACTIVE OPEN, PASSIVE OPEN, ESTABLISHED, CLOSING).
Receive Window	Amount of data in octets the local TCP entity is willing to receive.
Send Window	Amount of data in octets permitted to be sent to remote TCP entity.
Amount Awaiting ACK	Amount of previously transmitted data awaiting acknowledgment.
Amount Awaiting Receipt	Amount of data in octets buffered at local TCP entity pending receipt by local TCP user.
Urgent State	Indicates to the receiving TCP user whether there are urgent data available or whether all urgent data, if any, have been delivered to the user.

- **Reserved (6 bits):** Reserved for future use. RFC 3168 uses two of these bits for the explicit congestion notification function; a discussion of this function is beyond our scope.
- **Flags (6 bits):** For each flag, if set to 1, the meaning is as follows:

  URG: urgent pointer field significant

  ACK: acknowledgment field significant

  PSH: push function

  RST: reset the connection

SYN: synchronize the sequence numbers

FIN: no more data from sender

- **Window (16 bits):** Flow control credit allocation, in octets. Contains the number of data octets, beginning with the sequence number indicated in the acknowledgment field that the sender is willing to accept.

- **Checksum (16 bits):** The ones complement of the ones complement sum modulo of all the 16-bit words in the segment plus a pseudoheader, described subsequently.[2]

- **Urgent Pointer (16 bits):** This value, when added to the segment sequence number, contains the sequence number of the last octet in a sequence of urgent data. This allows the receiver to know how much urgent data is coming.

- **Options (Variable):** An example is the option that specifies the maximum segment size that will be accepted.

The *sequence number* and *acknowledgment number* are bound to octets rather than to entire segments. For example, if a segment contains sequence number 1001 and includes 600 octets of data, the sequence number refers to the first octet in the data field; the next segment in logical order will have sequence number 1601. Thus, TCP is logically stream oriented: It accepts a stream of octets from the user, groups them into segments as it sees fit, and numbers each octet in the stream.

The *checksum* field applies to the entire segment plus a pseudoheader prefixed to the header at the time of calculation (at both transmission and reception). The pseudoheader includes the following fields from the IP header: source and destination internet address and protocol, plus a segment length field. By including the pseudoheader, TCP protects itself from misdelivery by IP. That is, if IP delivers a packet to the wrong host, even if the packet contains no bit errors, the receiving TCP entity will detect the delivery error.

By comparing the TCP header to the TCP user interface defined in Tables 20.2 and 20.3, the reader may feel that some items are missing from the TCP header; that is indeed the case. TCP is designed specifically to work with IP. Hence, some TCP user parameters are passed down by TCP to IP for inclusion in the IP header. The relevant ones are as follows:

- Precedence: a 3-bit field
- Normal-delay/low-delay
- Normal-throughput/high-throughput
- Normal-reliability/high-reliability
- Security: an 11-bit field

It is worth observing that this TCP/IP linkage means that the required minimum overhead for every data unit is actually 40 octets.

---

[2] A discussion of this checksum is contained in a supporting document at this book's Web site.

TCP Mechanisms

We can group TCP mechanisms into the categories of connection establishment, data transfer, and connection termination.

Connection Establishment

Connection establishment in TCP always uses a three-way handshake. When the SYN flag is set, the segment is essentially a request for connection and functions as explained in Section 20.1. To initiate a connection, an entity sends a SYN, $SN = X$, where X is the initial sequence number. The receiver responds with SYN, $SN = Y$, $AN = X + 1$ by setting both the SYN and ACK flags. Note that the acknowledgment indicates that the receiver is now expecting to receive a segment beginning with data octet $X + 1$, acknowledging the SYN, which occupies $SN = X$. Finally, the initiator responds with $AN = Y + 1$. If the two sides issue crossing SYNs, no problem results: Both sides respond with SYN/ACKs (Figure 20.4).

A connection is uniquely determined by the source and destination sockets (host, port). Thus, at any one time, there can only be a single TCP connection between a unique pair of ports. However, a given port can support multiple connections, each with a different partner port.

Data Transfer

Although data are transferred in segments over a transport connection, data transfer is viewed logically as consisting of a stream of octets. Hence every octet is numbered, modulo 2^{32}. Each segment contains the sequence number of the first octet in the data field. Flow control is exercised using a credit allocation scheme in which the credit is a number of octets rather than a number of segments, as explained in Section 20.1.

Data are buffered by the transport entity on both transmission and reception. TCP normally exercises its own discretion as to when to construct a segment for transmission and when to release received data to the user. The PUSH flag is used to force the data so far accumulated to be sent by the transmitter and passed on by the receiver. This serves an end-of-block function.

The user may specify a block of data as urgent. TCP will designate the end of that block with an urgent pointer and send it out in the ordinary data stream. The receiving user is alerted that urgent data are being received.

If, during data exchange, a segment arrives that is apparently not meant for the current connection, the RST flag is set on an outgoing segment. Examples of this situation are delayed duplicate SYNs and an acknowledgment of data not yet sent.

Connection Termination

The normal means of terminating a connection is a graceful close. Each TCP user must issue a CLOSE primitive. The transport entity sets the FIN bit on the last segment that it sends out, which also contains the last of the data to be sent on this connection.

An abrupt termination occurs if the user issues an ABORT primitive. In this case, the entity abandons all attempts to send or receive data and discards data in its transmission and reception buffers. An RST segment is sent to the other side.

TCP Implementation Policy Options

The TCP standard provides a precise specification of the protocol to be used between TCP entities. However, certain aspects of the protocol admit several possible implementation options. Although two implementations that choose alternative options will be interoperable, there may be performance implications. The design areas for which options are specified are the following:

- Send policy
- Deliver policy
- Accept policy
- Retransmit policy
- Acknowledge policy

Send Policy

In the absence of both pushed data and a closed transmission window (see Figure 20.2a), a sending TCP entity is free to transmit data at its own convenience, within its current credit allocation. As data are issued by the user, they are buffered in the transmit buffer. TCP may construct a segment for each batch of data provided by its user or it may wait until a certain amount of data accumulates before constructing and sending a segment. The actual policy will depend on performance considerations. If transmissions are infrequent and large, there is low overhead in terms of segment generation and processing. On the other hand, if transmissions are frequent and small, the system is providing quick response.

Deliver Policy

In the absence of a Push, a receiving TCP entity is free to deliver data to the user at its own convenience. It may deliver data as each in-order segment is received, or it may buffer data from a number of segments in the receive buffer before delivery. The actual policy will depend on performance considerations. If deliveries are infrequent and large, the user is not receiving data as promptly as may be desirable. On the other hand, if deliveries are frequent and small, there may be unnecessary processing both in TCP and in the user software, as well as an unnecessary number of operating system interrupts.

Accept Policy

When all data segments arrive in order over a TCP connection, TCP places the data in a receive buffer for delivery to the user. It is possible, however, for segments to arrive out of order. In this case, the receiving TCP entity has two options:

- **In-order:** Accept only segments that arrive in order; any segment that arrives out of order is discarded.
- **In-window:** Accept all segments that are within the receive window (see Figure 20.2b).

The in-order policy makes for a simple implementation but places a burden on the networking facility, as the sending TCP must time out and retransmit segments that were successfully received but discarded because of misordering. Furthermore, if a single segment is lost in transit, then all subsequent segments must be retransmitted once the sending TCP times out on the lost segment.

The in-window policy may reduce transmissions but requires a more complex acceptance test and a more sophisticated data storage scheme to buffer and keep track of data accepted out of order.

Retransmit Policy

TCP maintains a queue of segments that have been sent but not yet acknowledged. The TCP specification states that TCP will retransmit a segment if it fails to receive an acknowledgment within a given time. A TCP implementation may employ one of three retransmission strategies:

- **First-only:** Maintain one retransmission timer for the entire queue. If an acknowledgment is received, remove the appropriate segment or segments from the queue and reset the timer. If the timer expires, retransmit the segment at the front of the queue and reset the timer.
- **Batch:** Maintain one retransmission timer for the entire queue. if an acknowledgment is received, remove the appropriate segment or segments from the queue and reset the timer. If the timer expires, retransmit all segments in the queue and reset the timer.
- **Individual:** Maintain one timer for each segment in the queue. If an acknowledgment is received, remove the appropriate segment or segments from the queue and destroy the corresponding timer or timers. If any timer expires, retransmit the corresponding segment individually and reset its timer.

The first-only policy is efficient in terms of traffic generated, because only lost segments (or segments whose ACK was lost) are retransmitted. Because the timer for the second segment in the queue is not set until the first segment is acknowledged, however, there can be considerable delays. The individual policy solves this problem at the expense of a more complex implementation. The batch policy also reduces the likelihood of long delays but may result in unnecessary retransmissions.

The actual effectiveness of the retransmit policy depends in part on the accept policy of the receiver. If the receiver is using an in-order accept policy, then it will discard segments received after a lost segment. This fits best with batch retransmission. If the receiver is using an in-window accept policy, then a first-only or individual retransmission policy is best. Of course, in a mixed network of computers, both accept policies may be in use.

Acknowledge Policy

When a data segment arrives that is in sequence, the receiving TCP entity has two options concerning the timing of acknowledgment:

- **Immediate:** When data are accepted, immediately transmit an empty (no data) segment containing the appropriate acknowledgment number.

- **Cumulative:** When data are accepted, record the need for acknowledgment, but wait for an outbound segment with data on which to piggyback the acknowledgment. To avoid long delay, set a window timer (Table 20.1); if the timer expires before an acknowledgment is sent, transmit an empty segment containing the appropriate acknowledgment number.

The immediate policy is simple and keeps the remote TCP entity fully informed, which limits unnecessary retransmissions. However, this policy results in extra segment transmissions, namely, empty segments used only to ACK. Furthermore, the policy can cause a further load on the network. Consider that a TCP entity receives a segment and immediately sends an ACK. Then the data in the segment are released to the application, which expands the receive window, triggering another empty TCP segment to provide additional credit to the sending TCP entity.

Because of the potential overhead of the immediate policy, the cumulative policy is typically used. Recognize, however, that the use of this policy requires more processing at the receiving end and complicates the task of estimating round-trip time by the sending TCP entity.

20.3 TCP CONGESTION CONTROL

The credit-based flow control mechanism of TCP was designed to enable a destination to restrict the flow of segments from a source to avoid buffer overflow at the destination. This same flow control mechanism is now used in ingenious ways to provide congestion control over the Internet between the source and destination. Congestion, as we have seen a number of times in this book, has two main effects. First, as congestion begins to occur, the transit time across a network or internetwork increases. Second, as congestion becomes severe, network or internet nodes drop packets. The TCP flow control mechanism can be used to recognize the onset of congestion (by recognizing increased delay times and dropped segments) and to react by reducing the flow of data. If many of the TCP entities operating across a network exercise this sort of restraint, internet congestion is relieved.

Since the publication of RFC 793, a number of techniques have been implemented that are intended to improve TCP congestion control characteristics. None of these techniques extend or violate the original TCP standard; rather they represent implementation policies that are within the scope of the TCP specification. Many of these techniques are mandated for use with TCP in RFC 1122, Requirements for Internet Hosts, while some of them are specified in RFC 2581. The techniques fall roughly into two categories: retransmission timer management and window management. In this section, we look at some of the most important and most widely implemented of these techniques.

Retransmission Timer Management

As network or internet conditions change, a static retransmission timer is likely to be either too long or too short. Accordingly, virtually all TCP implementations attempt to estimate the current round-trip time by observing the pattern of delay for recent segments, and then set the timer to a value somewhat greater than the estimated round-trip time.

Simple Average

One approach would be simply to take the average of observed round-trip times over a number of segments. If the average accurately predicts future round-trip times, then the resulting retransmission timer will yield good performance. The simple averaging method can be expressed as follows:

$$\text{ARTT}(K + 1) = \frac{1}{K + 1} \sum_{i=1}^{K+1} \text{RTT}(i) \tag{20.1}$$

where $\text{RTT}(i)$ is the round-trip time observed for the ith transmitted segment, and $\text{ARTT}(K)$ is the average round-trip time for the first K segments.

This expression can be rewritten as follows:

$$\text{ARTT}(K + 1) = \frac{K}{K + 1} \text{ARTT}(K) + \frac{1}{K + 1} \text{RTT}(K + 1) \tag{20.2}$$

With this formulation, it is not necessary to recalculate the entire summation each time.

Exponential Average

Note that each term in the summation is given equal weight; that is, each term is multiplied by the same constant $1/(K + 1)$. Typically, we would like to give greater weight to more recent instances because they are more likely to reflect future behavior. A common technique for predicting the next value on the basis of a time series of past values, and the one specified in RFC 793, is exponential averaging:

$$\text{SRTT}(K + 1) = \alpha \times \text{SRTT}(K) + (1 - \alpha) \times \text{RTT}(K + 1) \tag{20.3}$$

where $\text{SRTT}(K)$ is called the smoothed round-trip time estimate, and we define $\text{SRTT}(0) = 0$. Compare this with Equation (20.2). By using a constant value of $\alpha(0 < \alpha < 1)$, independent of the number of past observations, we have a circumstance in which all past values are considered, but the more distant ones have less weight. To see this more clearly, consider the following expansion of Equation (20.3):

$$\text{SRTT}(K + 1) = (1 - \alpha)\text{RTT}(K + 1) + \alpha(1 - \alpha)\text{RTT}(K) + \\ \alpha^2(1 - \alpha)\text{RTT}(K - 1) + \cdots + \alpha^K(1 - \alpha)\text{RTT}(1)$$

Because both α and $(1 - \alpha)$ are less than one, each successive term in the preceding equation is smaller. For example, for $\alpha = 0.8$, the expansion is

$$\text{SRTT}(K + 1) = (0.2)\text{RTT}(K + 1) + (0.16)\text{RTT}(K) + (0.128)\text{RTT}(K - 1) + \cdots$$

The older the observation, the less it is counted in the average.

The smaller the value of α, the greater the weight given to the more recent observations. For $\alpha = 0.5$, virtually all of the weight is given to the four or five most recent observations, whereas for $\alpha = 0.875$, the averaging is effectively spread out over the ten or so most recent observations. The advantage of using a small value of α is that the average will quickly reflect a rapid change in the observed quantity. The disadvantage is that if there is a brief surge in the value of the observed quantity and it then settles back to some relatively constant value, the use of a small value of α will result in jerky changes in the average.

Figure 20.11 compares simple averaging with exponential averaging (for two different values of α). In part (a) of the figure, the observed value begins at 1, grows gradually to a value of 10, and then stays there. In part (b) of the figure, the observed value begins at 20, declines gradually to 10, and then stays there. Note that exponential averaging tracks changes in process behavior faster than does simple averaging and that the smaller value of α results in a more rapid reaction to the change in the observed value.

Equation (20.3) is used in RFC 793 to estimate the current round-trip time. As was mentioned, the retransmission timer should be set at a value somewhat greater than the estimated round-trip time. One possibility is to use a constant value:

$$RTO(K + 1) = SRTT(K + 1) + \Delta$$

where RTO is the retransmission timer (also called the retransmission timeout) and Δ is a constant. The disadvantage of this is that Δ is not proportional to SRTT. For large values of SRTT, Δ is relatively small and fluctuations in the actual RTT will result in unnecessary retransmissions. For small values of SRTT, Δ is relatively large and causes unnecessary delays in retransmitting lost segments. Accordingly, RFC 793 specifies the use of a timer whose value is proportional to SRTT, within limits:

$$RTO(K + 1) = MIN(UBOUND, MAX(LBOUND, \beta \times SRTT(K + 1))) \quad (20.4)$$

where UBOUND and LBOUND are prechosen fixed upper and lower bounds on the timer value and β is a constant. RFC 793 does not recommend specific values but does list as "example values" the following: α between 0.8 and 0.9 and β between 1.3 and 2.0.

RTT Variance Estimation (Jacobson's Algorithm)

The technique specified in the TCP standard, and described in Equations (20.3) and (20.4), enables a TCP entity to adapt to changes in round-trip time. However, it does not cope well with a situation in which the round-trip time exhibits a relatively high variance. [ZHAN86] points out three sources of high variance:

1. If the data rate on the TCP connection is relatively low, then the transmission delay will be relatively large compared to propagation time and the variance in RTT due to variance in IP datagram size will be significant. Thus, the SRTT estimator is heavily influenced by characteristics that are a property of the data and not of the network.

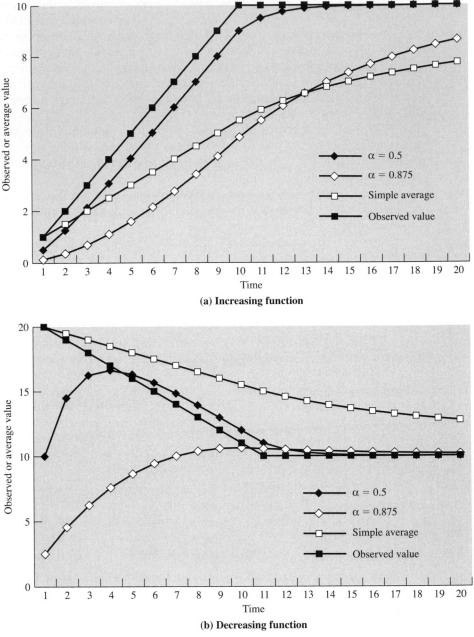

Figure 20.11 Use of Exponential Averaging

2. Internet traffic load and conditions may change abruptly due to traffic from other sources, causing abrupt changes in RTT.

3. The peer TCP entity may not acknowledge each segment immediately because of its own processing delays and because it exercises its privilege to use cumulative acknowledgments.

The original TCP specification tries to account for this variability by multiplying the RTT estimator by a constant factor, as shown in Equation (20.4). In a stable environment, with low variance of RTT, this formulation results in an unnecessarily high value of RTO, and in an unstable environment a value of $\beta = 2$ may be inadequate to protect against unnecessary retransmissions.

A more effective approach is to estimate the variability in RTT values and to use that as input into the calculation of an RTO. A variability measure that is easy to estimate is the mean deviation, defined as

$$\text{MDEV}(X) = \text{E}[|X - \text{E}[X]|]$$

where $\text{E}[X]$ is the expected value of X.

As with the estimate of RTT, a simple average could be used to estimate MDEV:

$$\text{AERR}(K + 1) = \text{RTT}(K + 1) - \text{ARTT}(K)$$
$$\text{ADEV}(K + 1) = \frac{1}{K + 1} \sum_{i=1}^{K+1} |\text{AERR}(i)|$$
$$= \frac{K}{K + 1} \text{ADEV}(K) + \frac{1}{K + 1} |\text{AERR}(K + 1)|$$

where $\text{ARTT}(K)$ is the simple average defined in Equation (20.1) and $\text{AERR}(K)$ is the sample mean deviation measured at time K.

As with the definition of ARRT, each term in the summation of ADEV is given equal weight; that is, each term is multiplied by the same constant $1/(K + 1)$. Again, we would like to give greater weight to more recent instances because they are more likely to reflect future behavior. Jacobson, who proposed the use of a dynamic estimate of variability in estimating RTT [JACO88], suggests using the same exponential smoothing technique as is used for the calculation of SRTT. The complete algorithm proposed by Jacobson can be expressed as follows:

$$\text{SRTT}(K + 1) = (1 - g) \times \text{SRTT}(K) + g \times \text{RTT}(K + 1)$$
$$\text{SERR}(K + 1) = \text{RTT}(K + 1) - \text{SRTT}(K) \tag{20.5}$$
$$\text{SDEV}(K + 1) = (1 - h) \times \text{SDEV}(K) + h \times |\text{SERR}(K + 1)|$$
$$\text{RTO}(K + 1) = \text{SRTT}(K + 1) + f \times \text{SDEV}(K + 1)$$

As in the RFC 793 definition [Equation (20.3)], SRTT is an exponentially smoothed estimate of RTT, with $(1 - g)$ equivalent to α. Now, however, instead of multiplying the estimate SRTT by a constant [Equation (20.4)], a multiple of the estimated mean deviation is added to SRTT to form the retransmission timer. Based on his timing experiments, Jacobson proposed the following values for the constants in his original paper [JACO88]:

$$g = 1/8 = 0.125$$
$$h = 1/4 = 0.25$$
$$f = 2$$

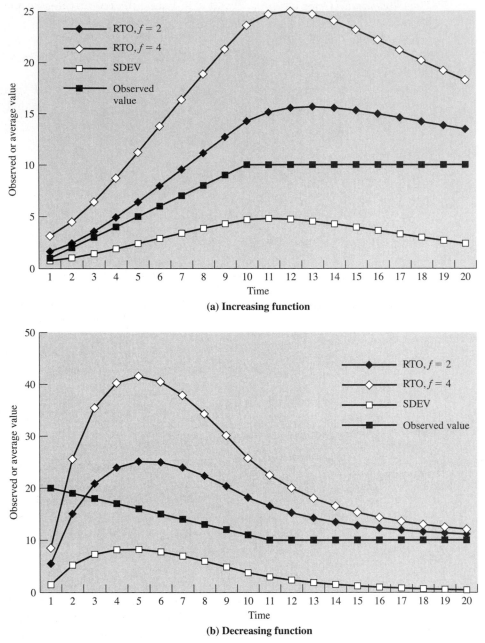

Figure 20.12 Jacobson's RTO Calculation

After further research [JACO90], he recommended changing the value of f to 4, and this is the standard value used in current implementations.

Figure 20.12 illustrates the use of Equation 20.5 on the same data set used in Figure 20.11. Once the arrival times stabilize, the variation estimate SDEV declines.

The values of RTO for both $f = 2$ and $f = 4$ are quite conservative as long as RTT is changing, but then begin to converge to RTT when it stabilizes.

Experience has shown that Jacobson's algorithm can significantly improve TCP performance. However, it does not stand by itself. Two other factors must be considered:

1. What RTO value should be used on a retransmitted segment? The exponential RTO backoff algorithm is used for this purpose.
2. Which round-trip samples should be used as input to Jacobson's algorithm? Karn's algorithm determines which samples to use.

Exponential RTO Backoff

When a TCP sender times out on a segment, it must retransmit that segment. RFC 793 assumes that the same RTO value will be used for this retransmitted segment. However, because the timeout is probably due to network congestion, manifested as a dropped packet or a long delay in round-trip time, maintaining the same RTO value is ill advised.

Consider the following scenario. There are a number of active TCP connections from various sources sending traffic into an internet. A region of congestion develops such that segments on many of these connections are lost or delayed past the RTO time of the connections. Therefore, at roughly the same time, many segments will be retransmitted into the internet, maintaining or even increasing the congestion. All of the sources then wait a local (to each connection) RTO time and retransmit yet again. This pattern of behavior could cause a sustained condition of congestion.

A more sensible policy dictates that a sending TCP entity increase its RTO each time the same segment is retransmitted; this is referred to as a *backoff* process. In the scenario of the preceding paragraph, after the first retransmission of a segment on each affected connection, the sending TCP entities will all wait a longer time before performing a second retransmission. This may give the internet time to clear the current congestion. If a second retransmission is required, each sending TCP entity will wait an even longer time before timing out for a third retransmission, giving the internet an even longer period to recover.

A simple technique for implementing RTO backoff is to multiply the RTO for a segment by a constant value for each retransmission:

$$\text{RTO} = q \times \text{RTO} \tag{20.6}$$

Equation (20.6) causes RTO to grow exponentially with each retransmission. The most commonly used value of q is 2. With this value, the technique is referred to as *binary exponential backoff*. This is the same technique used in the Ethernet CSMA/CD protocol (Chapter 16).

Karn's Algorithm

If no segments are retransmitted, the sampling process for Jacobson's algorithm is straightforward. The RTT for each segment can be included in the calculation. Suppose, however, that a segment times out and must be retransmitted. If an acknowledgment is subsequently received, there are two possibilities:

1. This is the ACK to the first transmission of the segment. In this case, the RTT is simply longer than expected but is an accurate reflection of network conditions.
2. This is the ACK to the second transmission.

The sending TCP entity cannot distinguish between these two cases. If the second case is true and the TCP entity simply measures the RTT from the first transmission until receipt of the ACK, the measured time will be much too long. The measured RTT will be on the order of the actual RTT plus the RTO. Feeding this false RTT into Jacobson's algorithm will produce an unnecessarily high value of SRTT and therefore RTO. Furthermore, this effect propagates forward a number of iterations, since the SRTT value of one iteration is an input value in the next iteration.

An even worse approach would be to measure the RTT from the *second* transmission to the receipt of the ACK. If this is in fact the ACK to the first transmission, then the measured RTT will be much too small, producing a too low value of SRTT and RTO. This is likely to have a positive feedback effect, causing additional retransmissions and additional false measurements.

Karn's algorithm [KARN91] solves this problem with the following rules:

1. Do not use the measured RTT for a retransmitted segment to update SRTT and SDEV [Equation (20.5)].
2. Calculate the backoff RTO using Equation 20.6 when a retransmission occurs.
3. Use the backoff RTO value for succeeding segments until an acknowledgment arrives for a segment that has not been retransmitted.

When an acknowledgment is received to an unretransmitted segment, Jacobson's algorithm is again activated to compute future RTO values.

Window Management

In addition to techniques for improving the effectiveness of the retransmission timer, a number of approaches to managing the send window have been examined. The size of TCP's send window can have a critical effect on whether TCP can be used efficiently without causing congestion. We discuss two techniques found in virtually all modern implementations of TCP: slow start and dynamic window sizing on congestion.[3]

Slow Start

The larger the send window used in TCP, the more segments that a sending TCP entity can send before it must wait for an acknowledgment. This can create a problem when a TCP connection is first established, because the TCP entity is free to dump the entire window of data onto the internet.

One strategy that could be followed is for the TCP sender to begin sending from some relatively large but not maximum window, hoping to approximate the window size that would ultimately be provided by the connection. This is risky be-

---

[3] These algorithms were developed by Van Jacobson [JACO88] and are also described in RFC 2581. Van Jacobson describes things in units of TCP segments, whereas RFC 2581 relies primarily on units of TCP data octets, with some reference to calculations in units of segments. We follow the development in [JACO88].

cause the sender might flood the internet with many segments before it realized from timeouts that the flow was excessive. Instead, some means is needed of gradually expanding the window until acknowledgments are received. This is the purpose of the slow start mechanism.

With slow start, TCP transmission is constrained by the following relationship:

$$awnd = \text{MIN}[credit, cwnd] \tag{20.7}$$

where

> $awnd$ = allowed window, in segments. This is the number of segments that TCP is currently allowed to send without receiving further acknowledgments.
>
> $cwnd$ = congestion window, in segments. A window used by TCP during startup and to reduce flow during periods of congestion.
>
> $credit$ = the amount of unused credit granted in the most recent acknowledgment, in segments. When an acknowledgment is received, this value is calculated as $window/segment\_size$, where $window$ is a field in the incoming TCP segment (the amount of data the peer TCP entity is willing to accept).

The TCP entity sets $cwnd = 1$ when a new connection is opened. That is, TCP is only allowed to send 1 segment and then must wait for an acknowledgment before transmitting a second segment. Each time an acknowledgment to new data is received, the value of $cwnd$ is increased by 1, up to some maximum value.

In effect, the slow-start mechanism probes the internet to make sure that the TCP entity is not sending too many segments into an already congested environment. As acknowledgments arrive, TCP is able to open up its window until the flow is controlled by the incoming ACKs rather than by $cwnd$.

The term *slow start* is a bit of a misnomer, because $cwnd$ actually grows exponentially. When the first ACK arrives, TCP opens $cwnd$ to 2 and can send two segments. When these two segments are acknowledged, TCP can slide the window 1 segment for each incoming ACK and can increase $cwnd$ by 1 for each incoming ACK. Therefore, at this point TCP can send four segments. When these four are acknowledged, TCP will be able to send eight segments.

Dynamic Window Sizing on Congestion

The slow-start algorithm has been found to work effectively for initializing a connection. It enables the TCP sender to determine quickly a reasonable window size for the connection. Might not the same technique be useful when there is a surge in congestion? In particular, suppose a TCP entity initiates a connection and goes through the slow-start procedure. At some point, either before or after $cwnd$ reaches the size of the credit allocated by the other side, a segment is lost (timeout). This is a signal that congestion is occurring. It is not clear how serious the congestion is. Therefore, a prudent procedure would be to reset $cwnd = 1$ and begin the slow-start process all over.

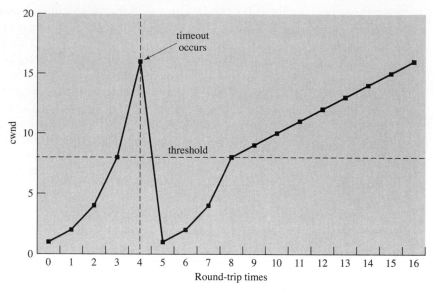

Figure 20.13 Illustration of Slow Start and Congestion Avoidance

This seems like a reasonable, conservative procedure, but in fact it is not conservative enough. Jacobson [JACO88] points out that "it is easy to drive a network into saturation but hard for the net to recover." In other words, once congestion occurs, it may take a long time for the congestion to clear.[4] Thus, the exponential growth of *cwnd* under slow start may be too aggressive and may worsen the congestion. Instead, Jacobson proposed the use of slow start to begin with, followed by a linear growth in *cwnd*. The rules are as follows. When a timeout occurs,

1. Set a slow-start threshold equal to half the current congestion window; that is, set *ssthresh* = *cwnd*/2.
2. Set *cwnd* = 1 and perform the slow-start process until *cwnd* = *ssthresh*. In this phase, *cwnd* is increased by 1 for every ACK received.
3. For *cwnd* ≥ *ssthresh*, increase *cwnd* by one for each round-trip time.

Figure 20.13 illustrates this behavior. Note that it takes 11 round-trip times to recover to the *cwnd* level that initially took 4 round-trip times to achieve.

20.4 UDP

In addition to TCP, there is one other transport-level protocol that is in common use as part of the TCP/IP protocol suite: the user datagram protocol (UDP), specified in RFC 768. UDP provides a connectionless service for application-level procedures. Thus, UDP is basically an unreliable service; delivery and duplicate protection are

---

[4] Kleinrock refers to this phenomenon as the long-tail effect during a rush-hour period. See Sections 2.7 and 2.10 of [KLEI76] for a detailed discussion.

not guaranteed. However, this does reduce the overhead of the protocol and may be adequate in many cases. An example of the use of UDP is in the context of network management, as described in Chapter 22.

The strengths of the connection-oriented approach are clear. It allows connection-related features such as flow control, error control, and sequenced delivery. Connectionless service, however, is more appropriate in some contexts. At lower layers (internet, network), a connectionless service is more robust (e.g., see discussion in Section 10.6). In addition, it represents a "least common denominator" of service to be expected at higher layers. Further, even at transport and above there is justification for a connectionless service. There are instances in which the overhead of connection establishment and termination is unjustified or even counterproductive. Examples are a follows:

- **Inward data collection:** Involves the periodic active or passive sampling of data sources, such as sensors, and automatic self-test reports from security equipment or network components. In a real-time monitoring situation, the loss of an occasional data unit would not cause distress, because the next report should arrive shortly.
- **Outward data dissemination:** Includes broadcast messages to network users, the announcement of a new node or the change of address of a service, and the distribution of real-time clock values.
- **Request-response:** Applications in which a transaction service is provided by a common server to a number of distributed TS users, and for which a single request-response sequence is typical. Use of the service is regulated at the application level, and lower-level connections are often unnecessary and cumbersome.
- **Real-time applications:** Such as voice and telemetry, involving a degree of redundancy and/or a real-time transmission requirement. These must not have connection-oriented functions such as retransmission.

Thus, there is a place at the transport level for both a connection-oriented and a connectionless type of service.

UDP sits on top of IP. Because it is connectionless, UDP has very little to do. Essentially, it adds a port addressing capability to IP. This is best seen by examining the UDP header, shown in Figure 20.14. The header includes a source port and destination port. The length field contains the length of the entire UDP segment, including header and data. The checksum is the same algorithm used for TCP and IP. For UDP, the checksum applies to the entire UDP segment plus a pseudoheader prefixed to the UDP header at the time of calculation and which is the same pseudoheader used for TCP. If an error is detected, the segment is discarded and no further action is taken.

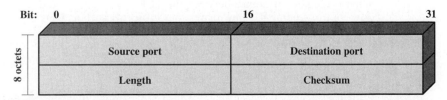

Figure 20.14 UDP Header

The checksum field in UDP is optional. If it is not used, it is set to zero. However, it should be pointed out that the IP checksum applies only to the IP header and not to the data field, which in this case consists of the UDP header and the user data. Thus, if no checksum calculation is performed by UDP, then no check is made on the user data.

20.5 RECOMMENDED READING

Perhaps the best coverage of the various TCP strategies for flow and congestion control is to be found in [STEV94]. An essential paper for understanding the issues involved is the classic [JACO88].

JACO88   Jacobson, V. "Congestion Avoidance and Control." *Proceedings, SIGCOMM '88, Computer Communication Review*, August 1988; reprinted in *Computer Communication Review*, January 1995; a slightly revised version is available at ftp.ee.lbl.gov/papers/congavoid.ps.Z.

STEV94   Stevens, W. *TCP/IP Illustrated, Volume 1: The Protocols*. Reading, MA: Addison-Wesley, 1994.

20.6 KEY TERMS, REVIEW QUESTIONS, AND PROBLEMS

Key Terms

checksum	port	Transmission Control
credit	retransmission strategy	Protocol (TCP)
data stream push	sequence number	transport protocol
duplicate detection	slow start	urgent data signaling
exponential average	socket	User Datagram Protocol
flow control	TCP congestion control	(UDP)
Karn's algorithm	TCP implementation policy	
multiplexing	options	

Review Questions

20.1 What addressing elements are needed to specify a target transport service (TS) user?

20.2 Describe four strategies by which a sending TS user can learn the address of a receiving TS user.

20.3 Explain the use of multiplexing in the context of a transport protocol.

20.4 Briefly describe the credit scheme used by TCP for flow control.

20.5 What is the key difference between the TCP credit scheme and the sliding-window flow control scheme used by many other protocols, such as HDLC?

20.6 Explain the two-way and three-way handshake mechanisms.

20.7 What is the benefit of the three-way handshake mechanism?

20.8 Define the urgent and push features of TCP.

20.9 What is a TCP implementation policy option?

20.10 How can TCP used to deal with network or internet congestion?

20.11 What does UDP provide that is not provided by IP?

Problems

20.1 It is common practice in most transport protocols (indeed, most protocols at all levels) for control and data to be multiplexed over the same logical channel on a per-user-connection basis. An alternative is to establish a single control transport connection between each pair of communicating transport entities. This connection would be used to carry control signals relating to all user transport connections between the two entities. Discuss the implications of this strategy.

20.2 The discussion of flow control with a reliable network service referred to a backpressure mechanism utilizing a lower-level flow control protocol. Discuss the disadvantages of this strategy.

20.3 Two transport entities communicate across a reliable network. Let the normalized time to transmit a segment equal 1. Assume that the end-to-end propagation delay is 3, and that it takes a time 2 to deliver data from a received segment to the transport user. The sender initially granted a credit of seven segments. The receiver uses a conservative flow control policy, and updates its credit allocation at every opportunity. What is the maximum achievable throughput?

20.4 Draw diagrams similar to Figure 20.4 for the following (assume a reliable sequenced network service):
   a. Connection termination: active/passive
   b. Connection termination: active/active
   c. Connection rejection
   d. Connection abortion: User issues an OPEN to a listening user, and then issues a CLOSE before any data are exchanged

20.5 With a reliable sequencing network service, are segment sequence numbers strictly necessary? What, if any, capability is lost without them?

20.6 Consider a connection-oriented network service that suffers a reset. How could this be dealt with by a transport protocol that assumes that the network service is reliable except for resets?

20.7 The discussion of retransmission strategy made reference to three problems associated with dynamic timer calculation. What modifications to the strategy would help to alleviate those problems?

20.8 Consider a transport protocol that uses a connection-oriented network service. Suppose that the transport protocol uses a credit allocation flow control scheme, and the network protocol uses a sliding-window scheme. What relationship, if any, should there be between the dynamic window of the transport protocol and the fixed window of the network protocol?

20.9 In a network that has a maximum packet size of 128 bytes, a maximum packet lifetime of 30 s, and an 8-bit packet sequence number, what is the maximum data rate per connection?

20.10 Is a deadlock possible using only a two-way handshake instead of a three-way handshake? Give an example or prove otherwise.

20.11 Listed are four strategies that can be used to provide a transport user with the address of the destination transport user. For each one, describe an analogy with the Postal Service user.
   a. Know the address ahead of time.
   b. Make use of a "well-known address."
   c. Use a name server.
   d. Addressee is spawned at request time.

20.12 In a credit flow control scheme such as that of TCP, what provision could be made for credit allocations that are lost or misordered in transit?

20.13 What happens in Figure 20.3 if a SYN comes in while the requested user is in CLOSED? Is there any way to get the attention of the user when it is not listening?

20.14 In discussing connection termination with reference to Figure 20.8, it was stated that in addition to receiving an acknowledgment of its FIN and sending an acknowledgment of the incoming FIN, a TCP entity must wait an interval equal to twice the maximum expected segment lifetime (the TIME WAIT state). Receiving an ACK to its FIN assures that all of the segments it sent have been received by the other side. Sending an ACK to the other side's FIN assures the other side that all its segments have been received. Give a reason why it is still necessary to wait before closing the connection.

20.15 Ordinarily, the Window field in the TCP header gives a credit allocation in octets. When the Window Scale option is in use, the value in the Window field is multiplied by a 2^F, where F is the value of the window scale option. The maximum value of F that TCP accepts if 14. Why is the option limited to 14?

20.16 One difficulty with the original TCP SRTT estimator is the choice of an initial value. In the absence of any special knowledge of network conditions, the typical approach is to pick an arbitrary value, such as 3 seconds, and hope that this will converge quickly to an accurate value. If this estimate is too small, TCP will perform unnecessary retransmissions. If it is too large, TCP will wait a long time before retransmitting if the first segment is lost. Also, the convergence may be slow, as this problem indicates.
  a. Choose $\alpha = 0.85$ and $SRTT(0) = 3$ seconds, and assume all measured RTT values $= 1$ second and no packet loss. What is $SRTT(19)$? *Hint:* Equation (20.3) can be rewritten to simplify the calculation, using the expression $(1 - \alpha^n)/(1 - \alpha)$.
  b. Now let $SRTT(0) = 1$ second and assume measured RTT values $= 3$ seconds and no packet loss. What is $SRTT(19)$?

20.17 A poor implementation of TCP's sliding-window scheme can lead to extremely poor performance. There is a phenomenon known as the Silly Window Syndrome (SWS), which can easily cause degradation in performance by several factors of 10. As an example of SWS, consider an application that is engaged in a lengthy file transfer, and that TCP is transferring this file in 200-octet segments. The receiver initially provides a credit of 1000. The sender uses up this window with 5 segments of 200 octets. Now suppose that the receiver returns an acknowledgment to each segment and provides an additional credit of 200 octets for every received segment. From the receiver's point of view, this opens the window back up to 1000 octets. However, from the sender's point of view, if the first acknowledgment arrives after five segments have been sent, a window of only 200 octets becomes available. Assume that at some point, the receiver calculates a window of 200 octets but has only 50 octets to send until it reaches a "push" point. It therefore sends 50 octets in one segment, followed by 150 octets in the next segment, and then resumes transmission of 200-octet segments. What might now happen to cause a performance problem? State the SWS in more general terms.

20.18 TCP mandates that both the receiver and the sender should incorporate mechanisms to cope with SWS.
  a. Suggest a strategy for the receiver. *Hint:* Let the receiver "lie" about how much buffer space is available under certain circumstances. State a reasonable rule of thumb for this.
  b. Suggest a strategy for the sender. *Hint:* Consider the relationship between the maximum possible send window and what is currently available to send.

20.19 In Equation (20.5), rewrite the definition of $SRTT(K + 1)$ so that it is a function of $SERR(K + 1)$. Interpret the result.

20.20 A TCP entity opens a connection and uses slow start. Approximately how many round-trip times are required before TCP can send N segments.

20.21 Although slow start with congestion avoidance is an effective technique for coping with congestion, it can result in long recovery times in high-speed networks, as this problem demonstrates.
  a. Assume a round-trip time of 60 ms (about what might occur across a continent) and a link with an available bandwidth of 1 Gbps and a segment size of 576 octets. Determine the window size needed to keep the pipe full and the time it will take to reach that window size after a timeout using Jacobson's approach.
  b. Repeat (a) for a segment size of 16 Kbytes.

CHAPTER **21**

NETWORK SECURITY

KEY POINTS

- Network security threats fall into two categories. **Passive threats**, sometimes referred to as eavesdropping, involve attempts by an attacker to obtain information relating to a communication. **Active threats** involve some modification of the transmitted data or the creation of false transmissions.

- By far the most important automated tool for network and communications security is **encryption**. With **symmetric encryption**, two parties share a single encryption/decryption key. The principal challenge with symmetric encryption is the distribution and protection of the keys. A **public-key encryption** scheme involves two keys, one for encryption and a paired key for decryption. The party that generated the key pair keeps one of the keys private and makes the other key public.

- Symmetric encryption and public-key encryption are often combined in secure networking applications. Symmetric encryption is used to encrypt transmitted data, using a one-time or short-term session key. The session key can be distributed by a trusted key distribution center or transmitted in encrypted form using public-key encryption. Public-key encryption is also used to create digital signatures, which can authenticate the source of transmitted messages.

- The Secure Sockets Layer (SSL) and the follow-on Internet standard known as Transport Layer Security (TLS) provide security services for Web transactions.

- A security enhancement used with both IPv4 and IPv6, called IPSec, provides both confidentiality and authentication mechanisms.

The requirements of **information security** within an organization have undergone two major changes in the last several decades. Before the widespread use of data processing equipment, the security of information felt to be valuable to an organization was provided primarily by physical and administrative means. An example of the former is the use of rugged filing cabinets with a combination lock for storing sensitive documents. An example of the latter is personnel screening procedures used during the hiring process.

With the introduction of the computer, the need for automated tools for protecting files and other information stored on the computer became evident. This is especially the case for a shared system, such as a time-sharing system, and the need is even more acute for systems that can be accessed over a public telephone or data network. The generic name for the collection of tools designed to protect data and to thwart hackers is **computer security**. Although this is an important topic, it is beyond the scope of this book.

The second major change that affected security is the introduction of distributed systems and the use of networks and communications facilities for carrying data between terminal user and computer and between computer and computer. **Network security** measures are needed to protect data during their transmission and to guarantee that data transmissions are authentic.

The essential technology underlying virtually all automated network and computer security applications is encryption. Two fundamental approaches are in use:

symmetric encryption and public-key encryption, also known as asymmetric encryption. As we look at the various approaches to network security, these two types of encryption will be explored.

The chapter begins with an overview of the requirements for network security. Next, we look at symmetric encryption and its use to provide confidentiality. This is followed by a discussion of message authentication. We then look at the use of public-key encryption and digital signatures. The chapter closes with an examination of security features in SSL and IPSec.

21.1 SECURITY REQUIREMENTS AND ATTACKS

To understand the types of threats to security that exist, we need to have a definition of security requirements. Computer and network security address four requirements:

- **Confidentiality:** Requires that data only be accessible by authorized parties. This type of access includes printing, displaying, and other forms of disclosure, including simply revealing the existence of an object.
- **Integrity:** Requires that data can be modified only by authorized parties. Modification includes writing, changing, changing status, deleting, and creating.
- **Availability:** Requires that data are available to authorized parties.
- **Authenticity:** Requires that a host or service be able to verify the identity of a user.

A useful means of classifying security attacks (RFC 2828) is in terms of *passive attacks* and *active attacks*. A passive attack attempts to learn or make use of information from the system but does not affect system resources. An active attack attempts to alter system resources or affect their operation.

Passive Attacks

Passive attacks are in the nature of eavesdropping on, or monitoring of, transmissions. The goal of the opponent is to obtain information that is being transmitted. Two types of passive attacks are release of message contents and traffic analysis.

The **release of message contents** is easily understood. A telephone conversation, an electronic mail message, or a transferred file may contain sensitive or confidential information. We would like to prevent an opponent from learning the contents of these transmissions.

A second type of passive attack, **traffic analysis**, is subtler. Suppose that we had a way of masking the contents of messages or other information traffic so that opponents, even if they captured the message, could not extract the information from the message. The common technique for masking contents is encryption. Even with encryption protection in place, an opponent might still be able to observe the pattern of these messages. The opponent could determine the location and identity of communicating hosts and could observe the frequency and length of messages being exchanged. This information might be useful in guessing the nature of the communication that was taking place.

Passive attacks are very difficult to detect because they do not involve any alteration of the data. Typically, the message traffic is sent and received in an apparently normal fashion and neither the sender nor receiver is aware that a third party has read the messages or observed the traffic pattern. However, it is feasible to prevent the success of these attacks, usually by means of encryption. Thus, the emphasis in dealing with passive attacks is on prevention rather than detection.

Active Attacks

Active attacks involve some modification of the data stream or the creation of a false stream and can be subdivided into four categories: masquerade, replay, modification of messages, and denial of service.

A **masquerade** takes place when one entity pretends to be a different entity. A masquerade attack usually includes one of the other forms of active attack. For example, authentication sequences can be captured and replayed after a valid authentication sequence has taken place, thus enabling an authorized entity with few privileges to obtain extra privileges by impersonating an entity that has those privileges.

Replay involves the passive capture of a data unit and its subsequent retransmission to produce an unauthorized effect.

Modification of messages simply means that some portion of a legitimate message is altered, or that messages are delayed or reordered, to produce an unauthorized effect. For example, a message meaning "Allow John Smith to read confidential file *accounts*" is modified to mean "Allow Fred Brown to read confidential file *accounts.*"

The **denial of service** prevents or inhibits the normal use or management of communications facilities. This attack may have a specific target; for example, an entity may suppress all messages directed to a particular destination (e.g., the security audit service). Another form of service denial is the disruption of an entire network or a server, either by disabling the network server, or by overloading it with messages so as to degrade performance.

Active attacks present the opposite characteristics of passive attacks. Whereas passive attacks are difficult to detect, measures are available to prevent their success. On the other hand, it is quite difficult to prevent active attacks absolutely, because to do so would require physical protection of all communications facilities and paths at all times. Instead, the goal is to detect them and to recover from any disruption or delays caused by them. Because the detection has a deterrent effect, it may also contribute to prevention.

21.2 CONFIDENTIALITY WITH SYMMETRIC ENCRYPTION

The universal technique for providing confidentiality for transmitted data is symmetric encryption. This section looks first at the basic concept of symmetric encryption, followed by a discussion of the two most important symmetric encryption algorithms: the Data Encryption Standard (DES) and the Advanced Encryption Standard (AES). We then examine the application of symmetric encryption to achieve confidentiality.

Symmetric Encryption

Symmetric encryption, also referred to as conventional encryption or single-key encryption, was the only type of encryption in use prior to the introduction of public-key encryption in the late 1970s. Countless individuals and groups, from Julius Caesar to the German U-boat force to present-day diplomatic, military, and commercial users, have used symmetric encryption for secret communication. It remains by far the more widely used of the two types of encryption.

A symmetric encryption scheme has five ingredients (Figure 21.1):

- **Plaintext:** This is the original message or data that is fed into the algorithm as input.
- **Encryption algorithm:** The encryption algorithm performs various substitutions and transformations on the plaintext.
- **Secret key:** The secret key is also input to the encryption algorithm. The exact substitutions and transformations performed by the algorithm depend on the key.
- **Ciphertext:** This is the scrambled message produced as output. It depends on the plaintext and the secret key. For a given message, two different keys will produce two different ciphertexts.
- **Decryption algorithm:** This is essentially the encryption algorithm run in reverse. It takes the ciphertext and the secret key and produces the original plaintext.

There are two requirements for secure use of symmetric encryption:

1. We need a strong encryption algorithm. At a minimum, we would like the algorithm to be such that an opponent who knows the algorithm and has access to one or more ciphertexts would be unable to decipher the ciphertext or figure out the key. This requirement is usually stated in a stronger form: The opponent should be unable to decrypt ciphertext or discover the key even if he or she is in possession of a number of ciphertexts together with the plaintext that produced each ciphertext.
2. Sender and receiver must have obtained copies of the secret key in a secure fashion and must keep the key secure. If someone can discover the key and knows the algorithm, all communication using this key is readable.

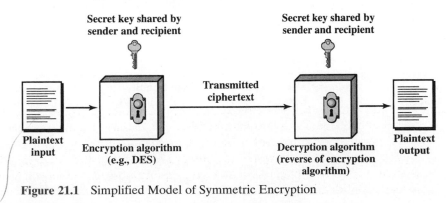

Figure 21.1 Simplified Model of Symmetric Encryption

There are two general approaches to attacking a symmetric encryption scheme. The first attack is known as **cryptanalysis**. Cryptanalytic attacks rely on the nature of the algorithm plus perhaps some knowledge of the general characteristics of the plaintext or even some sample plaintext-ciphertext pairs. This type of attack exploits the characteristics of the algorithm to attempt to deduce a specific plaintext or to deduce the key being used. If the attack succeeds in deducing the key, the effect is catastrophic: All future and past messages encrypted with that key are compromised.

The second method, known as the **brute-force** attack, is to try every possible key on a piece of ciphertext until an intelligible translation into plaintext is obtained. On average, half of all possible keys must be tried to achieve success. Table 21.1 shows how much time is involved for various key sizes. The table shows results for each key size, assuming that it takes 1 μs to perform a single decryption, a reasonable order of magnitude for today's computers. With the use of massively parallel organizations of microprocessors, it may be possible to achieve processing rates many orders of magnitude greater. The final column of the table considers the results for a system that can process 1 million keys per microsecond. As one can see, at this performance level, a 56-bit key can no longer be considered computationally secure.

Encryption Algorithms

The most commonly used symmetric encryption algorithms are block ciphers. A block cipher processes the plaintext input in fixed-size blocks and produces a block of ciphertext of equal size for each plaintext block. The two most important symmetric algorithms, both of which are block ciphers, are the Data Encryption Standard (DES) and the Advanced Encryption Standard (AES).

Data Encryption Standard

DES has been the dominant encryption algorithm since its introduction in 1977. However, because DES uses only a 56-bit key, it was only a matter of time before computer processing speed made DES obsolete. In 1998, the Electronic Frontier Foundation (EFF) announced that it had broken a DES challenge using a special-purpose "DES cracker" machine that was built for less than $250,000. The attack took less than three days. The EFF has published a detailed description of the machine, enabling others to build their own cracker [EFF98]. And, of course, hardware prices will continue to drop as speeds increase, making DES worthless.

Table 21.1 Average Time Required for Exhaustive Key Search

Key Size (bits)	Number of Alternative Keys	Time Required at 1 Encryption/μs	Time Required at 10^6 Encryptions/μs
32	$2^{32} = 4.3 \times 10^9$	2^{31} μs = 35.8 minutes	2.15 milliseconds
56	$2^{56} = 7.2 \times 10^{16}$	2^{55} μs = 1142 years	10.01 hours
128	$2^{128} = 3.4 \times 10^{38}$	2^{127} μs = 5.4×10^{24} years	5.4×10^{18} years
168	$2^{168} = 3.7 \times 10^{50}$	2^{167} μs = 5.9×10^{36} years	5.9×10^{30} years

The life of DES was extended by the use of triple DES (3DES), which involves repeating the basic DES algorithm three times, using either two or three unique keys, for a key size of 112 or 168 bits.

The principal drawback of 3DES is that the algorithm is relatively sluggish in software. A secondary drawback is that both DES and 3DES use a 64-bit block size. For reasons of both efficiency and security, a larger block size is desirable.

Advanced Encryption Standard

Because of these drawbacks, 3DES is not a reasonable candidate for long-term use. As a replacement, the National Institute of Standards and Technology (NIST) in 1997 issued a call for proposals for a new Advanced Encryption Standard (AES), which should have a security strength equal to or better than 3DES and significantly improved efficiency. In addition to these general requirements, NIST specified that AES must be a symmetric block cipher with a block length of 128 bits and support for key lengths of 128, 192, and 256 bits. Evaluation criteria include security, computational efficiency, memory requirements, hardware and software suitability, and flexibility. In 2001, AES was issued as a federal information processing standard (FIPS 197).

In the description of this section, we assume a key length of 128 bits, which is likely to be the one most commonly implemented.

Figure 21.2 shows the overall structure of AES. The input to the encryption and decryption algorithms is a single 128-bit block. In FIPS 197, this block is depicted as a square matrix of bytes. This block is copied into the **State** array, which is modified at each stage of encryption or decryption. After the final stage, **State** is copied to an output matrix. Similarly, the 128-bit key is depicted as a square matrix of bytes. This key is then expanded into an array of key schedule words; each word is four bytes and the total key schedule is 44 words for the 128-bit key. The ordering of bytes within a matrix is by column. So, for example, the first four bytes of a 128-bit plaintext input to the encryption cipher occupy the first column of the **in** matrix, the second four bytes occupy the second column, and so on. Similarly, the first four bytes of the expanded key, which form a word, occupy the first column of the **w** matrix.

The following comments give some insight into AES:

1. The key that is provided as input is expanded into an array of forty-four 32-bit words, $\mathbf{w}[i]$. Four distinct words (128 bits) serve as a round key for each round.
2. Four different stages are used, one of permutation and three of substitution:
   - **Substitute bytes:** Uses a table, referred to as an S-box[1] to perform a byte-by-byte substitution of the block
   - **Shift rows:** A simple permutation that is performed row by row
   - **Mix columns:** A substitution that alters each byte in a column as a function of all of the bytes in the column
   - **Add round key:** A simple bitwise XOR of the current block with a portion of the expanded key

---

[1] The term *S-box*, or substitution box, is commonly used in the description of symmetric ciphers to refer to a table used for a table-lookup type of substitution mechanism.

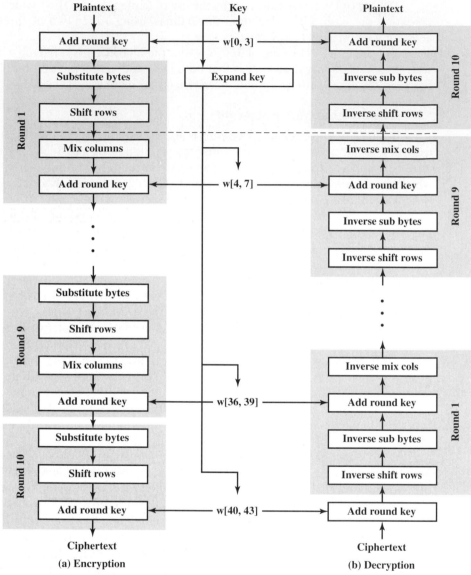

Figure 21.2 AES Encryption and Decryption

3. The structure is quite simple. For both encryption and decryption, the cipher begins with an Add Round Key stage, followed by nine rounds that each includes all four stages, followed by a tenth round of three stages. Figure 21.3 depicts the structure of a full encryption round.

4. Only the Add Round Key stage makes use of the key. For this reason, the cipher begins and ends with an Add Round Key stage. Any other stage, applied at the beginning or end, is reversible without knowledge of the key and so would add no security.

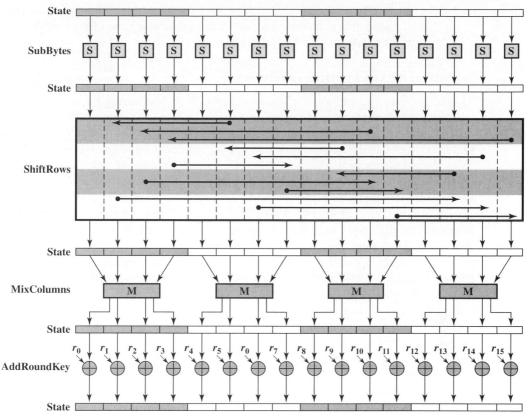

Figure 21.3 AES Encryption Round

5. The Add Round Key stage by itself would not be formidable. The other three stages together scramble the bits, but by themselves would provide no security because they do not use the key. We can view the cipher as alternating operations of XOR encryption (Add Round Key) of a block, followed by scrambling of the block (the other three stages), followed by XOR encryption, and so on. This scheme is both efficient and highly secure.

6. Each stage is easily reversible. For the Substitute Byte, Shift Row, and Mix Columns stages, an inverse function is used in the decryption algorithm. For the Add Round Key stage, the inverse is achieved by XORing the same round key to the block, using the result that $A \oplus A \oplus B = B$.

7. As with most block ciphers, the decryption algorithm makes use of the expanded key in reverse order. However, the decryption algorithm is not identical to the encryption algorithm. This is a consequence of the particular structure of AES.

8. Once it is established that all four stages are reversible, it is easy to verify that decryption does recover the plaintext. Figure 21.2 lays out encryption and decryption going in opposite vertical directions. At each horizontal point (e.g., the dashed line in the figure), **State** is the same for both encryption and decryption.

9. The final round of both encryption and decryption consists of only three stages. Again, this is a consequence of the particular structure of AES and is required to make the cipher reversible.

Location of Encryption Devices

The most powerful, and most common, approach to countering the threats to network security is encryption. In using encryption, we need to decide what to encrypt and where the encryption gear should be located. As Figure 21.4 indicates, there are two fundamental alternatives: link encryption and end-to-end encryption.

With link encryption, each vulnerable communications link is equipped on both ends with an encryption device. Thus, all traffic over all communications links is secured. Although this requires a lot of encryption devices in a large network, it provides a high level of security. One disadvantage of this approach is that the message must be decrypted each time it enters a packet switch; this is necessary because the switch must read the address (virtual circuit number) in the packet header to route the packet. Thus, the message is vulnerable at each switch. If this is a public packet-switching network, the user has no control over the security of the nodes.

With end-to-end encryption, the encryption process is carried out at the two end systems. The source host or terminal encrypts the data. The data, in encrypted form, are then transmitted unaltered across the network to the destination terminal or host. The destination shares a key with the source and so is able to decrypt the data. This approach would seem to secure the transmission against attacks on the network links or switches. There is, however, still a weak spot.

Consider the following situation. A host connects to an X.25 packet-switching network, sets up a virtual circuit to another host, and is prepared to transfer data to that other host using end-to-end encryption. Data are transmitted over such a network

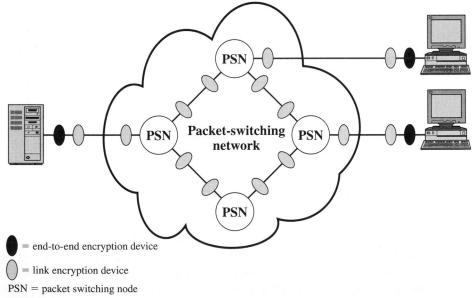

● = end-to-end encryption device

◗ = link encryption device

PSN = packet switching node

Figure 21.4   Encryption Across a Packet-Switching Network

in the form of packets, consisting of a header and some user data. What part of each packet will the host encrypt? Suppose that the host encrypts the entire packet, including the header. This will not work because, remember, only the other host can perform the decryption. The packet-switching node will receive an encrypted packet and be unable to read the header. Therefore, it will not be able to route the packet. It follows that the host may only encrypt the user data portion of the packet and must leave the header in the clear, so that the network can read it.

Thus, with end-to-end encryption, the user data are secure. However, the traffic pattern is not, because packet headers are transmitted in the clear. To achieve greater security, both link and end-to-end encryption are needed, as is shown in Figure 21.4.

To summarize, when both forms are employed, the host encrypts the user data portion of a packet using an end-to-end encryption key. The entire packet is then encrypted using a link encryption key. As the packet traverses the network, each switch decrypts the packet using a link encryption key to read the header and then encrypts the entire packet again for sending it out on the next link. Now the entire packet is secure except for the time that the packet is actually in the memory of a packet switch, at which time the packet header is in the clear.

Key Distribution

For symmetric encryption to work, the two parties to a secure exchange must have the same key, and that key must be protected from access by others. Furthermore, frequent key changes are usually desirable to limit the amount of data compromised if an attacker learns the key. Therefore, the strength of any cryptographic system rests with the key distribution technique, a term that refers to the means of delivering a key to two parties that wish to exchange data, without allowing others to see the key. Key distribution can be achieved in a number of ways. For two parties A and B,

1. A key could be selected by A and physically delivered to B.
2. A third party could select the key and physically deliver it to A and B.
3. If A and B have previously and recently used a key, one party could transmit the new key to the other, encrypted using the old key.
4. If A and B each have an encrypted connection to a third party C, C could deliver a key on the encrypted links to A and B.

Options 1 and 2 call for manual delivery of a key. For link encryption, this is a reasonable requirement, because each link encryption device is only going to be exchanging data with its partner on the other end of the link. However, for end-to-end encryption, manual delivery is awkward. In a distributed system, any given host or terminal may need to engage in exchanges with many other hosts and terminals over time. Thus, each device needs a number of keys, supplied dynamically. The problem is especially difficult in a wide area distributed system.

Option 3 is a possibility for either link encryption or end-to-end encryption, but if an attacker ever succeeds in gaining access to one key, then all subsequent keys are revealed. Even if frequent changes are made to the link encryption keys, these should be done manually. To provide keys for end-to-end encryption, option 4 is preferable.

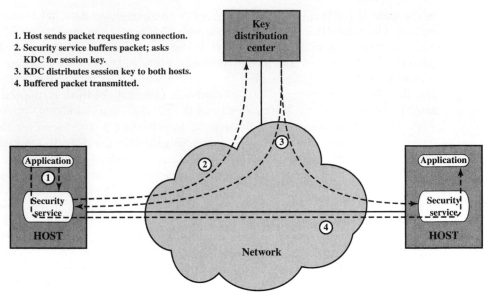

1. Host sends packet requesting connection.
2. Security service buffers packet; asks
   KDC for session key.
3. KDC distributes session key to both hosts.
4. Buffered packet transmitted.

Figure 21.5   Automatic Key Distribution for Connection-Oriented Protocol

Figure 21.5 illustrates an implementation of option 4 for end-to-end encryption. In the figure, link encryption is ignored. This can be added, or not, as required. For this scheme, two kinds of keys are identified:

- **Session key:** When two end systems (hosts, terminals, etc.) wish to communicate, they establish a logical connection (e.g., virtual circuit). For the duration of that logical connection, all user data are encrypted with a one-time session key. At the conclusion of the session, or connection, the session key is destroyed.

- **Permanent key:** A permanent key is a key used between entities for the purpose of distributing session keys.

The configuration consists of the following elements:

- **Key distribution center:** The key distribution center determines which systems are allowed to communicate with each other. When permission is granted for two systems to establish a connection, the key distribution center provides a one-time session key for that connection.

- **Security service module (SSM):** This module, which may consist of functionality at one protocol layer, performs end-to-end encryption and obtains session keys on behalf of users.

The steps involved in establishing a connection are shown in the figure. When one host wishes to set up a connection to another host, it transmits a connection-request packet (step 1). The SSM saves that packet and applies to the KDC for permission to establish the connection (step 2). The communication between the SSM and the KDC is encrypted using a master key shared only by this SSM and the KDC. If the KDC approves the connection request, it generates the session key and delivers it to the two appropriate SSMs, using a unique permanent key for each SSM (step 3). The requesting SSM can now release the connection request packet, and a connection is set up between the two end systems (step 4). All user data exchanged between the two end systems are encrypted by their respective SSMs using the one-time session key.

The automated key distribution approach provides the flexibility and dynamic characteristics needed to allow a number of terminal users to access a number of hosts and for the hosts to exchange data with each other.

Another approach to key distribution uses public-key encryption, which is discussed in Section 21.4.

Traffic Padding

We mentioned that, in some cases, users are concerned about security from traffic analysis. With the use of link encryption, packet headers are encrypted, reducing the opportunity for traffic analysis. However, it is still possible in those circumstances for an attacker to assess the amount of traffic on a network and to observe the amount of traffic entering and leaving each end system. An effective countermeasure to this attack is traffic padding.

Traffic padding is a function that produces ciphertext output continuously, even in the absence of plaintext. A continuous random data stream is generated. When plaintext is available, it is encrypted and transmitted. When input plaintext is not present, the random data are encrypted and transmitted. This makes it impossible for an attacker to distinguish between true data flow and noise and therefore impossible to deduce the amount of traffic.

21.3 MESSAGE AUTHENTICATION AND HASH FUNCTIONS

Encryption protects against passive attack (eavesdropping). A different requirement is to protect against active attack (falsification of data and transactions). Protection against such attacks is known as message authentication.

Approaches to Message Authentication

A message, file, document, or other collection of data is said to be authentic when it is genuine and came from its alleged source. Message authentication is a procedure that allows communicating parties to verify that received messages are authentic. The two important aspects are to verify that the contents of the message have not been altered and that the source is authentic. We may also wish to verify a message's timeliness (it has not been artificially delayed and replayed) and sequence relative to other messages flowing between two parties.

Authentication Using Symmetric Encryption

It is possible to perform authentication simply by the use of symmetric encryption. If we assume that only the sender and receiver share a key (which is as it should be), then only the genuine sender would be able successfully to encrypt a message for the other participant. Furthermore, if the message includes an error-detection code and a sequence number, the receiver is assured that no alterations have been made and that sequencing is proper. If the message also includes a time-stamp, the receiver is assured that the message has not been delayed beyond that normally expected for network transit.

Message Authentication without Message Encryption

In this section, we examine several approaches to message authentication that do not rely on message encryption. In all of these approaches, an authentication tag is generated and appended to each message for transmission. The message itself is not encrypted and can be read at the destination independent of the authentication function at the destination.

Because the approaches discussed in this section do not encrypt the message, message confidentiality is not provided. Because symmetric encryption will provide authentication, and because it is widely used with readily available products, why not simply use such an approach, which provides both confidentiality and authentication? [DAVI89] suggests three situations in which message authentication without confidentiality is preferable:

1. There are a number of applications in which the same message is broadcast to a number of destinations. For example, notification to users that the network is now unavailable or an alarm signal in a control center. It is cheaper and more reliable to have only one destination responsible for monitoring authenticity. Thus, the message must be broadcast in plaintext with an associated message authentication tag. The responsible system performs authentication. If a violation occurs, the other destination systems are alerted by a general alarm.

2. Another possible scenario is an exchange in which one side has a heavy load and cannot afford the time to decrypt all incoming messages. Authentication is carried out on a selective basis, with messages chosen at random for checking.

3. Authentication of a computer program in plaintext is an attractive service. The computer program can be executed without having to decrypt it every time, which would be wasteful of processor resources. However, if a message authentication tag were attached to the program, it could be checked whenever assurance is required of the integrity of the program.

Thus, there is a place for both authentication and encryption in meeting security requirements.

Message Authentication Code

One authentication technique involves the use of a secret key to generate a small block of data, known as a message authentication code, that is appended to the message. This technique assumes that two communicating parties, say A and B, share a common secret key K_{AB}. When A has a message M to send to B, it calculates the message authentication code as a function of the message and the key: $MAC_M = F(K_{AB}, M)$. The message plus code are transmitted to the intended recipient. The recipient performs the same calculation on the received message, using the same secret key, to generate a new message authentication code. The received

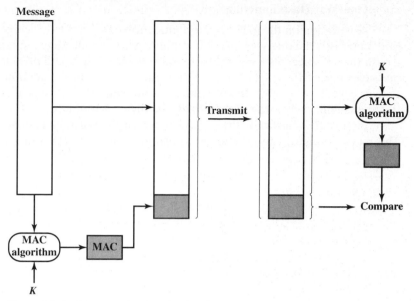

Figure 21.6 Message Authentication Using a Message Authentication Code (MAC)

code is compared to the calculated code (Figure 21.6). If we assume that only the receiver and the sender know the identity of the secret key, and if the received code matches the calculated code, then

1. The receiver is assured that the message has not been altered. If an attacker alters the message but does not alter the code, then the receiver's calculation of the code will differ from the received code. Because the attacker is assumed not to know the secret key, the attacker cannot alter the code to correspond to the alterations in the message.
2. The receiver is assured that the message is from the alleged sender. Because no one else knows the secret key, no one else could prepare a message with a proper code.
3. If the message includes a sequence number (such as is used with X.25, HDLC, and TCP), then the receiver can be assured of the proper sequence, because an attacker cannot successfully alter the sequence number.

A number of algorithms could be used to generate the code. The National Bureau of Standards, in its publication *DES Modes of Operation*, recommends the use of DES. DES is used to generate an encrypted version of the message, and the last number of bits of ciphertext are used as the code. A 16- or 32-bit code is typical.

The process just described is similar to encryption. One difference is that the authentication algorithm need not be reversible, as it must for decryption. It turns out that because of the mathematical properties of the authentication function, it is less vulnerable to being broken than encryption.

One-Way Hash Function

A variation on the message authentication code that has received much attention recently is the one-way hash function. As with the message authentication code, a hash function accepts a variable-size message M as input and produces a fixed-size message digest $H(M)$ as output. Unlike the MAC, a hash function does not also take a secret key as input. To authenticate a message, the message digest is sent with the message in such a way that the message digest is authentic.

Figure 21.7 illustrates three ways in which the message can be authenticated. The message digest can be encrypted using symmetric encryption (part a); if it is

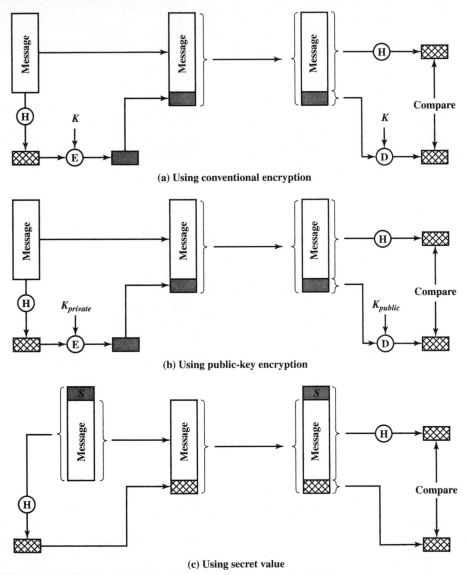

(a) Using conventional encryption

(b) Using public-key encryption

(c) Using secret value

Figure 21.7   Message Authentication Using a One-Way Hash Function

assumed that only the sender and receiver share the encryption key, then authenticity is assured. The message digest can also be encrypted using public-key encryption (part b); this is explained in Section 21.4. The public-key approach has two advantages: It provides a digital signature as well as message authentication, and it does not require the distribution of keys to communicating parties.

These two approaches have an advantage over approaches that encrypt the entire message in that less computation is required. Nevertheless, there has been interest in developing a technique that avoids encryption altogether. Several reasons for this interest are pointed out in [TSUD92]:

- Encryption software is quite slow. Even though the amount of data to be encrypted per message is small, there may be a steady stream of messages into and out of a system.

- Encryption hardware costs are nonnegligible. Low-cost chip implementations of DES are available, but the cost adds up if all nodes in a network must have this capability.

- Encryption hardware is optimized toward large data sizes. For small blocks of data, a high proportion of the time is spent in initialization/invocation overhead.

- Encryption algorithms may be covered by patents. Some encryption algorithms, such as the RSA public-key algorithm, are patented and must be licensed, adding a cost.

- Encryption algorithms may be subject to export control.

Figure 21.7c shows a technique that uses a hash function but no encryption for message authentication. This technique assumes that two communicating parties, say A and B, share a common secret value S_{AB}. When A has a message to send to B, it calculates the hash function over the concatenation of the secret value and the message: $MD_M = H(S_{AB} \| M)$.[2] It then sends $[M \| MD_M]$ to B. Because B possesses S_{AB}, it can recompute $H(S_{AB} \| M)$ and verify MD_M. Because the secret value itself is not sent, it is not possible for an attacker to modify an intercepted message. As long as the secret value remains secret, it is also not possible for an attacker to generate a false message.

This third technique, using a shared secret value, is the one adopted for IP security; it has also been specified for SNMPv3, discussed in Chapter 22.

Secure Hash Functions

The one-way hash function, or secure hash function, is important not only in message authentication but in digital signatures. In this section, we begin with a discussion of requirements for a secure hash function. Then we look at one of the most important hash functions, SHA-1.

---

[2] $\|$ denotes concatenation.

Hash Function Requirements

The purpose of a hash function is to produce a "fingerprint" of a file, message, or other block of data. To be useful for message authentication, a hash function H must have the following properties:

1. H can be applied to a block of data of any size.
2. H produces a fixed-length output.
3. $H(x)$ is relatively easy to compute for any given x, making both hardware and software implementations practical.
4. For any given code h, it is computationally infeasible to find x such that $H(x) = h$.
5. For any given block x, it is computationally infeasible to find $y \neq x$ with $H(y) = H(x)$.
6. It is computationally infeasible to find any pair (x, y) such that $H(x) = H(y)$.

The first three properties are requirements for the practical application of a hash function to message authentication.

The fourth property is the one-way property: It is easy to generate a code given a message, but virtually impossible to generate a message given a code. This property is important if the authentication technique involves the use of a secret value (Figure 21.7c). The secret value itself is not sent; however, if the hash function is not one way, an attacker can easily discover the secret value: If the attacker can observe or intercept a transmission, the attacker obtains the message M and the hash code $MD_M = H(S_{AB} \| M)$. The attacker then inverts the hash function to obtain $S_{AB} \| M = H^{-1}(MD_M)$. Because the attacker now has both M and $S_{AB} \| M$, it is a trivial matter to recover S_{AB}.

The fifth property guarantees that it is impossible to find an alternative message with the same hash value as a given message. This prevents forgery when an encrypted hash code is used (Figures 21.7a and b). If this property were not true, an attacker would be capable of the following sequence: First, observe or intercept a message plus its encrypted hash code; second, generate an unencrypted hash code from the message; third, generate an alternate message with the same hash code.

A hash function that satisfies the first five properties in the preceding list is referred to as a weak hash function. If the sixth property is also satisfied, then it is referred to as a strong hash function. The sixth property protects against a sophisticated class of attack known as the birthday attack.[3]

In addition to providing authentication, a message digest also provides data integrity. It performs the same function as a frame check sequence: If any bits in the message are accidentally altered in transit, the message digest will be in error.

The SHA-1 Secure Hash Function

The Secure Hash Algorithm (SHA) was developed by NIST and published as a federal information processing standard (FIPS 180) in 1993; a revised version was issued as FIPS 180-1 in 1995 and is generally referred to as SHA-1.

---

[3] See [STAL03] for a discussion of birthday attacks.

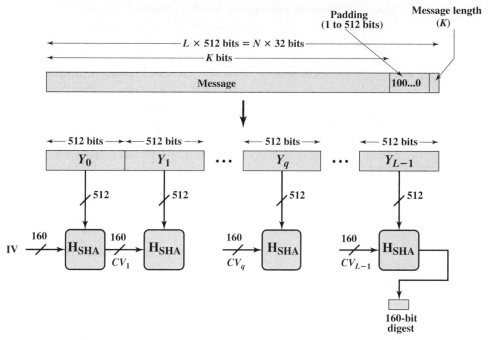

Figure 21.8   Message Digest Generation Using SHA-1

The algorithm takes as input a message with a maximum length of less than 2^{64} bits and produces as output a 160-bit message digest. The input is processed in 512-bit blocks. Figure 21.8 depicts the overall processing of a message to produce a digest. The processing consists of the following steps:

Step 1: Append padding bits. The message is padded so that its length is congruent to 448 modulo 512 (length = 448 mod 512). That is, the length of the padded message is 64 bits less than a multiple of 512 bits. Padding is always added, even if the message is already of the desired length. Thus, the number of padding bits is in the range of 1 to 512. The padding consists of a single 1-bit followed by the necessary number of 0-bits.

Step 2: Append length. A block of 64 bits is appended to the message. This block is treated as an unsigned 64-bit integer (most significant byte first) and contains the length of the original message (before the padding). The inclusion of a length value makes more difficult a kind of attack known as a padding attack [TSUD92].

The outcome of the first two steps yields a message that is an integer multiple of 512 bits in length. In Figure 21.8, the expanded message is represented as the sequence of 512-bit blocks $Y_0, Y_1, \ldots, Y_{L-1}$, so that the total length of the expanded message is $L \times 512$ bits. Equivalently, the result is a multiple of 16 32-bit words.

Step 3: Initialize MD buffer. A 160-bit buffer is used to hold intermediate and final results of the hash function.

Step 4: Process message in 512-bit (16-word) blocks. The heart of the algorithm is a module that consists of four rounds of processing of 20 steps each. The four rounds have a similar structure, but each uses a different primitive logical function. Each round takes as input the current 512-bit block being processed (Y_q) and the 160-bit buffer value and updates the contents of the buffer.

Step 5: Output. After all L 512-bit blocks have been processed, the output from the Lth stage is the 160-bit message digest.

The SHA-1 algorithm has the property that every bit of the hash code is a function of every bit in the input. The algorithm produces results that are well mixed; that is, it is unlikely that two messages chosen at random, even if they exhibit similar regularities, will have the same hash code. Unless there is some hidden weakness in SHA-1, which has not so far been published, the difficulty of coming up with two messages having the same message digest is on the order of 2^{80} operations, while the difficulty of finding a message with a given digest is on the order of 2^{160} operations.

21.4 PUBLIC-KEY ENCRYPTION AND DIGITAL SIGNATURES

Of equal importance to symmetric encryption is public-key encryption, which finds use in message authentication and key distribution. This section looks first at the basic concept of public-key encryption, followed by a discussion of digital signatures. Then we discuss the most widely-used public-key algorithm: RSA. We then look at the problem of key distribution.

Public–Key Encryption

Public-key encryption, first publicly proposed by Diffie and Hellman in 1976 [DIFF76], is the first truly revolutionary advance in encryption in literally thousands of years. For one thing, public-key algorithms are based on mathematical functions rather than on simple operations on bit patterns. More important, public-key cryptography is asymmetric, involving the use of two separate keys, in contrast to symmetric encryption, which uses only one key. The use of two keys has profound consequences in the areas of confidentiality, key distribution, and authentication.

Before proceeding, we should first mention several common misconceptions concerning public-key encryption. One is that public-key encryption is more secure from cryptanalysis than symmetric encryption. In fact, the security of any encryption scheme depends on (1) the length of the key and (2) the computational work involved in breaking a cipher. There is nothing in principle about either symmetric or public-key encryption that makes one superior to another from the viewpoint of resisting cryptanalysis. A second misconception is that public-key encryption is a general-purpose technique that has made symmetric encryption obsolete. On the contrary, because of the computational overhead of current public-key encryption schemes, there seems no foreseeable likelihood that symmetric encryption will be abandoned. Finally, there is a feeling that key distribution is trivial when using public-

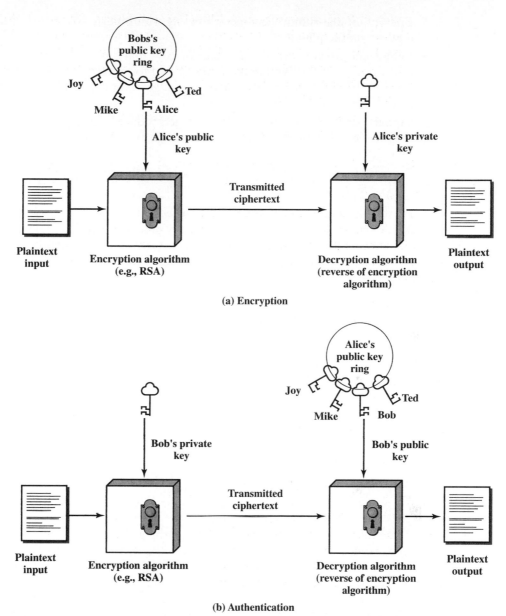

Figure 21.9 Public-Key Encryption

key encryption, compared to the rather cumbersome handshaking involved with key distribution centers for symmetric encryption. In fact, some form of protocol is needed, often involving a central agent, and the procedures involved are no simpler or any more efficient than those required for symmetric encryption.

A public-key encryption scheme has six ingredients (Figure 21.9):

- **Plaintext:** This is the readable message or data that is fed into the algorithm as input.

- **Encryption algorithm:** The encryption algorithm performs various transformations on the plaintext.
- **Public and private key:** This is a pair of keys that have been selected so that if one is used for encryption the other is used for decryption. The exact transformations performed by the encryption algorithm depend on the public or private key that is provided as input.
- **Ciphertext:** This is the scrambled message produced as output. It depends on the plaintext and the key. For a given message, two different keys will produce two different ciphertexts.
- **Decryption algorithm:** This algorithm accepts the ciphertext and the matching key and produces the original plaintext.

As the names suggest, the public key of the pair is made public for others to use, while the private key is known only to its owner. A general-purpose public-key cryptographic algorithm relies on one key for encryption and a different but related key for decryption. Furthermore, these algorithms have the following important characteristics:

- It is computationally infeasible to determine the decryption key given only knowledge of the cryptographic algorithm and the encryption key.
- For most public-key schemes, either of the two related keys can be used for encryption, with the other used for decryption.

The essential steps are the following:

1. Each user generates a pair of keys to be used for the encryption and decryption of messages.
2. Each user places one of the two keys in a public register or other accessible file. This is the public key. The companion key is kept private. As Figure 21.9 suggests, each user maintains a collection of public keys obtained from others.
3. If Bob wishes to send a private message to Alice, Bob encrypts the message using Alice's public key.
4. When Alice receives the message, she decrypts it using her private key. No other recipient can decrypt the message because only Alice knows Alice's private key.

With this approach, all participants have access to public keys, and private keys are generated locally by each participant and therefore need never be distributed. As long as a user protects his or her private key, incoming communication is secure. At any time, a user can change the private key and publish the companion public key to replace the old public key.

Digital Signature

Public-key encryption can be used in another way, as illustrated in Figure 21.9b. Suppose that Bob wants to send a message to Alice and, although it is not important that the message be kept secret, he wants Alice to be certain that the message is indeed from him. In this case Bob uses his own private key to encrypt the message. When Alice receives the ciphertext, she finds that she can decrypt it with Bob's public key, thus proving that the message must have been encrypted by Bob. No one else has Bob's private key and therefore no one else could have created a ciphertext that could be decrypted with Bob's public key. Therefore, the entire encrypted message serves as a **digital signature**. In addition, it is impossible to alter the message without access to Bob's private key, so the message is authenticated both in terms of source and in terms of data integrity.

In the preceding scheme, the entire message is encrypted, which, although validating both author and contents, requires a great deal of storage. Each document must be kept in plaintext to be used for practical purposes. A copy also must be stored in ciphertext so that the origin and contents can be verified in case of a dispute. A more efficient way of achieving the same results is to encrypt a small block of bits that is a function of the document. Such a block, called an authenticator, must have the property that it is infeasible to change the document without changing the authenticator. If the authenticator is encrypted with the sender's private key, it serves as a signature that verifies origin, content, and sequencing. A secure hash code such as SHA-1 can serve this function.

It is important to emphasize that the digital signature does not provide confidentiality. That is, the message being sent is safe from alteration but not safe from eavesdropping. This is obvious in the case of a signature based on a portion of the message, because the rest of the message is transmitted in the clear. Even in the case of complete encryption, there is no protection of confidentiality because any observer can decrypt the message by using the sender's public key.

The RSA Public-Key Encryption Algorithm

One of the first public-key schemes was developed in 1977 by Ron Rivest, Adi Shamir, and Len Adleman at MIT and first published in 1978 [RIVE78]. The RSA scheme has since that time reigned supreme as the only widely accepted and implemented approach to public-key encryption. RSA is a block cipher in which the plaintext and ciphertext are integers between 0 and $n - 1$ for some n.

Encryption and decryption are of the following form, for some plaintext block M and ciphertext block C:

$$C = M^e \bmod n$$
$$M = C^d \bmod n = (M^e)^d \bmod n = M^{ed} \bmod n$$

Both sender and receiver must know the values of n and e, and only the receiver knows the value of d. This is a public-key encryption algorithm with a public key of $KU = \{e, n\}$ and a private key of $KR = \{d, n\}$. For this algorithm to be satisfactory for public-key encryption, the following requirements must be met:

1. It is possible to find values of e, d, n such that $M^{ed} = M \bmod n$ for all $M < n$.
2. It is relatively easy to calculate M^e and C^d for all values of $M < n$.
3. It is infeasible to determine d given e and n.

The first two requirements are easily met. The third requirement can be met for large values of e and n.

Key Generation

Select p, q	p and q both prime, $p \neq q$
Calculate $n = p \times q$	
Calculate $\phi(n) = (p - 1)(q - 1)$	
Select integer e	$\gcd(\phi(n), e) = 1; 1 < e < \phi(n)$
Calculate d	$de \bmod \phi(n) = 1$
Public key	$KU = \{e, n\}$
Private key	$KR = \{d, n\}$

Encryption

Plaintext:	$M < n$
Ciphertext:	$C = M^e \pmod{n}$

Decryption

Ciphertext:	C
Plaintext:	$M = C^d \pmod{n}$

Figure 21.10   The RSA Algorithm

Figure 21.10 summarizes the RSA algorithm. Begin by selecting two prime numbers, p and q and calculating their product n, which is the modulus for encryption and decryption. Next, we need the quantity $\phi(n)$, referred to as the Euler totient of n, which is the number of positive integers less than n and relatively prime to n.[4] Then select an integer e that is relatively prime to $\phi(n)$ [i.e., the greatest common divisor of e and $\phi(n)$ is 1]. Finally, calculate d such that $de \bmod \phi(n) = 1$. It can be shown that d and e have the desired properties.

Suppose that user A has published its public key and that user B wishes to send the message M to A. Then B calculates $C = M^e \pmod{n}$ and transmits C. On receipt of this ciphertext, user A decrypts by calculating $M = C^d \pmod{n}$.

An example, from [SING99], is shown in Figure 21.11. For this example, the keys were generated as follows:

1. Select two prime numbers, $p = 17$ and $q = 11$.
2. Calculate $n = pq = 17 \times 11 = 187$.
3. Calculate $\phi(n) = (p - 1)(q - 1) = 16 \times 10 = 160$.

---

[4] It can be shown that when n is a product of two primes, pq, then $\phi(n) = (p - 1)(q - 1)$.

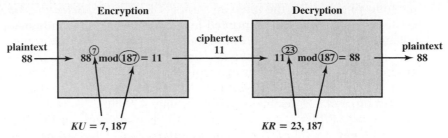

Figure 21.11 Example of RSA Algorithm

4. Select e such that e is relatively prime to $\phi(n) = 160$ and less than $\phi(n)$; we choose $e = 7$.
5. Determine d such that de mod $160 = 1$ and $d < 160$. The correct value is $d = 23$, because $23 \times 7 = 161 = 10 \times 160 + 1$.

The resulting keys are public key $KU = [7, 187]$ and private key $KR = [23, 187]$. The example shows the use of these keys for a plaintext input of $M = 88$. For encryption, we need to calculate $C = 88^7$ mod 187. Exploiting the properties of modular arithmetic, we can do this is follows:

88^7 mod $187 = [(88^4$ mod $187) \times (88^2$ mod $187) \times (88^1$ mod $187)]$ mod 187
88^1 mod $187 = 88$
88^2 mod $187 = 7744$ mod $187 = 77$
88^4 mod $187 = 59{,}969{,}536$ mod $187 = 132$
88^7 mod $187 = (88 \times 77 \times 132)$ mod $187 = 894{,}432$ mod $187 = 11$

For decryption, we calculate $M = 11^{23}$ mod 187:

11^{23} mod $187 = [(11^1$ mod $187) \times (11^2$ mod $187) \times (11^4$ mod $187) \times$
$\qquad\qquad (11^8$ mod $187) \times (11^8$ mod $187)]$ mod 187
11^1 mod $187 = 11$
11^2 mod $187 = 121$
11^4 mod $187 = 14{,}641$ mod $187 = 55$
11^8 mod $187 = 214{,}358{,}881$ mod $187 = 33$
11^{23} mod $187 = (11 \times 121 \times 55 \times 33 \times 33)$ mod $187 = 79{,}720{,}245$ mod $187 = 88$

There are two possible approaches to defeating the RSA algorithm. The first is the brute force approach: Try all possible private keys. Thus, the larger the number of bits in e and d, the more secure the algorithm. However, because the calculations involved, both in key generation and in encryption/decryption, are complex, the larger the size of the key, the slower the system will run.

Most discussions of the cryptanalysis of RSA have focused on the task of factoring n into its two prime factors. For a large n with large prime factors, factoring is a hard problem, but not as hard as it used to be. A striking illustration of this is the following. In 1977, the three inventors of RSA dared *Scientific American* readers to decode a cipher they printed in Martin Gardner's "Mathematical Games" column. They offered a $100 reward for the return of a plaintext sentence, an event they predicted might not occur for some 40 quadrillion years. In April of 1994, a group working over the Internet and using over 1600 computers claimed the prize after only eight months of work [LEUT94]. This challenge used a public-key size (length of n) of 129 decimal digits, or around 428 bits. This result does not invalidate the use of RSA; it simply means that larger key sizes must be used. Currently, a 1024-bit key size (about 300 decimal digits) is considered strong enough for virtually all applications.

Key Management

With symmetric encryption, a fundamental requirement for two parties to communicate securely is that they share a secret key. Suppose Bob wants to create a messaging application that will enable him to exchange e-mail securely with anyone who has access to the Internet or to some other network that the two of them share. Suppose Bob wants to do this using only symmetric encryption. With symmetric encryption, Bob and his correspondent, say, Alice, must come up with a way to share a unique secret key that no one else knows. How are they going to do that? If Alice is in the next room from Bob, Bob could generate a key and write it down on a piece of paper or store it on a diskette and hand it to Alice. But if Alice is on the other side of the continent or the world, what can Bob do? Well, he could encrypt this key using symmetric encryption and e-mail it to Alice, but this means that Bob and Alice must share a secret key to encrypt this new secret key. Furthermore, Bob and everyone else who uses this new e-mail package faces the same problem with every potential correspondent: Each pair of correspondents must share a unique secret key.

How to distribute secret keys securely is the most difficult problem for symmetric encryption. This problem is wiped away with public-key encryption by the simple fact that the private key is never distributed. If Bob wants to correspond with Alice and other people, he generates a single pair of keys, one private and one public. He keeps the private key secure and broadcasts the public key to all and sundry. If Alice does the same, then Bob has Alice's public key, Alice has Bob's public key, and they can now communicate securely. When Bob wishes to communicate with Alice, Bob can do the following:

1. Prepare a message.
2. Encrypt that message using symmetric encryption with a one-time symmetric session key.
3. Encrypt the session key using public-key encryption with Alice's public key.
4. Attach the encrypted session key to the message and send it to Alice.

Only Alice is capable of decrypting the session key and therefore of recovering the original message.

It is only fair to point out, however, that we have replaced one problem with another. Alice's private key is secure because she need never reveal it; however, Bob must be sure that the public key with Alice's name written all over it is in fact Alice's public key. Someone else could have broadcast a public key and said it was Alice's.

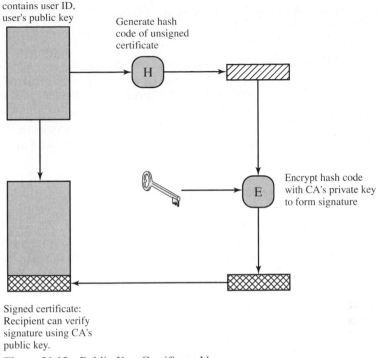

Unsigned certificate:
contains user ID,
user's public key

Generate hash
code of unsigned
certificate

Encrypt hash code
with CA's private key
to form signature

Signed certificate:
Recipient can verify
signature using CA's
public key.

Figure 21.12   Public-Key Certificate Use

The solution to this problem is the **public-key certificate**. In essence, a certificate consists of a public key plus a User ID of the key owner, with the whole block signed by a trusted third party. Typically, the third party is a certificate authority (CA) that is trusted by the user community, such as a government agency or a financial institution. A user can present his or her public key to the authority in a secure manner and obtain a certificate. The user can then publish the certificate. Anyone needing this user's public key can obtain the certificate and verify that it is valid by way of the attached trusted signature. Figure 21.12 illustrates the process.

21.5 SECURE SOCKET LAYER AND TRANSPORT LAYER SECURITY

One of the most widely used security services is the Secure Sockets Layer (SSL) and the follow-on Internet standard known as Transport Layer Security (TLS), the latter defined in RFC 2246. SSL is a general-purpose service implemented as a set of protocols that rely on TCP. At this level, there are two implementation choices. For full generality, SSL (or TLS) could be provided as part of the underlying protocol suite and therefore be transparent to applications. Alternatively, SSL can be embedded in specific packages. For example, Netscape and Microsoft Explorer browsers come equipped with SSL, and most Web servers have implemented the protocol.

This section discusses SSLv3. Only minor changes are found in TLS.

SSL Architecture

SSL is designed to make use of TCP to provide a reliable end-to-end secure service. SSL is not a single protocol but rather two layers of protocols, as illustrated in Figure 21.13.

The SSL Record Protocol provides basic security services to various higher-layer protocols. In particular, the Hypertext Transfer Protocol (HTTP), which provides the transfer service for Web client/server interaction, can operate on top of SSL. Three higher-layer protocols are defined as part of SSL: the Handshake Protocol, The Change Cipher Spec Protocol, and the Alert Protocol. These SSL-specific protocols are used in the management of SSL exchanges and are examined later in this section.

Two important SSL concepts are the SSL session and the SSL connection, which are defined in the specification as follows:

- **Connection:** A connection is a transport (in the OSI layering model definition) that provides a suitable type of service. For SSL, such connections are peer-to-peer relationships. The connections are transient. Every connection is associated with one session.
- **Session:** An SSL session is an association between a client and a server. Sessions are created by the Handshake Protocol. Sessions define a set of cryptographic security parameters, which can be shared among multiple connections. Sessions are used to avoid the expensive negotiation of new security parameters for each connection.

Between any pair of parties (applications such as HTTP on client and server), there may be multiple secure connections. In theory, there may also be multiple simultaneous sessions between parties, but this feature is not used in practice.

SSL Record Protocol

The SSL Record Protocol provides two services for SSL connections:

- **Confidentiality:** The Handshake Protocol defines a shared secret key that is used for symmetric encryption of SSL payloads.

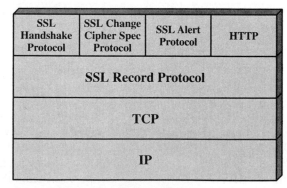

Figure 21.13 SSL Protocol Stack

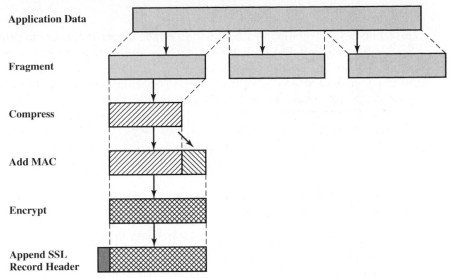

Figure 21.14   SSL Record Protocol Operation

- **Message Integrity:** The Handshake Protocol also defines a shared secret key that is used to form a message authentication code (MAC).

Figure 21.14 indicates the overall operation of the SSL Record Protocol. The first step is **fragmentation**. Each upper-layer message is fragmented into blocks of 2^{14} bytes (16384 bytes) or less. Next, **compression** is optionally applied. The next step in processing is to compute a **message authentication code** over the compressed data. Next, the compressed message plus the MAC are **encrypted** using symmetric encryption.

The final step of SSL Record Protocol processing is to prepend a header, consisting of the following fields:

- **Content Type (8 bits):** The higher-layer protocol used to process the enclosed fragment.
- **Major Version (8 bits):** Indicates major version of SSL in use. For SSLv3, the value is 3.
- **Minor Version (8 bits):** Indicates minor version in use. For SSLv3, the value is 0.
- **Compressed Length (16 bits):** The length in bytes of the plaintext fragment (or compressed fragment if compression is used). The maximum value is $2^{14} + 2048$.

The content types that have been defined are change_cipher_spec, alert, handshake, and application_data. The first three are the SSL-specific protocols, discussed next. Note that no distinction is made among the various applications (e.g., HTTP) that might use SSL; the content of the data created by such applications is opaque to SSL.

The Record Protocol then transmits the resulting unit in a TCP segment. Received data are decrypted, verified, decompressed, and reassembled and then delivered to higher-level users.

Change Cipher Spec Protocol

The Change Cipher Spec Protocol is one of the three SSL-specific protocols that use the SSL Record Protocol, and it is the simplest. This protocol consists of a single message, which consists of a single byte with the value 1. The sole purpose of this message is to cause the pending state to be copied into the current state, which updates the cipher suite to be used on this connection.

Alert Protocol

The Alert Protocol is used to convey SSL-related alerts to the peer entity. As with other applications that use SSL, alert messages are compressed and encrypted, as specified by the current state.

Each message in this protocol consists of two bytes. The first byte takes the value warning(1) or fatal(2) to convey the severity of the message. If the level is fatal, SSL immediately terminates the connection. Other connections on the same session may continue, but no new connections on this session may be established. The second byte contains a code that indicates the specific alert. An example of a fatal alert is an incorrect MAC. An example of a nonfatal alert is a close_notify message, which notifies the recipient that the sender will not send any more messages on this connection.

Handshake Protocol

The most complex part of SSL is the Handshake Protocol. This protocol allows the server and client to authenticate each other and to negotiate an encryption and MAC algorithm and cryptographic keys to be used to protect data sent in an SSL record. The Handshake Protocol is used before any application data is transmitted.

The Handshake Protocol consists of a series of messages exchanged by client and server. Figure 21.15 shows the initial exchange needed to establish a logical connection between client and server. The exchange can be viewed as having four phases.

Phase 1 is used to initiate a logical connection and to establish the security capabilities that will be associated with it. The exchange is initiated by the client, which sends a client_hello message with the following parameters:

- **Version:** The highest SSL version understood by the client.
- **Random:** A client-generated random structure, consisting of a 32-bit timestamp and 28 bytes generated by a secure random number generator. These values are used during key exchange to prevent replay attacks.
- **Session ID:** A variable-length session identifier. A nonzero value indicates that the client wishes to update the parameters of an existing connection or create a new connection on this session. A zero value indicates that the client wishes to establish a new connection on a new session.
- **CipherSuite:** This is a list that contains the combinations of cryptographic algorithms supported by the client, in decreasing order of preference. Each element of the list (each cipher suite) defines both a key exchange algorithm and a CipherSpec.
- **Compression Method:** This is a list of the compression methods the client supports.

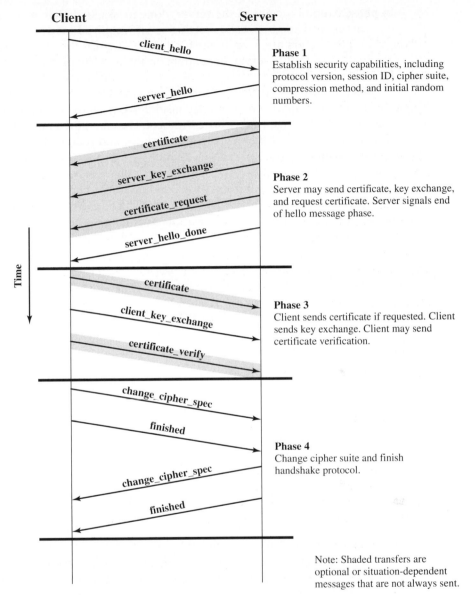

Figure 21.15   Handshake Protocol Action

After sending the client_hello message, the client waits for the server_hello message, which contains the same parameters as the client_hello message.

The details of **phase 2** depend on the underlying public-key encryption scheme that is used. In some cases, the server passes a certificate to the client, possibly additional key information, and a request for a certificate from the client.

The final message in Phase 2, and one that is always required, is the server_done message, which is sent by the server to indicate the end of the server hello and associated messages. After sending this message, the server will wait for a client response.

In **phase 3**, upon receipt of the server_done message, the client should verify that the server provided a valid certificate if required and check that the server_hello parameters are acceptable. If all is satisfactory, the client sends one or more messages back to the server, depending on the underlying public-key scheme.

Phase 4 completes the setting up of a secure connection. The client sends a change_cipher_spec message and copies the pending CipherSpec into the current CipherSpec. Note that this message is not considered part of the Handshake Protocol but is sent using the Change Cipher Spec Protocol. The client then immediately sends the finished message under the new algorithms, keys, and secrets. The finished message verifies that the key exchange and authentication processes were successful.

In response to these two messages, the server sends its own change_cipher_spec message, transfers the pending to the current CipherSpec, and sends its finished message. At this point the handshake is complete and the client and server may begin to exchange application layer data.

21.6 IPV4 AND IPV6 SECURITY

In 1994, the Internet Architecture Board (IAB) issued a report entitled *Security in the Internet Architecture* (RFC 1636). The report stated the general consensus that the Internet needs more and better security, and it identified key areas for security mechanisms. Among these were the need to secure the network infrastructure from unauthorized monitoring and control of network traffic and the need to secure end-user-to-end-user traffic using authentication and encryption mechanisms.

These concerns are fully justified. As confirmation, the 2002 annual report from the Computer Emergency Response Team (CERT) lists over 82,000 reported security incidents [CERT03]. The most serious types of attacks included IP spoofing, in which intruders create packets with false IP addresses and exploit applications that use authentication based on IP; and various forms of eavesdropping and packet sniffing, in which attackers read transmitted information, including logon information and database contents.

In response to these issues, the IAB included authentication and encryption as necessary security features in the next-generation IP, which has been issued as IPv6. Fortunately, these security capabilities were designed to be usable both with IPv4 and IPv6. This means that vendors can begin offering these features now, and many vendors do now have some IPSec capability in their products.

Applications of IPSec

IPSec provides the capability to secure communications across a LAN, across private and public WANs, and across the Internet. Examples of its use include the following:

- **Secure branch office connectivity over the Internet:** A company can build a secure virtual private network over the Internet or over a public WAN. This enables a business to rely heavily on the Internet and reduce its need for private networks, saving costs and network management overhead.

- **Secure remote access over the Internet:** An end user whose system is equipped with IP security protocols can make a local call to an Internet service provider (ISP) and gain secure access to a company network. This reduces the cost of toll charges for traveling employees and telecommuters.
- **Establishing extranet and intranet connectivity with partners:** IPSec can be used to secure communication with other organizations, ensuring authentication and confidentiality and providing a key exchange mechanism.
- **Enhancing electronic commerce security:** Even though some Web and electronic commerce applications have built-in security protocols, the use of IPSec enhances that security.

The principal feature of IPSec that enables it to support these varied applications is that it can encrypt and/or authenticate *all* traffic at the IP level. Thus, all distributed applications, including remote logon, client/server, e-mail, file transfer, Web access, and so on, can be secured.

The Scope of IPSec

IPSec provides three main facilities: an authentication-only function referred to as Authentication Header (AH), a combined authentication/encryption function called Encapsulating Security Payload (ESP), and a key exchange function. For virtual private networks, both authentication and encryption are generally desired, because it is important both to (1) assure that unauthorized users do not penetrate the virtual private network and (2) assure that eavesdroppers on the Internet cannot read messages sent over the virtual private network. Because both features are generally desirable, most implementations are likely to use ESP rather than AH. The key exchange function allows for manual exchange of keys as well as an automated scheme.

The IPSec specification is quite complex and covers numerous documents. The most important of these, issued in November of 1998, are RFCs 2401, 2402, 2406, and 2408. In this section, we provide an overview of some of the most important elements of IPSec.

Security Associations

A key concept that appears in both the authentication and confidentiality mechanisms for IP is the security association (SA). An association is a one-way relationship between a sender and a receiver that affords security services to the traffic carried on it. If a peer relationship is needed, for two-way secure exchange, then two security associations are required. Security services are afforded to an SA for the use of AH or ESP, but not both.

A security association is uniquely identified by three parameters:

- **Security parameters index (SPI):** A bit string assigned to this SA and having local significance only. The SPI is carried in AH and ESP headers to enable the receiving system to select the SA under which a received packet will be processed.

- **IP destination address:** Currently, only unicast addresses are allowed; this is the address of the destination endpoint of the SA, which may be an end user system or a network system such as a firewall or router.
- **Security protocol identifier:** This indicates whether the association is an AH or ESP security association.

Hence, in any IP packet, the security association is uniquely identified by the Destination Address in the IPv4 or IPv6 header and the SPI in the enclosed extension header (AH or ESP).

An IPSec implementation includes a security association data base that defines the parameters associated with each SA. A security association is defined by the following parameters:

- **Sequence number counter:** A 32-bit value used to generate the sequence number field in AH or ESP headers.
- **Sequence counter overflow:** A flag indicating whether overflow of the sequence number counter should generate an auditable event and prevent further transmission of packets on this SA.
- **Anti-replay window:** Used to determine whether an inbound AH or ESP packet is a replay, by defining a sliding window within which the sequence number must fall.
- **AH information:** Authentication algorithm, keys, key lifetimes, and related parameters being used with AH.
- **ESP information:** Encryption and authentication algorithm, keys, initialization values, key lifetimes, and related parameters being used with ESP.
- **Lifetime of this security association:** A time interval or byte count after which an SA must be replaced with a new SA (and new SPI) or terminated, plus an indication of which of these actions should occur.
- **IPSec protocol mode:** Tunnel, transport, or wildcard (required for all implementations). These modes are discussed later in this section.
- **Path MTU:** Any observed path maximum transmission unit (maximum size of a packet that can be transmitted without fragmentation) and aging variables (required for all implementations).

The key management mechanism that is used to distribute keys is coupled to the authentication and privacy mechanisms only by way of the security parameters index. Hence, authentication and privacy have been specified independent of any specific key management mechanism.

Authentication Header

The authentication header provides support for data integrity and authentication of IP packets. The data integrity feature ensures that undetected modification to a packet's content in transit is not possible. The authentication feature enables an end system or network device to authenticate the user or application and filter traffic

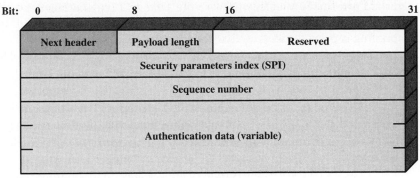

Figure 21.16 IPSec Authentication Header

accordingly; it also prevents the address spoofing attacks observed in today's Internet. The AH also guards against the replay attack described later in this section.

Authentication is based on the use of a message authentication code (MAC), as described in Section 21.3; hence the two parties must share a secret key.

The authentication header consists of the following fields (Figure 21.16):

- **Next Header (8 bits):** Identifies the type of header immediately following this header.
- **Payload Length (8 bits):** Length of authentication header in 32-bit words, minus 2. For example, the default length of the authentication data field is 96 bits, or three 32-bit words. With a three-word fixed header, there are a total of six words in the header, and the Payload Length field has a value of 4.
- **Reserved (16 bits):** For future use.
- **Security Parameters Index (32 bits):** Identifies a security association.
- **Sequence Number (32 bits):** A monotonically increasing counter value.
- **Authentication Data (variable):** A variable-length field (must be an integral number of 32-bit words) that contains the integrity check value (ICV), or MAC, for this packet.

The authentication data field is calculated over the following:

- IP header fields that either do not change in transit (immutable) or that are predictable in value upon arrival at the endpoint for the AH SA. Fields that may change in transit and whose value on arrival are unpredictable are set to zero for purposes of calculation at both source and destination.
- The AH header other than the Authentication Data field. The Authentication Data field is set to zero for purposes of calculation at both source and destination.
- The entire upper-level protocol data, which is assumed to be immutable in transit.

For IPv4, examples of immutable fields are Internet Header Length and Source Address. An example of a mutable but predictable field is the Destination Address (with loose or strict source routing). Examples of mutable fields that are zeroed prior to ICV calculation are the Time to Live and Header Checksum fields. Note that both source and destination address fields are protected, so that address spoofing is prevented.

For IPv6, examples in the base header are Version (immutable), Destination Address (mutable but predictable), and Flow Label (mutable and zeroed for calculation).

Encapsulating Security Payload

The encapsulating security payload provides confidentiality services, including confidentiality of message contents and limited traffic flow confidentiality. As an optional feature, ESP can also provide an authentication service.

Figure 21.17 shows the format of an ESP packet. It contains the following fields:

- **Security Parameters Index (32 bits):** Identifies a security association.
- **Sequence Number (32 bits):** A monotonically increasing counter value.
- **Payload Data (variable):** This is a upper-level segment protected by encryption.
- **Padding (0–255 bytes):** May be required if the encryption algorithm requires the plaintext to be a multiple of some number of octets.
- **Pad Length (8 bits):** Indicates the number of pad bytes immediately preceding this field.
- **Next Header (8 bits):** Identifies the type of data contained in the payload data field by identifying the first header in that payload (for example, an extension header in IPv6, or an upper-layer protocol such as TCP).
- **Authentication Data (variable):** A variable-length field (must be an integral number of 32-bit words) that contains the integrity check value computed over the ESP packet minus the Authentication Data field.

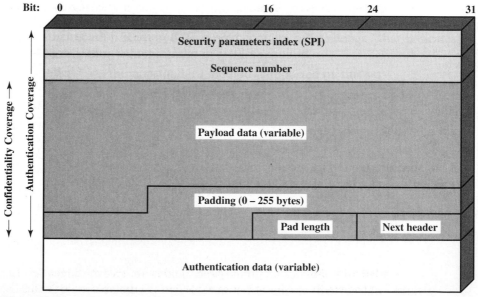

Figure 21.17   IPSec ESP Format

21.7 RECOMMENDED READING AND WEB SITES

The topics in this chapter are covered in greater detail in [STAL03]. For coverage of cryptographic algorithms, [SCHN96] is an essential reference work; it contains descriptions of virtually every cryptographic algorithm and protocol published in the last 15 years.

SCHN96   Schneier, B. *Applied Cryptography.* New York: Wiley, 1996.

STAL03   Stallings, W. *Cryptography and Network Security: Principles and Practice, 3rd ed..* Upper Saddle River, NJ: Prentice Hall, 2003.

Recommended Web Sites:

- **COAST:** Comprehensive set of links related to cryptography and network security
- **IETF Security Area:** Provides up-to-date information on Internet security standardization efforts
- **IEEE Technical Committee on Security and Privacy:** Provides copies of IEEE's newsletter and information on IEEE-related activities

21.8 KEY TERMS, REVIEW QUESTIONS, AND PROBLEMS

Key Terms

active attack	hash function	public-key certificate
authenticity	integrity	public-key encryption
availability	IP Security (IPSec)	replay
Advanced Encryption Standard (AES)	key distribution	RSA
brute-force attack	key distribution center	secret key
ciphertext	key management	secure hash function
confidentiality	masquerade	Secure Socket Layer (SSL)
cryptanalysis	message authentication	session key
Data Encryption Standard (DES)	message authentication code (MAC)	SHA-1
decryption algorithm	one-way hash function	symmetric encryption
denial of service	passive attack	traffic analysis
digital signature	plaintext	traffic padding
encryption algorithm	private key	Transport Layer Security (TLS)
	public key	

Review Questions

21.1 What is the difference between passive and active security threats?

21.2 List and briefly define categories of passive and active security threats.

21.3 What are DES and triple DES?

21.4   How is the AES expected to be an improvement over triple DES?

21.5   Explain traffic padding.

21.6   List and briefly define various approaches to message authentication.

21.7   What is a secure hash function?

21.8   Explain the difference between symmetric encryption and public-key encryption.

21.9   What are the distinctions among the terms *public key*, *private key*, *secret key*?

21.10   What is a digital signature?

21.11   What is a public-key certificate?

21.12   What protocols comprise SSL?

21.13   What is the difference between and SSL connection and an SSL session?

21.14   What services are provided by the SSL Record Protocol?

21.15   What services are provided by IPSec?

Problems

21.1   Give some examples where traffic analysis could jeopardize security. Describe situations where end-to-end encryption combined with link encryption would still allow enough traffic analysis to be dangerous.

21.2   Key distribution schemes using an access control center and/or a key distribution center have central points vulnerable to attack. Discuss the security implications of such centralization.

21.3   Suppose that someone suggests the following way to confirm that the two of you are both in possession of the same secret key. You create a random bit string the length of the key, XOR it with the key, and send the result over the channel. Your partner XORs the incoming block with the key (which should be the same as your key) and sends it back. You check and if what you receive is your original random string, you have verified that your partner has the same secret key, yet neither of you has ever transmitted the key. Is there a flaw in this scheme?

21.4   Prior to the discovery of any specific public-key schemes, such as RSA, an existence proof was developed whose purpose was to demonstrate that public-key encryption is possible in theory. Consider the functions $f_1(x_1) = z_1$; $f_2(x_2, y_2) = z_2$; $f_3(x_3, y_3) = z_3$, where all values are integers with $1 \leq x_i, y_i, z_i \leq N$. Function f_1 can be represented by a vector M1 of length N, in which the kth entry is the value of $f_1(k)$. Similarly, f_2 and f_3 can be represented by $N \times N$ matrices M2 and M3. The intent is to represent the encryption/decryption process by table lookups for tables with very large values of N. Such tables would be impractically huge but could, in principle, be constructed. The scheme works as follows: Construct M1 with a random permutation of all integers between 1 and N; that is, each integer appears exactly once in M1. Construct M2 so that each row contains a random permutation of the first N integers. Finally, fill in M3 to satisfy the following condition:

$$f_3(f_2(f_1(k), p), k) = p \text{ for all } k, p \text{ with } 1 \leq k, p \leq N$$

In words,

1. M1 takes an input k and produces an output x.
2. M2 takes inputs x and p giving output z.
3. M3 takes inputs z and k and produces p.

The three tables, once constructed, are made public.
  a. It should be clear that it is possible to construct M3 to satisfy the preceding condition. As an example, fill in M3 for the following simple case:

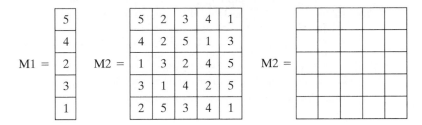

Convention: The ith element of M1 corresponds to $k = i$. The ith row of M2
corresponds to $x = i$; the jth column of M2 corresponds to $p = j$. The ith row of M3
corresponds to $z = i$; the jth column of M3 corresponds to $k = j$.
  b. Describe the use of this set of tables to perform encryption and decryption between two users.
  c. Argue that this is a secure scheme.

21.5 Perform encryption and decryption using the RSA algorithm, as in Figure 21.11, for
the following:
  a. $p = 3; q = 11, d = 7; M = 5$
  b. $p = 5; q = 11, e = 3; M = 9$
  c. $p = 7; q = 11, e = 17; M = 8$
  d. $p = 11; q = 13, e = 11; M = 7$
  e. $p = 17; q = 31, e = 7; M = 2$. *Hint:* Decryption is not as hard as you think; use
  some finesse.

21.6 In a public-key system using RSA, you intercept the ciphertext $C = 10$ sent to a user
whose public key is $e = 5, n = 35$. What is the plaintext M?

21.7 In an RSA system, the public key of a given user is $e = 31, n = 3599$. What is the private key of this user?

21.8 Suppose we have a set of blocks encoded with the RSA algorithm and we don't have
the private key. Assume $n = pq$, e is the public key. Suppose also someone tells us
they know one of the plaintext blocks has a common factor with n. Does this help us
in any way?

21.9 Show how RSA can be represented by matrices M1, M2, and M3 of Problem 21.4.

21.10 Consider the following scheme:
  1. Pick an odd number, E.
  2. Pick two prime numbers, P and Q, where $(P - 1)(Q - 1) - 1$ is evenly divisible
  by E.
  3. Multiply P and Q to get N.
  4. Calculate $D = \dfrac{(P - 1)(Q - 1)(E - 1) + 1}{E}$.

Is this scheme equivalent to RSA? Show why or why not.

21.11 Consider using RSA with a known key to construct a one-way hash function. Then
process a message consisting of a sequence of blocks as follows: Encrypt the first
block, XOR the result with the second block and encrypt again, and so on. Show that
this scheme is not secure by solving the following problem. Given a two-block message B1, B2, and its hash

$$\mathrm{RSAH}(B1, B2) = \mathrm{RSA}(\mathrm{RSA}(B1) \oplus B2)$$

and given an arbitrary block C1, choose C2 so that RSAH(C1, C2) = RSAH(B1, B2).

21.12 In SSL and TLS, why is there a separate Change Cipher Spec Protocol rather than including a change_cipher_spec message in the Handshake Protocol?

21.13 In discussing AH processing, it was mentioned that not all of the fields in an IP header are included in MAC calculation.

  a. For each of the fields in the IPv4 header, indicate whether the field is immutable, mutable but predictable, or mutable (zeroed prior to ICV calculation).

  b. Do the same for the IPv6 header.

  c. Do the same for the IPv6 extension headers.

In each case, justify your decision for each field.

CHAPTER 22

DISTRIBUTED APPLICATIONS

KEY POINTS

- The most widely used protocol for the transmission of electronic mail is SMTP. SMTP assumes that the content of the message is a simple text block. The recent MIME standard expands SMTP to support transmission of multimedia information.

- The rapid growth in the use of the Web is due to the standardization of all the elements that support Web applications. A key element is HTTP, which is the protocol for the exchange of Web-based information between Web browsers and Web servers.

- The most important standardized scheme for supporting network management applications is the Simple Network Management Protocol (SNMP). The original version of SNMP is available on a wide array of products and is widely used. SNMPv2 contains a number of functional enhancements to SNMP and is supplanting it. SNMPv3 provides security features that are added on to SNMPv2.

All of the protocols and functions described so far in Part Five are geared toward one objective: the support of distributed applications that involve the interaction of multiple independent systems. In the OSI model, such applications occupy the application layer and are directly supported by the presentation layer. In the TCP/IP suite, such applications typically rely on TCP or UDP for support.

In this chapter, we examine three applications that give the reader a feel for the range and diversity of applications supported by a communications architecture. The chapter begins with electronic mail, with the SMTP and MIME standards as examples; SMTP provides a basic e-mail service, while MIME adds multimedia capability to SMTP. Next, we look at HTTP, which is the support protocol on which the World Wide Web (WWW) operates. Finally, network management, is a support-type application, designed to assure the effective monitoring and control of a distributed system. The specific protocol that is examined is the Simple Network Management Protocol (SNMP), which is designed to operate in both the TCP/IP and OSI environments.

Refer to Figure 2.15 to see the position within the TCP/IP suite of the protocols discussed in this chapter.

22.1 ELECTRONIC MAIL—SMTP AND MIME

The most heavily used application in virtually any distributed system is electronic mail. The Simple Mail Transfer Protocol (SMTP) has always been the workhorse of the TCP/IP suite. However, SMTP has traditionally been limited to the delivery of simple text messages. In recent years, there has been a demand for the capability of delivery mail containing various types of data, including voice, images, and video clips. To satisfy this requirement, a new electronic mail standard, which builds on SMTP, has been defined: the Multi-Purpose Internet Mail Extension (MIME). In this section, we first examine SMTP, and then look at MIME.

Simple Mail Transfer Protocol (SMTP)

SMTP is the standard protocol for transferring mail between hosts in the TCP/IP suite; it is defined in RFC 821.

Although messages transferred by SMTP usually follow the format defined in RFC 822, described later, SMTP is not concerned with the format or content of messages themselves, with two exceptions. This concept is often expressed by saying that SMTP uses information written on the *envelope* of the mail (message header), but does not look at the contents (message body) of the envelope. The two exceptions are as follows:

1. SMTP standardizes the message character set as 7-bit ASCII.
2. SMTP adds log information to the start of the delivered message that indicates the path the message took.

Basic Electronic Mail Operation

Figure 22.1 illustrates the overall flow of mail in a typical system. Although much of this activity is outside the scope of SMTP, the figure illustrates the context within which SMTP typically operates.

To begin, mail is created by a user agent program in response to user input. Each created message consists of a header that includes the recipient's e-mail address and other information, and a body containing the message to be sent. These messages are then queued in some fashion and provided as input to an SMTP Sender program, which is typically an always-present server program on the host.

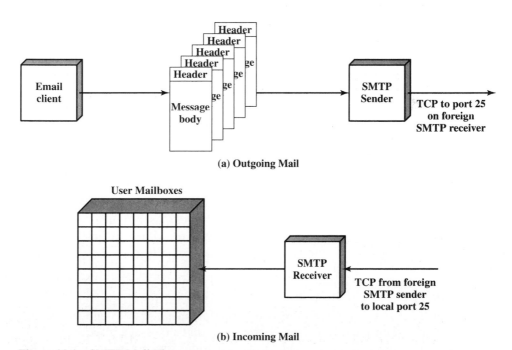

Figure 22.1 SMTP Mail Flow

Although the structure of the outgoing mail queue will differ depending on the host's operating system, each queued message conceptually has two parts:

1. The message text, consisting of
   - The RFC 822 header: This constitutes the message envelope and includes an indication of the intended recipient or recipients.
   - The body of the message, composed by the user.
2. A list of mail destinations.

The list of mail destinations for the message is derived by the user agent from the 822 message header. In some cases, the destination or destinations are literally specified in the message header. In other cases, the user agent may need to expand mailing list names, remove duplicates, and replace mnemonic names with actual mailbox names. If any blind carbon copies (BCCs) are indicated, the user agent needs to prepare messages that conform to this requirement. The basic idea is that the multiple formats and styles preferred by humans in the user interface are replaced by a standardized list suitable for the SMTP send program.

The **SMTP sender** takes messages from the outgoing mail queue and transmits them to the proper destination host via SMTP transactions over one or more TCP connections to port 25 on the target hosts. A host may have multiple SMTP senders active simultaneously if it has a large volume of outgoing mail, and should also have the capability of creating SMTP receivers on demand so that mail from one host cannot delay mail from another.

Whenever the SMTP sender completes delivery of a particular message to one or more users on a specific host, it deletes the corresponding destinations from that message's destination list. When all destinations for a particular message are processed, the message is deleted from the queue. In processing a queue, the SMTP sender can perform a variety of optimizations. If a particular message is sent to multiple users on a single host, the message text need be sent only once. If multiple messages are ready to send to the same host, the SMTP sender can open a TCP connection, transfer the multiple messages, and then close the connection, rather than opening and closing a connection for each message.

The SMTP sender must deal with a variety of errors. The destination host may be unreachable, out of operation, or the TCP connection may fail while mail is being transferred. The sender can requeue the mail for later delivery, but give up after some period rather than keep the message in the queue indefinitely. A common error is a faulty destination address, which can occur due to user input error or because the intended destination user has a new address on a different host. The SMTP sender must either redirect the message if possible or return an error notification to the message's originator.

The **SMTP protocol** is used to transfer a message from the SMTP sender to the SMTP receiver over a TCP connection. SMTP attempts to provide reliable operation but does not guarantee to recover from lost messages. No end-to-end acknowledgment is returned to a message's originator that a message is successfully delivered to the message's recipient, and error indications are not guaranteed to be returned either. However, the SMTP-based mail system is generally considered reliable.

The **SMTP receiver** accepts each arriving message and either places it in the appropriate user mailbox or copies it to the local outgoing mail queue if forwarding is required. The SMTP receiver must be able to verify local mail destinations and deal with errors, including transmission errors and lack of storage capacity.

The SMTP sender is responsible for a message up to the point where the SMTP receiver indicates that the transfer is complete; however, this simply means that the message has arrived at the SMTP receiver, not that the message has been delivered to and retrieved by the intended final recipient. The SMTP receiver's error-handling responsibilities are generally limited to giving up on TCP connections that fail or are inactive for very long periods. Thus, the sender has most of the error recovery responsibility. Errors during completion indication may cause duplicate, but not lost, messages.

In most cases, messages go directly from the mail originator's machine to the destination machine over a single TCP connection. However, mail will occasionally go through intermediate machines via an SMTP forwarding capability, in which case the message must traverse a series of TCP connections between source and destination. One way for this to happen is for the sender to specify a route to the destination in the form of a sequence of servers. A more common event is forwarding required because a user has moved.

It is important to note that the SMTP protocol is limited to the conversation that takes place between the SMTP sender and the SMTP receiver. SMTP's main function is the transfer of messages, although there are some ancillary functions dealing with mail destination verification and handling. The rest of the mail-handling apparatus depicted in Figure 22.1 is beyond the scope of SMTP and may differ from one system to another.

We now turn to a discussion of the main elements of SMTP.

SMTP Overview

The operation of SMTP consists of a series of commands and responses exchanged between the SMTP sender and receiver. The initiative is with the SMTP sender, who establishes the TCP connection. Once the connection is established, the SMTP sender sends commands over the connection to the receiver. Each command generates exactly one reply from the SMTP receiver.

Table 22.1 lists the **SMTP commands**. Each command consists of a single line of text, beginning with a four-letter command code followed in some cases by an argument field. Most replies are a single-line, although multiple-line replies are possible. The table indicates those commands that all receivers must be able to recognize. The other commands are optional and may be ignored by the receiver.

SMTP replies are listed in Table 22.2. Each reply begins with a three-digit code and may be followed by additional information. The leading digit indicates the category of the reply:

- **Positive Completion reply:** The requested action has been successfully completed. A new request may be initiated.
- **Positive Intermediate reply:** The command has been accepted, but the requested action is being held in abeyance, pending receipt of further information. The sender-SMTP should send another command specifying this information. This reply is used in command sequence groups.

Table 22.1 SMTP Commands

Name	Command Form	Description
HELO	HELO <SP> <domain> <CRLF>	Send identification
MAIL	MAIL <SP> FROM:<reverse-path> <CRLF>	Identifies originator of mail
RCPT	RCPT <SP> TO:<forward-path> <CRLF>	Identifies recipient of mail
DATA	DATA <CRLF>	Transfer message text
RSET	RSET <CRLF>	Abort current mail transaction
NOOP	NOOP <CRLF>	No operation
QUIT	QUIT <CRLF>	Close TCP connection
SEND	SEND <SP> FROM:<reverse-path> <CRLF>	Send mail to terminal
SOML	SOML <SP> FROM:<reverse-path> <CRLF>	Send mail to terminal if possible; otherwise to mailbox
SAML	SAML <SP> FROM:<reverse-path> <CRLF>	Send mail to terminal and mailbox
VRFY	VRFY <SP> <string> <CRLF>	Confirm user name
EXPN	EXPN <SP> <string> <CRLF>	Return membership of mailing list
HELP	HELP [<SP> <string>] <CRLF>	Send system-specific documentation
TURN	TURN <CRLF>	Reverse role of sender and receiver

<CRLF> = carriage return, line feed
<SP> = space
Square brackets denote optional elements.
Shaded commands are optional in a conformant SMTP implementation.

- **Transient Negative Completion reply:** The command was not accepted and the requested action did not occur. However, the error condition is temporary and the action may be requested again.
- **Permanent Negative Completion reply:** The command was not accepted and the requested action did not occur.

Basic SMTP operation occurs in three phases: connection setup, exchange of one or more command-response pairs, and connection termination. We examine each phase in turn.

Connection Setup

An SMTP sender will attempt to set up a TCP connection with a target host when it has one or more mail messages to deliver to that host. The sequence is quite simple:

1. The sender opens a TCP connection with the receiver.
2. Once the connection is established, the receiver identifies itself with "220 Service Ready".
3. The sender identifies itself with the HELO command.
4. The receiver accepts the sender's identification with "250 OK".

If the mail service on the destination is unavailable, the destination host returns a "421 Service Not Available" reply in step 2 and the process is terminated.

Table 22.2 SMTP Replies

Code	Description
Positive Completion Reply	
211	System status, or system help reply
214	Help message (Information on how to use the receiver or the meaning of a particular non-standard command; this reply is useful only to the human user)
220	\<domain\> Service ready
221	\<domain\> Service closing transmission channel
250	Requested mail action okay, completed
251	User not local; will forward to \<forward-path\>
Positive Intermediate Reply	
354	Start mail input; end with \<CRLF\>.\<CRLF\>
Transient Negative Completion Reply	
421	\<domain\> Service not available, losing transmission channel (This may be a reply to any command if the service knows it must shut down)
450	Requested mail action not taken: mailbox unavailable (e.g., mailbox busy)
451	Requested action aborted: local error in processing
452	Requested action not taken: insufficient system storage
Permanent Negative Completion Reply	
500	Syntax error, command unrecognized (This may include errors such as command line too long)
501	Syntax error in parameters or arguments
502	Command not implemented
503	Bad sequence of commands
504	Command parameter not implemented
550	Requested action not taken: mailbox unavailable (e.g., mailbox not found, no access)
551	User not local; please try \<forward-path\>
552	Requested mail action aborted: exceeded storage allocation
553	Requested action not taken: mailbox name not allowed (e.g., mailbox syntax incorrect)
554	Transaction failed

Mail Transfer

Once a connection has been established, the SMTP sender may send one or more messages to the SMTP receiver. There are three logical phases to the transfer of a message:

1. A MAIL command identifies the originator of the message.
2. One or more RCPT commands identify the recipients for this message.
3. A DATA command transfers the message text.

The **MAIL command** gives the reverse path, which can be used to report errors. If the receiver is prepared to accept messages from this originator, it returns a "250 OK" reply. Otherwise the receiver returns a reply indicating failure to execute the command (codes 451, 452, 552) or an error in the command (codes 421, 500, 501).

The **RCPT command** identifies an individual recipient of the mail data; multiple recipients are specified by multiple use of this command. A separate reply is returned for each RCPT command, with one of the following possibilities:

1. The receiver accepts the destination with a 250 reply; this indicates that the designated mailbox is on the receiver's system.
2. The destination will require forwarding and the receiver will forward (251).
3. The destination requires forwarding but the receiver will not forward; the sender must resend to the forwarding address (551).
4. A mailbox does not exist for this recipient at this host (550).
5. The destination is rejected due to some other failure to execute (codes 450, 451, 452, 552, 553) or an error in the command (codes 421, 500, 501, 503).

The advantage of using a separate RCPT phase is that the sender will not send the message until it is assured that the receiver is prepared to receive the message for at least one recipient, thereby avoiding the overhead of sending an entire message only to learn that the destination is unknown. Once the SMTP receiver has agreed to receive the mail message for at least one recipient, the SMTP sender uses the **DATA command** to initiate the transfer of the message. If the SMTP receiver is still prepared to receive the message, it returns a 354 message; otherwise the receiver returns a reply indicating failure to execute the command (codes 451, 554) or an error in the command (codes 421, 500, 501, 503). If the 354 reply is returned, the SMTP sender proceeds to send the message over the TCP connection as a sequence of ASCII lines. The end of the message is indicated by a line containing only a period. The SMTP receiver responds with a 250 OK reply if the message is accepted or with the appropriate error code (451, 452, 552, 554).

An example, taken from RFC 821, illustrates the process:

```
S: MAIL FROM:<Smith@Alpha.ARPA>
R: 250 OK

S: RCPT TO: <Jones@Beta.ARPA>
R: 250 OK

S: RCPT TO: <Green@Beta.ARPA>
R: 550 No such user here

S: RCPT TO: <Brown@Beta.ARPA>
R: 250 OK

S: DATA
R: 354 Start mail input; end with <CRLF>.<CRLF>
S: Blah blah blah ...
S: ... etc. etc. etc.

S: <CRLF>.<CRLF>
R: 250 OK
```

The SMTP sender is transmitting mail that originates with the user Smith@ Alpha.ARPA. The message is addressed to three users on machine Beta.ARPA, namely, Jones, Green, and Brown. The SMTP receiver indicates that it has mailboxes for Jones and Brown but does not have information on Green. Because at least one of the intended recipients has been verified, the sender proceeds to send the text message.

Connection Closing

The SMTP sender closes the connection in two steps. First, the sender sends a QUIT command and waits for a reply. The second step is to initiate a TCP close operation for the TCP connection. The receiver initiates its TCP close after sending its reply to the QUIT command.

RFC 822

RFC 822 defines a format for text messages that are sent using electronic mail. The SMTP standard adopts RFC 822 as the format for use in constructing messages for transmission via SMTP. In the RFC 822 context, messages are viewed as having an envelope and contents. The envelope contains whatever information is needed to accomplish transmission and delivery. The contents comprise the object to be delivered to the recipient. The RFC 822 standard applies only to the contents. However, the content standard includes a set of header fields that may be used by the mail system to create the envelope, and the standard is intended to facilitate the acquisition of such information by programs.

An RFC 822 message consists of a sequence of lines of text and uses a general "memo" framework. That is, a message consists of some number of header lines, which follow a rigid format, followed by a body portion consisting of arbitrary text.

A header line usually consists of a keyword, followed by a colon, followed by the keyword's arguments; the format allows a long line to be broken up into several lines. The most frequently used keywords are From, To, Subject, and Date. Here is an example message:

> Date: Tue, 16 Jan 1996 10:37:17 (EST)
>
> From: "William Stallings" <ws@host.com>
>
> Subject: The Syntax in RFC 822
>
> To: Smith@Other-host.com
> Cc: Jones@Yet-Another-Host.com
>
> Hello. This section begins the actual message body, which is delimited from the message heading by a blank line.

Another field that is commonly found in RFC 822 headers is Message-ID. This field contains a unique identifier associated with this message.

Multipurpose Internet Mail Extensions (MIME)

MIME is an extension to the RFC 822 framework that is intended to address some of the problems and limitations of the use of SMTP and RFC 822 for electronic mail. [RODR02] lists the following limitations of the SMTP/822 scheme:

1. SMTP cannot transmit executable files or other binary objects. A number of schemes are in use for converting binary files into a text form that can be used by SMTP mail systems, including the popular UNIX UUencode/UUdecode scheme. However, none of these is a standard or even a de facto standard.
2. SMTP cannot transmit text data that includes national language characters because these are represented by 8-bit codes with values of 128 decimal or higher, and SMTP is limited to 7-bit ASCII.
3. SMTP servers may reject mail messages over a certain size.
4. SMTP gateways that translate between the character codes ASCII and EBCDIC do not use a consistent set of mappings, resulting in translation problems.
5. SMTP gateways to X.400 electronic mail networks cannot handle nontextual data included in X.400 messages.
6. Some SMTP implementations do not adhere completely to the SMTP standards defined in RFC 821. Common problems include the following:
   - Deletion, addition, or reordering of carriage return and linefeed
   - Truncating or wrapping lines longer than 76 characters
   - Removal of trailing white space (tab and space characters)
   - Padding of lines in a message to the same length
   - Conversion of tab characters into multiple space characters

MIME is intended to resolve these problems in a manner that is compatible with existing RFC 822 implementations. The specification is provided in RFCs 2045 through 2049.

Overview

The MIME specification includes the following elements:

1. Five new message header fields are defined, which may be included in an RFC 822 header. These fields provide information about the body of the message.
2. A number of content formats are defined, thus standardizing representations that support multimedia electronic mail.
3. Transfer encodings are defined that enable the conversion of any content format into a form that is protected from alteration by the mail system.

In this subsection, we introduce the five message header fields. The next two subsections deal with content formats and transfer encodings. The five header fields defined in MIME are as follows:

- **MIME-Version:** Must have the parameter value 1.0. This field indicates that the message conforms to the RFCs.

- **Content-Type:** Describes the data contained in the body with sufficient detail that the receiving user agent can pick an appropriate agent or mechanism to present the data to the user or otherwise deal with the data in an appropriate manner.
- **Content-Transfer-Encoding:** Indicates the type of transformation that has been used to represent the body of the message in a way that is acceptable for mail transport.
- **Content-ID:** Used to uniquely identify MIME entities in multiple contexts.
- **Content-Description:** A plaintext description of the object with the body; this is useful when the object is not displayable (e.g., audio data).

Any or all of these fields may appear in a normal RFC 822 header. A compliant implementation must support the MIME-Version, Content-Type, and Content-Transfer-Encoding fields; the Content-ID and Content-Description fields are optional and may be ignored by the recipient implementation.

MIME Content Types

The bulk of the MIME specification is concerned with the definition of a variety of content types. This reflects the need to provide standardized ways of dealing with a wide variety of information representations in a multimedia environment.

Table 22.3 lists the MIME content types. There are seven different major types of content and a total of 14 subtypes. In general, a content type declares the general type of data, and the subtype specifies a particular format for that type of data.

Table 22.3 MIME Content Types

Type	Subtype	Description
Text	Plain	Unformatted text; may be ASCII or ISO 8859.
Multipart	Mixed	The different parts are independent but are to be transmitted together. They should be presented to the receiver in the order that they appear in the mail message.
	Parallel	Differs from Mixed only in that no order is defined for delivering the parts to the receiver.
	Alternative	The different parts are alternative versions of the same information. They are ordered in increasing faithfulness to the original and the recipient's mail system should display the "best" version to the user.
	Digest	Similar to Mixed, but the default type/subtype of each part is message/rfc822.
Message	rfc822	The body is itself an encapsulated message that conforms to RFC 822.
	Partial	Used to allow fragmentation of large mail items, in a way that is transparent to the recipient.
	External-body	Contains a pointer to an object that exists elsewhere.
Image	jpeg	The image is in JPEG format, JFIF encoding.
	gif	The image is in GIF format.
Video	mpeg	MPEG format.
Audio	Basic	Single-channel 8-bit ISDN mu-law encoding at a sample rate of 8 kHz.
Application	PostScript	Adobe Postscript.
	octet-stream	General binary data consisting of 8-bit bytes.

For the **text type** of body, no special software is required to get the full meaning of the text, aside from support of the indicated character set. The only defined subtype is plaintext, which is simply a string of ASCII characters or ISO 8859 characters. An earlier version of the MIME specification included a *richtext* subtype, which allows greater formatting flexibility. It is expected that this subtype will reappear in a later RFC.

The **multipart type** indicates that the body contains multiple, independent parts. The Content-Type header field includes a parameter, called boundary, that defines the delimiter between body parts. This boundary should not appear in any parts of the message. Each boundary starts on a new line and consists of two hyphens followed by the boundary value. The final boundary, which indicates the end of the last part, also has a suffix of two hyphens. Within each part, there may be an optional ordinary MIME header.

Here is a simple example of a multipart message, containing two parts both consisting of simple text:

From: John Smith <js@company.com>
To: Ned Jones <ned@soft.com>
Subject: Sample message
MIME-Version: 1.0
Content-type: multipart/mixed; boundary = "simple boundary"

This is the preamble. It is to be ignored, though it is a handy place for mail composers to include an explanatory note to non-MIME conformant readers.
– simple boundary

This is implicitly typed plain ASCII text. It does NOT end with a linebreak.
– simple boundary
Content-type: text/plain; charset = us-ascii

This is explicitly typed plain ASCII text. It DOES end with a linebreak.

– simple boundary –
This is the epilogue. It is also to be ignored.

There are four subtypes of the multipart type, all of which have the same overall syntax. The **multipart/mixed subtype** is used when there are multiple independent body parts that need to be bundled in a particular order. For the **multipart/ parallel subtype**, the order of the parts is not significant. If the recipient's system is appropriate, the multiple parts can be presented in parallel. For example, a picture or text part could be accompanied by a voice commentary that is played while the picture or text is displayed.

For the **multipart/alternative subtype**, the various parts are different representations of the same information. The following is an example:

```
From: John Smith <js@company.com>
To: Ned Jones <ned@soft.com>
Subject: Formatted text mail
MIME-Version: 1.0
Content-Type: multipart/alternative; boundary = "boundary42"

– boundary42

Content-Type: text/plain; charset = us-ascii

... plaintext version of message goes here ...
– boundary42
Content-Type: text/richtext

... RFC 1341 richtext version of same message goes here ...
– boundary42 –
```

In this subtype, the body parts are ordered in terms of increasing preference. For this example, if the recipient system is capable of displaying the message in the richtext format, this is done; otherwise, the plaintext format is used.

The **multipart/digest subtype** is used when each of the body parts is interpreted as an RFC 822 message with headers. This subtype enables the construction of a message whose parts are individual messages. For example, the moderator of a group might collect e-mail messages from participants, bundle these messages, and send them out in one encapsulating MIME message.

The **message type** provides a number of important capabilities in MIME. The **message/rfc822 subtype** indicates that the body is an entire message, including header and body. Despite the name of this subtype, the encapsulated message may be not only a simple RFC 822 message, but any MIME message.

The **message/partial subtype** enables fragmentation of a large message into a number of parts, which must be reassembled at the destination. For this subtype, three parameters are specified in the Content-Type: Message/Partial field:

id: A value that is common to each fragment of the same message, so that the fragments can be identified at the recipient for reassembly, but unique across different messages.

number: A sequence number that indicates the position of this fragment in the original message. The first fragment is numbered 1, the second 2, and so on.

total: The total number of parts. The last fragment is identified by having the same value for the *number* and *total* parameters.

The **message/external-body subtype** indicates that the actual data to be conveyed in this message are not contained in the body. Instead, the body contains the information needed to access the data. As with the other message types, the message/

external-body subtype has an outer header and an encapsulated message with its own header. The only necessary field in the outer header is the Content-Type field, which identifies this as a message/external-body subtype. The inner header is the message header for the encapsulated message.

The Content-Type field in the outer header must include an access-type parameter, which has one of the following values:

- **FTP:** The message body is accessible as a file using the file transfer protocol (FTP). For this access type, the following additional parameters are mandatory: name, the name of the file; and site, the domain name of the host where the file resides. Optional parameters are directory, the directory in which the file is located; and mode, which indicates how FTP should retrieve the file (e.g., ASCII, image). Before the file transfer can take place, the user will need to provide a user id and password. These are not transmitted with the message for security reasons.
- **TFTP:** The message body is accessible as a file using the trivial file transfer protocol (TFTP). The same parameters as for FTP are used, and the user id and password must also be supplied.
- **Anon-FTP:** Identical to FTP, except that the user is not asked to supply a user id and password. The parameter name supplies the name of the file.
- **local-file:** The message body is accessible as a file on the recipient's machine.
- **AFS:** The message body is accessible as a file via the global AFS (Andrew File System). The parameter name supplies the name of the file.
- **mail-server:** The message body is accessible by sending an e-mail message to a mail server. A *server* parameter must be included that gives the e-mail address of the server. The body of the original message, known as the phantom body, should contain the exact command to be sent to the mail server.

The **image type** indicates that the body contains a displayable image. The subtype, jpeg or gif, specifies the image format. In the future, more subtypes will be added to this list.

The **video type** indicates that the body contains a time-varying picture image, possibly with color and coordinated sound. The only subtype so far specified is mpeg.

The **audio type** indicates that the body contains audio data. The only subtype, basic, conforms to an ISDN service known as "64-kbps, 8-kHz Structured, Usable for Speech Information," with a digitized speech algorithm referred to as μ-law PCM (pulse code modulation). This general type is the typical way of transmitting speech signals over a digital network. The term μ-law refers to the specific encoding technique; it is the standard technique used in North America and Japan. A competing system, known as A-law, is standard in Europe.

The **application type** refers to other kinds of data, typically either uninterpreted binary data or information to be processed by a mail-based application. The **application/octet-stream subtype** indicates general binary data in a sequence of octets. RFC 2045 recommends that the receiving implementation should offer to put the data in a file or use the data as input to a program.

The **application/Postscript subtype** indicates the use of Adobe Postscript.

MIME Transfer Encodings

The other major component of the MIME specification, in addition to content type specification, is a definition of transfer encodings for message bodies. The objective is to provide reliable delivery across the largest range of environments.

The MIME standard defines two methods of encoding data. The Content-Transfer-Encoding field can actually take on six values, as listed in Table 22.4. However, three of these values (7bit, 8bit, and binary) indicate that no encoding has been done but provide some information about the nature of the data. For SMTP transfer, it is safe to use the 7bit form. The 8bit and binary forms may be usable in other mail transport contexts. Another Content-Transfer-Encoding value is x-token, which indicates that some other encoding scheme is used, for which a name is to be supplied. This could be a vendor-specific or application-specific scheme. The two actual encoding schemes defined are quoted-printable and base64. Two schemes are defined to provide a choice between a transfer technique that is essentially human readable, and one that is safe for all types of data in a way that is reasonably compact.

The **quoted-printable** transfer encoding is useful when the data consist largely of octets that correspond to printable ASCII characters. In essence, it represents nonsafe characters by the hexadecimal representation of their code and introduces reversible (soft) line breaks to limit message lines to 76 characters. The encoding rules are as follows:

1. General 8-bit representation: This rule is to be used when none of the other rules apply. Any character is represented by an equal sign followed by a two-digit hexadecimal representation of the octet's value. For example, the ASCII form feed, which has an 8-bit value of decimal 12, is represented by "=0C".

2. Literal representation: Any character in the range decimal 33 ("!") through decimal 126 ("~"), except decimal 61 ("="), is represented as that ASCII character.

3. White space: Octets with the values 9 and 32 may be represented as ASCII tab and space characters, respectively, except at the end of a line. Any white space (tab or blank) at the end of a line must be represented by rule 1. On decoding, any trailing white space on a line is deleted. This eliminates any white space added by intermediate transport agents.

4. Line breaks: Any line break, regardless of its initial representation, is represented by the RFC 822 line break, which is a carriage-return/line-feed combination.

Table 22.4 MIME Transfer Encodings

7bit	The data are all represented by short lines of ASCII characters.
8bit	The lines are short, but there may be non-ASCII characters (octets with the high-order bit set).
binary	Not only may non-ASCII characters be present but the lines are not necessarily short enough for SMTP transport.
quoted-printable	Encodes the data in such a way that if the data being encoded are mostly ASCII text, the encoded form of the data remains largely recognizable by humans.
base64	Encodes data by mapping 6-bit blocks of input to 8-bit blocks of output, all of which are printable ASCII characters.
x-token	A named nonstandard encoding.

5. Soft line breaks: If an encoded line would be longer than 76 characters (excluding <CRLF>), a soft line break must be inserted at or before character position 75. A soft line break consists of the hexadecimal sequence 3D0D0A, which is the ASCII code for an equal sign followed by carriage return, line feed.

The **base64 transfer encoding**, also known as radix-64 encoding, is a common one for encoding arbitrary binary data in such a way as to be invulnerable to the processing by mail transport programs. This technique maps arbitrary binary input into printable character output. The form of encoding has the following relevant characteristics:

1. The range of the function is a character set that is universally representable at all sites, not a specific binary encoding of that character set. Thus, the characters themselves can be encoded into whatever form is needed by a specific system. For example, the character "E" is represented in an ASCII-based system as hexadecimal 45 and in an EBCDIC-based system as hexadecimal C5.

2. The character set consists of 65 printable characters, one of which is used for padding. With $2^6 = 64$ available characters, each character can be used to represent 6 bits of input.

3. No control characters are included in the set. Thus, a message encoded in radix 64 can traverse mail handling systems that scan the data stream for control characters.

4. The hyphen character ("-") is not used. This character has significance in the RFC 822 format and should therefore be avoided.

Table 22.5 shows the mapping of 6-bit input values to characters. The character set consists of the alphanumeric characters plus "+" and "/". The " = " character is used as the padding character.

Figure 22.2 illustrates the simple mapping scheme. Binary input is processed in blocks of 3 octets, or 24 bits. Each set of 6 bits in the 24-bit block is mapped into a

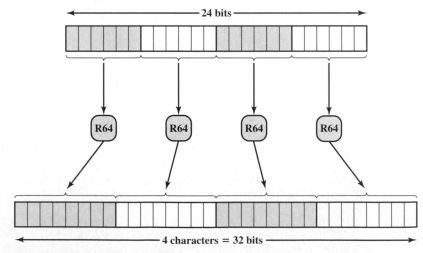

Figure 22.2   Printable Encoding of Binary Data into Radix-64 Format

Table 22.5 Radix-64 Encoding

6-Bit Value	Character Encoding	6-Bit Value	Character Encoding	6-Bit Value	Character Encoding	6-Bit Value	Character Encoding
0	A	16	Q	32	g	48	w
1	B	17	R	33	h	49	x
2	C	18	S	34	i	50	y
3	D	19	T	35	j	51	z
4	E	20	U	36	k	52	0
5	F	21	V	37	l	53	1
6	G	22	W	38	m	54	2
7	H	23	X	39	n	55	3
8	I	24	Y	40	o	56	4
9	J	25	Z	41	p	57	5
10	K	26	a	42	q	58	6
11	L	27	b	43	r	59	7
12	M	28	c	44	s	60	8
13	N	29	d	45	t	61	9
14	O	30	e	46	u	62	+
15	P	31	f	47	v	63	/
						(pad)	=

character. In the figure, the characters are shown encoded as 8-bit quantities. In this typical case, each 24-bit input is expanded to 32 bits of output.

For example, consider the 24-bit raw text sequence 00100011 01011100 10010001, which can be expressed in hexadecimal as 235C91. We arrange this input in blocks of 6 bits:

$$001000\ 110101\ 110010\ 010001$$

The extracted 6-bit decimal values are 8, 53, 50, and 17. Looking these up in Table 22.5 yields the radix-64 encoding as the following characters: I1yR. If these characters are stored in 8-bit ASCII format with parity bit set to zero, we have

$$01001001\ 00110001\ 01111001\ 01010010$$

In hexadecimal, this is 49317952. To summarize,

Input Data		
Binary representation		00100011 01011100 10010001
Hexadecimal representation		235C91
Radix-64 Encoding of Input Data		
Character representation		I1yR
ASCII code (8 bit, zero parity)		01001001 00110001 01111001 01010010
Hexadecimal representation		49317952

22.2 HYPERTEXT TRANSFER PROTOCOL (HTTP)

The Hypertext Transfer Protocol (HTTP) is the foundation protocol of the World Wide Web (WWW) and can be used in any client/server application involving hypertext. The name is somewhat misleading in that HTTP is not a protocol for transferring hypertext; rather it is a protocol for transmitting information with the efficiency necessary for making hypertext jumps. The data transferred by the protocol can be plaintext, hypertext, audio, images, or any Internet-accessible information.

We begin with an overview of HTTP concepts and operation and then look at some of the details, basing our discussion on the most recent version to be put on the Internet standards track, HTTP 1.1 (RFC 2616). A number of important terms defined in the HTTP specification are summarized in Table 22.6; these will be introduced as the discussion proceeds.

HTTP Overview

HTTP is a transaction-oriented client/server protocol. The most typical use of HTTP is between a Web browser and a Web server. To provide reliability, HTTP makes use of TCP. Nevertheless, HTTP is a "stateless" protocol: Each transaction is treated independently. Accordingly, a typical implementation will create a new TCP connection between client and server for each transaction and then terminate the connection as soon as the transaction completes, although the specification does not dictate this one-to-one relationship between transaction and connection lifetimes.

The stateless nature of HTTP is well suited to its typical application. A normal session of a user with a Web browser involves retrieving a sequence of Web pages and documents. The sequence is, ideally, performed rapidly, and the locations of the various pages and documents may be a number of widely distributed servers.

Another important feature of HTTP is that it is flexible in the formats that it can handle. When a client issues a request to a server, it may include a prioritized list of formats that it can handle, and the server replies with the appropriate format. For example, a lynx browser cannot handle images, so a Web server need not transmit any images on Web pages. This arrangement prevents the transmission of unnecessary information and provides the basis for extending the set of formats with new standardized and proprietary specifications.

Figure 22.3 illustrates three examples of HTTP operation. The simplest case is one in which a user agent establishes a direct connection with an origin server. The *user agent* is the client that initiates the request, such as a Web browser being run on behalf of an end user. The *origin server* is the server on which a resource of interest resides; an example is a Web server at which a desired Web home page resides. For this case, the client opens a TCP connection that is end-to-end between the client and the server. The client then issues an HTTP request. The request consists of a specific command, referred to as a method, a URL, and a MIME-like message containing request parameters, information about the client, and perhaps some additional content information.

When the server receives the request, it attempts to perform the requested action and then returns an HTTP response. The response includes status information,

Table 22.6 Key Terms Related to HTTP

Cache A program's local store of response messages and the subsystem that controls its message storage, retrieval, and deletion. A cache stores cacheable responses in order to reduce the response time and network bandwidth consumption on future, equivalent requests. Any client or server may include a cache, though a cache cannot be used by a server while it is acting as a tunnel. **Client** An application program that establishes connections for the purpose of sending requests. **Connection** A transport layer virtual circuit established between two application programs for the purposes of communication. **Entity** A particular representation or rendition of a data resource, or reply from a service resource, that may be enclosed within a request or response message. An entity consists of entity headers and an entity body. **Gateway** A server that acts as an intermediary for some other server. Unlike a proxy, a gateway receives requests as if it were the original server for the requested resource; the requesting client may not be aware that it is communicating with a gateway. Gateways are often used as server-side portals through network firewalls and as protocol translators for access to resources stored on non-HTTP systems. **Message** The basic unit of HTTP communication, consisting of a structured sequence of octets transmitted via the connection.	**Origin Server** The server on which a given resource resides or is to be created. **Proxy** An intermediary program that acts as both a server and a client for the purpose of making requests on behalf of other clients. Requests are serviced internally or by passing them, with possible translation, on to other servers. A proxy must interpret and, if necessary, rewrite a request message before forwarding it. Proxies are often used as client-side portals through network firewalls and as helper applications for handling requests via protocols not implemented by the user agent. **Resource** A network data object or service which can be identified by a URI. **Server** An application program that accepts connections in order to service requests by sending back responses. **Tunnel** An intermediary program that is acting as a blind relay between two connections. Once active, a tunnel is not considered a party to the HTTP communication, though the tunnel may have been initiated by an HTTP request. A tunnel ceases to exist when both ends of the relayed connections are closed. Tunnels are used when a portal is necessary and the intermediary cannot, or should not, interpret the relayed communication. **User Agent** The client that initiates a request. These are often browsers, editors, spiders, or other end-user tools.

a success/error code, and a MIME-like message containing information about the server, information about the response itself, and possible body content. The TCP connection is then closed.

The middle part of Figure 22.3 shows a case in which there is not an end-to-end TCP connection between the user agent and the origin server. Instead, there are one or more intermediate systems with TCP connections between logically adjacent systems. Each intermediate system acts as a relay, so that a request initiated by the client is relayed through the intermediate systems to the server, and the response from the server is relayed back to the client.

Three forms of intermediate system are defined in the HTTP specification: proxy, gateway, and tunnel, all of which are illustrated in Figure 22.4.

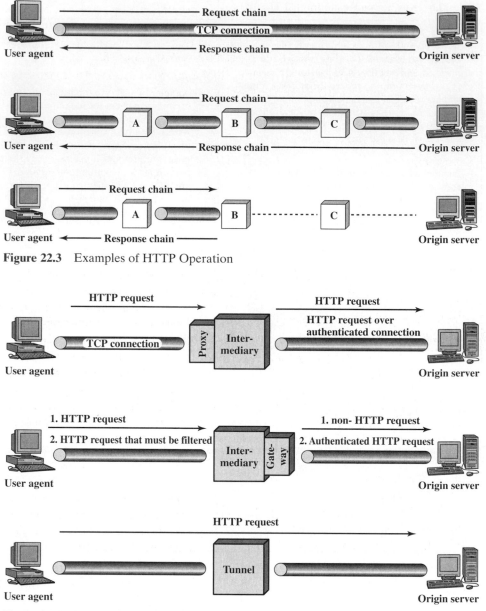

Figure 22.3 Examples of HTTP Operation

Figure 22.4 Intermediate HTTP Systems

Proxy

A proxy acts on behalf of other clients and presents requests from other clients to a server. The proxy acts as a server in interacting with a client and as a client in interacting with a server. There are two scenarios that call for the use of a proxy:

- **Security intermediary:** The client and server may be separated by a security intermediary such as a firewall, with the proxy on the client side of the firewall.

Typically, the client is part of a network secured by a firewall and the server is external to the secured network. In this case, the server must authenticate itself to the firewall to set up a connection with the proxy. The proxy accepts responses after they have passed through the firewall.

- **Different versions of HTTP:** If the client and server are running different versions of HTTP, then the proxy can implement both versions and perform the required mapping.

In summary, a proxy is a forwarding agent, receiving a request for a URL object, modifying the request, and forwarding the request toward the server identified in the URL.

Gateway

A gateway is a server that appears to the client as if it were an origin server. It acts on behalf of other servers that may not be able to communicate directly with a client. There are two scenarios in which gateways can be used.

- **Security intermediary:** The client and server may be separated by a security intermediary such as a firewall, with the gateway on the server side of the firewall. Typically, the server is connected to a network protected by a firewall, with the client external to the network. In this case the client must authenticate itself to the gateway, which can then pass the request on to the server.
- **Non-HTTP server:** Web browsers have built into them the capability to contact servers for protocols other than HTTP, such as FTP and Gopher servers. This capability can also be provided by a gateway. The client makes an HTTP request to a gateway server. The gateway server then contacts the relevant FTP or Gopher server to obtain the desired result. This result is then converted into a form suitable for HTTP and transmitted back to the client.

Tunnel

Unlike the proxy and the gateway, the tunnel performs no operations on HTTP requests and responses. Instead, a tunnel is simply a relay point between two TCP connections, and the HTTP messages are passed unchanged as if there were a single HTTP connection between user agent and origin server. Tunnels are used when there must be an intermediary system between client and server but it is not necessary for that system to understand the contents of messages. An example is a firewall in which a client or server external to a protected network can establish an authenticated connection and then maintain that connection for purposes of HTTP transactions.

Cache

Returning to Figure 22.3, the lowest portion of the figure shows an example of a cache. A cache is a facility that may store previous requests and responses for handling new requests. If a new request arrives that is the same as a stored request, then the cache can supply the stored response rather than accessing the resource indicated in the URL. The cache can operate on a client or server or on an intermediate

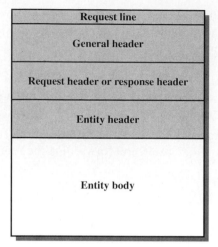

Figure 22.5 General Structure of HTTP Messages

system other than a tunnel. In the figure, intermediary B has cached a request/response transaction, so that a corresponding new request from the client need not travel the entire chain to the origin server, but is handled by B.

Not all transactions can be cached, and a client or server can dictate that a certain transaction may be cached only for a given time limit.

Messages

The best way to describe the functionality of HTTP is to describe the individual elements of the HTTP message. HTTP consists of two types of messages: requests from clients to servers, and responses from servers to clients. The general structure of such messages is shown in Figure 22.5. More formally, using enhanced BNF (Backus-Naur Form) notation (Table 22.7), we have

```
HTTP-Message = Simple-Request | Simple-Response | Full-Request
| Full-Response
Full-Request = Request-Line
  *( General-Header | Request-Header | Entity-Header )
  CRLF
  [ Entity-Body ]
Full-Response = Status-Line
  *( General-Header | Response-Header | Entity-Header )
  CRLF
  [ Entity-Body ]
Simple-Request = "GET" SP Request-URL CRLF
Simple-Response = [ Entity-Body ]
```

The Simple-Request and Simple-Response messages were defined in HTTP/0.9. The request is a simple GET command with the requested URL; the response is simply a block containing the information identified in the URL. In HTTP/1.1,

Table 22.7   Augmented BNF Notation Used in URL and HTTP Specifications

- Words in lower case represent variables or names of rules.
- A rule has the form

    name = definition

- DIGIT is any decimal digit; CRLF is carriage return, line feed; SP is one or more spaces.
- Quotation marks enclose literal text.
- Angle brackets, "<" ">", may be used within a definition to enclose a rule name when their presence will facilitate clarity.
- Elements separated by bar ("|") are alternatives.
- Ordinary parentheses are used simply for grouping.
- The character "*" preceding an element indicates repetition. The full form is

    <I>*<J>element

    indicating at least I and at most J occurrences of element. *element allows any number, including 0; 1*element requires at least one element; and 1*2element allows 1 or 2 elements; <N>element means exactly N elements.
- Square brackets, "[" "]", enclose optional elements.
- The construct "#" is used to define, with the following form:

    <I>#<J>element

    indicating at least I and at most J elements, each separated by a comma and optional linear white space.
- A semicolon at the right of a rule starts a comment that continues to the end of the line.

the use of these simple forms is discouraged because it prevents the client from using content negotiation and the server from identifying the media type of the returned entity.

With full requests and responses, the following fields are used:

- **Request-Line:** Identifies the message type and the requested resource
- **Response-Line:** Provides status information about this response
- **General-Header:** Contains fields that are applicable to both request and response messages but that do not apply to the entity being transferred
- **Request-Header:** Contains information about the request and the client
- **Response-Header:** Contains information about the response
- **Entity-Header:** Contains information about the resource identified by the request and information about the entity body
- **Entity-Body:** The body of the message

All of the HTTP headers consist of a sequence of fields, following the same generic format as RFC 822 (described in Section 22.1). Each field begins on a new line and consists of the field name followed by a colon and the field value.

Although the basic transaction mechanism is simple, there are a large number of fields and parameters defined in HTTP; these are listed in Table 22.8. In the remainder of this section, we look at the general header fields. Following sections describe request headers, response headers, and entities.

Table 22.8   HTTP Elements

ALL MESSAGES			
General Header Fields		**Entity Header Fields**	
Cache-Control	Keep-Alive	Allow	Derived-From
Connection	MIME-Version	Content-Encoding	Expires
Date	Pragma	Content-Language	Last-Modified
Forwarded	Upgrade	Content-Length	Link
		Content-MD5	Title
		Content-Range	Transfer-Encoding
		Content-Type	URI-Header
		Content-Version	extension-header

REQUEST MESSAGES			
Request Methods		**Request Header Fields**	
OPTIONS	MOVE	Accept	If-Modified-Since
GET	DELETE	Accept-Charset	Proxy-Authorization
HEAD	LINK	Accept-Encoding	Range
POST	UNLINK	Accept-Language	Referer
PUT	TRACE	Authorization	Unless
PATCH	WRAPPED	From	User-Agent
COPY	extension-method	Host	

RESPONSE MESSAGES			
Response Status Codes			**Response Header Fields**
Continue	Moved Temporarily	Request Timeout	Location
Switching Protocols	See Other	Conflict	Proxy-Authenticate
OK	Not Modified	Gone	Public
Created	Use Proxy	Length Required	Retry-After
Accepted	Bad Request	Unless True	Server
Non-Authoritative	Unauthorized	Internal Server Error	WWW-Authenticate
Information	Payment Required	Not Implemented	
No Content	Forbidden	Bad Gateway	
Reset Content	Not Found	Service Unavailable	
Partial Content	Method Not Allowed	Gateway Timeout	
Multiple Choices	None Acceptable	extension code	
Moved Permanently	Proxy Authentication Required		

General Header Fields

General header fields can be used in both request and response messages. These fields are applicable in both types of messages and contain information that does not directly apply to the entity being transferred. The fields are as follows:

- **Cache-Control:** Specifies directives that must be obeyed by any caching mechanisms along the request/response chain. The purpose is to prevent a cache from adversely interfering with this particular request or response.
- **Connection:** Contains a list of keywords and header field names that only apply to this TCP connection between the sender and the nearest nontunnel recipient.
- **Date:** Date and time at which the message originated.
- **Forwarded:** Used by gateways and proxies to indicate intermediate steps along a request or response chain. Each gateway or proxy that handles a message may attach a Forwarded field that gives its URL.
- **Keep-Alive:** May be present if the keep-alive keyword is present in an incoming Connection field, to provide information to the requester of the persistent connection. This field may indicate a maximum time that the sender will keep the connection open waiting for the next request or the maximum number of additional requests that will be allowed on the current persistent connection.
- **MIME-Version:** Indicates that the message complies with the indicated version of MIME.
- **Pragma:** Contains implementation-specific directives that may apply to any recipient along the request/response chain.
- **Upgrade:** Used in a request to specify what additional protocols the client supports and would like to use; used in a response to indicate which protocol will be used.

Request Messages

A full request message consists of a status line followed by one or more general, request, and entity headers, followed by an optional entity body.

Request Methods

A full request message always begins with a Request-Line, which has the following format:

Request-Line = Method SP Request-URL SP HTTP-Version CRLF

The Method parameter indicates the actual request command, called a method in HTTP. Request-URL is the URL of the requested resource, and HTTP-Version is the version number of HTTP used by the sender.

The following request methods are defined in HTTP/1.1:

- **OPTIONS:** A request for information about the options available for the request/response chain identified by this URL.
- **GET:** A request to retrieve the information identified in the URL and return it in a entity body. A GET is conditional if the If-Modified-Since header field is included and is partial if a Range header field is included.

- **HEAD:** This request is identical to a GET, except that the server's response must not include an entity body; all of the header fields in the response are the same as if the entity body were present. This enables a client to get information about a resource without transferring the entity body.

- **POST:** A request to accept the attached entity as a new subordinate to the identified URL. The posted entity is subordinate to that URL in the same way that a file is subordinate to a directory containing it, a news article is subordinate to a newsgroup to which it is posted, or a record is subordinate to a database.

- **PUT:** A request to accept the attached entity and store it under the supplied URL. This may be a new resource with a new URL or a replacement of the contents of an existing resource with an existing URL.

- **PATCH:** Similar to a PUT, except that the entity contains a list of differences from the content of the original resource identified in the URL.

- **COPY:** Requests that a copy of the resource identified by the URL in the Request-Line be copied to the location(s) given in the URL-Header field in the Entity-Header of this message.

- **MOVE:** Requests that the resource identified by the URL in the Request-Line be moved to the location(s) given in the URL-Header field in the Entity-Header of this message. Equivalent to a COPY followed by a DELETE.

- **DELETE:** Requests that the origin server delete the resource identified by the URL in the Request-Line.

- **LINK:** Establishes one or more link relationships from the resource identified in the Request-Line. The links are defined in the Link field in the Entity-Header.

- **UNLINK:** Removes one or more link relationships from the resource identified in the Request-Line. The links are defined in the Link field in the Entity-Header.

- **TRACE:** Requests that the server return whatever is received as the entity body of the response. This can be used for testing and diagnostic purposes.

- **WRAPPED:** Allows a client to send one or more encapsulated requests. The requests may be encrypted or otherwise processed. The server must unwrap the requests and process accordingly.

- **Extension-method:** Allows additional methods to be defined without changing the protocol, but these methods cannot be assumed to be recognizable by the recipient.

Request Header Fields

Request header fields function as request modifiers, providing additional information and parameters related to the request. The following fields are defined in HTTP/1.1:

- **Accept:** A list of media types and ranges that are acceptable as a response to this request.

- **Accept-Charset:** A list of character sets acceptable for the response.

- **Accept-Encoding:** List of acceptable content encodings for the entity body. Content encodings are primarily used to allow a document to be compressed or encrypted. Typically, the resource is stored in this encoding and only decoded before actual use.
- **Accept-Language:** Restricts the set of natural languages that are preferred for the response.
- **Authorization:** Contains a field value, referred to as *credentials*, used by the client to authenticate itself to the server.
- **From:** The Internet e-mail address for the human user who controls the requesting user agent.
- **Host:** Specifies the Internet host of the resource being requested.
- **If-Modified-Since:** Used with the GET method. This header includes a date/time parameter; the resource is to be transferred only if it has been modified since the date/time specified. This feature allows for efficient cache update. A caching mechanism can periodically issue GET messages to an origin server, and will receive only a small response message unless an update is needed.
- **Proxy-Authorization:** Allows the client to identify itself to a proxy that requires authentication.
- **Range:** For future study. The intent is that, in a GET message, a client can request only a portion of the identified resource.
- **Referrer:** The URL of the resource from which the Request-URL was obtained. This enables a server to generate lists of back-links.
- **Unless:** Similar in function to the If-Modified-Since field, with two differences: (1) It is not restricted to the GET method, and (2) comparison is based on any Entity-Header field value rather than a date/time value.
- **User-Agent:** Contains information about the user agent originating this request. This is used for statistical purposes, the tracing of protocol violations, and automated recognition of user agents for the sake of tailoring responses to avoid particular user agent limitations.

Response Messages

A full response message consists of a status line followed by one or more general, response, and entity headers, followed by an optional entity body.

Status Codes

A full response message always begins with a Status-Line, which has the following format:

Status-Line = HTTP-Version SP Status-Code SP Reason-Phrase CRLF

The HTTP-Version value is the version number of HTTP used by the sender. The Status-Code is a three-digit integer that indicates the response to a received request, and the Reason-Phrase provides a short textual explanation of the status code.

The are a rather large number of status codes defined in HTTP/1.1; these are listed in Table 22.9, together with a brief definition. The codes are organized into the following categories:

- **Informational:** The request has been received and processing continues. No entity body accompanies this response.
- **Successful:** The request was successfully received, understood, and accepted. The information returned in the response message depends on the request method, as follows:
    - GET: The contents of the entity-body corresponds to the requested resource.
    - HEAD: No entity body is returned.
    - POST: The entity describes or contains the result of the action.
    - TRACE: The entity contains the request message.
    - Other methods: The entity describes the result of the action.
- **Redirection:** Further action is required to complete the request.
- **Client Error:** The request contains a syntax error or the request cannot be fulfilled.
- **Server Error:** The server failed to fulfill an apparently valid request.

Response Header Fields

Response header fields provide additional information related to the response that cannot be placed in the Status-Line. The following fields are defined in HTTP/1.1:

- **Location:** Defines the exact location of the resource identified by the Request-URL.
- **Proxy-Authenticate:** Included with a response that has a status code of Proxy Authentication Required. This field contains a "challenge" that indicates the authentication scheme and parameters required.
- **Public:** Lists the nonstandard methods supported by this server.
- **Retry-After:** Included with a response that has a status code of Service Unavailable, and indicates how long the service is expected to be unavailable.
- **Server:** Identifies the software product used by the origin server to handle the request.
- **WWW-Authenticate:** Included with a response that has a status code of Unauthorized. This field contains a "challenge" that indicates the authentication scheme and parameters required.

Entities

An entity consists of an entity header and an entity body in a request or response message. An entity may represent a data resource, or it may constitute other information supplied with a request or response.

Table 22.9   HTTP Status Codes

Informational	
Continue	Initial part of request received; client may continue with request.
Switching Protocols	Server will switch to requested new application protocol.
Successful	
OK	Request has succeeded and the appropriate response information is included.
Created	Request fulfilled and a new resource has been created; the URI(s) are included.
Accepted	Request accepted but processing not completed. The request may or may not eventually be acted upon.
Non-Authoritative Information	Returned contents of entity header is not the definitive set available from origin server, but is gathered from a local or third-party copy.
No Content	Server has fulfilled request but there is no information to send back.
Reset Content	Request has succeeded and the user agent should reset the document view that caused the request to be generated.
Partial Content	Server has fulfilled the partial GET request and the corresponding information is included.
Redirection	
Multiple Choices	Requested resource is available at multiple locations and a preferred location could not be determined.
Moved Permanently	Requested resource has been assigned a new permanent URI; future reference should use this URI
Moved Temporarily	Requested resource resides temporarily under a different URI.
See Other	Response to the request can be found under a different URI and should be retrieved using a GET on that resource.
Not Modified	The client has performed a conditional GET, access is allowed, and the document has not been modified since the date/time specified in the request.
Use Proxy	Requested resource must be accessed through the proxy indicated in the Location field.
Client Error	
Bad Request	Malformed syntax in request.
Unauthorized	Request requires user authentication.
Payment Required	Reserved for future use.
Forbidden	Server refuses to fulfill request; used when server does not wish to reveal why the request was refused.
Not Found	Requested URI not found.
Method Not Allowed	Method (command) not allowed for the requested resource.
None Acceptable	Resource found that matches requested URI, but does not satisfy conditions specified in the request.
Proxy Authentication Required	Client must first authenticate itself with the proxy.
Request Timeout	Client did not produce a request within the time that the server was prepared to wait.
Conflict	Request could not be completed due to a conflict with the current state of the resource.
Gone	Requested resource no longer available at the server and no forwarding address is known.
Length Required	Server refuses to accept request without a defined content length.
Unless True	Condition given in the Unless field was true when tested on server.
Server Error	
Internal Server Error	Server encountered an unexpected condition that prevented it from fulfilling the request.
Not Implemented	Server does not support the functionality required to fulfill the request.
Bad Gateway	Server, while acting as a gateway or proxy, received an invalid response from the upstream server it accessed to fulfill the request.
Service Unavailable	Server unable to handle request due to temporary overloading or maintenance of the server.
Gateway Timeout	Server, while acting as a gateway or proxy, did not receive a timely response from the upstream server it accessed to fulfill the request.

Entity Header Fields

Entity header fields provide optional information about the entity body or, if no body is present, about the resource identified by the request. The following fields are defined in HTTP/1.1:

- **Allow:** Lists methods supported by the resource identified in the Request-URL. This field must be included with a response that has a status code of Method Not Allowed and may be included in other responses.
- **Content-Encoding:** Indicates what content encodings have been applied to the resource. The only encoding currently defined is zip compression.
- **Content-Language:** Identifies the natural language(s) of the intended audience of the enclosed entity.
- **Content-Length:** The size of the entity body in octets.
- **Content-MD5:** For future study. MD5 refers to the MD5 hash code function, described in Chapter 21.
- **Content-Range:** For future study. The intent is that this will indicate a portion of the identified resource that is included in this response.
- **Content-Type:** Indicates the media type of the entity body.
- **Content-Version:** A version tag associated with an evolving entity.
- **Derived-From:** Indicates the version tag of the resource from which this entity was derived before modifications were made by the sender. This field and the Content-Version field can be used to manage multiple updates by a group of users.
- **Expires:** Date/time after which the entity should be considered stale.
- **Last-Modified:** Date/time that the sender believes the resource was last modified.
- **Link:** Defines links to other resources.
- **Title:** A textual title for the entity.
- **Transfer-Encoding:** Indicates what type of transformation has been applied to the message body to transfer it safely between the sender and the recipient. The only encoding defined in the standard is *chunked*. The chunked option defines a procedure for breaking an entity body into labeled chunks that are transmitted separately.
- **URL-Header:** Informs the recipient of other URLs by which the resource can be identified.
- **Extension-Header:** Allows additional fields to be defined without changing the protocol, but these fields cannot be assumed to be recognizable by the recipient.

Entity Body

An entity body consists of an arbitrary sequence of octets. HTTP is designed to be able to transfer any type of content, including text, binary data, audio, images, and video. When an entity body is present in a message, the interpretation of the octets in the body is determined by the entity header fields Content-Encoding, Content-Type, and Transfer-Encoding. These define a three-layer, ordered encoding model:

entity-body := Transfer-Encoding(Content-Encoding(Content-Type(data)))

The data are the content of a resource identified by a URL. The Content-Type field determines the way in which the data are interpreted. A Content-Encoding may be applied to the data and stored at the URL instead of the data. Finally, on transfer, a Transfer-Encoding may be applied to form the entity body of the message.

22.3 NETWORK MANAGEMENT—SNMP

Networks and distributed processing systems are of critical and growing importance in business, government, and other organizations. Within a given organization, the trend is toward larger, more complex networks supporting more applications and more users. As these networks grow in scale, two facts become painfully evident:

- The network and its associated resources and distributed applications become indispensable to the organization.
- More things can go wrong, disabling the network or a portion of the network or degrading performance to an unacceptable level.

A large, reliable network cannot be put together and managed by human effort alone. The complexity of such a system dictates the use of automated network management tools. The urgency of the need for such tools is increased, and the difficulty of supplying such tools is also increased, if the network includes equipment from multiple vendors. In response, standards that deal with network management have been developed, covering services, protocols, and management information base.

This section begins with an introduction to the overall concepts of standardized network management. The remainder of the section is devoted to a discussion of SNMP, the most widely used network management standard.

Network Management Systems

A network management system is a collection of tools for network monitoring and control that is integrated in the following senses:

- A single operator interface with a powerful but user-friendly set of commands for performing most or all network management tasks.
- A minimal amount of additional equipment. That is, most of the hardware and software required for network management is incorporated into the existing user equipment.

A network management system consists of incremental hardware and software additions implemented among existing network components. The software used in accomplishing the network management tasks resides in the host computers and communications processors (e.g., networks switches, routers). A network management system is designed to view the entire network as a unified architecture, with addresses and labels assigned to each point and the specific attributes of each element and link known to the system. The active elements of the network provide regular feedback of status information to the network control center.

Simple Network Management Protocol Version 1 (SNMPv1)

SNMP was developed for use as a network management tool for networks and internetworks operating TCP/IP. It has since been expanded for use in all types of networking environments. The term *simple network management protocol (SNMP)* is actually used to refer to a collection of specifications for network management that include the protocol itself, the definition of a database, and associated concepts.

Basic Concepts

The model of network management that is used for SNMP includes the following key elements:

- Management station, or manager
- Agent
- Management information base
- Network management protocol

The **management station** is typically a standalone device, but may be a capability implemented on a shared system. In either case, the management station serves as the interface for the human network manager into the network management system. The management station will have, at minimum,

- A set of management applications for data analysis, fault recovery, and so on
- An interface by which the network manager may monitor and control the network
- The capability of translating the network manager's requirements into the actual monitoring and control of remote elements in the network
- A database of network management information extracted from the databases of all the managed entities in the network

Only the last two elements are the subject of SNMP standardization. The other active element in the network management system is the **management agent**. Key platforms, such as hosts, bridges, routers, and hubs, may be equipped with agent software so that they may be managed from a management station. The agent responds to requests for information from a management station, responds to requests for actions from the management station, and may asynchronously provide the management station with important but unsolicited information.

To manage resources in the network, each resource is represented as an object. An object is, essentially, a data variable that represents one aspect of the managed agent. The collection of objects is referred to as a **management information base** (MIB). The MIB functions as a collection of access points at the agent for the management station. These objects are standardized across systems of a particular class (e.g., bridges all support the same management objects). A management station performs the monitoring function by retrieving the value of MIB objects. A management station can cause an action to take place at an agent or can change the configuration settings of an agent by modifying the value of specific variables.

The management station and agents are linked by a **network management protocol**. The protocol used for the management of TCP/IP networks is the Simple

Network Management Protocol (SNMP). An enhanced version of SNMP, known as SNMPv2, is intended for both TCP/IP- and OSI-based networks. Each of these protocols includes the following key capabilities:

- **Get:** Enables the management station to retrieve the value of objects at the agent
- **Set:** Enables the management station to set the value of objects at the agent
- **Notify:** Enables an agent to send unsolicited notifications to the management station of significant events

In a traditional centralized network management scheme, one host in the configuration has the role of a network management station; there may be one or two other management stations in a backup role. The remainder of the devices on the network contain agent software and a MIB, to allow monitoring and control from the management station. As networks grow in size and traffic load, such a centralized system is unworkable. Too much burden is placed on the management station, and there is too much traffic, with reports from every single agent having to wend their way across the entire network to headquarters. In such circumstances, a decentralized, distributed approach works best (e.g., Figure 22.6). In a decentralized network management scheme, there may be multiple top-level management stations, which might be referred to as management servers. Each such server might directly manage a portion of the total pool of agents. However, for many of the agents, the

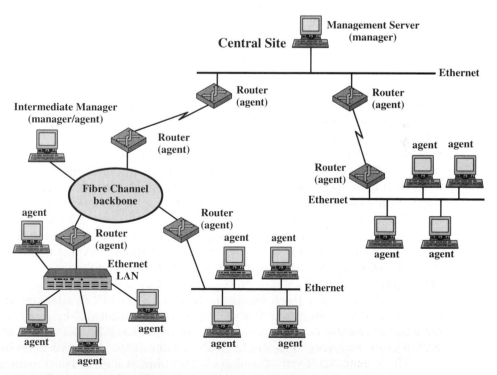

Figure 22.6   Example of Distributed Network Management Configuration

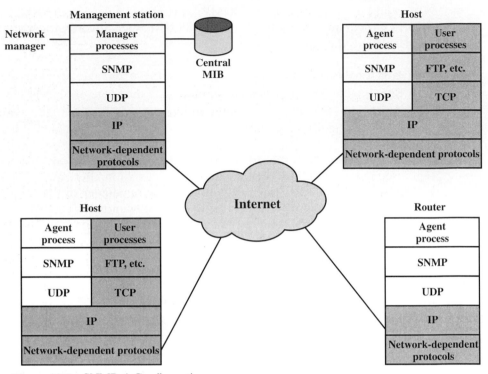

Figure 22.7   SNMPv1 Configuration

management server delegates responsibility to an intermediate manager. The intermediate manager plays the role of manager to monitor and control the agents under its responsibility. It also plays an agent role to provide information and accept control from a higher-level management server. This type of architecture spreads the processing burden and reduces total network traffic.

Network Management Protocol Architecture

SNMP is an application-level protocol that is part of the TCP/IP protocol suite. It is intended to operate over the user datagram protocol (UDP). Figure 22.7 suggests the typical configuration of protocols for SNMPv1. For a standalone management station, a manager process controls access to a central MIB at the management station and provides an interface to the network manager. The manager process achieves network management by using SNMP, which is implemented on top of UDP, IP, and the relevant network-dependent protocols (e.g., Ethernet, ATM, frame relay).

Each agent must also implement SNMP, UDP, and IP. In addition, there is an agent process that interprets the SNMP messages and controls the agent's MIB. For an agent device that supports other applications, such as FTP, TCP as well as UDP is required. In Figure 22.7, the shaded portions depict the operational environment: that which is to be managed. The unshaded portions provide support to the network management function.

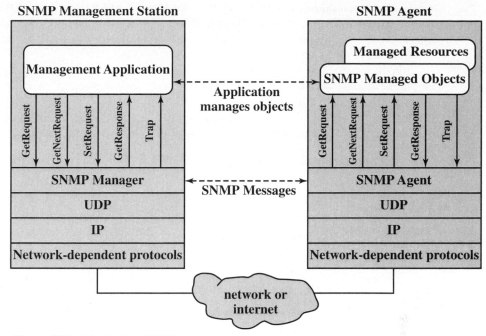

Figure 22.8 The Role of SNMPv1

Figure 22.8 provides a somewhat closer look at the protocol context of SNMP. From a management station, three types of SNMP messages are issued on behalf of a management applications: GetRequest, GetNextRequest, and SetRequest. The first two are two variations of the get function. All three messages are acknowledged by the agent in the form of a GetResponse message, which is passed up to the management application. In addition, an agent may issue a trap message in response to an event that affects the MIB and the underlying managed resources. Management requests are sent to UDP port 161, while the agent sends traps to UDP port 162.

Because SNMP relies on UDP, which is a connectionless protocol, SNMP is itself connectionless. No ongoing connections are maintained between a management station and its agents. Instead, each exchange is a separate transaction between a management station and an agent.

Simple Network Management Protocol Version 2 (SNMPv2)

In August of 1988, the specification for SNMP was issued and rapidly became the dominant network management standard. A number of vendors offer standalone network management workstations based on SNMP, and most vendors of bridges, routers, workstations, and PCs offer SNMP agent packages that allow their products to be managed by an SNMP management station.

As the name suggests, SNMP is a simple tool for network management. It defines a limited, easily implemented management information base (MIB) of scalar variables and two-dimensional tables, and it defines a streamlined protocol to enable a manager to get and set MIB variables and to enable an agent to issue unsolicited notifications, called *traps*. This simplicity is the strength of SNMP. SNMP is easily implemented and consumes modest processor and network resources. Also, the structure of the protocol and the MIB are sufficiently straightforward that it is not difficult to achieve interoperability among management stations and agent software from a mix of vendors.

With its widespread use, the deficiencies of SNMP became increasingly apparent; these include both functional deficiencies and a lack of a security facility. As a result, an enhanced version, known as SNMPv2, was issued (RFCs 1901, 1905 through 1909, and 2578 through 2580). SNMPv2 has quickly gained support, and a number of vendors announced products within months of the issuance of the standard.

The Elements of SNMPv2

Surprisingly, SNMPv2 does not provide network management at all. SNMPv2 instead provides a framework on which network management applications can be built. Those applications, such as fault management, performance monitoring, accounting, and so on, are outside the scope of the standard.

SNMPv2 provides the infrastructure for network management. Figure 22.9 is an example of a configuration that illustrates that infrastructure.

The essence of SNMPv2 is a protocol that is used to exchange management information. Each "player" in the network management system maintains a local database of information relevant to network management, known as the management information base (MIB). The SNMPv2 standard defines the structure of this information and the allowable data types; this definition is known as the structure of management information (SMI). We can think of this as the language for defining management information. The standard also supplies a number of MIBs that are generally useful for network management.[1] In addition, new MIBs may be defined by vendors and user groups.

At least one system in the configuration must be responsible for network management. It is here that any network management applications are hosted. There may be more than one of these management stations, to provide redundancy or simply to split up the duties in a large network. Most other systems act in the role of agent. An agent collects information locally and stores it for later access by a manager. The information includes data about the system itself and may also include traffic information for the network or networks to which the agent attaches.

SNMPv2 will support either a highly centralized network management strategy or a distributed one. In the latter case, some systems operate both in the role of manager and of agent. In its agent role, such a system will accept commands from a superior management system. Some of those commands relate to the local MIB at the agent. Other commands require the agent to act as a proxy for remote devices. In this case, the proxy agent assumes the role of manager to access information at a remote agent, and then assumes the role of an agent to pass that information on to a superior manager.

---

[1] There is a slight fuzziness about the term *MIB*. In its singular form, the term *MIB* can be used to refer to the entire database of management information at a manager or an agent. It can also be used in singular or plural form to refer to a specific defined collection of management information that is part of an overall MIB. Thus, the SNMPv2 standard includes the definition of several MIBs and incorporates, by reference, MIBs defined in SNMPv1.

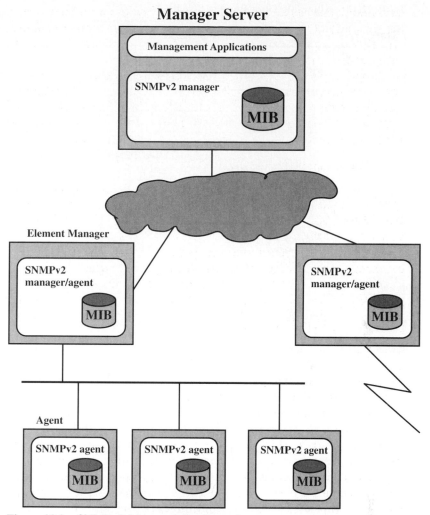

Figure 22.9   SNMPv2-Managed Configuration

All of these exchanges take place using the SNMPv2 protocol, which is a simple request/response type of protocol. Typically, SNMPv2 is implemented on top of the user datagram protocol (UDP), which is part of the TCP/IP suite. Because SNMPv2 exchanges are in the nature of discrete request-response pairs, an ongoing reliable connection is not required.

Structure of Management Information

The structure of management information (SMI) defines the general framework within which a MIB can be defined and constructed. The SMI identifies the data types that can be used in the MIB, and how resources within the MIB are represented and named. The philosophy behind SMI is to encourage simplicity and extensibility within the MIB. Thus, the MIB can store only simple data types: scalars and two-dimensional arrays of scalars, called tables. The SMI does not support the

Table 22.10 Allowable Data Types in SNMPv2

Data Type	Description
INTEGER	Integers in the range of -2^{31} to $2^{31} - 1$,
UInteger32	Integers in the range of 0 to $2^{32} - 1$,
Counter32	A nonnegative integer that may be incremented modulo 2^{32}.
Counter64	A nonnegative integer that may be incremented modulo 2^{64}.
Gauge32	A nonnegative integer that may increase or decrease, but shall not exceed a maximum value. The maximum value cannot be greater than $2^{32} - 1$.
TimeTicks	A nonnegative integer that represents the time, modulo 2^{32}, in hundredths of a second.
OCTET STRING	Octet strings for arbitrary binary or textual data; may be limited to 255 octets.
IpAddress	A 32-bit internet address.
Opaque	An arbitrary bit field.
BIT STRING	An enumeration of named bits.
OBJECT IDENTIFIER	Administratively assigned name to object or other standardized element. Value is a sequence of up to 128 nonnegative integers.

creation or retrieval of complex data structures. This philosophy is in contrast to that used with OSI systems management, which provides for complex data structures and retrieval modes to support greater functionality. SMI avoids complex data types and structures to simplify the task of implementation and to enhance interoperability. MIBs will inevitably contain vendor-created data types and, unless tight restrictions are placed on the definition of such data types, interoperability will suffer.

There are three key elements in the SMI specification. At the lowest level, the SMI specifies the data types that may be stored. Then the SMI specifies a formal technique for defining objects and tables of objects. Finally, the SMI provides a scheme for associating a unique identifier with each actual object in a system, so that data at an agent can be referenced by a manager.

Table 22.10 shows the data types that are allowed by the SMI. This is a fairly restricted set of types. For example, real numbers are not supported. However, it is rich enough to support most network management requirements.

Protocol Operation

The heart of the SNMPv2 framework is the protocol itself. The protocol provides a straightforward, basic mechanism for the exchange of management information between manager and agent.

The basic unit of exchange is the message, which consists of an outer message wrapper and an inner protocol data unit (PDU). The outer message header deals with security and is discussed later in this section.

Seven types of PDUs may be carried in an SNMP message. The general formats for these are illustrated informally in Figure 22.10. Several fields are common

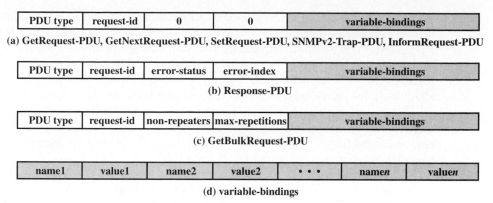

PDU type	request-id	0	0	variable-bindings

(a) GetRequest-PDU, GetNextRequest-PDU, SetRequest-PDU, SNMPv2-Trap-PDU, InformRequest-PDU

PDU type	request-id	error-status	error-index	variable-bindings

(b) Response-PDU

PDU type	request-id	non-repeaters	max-repetitions	variable-bindings

(c) GetBulkRequest-PDU

name1	value1	name2	value2	• • •	name$n$	value$n$

(d) variable-bindings

Figure 22.10   SNMPv2 PDU Format

to a number of PDUs. The request-id field is an integer assigned such that each out-standing request can be uniquely identified. This enables a manager to correlate incoming responses with outstanding requests. It also enables an agent to cope with duplicate PDUs generated by an unreliable transport service. The variable-bindings field contains a list of object identifiers; depending on the PDU, the list may also include a value for each object.

The GetRequest-PDU, issued by a manager, includes a list of one or more object names for which values are requested. If the get operation is successful, then the responding agent will send a Response-PDU. The variable-bindings list will contain the identifier and value of all retrieved objects. For any variables that are not in the relevant MIB view, its identifier and an error code are returned in the variable-bindings list. Thus, SNMPv2 permits partial responses to a GetRequest, which is a significant improvement over SNMP. In SNMP, if one or more of the variables in a GetRequest is not supported, the agent returns an error message with a status of noSuchName. To cope with such an error, the SNMP manager must either return no values to the requesting application, or it must include an algorithm that responds to an error by removing the missing variables, resending the request, and then sending a partial result to the application.

The GetNextRequest-PDU also is issued by a manager and includes a list of one or more objects. In this case, for each object named in the variable-bindings field, a value is to be returned for the object that is next in lexicographic order, which is equivalent to saying next in the MIB in terms of its position in the tree structure of object identifiers. As with the GetRequest-PDU, the agent will return values for as many variables as possible. One of the strengths of the GetNextRequest-PDU is that it enables a manager entity to discover the structure of a MIB view dynamically. This is useful if the manager does not know a priori the set of objects that are supported by an agent or that are in a particular MIB view.

One of the major enhancements provided in SNMPv2 is the GetBulkRequest PDU. The purpose of this PDU is to minimize the number of protocol exchanges required to retrieve a large amount of management information. The GetBulkRequest PDU allows an SNMPv2 manager to request that the response be as large as possible given the constraints on message size.

The SetRequest-PDU is issued by a manager to request that the values of one or more objects be altered. The receiving SNMPv2 entity responds with a Response-PDU containing the same request-id. The SetRequest operation is atomic: Either all of the variables are updated or none are. If the responding entity is able to set values for all of the variables listed in the incoming variable-bindings list, then the Response-PDU includes the variable-bindings field, with a value supplied for each variable. If at least one of the variable values cannot be supplied, then no values are returned, and no values are updated. In the latter case, the error-status code indicates the reason for the failure, and the error-index field indicates the variable in the variable-bindings list that caused the failure.

The SNMPv2-Trap-PDU is generated and transmitted by an SNMPv2 entity acting in an agent role when an unusual event occurs. It is used to provide the management station with an asynchronous notification of some significant event. The variable-bindings list is used to contain the information associated with the trap message. Unlike the GetRequest, GetNextRequest, GetBulkRequest, SetRequest, and InformRequest-PDUs, the SNMPv2-Trap-PDU does not elicit a response from the receiving entity; it is an unconfirmed message.

The InformRequest-PDU is sent by an SNMPv2 entity acting in a manager role, on behalf of an application, to another SNMPv2 entity acting in a manager role, to provide management information to an application using the latter entity. As with the SNMPv2-Trap-PDU, the variable-bindings field is used to convey the associated information. The manager receiving an InformRequest acknowledges receipt with a Response-PDU.

For both the SNMPv2-Trap and the InformRequest, various conditions can be defined that indicate when the notification is generated; the information to be sent is also specified.

Simple Network Management Protocol Version 3 (SNMPv3)

Many of the functional deficiencies of SNMP were addressed in SNMPv2. To correct the security deficiencies of SNMPv1/v2, SNMPv3 was issued as a set of Proposed Standards in January 1998 (currently RFCs 2570 through 2575). This set of documents does not provide a complete SNMP capability but rather defines an overall SNMP architecture and a set of security capabilities. These are intended to be used with the existing SNMPv2.

SNMPv3 provides three important services: authentication, privacy, and access control. The first two are part of the User-Based Security (USM) model, and the last is defined in the View-Based Access Control Model (VACM). Security services are governed by the identity of the user requesting the service; this identity is expressed as a principal, which may be an individual or an application or a group of individuals or applications.

The authentication mechanism in USM assures that a received message was transmitted by the principal whose identifier appears as the source in the message header. This mechanism also assures that the message has not been altered in transit and has not been artificially delayed or replayed. The sending principal provides authentication by including a message authentication code with the SNMP message it is sending. This code is a function of the contents of the message, the identity of the sending and receiving parties, the time of transmission, and a secret key that should be known only to sender and receiver. The secret key must be set up outside of USM as a configuration function. That is, the configuration manager or network manager is responsible for distributing secret keys to be loaded into the databases of the various SNMP managers and agents. This can be done manually or using some form of secure data transfer outside of USM. When the receiving principal gets the message, it uses the same secret key to calculate the message authentication code once again. If the receiver's version of the code matches the value appended to the incoming message, then the receiver knows that the message can only have originated from the authorized manager and that the message was not altered in transit. The shared secret key between sending and receiving parties must be preconfigured. The actual authentication code used is known as HMAC, which is an Internet-standard authentication mechanism.

The privacy facility of USM enables managers and agents to encrypt messages. Again, manager principal and agent principal must share a secret key. In this case, if the two are configured to use the privacy facility, all traffic between them is encrypted using the Data Encryption Standard (DES). The sending principal encrypts the message using the DES algorithm and its secret key, and sends the message to the receiving principal, which decrypts it using the DES algorithm and the same secret key.

The access control facility makes it possible to configure agents to provide different levels of access to the agent's management information base (MIB) to different managers. An agent principal can restrict access to its MIB for a particular manager principal in two ways. First, it can restrict access to a certain portion of its MIB. For example, an agent may restrict most manager parties to viewing performance-related statistics and only allow a single designated manager principal to view and update configuration parameters. Second, the agent can limit the operations that a manager can use on that portion of the MIB. For example, a particular manager principal could be limited to read-only access to a portion of an agent's MIB. The access control policy to be used by an agent for each manager must be preconfigured and essentially consists of a table that detail the access privileges of the various authorized managers.

22.4 RECOMMENDED READING AND WEB SITES

[ROSE98] provides a book-length treatment of electronic mail, including some coverage of SMTP and MIME. [KRIS01] provides good coverage of HTTP. [STAL99] provides a comprehensive and detailed examination of SNMP, SNMPv2, and SNMPv3; the book also provides an overview of network management technology.

KRIS01	Krishnamurthy, B., and Rexford, J. *Web Protocols and Practice: HTTP/1.1, Networking Protocols, Caching, and Traffic Measurement.* Upper Saddle River, NJ: Prentice Hall, 2001.
ROSE98	Rose, M., and Strom, D. *Internet Messaging: From the Desktop to the Enterprise.* Upper Saddle River, NJ: Prentice Hall, 1998.
STAL99	Stallings, W. *SNMP, SNMPv2, SNMPv3, and RMON 1 and 2.* Reading, MA: Addison-Wesley, 1999.

Recommended Web Sites:

- **WWW Consortium:** Contains up-to-date information on HTTP and related topics.
- **Simple Web Site:** Maintained by the University of Twente. It is a good source of information on SNMP, including pointers to many public-domain implementations and lists of books and articles.

22.5 KEY TERMS, REVIEW QUESTIONS, AND PROBLEMS

Key Terms

agent base64 electronic mail Hypertext Transfer Protocol (HTTP) management information base (MIB)	management station Multipurpose Internet Mail Extension (MIME) network management protocol network management system	proxy radix-64 encoding Simple Mail Transfer Protocol (SMTP) Simple Network Management Protocol (SNMP)

Review Questions

22.1 What is the difference between the RFC 821 and RFC 822?

22.2 What are the SMTP and MIME standards?

22.3 What is the difference between a MIME content type and a MIME transfer encoding?

22.4 Briefly explain radix-64 encoding.

22.5 Explain the differences among http proxy, gateway, and tunnel.

22.6 What is a network management system?

22.7 List and briefly define the key elements of SNMP.

22.8 What functions are provided by SNMP?

22.9 What are the differences among SNMPv1, SNMPv2, and SNMPv3?

Problems

22.1 Electronic mail systems differ in the manner in which multiple recipients are handled. In some systems, the originating user agent or mail sender makes all the necessary copies and these are sent out independently. An alternative approach is to determine the route for each destination first. Then a single message is sent out on a common portion of the route and copies are only made when the routes diverge; this process is referred to as mail-bagging. Discuss the relative advantages and disadvantages of the two methods.

22.2 The original (version 1) specification of SNMP has the following definition of a new type:
Gauge: ≔ [APPLICATION 2] IMPLICIT INTEGER (0..4294967295)

The standard includes the following explanation of the semantics of this type:

> This application-wide type represents a non-negative integer, which may increase or decrease, but which latches at a maximum value. This standard specifies a maximum value of $2^{23} - 1$ (4294967295 decimal) for gauges.

Unfortunately, the word *latch* is not defined, and this has resulted in two different interpretations. The SNMPv2 standard cleared up the ambiguity with the following definition:

> The value of a Gauge has its maximum value whenever the information being modeled is greater than or equal to that maximum value; if the information being modeled subsequently decreases below the maximum value, the Gauge also decreases.

    a. What is the alternative interpretation?
    b. Discuss the pros and cons of the two interpretations.

22.3 Excluding the connection establishment and termination, what is the minimum number of network round trips to send a small email message using SMTP?

22.4 Although TCP is a full-duplex protocol, SMTP uses TCP in a half-duplex fashion. The client sends a command and then stops and waits for the reply. How can this half-duplex operation fool the TCP slow start mechanism when the network is running near capacity?

22.5 Because SNMP uses two different port numbers (UDP ports 161 and 162), a single system can easily run both a manager and an agent. What would happen if the same port number were used for both?

APPENDIX A

RFCs Cited in This Book

Number	Title	Date
768	User Datagram Protocol (UDP)	1980
791	Internet Protocol (IP)	1981
792	Internet Control Message Protocol (ICMP)	1981
793	Transmission Control Protocol (TCP)	1981
821	Simple Mail Transfer Protocol (SMTP)	1982
822	Standard for the Format of ARPA Internet Text Messages	1982
959	File Transfer Protocol	1985
1350	Trivial File Transfer Protocol (Revision 2)	1992
1633	Integrated Service in the Internet Architecture: An Overview	1994
1636	Security in the Internet Architecture	1994
1752	The Recommendation for the IP Next Generation Protocol	1995
1771	A Border Gateway Protocol 4 (BGP-4)	1995
1812	Requirements for IP Version 4 Routers	1995
1901	Introduction to Community-Based SNMPv2	1996
1905	Protocol Operations for SNMPv2	1996
1906	Transport Mappings for SNMPv2	1996
1907	Management Information Base for SNMPv2	1996
1908	Coexistence Between Version 1 and Version 2 of the Internet-Standard Network Management Framework	1996
1909	An Administrative Infrastructure for SNMPv2	1996
2045	Multipurpose Internet Mail Extensions (MIME) Part One: Format of Internet Message Bodies	1996
2046	Multipurpose Internet Mail Extensions (MIME) Part Two: Media Types	1996

Number	Title	Date
2047	MIME (Multipurpose Internet Mail Extensions) Part Three: Message Header Extensions for Non-ASCII Text	1996
2048	Multipurpose Internet Mail Extensions (MIME) Part Four: Registration Procedures	1996
2049	Multipurpose Internet Mail Extensions (MIME) Part Five: Conformance Criteria and Examples	1996
2205	Resource ReSerVation Protocol (RSVP)—Version 1 Functional Specification	1997
2328	Open Shortest Path First (OSPF) Version 2	1998
2246	The TLS Protocol	1999
2373	IP Version 6 Addressing Architecture	1998
2401	Security Architecture for the Internet Protocol	1998
2402	IP Authentication Header	1998
2406	IP Encapsulating Security Payload (ESP)	1998
2408	Internet Security Association and Key Management Protocol	1998
2460	Internet Protocol, Version 6 Specification	1998
2474	Definition of the Differentiated Services Field in the IPv4 and IPv6 Headers	1998
2475	An Architecture for Differentiated Services	1998
2570	Introduction to Version 3 of the Internet-Standard Network Management Framework	1999
2571	An Architecture for Describing SNMP Management Frameworks	1999
2572	Message Processing and Dispatching for SNMP	1999
2573	SNMP Applications	1999
2574	User-Based Security Model for SNMPv3	1999
2575	View-Based Access Control Model (VACM) for SNMP	1999
2578	Structure of Management Information Version 2 (SMIv2)	1999
2579	Textual Conventions for SMIv2	1999
2580	Conformance Statements for SMIv2	1999
2597	Assured Forwarding PHB Group	1999
2581	TCP Congestion Control	1999
2616	Hypertext Transfer Protocol—HTTP/1.1	1999
2828	Internet Security Glossary	2000
3015	Media Gateway Control Protocol	2000
3168	The Addition of Explicit Congestion Notification (ECN) to IP	2001
3246	An Expedited Forwarding (PHB Per-Hop Behavior)	2002
3376	Internet Group Management Protocol, Version 3	2002

APPENDIX B

FOURIER ANALYSIS

In this appendix, we provide an overview of key concepts in Fourier analysis.

B.1 FOURIER SERIES REPRESENTATION OF PERIODIC SIGNALS

With the aid of a good table of integrals, it is a remarkably simple task to determine the frequency domain nature of many signals. We begin with periodic signals. Any periodic signal can be represented as a sum of sinusoids, known as a Fourier series:[1]

$$x(t) = \frac{A_0}{2} + \sum_{n=1}^{\infty} [A_n \cos(2\pi n f_0 t) + B_n \sin(2\pi n f_0 t)]$$

where f_0 is the reciprocal of the period of the signal ($f_0 = 1/T$). The frequency f_0 is referred to as the **fundamental frequency** or **fundamental harmonic**; integer multiples of f_0 are referred to as **harmonics**. Thus a periodic signal with period T consists of the fundamental frequency $f_0 = 1/T$ plus integer multiples of that frequency. If $A_0 \neq 0$, then $x(t)$ has a **dc component**.

The values of the coefficients are calculated as follows:

$$A_0 = \frac{2}{T} \int_0^T x(t)\, dt$$

$$A_n = \frac{2}{T} \int_0^T x(t) \cos(2\pi n f_0 t)\, dt$$

$$B_n = \frac{2}{T} \int_0^T x(t) \sin(2\pi n f_0 t)\, dt$$

[1] Mathematicians typically write Fourier series and transform expressions using the variable w_0, which has a dimension of radians per second and where $w_0 = 2\pi f_0$. For physics and engineering, the f_0 formulation is preferred; it makes for simpler expressions, and is it intuitively more satisfying to have frequency expressed in Hz rather than radians per second.

This form of representation, known as the sine-cosine representation, is the easiest form to compute but suffers from the fact that there are two components at each frequency. A more meaningful representation, the amplitude-phase representation, takes the form

$$x(t) = \frac{C_0}{2} + \sum_{n=1}^{\infty} C_n \cos(2\pi n f_0 t + \theta_n)$$

This relates to the earlier representation as follows:

$$C_0 = A_0$$

$$C_n = \sqrt{A_n^2 + B_n^2}$$

$$\theta_n = \tan^{-1}\left(\frac{-B_n}{A_n}\right)$$

Examples of the Fourier series for periodic signals are shown in Figure B.1.

B.2 FOURIER TRANSFORM REPRESENTATION OF APERIODIC SIGNALS

For a periodic signal, we have seen that its spectrum consists of discrete frequency components, at the fundamental frequency and its harmonics. For an aperiodic signal, the spectrum consists of a continuum of frequencies. This spectrum can be defined by the Fourier transform. For a signal $x(t)$ with a spectrum $X(f)$, the following relationships hold:

$$x(t) = \int_{-\infty}^{\infty} X(f) e^{j2\pi ft}\, df$$

$$X(f) = \int_{-\infty}^{\infty} x(t) e^{-j2\pi ft}\, dt$$

where $j = \sqrt{-1}$. The presence of an imaginary number in the equations is a matter of convenience. The imaginary component has a physical interpretation having to do with the phase of a waveform, and a discussion of this topic is beyond the scope of this book.

Figure B.2 presents some examples of Fourier transform pairs.

Power Spectral Density and Bandwidth

The absolute bandwidth of any time-limited signal is infinite. In practical terms, however, most of the power in a signal is concentrated in some finite band, and the effective bandwidth consists of that portion of the spectrum that contains most of

Signal	Fourier Series

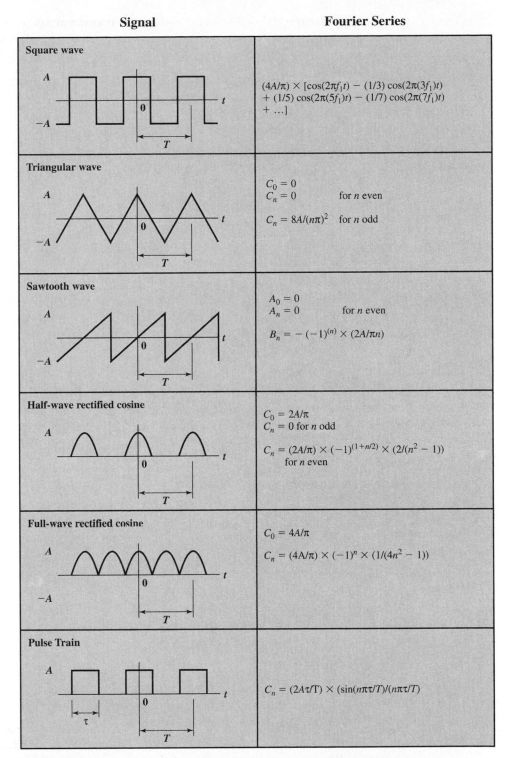

Square wave

$(4A/\pi) \times [\cos(2\pi f_1 t) - (1/3)\cos(2\pi(3f_1)t)$
$+ (1/5)\cos(2\pi(5f_1)t) - (1/7)\cos(2\pi(7f_1)t)$
$+ \ldots]$

Triangular wave

$C_0 = 0$
$C_n = 0 \qquad$ for n even

$C_n = 8A/(n\pi)^2 \quad$ for n odd

Sawtooth wave

$A_0 = 0$
$A_n = 0 \qquad$ for n even

$B_n = -(-1)^{(n)} \times (2A/\pi n)$

Half-wave rectified cosine

$C_0 = 2A/\pi$
$C_n = 0$ for n odd

$C_n = (2A/\pi) \times (-1)^{(1+n/2)} \times (2/(n^2 - 1))$
$\qquad$ for n even

Full-wave rectified cosine

$C_0 = 4A/\pi$

$C_n = (4A/\pi) \times (-1)^n \times (1/(4n^2 - 1))$

Pulse Train

$C_n = (2A\tau/T) \times (\sin(n\pi\tau/T)/(n\pi\tau/T))$

Figure B.1 Some Common Periodic Signals and Their Fourier Series

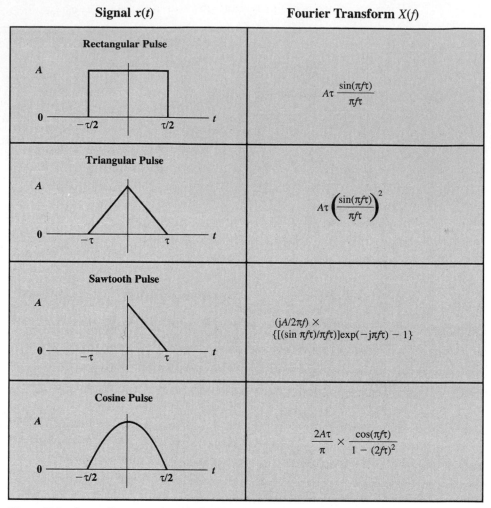

Figure B.2   Some Common Aperiodic Signals and Their Fourier Transforms

the power. To make this concept precise, we need to define the power spectral density (PSD). In essence, the PSD describes the power content of a signal as a function of frequency, so that it shows how much power is present over various frequency bands.

First, we observe the power in the time domain. A function $x(t)$ usually specifies a signal in terms of either voltage or current. In either case, the instantaneous power in the signal is proportional to $|x(t)|^2$. We define the average power of a time-limited signal as

$$P = \frac{1}{t_1 - t_2} \int_{t_1}^{t_2} |x(t)|^2 \, dt$$

For a periodic signal the average power in one period is

$$P = \frac{1}{T} \int_0^T |x(t)|^2 \, dt$$

We would like to know the distribution of power as a function of frequency. For periodic signals, this is easily expressed in terms of the coefficients of the Fourier series. The power spectral density $S(f)$ obeys

$$S(f) = \sum_{n=-\infty}^{\infty} |C_n|^2 \delta(f - nf_0)$$

where f_0 is the inverse of the period of the signal $(f_0 = 1/T)$, C_n is the coefficient in the amplitude-phase representation of a Fourier series, and $\delta(t)$ is the unit impulse, or delta, function, defined as

$$\delta(t) = \begin{cases} 0 & \text{if } t \neq 0 \\ \infty & \text{if } t = 0 \end{cases}$$

$$\int_{-\infty}^{\infty} \delta(t) \, dt = 1$$

The power spectral density $S(f)$ for aperiodic functions is more difficult to define. In essence, it is obtained by defining a "period" T_0 and allowing T_0 to increase without limit.

For a continuous valued function $S(f)$, the power contained in a band of frequencies, $f_1 < f < f_2$, is

$$P = 2 \int_{f_1}^{f_2} S(f) \, df$$

For a periodic waveform, the power through the first j harmonics is

$$P = \frac{1}{4} C_0^2 + \frac{1}{2} \sum_{n=1}^{j} C_n^2$$

With these concepts, we can now define the half-power bandwidth, which is perhaps the most common bandwidth definition. The half-power bandwidth is the interval between frequencies at which $S(f)$ has dropped to half of its maximum value of power, or 3 dB below the peak value.

B.3 RECOMMENDED READING

A very accessible treatment of Fourier series and Fourier transforms is [JAME01]. For a thorough understanding of Fourier series and transforms, the book to read is [KAMM00].

JAME01   James, J. *A Student's Guide to Fourier Transforms.* Cambridge, England: Cambridge University Press, 2001.

KAMM00   Kammler, D. *A First Course in Fourier Analysis.* Upper Saddle River, NJ: Prentice Hall, 2000.

APPENDIX C

SOCKETS PROGRAMMING

The concept of sockets and sockets programming was developed in the 1980s in the Unix environment as the Berkeley Sockets Interface. In essence, a socket enables communications between a client and server process and may be either connection-oriented or connectionless. A socket can be considered an endpoint in a communication. A client socket in one computer uses an address to call a server socket on another computer. Once the appropriate sockets are engaged, the two computers can exchange data.

Typically, computers with server sockets keep a TCP or UDP port open, ready for unscheduled incoming calls. The client typically determines the socket identification of the desired server by finding it in a Domain Name System (DNS) database. Once a connection is made, the server switches the dialogue to a different port number to free up the main port number for additional incoming calls.

Internet applications, such as TELNET and remote login (rlogin), make use of sockets, with the details hidden from the user. However, sockets can be constructed from within a program (in a language such as C or Java), enabling the programmer to easily support networking functions and applications. The sockets programming mechanism includes sufficient semantics to permit unrelated processes on different hosts to communicate.

The Berkeley Sockets Interface is the de facto standard application programming interface (API) for developing networking applications, spanning a wide range of operating systems. The sockets API provides generic access to interprocess communications services. Thus, the sockets capability is ideally suited for students to learn the principles of protocols and distributed applications by hands-on program development.

The Web site for this course includes an overview of sockets programming plus links to sites with more information on the subject. In addition, the instructor's manual includes a set of programming projects.

APPENDIX D

PROJECTS FOR TEACHING DATA AND COMPUTER COMMUNICATIONS

Many instructors believe that research or implementation projects are crucial to the clear understanding of the concepts of data and computer communications. Without projects, it may be difficult for students to grasp some of the basic concepts and interactions among components. Projects reinforce the concepts introduced in the book, give the student a greater appreciation of the how protocols and transmission schemes work, and can motivate students and give them confidence that they have mastered the material.

In this text, I have tried to present the concepts as clearly as possible and have provided over 270 homework problems to reinforce those concepts. Many instructors will wish to supplement this material with projects. This appendix provides some guidance in that regard and describes support material available in the instructor's manual. The support material covers four types of projects:

- Simulation projects
- Performance modeling projects
- Research projects
- Reading/report assignments

D.1 SIMULATION PROJECTS

An excellent way to obtain a grasp of the operation of communication protocols and network configurations, and to study and appreciate some of the design tradeoffs and performance implications, is by simulating key elements. A tool that is useful for this purpose is *cnet*.

Compared to actual hardware/software implementation, simulation provides several advantages for both research and educational use:

- With simulation, it is easy to modify various elements of a network configuration or various features of a protocol, to vary the performance characteristics of various components, and then to analyze the effects of such modifications.
- Simulation provides for detailed performance statistics collection, which can be used to understand performance tradeoffs.

The *cnet* network simulator [MCDO91] enables experimentation with various data link layer, network layer, routing and transport layer protocols, and with various network configurations. It has been specifically designed for undergraduate computer networking courses and used worldwide by thousands of students since 1991.

The *cnet* simulator was developed by Professor Chris McDonald at the University of Western Australia. Professor McDonald has developed a Student User's Manual and a set of project assignments specifically for use with Data and Computer Communications and available to professors on request.

The *cnet* simulator runs under a variety of UNIX and LINUX platforms. The software can be downloaded from the *cnet* Web site. It is available at no cost for noncommercial use.

D.2 PERFORMANCE MODELING

An alternative to simulation for assessing the performance of a communications system or networking protocol is analytic modeling. As used here, analytic modeling refers to tools for doing queuing analysis, as well as tools for doing simple statistical tests on network traffic data and tools for generating time series for analysis.

A powerful and easy-to-use set of tools has been developed by Professor Kenneth Christensen at the University of South Florida. His *tools page* contains downloadable tools primarily related to performance evaluation of computer networks and to TCP/IP sockets programming. Each tool is written in ANSI C. The format for each tool is the same, with the program header describing tool purpose, general notes, sample input, sample output, build instructions, execution instructions, and author/contact information. The code is documented with extensive inline comments and header blocks for all functions. The goal for each tool is that it can serve as a teaching tool for the concept implemented by the tool (and as a model for good programming practices). Thus, the emphasis is on simplicity and clarity. It is assumed that the student will have access to a C compiler and have at least moderate experience in C programming.

Professor Christensen has developed a Student User's Manual and a set of project assignments specifically for use with Data and Computer Communications and available to professors on request. The software can be downloaded from the *tools* Web site. It is available at no cost for noncommercial use.

D.3 RESEARCH PROJECTS

An effective way of reinforcing basic concepts from the course and for teaching students research skills is to assign a research project. Such a project could involve a literature search as well as a Web search of vendor products, research lab activities, and standardization efforts. Projects could be assigned to teams or, for smaller projects, to individuals. In any case, it is best to require some sort of project proposal early in the term, giving the instructor time to evaluate the proposal for appropriate topic and appropriate level of effort. Student handouts for research projects should include

- A format for the proposal
- A format for the final report
- A schedule with intermediate and final deadlines
- A list of possible project topics

The students can select one of the listed topics or devise their own comparable project. The instructor's manual includes a suggested format for the proposal and final report plus a list of possible research topics.

D.4 READING/REPORT ASSIGNMENTS

Another excellent way to rcinforce concepts from the course and to give students research experience is to assign papers from the literature to be read and analyzed. The instructor's manual includes a suggested list of papers to be assigned. All of the papers are readily available either via the Internet or in any good college technical library. The manual also includes a suggested assignment wording.

GLOSSARY

Some of the definitions in this glossary are from the *American National Standard Dictionary of Information Technology*, ANSI Standard X3.172, 1995. These are marked with an asterisk.

Abstract Syntax Notation One (ASN.1)   A formal language used to define syntax. In the case of SNMP, ASN.1 notation is used to defined the format of SNMP protocol data units and of objects.

Aloha   A medium access control technique for multiple access transmission media. A station transmits whenever it has data to send. Unacknowledged transmissions are repeated.

Amplitude   The size or magnitude of a voltage or current waveform.

Amplitude modulation*   A form of modulation in which the amplitude of a carrier wave is varied in accordance with some characteristic of the modulating signal.

Amplitude-shift keying   Modulation in which the two binary values are represented by two different amplitudes of the carrier frequency.

Analog data*   Data represented by a physical quantity that is considered to be continuously variable and whose magnitude is made directly proportional to the data or to a suitable function of the data.

Analog signal   A continuously varying electromagnetic wave that may be propagated over a variety of media.

Analog transmission   The transmission of analog signals without regard to content. The signal may be amplified, but there is no intermediate attempt to recover the data from the signal.

Angle modulation*   Modulation in which the angle of a sine wave carrier is varied. Phase and frequency modulation are particular forms of angle modulation.

Application layer   Layer 7 of the OSI model. This layer determines the interface of the system with the user.

Asymmetric encryption   A form of cryptosystem in which encryption and decryption are performed using two different keys, one of which is referred to as the public key and one of which is referred to as the private key. Also known as public-key encryption.

Asynchronous transfer mode (ATM)   A form of packet transmission using fixed-size packets, called cells. ATM is the data transfer interface for B-ISDN. Unlike X.25, ATM does not provide error control and flow control mechanisms.

Asynchronous transmission   Transmission in which each information character is individually synchronized (usually by the use of start elements and stop elements).

Attenuation   A decrease in magnitude of current, voltage, or power of a signal in transmission between points.

ATM Adaptation Layer (AAL)   The layer that maps information transfer protocols onto ATM.

Authentication*   A process used to verify the integrity of transmitted data, especially a message.

Automatic repeat request   A feature that automatically initiates a request for retransmission when an error in transmission is detected.

Balanced transmission   A transmission mode in which signals are transmitted as a current that travels down one conductor and returns on the other. For digital signals, this technique is known as differential signaling, with the binary value depending on the voltage difference.

Bandlimited signal   A signal all of whose energy is contained within a finite frequency range.

Bandwidth*   The difference between the limiting (upper and lower) frequencies of a continuous frequency spectrum.

Baseband   Transmission of signals without modulation. In a baseband local network, digital signals (1s and 0s) are inserted directly onto the cable as voltage pulses. The entire spectrum of the cable is consumed by the signal. This scheme does not allow frequency division multiplexing.

Baud   A unit of signaling speed equal to the number of discrete conditions or signal events per second, or the reciprocal of the time of the shortest signal element.

Bit error rate   The probability that a transmitted bit is received in error.

Bit stuffing   The insertion of extra bits into a data stream to avoid the appearance of unintended control sequences.

Bridge*   A functional unit that interconnects two local area networks (LANs) that use the same logical link control protocol but may use different medium access control protocols.

Broadband   In general, wide bandwidth equipment or systems that can carry signals occupying a large portion of the electromagnetic spectrum. Typically, a broadband communication system can simultaneously accommodate voice, data, video, and other services. In digital transmission systems, the term connotes high data rate.

Broadband ISDN (B-ISDN)   A second generation of ISDN. The key characteristic of broadband ISDN is that it provides transmission channels capable of supporting rates greater than the primary ISDN rate.

Broadband LAN   The use of coaxial cable for providing data transfer by means of analog (radio-frequency) signals. Digital signals are passed through a modem and transmitted over one of the frequency bands of the cable.

Broadcast   The simultaneous transmission of data to a number of stations.

Broadcast address   An address that designates all entities within a domain (e.g., network, internet).

Broadcast communication network   A communication network in which a transmission from one station is broadcast to and received by all other stations.

Bus*   One or more conductors that serve as a common connection for a related group of devices.

Byte   A group of bits, usually eight, used to represent a character of other data.

Carrier   A continuous frequency capable of being modulated or impressed with a second (information-carrying) signal.

CATV   Community Antenna Television. CATV cable is used for broadband local networks, and broadcast TV distribution.

Cell relay   The packet-switching mechanism used for the fixed-size packets called cells. ATM is based on cell relay technology.

Checksum   An error-detecting code based on a summation operation performed on the bits to be checked.

Ciphertext   The output of an encryption algorithm; the encrypted form of a message or data.

Circuit switching   A method of communicating in which a dedicated communications path is established between two devices through one or more intermediate switching nodes. Unlike packet switching, digital data are sent as a continuous stream of bits. Bandwidth is guaranteed, and delay is essentially limited to propagation time. The telephone system uses circuit switching.

Coaxial cable   A cable consisting of one conductor, usually a small copper tube or wire, within and insulated from another conductor of larger diameter, usually copper tubing or copper braid.

Codec (Coder-decoder)   Transforms analog data into a digital bit stream (coder), and digital signals into analog data (decoder).

Collision   A condition in which two packets are being transmitted over a medium at the same time. Their interference makes both unintelligible.

Common carrier   In the United States, companies that furnish communication services to the public. The usual connotation is for long-distance telecommunications services. Common carriers are subject to regulation by federal and state regulatory commissions.

Common channel signaling   Technique in which network control signals (e.g., call request) are separated from the associated voice or data path by placing the signaling from a group of voice or data paths on a separate channel dedicated to signaling only.

Communications architecture   The hardware and software structure that implements the communications function.

Communication network   A collection of interconnected functional units that provides a data communications service among stations attached to the network.

Connectionless data transfer   A protocol for exchanging data in an unplanned fashion and without prior coordination (e.g., datagram).

Connection-oriented data transfer   A protocol for exchanging data in which a logical connection is established between the endpoints (e.g., virtual circuit).

Contention   The condition when two or more stations attempt to use the same channel at the same time.

Conventional encryption   Symmetric encryption.

Crosstalk*   The phenomenon in which a signal transmitted on one circuit or channel of a transmission system creates an undesired effect in another circuit or channel.

CSMA (Carrier Sense Multiple Access)   A medium access control technique for multiple-access transmission media. A station wishing to transmit first senses the medium and transmits only if the medium is idle.

CSMA/CD (Carrier Sense Multiple Access with Collision Detection)   A refinement of CSMA in which a station ceases transmission if it detects a collision.

Current-mode transmission   A transmission mode in which the transmitter alternately applies current to each of two conductors in a twisted pair to represent logic 1 or 0. The total current is constant and always in the same direction.

Cyclic redundancy check   An error detecting code in which the code is the remainder resulting from dividing the bits to be checked by a predetermined binary number.

Data circuit-terminating equipment (DCE)   In a data station, the equipment that provides the signal conversion and coding between the data terminal equipment (DTE) and the line. The DCE may be separate equipment or an integral part of the DTE or of intermediate equipment. The DCE may perform other functions that are normally performed at the network end of the line.

Datagram*   In packet switching, a packet, independent of other packets, that carries information sufficient for routing from the originating data terminal equipment (DTE) to the destination DTE without the necessity of establishing a connection between the DTEs and the network.

Data Link Layer* In OSI, the layer that provides service to transfer data between network layer entities, usually in adjacent nodes. The data link layer detects and possibly corrects errors that may occur in the physical layer.

Data terminal equipment (DTE)* Equipment consisting of digital end instruments that convert the user information into data signals for transmission, or reconvert the received data signals into user information.

Decibel A measure of the relative strength of two signals. The number of decibels is 10 times the log of the ratio of the power of two signals, or 20 times the log of the ratio of the voltage of two signals.

Decryption The translation of encrypted text or data (called ciphertext) into original text or data (called plaintext). Also called deciphering.

Delay distortion Distortion of a signal occurring when the propagation delay for the transmission medium is not constant over the frequency range of the signal.

Demand-assignment multiple access A technique for allocating satellite capacity, based on either FDM or TDM, in which capacity is granted on demand.

Differential encoding A means of encoding digital data on a digital or analog signal such that the binary value is determined by a signal change rather than a signal level.

Digital data Data consisting of a sequence of discrete elements.

Digital signal A discrete or discontinuous signal, such as voltage pulses.

Digital signature An authentication mechanism that enables the creator of a message to attach a code that acts as a signature. The signature guarantees the source and integrity of the message.

Digital switch A star topology local network. Usually refers to a system that handles only data but not voice.

Digital transmission The transmission of digital data, using either an analog or digital signal, in which the digital data are recovered and repeated at intermediate points to reduce the effects of noise.

Digitize* To convert an analog signal to a digital signal.

Encapsulation The addition of control information by a protocol entity to data obtained from a protocol user.

Encrypt* To convert plaintext or data into unintelligible form by the use of a code in such a manner that reconversion to the original form is possible.

Error-detecting code* A code in which each expression conforms to specific rules of construction, so that if certain errors occur in an expression, the resulting expression will not conform to the rules of construction and thus the presence of the errors is detected.

Error rate* The ratio of the number of data units in error to the total number of data units.

Flow control   The function performed by a receiving entity to limit the amount or rate of data that is sent by a transmitting entity.

Frame   A group of bits that includes data plus one or more addresses and other protocol control information. Generally refers to a link layer (OSI layer 2) protocol data unit.

Frame check sequence   An error-detecting code inserted as a field in a block of data to be transmitted. The code serves to check for errors upon reception of the data.

Frame relay   A form of packet switching based on the use of variable-length link-layer frames. There is no network layer and many of the basic functions have been streamlined or eliminated to provide for greater throughput.

Frequency   Rate of signal oscillation in hertz.

Frequency division multiplexing   The division of a transmission facility into two or more channels by splitting the frequency band transmitted by the facility into narrower bands, each of which is used to constitute a distinct channel.

Frequency modulation   Modulation in which the frequency of an alternating current is the characteristic varied.

Frequency shift keying   Modulation in which the two binary values are represented by two different frequencies near the carrier frequency.

Full-duplex transmission   Data transmission in both directions at the same time.

Half-duplex transmission   Data transmission in either direction, one direction at a time.

Hash function   A function that maps a variable length data block or message into a fixed-length value called a hash code. The function is designed in such a way that, when protected, it provides an authenticator to the data or message. Also referred to as a message digest.

HDLC (high-level data link control)   A very common bit-oriented data link protocol (OSI layer 2) issued by ISO. Similar protocols are LAPB, LAPD, and LLC.

Header   System-defined control information that precedes user data.

Hop count   The number of hops along a path from a given source to a given destination is the number of network nodes (packet-switching nodes, ATM switches, routers, etc.) that a packet encounters along that path.

Impulse noise   A high-amplitude, short-duration noise pulse.

Integrated services digital network   A worldwide telecommunication service that uses digital transmission and switching technology to support voice and digital data communication.

Intermediate system (IS)   A device attached to two or more networks in an internet and that performs routing and relaying of data between end systems. Examples of intermediate systems are bridges and routers.

Intermodulation noise   Noise due to the nonlinear combination of signals of different frequencies.

Internetwork   A collection of packet-switching and broadcast networks that are connected via routers.

Internet protocol   An internetworking protocol that provides connectionless service across multiple packet-switching networks.

Internetworking   Communication among devices across multiple networks.

Layer*   A group of services, functions, and protocols that is complete from a conceptual point of view, that is one out of a set of hierarchically arranged groups, and that extends across all systems that conform to the network architecture.

Local area network   A communication network that provides interconnection of a variety of data communicating devices within a small area.

Local loop   Transmission path, generally twisted pair, between the individual subscriber and the nearest switching center of the public telecommunications network.

Longitudinal redundancy check   The use of a set of parity bits for a block of characters such that there is a parity bit for each bit position in the characters.

Manchester encoding   A digital signaling technique in which there is a transition in the middle of each bit time. A 1 is encoded with a high level during the first half of the bit time; a 0 is encoded with a low level during the first half of the bit time.

Medium access control (MAC)   For broadcast networks, the method of determining which device has access to the transmission medium at any time. CSMA/CD and token are common access methods.

Microwave   Electromagnetic waves in the frequency range of about 2 to 40 GHz.

Modem (modulator/demodulator)   Transforms a digital bit stream into an analog signal (modulator), and vice versa (demodulator).

Modulation*   The process, or result of the process, of varying certain characteristics of a signal, called a carrier, in accordance with a message signal.

Multicast address   An address that designates a group of entities within a domain (e.g., network, internet).

Multiplexing   In data transmission, a function that permits two or more data sources to share a common transmission medium such that each data source has its own channel.

Multipoint   A configuration in which more than two stations share a transmission path.

Network layer   Layer 3 of the OSI model. Responsible for routing data through a communication network.

Network terminating equipment   Grouping of ISDN functions at the boundary between the ISDN and the subscriber.

Noise   Unwanted signals that combine with and hence distort the signal intended for transmission and reception.

Nonreturn to zero   A digital signaling technique in which the signal is at a constant level for the duration of a bit time.

Octet   A group of eight bits, usually operated upon as an entity.

Open Systems Interconnection (OSI) Reference Model   A model of communications between cooperating devices. It defines a seven-layer architecture of communication functions.

Optical fiber   A thin filament of glass or other transparent material through which a signal-encoded light beam may be transmitted by means of total internal reflection.

Packet   A group of bits that includes data plus control information. Generally refers to a network layer (OSI layer 3) protocol data unit.

Packet switching   A method of transmitting messages through a communication network, in which long messages are subdivided into short packets. The packets are then transmitted as in message switching.

Parity bit*   A check bit appended to an array of binary digits to make the sum of all the binary digits, including the check bit, always odd (odd parity) or always even (even parity).

PBX   Private branch exchange. A telephone exchange on the user's premises. Provides a switching facility for telephones on extension lines within the building and access to the public telephone network.

Period   The absolute value of the minimum interval after which the same characteristics of a periodic waveform recur.

Periodic waveform   A waveform $f(t)$ that satisfies $f(t) = f(t + nk)$ for all integers n, with k being a constant.

Phase   For a periodic signal $f(t)$, the fractional part t/P of the period P through which t has advanced relative to an arbitrary origin. The origin is usually taken at the last previous passage through zero from the negative to the positive direction.

Phase modulation   Modulation in which the phase angle of a carrier is the characteristic varied.

Phase-shift keying   Modulation in which the phase of the carrier signal is shifted to represent digital data.

Physical layer   Layer 1 of the OSI model. Concerned with the electrical, mechanical, and timing aspects of signal transmission over a medium.

Piggybacking The inclusion of an acknowledgment to a previously received packet in an outgoing data packet.

Plaintext The input to an encryption function or the output of a decryption function.

Point-to-point A configuration in which two stations share a transmission path.

Poll and select The process by which a primary station invites secondary stations, one at a time, to transmit (poll), and by which a primary station requests that a secondary receive data (select).

Power spectral density (PSD) The PSD of a signal is a function of frequency that represents the power per unit bandwidth of the spectral components at each frequency.

Presentation layer* Layer 6 of the OSI model. Provides for the selection of a common syntax for representing data and for transformation of application data into and from the common syntax.

Private Key One of the two keys used in an asymmetric encryption system. For secure communication, the private key should only be known to its creator.

Propagation Delay The delay between the time a signal enters a channel and the time it is received.

Protocol A set of rules that govern the operation of functional units to achieve communication.

Protocol control information* Information exchanged between entities of a given layer, via the service provided by the next lower layer, to coordinate their joint operation.

Protocol data unit (PDU)* A set of data specified in a protocol of a given layer and consisting of protocol control information of that layer, and possibly user data of that layer.

Public data network A government-controlled or national-monopoly packet-switching network. This service is publicly available to data processing users.

Public key One of the two keys used in an asymmetric encryption system. The public key is made public, to be used in conjunction with a corresponding private key.

Public-key encryption Asymmetric encryption.

Pulse code modulation A process in which a signal is sampled, and the magnitude of each sample with respect to a fixed reference is quantized and converted by coding to a digital signal.

Residual error rate The error rate remaining after attempts at correction are made.

Repeater A device that receives data on one communication link and transmits it, bit by bit, on another link as fast as the data are received, without buffering.

Ring A local network topology in which stations are attached to repeaters connected in a closed loop. Data are transmitted in one direction around the ring and can be read by all attached stations.

Router An internetworking device that connects two computer networks. It makes use of an internet protocol and assumes that all of the attached devices on the networks use the same communications architecture and protocols. A router operates at OSI layer 3.

Routing The determination of a path that a data unit (frame, packet, message) will traverse from source to destination.

Scattering **(1) (fiber optics)** The change in direction of light rays after striking a small particle or particles, or due to minute variations in the density of glass. **(2) (radio-wave propagation)** The production of waves of changed direction or frequency when radio waves encounter matter.

Service access point A means of identifying a user of the services of a protocol entity. A protocol entity provides one or more SAPs for use by higher-level entities.

Session layer Layer 5 of the OSI model. Manages a logical connection (session) between two communicating processes or applications.

Signal element The part of a signal that occupies the shortest time interval of a signaling code. It is the smallest element recognized by a receiver and can correspond to a single bit, a part of a bit, or multiple bits.

Signaling The exchange of information specifically concerned with the establishment and control of connections, and with management, in a telecommunication network.

Simplex transmission Data transmission in one preassigned direction only.

Sliding-window technique A method of flow control in which a transmitting station may send numbered packets within a window of numbers. The window changes dynamically to allow additional packets to be sent.

Space division switching A circuit-switching technique in which each connection through the switch takes a physically separate and dedicated path.

Spectrum Refers to an absolute range of frequencies. For example, the spectrum of CATV cable is now about 5 to 400 MHz.

Star A topology in which all stations are connected to a central switch. Two stations communicate via circuit switching.

Statistical time division multiplexing A method of TDM in which time slots on a shared transmission line are allocated to I/O channels on demand.

Stop and wait A flow control protocol in which the sender transmits a block of data and then awaits an acknowledgment before transmitting the next block.

Switched communication network A communication network consisting of a network of nodes connected by point-to-point links. Data are transmitted from source to destination through intermediate nodes.

Symmetric encryption   A form of cryptosystem in which encryption and decryption are performed using the same key. Also known as conventional encryption.

Synchronous time division multiplexing   A method of TDM in which time slots on a shared transmission line are assigned to I/O channels on a fixed, predetermined basis.

Synchronous transmission   Data transmission in which the time of occurrence of each signal representing a bit is related to a fixed time frame.

Telematics   User-oriented information transmission services. Includes teletex, videotex, and facsimile.

Thermal noise   Statistically uniform noise due to the temperature of the transmission medium.

Time division multiplexing   The division of a transmission facility into two or more channels by allotting the facility to several different information channels, one at a time.

Time division switching   A circuit-switching technique in which time slots in a time multiplexed stream of data are manipulated to pass data from an input to an output.

Token bus   A medium access control technique for bus/tree. Stations form a logical ring, around which a token is passed. A station receiving the token may transmit data and then must pass the token on to the next station in the ring.

Token ring   A medium access control technique for rings. A token circulates around the ring. A station may transmit by seizing the token, inserting a packet onto the ring, and then retransmitting the token.

Topology   The structure, consisting of paths and switches, that provides the communications interconnection among nodes of a network.

Transmission medium   The physical path between transmitters and receivers in a communications system.

Transport layer   Layer 4 of the OSI model. Provides reliable, transparent transfer of data between endpoints.

Twisted pair   A transmission medium consisting of two insulated wires arranged in a regular spiral pattern.

Unbalanced transmission   A transmission mode in which signals are transmitted on a single conductor. Transmitter and receiver share a common ground.

Value-added network   A privately owned packet-switching network whose services are sold to the public.

Virtual circuit   A packet-switching service in which a connection (virtual circuit) is established between two stations at the start of transmission. All packets follow the same route, need not carry a complete address, and arrive in sequence.

White noise   Noise that has a flat, or uniform, frequency spectrum in the frequency range of interest.

REFERENCES

ABBREVIATIONS

ACM   Association for Computing Machinery
IEEE   Institute of Electrical and Electronics Engineers
NIST   National Institute of Standards and Technology

10GE02   10 Gigabit Ethernet Alliance. *10 Gigabit Ethernet—Technology Overview.* White paper, April 2002.

ADAM91   Adamek, J. *Foundations of Coding.* New York: Wiley, 1991.

ANDE95   Anderson, J.; Rappaport, T.; and Yoshida, S. "Propagation Measurements and Models for Wireless Communications Channels." *IEEE Communications Magazine*, January 1995.

ANDR99   Andrikopoulos, I.; Liakopoulous, A.; Pavlou, G.; and Sun, Z. "Providing Rate Guarantees for Internet Application Traffic Across ATM Networks." *IEEE Communications Surveys*, Third Quarter 1999. http://www.comsoc.org/pubs/surveys.

ARMI93   Armitage, G., and Adams, K. "Packet Reassembly During Cell Loss." *IEEE Network*, September 1995.

ARMI00   Armitage, G. *Quality of Service in IP Networks.* Indianapolis, IN: Macmillan Technical Publishing, 2000.

ASH90   Ash, R. *Information Theory.* New York: Dover, 1990.

BANT94   Bantz, D., and Bauchot, F. "Wireless LAN Design Alternatives." *IEEE Network*, March/April, 1994.

BELL00   Bellamy, J. *Digital Telephony.* New York: Wiley, 2000.

BELL90   Bellcore (Bell Communications Research). *Telecommunications Transmission Engineering, Volume 2: Facilities.* 1990.

BENE64   Benice, R. "An Analysis of Retransmission Systems." *IEEE Transactions on Communication Technology*, December 1964.

BERG91   Bergman, W. "Narrowband Frame Relay Congestion Control." *Proceedings of the Tenth Annual Phoenix Conference of Computers and Communications*, March 1991.

BERG96   Bergmans, J. *Digital Baseband Transmission and Recording.* Boston: Kluwer, 1996.

BERL87   Berlekamp, E.; Peile, R.; and Pope, S. "The Application of Error Control to Communications." *IEEE Communications Magazine*, April 1987.

BERN00   Bernet, Y. "The Complementary Roles of RSVP and Differentiated Services in the Full-Service QoS Network." *IEEE Communications Magazine*, February 2000.

BERT92 Bertsekas, D., and Gallager, R. *Data Networks.* Englewood Cliffs, NJ: Prentice Hall, 1992.

BERT94 Bertoni, H.; Honcharenko, W.; Maciel, L.; and Xia, H. "UHF Propagation Prediction for Wireless Personal Communications." *Proceedings of the IEEE*, September 1994.

BHAR83 Bhargava, V. "Forward Error Correction Schemes for Digital Communications." *IEEE Communications Magazine*, January 1983.

BHAT97 Bhatnagar, P. *Engineering Networks for Synchronization, CCS 7 and ISDN.* New York: IEEE Press, 1997.

BLAC93 Black, U. *Data Link Protocols.* Englewood Cliffs, NJ: Prentice Hall, 1993.

BLAC95 Black, U. *The V Series Recommendations: Standards for Data Communications Over the Telephone Network.* New York: McGraw-Hill, 1996.

BLAC96 Black, U. *Physical Level Interfaces and Protocols.* Los Alamitos, CA: IEEE Computer Society Press, 1996.

BLAC97 Black, U. *ISDN and SS7: Architectures for Digital Signaling Networks.* Upper Saddle River, NJ: Prentice Hall, 1997.

BLAC99a Black, U. *ATM Volume I: Foundation for Broadband Networks.* Upper Saddle River, NJ: Prentice Hall, 1992.

BLAC99b Black, U. *Second-generation Mobile and Wireless Networks.* Upper Saddle River, NJ: Prentice Hall, 1999.

BLAC00 Black, U. *IP Routing Protocols: RIP, OSPF, BGP, PNNI & Cisco Routing Protocols.* Upper Saddle River, NJ: Prentice Hall, 2000.

BORE97 Borella, M., et al., "Optical Components for WDM Lightwave Networks." *Proceedings of the IEEE*, August 1997.

BOSS98 Bosse, J. *Signaling in Telecommunication Networks.* New York: Wiley, 1998.

BREY99 Breyer, R., and Riley, S. *Switched, Fast, and Gigabit Ethernet.* New York: Macmillan Technical Publishing, 1999.

BUCK00 Buckwalter, J. *Frame Relay: Technology and Practice.* Reading, MA: Addison-Wesley, 2000.

BURG91 Burg, J., and Dorman, D. "Broadband ISDN Resource Management: The Role of Virtual Paths." *IEEE Communications Magazine*, September 1991.

BUX80 Bux, W.; Kummerle, K.; and Truong, H. "Balanced HDLC Procedures: A Performance Analysis." *IEEE Transactions on Communications*, November 1980.

CARN99 Carne, E. *Telecommunications Primer: Data, Voice, and Video Communications.* Upper Saddle River, NJ: Prentice Hall, 1999.

CARP02 Carpenter, B., and Nichols, K. "Differentiated Services in the Internet." *Proceedings of the IEEE*, September 2002.

CERT03 CERT Coordination Center. *CERT Coordination Center 2002 Annual Report.* Carnegie-Mellon University, 2003. http://www.cert.org/annual_rpts/cert_rpt_02.html.

CLAR92 Clark, D.; Shenker, S.; and Zhang, L. "Supporting Real-Time Applications in an Integrated Services Packet Network: Architecture and Mechanism" *Proceedings, SIGCOMM '92*, August 1992.

CLAR95 Clark, D. *Adding Service Discrimination to the Internet.* MIT Laboratory for Computer Science Technical Report, September 1995. Available at http://ana-www.lcs.mit.edu/anaWeb/papers.html.

CLAR98 Clark, D., and Fang, W. "Explicit Allocation of Best-Effort Packet Delivery Service." *IEEE/ACM Transactions on Networking*, August 1998.

COME99 Comer, D., and Stevens, D. *Internetworking with TCP/IP, Volume II: Design Implementation, and Internals.* Upper Saddle River, NJ: Prentice Hall, 1994.

COME00 Comer, D. *Internetworking with TCP/IP, Volume I: Principles, Protocols, and Architecture.* Upper Saddle River, NJ: Prentice Hall, 2000.

COME01 Comer, D., and Stevens, D. *Internetworking with TCP/IP, Volume III: Client-Server Programming and Applications.* Upper Saddle River, NJ: Prentice Hall, 2001.

CORM01 Cormen, T., et al., *Introduction to Algorithms.* Cambridge, MA: MIT Press, 2001.

COUC01 Couch, L. *Digital and Analog Communication Systems.* Upper Saddle River, NJ: Prentice Hall, 2001.

CROW97 Crow, B., et al., "IEEE 802.11 Wireless Local Area Networks." *IEEE Communications Magazine*, September 1997.

DAVI89 Davies, D., and Price, W. *Security for Computer Networks.* New York: Wiley, 1989.

DIFF76 Diffie, W., and Hellman, M. "Multiuser Cryptographic Techniques." *IEEE Transactions on Information Theory*, November 1976.

DIJK59 Dijkstra, E. "A Note on Two Problems in Connection with Graphs." *Numerical Mathematics*, October 1959.

DINA98 Dinan, E., and Jabbari, B. "Spreading Codes for Direct Sequence CDMA and Wideband CDMA Cellular Networks." *IEEE Communications Magazine*, September 1998.

DIXO94 Dixon, R. *Spread Spectrum Systems with Commercial Applications.* New York: Wiley, 1994.

DUTT99 Dutta-Roy, A. "Cable: It's Not Just for TV." *IEEE Spectrum*, May 1999.

EFF98 Electronic Frontier Foundation. *Cracking DES: Secrets of Encryption Research, Wiretap Politics, and Chip Design.* Sebastopol, CA: O'Reilly, 1998.

FCIA98 Fibre Channel Industry Association. *Fibre Channel Storage Area Networks.* San Francisco: Fibre Channel Industry Association, 2001.

FIOR95 Fiorini, D.; Chiani, M.; Tralli, V.; and Salati, C. "Can We Trust HDLC?" *Computer Communications Review*, October 1995.

FORD62 Ford, L. and Fulkerson, D. *Flows in Networks.* Princeton, NJ: Princeton University Press, 1962.

FRAZ99 Frazier, H., and Johnson, H. "Gigabit Ethernet: From 100 to 1,000 Mbps." *IEEE Internet Computing*, January/February 1999.

FREE96 Freeman, R. *Telecommunication System Engineering.* New York: Wiley, 1996.

FREE97 Freeman, R. *Radio System Design for Telecommunications.* New York: Wiley, 1997.

FREE98a Freeman, R. *Telecommunication Transmission Handbook.* New York: Wiley, 1998.

FREE98b Freeman, R. "Bits, Symbols, Baud, and Bandwidth." *IEEE Communications Magazine*, April 1998.

FREE99 Freeman, R. *Fundamentals of Telecommunications.* New York: Wiley, 1999.

FREE02 Freeman, R. *Fiber-Optic Systems for Telecommunications.* New York: Wiley, 2002.

GARR96 Garrett, M. "A Service Architecture for ATM: From Applications to Scheduling." *IEEE Network*, May/June 1996.

GEIE99 Geier, J. *Wireless LANs.* New York: Macmillan Technical Publishing, 1999.

GEIE01 Geier, J. "Enabling Fast Wireless Networks with OFDM." *Communications System Design*, February 2001. (www.csdmag.com)

GERS91 Gersht, A. and Lee, K. "A Congestion Control Framework for ATM Networks." *IEEE Journal on Selected Areas in Communications*, September 1991.

GIBS93 Gibson, J. *Principles of Digital and Analog Communications.* New York: Macmillan, 1993.

GIBS97 Gibson, J. ed. *The Communications Handbook.* Boca Raton, FL: CRC Press, 1997.

GIRA90 Girard, A. *Routing and Dimensioning in Circuit-switching Networks.* Reading, MA: Addison-Wesley, 1990.

GLOV98 Glover, I., and Grant, P. *Digital Communications.* Upper Saddle River, NJ: Prentice Hall, 1998.

GOYA98 Goyal, R., et al., "Providing Rate Guarantees to TCP over the ATM GFR Service." *Proceedings of the Local Computer Networks Conference,* October 1998.

HAAS00 Haas, Z. "Wireless and Mobile Networks." In [TERP00].

HARB92 Harbison, R. "Frame Relay: Technology for Our Time." *LAN Technology,* December 1992.

HARJ00 Harju, J., and Kivimaki, P. "Cooperation and Comparison of DiffServ and IntServ: Performance Measurements." *Proceedings, 23rd Annual IEEE Conference on Local Computer Networks,* November 2000.

HATA80 Hata, M. "Empirical Formula for Propagation Loss in Land Mobile Radio Services." *IEEE Transactions on Vehicular Technology,* March 1980.

HAWL97 Hawley, G. "Systems Considerations for the Use of xDSL Technology for Data Access." *IEEE Communications Magazine,* March 1997.

HAYK01 Haykin, S. *Communication Systems.* New York: Wiley, 2001.

HIND83 Hinden, R., Haverty, J. and Sheltzer, A. "The DARPA Internet: Interconnecting Heterogeneous Computer Networks with Gateways." *Computer,* September 1983.

HIND95 Hinden, R. "IP Next Generation Overview." *Connexions,* March 1995.

HUIT98 Huitema, C. *IPv6: The New Internet Protocol.* Upper Saddle River, NJ: Prentice Hall, 1998.

HUIT00 Huitema, C. *Routing in the Internet.* Upper Saddle River, NJ: Prentice Hall, 2000.

HUMP97 Humphrey, M., and Freeman, J. "How xDSL Supports Broadband Services to the Home." *IEEE Network,* January/March 1997.

HURW98 Hurwicz, M. "Fibre Channel: More Vision Than Reality?" *Network Magazine,* June 1998.

JACO88 Jacobson, V. "Congestion Avoidance and Control." *Proceedings, SIGCOMM '88, Computer Communication Review,* August 1988; reprinted in *Computer Communication Review,* January 1995; a slightly revised version is available at ftp.ee.lbl.gov/papers/congavoid.ps.Z.

JACO90 Jacobson, V. "Berkeley TCP Evolution from 4.3 Tahoe to 4.3-Reno." *Proceedings of the Eighteenth Internet Engineering Task Force,* September 1990.

JAIN91 Jain, R. *The Art of Computer Systems Performance Analysis: Techniques for Experimental Design, Measurement, Simulation, and Modeling.* New York: Wiley, 1991.

JAIN92 Jain, R. "Myths About Congestion Management in High-Speed Networks." *Internetworking: Research and Experience,* Volume 3, 1993.

JAME01 James, J. *A Student's Guide to Fourier Transforms.* Cambridge, England: Cambridge University Press, 2001.

JOHN98 Johnston, M. *An Up-to-Date Review of Physical Layer Measurements, Cabling Standards, Troubleshooting Practices, and Certification Techniques.* Phoenix, AZ: Microtest Inc. 1998.

KADA98 Kadambi, J.; Crayford, I.; and Kalkunte, M. *Gigabit Ethernet.* Upper Saddle River, NJ: Prentice Hall, 1998.

KAMM00 Kammler, D. *A First Course in Fourier Analysis.* Upper Saddle River, NJ: Prentice Hall, 2000.

KARN91 Karn, P., and Partridge, C. "Improving Round-Trip Estimates in Reliable Transport Protocols." *ACM Transactions on Computer Systems,* November 1991.

KHAN89 Khanna, A., and Zinky, J. "The Revised ARPANET Routing Metric." *Proceedings, SIGCOMM '89 Sypmosium,* 1989.

KAHN97 Kahn, J., and Barry, J. "Wireless Infrared Communications." *Proceedings of the IEEE,* February 1997.

KESH98   Keshav, S., and Sharma, R. "Issues and Trends in Router Design." *IEEE Communications Magazine*, May 1998.

KILK99   Kilkki, K. *Differentiated Services for the Internet.* Indianapolis, IN: Macmillan Technical Publishing, 1999.

KLEI76   Kleinrock, L. *Queuing Systems, Volume II: Computer Applications.* New York: Wiley, 1976.

KLEI92   Kleinrock, L. "The Latency/Bandwidth Tradeoff in Gigabit Networks." *IEEE Communications Magazine*, April 1992.

KLEI93   Kleinrock, L. "On the Modeling and Analysis of Computer Networks." *Proceedings of the IEEE*, August 1993.

KNUT98   Knuth, D. *The Art of Computer Programming, Volume 2: Seminumerical Algorithms.* Reading, MA: Addison-Wesley, 1998.

KONH80   Konheim, A. "A Queuing Analysis of Two ARQ Protocols." *IEEE Transactions on Communications*, July 1980.

KRIS01   Krishnamurthy, B., and Rexford, J. *Web Protocols and Practice: HTTP/1.1, Networking Protocols, Caching, and Traffic Measurement.* Upper Saddle River, NJ: Prentice Hall, 2001.

KUMA98   Kumar, V.; Lakshman, T.; and Stiliadis, D. "Beyond Best Effort: Router Architectures for the Differentiated Services of Tomorrow's Internet." *IEEE Communications Magazine*, May 1998.

KURO01   Kurose, J., and Ross, K. *Computer Networking.* Reading, MA: Addison-Wesley, 2001.

LARO02   LaRocca, J., and LaRocca, R. *802.11 Demystified.* New York: McGraw-Hill, 2002.

LEBO98   Lebow, I. *Understanding Digital Transmission and Recording.* New York: IEEE Press, 1998.

LEON00   Leon-Garcie, A., and Widjaja, I. *Communication Networks: Fundamental Concepts and Key Architectures.* New York: McGraw-Hill, 2000.

LEUT94   Leutwyler, K. "Superhack." *Scientific American*, July 1994.

LIN84   Lin, S.; Costello, D; and Miller, M. "Automatic-Repeat-Request Error-Control Schemes." *IEEE Communications Magazine*, December 1984.

LUIN97   Luinen, S., Budrikis, Z.; and Cantoni, A. "The Controlled Cell Transfer Capability." *Computer Communications Review*, January 1997.

MAXW96   Maxwell, K. "Asymmetric Digital Subscriber Line: Interim Technology for the Next Forty Years." *IEEE Communications Magazine*, October 1996.

MCDO91   McDonald, C. "A Network Specification Language and Execution Environment for Undergraduate Teaching." *Proceedings of the ACM Computer Science Educational Technical Symposium*, March 1991.

MCDY99   McDysan, D., and Spohn, D. *ATM: Theory and Application.* New York: McGraw-Hill, 1999.

MCQU80   McQuillan, J., Richer, I. and Rosen, E. "The New Routing Algorithm for the ARPANET." *IEEE Transactions on Communications*, May 1980.

METZ99   Metzler, J., and DeNoia, L. *Layer 2 Switching.* Upper Saddle River, NJ: Prentice Hall, 1999.

MOSH89   Moshos, G. *Data Communications: Principles and Problems.* New York: West Publishing Co., 1989.

MOY98   Moy, J. *OSPF: Anatomy of an Internet Routing Protocol.* Reading, MA: Addison-Wesley, 1998.

OHAR99   Ohara, B., and Petrick, A. *IEEE 802.11 Handbook: A Designer's Companion.* New York: IEEE Press, 1999.

OJAN98   Ojanpera, T., and Prasad, G. "An Overview of Air Interface Multiple Access for IMT-2000/UMTS." *IEEE Communications Magazine*, September 1998.

OKUM68 Okumura, T., et. al., "Field Strength and Its Variability in VHF and UHF Land Mobile Radio Service." *Rev. Elec. Communication Lab.* 1968.

PAHL95 Pahlavan, K.; Probert, T.; and Chase, M. "Trends in Local Wireless Networks." *IEEE Communications Magazine*, March 1995.

PARK88 Park, S., and Miller, K. "Random Number Generators: Good Ones are Hard to Find." *Communications of the ACM*, October 1988.

PARE88 Parekh, S., and Sohraby, K. "Some Performance Trade-Offs Associated with ATM Fixed-Length Vs. Variable-Length Cell Formats." *Proceedings, GlobeCom*, November 1988.

PEAR92 Pearson, J. *Basic Communication Theory.* Englewood Cliffs, NJ: Prentice Hall, 1992.

PERL00 Perlman, R. *Interconnections: Bridges, Routers, Switches, and Internetworking Protocols.* Reading, MA: Addison-Wesley, 2000.

PETE95 Peterson, R.; Ziemer, R.; and Borth, D. *Introduction to Spread Spectrum Communications.* Englewood Cliffs, NJ: Prentice Hall, 1995.

PETE61 Peterson, W., and Brown, D. "Cyclic Codes for Error Detection." *Proceedings of the IEEE*, January 1961.

PETE00 Peterson, L., and Davie, B. *Computer Networks: A Systems Approach.* San Francisco: Morgan Kaufmann, 2000.

PICK82 Pickholtz, R.; Schilling, D.; and Milstein, L. "Theory of Spread Spectrum Communications—A Tutorial." IEEE Transactions on Communications, May 1982. Reprinted in [TANT98].

PRAS98 Prasad, R., and Ojanpera, T. "An Overview of CDMA Evolution: Toward Wideband CDMA." *IEEE Communications Surveys*, Fourth Quarter 1998. Available at www.comsoc.org.

PRAS00 Prasad, R.; Mohr, W.; and Konhauser, W., eds. *Third-Generation Mobile Communication Systems.* Boston: Artech House, 2000.

PROA02 Proakis, J. *Communication Systems Engineering.* Upper Saddle River, NJ: Prentice Hall, 2002.

RAMA88 Ramabadran, T., and Gaitonde, S. "A Tutorial on CRC Computations." *IEEE Micro*, August 1988.

RAPP96 Rappaport, T. *Wireless Communications.* Upper Saddle River, NJ: Prentice Hall, 1996.

RAPP97 Rappaport, T.; Rias, M.; and Kapoor, V. "Propagation Models." In [GIBS97].

REEV95 Reeve, W. *Subscriber Loop Signaling and Transmission Handbook.* Piscataway, NJ: IEEE Press, 1995.

RIVE78 Rivest, R.; Shamir, A.; and Adleman, L. "A Method for Obtaining Digital Signatures and Public Key Cryptosystems." *Communications of the ACM*, February 1978.

RODR02 Rodriguez, A., et al., *TCP/IP Tutorial and Technical Overview.* Upper Saddle River: NJ: Prentice Hall, 2002.

ROSE98 Rose, M., and Strom, D. *Internet Messaging: From the Desktop to the Enterprise.* Upper Saddle River, NJ: Prentice Hall, 1998.

RUSS95 Russell, R. *Signaling System #7.* New York: McGraw-Hill, 1995.

SACH96 Sachs, M., and Varma, A. "Fibre Channel and Related Standards." *IEEE Communications Magazine*, August 1996.

SATO90 Sato, K.; Ohta, S.; and Tokizawa, I. "Broad-Band ATM Network Architecture Based on Virtual Paths." *IEEE Transactions on Communications*, August 1990.

SATO91 Sato, K.; Ueda, H.; and Yoshikai, M. "The Role of Virtual Path Crossconnection." *IEEE LTS*, August 1991.

SCHN96 Schneier, B. *Applied Cryptography.* New York: Wiley, 1996.

SEIF98 Seifert, R. *Gigabit Ethernet.* Reading, MA: Addison-Wesley, 1998.

SEIF00   Seifert, R. *The Switch Book.* New York: Wiley, 2000.

SHEN95   Shenker, S. "Fundamental Design Issues for the Future Internet." *IEEE Journal on Selected Areas in Communications*, September 1995.

SING99   Singh, S. *The Code Book: The Science of Secrecy from Ancient Egypt to Quantum Cryptography.* New York: Anchor Books, 1999.

SKLA93   Sklar, B. "Defining, Designing, and Evaluating Digital Communication Systems." *IEEE Communications Magazine*, November 1993.

SKLA01   Sklar, B. *Digital Communications: Fundamentals and Applications.* Upper Saddle River, NJ: Prentice Hall, 2001.

SPOH02   Spohn, D. *Data Network Design.* New York: McGraw-Hill, 2002.

SPUR00   Spurgeon, C. *Ethernet: The Definitive Guide.* Cambridge, MA: O'Reilly and Associates, 2000.

SPRA91   Spragins, J.; Hammond, J.; and Pawlikowski, K. *Telecommunications: Protocols and Design.* Reading, MA: Addison-Wesley, 1991.

STAL99a   Stallings, W. *ISDN and Broadband ISDN, with Frame Relay and ATM.* Upper Saddle River, NJ: Prentice Hall, 1999.

STAL99b   Stallings, W. *SNMP, SNMPv2, SNMPv3, and RMON 1 and 2.* Reading, MA: Addison-Wesley, 1999.

STAL00   Stallings, W. *Local and Metropolitan Area Networks, 6th ed.* Upper Saddle River, NJ: Prentice Hall, 2000.

STAL02   Stallings, W. *Wireless Communications and Networks.* Upper Saddle River, NJ: Prentice Hall, 2002.

STAL03   Stallings, W. *Cryptography and Network Security: Principles and Practice, 3rd ed.* Upper Saddle River, NJ: Prentice Hall, 2003.

STEI95   Steinke, S. "IP Addresses and Subnet Masks." *LAN Magazine*, October 1995.

STEV94   Stevens, W. *TCP/IP Illustrated, Volume 1: The Protocols.* Reading, MA: Addison-Wesley, 1994.

STEV96   Stevens, W. *TCP/IP Illustrated, Volume 3: TCP for Transactions, HTTP, NNTP, and the UNIX(R) Domain Protocol.* Reading, MA: Addison-Wesley, 1996.

SUZU94   Suzuki, T. "ATM Adaptation Layer Protocol." *IEEE Communications Magazine*, April 1995.

TANE03   Tanenbaum, A. *Computer Networks.* Upper Saddle River, NJ: Prentice Hall, 2003.

TANT98   Tantaratana, S, and Ahmed, K., eds. *Wireless Applications of Spread Spectrum Systems: Selected Readings.* Piscataway, NJ: IEEE Press, 1998.

TERP00   Terplan, K., and Morreale, P. eds. *The Telecommunications Handbook.* Boca Raton, FL: CRC Press, 2000.

TSUD92   Tsudik, G. "Message Authentication with One-Way Hash Functions." *Proceedings, INFOCOM '92*, May 1992.

WALR98   Walrand, J. *Communication Networks: A First Course.* New York: McGraw-Hill, 1998.

WALR00   Walrand, J., and Varaiya, P. *High-Performance Communication Networks.* San Francisco, CA: Morgan Kaufmann, 2000.

WANG92   Wang, Z., and Crowcroft, J. "SEAL Detects Cell Misordering." *IEEE Network*, July 1992.

WEIS98   Weiss, W. "QoS with Differentiated Services." *Bell Labs Technical Journal*, October–December 1998.

WHIT97   White, P., and Crowcroft, J. "The Integrated Services in the Internet: State of the Art." *Proceedings of the IEEE*, December 1997.

WIDM83   Widmer, A. and Franaszek, P. "A DC-Balanced, Partitioned, 8B/10B Transmission Code." *IBM Journal of Research and Development*, September 1983.

WRIG95   Wright, G., and Stevens, W. *TCP/IP Illustrated, Volume 2: The Implementation.* Reading, MA: Addison-Wesley, 1995.

WILL97   Willner, A. "Mining the Optical Bandwidth for a Terabit per Second." *IEEE Spectrum*, April 1997.

XIAO99   Xiao, X., and Ni, L. "Internet QoS: A Big Picture." *IEEE Network*, March/April 1999.

XION00   Xiong, F. *Digital Modulation Techniques.* Boston: Artech House, 2000.

ZENG00   Zeng, M.; Annamalai, A.; and Bhargava, V. "Harmonization of Global Third-Generation Mobile Systems. *IEEE Communications Magazine*, December 2000.

ZHAN86   Zhang, L. "Why TCP Timers Don't Work Well." *Proceedings, SIGCOMM '86 Symposium*, August 1986.

ZHAN93   Zhang, L.; Deering, S.; Estrin, D.; Shenker, S.; and Zappala, D. "RSVP: A New Resource ReSerVation Protocol." *IEEE Network*, September 1993.

ZHAN95   Zhang, H. "Service Disciplines for Guaranteed Performance Service in Packet-Switching Networks." *Proceedings of the IEEE*, October 1995.

ZORZ96   Zorzi, M., and Rao, R. "On the Use of Renewal Theory in the Analysis of ARQ Protocols." *IEEE Transactions on Communications*, September 1996.

INDEX

N

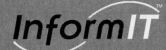
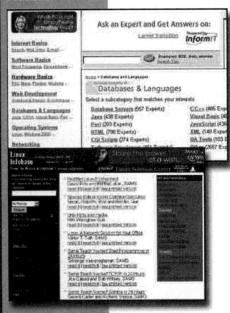

ACRONYMS

AAL	ATM Adaptation Layer
ADSL	Asymmetric Digital Subscriber Line
AES	Advanced Encryption Standard
AM	Amplitude Modulation
AMI	Alternate Mark Inversion
ANS	American National Standard
ANSI	American National Standard Institute
ARQ	Automatic Repeat Request
ASCII	American Standard Code for Information Interchange
ASK	Amplitude-Shift Keying
ATM	Asynchronous Transfer Mode
BER	Bit Error Rate
B-ISDN	Broadband ISDN
BGP	Border Gateway Protocol
BOC	Bell Operating Company
CBR	Constant Bit Rate
CCITT	International Consultative Committee on Telegraphy and Telephony
CIR	Committed Information Rate
CMI	Coded Mark Inversion
CRC	Cyclic Redundancy Check
CSMA/CD	Carrier Sense Multiple Access with Collision Detection
DCE	Data Circuit-Terminating Equipment
DEA	Data Encryption Algorithm
DES	Data Encryption Standard
DS	Differentiated Services
DTE	Data Terminal Equipment
FCC	Federal Communications Commission
FCS	Frame Check Sequence
FDM	Frequency-Division Multiplexing
FSK	Frequency-Shift Keying
FTP	File Transfer Protocol
FM	Frequency Modulation
GFR	Guaranteed Frame Rate
HDLC	High-Level Data Link Control
HTML	Hypertext Markup Language
HTTP	Hypertext Transfer Protocol
IAB	Internet Architecture Board
ICMP	Internet Control Message Protocol
IDN	Integrated Digital Network
IEEE	Institute of Electrical and Electronics Engineers
IETF	Internet Engineering Task Force
IGMP	Internet Group Management Protocol
IP	Internet Protocol
IPng	Internet Protocol - Next Generation
IRA	International Reference Alphabet
ISA	Integrated Services Architecture
ISDN	Integrated Services Digital Network

ISO	International Organization for Standardization
ITU	International Telecommunication Union
ITU-T	ITU Telecommunication Standardization Sector
LAN	Local Area Network
LAPB	Link Access Procedure - Balanced
LAPD	Link Access Procedure on the D Channel
LAPF	Link Access Procedure for Frame Mode Bearer Services
LLC	Logical Link Control
MAC	Medium Access Control
MAN	Metropolitan Area Network
MIME	Multi-Purpose Internet Mail Extension
NRZI	Nonreturn to Zero, Inverted
NRZL	Nonreturn to Zero, Level
NT	Network Termination
OSI	Open Systems Interconnection
OSPF	Open Shortest Path First
PBX	Private Branch Exchange
PCM	Pulse-Code Modulation
PDU	Protocol Data Unit
PSK	Phase-Shift Keying
PTT	Postal, Telegraph, and Telephone
PM	Phase Modulation
QAM	Quadrature Amplitude Modulation
QoS	Quality of Service
QPSK	Quadrature Phase Shift Keying
RBOC	Regional Bell Operating Company
RF	Radio Frequency
RSA	Rivest, Shamir, Adleman Algorithm
RSVP	Resource ReSerVation Protocol
SAP	Service Access Point
SDH	Synchronous Digital Hierarchy
SDU	Service Data Unit
SMTP	Simple Mail Transfer Protocol
SNMP	Simple Network Management Protocol
SONET	Synchronous Optical Network
SS7	Signaling System Number 7
STP	Shielded Twisted Pair
TCP	Transmission Control Protocol
TDM	Time-Division Multiplexing
TE	Terminal Equipment
UBR	Unspecified Bit Rate
UDP	User Datagram Protocol
UNI	User-Network Interface
UTP	Unshielded Twisted Pair
VAN	Value-Added Network
VBR	Variable Bit Rate
VCC	Virtual Channel Connection
VPC	Virtual Path Connection
WDM	Wavelength Division Multiplexing
WWW	World Wide Web